THE INTERNATIONAL HANDBOOK ON SOCIAL INNOVATION

The International Handbook on Social Innovation

Collective Action, Social Learning and Transdisciplinary Research

Edited by

Frank Moulaert

KU Leuven, Belgium

Diana MacCallum

Curtin University, Australia

Abid Mehmood

Cardiff University, UK

Abdelillah Hamdouch

University of Tours, France

Edward Elgar
Cheltenham, UK • Northampton, MA, USA

Published by
Edward Elgar Publishing Limited
The Lypiatts
15 Lansdown Road
Cheltenham
Glos GL50 2JA
UK

Edward Elgar Publishing, Inc.
William Pratt House
9 Dewey Court
Northampton
Massachusetts 01060
USA

Paperback edition 2014
Cased edition reprinted 2014
Paperback edition reprinted 2015

A catalogue record for this book
is available from the British Library

Library of Congress Control Number: 2012955457

This book is available electronically in the ElgarOnline.com Social and Political Science Subject Collection E-ISBN 978 1 84980 999 3

ISBN   978 1 84980 998 6 (cased)
       978 1 78254 559 0 (paperback)

Printed and bound in Great Britain by T.J. International Ltd, Padstow

To Julie Graham, teacher, scientist, activist and friend
who taught us to learn from solidarity

Contents

Figures

Tables

Contributors

Alexandre Abreu is a Researcher at the Centre for Geographical Studies (CEG – University of Lisbon) and has recently finished his doctorate at the School of Oriental and African Studies (SOAS – University of London). He has been involved in the European Actions *KATARSIS* and *Social Polis*, in addition to several national-level projects with EU funding in Portugal. His research interests include the political economy of development, migration, social exclusion and social innovation.

John Andersen is a sociologist, Professor and Director of Planning Studies at Roskilde University in Denmark. He has worked as a consultant in the EU Poverty 3 Program, and over the last two decades as researcher with a focus on strategies and practices against urban poverty and social exclusion. Recently he has participated in the KATARSIS network. His research interest is focused on critique of neoliberalism and on empowerment planning, action research and social innovation.

Isabel André is Associate Professor of the Institute of Geography and Spatial Planning of the University of Lisbon (IGOT-UL) and senior researcher at the Centre for Geographical Studies (CEG-UL). She has co-ordinated and/or participated in numerous research projects in the areas of labour market and gender, social innovation and cultural studies. She has worked as a consultant to several urban and regional development projects, and as an evaluator of public policies and programmes in these domains.

Len Arthur is now a retired academic. His discipline area was largely sociology and social history. He worked in colleges and universities in Wales from 1974 until his retirement in 2010. In the late 1990s he started to research and publish on cooperatives as social movements and linked this to his earlier research on trade unions. Since leaving school in the 1960s he has been a political, trade union and community activist – this continues. Background traces of this experience may be seen in his chapter.

Arvind Ashta holds the Banque Populaire Chair in Microfinance at the Burgundy School of Business (Groupe ESC Dijon-Bourgogne), France. He offers courses in microfinance and has taught microfinance as visiting faculty in Chicago (US), Pforzheim (Germany) and Brussels (Belgium). He has a number of publications in international journals and guest edits special editions of various journals devoted to microfinance. He has recently edited a book on *Advanced Technologies for Microfinance* (IGI Global, 2011).

Annette Bilfeldt is currently Associate Professor in social science and social innovation at the Department of Learning and Philosophy, Aalborg University. She is also affiliated with the Centre for Action Research and Democratic Social Change at Roskilde University in Denmark. Her research over the last decade has focused on critical sociology and critical utopian action research in public welfare institutions and public elder care in cooperation with trade unions and employees.

Igor Calzada is Research Fellow at the University of Oxford's (UK) 'Future of Cities' Programme, and Postdoctoral Fellow at Ikerbasque, the Basque Foundation for Science, as Scientific Director of the City Region Congress organized by the Basque Government. He also works as 'Networks and Territory' Lecturer at the University of Mondragón (Spain). He has worked in the academic, political, institutional and international business fields, specifically in the area of Social Innovation under the EU's Framework Programme, and spent 10 years in the Mondragón Corporación Cooperativa group (at the Innovation Research Centre and University of Mondragón).

Stuart Cameron is Senior Lecturer in the School of Architecture, Planning and Landscape, Newcastle University. His academic background is in sociology and urban planning, and his research and publications are in the areas of urban regeneration and housing. He has participated in several EU research programmes on issues of cities, social innovation and social cohesion.

André Carmo holds a Masters degree in Modernity, Space and Place from University College London. He is a researcher at the Centre for Geographical Studies and a PhD candidate at the Institute of Geography and Spatial Planning (University of Lisbon). His research interests include citizenship, spatial injustice, urban segregations, and social art.

Karl Dayson is Professor and Director of Sociology and Criminology, and the Executive Director of the research and development unit Community Finance Solutions at the University of Salford, UK. Karl's research is in the fields of community finance, financial exclusion and institutional forms of collective and communal ownership. His current work includes research on credit cards and assessing the social impact of microfinance initiatives. He has advised various UK government departments and local authorities, and has just completed the European Code of Conduct for Microcredit Providers on behalf of the European Commission.

Pascal Debruyne is a PhD researcher at the Middle East and North African Research Group (MENARG) at Ghent University. He is working on urbanization and state transformation in Jordan. He has also published on urban transformation and cultural diversity in Flanders.

Jacques Defourny is Professor of non-profit and cooperative economics as well as comparative economic systems at HEC-ULg (Management School, University of Liège), where he has also served as a director of the Centre for Social Economy since 1992. A founding member of the EMES European Research Network, he was also the first president of the network (2002–2010). His research focuses mainly on the economic analysis of Third sector organizations and the comparative analysis of social enterprise models throughout the world.

Kristian Delica is Assistant Professor in Planning and Health Promotion Studies at Roskilde University in Denmark. His research interests include urban sociology, public libraries, the organization of public sector institutions, critical studies of social innovation and methodologies of social science (field analysis and ethnography). He has published on contemporary forms of urban marginalization, social innovation and territorial development and on the sociology of Pierre Bourdieu and Loíc Wacquant.

Ana Dubeux has a PhD in Sociology from the University of Paris I and is currently Professor at the Federal Rural University of Pernambuco, Recife, Brazil. She is a member of the incubator UFRPE and coordinator of the Training Centre in Solidarity Economy of the Northeast in Brazil. Her research focuses on the territorial dynamics of the solidarity economy and crosses the fields of sociology and education, always from an action research perspective. A key aim of her work is to revisit and re-imagine the paradigm of knowledge production at the university, drawing constantly on relationships with wider society.

Santiago Eizaguirre Anglada is a PhD candidate in the department of Sociological Theory in the University of Barcelona. His research focuses on innovation against social exclusion from the perspective of urban sociology. He has analysed the impact of bottom-up strategies oriented to combat social exclusion on multilevel urban governance. He has also analysed social policies focusing on territorial planning, the social construction of participation, the institutionalization of citizenship practices and multilevel governance of social innovation.

Vicente Espinoza is Professor in the Universidad de Santiago de Chile (USACH) and Senior researcher at IDEA (Institute for Advanced Studies). His research has focused on public policies, social inequality and political processes. His published books (in Spanish) include *Social History of Santiago de Chile* (1988); *Approaches and Applications of Social Networks Analysis* (2005); *The emerging political elite in Chile: Trajectory and efficacy of young party militants* (2009).

Ana Cristina Fernandes is Professor at the Federal University of Pernambuco, Brazil, where she teaches Economic Geography and Urban and Regional Studies. She is also a CNPq (National Council of Technological and Scientific Development) researcher and has published and supervised graduate students on regional development and technological as well as social innovation and innovation policies. She has been involved in national and transnational research projects and has supported Brazilian local and regional authorities on innovation policies.

Jean-Marc Fontan is Professor of Sociology at Université du Québec à Montréal (UQAM). He has over 20 years experience in research on local and community development and has an important number of publications in this field. He is a member of the Centre de recherche sur les innovations sociales (CRISES) and director of an important community based research centre, l'Incubateur universitaire *Parole d'excluEs*, associated with CRISES.

Laurent Fraisse has been a member of the Laboratoire Interdisciplinaire pour la Sociologie Economique (LISE / CNAM CNRS) since 2004. A socio-economist, he took part in several European research programmes on social innovation, on non-profit, social and solidarity-based economy organisations and movements, on public policies and the third sector, on the governance of welfare policies and social cohesion.

Martin Severin Frandsen is affiliated to the Centre for Action Research and Democratic Social Change at Roskilde University and a member of the grassroots urban laboratory Supertanker based in Copenhagen. His research focuses on theory of democracy, urban sociology, community development, social innovation and action research. Over nearly a decade he has combined his university-based research with practical experimentations collaborating with civil society organizations, local residents, public institutions, business communities and local levels of government.

Marisol García Cabeza is Professor of Sociology at the University of Barcelona. Her research has covered areas such as: urban social inequality and citizenship, governance and social innovation and urban regeneration. Since the mid-1990s, she has focussed particularly on Southern European welfare regimes, multi-level governance and democracy. She has been the Spanish coordinator of several European projects financed by subsequent EU framework programs (IV–VII). She has published her work in several international journals, such as *The International Journal of Urban and Regional Research* and *Urban Studies* as well as in books published by Oxford University Press, Blackwell and Sage.

Rajat Gera is an Associate Professor in Marketing at Institute of Management Technology, Ghaziabad, India and visiting faculty at Fontys University, Netherlands and Summer school KIMEP, Kazakasthan. He teaches courses in Marketing Management, Marketing of Services, Marketing of Financial Services, New Product Management and Product Management. His research interests are in modelling of service quality and its consumer consequences in financial services, microfinance, e-learning and e-service quality. He has over 20 international publications.

J.K Gibson-Graham is the pen-name of Katherine Gibson and the late Julie Graham, feminist political economists and economic geographers based at the University of Western Sydney, Australia and the University of Massachusetts Amherst, USA. They are founding members of the Community Economies Collective www.communityeconomies.org (last accessed 6 December 2012). Their 1996 book *The End of Capitalism (As We Knew It): A Feminist Critique of Political Economy* was republished in 2006 by University of Minnesota Press along with its sequel *A Postcapitalist Politics*.

Sarah Habersack was Research Assistant in Social Polis and Ungleiche Vielfalt and is the coordinator of a network for development politics (Enchada – Network of development politics of the Catholic Youth Austria). She also works in organizational development and her current research focus is interorganizational cooperation between civil society, public administration and the private sector.

Abdelillah Hamdouch is currently Professor of Urban and Regional Planning and Vice-Dean of the Planning Department at the Polytechnic School of the University of Tours, France and Senior Researcher at the CNRS research unit CITERES (CIties, TERritories, Environment and Society). Co-founder of the Research Network on Innovation and Associate Editor of the Revue d'Economie Régionale et Urbaine, his main research topics focus on the territorial dynamics of innovation and the role of universities, the integration of sustainable development in spatial planning approaches, and the socio-economic development models of small and medium sized towns.

Denis Harrisson is Professor at the Department of Organization & Human Resources at the School of Management, Université du Québec à Montréal (UQAM). He was the director of the Centre de recherche sur l'innovation sociale (CRISES) between 2003 and 2009. His research interests concern new forms of partnership between trade unions and associations, public enterprises and civil society. His publications have appeared in *Economic And Industrial Democracy, Human Relations, Journal of Management Studies, British Journal of Industrial Relations, Handbook on Innovations in Services* and many others.

Samanthala Hettihewa, a Senior Lecturer in Finance at the University of Ballarat (Australia), has taught in four countries (Australia, Canada, Sri Lanka and New Zealand) and has published extensively (including such venues as the *Journal of Business Ethics, Small Business Economics* and *Journal of International Business Studies*). She is a senior fellow in FINSIA (the Financial Services Institute of Australasia), a Chartered Financial Analyst (CFA), and a Financial Planner Australia (FPA).

Jean Hillier is Chair and Associate Dean of Sustainability and Urban Planning at RMIT University, Melbourne, Australia. Research interests include poststructuralist planning theory, decision-making analyses and methodology for strategic practice in conditions of uncertainty. Recent books include *Critical Essays in Planning Theory* (3 volumes, with Patsy Healey, 2008) and *Conceptual Challenges for Planning Theory* (with Patsy Healey, 2010). Jean's work has been translated into Chinese, Italian and Danish.

Lars Hulgård is Professor at Roskilde University, Denmark, co-founder of EMES European Research Network and founder of CINEFOGO Network of Excellence (FP6) and Centre for Social Entrepreneurship at Roskilde University. His research interests include social and solidarity economy, the political dimension of civil society, social innovation and social entrepreneurship especially related to the Third sector.

Bob Jessop is Distinguished Professor of Sociology and Co-Director (with Ngai-Ling Sum) of the Cultural Political Economy Research Centre at Lancaster University, UK. He holds a three-year research professorship financed by the Economic and Social Science Research Council (UK) to research crises of crisis-management in the North Atlantic Financial Crisis (2010–2013). His other research interests include critical political economy, social theory, and state theory. His recent books include *The Future of the Capitalist State* (2002), *Beyond the Regulation Approach: Putting Capitalist Economies in their Place* (2006, co-authored with Ngai-Ling Sum), and *State Power: A Strategic-Relational Approach* (2007).

Juan-Luis Klein is Professor at the Department of Geography and, since 2009, the Director of the Centre de recherche sur l'innovation sociale (CRISES) at the Université du Québec à Montréal (UQAM). He is also in charge of the Series on Géographie contemporaine, published by the Presses de l'Université du Québec and has authored and co-authored several books and articles on the topics of economic geography, local development and socio-territorial innovation.

Haris Konstantatos is a political scientist, MA in Urban and Regional Planning (NTUA), and a PhD Candidate on Governance and Unequal Development in the Department of Geography, Harokopio University of Athens. He has worked on issues of local politics, sustainable development and social services for Greek municipalities and NGOs. He was a participant in the FP6 coordination action KATARSIS and other research projects on social innovation.

N.V. Krishna is a Director of Microsense, an internet services company based in India, and serves as the Chairman of TIDE, a not-for-profit enterprise focused on technological interventions to solve social problems. Krishna has a long standing interest in the role of technology in society, and has several publications in this area. He holds a degree in engineering from the Indian Institute of Technology, Madras and a postgraduate diploma in management from the Indian Institute of Management, Calcutta.

Nola Kunnen has 30 years experience as a community development researcher, educator and practitioner in Western Australia, with particular interest in collaborative methods, action research and strengths-based approaches to community development and research. She taught community development in undergraduate and postgraduate courses at Curtin University for 20 years and has been principal researcher on projects funded by national, state and non-government funding programs. Her research interests and publications address social housing, homelessness, community development, community based service delivery and inclusive research practice. She retired from full time employment in January 2012.

Benoît Lévesque is Professor Emeritus at the Université du Québec à Montréal (UQAM) and Associate Professor at Ecole nationale d'administration publique (ENAP). He is a member and co-founder (1986–2001) of the Centre de recherche sur les innovations sociales (CRISES) and the Alliance of Research Universities and Communities Social Economy (CURA-SE). From 2002 to 2010, he was the Chairman of the International Scientific Council of the International Centre for Research and Information on the Public, Social and Cooperative Economy (CIRIEC). He has published numerous articles and books primarily in the areas of governance, public administration, social economy and economic sociology.

Diana MacCallum is Lecturer in Urban and Regional Planning at Curtin University, Western Australia. Her research interests centre on urban development in its social aspects: governance practices and discourses, grass-roots action, community development, and the eco-social justice dimensions of urban and environmental policy.

Flavia Martinelli is Professor of Analysis of Urban and Territorial Systems at the DArTe – Department of Architecture and Territory of the University of Reggio Calabria, Italy. She holds a PhD in City and Regional Planning, (University of California, Berkeley). Her research focuses on urban and regional, spatial development trajectories and cohesion policies, with particular attention to the service sector and the Mezzogiorno of Italy. She has participated in several European FP projects and is currently coordinating the COST Action IS1102 'Social Services, Welfare State and Places'. Recent publications include *Can Neighbourhoods save the City* (2010, edited with F. Moulaert, Erik Swyngedouw and Sara González) and *Urban and Regional Development Trajectories in Contemporary Capitalism* (2012, edited with Frank Moulaert and Andreas Novy).

Abid Mehmood is Research Fellow at the Sustainable Places Research Institute, Cardiff University. His current research focuses on sustainability governance, local and regional development, social innovation, social inclusion, and sustainable place-making. Other research interests include human-nature relationships and community resilience.

xviii *The international handbook on social innovation*

Andrea Membretti has a PhD in Sociology (University of Milano Statale), and is Research Fellow in Sociology at the University of Milano-Bicocca, where he is involved in qualitative research on urban segregation. Previously, he taught for several years in Urban Sociology at the University of Pavia; working also as a consultant for municipalities, NGO and private organizations in the field of participation and local governance. He is member of the networks of researchers 'SQEK' ('Squatting in Europe') and 'EURoma' (European network of scholars interested in Roma studies).

Emmanuel Midheme is a PhD student in Spatial Planning and Urban Development at the Catholic University of Leuven, Belgium. His current research focuses on the role of social innovation in the production of urban space within rapidly growing cities and towns of Kenya.

Frank Moulaert is Professor of Spatial Planning, Head of the Planning and Development Unit ASRO, and Chairman of the Leuven Research Centre on Space and Society, Faculty of Engineering, KU Leuven, Belgium. His research covers urban and regional development, social science theories and methods, but especially social innovation.

Andreas Novy is Associate Professor at the Institute for the Environment and Regional Development (RUW) at Wirtschaftsuniversität Vienna. He has published widely in the fields of political economy, development studies and urban and regional development. He has been involved in European research projects (URSPIC, SINGOCOM, DEMOLOGOS, KATARSIS, Social Polis) as well as transdisciplinary research in the field of urban development and development cooperation.

Marthe Nyssens is Professor at UC Louvain and chair of the interdsiciplinary research centre 'Labour, State and Society' (CIRTES). Her research work focuses on conceptual approaches to the third sector (associations, cooperatives, social enterprises . . .), both in developed and developing countries, as well as on the links between third sector organizations and public policies. She investigates the role of these kinds of organizations in comparison with business and public bodies in several fields such as socio-professional integration, social services or social entrepreneurship. She is a founding member of the EMES research network.

Stijn Oosterlynck is Assistant Professor in Urban Sociology at the Department of Sociology, University of Antwerp. His main research interests are the political sociology of urban development, social innovation and its relation to the welfare state, urban planning and globalization and the spatial restructuring of the welfare state.

Constanza Parra is Assistant Professor and Rosalind Franklin Fellow in the Department of Spatial Planning & Environment at the University of Groningen, The Netherlands, and a FWO fellow at ASRO-P&D group, K.U. Leuven, Belgium. Between 2010 and 2011, she was an AFR/Marie Curie postdoctoral fellow at the University of Luxembourg. Her current research focuses on social sustainability, nature-culture nexus in socio-ecological systems, and multi-level governance of protected areas.

Thomas Pilati has a degree in architecture from the University of Florence. After gaining his Master of Arts and Culture Management in 2005, he participated in various research projects on culture and local development and on the creative city.

He deals with the conception of exhibit design: in 2002 with the Fondation Cartier for the Biennale de Montréal in 2007 and the European Biennial of Contemporary Art Manifesta in 2008. At present he works freelance for different museums and contemporary art galleries.

Marc Pradel Miquel is Assistant Professor and PhD candidate in the department of Sociological Theory, Universitat de Barcelona. His research focuses on multi-level governance and the development of new forms of regulation at the local and regional levels. He has also been involved in different research projects focusing on the influence of the European Union in national policy-making processes (EURopub, 2002–2004), creativity as an engine for economic growth (ACRE, 2006–2010) and social creativity as a way to tackle social exclusion (KATARSIS, 2007–2009).

Gerda Roelvink is a Research Fellow in the School of Humanities and Communication Arts at the University of Western Sydney. Her research explores collective action centred on contemporary economic concerns, particularly climate change. She has published a range of articles in journals such as *Antipode, Emotion, Space and Society, Progress in Human Geography, Journal of Cultural Economy, Australian Humanities Review, Rethinking Marxism, Angelaki* and *Social Identities*.

Barbara Schaller is about to finish her PhD studies at POLSIS, University of Birmingham, UK. Her current research focus is on post-Keynesian and institutionalist economics and the coexistence of abundance and poverty in advanced capitalist economies.

P.K. Shajahan is Associate Professor and Chairperson of the South Asia Centre for Studies in Conflicts, Peace and Human Security, School of Social Work, Tata Institute of Social Sciences (TISS), Mumbai. He teaches community organization, social action, disaster management and conflicts and peace at TISS. He is an academic with a strong practice orientation in the field of minority rights and peace processes. His research interests include communal expressions, social cohesion, conflicts and peace.

Dimitra Siatitsa is an architect with an MA in Architecture and Urban Theory (UPC), and a PhD candidate at the Department of Urban and Regional Planning of the National Technical University of Athens (NTUA). Her research interests include housing and welfare in Southern Europe, urban social movements, urban and sustainable development. She has participated in the Coordination Action KATARSIS and other EU-funded projects.

Paul Singer is Professor Emeritus of Economics at the Universidade de São Paulo. He has published widely in the field of development studies, urban and international economics. He has been State Secretary for solidarity economics at the Brazilian Ministry of Labour since 2003.

Chiara Tornaghi is currently ESRC Research Fellow at the Cities and Social Justice research cluster, School of Geography, University of Leeds, developing an action research project on urban agriculture, social cohesion and environmental justice in the UK. She has been Lecturer in Urban Sociology (Politecnico di Milano) and Critical Human Geography (University of Leeds) and visiting junior professor at the Interdisciplinary Centre for Urban Cultures and Public Space (SKuOR), TU Vienna.

Diane-Gabrielle Tremblay is the Canada Research Chair on the socio-organizational challenges of the Knowledge Economy and director of the Community-University Research Alliance on Work-Life over the Lifecourse (www.teluq.ca/aruc-gats) as well as professor at the Business School of the Télé-université of the Université du Québec. She has published many articles and books on governance, local development, employment issues, innovation in the workplace and work organization, as well as the articulation between work and family life.

Dina Vaiou teaches urban analysis and gender studies at the Department of Urban and Regional Planning of the National Technical University of Athens (NTUA). Her research interests include the feminist critique of urban analysis, the changing features of local labour markets, with special emphasis on women's work and informalization processes, the impact of mass migration on Southern European cities and women's migration in particular. She has coordinated several national and European projects.

Pieter Van den Broeck has for the last 16 years been a planning practitioner in OMGEVING, a Belgian private consultancy firm in the field of spatial planning, landscape planning and architecture. He has worked on integrated area development and strategic spatial planning. Since 2005 he has been a part-time researcher at the Catholic University of Leuven (K.U. Leuven) where he finished a PhD on the social construction of planning instruments. His current research interests are in planning instruments and planning systems, institutionalist planning theory, social innovation and territorial governance of socio-ecological systems.

Barbara Van Dyck is a post-doctoral researcher. Motivated by a concern to understand and impact on spatial transformation practices, her research focuses on the political economy of spatial development, social innovation and local development, urban waste land and social movements. In her PhD research at the University of Antwerp (2010) she undertook international comparative research on social innovation in and through urban transformation projects.

Serena Vicari Haddock is currently Senior Associate Professor, Dipartimento di Sociologia e Ricerca Sociale, Università degli Studi di Milano-Bicocca (Italy). Her primary research interests are urban development, regeneration policies in Italian cities from a comparative perspective; her specific focus is on bottom-up and inclusive decision-making processes, social innovation and urban culture.

Tommaso Vitale has a Masters in Political Science (1999) and PhD in Sociology (2002) at the Università degli Studi di Milano, Certificate of Achievement awarded in the Program for Advanced Study in Comparative Institutional Analysis and Design at the Indiana University, Bloomington (2004). He is Associate Professor of Sociology at Sciences Po (Paris, France), where he is the scientific director of the biannual master 'Governing the Large Metropolis' and member of the Centre d'études européennes (CEE) and of the research program 'Cities are back in town'.

Christopher Wright is an Associate Professor with the University of Adelaide Business School, has a multi-disciplinary PhD from Simon Fraser University, was Head of the School of Business (Melbourne Institute of Technology) and Professor of Accounting at Lincoln University (NZ). His industry qualifications include: FCPA (Australia), CMA

(Canada) and FRSA (UK) and his research interests are in accounting theory, micro and small business, microfinance, teaching and finance.

Susan Young is Lecturer in Social Work and Social Policy at the University of Western Australia where she teaches Community Development. She has a long term interest in local developmental practices in various locations around the state and is currently involved in research and developmental work in remote WA and with an innovative school in the metropolitan area of Perth. She has recently co-written a chapter on capacity building in indigenous communities which illustrates some of these developmental practices.

Acknowledgements

The cover image photograph shows a detail from Paolo Ferrari's *Raddoppio in-Cavaliere errante*, part of The Wandering Knight installation at the entrance to *Il Dado* (The Dice) Roma housing initiative, Turin, photographed by Simona Riboni. It is reproduced with the kind permission of the artist and the photographer.

Chapter 34 has been developed from an earlier paper published in MacCallum, Moulaert, Hillier and Vicari Haddock (2009), *Social Innovation and Territorial Development*, with the permission of Ashgate Publishing.

The editors would like to thank the colleagues who reviewed and provided comments on draft chapters for this book: John Andersen, Isabel Andre, Len Arthur, Stuart Cameron, André Carmo, Kristian Delica, Ana Dubeux, Santi Eizaguirre Anglada, Laurent Fraisse, Marisol García Cabeza, Juan-Luis Klein, Flavia Martinelli, Andreas Novy, Marthe Nyssens, Stijn Oosterlynck, Constanza Parra, Marc Pradel Miquel, Dimitra Siatitsa, Pieter Van den Broeck, Dina Vaiou, Barbara Van Dyck, Serena Vicari Haddock.

We also wish to thank the more than hundred participants in the Social Polis and KATARSIS workshops who discussed and commented upon working documents preceding many of the chapters in this book.

General introduction: the return of social innovation as a scientific concept and a social practice

Frank Moulaert, Diana MacCallum, Abid Mehmood and Abdelillah Hamdouch

In recent years, social innovation has become increasingly influential in both scholarship and policy. It is the conceptual foundation for community-based trusts, think tanks, corporate management practices and government funding programs in every continent, leading to a wide range of projects and international networks which recognize past failures of conventional service delivery to tackle poverty and social exclusion, and seek to promote new ways of doing things, grounded in the social relations and experiences of those in need. It is the great inspiration for many social movements, associations, bottom-up initiatives to claim improvements in their human conditions, their community life and their place in society. It has found a home in policy at the highest level, for example in the US Whitehouse's Office for Social Innovation and Civic Participation, through the creation of the National Secretariat for Solidarity Economy in Brazil and in the European Commission's Innovation Policy programmes. It has become a lead term for corporate social responsibility, business ethics and the revisiting of the role of social enterprise and the social economy in socioeconomic development. The growing importance of the idea reflects wide and profound dissatisfaction with recent directions and outcomes of 'innovation' in technology, markets, policy and governance systems, and particularly a sense – to remain polite – that the benefits of such innovations have not been distributed as generally or as equitably as they should (see Jessop et al., Chapter 8). This also holds for changes in socio-political regimes. Social innovation as a governance change with more bottom-up participation, protection of the rights of 'common' citizens and collective decision-making systems has indeed increasingly become a mirror to reflect on the consequences of macro-institutional changes such as the privatization of banks and social services, deregulation of markets at the expense of the satisfaction of collective needs, the heralding of elite consumerism as a value system, etc.

In much policy and management discourse, social innovation refers broadly to innovation in meeting social needs of, or delivering social benefits to, communities – the creation of new products, services, organizational structures or activities that are 'better' or 'more effective' than traditional public sector, philanthropic or market-reliant approaches in responding to social exclusion. Particularly successful forms of social innovation in this sense, which to many people represent 'iconic' examples, include microfinance and popular education – game-changing initiatives which have travelled well beyond their original geographical and social contexts to find permanent institutional homes in the public services of many countries (see for example Ashta et al., Chapter 6; Dubeux, Chapter 22; Fernandes et al., Chapter 29). Equally important, and part

1

of the continuously evolving dynamic nature of social innovation, are practical lessons drawn from social enterprises and the third sector economy, as several chapters in this volume demonstrate (e.g. Defourny and Nyssens, Chapter 3; Calzada, Chapter 16; Fraisse, Chapter 27; Klein et al., Chapter 28).

THE PURPOSE OF THE HANDBOOK

The purpose of this handbook is, in part, to honour such initiatives. However, it is also to present a coherent methodological perspective on social innovation, one which attends – both conceptually and practically – to multi-scalar structural, political and cultural forces which produce social exclusion but also hold the potential for social change and socially innovative initiatives. As such, it develops a line of thought, investigated and progressively enriched collectively by many of the contributors to this volume over the past thirty years (see Moulaert et al., Chapter 1), which connects societal wellbeing and progress with the shape and organization of society – relations of power, solidarity and affect between individuals and social groups.

Fundamental to the understanding of social innovation that we present here is that it means *innovation in social relations*. As such, we see the term as referring not just to particular actions, but also to the mobilization-participation processes and to the *outcome* of actions which lead to improvements in social relations, structures of governance, greater collective empowerment, and so on. Thus many of the chapters refer to such actions as 'socially innovative strategies' and at the same time consider their processual nature, the way they contribute to the

transformation of governance systems and community dynamics in different life spheres (biosystem, economy, society and polity) as well as the articulations between them (see for example Lévesque, Chapter 2; Hulgård and Shajahan, Chapter 7; Van Dyck and Van den Broeck, Chapter 9; Parra, Chapter 10; Andersen et al., Chapter 14; Andersen and Bifeldt, Chapter 24; Martinelli, Chapter 26; Espinoza, Chapter 30; André, Chapter 31).

The handbook is framed by three generic and interrelated features of social innovation: satisfaction of needs, reconfigured social relations and empowerment or political mobilization. The power of this three dimensional framework rests with its ability to simultaneously acknowledge and connect the material, social, political and discursive dimensions of exclusion processes with collective action to the benefit of human development in different life spheres of the human world. We are concerned with social innovation (SI) not only as a descriptor for a set of practices but, more importantly, as an emerging phenomenon, a theoretical construct and an ongoing field of research within a world of social transformation.

SI occurs because socially innovative actions, strategies, practices and processes arise whenever problems of poverty, exclusion, segregation and deprivation or opportunities for improving living conditions cannot find satisfactory solutions in the 'institutionalized field' of public or private action. As demonstrated in many chapters of the handbook (for example Tremblay and Pilati, Chapter 5; Vitale and Membretti, Chapter 13; Midheme, Chapter 15; André et al., Chapter 18; Kunnen et al., Chapter 21; Gibson-Graham and Roelvink, Chapter 33) in all continents, most countries, regions, cities or even urban districts where socio-economic-political-cultural-environmental problems or opportunities for improvement touching the existential and living conditions of people have arisen, socially innovative approaches and solutions emerged that shared a common profile, one in which the social and political empowerment of people is fundamental to meeting their unmet needs; in which improving material conditions and changing social relations are intimately and necessarily connected. Accordingly, social innovation can also be viewed as a general, shared 'consciousness' about the nature of problems that modern societies face and the ways that they should be confronted. It is from this perspective a real challenge to the reading of innovation in technological and organizational terms only (see Jessop et al., Chapter 8).

Social Innovation is also a scientific construct as the concept has not only emerged 'spontaneously' from the social field per se or from the practices of certain actors, but also from the need for researchers investigating the phenomena described above to capture analytically the essence of innovative initiatives, experiences and processes that have been historically or more recently engaged for facing structural problems of social exclusion and inequality. Several chapters in the book address the (need for) theorization of social innovation. Chapters 1 and 8 explain the genesis of the concept and how in different periods and contexts it has received a more disciplinary or interdisciplinary content; a more process or agency-based interpretation; how it is connected to social change, to societal challenges and to micro-logical behaviour addressing very particular needs. All chapters in Part II explain the need for theoretical *particularity* according to the role of social innovation in territorial development (Van Dyck and Van den Broeck, Chapter 9; also Oosterlynck and Debruyne, Chapter 17), sustainable development (Mehmood

and Parra, Chapter 4; Parra, Chapter 10), multi-level governance and political transformation (Pradel et al., Chapter 11). Methodological improvements – including revisiting the different roles of theory – are addressed in Chapter 12 (Hillier presenting a Deleuzean perspective), the chapters on action research in Part IV (Chapters 19–25) and the methodological chapters in Part VI (Chapters 32–35) which establish transdisciplinary methods for SI research in which theory-building as a component of action research plays an important part.

SI research is an ongoing field of research for at least three key reasons. Firstly, most of the social problems in our societies are far from being solved, and new ones are likely to arise as globalization, competitive pressures and free-market policies will continue to shape the socio-economic functioning of the society. At the same time constructive visions on how human development can be furthered are revealed on a daily basis and need collective action and implementation. Consequently, new socially creative approaches and initiatives will be needed and will continue to emerge and feed the knowledge accumulated by the researchers. Secondly, research methodologies on social innovation are far from being stabilized or agreed upon by all researchers and stakeholders, and debate, controversy and imagination will be the key to methodological improvement. But perhaps this is a normal condition if researchers and field actors endeavour to improve their knowledge of 'what is going on' in society and step forward, together with other SI actors, to design, negotiate and implement new solutions. The final reason is probably the most important and also the most challenging for researchers: it is about how to position themselves in the 'social arena' and how to contribute to its transformation. Here, undoubtedly, cross learning and dialogue among researchers and field actors should continue.

OUTLINE OF THE BOOK

The concerns outlined above are reflected in the way the book unfolds. We have divided the chapters into six parts, each of which has its own introduction outlining the individual chapters and the relations between them in more detail.

Part I ('Social innovation: from concept to theory and practice') demonstrates the relevance and prospects of the social innovation concept and its theorization to a range of topical life spheres, policy fields and practices. The increased proliferation of social innovation discourse is closely linked with the absence of an integrative framework for social innovation approaches. As a result, social innovation is often seen as a set of tools to provide instant solutions to pressing problems. The assortment of perspectives, coupled with the propensity for reductionist views and the need to overcome this propensity, has been the inspiration for the chapters in this part. The part explores social innovation from an epistemological perspective and highlights the social, economic, political, environmental and ethical importance of asserting its place as a key element of an alternative development strategy. In that sense, social innovation is presented as a driver of transdisciplinary research as well as a guide for steering collective action in a diversity of life spheres.

Part II ('Social innovation theory: its role in knowledge building') presents a series of theoretical dialogues which place social innovation in relation to various fields of scholarship. Social innovation has a deep and complex conceptual heritage, which has been informed by – and has informed – debates within sociology, economics, geography, urban studies, political science, philosophy and more. Social innovation, in this sense, has become a key concept driving a body of knowledge with a strong interdisciplinary and transdisciplinary character. The contributions in this part address the value of theorizing social innovation and putting it in dialogue with related concepts (territorialization, sustainable development, multilevel governance, strategic planning, etc.). The chapters in this part do not intend to formulate a definitive theory of social innovation; this would indeed be contradictory to the epistemic diversity that is inherent in the transdisciplinary reflexive methodology that is adopted. Instead they discuss a number of conceptual elaborations and theoretical explorations that provide building stones for this methodology – summarized especially in Chapter 8 but also in Part VI of the book.

Part III ('Instructive case studies in social innovation analysis') supports the aim of this handbook to help refine conceptual and analytical instruments by utilizing them in empirical research especially addressing questions of how socially creative strategies can develop to address social exclusion or materialize opportunities for human development of various kinds. The focus here is on practice, in the form of six case studies which nicely capture some characteristics of socially innovative action. Of particular interest in this part is how widely varying actors and strategies, in a diversity of sociocultural and socio-political contexts, can materialize social innovation (in all its dimensions) at the local and regional levels. These case studies provide inspiring tales of tribulations and triumphs in the initiation of socially creative strategies. They also go beyond mere storytelling by analysing the societal dynamics, change potentials and actual impacts of these socially innovative actions and processes.

Part IV ('Social innovation analysis: methodologies') is about the conduct of research. It emphasizes throughout the importance of the researcher's position in relation to the 'what', the 'how' and the 'who' of the research. That is, social innovation, as a form of social change and empowerment, cannot be understood 'objectively' – and no more can our analysis of it. As such, the part pays special attention to various forms of participatory and action research. Such approaches see the creative production of knowledge and the pursuit of social goals as intrinsically linked, and as such they problematize the 'researcher's' relationships (of power and affect) with those 'researched'. Ongoing reflection on whose knowledge researchers and other SI actors are producing and using, to what end and for whose benefit, becomes central to the process of enquiry.

Part V ('Collective action, institutional leverage and public policy') explores a crucial issue at the interface between social innovation research and social innovation action and processes in the 'real world': SI's capacity to mobilize collective action and leverage institutional resources at a broad scale or to feed into society-wide dynamics (social services, social economy, regional governance model, social movements, diversity policies). The relationship between state institutions and social innovation is complex and can be fraught with tensions as well as opportunities. Certainly, both policy and public funding are crucial to the emergence and success of many socially innovative actions and practices; moreover the sustainability of such practices often requires institutionalization at a higher scale or level which, in turn, may both shape the path for local development and allow for other people, in other places and social contexts, to learn from situated experience. Documentation and analysis, as represented by these chapters, can make an important contribution to these collective learning and (mainly tacit) knowledge diffusion processes.

Part VI ('Frontiers in social innovation research') considers new directions in social innovation research, with particular reference to *meta-theoretical* frameworks that shape our understanding of what it is that we – as researchers interested in social change across multiple fields and spatial scales – are doing and in which society and social change processes we are doing it. Trandisciplinarity, holistic research methodologies, pragmatic collective action and more are discussed as to their potential contribution to better integrating the 'research side' (understanding the reality) and the 'action side' (changing the reality) of SI. Highlighted throughout this part is the question of ethics – not the formal research ethics that form part of academic governance, but a more reflexive ethics that places research foci, discourses and methods in the context of the world that we live in, and the one that we wish to live in. This question of ethics cannot be handled by researchers by themselves but should be addressed in collaboration with all actors involved in a SI initiative or change process (Chapter 34). This is why we have summarized the basic methodological style in SI research as 'trandisciplinary reflexivity' (Chapter 32). Methodologies enacting this style such as holism in the old institutionalist tradition (Chapter 33) and an enriched sociology of knowledge and practice approach (Chapter 35) would fit this style.

OPENING THE FIELD

The chapters in this handbook illustrate the extraordinary richness of social innovation as an area of research, action and social change. They also show the non-trivial relationships between 'knowing' and 'theorizing', 'hoping' and 'doing', 'experiencing' and 'institutionalizing' whenever the 'social matter' and its possible transformation through research and action are the focus.

The conviction shared by the editors and contributors is that this handbook is a step in consolidating our understanding and promotion of social innovation. As such, we believe that it provides material, analysis and insights to demonstrate that social innovation is neither a 'miracle' or a 'chimera', nor a vain quest. It is at the heart of our *present and future core societal concerns*, and it challenges all of us, be we 'committed academics', 'social and political actors', 'activists' or 'ordinary people' (i.e. the people and communities who are precisely the most affected by social problems or preoccupied by fostering new modes of human development). Research and action together have opened the window on new beliefs and practices by providing documented insights on 'how things may change'; we maintain that this implies a commitment to finding the 'right' balance between 'research on action', 'action in research' and 'research through and by action'. A vast program indeed, challenging for generations of researchers, but a genuinely promising one.

We hope that the varied, complementary contributions to this handbook inspire readers by showing a positive, practical and analytically forceful alternative to many contemporary discourses and practices of market-led innovation and economic development. While social innovation analysis is by necessity rigorously critical of these often dominant discourses and processes, it highlights at the same time the capacities and commitment of the thousands of organizations, networks, social enterprises and movements representing millions of people working for SI. In providing a collection of SI research, this handbook reflects upon what has been learnt through more than three decades of social innovation research efforts, socially creative initiatives and their relationship to social change processes; it also opens questions and raises challenges for further creative research. We therefore hope that it will encourage many of our peers and students to continue 'the good work'.

PART I

SOCIAL INNOVATION: FROM CONCEPT TO THEORY AND PRACTICE

Introduction: social innovation at the crossroads between science, economy and society
Juan-Luis Klein

As the general introduction and many chapters in this handbook show, social innovation is in vogue. Up until some years ago, the very idea of social innovation was, at best, seen as a part of the organizational changes necessary for implementing technological innovations or, at worst, virtually unheard of. However, of late there has been a proliferation of literature that refers to social innovation. Public institutions at all levels (international, national, regional and local) are launching new programs to promote social innovations, alongside organizations in support of these efforts and studies that describe and explain them.[1] What is all the buzz about? The failings and inconsistencies of the neoliberal growth model that has prevailed worldwide since the 1980s are certainly a key factor.

However, such a proliferation of discourse and works on social innovation shows the absence of an integrative framework and a great diversity of approaches. Among the latter, many see social innovation as a tool box that could provide rapid solutions to pressing problems. It is this diversity, together with the propensity for reductionist views – which in fact renders social innovation contributive to neoliberalism – that inspired the writing of this book that aims to establish an analytical framework of the principles and orientations required to approach social innovation from a societal rather than just a utilitarian perspective. The section of the book we introduce here analyses social innovation from an epistemological perspective and highlights the political and social importance of asserting the place of social innovation as an ingredient of an alternative development strategy. In that sense, social innovation will be presented as a driver of transdisciplinary research and a guide for collective action, both interrelated.

The first chapter, written by Moulaert, MacCallum and Hillier, examines the wide range of definitions of social innovation and their theoretical basis, criticizing the reductionist visions that regard social innovation simply as a means to deal with the most pressing problems of the most vulnerable segments of society. It presents social innovation as a force that upholds the values of solidarity and equity, fostering research and actions that aims at building a more socially inclusive society. But, as the authors say, social innovation is not a recipe that can be applied in any conditions. It is path dependent and contextual, therefore social innovation oriented researchers and actors should consider the global and the local and a solid interaction between theory and practice in order to contribute to social change. According to Moulaert et al. social innovation research should be engaged with complexity, in theory as well as in action terms, and give a place to social actors in the building of a theoretical framework. The compilation of texts included in this section of the book contributes to further developing this vision.

Chapter 2, written by Lévesque, discusses social innovation with regard to the governance of public administration. The changes that governments have realized to adapt to the demands of the market, by adopting management principles derived from private business practice, are compared with the implementation of a collaborative mode of governance. What was hailed as the 'new public management' is juxtaposed against the 'new public value', a management method based on participatory governance and the networking of all actors involved in the production of services, including the users. Such a management method can only be implemented if coalitions of social and economic actors become mobilized, undertake collective actions and ensure that the method is not undermined for the sake of short-term profitability.

In Chapter 3, Defourny and Nyssens present social innovation in relation to the social economy and the new social entrepreneurship. The text presents the social actors as crucial for the implementation of inclusive networks that promote collaboration between diverse types of actors, namely social economy organizations and businesses. The social economy, comprised of diverse types of organizations that are not driven by personal gain and return on investment but that nevertheless play a considerable economic role, becomes increasingly important in a welfare state characterized by crisis. The social economy sector participates in the provision of services and addresses the needs neglected by private capital or public bodies, while interlinking diverse categories of actors and supporting social experimentation. Governed by a hybrid rationale combining the market, personal development and public interest, social economy organizations and businesses are a breeding ground for social experiments

that, through their dissemination, contribute to the construction of public policies.

Chapter 4, by Mehmood and Parra, frames social innovation as the necessary motor for a sustainable development vision that includes the social dimension. Criticizing the too-technical and reductionist perspective that prevails in sustainable development theories, the chapter insists on the advantages of cross-fertilization between the environmental and the social options. However, achieving this requires avoiding the traps of technical normativeness and localism. The capacity of collective reflection, to which Moulaert et al. appeal, and the implementation of a collaborative governance, invoked by Lévesque, here merge with the need for an approach that is both trans-sectoral and trans-scalar and that takes account of the holistic and comprehensive dimension required to reach a sustainable human development.

Chapter 5, by Tremblay and Pilati, is concerned with social innovation in the arts. The chapter underlines the new importance acquired by culture with regard to human resources development and the strengthening of the social capital of communities. Cultural projects also have an economic importance because they intervene in the creation of value and in the networking of productive and non-productive activities. Moreover, they build capacities that allow the improvement of the living conditions of those in low-income neighbourhoods, and develop bridges between these neighbourhoods and other neighbourhoods of the city, thereby strengthening socio-territorial cohesion.

Chapter 6 focuses on microfinancing as an innovative response to poverty and the incapability of the most disempowered to obtain the necessary loans to launch projects that would improve their living environments, provide services or create productive businesses. Because the main beneficiaries of microcredits are women, microfinancing also contributes to the social and economic empowerment of women, and thereby to improving the living conditions of the whole family. Microcredits thus have positive effects on the entire collectivity, integrating the excluded into production and consumption. Largely based on trust, which makes for its local and community rootedness, microcredits allow the construction of social and productive networks that go far beyond the local and that, linking up with other more traditional financial networks, contribute to a more inclusive regional and national economic development.

The last chapter of this part (Chapter 7), by Hulgård and Shajahan, presents the characteristics of an integrative model referred to as 'people-centred development', which includes knowledge production and social intervention. Developed in response to the needs in Mumbai, a city marked by urban and social vulnerability, this model offers the possibility of spreading and adapting in diverse societies. It is based on the collaboration between researchers and community actors in the production of knowledge that is applicable to community development. The model embodies a new paradigm in which the collaboration between actors involves a fusion of cultures and a common understanding of the stakes. This allows marginalized communities to build a knowledge framework in which the actors learn collectively and promote open innovation based on sharing and solidarity.

Social innovation thus appears as the foundation for an alternative to the neoliberalist societal vision. Favouring solidarity over individualism, integration over sectoralization, and collaboration over division, it distinguishes itself through epistemological, ethical and strategic approaches.

At the epistemological level, this alternative vision considers social innovation as part of a paradigm shift. Knowledge is to be the result of a co-construction, a collaborative effort of researchers and actors, and should take account of local and global factors in a holistic and sustainable perspective. At the ethical level, social innovations function as a means to learn collectively and to increase the capabilities of the most vulnerable people to better their living conditions. This latter aspect also includes the improvement of the capabilities for transforming the institutional environment that keeps this segment of society in a state of precariousness and that widens the social and economic gaps. At the strategic level, social innovation becomes the driver of an inclusive project in which wealth is produced and shared thanks to the networking of political, economic, environmental and social actors of the collectivity. For this, as the chapters of this part show, it is important to integrate the global, national and local levels, as well as the diverse spheres of human activity, namely the public, social and private spheres. Public institutions should play a key role here, albeit in consideration of the specificities of the civil society actors who, as shown by analyses of the social economy, the environment, culture, microcredits and anti-poverty actions, are an endless source of innovation.

NOTE

1. Concerning recent works that explicitly refer to social innovation, see Klein and Harrisson 2007; Moulaert and Nussbaumer 2008; Drewe, Klein and Hulsbergen, 2008; MacCallum et al. 2009; Gallouj and Djellal 2010; and, Richez-Battesti et al., 2012. To that we should add the works created in the framework of centres and work groups that dedicate their efforts to the description and analysis of social innovation, such as KATARSIS (http://katarsis.ncl.

ac.uk), CRISES (http://www.crises.uqam.ca/) or Innobasque (http://www.innobasque.com/home.aspx?tabid=811) to name just a few (all websites last accessed 7 January 2013).

REFERENCES

Drewe, P., J.-L. Klein and E. Hulsbergen (eds) (2008), *The Challenge of Social Innovation in Urban Revitalization,* Amsterdam: Techne Press.

Gallouj, F. and F. Djellal (eds) (2010), *The Handbook of Innovation and Services,* Cheltenham, UK: Edward Elgar Publishing.

Klein, J.-L. and D. Harrison (eds) (2007), *L'innovation sociale. Émergence et effets sur la transformation des sociétés,* Québec: Presses de l'Université du Québec.

MacCallum, D., F. Moulaert, J. Hillier and S. Vicari Haddock (eds) (2009), *Social Innovation and Territorial Development,* Farnham: Ashgate.

Moulaert, F. and J. Nussbaumer (2008), *La logique sociale du développement territorial,* Québec: Presses de l'Université du Québec.

Richez-Battesti, N., F. Petrella and D. Vallade (eds) (2012), 'L'innovation sociale. Acteurs et Système', *Innovations, Cahiers d'Économie de l'Innovation,* **38**, 2.

1. Social innovation: intuition, precept, concept, theory and practice

Frank Moulaert, Diana MacCallum and Jean Hillier

1.1 INTRODUCTION

Reading and talking about social innovation, as the authors of this chapter have done for many years, do not necessarily make its scientific meaning unambiguously clear. In our opinion, the lack of clarity about the term 'social innovation' can be attributed not only to its evolving analytical status but also to its over-simplistic use as a buzzword in a multiplicity of policy practices associated, for example, with the rationalization of the welfare state and the commodification of sociocultural wellbeing. The appropriation of the term by 'caring liberalism', in one of its new incarnations, has added to a Babel-like terminological confusion. For example, several of the roll-out neoliberalization strategies, like 'new governance' and 'experimental reregulation', if not critically examined, could be considered as forms of social innovation (Peck 2013).

Social innovation (SI), appropriately utilized, is a driver of interdisciplinarity and transdisciplinarity[1] in scientific research whose epistemological and methodological stances are in continuous development. It is used as a label to indicate significant changes in the way society evolves, how its structures are modified, its ethical norms revisited, etc. Such changes are, in the first place, the concern of collective action, public policy, socio-political movements, public uprising, spontaneous organization, etc. But they are also important issues in philosophical and ethical debates, in social theory and in the search for new social science methodologies capable of addressing emerging SI questions. Cooperrider and Pasmore predicted in 1991 that 'the 1990s will be known as the decade of global social innovation' (1991, p. 1037). This may be an overstatement, granting too much honour to the 1990s as a turning-point decade; but these authors nevertheless point to a changing dynamic in efforts to improve the quality of life throughout the world.

Innovative forms of organizing across traditional boundaries of geography, cultures, and politics are springing to life to address long-standing global problems such as hunger, poverty, conflict, political imprisonment, pollution, illiteracy, economic oppression, racism, classism, sexism, and environmental degradation. These innovative forms of organization represent an emerging type of social behaviour that has no historical precedent (Cooperrider and Pasmore 1991, p. 1038).

What Cooperrider and Pasmore refer to here is the new organizational form of 'Global Social Change Organizations' (GSCO) operating internationally in the above problem areas. Of course, there have been historical precedents in social transformation and collective action. Before the GSCO there were the labour unions, human rights organizations, socio-political movements for independence: a great variety of organizations that in different socio-political contexts and epochs addressed social problems and desires and strived for a 'better world'; an improvement of the 'human condition' etc.

The confused status of the term 'social innovation' in both collective action and research is expressed in the summative title of this chapter, which articulates a growing degree of rational reflection about, as well as rationally organized mobilization inspired by, the concept. But in choosing this title, we reflect the way John Commons – one of the main US economists working in the old institutionalist tradition and also considered both a holist and a pragmatist (see Moulaert and Mehmood, Chapter 33) – developed his holistic definitions and theories (Moulaert and Nussbaumer 2005).[2] Commons' intellectual constructions were not linear but interactive. 'Precept' refers to ethical principles inspiring human behaviour. It thus evokes the ethics not only of collective action, but also of the process of pragmatist-holistic scientific inquiry, which, according to its epistemological premises, should be to the benefit of humans and humanity. But 'precept' also refers to 'pre'-concept, the intuitive maturation of what may become a 'concept' or a 'theme' later on in the research and/or collective action. Concepts or themes then, through their relations with other themes and within a diversity of comparative contexts, are potential building blocks of theories. Thus themes and theories are built through collective or shared intuitions, concerns about human progress and how collective action to achieve such progress should be organized and materialized as a going concern. This 'old' institutionalist reading of scientific practice resonates with the concerns we are trying to address in inter- and transdisciplinary research in social science today. As such, SI, as one of the most frequently discussed topics in social analysis, collective action and policy, is a lever for 'post' disciplinary research, because it forces us

to bypass the delimitations between problems and fields of knowledge or practice in the methodologies to be used (Moulaert et al. 2011). This book demonstrates that SI research is never 'purely scientific', but is always about human development ambitions as represented by a diversity of social actors and individuals. It also clearly shows that research cannot be the responsibility of a single social science discipline, nor entrusted to theoretical and empirical analysis only, but that it has, instead, a strong action orientation (see in particular Parts I and IV).

'Social Innovation' as the new dimension of management science (Drucker 1987), has defended collective action and new global social change organizations as key modes of coordination for the contemporary provision of social services (Young Foundation 2010; BEPA 2010), as suspect reformist 'solutions' for the scarcity of resources in the welfare state (see Martinelli, Chapter 26). This diversity of often contradictory meanings has even caused some scholars to drop it as a scientific concept, because they believe that its chameleonic character would not serve any progress in the analysis of social change. We do not share this sceptical viewpoint. Instead we want to show how SI has been a driver of social science analysis and that the various entry points to the use of the term reflect well the societal challenges of our and previous times.

In the next section we recount the history of definitions of SI, their theoretical underpinnings and their connections with other concepts of social change and invention. Next, we briefly address the ideological-political significance of SI as a reformist approach to solve social problems – an expression of 'soft or caring neoliberalism', but more pertinently as an ideological reaction against an economistic and technologist view of socioeconomic and socio-political development. In the subsequent section we explain how our work on SI, especially addressing its socially and spatially embedded nature, has contributed to progress in SI analysis. The final section suggests some important (new) methodological avenues in SI analysis and theory building, including granting new roles for theory, such as meta-theoretical frameworks and holistic theory building.

1.2   WHAT IS SOCIAL INNOVATION?

It is not clear who first used the term 'social innovation'. Some argue it was James Taylor in 1970 in his analysis of community development dynamics in Topeka, Kansas. We believe that the term was coined on the European continent, amidst the social revolts of the late 1960s. The 'competing' term 'social invention' was in use much earlier, launched by Max Weber (1947[1920]) in the early 1900s. James Coleman (1970) uses the term 'social invention' to describe new forms of social relationship and social organization, while Stuart Conger (1973) makes three distinctions in social invention: organizational social inventions; social inventions in the form of laws; and procedural social inventions. Affiliated concepts, such as social change and transformation, and innovations with a social meaning, were introduced and reintroduced at different points in time. Important also are the authors who interpret social changes in terms of SI, as Peter Drucker (1987) does for management and mass movements; or Michael Mumford (2002) for the innovations which Benjamin Franklin introduced in 19th-century Philadelphia.

What is important for our analysis is that 'social innovation' has been launched as a term for many different reasons and in a diversity of contexts. For example, in the 1960s and early 1970s with the student and workers' movements in Paris, Berlin, and other European and American cities, SI was used as a kind of common denominator for the different types of collective actions and social transformations that would lead us from a top down economy and society into a more bottom up, creative and participative society that would also recognize, almost in a progressive-liberal way, the different individual rights of people in all segments of the population (Chambon et al. 1982). It was a time when discussions about students' and workers' democracy, gender and emancipation issues were taken on board in public debate. Chambon, David and Devevey (1982) build on most of the issues highlighted in this debate. Their 128-page book remains the most complete 'open' synthesis on the subject of SI to this day. In brief, the authors examine the relationship between SI and the pressures brought by societal changes, and show how the mechanisms of crisis and recovery both provoke and accelerate SI. Much of the debate was echoed in the columns of the journal *Autrement* in the 1970s with contributions from such prominent figures as Pierre Rosanvallon, Jacques Fournier and Jacques Attali.

Peter Drucker (1987) uses 'social innovation' as a hinge term to refer to the need for organizational slimness and human synergies within management. In this context, he also refers to a grand societal challenge, namely to overcome the unwieldiness of large bureaucracies in business and government – a discourse which in more recent times has been unfortunately misused in defence of New Public Management styles and models (see Lévesque, Chapter 2). Drucker also refers to other SIs in business and public life, such as mass movements, the farm agent and management – historical examples which should continue to play a role within the academic debate. Another use of the term SI is due to Jonathan Gershuny in his article on 'Technology, Social Innovation and the Informal Economy' (1987). Gershuny, one of the main authorities in the study of the service economy, refers to the substitution of domestic appliances for domestic labour time as a major SI as in this way people can liberate housework time in favour of leisure activities – a large number of which, again thanks to technological progress, can be enjoyed at home (home video, TV, . . .). Obviously this is a significant social transformation. But is it also a social innovation?

As noted above, several authors have addressed dimensions of SI without using the term. Among the most important we consider the following. As far back as the 18th century, Benjamin Franklin evoked SI in proposing minor modifications within the social organization of communities (Mumford 2002) and in 1893 Émile Durkheim highlighted the importance of social regulation in the development of the division of labour which accompanies technical change. Indeed, technical change itself can only be understood within the framework of an innovation or renovation of the social order to which it is relevant. At the start of the 20th century, Max Weber (1947[1920]) demonstrated the power of rationalization in his work on the capitalist system. He examined the relationship between social order and innovation, a theme which was revisited by philosophers in the 1960s. Among other things, he affirmed that changes in living conditions are not the only determinants of social change. Individuals who introduce behavioural variants, often initially considered deviant, can exert a decisive influence; if the new behaviour spreads and develops, it can become established social usage. In the 1930s, Joseph Schumpeter considered

innovation as including structural change in the organization of society, or within the network of organizational forms of enterprise or business. Schumpeter's theory of innovation went far beyond the usual economic logic, and appealed to an ensemble of sociologies (cultural, artistic, economic, political, and so on), which he sought to integrate into a comprehensive social theory – a Sociology of Knowledge – that would allow the analysis of both development and innovation (Schumpeter 2005[1932]).

Today, and certainly in this book, when we talk about SI we refer to finding acceptable progressive solutions for a whole range of problems of exclusion, deprivation, alienation, lack of wellbeing, and also to those actions that contribute positively to significant human progress and development. SI means fostering inclusion and wellbeing through improving social relations and empowerment processes: imagining and pursuing a world, a nation, a region, a locality, a community that would grant universal rights and be more socially inclusive. Socially innovative change means the improvement of social relations – micro relations between individuals and people, but also macro relations between classes and other social groups. It also means a focus on the different skills by which collective actors and groups play their roles in society.

If SI is about addressing problems, improving the human condition, satisfying the needs of humans, setting agendas for a better future, and so on, then as a scientific concept it should include the search for improvement or fulfilment of human existence, a better equilibrium in living together, together with the evolution of relations between human beings and the initiation of actions to improve the human condition. Several more contemporary definitions cover all or part of these concerns, as in the SINGOCOM project (explained in Section 1.4).

SI is considered as path dependent and contextual. It refers to the changes and agendas, agency and institutions that lead to a better inclusion of excluded groups and individuals into various fields of societies at various spatial scales. SI is very strongly a matter of process innovation of changes and the dynamics of social relations including power relations. Therefore, SI is about social inclusion and about countering or overcoming conservative forces that are eager to strengthen or preserve social exclusion situations. SI, therefore, explicitly refers to an ethical position of social justice; the latter is, of course, susceptible to a variety of interpretations and will in practice often be the outcome of social construction (Moulaert et al. 2010).

Other definitions stress the role of SI in building workable 'utopias'. For Gilles Deleuze, for example, SI takes place through windows of opportunity for social creativity along lines of life, lines of imagination, lines of bringing in assets for a better future. All these are windows of opportunity for social creativity which may emerge from challenges to institutional practices. Innovation often emerges from conflict: opportunity spaces at micro scales may make creative strategies possible at macro scales. Here, we already see the announcement of the very important relationship between the initiatives of individuals and groups in small communities, and its logic of continuation in the construction and facilitation of institutions that could enable socially creative strategies at macro/micro scales.

We can see in these definitions, as we pointed out before, that there is always concern about the human condition: to overcome social exclusion, to improve the quality of service provision, to improve the quality of human life and of wellbeing.

This means of course that SI cannot be separated either from its social-cultural, or from its social-political context. But at the same time it implies a commitment to engage with SI research itself in a democratic way, by involving all actors concerned with improving the human condition and by building transdisciplinary action research models to allow this.

1.3   THE POLITICO-IDEOLOGICAL SIGNIFICANCE OF SOCIAL INNOVATION

SI has a very strong politico-ideological significance. We have already noted the contribution of the students' and workers' revolts of the 1960s and the different types of collective action that work against social exclusion in contemporary times. In the 1990s, this especially meant addressing social exclusion not only in deprived urban neighbourhoods, but also in rural localities where decline due to socioeconomic problems had gone almost unnoticed for decades (Moulaert and Nussbaumer 2007).

Today, the social problematic addressed through SI has become much more complex, due to the deepening of mutually-reinforcing socioeconomic, socio-political and socio-ecological crises (Swyngedouw 2009). Today's use of the term has become quite ambiguous, as we have noted (see also Jessop et al., Chapter 8). On the one hand it remains a powerful guide for social and political movements pursuing human development. But on the other hand SI is increasingly embraced as a 'new' approach to solving the crisis of the welfare state, by creating new jobs in the 'cheap' social economy and reorganizing the welfare system through commodification and privatization of some of its services and the more efficient restructure of others. Jamie Peck (2013) demonstrates the Janus face of many strategies of 'rolling out' neoliberalism. Many of these strategies are realized in the form of 'fast policy' programs, spreading rapidly across the globe; a phenomenon that brings a risk that SI can become packaged as part of the pervasive language of 'best practice' that can be applied anywhere in the world. The problem of this fast policy approach is that it follows a micro-logic of a 'silver bullet', ubiquitously applicable, while in reality all conditions are different, context matters and institutional embedding – including 'taking to scale' – are essential if socially innovative policies and collective strategies are to succeed (Peck 2013, pp. 18–19).

This is why it so important to focus on the role of SI in developing alternative socio-political discourses and on its potential for social change in particular contexts. In any case, SI as a principle, as a slogan, as a *mot d'ordre* as Deleuze would say, has a clear mobilizing power in reaction to economic and technologist interpretations and applications of innovation. From a scientific point of view, particularly in the light of our ambition to develop a more action-oriented research methodology, this means that we must analyse the relationship between the system to which many of the SI actors are reacting and the political significance of their SI initiatives. What are the exclusionary and alienating dynamics of the economic system against which SI is reacting? What dynamics feed into the improvement of the human condition? What social or political movements are of relevance for social change? What socio-political dynamics and institutional transformations are needed in order to make SI a success in the streets, the local communities, the enterprises?

There are many possible answers to these questions, and thus many dimensions to SI as a politico-ideological alternative. It has been deliberately mobilized in reaction to privatization discourse and practice (Moulaert and Nussbaumer 2005): it offers an antithesis to the thesis of privatization, and inspires a counter-ideology of solidarity. But SI has also frequently been a matter of spontaneous mobilization of people against their exclusion, their alienation, the deprivation of resources caused by capitalism, by personal isolation, by difficult social circumstances, by environmental and economic changes, and so on. Reacting against often oppressive mainstream institutionalization and legitimatization which confirm the power of already-empowered agents and organizations – think for example of the world food crisis through which food multinationals have reinforced their positions in the world market – is a very important aspect of SI. Mobilization matters. Mobilization, throughout this book, also means collectively fostering a better understanding of the role of different actors and stakeholders in SI analysis and practice. In this respect, SI also concerns collaboratively imagining, mapping, designing, constructing views of the future and strategies to achieve those views. Putting in place an *équipement* (infrastructure), as Deleuze would suggest, is very important in SI processes. What might an *équipement* of SI look like? It could be tangible policies or support in terms of resources – especially finance and information, but also intangibles such as open-mindedness, flexibility and a willingness to take risks.

1.4   SOCIO-SPATIALLY EMBEDDED AND TIME-BOUND SOCIAL INNOVATION

A key task of SI theory in this context, as we see it, is to help define the types of collective action and social transformation which we believe are needed to respond in an appropriate way to situations of exclusion, to situations of need, to situations of desire for improvement of the human condition. There is today a host of theories that address, for example, empowerment, improvement of governance structures, creation of human development agencies, modes of participation and shared decision-making, ... (MacCallum et al. 2009). In addition there is a whole range of theories that deal with relationships between agency, structure, institutions, culture and discourse (Moulaert and Jessop 2012) and between globalization and SI processes and strategies (Cooperrider and Pasmore 1991; Klein and Roy 2013). These theories connect path dependence and the shape of development to the role of agency and organization. They link such 'big-picture' issues with situated strategies for imagining new futures, design scenarios, political participation and mobilization. They point to the interaction between globalization and SI, for example, by analysing the socially innovative dynamics of new global NGOs and how, through their innovative agendas and modes of organization, these address 'new' global challenges such as climate change or economic crisis. In sum, they identify key concepts for the analysis and building of SI, both connecting these, on the one hand, to problematic features of the world and, on the other hand, to the necessary institutional transformations at different spatial scales to make SI possible.

Our politico-ideological ambition, as part of a growing network of SI researchers, is to mobilize such theories to offer an alternative to the technology-based and business-oriented discourses which have long dominated innovation and development policy – particularly in the context of the 'knowledge-based economy' – and to develop an analytical framework which connects precepts, concepts, theories and strategies of SI. This work has been ongoing since 1989, in particular through four projects on the role of SI in community development and societal transformation, in which almost half of the authors in this Handbook have been involved (see www.socialpolis.eu).

The first of these projects explored Integrated Area Development (IAD) as a mode of needs satisfaction for populations in defined local areas (Moulaert 2000). IAD responds to particular challenges and opportunities faced by neighbourhoods within a framework of participatory democracy, and it provides an alternative to the more prevalent forms of market-led economic development. Drawing explicitly on the three dimensions which have been systematically attributed to SI in these four projects (needs satisfaction, social relations and empowerment; see General Introduction), IAD adds a spatial dimension to SI, showing how empowerment, or socio-political mobilization, is effected at 'higher' scales than the neighbourhood (such as the city or state) and drawing attention to the trans-scalar and multi-faceted nature of relations that affect conditions of existence in particular places. In addition, the IAD project conceptualized the relationship between SI and social exclusion, noting that SI can emerge from the actions that communities take to alleviate social, political and/or material problems. A sort of dialectic is at work, which lends form to the dynamics of innovation.

The second project which played a significant role in the development of an analytical framework capable of dealing with complexity of SI was SINGOCOM (Social Innovation, Governance and Community Building) (Moulaert et al. 2010). SINGOCOM extended the gaze of the IAD project to the social relations and strategic agencies of territorial development dynamics more broadly, bringing together theoretical perspectives from various disciplines to analyse 32 local development case studies, with a particular focus on institutional and governance dynamics. This research project confirmed that needs satisfaction involves a number of different dimensions – not only in the material and economic realms, but also in relation to culture, social connection and (individual and collective) identity. As such, SINGOCOM reaffirmed the importance of cultural and political activities in local and regional development, and provided a powerful counterpoint to the science- and technology-driven approaches to innovation that had traditionally dominated development policy. In addition, SINGOCOM dynamized the IAD model in both its spatial and temporal aspects: spatially, by paying explicit attention to how institutional and social networks and interactions between levels of governance can work to enable or constrain local innovation; temporally, by introducing the notion of path dependence – not as a form of 'institutional determinism' but as a recognition of the conditions of possibility that are shaped by an area's own history. Both multi-level governance and path dependence, then, may be either limiting or empowering – they are the foundations or assets which can often be creatively recombined into new opportunities for the future.

The third project, KATARSIS, further extended SI analysis by placing local initiatives in a broader spatial and conceptual ambit. Rather than focussing on territory or place as a basis for innovation, it explored the nature of the relationship between social exclusion and agency in SI across various fields of experience – health, education, employment, environment and so on. It drew upon a large number of what it termed 'socially creative strategies'

– initiatives which responded to inequality or exclusion in novel ways – which operated at a range of scales (local to global) and were initiated by different sectors of society (government, non-government, private). Key themes guiding this work were the role of culture, the nature of 'innovative' governance, and implications for research methodology. As such, the project raised some new challenges for SI analysis: questions about path dependence and the relationship between existing cultures and governance systems and 'desirable' systems which create spaces for SI; questions about what socially creative strategies can teach us, not only in relation to their substance, but in relation to the conduct of research into social exclusion.

The fourth project is Social Polis – not in itself a research project, but a 'social platform' built to enable dialogue across disciplines, sectors and countries about priorities for future research on urban social cohesion, and to build a transdisciplinary research methodology for SI analysis (see also Novy et al., Chapter 32). Social Polis has established methods to facilitate cooperation between social scientists, community organizations, political activists, policy makers, service delivery agencies and businesses, at the same time developing SI research as a response to the complexity of social phenomena (such as social exclusion/cohesion) by bringing diverse forms of knowledge (both academic and non-academic) into mutual interaction.

In sum, these four projects, which span a period from 1989 to 2011, represent not only a rich collection of stories reflecting their changing socio-political contexts, but also an evolution in theory building and methodology. Throughout this period, the interdisciplinarity of the network has allowed its participants to exchange understandings of the situated dynamics of exclusion, grass-roots action, governance and SI. At the same time, the extraordinary depth and variety of the case studies examined has facilitated a degree of comparative and holistic analysis through which these understandings have been further developed, taking into account the multi-scalar, multi-dimensional interactions that shape the 'local' as well as the tensions – both constraining and productive – between path dependence and radical change agendas. Most recently, this work has begun to shift towards more transdisciplinary approaches in which the analysis, design and practice of socially innovative strategies have strengthened their links, not only at the level of particular actions/institutions but also between countries and sectors across Europe and, to a lesser extent, other continents. With this commitment, there has also been a stronger focus on the meta-theoretical and ontological frameworks that shape these relationships and knowledge-building practices, as the following section will elaborate.

1.5 POTENTIAL DIRECTIONS FOR SI ANALYSIS

If the core of SI research is to respond in both an analytical and an activist way to poor or improvable conditions of human development, this poses a particular epistemological challenge. That is, our processes for knowledge making have not only to interrogate critically the relationships between the politico-ideological system, oppressive institutionalization and collective behaviour, but also, in themselves, to identify and sustain opportunities for alternative strategies and development processes. To do this, we need to ask not only what to analyse and how to analyse it, but also how our knowledge production system should be organized and

legitimized. This means unveiling and substituting those aspects of the dominant paradigm of academic research that are incoherent with the emancipatory intent of SI. To this end, we propose several possible directions for SI methodology and theory; directions to which we believe this book makes a significant contribution.

First, we propose a theoretical engagement with complexity: the uncertainty and complexity of the social world; and the complexity of our approaches to understanding and changing it. Complexity, as currently theorized, focuses on the dynamic properties and structural transformation of discontinuous and unpredictable systems in flux (Martin and Sunley 2007, p. 575). It recognizes the idea of holistic, emergent order; qualities as much as quantities, and asserts the primacy of processes over events, of relationships over entities and of development over structure (Thrift 1999, cited in Hillier 2012, p. 38). In SI research, such an understanding can help in recognizing the potentialities in historically constituted relations, to tease out paths between the world as it is and the emerging world as we would like it to be (from 'ontology' to 'ontogenesis', in the terms of Gilbert Simondon, who directly influenced Deleuze (1994[1968])). In relation to the research process, complexity also highlights the relationships between researchers-as-actors and the social world in which they are acting; the ways in which these and other relations can be changed (in iterative, non-linear fashion) by the analytical events which draw attention to them. The following points elaborate this potential.

Second, action research should be reaffirmed as a methodology, both within particular case-studies and also by reconstructing its history and returning to its roots (see Arthur, Chapter 25). It should go beyond this ambition, however. Action research can build a trajectory of shared research activities, including the formulation of relevant research questions – which problems to address; which theories and methods to be used; the role of SI analysis (see Novy et al., Chapter 32). This trajectory should be developed collaboratively between all actors, in a process of 'transdisciplinary problematization' (Miciukiewicz et al. 2012).

Third, the problematization approach needs the inclusive, collaborative development of a theoretical framework which includes both a meta-framework capable of showing the complexity of the world and also theories enlightening particular aspects of the SI challenges. Such a meta-theoretical framework would perform several functions, such as representing the major ontological features of the world to be potentially changed, but also highlighting the dynamics and cracks in the system from which SI may emerge. Such analysis can take advantage of a holistic methodology (as in pragmatism) which allows theoretical perspectives to engage in dialogue with empirical observations from an ethical position (see Moulaert and Mehmood, Chapter 33).

Finally, SI analysis should be reflexive and, to this end, coherent with its own ontological premises. It should give a place to the role of critically thinking participating actors in the research and action process – not only in the meta-theoretical framework, but especially by submitting any scientific methodology to reflexive, sociological assessment – that is, through a Sociology of Knowledge (SoK) approach (see Moulaert and Van Dyck, Chapter 35). We believe that this step, of assessing theories and methods in relation to the context of their development, is central to ensuring the continued relevance of SI analysis in constantly evolving, ever-complex sociopolitical and academic worlds.

1.6 CONCLUSION

The current appeal of SI is, in part, a function of its wide applicability to a range of strategies responding to conditions of rapid economic and social change, and to the inequities and exclusion but also opportunities that such change brings. We believe that the concept is best understood and mobilized in the context of a sociological heritage that challenges conventional economic approaches to development, and that has at its heart a desire for emancipatory macro-social change. New directions in SI analysis, a field of expanding diversity, are set within this general framing, which we see as the basis for building a more comprehensive meta-theoretical framework that can host the many partial theories, methodologies and practices that characterize and enrich SI. In making this proposal, we emphasize the importance of attention to context, both of the practical actions that ground research and of the theoretical orientations that research itself takes. Any 'grand' meta-theory must speak across social-cultural-economic differences and spatial-temporal scales to realize its socially innovative potential.

1.7 QUESTIONS FOR DISCUSSION

- Can you think of an example of a socially innovative practice being 'copied' from one socio-political context to another? What were some of the benefits and problems associated with this translation?
- How important is it for actors engaged in SI strategies to understand social theory?
- Can scientists and actors from different disciplinary backgrounds

hope to agree on a meta-theoretical framework for their work?

NOTES

1. *Interdisciplinarity* describes research which uses methodologies transferred between several established disciplines. For instance, substandard housing may be examined in one project from the methodologies of construction, public health, spatial planning, politics, geography, sociology, community development etc. *Transdisciplinary* research takes place between, across and beyond disciplinary boundaries and involves both scientists and practitioners in non scientific fields. Its goal is the holistic understanding of the world through the connections and unity of knowledge (Nicolescu 2002). In other words, researchers *modify* or *adapt* their approaches so that they are more appropriate to the practical issues studied.
2. Commons (1961[1934]), p. 55 for an example of a holistic definition, i.e. the definition of transactions.

REFERENCES

(References in bold are recommended reading.)

Bureau of European Policy Advisors (BEPA) (2010), *Empowering people, driving change: Social Innovation in The European Union*, Brussels: EC.

Chambon, J.-L., A. David and J.-M. Devevey (1982), *Les innovations sociales*, Paris: Presses universitaires de France.

Coleman, J. (1970), 'Social Inventions', *Social Forces*, **49** (2), 163–173

Commons, J. (1961[1934]), *Institutional Economics*, Part One. Madison: The University of Wisconsin Press.

Conger, S. (1973), *Social Inventions – Saskatchewan Newstart Incorporated*, Prince Albert: Saskatchewan NewStart.

Cooperrider, L. and W.A. Pasmore (1991), 'Global Social Change: A New Agenda for Social Science?', *Human Relations*, **44** (10), 1037–1055.

Deleuze, G. (1994[1968]), *Difference and Repetition* (trans. P. Patton), New York: Columbia University Press.

Drucker, P. (1987), 'Social innovation: management's new dimension', *Long Range Planning*, **20** (6), 29–34.

Gershuny, J. (1987), 'Technology, Social Innovation and the Informal Economy', *The Annals of the American Academy of Political and Social Science*, **493**, 47–63.

Hillier, J. (2012), 'Baroque Complexity: "If Things were Simple, Word Would Have Gotten Round"', in G. de Roo, J. Hillier and J. Van Wezemael (eds), *Complexity and Planning: Systems, Assemblages and Simulations*, Farnham: Ashgate, pp. 37–73.

Klein J.L. and M. Roy (eds) (2013), *Pour une nouvelle mondialisation: le défi d'innover*, Québec: Presses de l'Université du Québec.

MacCallum, D., F. Moulaert, J. Hillier and S. Vicari Haddock (eds) (2009), *Social Innovation and Territorial Development*, Aldershot: Ashgate.

Martin, R. and Sunley, P. (2007), 'Complexity thinking and evolutionary economic geography', *Journal of Economic Geography*, **7**, 573–601.

Miciukiewicz, K., F. Moulaert, A. Novy, S. Musterd and J. Hillier (2012), 'Introduction: Problematising Urban Social Cohesion: A Transdisciplinary Endeavour', *Urban Studies*, 49 (9), 1855–1872.

Moulaert, F. (2000), *Globalization and Integrated Area Development in European Cities*, Oxford: Oxford University Press. Moulaert, F. and J. Nussbaumer (2005), 'The Social Region: beyond the territorial dynamics of the learning economy', *European Urban and Regional Studies*, **12** (1), 45–64.

Moulaert, F. and J. Nussbaumer (2007), 'L'innovation sociale au coeur des débats publics et scientifiques. Un essai de déprivatisation de la société', in J.L. Klein and D Harisson (eds), *L'innovation sociale: émergence et effets sur la transformation des sociétés*, Québec: Presses de l'Université du Québec.

Moulaert, F. and B. Jessop (2012), 'Theoretical foundations for the analysis of socio-economic development in space', in F. Martinelli, F. Moulaert and A. Novy (eds), *Urban and Regional Development Trajectories in Contemporary Capitalism*, London: Routledge (in press).

Moulaert, F., E. Swyngedouw, F. Martinelli and S. Gonzalez (eds) (2010), *Can Neighbourhoods Save the City? Community Development and Social Innovation*, London: Routledge.

Moulaert, F., D. Cassinari, J. Hillier, K. Miciukiewicz, A. Novy, S. Habersack and D. MacCallum (2011), *Transdisciplinary Research in Social Polis*, Leuven: Social Polis, http://www.socialpolis.eu/the-social-polisapproach/transdisciplinarity/ (accessed 15 August 2012).

Mumford, M.D. (2002), 'Social Innovation: Ten cases from Benjamin Franklin'. *Creativity Research Journal*, **14** (2), 253–266.

Nicolescu, B. (2002), *Manifesto of Transdisciplinarity* (trans. K-C. Voss), New York: SUNY Press.

Peck, J. (2013), 'Innovation sociale . . . aux limites du néoberalisme', in Klein and Roy (eds).

Schumpeter, J. (2005[1932]), 'Development' ['Entwicklung'] trans. and introduction M.C. Becker and T. Knudsen, *Journal of Economic Literature*, **43** (1), 108–120.

Swyngedouw, E. (2009) 'The Political Economy and Political Ecology of the Hydro-Social Cycle',

Journal of Contemporary Water Research & Education, **142** (1), 56–60.

Taylor, J. (1970), 'Introducing social innovation', *Journal of Applied Behavioral Science*, **6** (1), 68–77.

Thrift, N. (1999), 'The place of complexity', *Theory, Culture & Society*, **16** (3), 31–70.

Weber, M. (1947[1920]), *The Theory of Social and Economic Organization* (trans. M. Henderson and Talcott Parsons), New York: Oxford University Press.

Young Foundation (2010), *Study on Social Innovation*, Study for BEPA in cooperation with Social Innovation Exchange (SIX), Brussels: EC.

2. Social innovation in governance and public management systems: toward a new paradigm?

Benoît Lévesque[1]

2.1 INTRODUCTION

While the decades following the Second World War saw a proliferation of social innovations in public administration,[2] the term 'innovation' as such was rarely mentioned. Instead, emphasis was placed on the main political reforms that led, among others, to the establishment of diverse types of welfare states in the developed countries, in particular through defamilialization and decommodification of public services (Esping-Andersen 1990). However, over the past two decades, reference to innovations in public administration and public services management has become more commonplace. This growing interest in social innovations can be largely explained as the outcome of reforms inspired by New Public Management (NPM), a new paradigm that emerged in the 1980s (Osborne and Gaebler 1993).

In this chapter we begin by providing an overview of social innovations and show how a great number of these have in fact emerged from the new NPM approach. Thereafter, we take a more critical look at these innovations and discuss alternative views of innovation and governance. In conclusion, we comment on, among others, the specificity of social innovations in public administration and how this topic merits further research.

2.2 SOCIAL INNOVATION: SOCIETAL PARADIGM AND NEW CLUSTER OF INNOVATIONS

Public administration has become a fertile ground for social innovation, a phenomenon that has been approached from different angles. In most chapters of this book, for example, social innovation carries a more general meaning and is viewed mainly as a process that aims to contribute new solutions to unresolved social problems. A further notion of social innovation focuses on the type of social relationships generated by these innovations, such as organizational innovations (management and coordination relationships) and institutional innovations (power and regulatory relationships) (Lévesque 2006). In this chapter, we subscribe mostly to the first meaning given to the term, although we do at times make use of the second meaning when it appears expedient, in particular with regard to public services.

Social innovations in public administration and in most public services spread more through institutionalization, namely through the recognition and support of public authorities, than through market forces. Moreover, the role of the state remains significant in market or quasi-market situations, and state-regulated redistribution consolidates the demand for services deemed essential. In public services, product innovations often become organizational innovations, because [translation] 'the division of tasks, their content, the nature of competencies, the coordination procedures are heavily processed and reconfigured when the content of the service is modified' (Callon et al. 1997, p. 35).

Moreover, some geographical areas are more receptive and conducive than others to social innovations (Moulaert 2009), explaining why the NPM approach has spread differently in different countries (Bezes 2009, p. 41). Certain historical periods have also been more favourable than others, such as major crises, which are generally overcome through the adoption of generic innovations (transversally, in many sectors of activities). This latter phenomenon generally gives way to clusters of innovation, as shown by Schumpeter. However, innovations following major crises do not spread randomly, but rather in keeping with a socio-technical paradigm that promulgates a new vision of the problems, methods and possible solutions (Freeman 1991).

This socio-technical paradigm, which applies to technological innovations, is correlated by a societal paradigm that applies to social innovations (Lévesque 2005). This new type of paradigm promotes the emergence of radical innovations, such as social innovations that break into new knowledge domains, but also incremental or 'ordinary' innovations.[3] The societal paradigm also promotes the creation of a path that renders innovations increasingly irreversible.

For a new paradigm to gain foothold, the old paradigm must first have proven itself incapable of providing solutions and responses to the current social problems and demands. Moreover, a transition to a new paradigm requires the building of political and social alliances as well as a change in the sites of power. Further, these changes also presuppose distinct realizations that promote learning and the assim-

ilation of new approaches and the use of new tools (Hall 1993). For a new societal paradigm to manifest in innovations thus requires not only coalitions and alliances but also entrepreneurs and 'intrapreneurs', including in public administration (Bernier and Hafsi 2007).

2.3   NEW PUBLIC MANAGEMENT: A NEW SOCIETAL PARADIGM AND A NEW WAVE OF SOCIAL INNOVATION

In this section we show how the New Public Management (NPM) approach has promoted the deployment of social innovations, in particular of the organizational type and the institutional type. For this, we proceed in three steps: 1) we specify the context in which government reforms emerged, including the alliances that allowed for them, 2) we then define NPM in relation to the innovations, and 3) we characterize the main innovation clusters in their relation to governance.

2.3.1   The Reform Movement of the State: Political Parties and Political and Social Alliances

According to Kamarck (2003, p. 2), '[a]t the beginning of the twenty first century many of the world's nation states are engaged in serious efforts to reform their government and inject a culture of innovation into their government's bureaucracies.' The arrival to power of Margaret Thatcher in 1979 and Ronald Reagan in 1980 could be seen as the turning point that ushered in those state reforms. Although these reforms were driven by right-wing and neoliberal thinking, they are not the exclusive brainchild of right-wing political parties because they were also pushed by leftist and left-of-centre governments, such as the labour government in New Zealand in 1984 and in Australia in 1983, and then by Bill Clinton in 1992 and Tony Blair in 1997. In some countries such as Sweden and the Netherlands, the reforms were less ideological and more pragmatic. And in other countries such as Germany, France and Japan, the effects of the reform movement were more limited than elsewhere, at least until the mid-1990s (Pollit and Dan 2011, p. 7).

Some analyses have well captured the coalitions and alliances behind those reforms. Wood (1995, p. 102), for example, identifies the formation of a coalition bringing together 'accounting firms, financial intermediaries, management consultants and business schools,' in sum, a 'coalition of professional and corporate interest.' However, the push in that direction also came from within the state. In that context, a new class of 'top public managers' with a background in neoclassic economics rather than in the social sciences and humanities were predisposed to take on 'analytic work in collegial elite units and to distance themselves from front-line supervisory role in favour of a super-control position which offers more job satisfaction and less tedious routine' (Wood 1995).

At the level of the nation states, one portion of the middle class displayed an interest in an improvement of public services combined with a reduction of taxes, and was amenable to the idea of involving the market in order to get there. For different reasons, other segments of society involved in the new social movements were also favourable to reforms likely to ensure a democratization of public services based on the participation of the users, thereby expressing a lack of confidence in the ability of the bureaucratic state to provide democratic accountability (Aucoin 1995, p. 188 et seq). In addition, citizens' groups

in certain regions even submitted formal appeals for a decentralization of public administration (Moulaert 2009; Klein 2008).

The government reform movement was supported by most of the big international institutions such as the World Bank, the IMF, the United Nations (Department of Economics and Social Affairs) and the OECD (United Nations 2006). Innovations in public services were encouraged by competitions in many countries, the most known being the American Government Awards Program of the John Kennedy School of Government, which received financial support from the Ford Foundation starting from 1985. Such initiatives were reproduced in Brazil, Chile, China, East Africa, Mexico, Peru, the Philippines and South Africa (Borins 2008, p. 2),

2.3.2 The NPM Approach: Ideas and Axioms Favourable to Innovation

NPM can be considered a set of 'new ideas about the role of government' as well as a set of 'managerial innovations' in the public sector (Van de Walle and Hammerschmid 2011, pp. 191–193). At the level of ideas, NPM has eclipsed other management approaches. However, the implementation of the NPM approach presupposes the existence of: 1) the new institutional economy, comprised of public choice, monetarism, and a supply side economy, alongside 2) new management trends characterized by a 'mixture of management theories and business motivation psychology' (König, quoted by Van de Walle and Hammerschmid 2011, p. 191) as well as a penchant for 'pop management stardom' (Hood 1991, p. 6).

Both of these theoretical approaches are amenable to the introduction of private business into the public sector and are in essence favourable to innovation. Each also questions the traditional values of public administration in favour of those of efficiency, creativity and risk-taking. However, they differ with regard to the degree of autonomy they accord to managers. The first, the new institutional economy, views competition and financial incentives as the key to ensuring compliance to the principal; while the second, new public management, seeks to entrust managers with greater autonomy and leeway so that these can innovate (Pollitt and Dan 2011, p. 7).

Hood (1991 pp. 4–5) was the first to characterize NPM as an ideal type that included the following elements:

1. 'Hands-on professional management in the public sector': this refers to giving more autonomy to those at the head of a public organization by means of a clear sharing of responsibilities and a better accountability.
2. 'Explicit standards and measures of performance': to this end, the targets, objectives and indicators must be better defined if one wants quantitative evaluations of the performance and a superior accountability.
3. 'Greater emphasis on output controls': diverse innovations could be proposed to implement incentives for an improved performance.
4. 'Shift to *disaggregation* of units in the public sectors': which aims for a decentralization of administrations and management systems alongside relatively independent operational units with budgets leaving great leeway to managers, the whole with a view to greater effectiveness.
5. 'Shift to a greater *competition* in public sector': the aim here is to achieve cost reduction and greater effectiveness by introducing competition among units

within or outside of the public sector through tendering procedures.
6. '*Stress on private-sector styles of management practice*': through the introduction of private sector management tools in the public sector, leading to, among other results, more flexibility in the hiring of personnel.
7. 'Stress on greater *discipline* and *parsimony* in resource use': following the example of the private sector, public administration is encouraged to be more frugal and to reduce costs, in particular concerning human resources.

This definition of NPM, inspired mainly by the British experience, provides elements found in many government documents, in particular in those of Anglo-Saxon countries. However, that definition can be retained as a starting point, especially as it is the first to have been formulated. As indicated by Bernier and Angers (2010), many other researchers thereafter developed their own definition; however, the added elements such as client orientation have not substantially modified the vision imparted by this first definition (Bezes 2009; Emery and Giauque 2005; Osborne and Gaebler 1992; Pollitt and Dan 2011). Lastly, as we shall see in the following section, that paradigm gives way to a new space for social innovations in public administration.

2.3.3   A New Wave of Social Innovations

The state reforms and the wave of innovation resulting from these took place in two stages. The first, from the 1980s, was centered on economic liberalization, the privatization of state corporations and the reduction of public spending, all in compliance with the goals of monetarism and supply side economics (Bezes 2009,

p. 23). The second stage, from the 1990s and 2000s, was focused more on administrative reforms and the modernization of the state, with the goal to make services more efficient and more responsible with regard to users. This latter stage also generated a 'set of managerial and service delivery innovations' (Van de Walle and Hammerschmid 2011, pp. 3–6).

In keeping with the characteristics of NPM already discussed, social innovations branch off into many different directions. In the framework of a greater autonomy for managers, the distinction between steering and rowing, and an orientation given by the mission (mission driven), many innovations will be pursued. The quest for performance and efficiency opens up a large space for defining new indicators for measuring outputs and for conceiving innovative methods and procedures for performance-based management and budgeting. Similarly, the emphasis on monitoring results rather than processes has led to innovations concerning client orientation, the improvement of the quality of services (e.g., TQM), significant modalities for resource allocation and evaluation, not to mention 'a focus on organizational capacity building' (Levy 2011, p. 20). The disaggregation of public services administration as a whole into specialized service units opens up a territory of innovation that features relatively independent agencies, partnerships such as public-private partnerships (PPP), decentralization toward regions and local communities, non-profit organizations and devolutions. The transition to greater competition in the public sector promotes 1) a redesign of the contractual and quasi-contractual processes entered into between the central directions and the agencies, and even between the units of independent agencies, 2) a proliferation of calls for tenders, 3) the

establishment of quasi-markets open to both the private and the non-profit sector as well as the social economy. The emphasis on private sector-based management and on a 'customer driven government' encourages innovation to embrace new management modes, new organizational forms (lean organization), new ways of recruiting and remunerating personnel, business processes renewing, new forms of work organization, and new relationships to users. Lastly, the accent on greater discipline and parsimony in the use of public resources has generated a greater awareness for the need to achieve greater productivity alongside cost reductions. In particular human resources costs have been targeted for reductions, usually by encouraging staff to take voluntary retirement (here, the public sector appears to have taken the cue from the private sector).

Diverse listings of innovations in public administration exist, for example those based on the many applications submitted to award competitions, which allows to identify achievements from the point of view of both the actors and the experts (Bernier et al. 2011; Borins 2008). There are also typologies that highlight the scope of innovations in public administration and public services, namely incremental innovations (e.g., providing a service to a larger clientele, or providing more choices for a service), radical innovations (participation of users in the development of a policy on home care services) and 'systemic and transformative innovations' (e.g., creation of autonomous agencies) (Mulgan and Albury 2003).

For our part, we find it useful to distinguish, within social innovations, organizational innovations from institutional institutions, in particular in public administration, where NPM tends to separate what belongs to steering from what belongs to rowing. In this way we find, among the organizational innovations in public services, innovations concerning flexibility in management, new modes of work organization, modalities for recruiting functionaries and promotion, new modalities of accountability, the use and control of allocated budgets, new performance management tools, evaluation methods, initiatives for providing users with more choices, charters for citizens or users, and modalities for the provision of services. The institutional innovations comprise everything else from the political domain as such, including: the revision of the field of competency of the state apparatus; the reciprocal role of elected government officials and managers; the modalities for distinguishing between steering and rowing; the decentralization or delegation of public services; the creation of relatively independent administrative entities such as the agencies; externalization; and the delegation of power, partnership and privatization (Bezes 2009, pp. 23–24).

As it would go beyond the scope of this chapter to present all innovations in public administration, we shall conclude with an examination of two categories of innovations that appear to us as the most significant, namely the creation of the independent agencies and the Alternative Services Delivery approach. The creation of agencies that are [translation] 'at the heart of the NPM reforms' (Emery and Giauque 2005, p. 138) responds to many objectives, such as breaking the monolithic block represented by the bureaucracy, providing managers with more autonomy in view of promoting innovation, creating more direct relationships with users, and improving efficiency and the accountability of services.

The programs Next Steps (1988) in England, Public Service 2000 (1989) in Canada and Renouveau du Service public (1989) in France constitute programs for rethinking public services alongside the structures intended to ensure delivery. As Figure 2.1 shows, service delivery can be provided by four clusters of organizations, namely the public sector (including Line organizations and SOAs, or devolution to other levels of government), the private sector (through independent entities, such as the associations and social economy businesses, businesses taken over employees), and state-run organizations, through licenses, contracting out and government-owned contractors operated (GOCOs). The partnerships serve to interlink organizations that are exclusively public (between agencies, for example) or that are private and public, as is the case with public-private partnerships (PPP).

What is new in the case of the ASD is a question grid that allows us to choose the most appropriate institutional form on the basis of a bottom-up, case-by-case approach. The institutional innovations resulting from these restructurings or the decisions to implement improvements can lead to a full-fledged series of organizational innovations. The diversity of the institutions and organizations involved in the delivery of services (see Figure 2.1) and in the integration of the value chain in the production of services, including through the mobilization of stakeholders (suppliers, users and the affected community), constitutes a matrix of innovation. Apart from the institutional innovations already mentioned and the organizational innovations around the improvement of services, governance appears 'at the heart of ASD' (Wilkins 2011: 9) and, in the best of cases, manifests as shared governance.

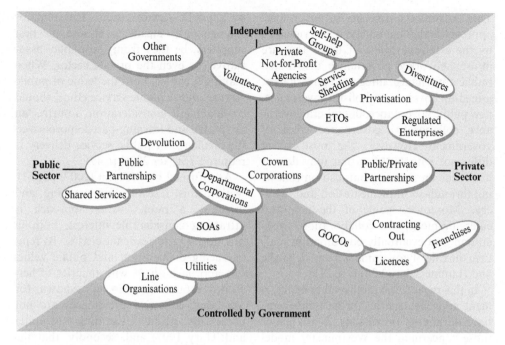

Source: John Wilkins, Commonwealth Secretariat (2011: 3).

Figure 2.1   Delivery options

2.4   SEARCH FOR ALTERNATIVES

For over a decade, NPM seems have reached its peak, 'thus requiring us to look beyond or transcend NPM' (Christensen and Laegreid 2011, p. 12). Of the new avenues, the three that are most often mentioned are: 'the new Weberian state which aims to restore the legitimacy of the state by placing more emphasis on non-economic value and societal problem'; the theories concerning the relationships between 'the state, civil society and the market'; and 'the government-governance theory about vertical and horizontal steering with the so-called network society' (Vries 2010, p. 3). As evidenced by the 'public value management' approach, these diverse visions overlap in many regards, in particular concerning governance and innovations (Benington

and Moore 2011; Moore 1995). In the following, we will examine the possible alternatives in terms of governance and innovation.

2.4.1   Toward a Collaborative Governance

Concerning public administration, Paradeise et al. (2009, p. 89) advance that 'an emergent model is best represented in the mid-2000s as integrating governance.' The NPM-inspired reforms have turned the welfare state into a kind of 'welfare pluralism' or 'welfare mix' that features a diversity of relatively independent actors in the delivery of services (Evers and Laville 2004). As a result of contrasting, if not conflicting, institutional arrangements, the governments have had to become involved in networks to ensure the realization of activities that pertain to the public interest.

This explains the diversity of governance approaches that has emerged, as evidenced by the extensive range of terms that are in use: networked governance, distributed public governance, integrated governance, joined-up governance, holistic governance, new public governance, digital-era governance, collaborative governance, whole-of government. However, 'the most crucial difference with NPM is that they do not just focus on steering, but also on following through to implementation and delivery.' Moreover, 'some of the new and emerging models for collaboration, cooperation and eventually coordination reaffirm the role of government' (Van de Walle and Hammerschmid 2011, p. 22).

In this regard, the public value management approach merits further consideration, despite its drawbacks, in particular those concerning the Westminster model and the roles of elected government officials and public servants (Rhodes and Wanna 2011). According to this approach, which was first formalized by Moore (1995), 'the governance of the public realm involves networks of deliberation and delivery in pursuit of public value' (Stoker 2006, p. 47). This new understanding can be characterized by the following four recommendations. First, 'public interventions are defined by the search for public value.' The meaning and need for the delivery of services is shaped by the framework of exchanges between the stakeholders and the government officials, among other reasons because the collective preferences and the public value have not yet solidified into coherent entities and have yet to be established (Côté and Lévesque 2009, p. 37 sq.). Second, the legitimacy of a large range of stakeholders must be recognized and appropriate means must be found for obtaining their participation. Third, 'an open-minded, relationship approach to the procurement of services is framed by a public service ethos.' This requires acquiring the means to choose the best suppliers, be they from the public, associative, or even the private sector. When making a choice, both the 'ethic of public service' and 'a public service ethos' should be taken into consideration. Fourth, 'an adaptable and learning-based approach to the challenge of public service delivery is required' (Stoker 2006, p. 49).

As affirmed by O'Flynn (2007, p. 353), 'within this research for meaning and direction a public value approach is attracting considerable interest, both in practitioner and academic circles.' By reintroducing deliberation and public value, this approach aligns with theories of heterodox economists who have shown, for one, that collective preferences are not necessarily readily discernible (Monnier and Thiry 1997) and, secondly, that the range of rationales for action extends far beyond mere self-interest, without denying the importance of the latter (Boltanski and Chapiello 1999; Enjolras 2008). Moreover, unlike hierarchical coordination and market coordination, coordination through networks can be based on both horizontality, as in market coordination, and on involvement, as in hierarchical coordination (Hollingsworth and Boyer 1997). The network thereby functions as a specific form of coordination, although, to become a mode of governance, it must be able to 'play a role in steering, setting directions and influencing behaviour.' And that role cannot be fully assumed without an identity and mutually shared trust (Parker 2007, p. 4).

As we shall see in the chapter on social innovations in Québec (see Klein et al., Chapter 28), the actors involved in public services in the framework of a governance qualified as partnership-based cannot only participate in the co-production of a service (as is the case with parents involved

Table 2.1   Three theories of public administration and governance

	Traditional public administration	New public management (NPM)	Public value management
State	Inserted and generally interventionist	Limited (privatization and deregulation)	Located (no exterior) and partner
Governance through actors	Hierarchies Public servants	Markets Purchasers and providers Clients to contractors	Networks and partnerships Collaborative governance Civil leadership
Role of policy-makers	'Commanders'	'Announcers/ commissioners'	'Leaders and interpreters'
Role of public managers	'Clerks and martyrs'	Efficiency and market maximizers	'Explorers'
Role of the population	Citizen user	Customers	Co-producers and citizens
Strategy	State and producer-centred	Market and customer-centred	Shaped by civil society and state
Key concepts	Public goods	Public choice	Public value
Needs/problems	'Straightforward, defined by professionals'	'Wants, expressed through the market'	'Complex, volatile and prone to risk'
Innovation	Some large-scale, national and universal innovations (compare social net in welfare state)	Innovation in organizational form more than content	Innovation at both central and local levels
		Process	Collaborative and incremental innovation
		Radical innovation	innovation

Source: Adapted from Hartley (2005, pp. 28 and 29), Stoker (2006) and Lévesque (2005).

in a school committee), but also co-develop or co-build a public policy starting from a consultation with elected government officials and representatives from senior public administration (Vaillancourt 2009; Côté and Lévesque 2009). As concerns managers and public administrators, this form of governance presupposes major learning investments and 'longer-term relationship management skills' due to the emphasis put on the deliberation and collaborative construction of the public value (O'Flynn 2007, p. 362). This comprises significant challenges, the importance of which should not be under-estimated. Very critical of this approach, Rhodes and Wanna (2007, p. 417) nevertheless write: 'Such a philosophical challenge has not been seen since neo-liberal and public choice theories revolutionized public management in the 1980s.' Table 2.1 demonstrates how public value management (Moore 1995) differs from both traditional public administration and from NPM.

2.4.2   Open Innovations and Collaborative Innovations

According to the NPM perspective, innovation is initiated and conducted by the producers. To get there, NPM makes two requests (Verhoest et al. 2007, pp. 470–471). One, 'Let public managers innovate' in compliance with the managerial approach, and two, aligned with public choice theory, 'Make public managers innovate' namely by exerting internal pressure (control) on the latter and external pressure by creating competition. In sum, for innovation, NPM looks to the capitalist entrepreneur as a reference, while ignoring the specificity of 'political-administrative pressure-responses' (Verhoest et al. 2007, pp. 484–489). From this angle, innovation could be categorized more as closed than as open innovation (Chesbrough 2003).

In the framework of collaborative governance, innovation that involves and integrates users represents a form of open innovation. Thereby, collaborative innovation can be defined as:

> an externally focused, collaborative approach to innovation and problem solving in the public sector that relies on harnessing the resources and the creativity of external networks and communities (including citizen networks as well as networks of nonprofits and private corporations) to amplify or enhance the innovation speed as well as the range and quality of innovation outcomes (or solutions). (Nambisan 2008, p. 11)

More broadly, it can be specified by 1) shared objectives and goals that strengthen the network while giving it a direction, 2) a shared vision of the world and a social conscience for interpreting the dynamic of the external environment in a consistent way, 3) the capacity to create social knowledge through interactions and dialogue among the members of the network, 4) an architecture of participation that supplies governance mechanisms allowing users to participate in discussions or deliberation, and an integration that ensures that the benefits and spinoffs benefit all members (Nambisan 2008, p. 12).

From the point of view of the relationship to the state and the community, collaborative innovations can be distinguished on the basis of two dimensions, one being the nature of innovation or the problem (whether well defined or little defined) to be solved, and the second being the nature of the leadership and the arrangements of collaboration (leadership ensured by the government or by the community). Concerning a cross-over of these two dimensions and the two possibilities that each offer, Nambisan (2008) identifies four types of contributions from public administration. When the problem is not well defined and the services relatively new, two scenarios can take place. In one, the government exerts leadership as 'innovation seeker' in the search of new ideas with citizens and researchers, and in the second, leadership comes from within the community in an informal structure, with the government acting as 'champion innovator' by interconnecting the partners (e.g., citizens and non-profit associations) to find innovative solutions. Cases where the problem is well defined and services already in place also result in two scenarios. In the first, the government exerts leadership by acting as 'innovation integrator' by facilitating the integration of diverse contributions for a final production, and in the second, the community exerts leadership in an informal structure while the government acts as 'innovation catalyst'.

Collaborative innovation undoubtedly allows for innovations that are better adapted to the users and their community. Apart from the case of downright failure, innovations that spread do not necessarily constitute improvements, be it from the point of view of the organization or the users, explaining the importance of collaborative governance (Hartley 2011). As was observed in United Kingdom, innovation encouraged only for the sake of performance sometimes leads to 'hyper-innovation', which can be as harmful as 'a shortage of innovation' (Hartley 2011, p. 171).

Lastly, collaborative innovations in the framework of a networked governance (collaborative) can reduce risk in various ways (Hartley 2011, p. 181). First, they promote information sharing and good practices between organizations, thereby contributing to the success of the experiments and the reduction of failures. Secondly, by focusing on the process and its development stages and by considering that '[h]ow services are provided has an impact on the public sphere as well as what is provided', collaborative innovations allow not only to reduce costs but also to anticipate what is feasible from one stage to the next. Thirdly, from the point of view of risk reduction, such innovations are well adapted to public services that are multidimensional and that comprise a high number of stakeholders, namely users, citizens, managers and personnel, politicians and their advisers, the media, interest groups, and lobbies. In sum, to the extent that they encourage deliberation and even co-construction, collaborative innovation ensures not only greater support but also better conditions for success due to, in particular, the mobilized tangible and intangible resources, in particular for the production of services normally provided by a welfare state (Von Hippel 2005, p. 73).

2.5 CONCLUSION

Two conclusions can be drawn from the above discussion. The first concerns the course of social innovations in public administration over the three past decades. The second concerns the specificity of social innovations in that domain combined with the importance of giving these more attention if aiming for a theory of innovation that is not limited to the private sector.

While public administration has traditionally been considered not very favourable to innovation, it has became rather fertile subsequent to the adoption of a vision and of reforms and by looking to private enterprise for not only organizational innovations (e.g., management modes and incentives for innovation) but also for institutional innovations such as the creation of internal independent entities and the provision of external entities (quasi public, private and non-profit associative). Some of these innovations represent imitations of what the private sector had already realized and constitute 'creative destructions'. This vision and its associated concepts has spread to all developed countries and even beyond, although with contrasting configurations, an analysis of which would exceed the scope this chapter.

NPM here represents a paradigm for putting this set of innovations into a coherent framework and for promoting their spread. With time, the reforms adopted have revealed their limit from the point of view of governance and the relative loss of control and expertise of the state. Thereby, new avenues of thinking have emerged. And although NPM continues to be predominant for the moment, these new avenues are spurring new waves of innovation that call for a reframing and redefinition of the public value, deliberation and user participation with the view to improving governance and creating a more collaborative innovation. It would be premature to advance that these new avenues will one day become as dominant as NPM, especially since such avenues could only take root if new alliances were forged both within and outside the state. However, predominant or not, these new avenues are nevertheless provoking changes in public services and are giving way to new relationships between the state, the market and civil society (Lévesque 2003). This prompts us to find out whether these new innovations will promote the emergence of a renewed administration by hybridization with the existing one or whether they will lead to a form of sedimentation, which would have a more limited impact (Thelen 2004). We tend to argue that hybridization could prevail in some societies and sedimentation in others, depending on the country.

Lastly, despite a certain mimetism of NPM with regard to the private, we wish to underline that the course of innovation taken in the public sector reveals significant specificities. The sector is subjected to the same economic constraints to innovation facing other sectors, albeit with a certain delay. In addition, it must deal with additional constraints pertaining to the political realm and public opinion. Moreover, the spread of innovations in the public sector is not ensured by the market but by institutionalization, which essentially consists of the recognition and support of public authorities. Here as well, radical innovations must be justified before being adopted, explaining the role, undoubtedly more determining here than elsewhere, of a societal paradigm and a narrative thread that gives them not only direction but also meaning. However, such a societal paradigm only establishes itself in a sector such as public administration if it is carried by large

social alliances. Moreover, while in the private sector innovations are considered to be good if they make a profit, the same cannot be said for the public sector, where they are not only expected to be beneficial to the organization but also to make improvements to public value, or to contribute to the creation of public value. In that context, public administration cannot pursue 'creative destructions' as if the negative consequences were externalities (in the domain of public value, there are no externalities strictly speaking), explaining its penchant for pilot projects as well as open and incremental innovations. Innovations of rupture are normally preceded by debates within society. In sum, innovations in public administration would be a lot more complex from the point of view of processes. For all these reasons, it appears to us that researchers and professionals specialized in innovation can no longer ignore the domain of public administration, especially if they want to contribute to building an innovation theory that would be applicable to more than just the private sector.

2.6   QUESTIONS FOR DISCUSSION

In this chapter, the author explains that public administration has not been perceived as innovative but that it has become so over the two past decades, giving rise to the following questions:

- How has public administration become a more fertile ground for social innovations over the past decades?
- What are the main types of social innovation generated by public administration and public services?
- What are the consequences of the new alternative approaches to New

Public Management for innovations and the type of governance?

NOTES

1. We wish to thank Luc Bernier, Director of CERGO (Centre de recherche sur la gouvernance), and Louis Côté, Director of L'Observatoire de l'administration publique (ENAP), for their suggestions and advice concerning, among others, NPM and the public value approach. We also thank Nicolas Charest from ENAP's Observatoire de l'Administration publique for his suggestions concerning the documentation on innovations in public administration. We nevertheless assume full responsibility for the choice of the documents retained as well as for the analyses proposed.
2. This latter can be defined as [translation] 'the entirety of administrative power controlled by the state (directly by departments or by public enterprises),' which is based on 'a network of organizations tasked to accomplish the different missions of the State' and that are oriented toward the general interest (Simard and Bernier, 1992, p. 15). For a more international definition, we refer to the definition proposed by the United Nations (2006).
3. Ordinary innovation is moreover the title of a book by Alter (2005), who shows well the importance of incremental innovations. The distinction between radical innovation and incremental innovation is generalized in the literature. The few researchers who reserve the term innovation for change that 'represents discontinuity with the past' are an exception (Osborne 1994; Osborne and Brown 2005, pp. 4–6; also Hartley 2011). As Bezes (2009) shows for France, Bernier and Hafsi (2010) for Canada, and Hall and Soskice (2001) for Germany and the United States, change is sometimes based mainly on incremental rather than radical innovation.

REFERENCES

(References in bold are recommended reading.)

Alter, N. (2005), *L'innovation ordinaire*, Paris: P.U.F.
Aucoin, P. (1995), *The New Public Management: Canada in Comparative Perspective*, Montreal: Institute for Research on Public Policy.
Benington, J. and M.H. Moore (eds) (2011), *Public Value. Theory and Practice*, New York: Palgrave Macmillan.

Bernier, L. and T. Hafsi (2007), 'The changing Nature of Public Entrepreneurship', *Public Administration Review*, **66** (3), 488–503.
Bernier, L. and S. Angers (2010), 'Le NMP ou le nouveau management public', in Paquin, Stéphane, Luc Bernier and Guy Lachapelle (eds), *L'analyse des politiques publiques*, Montréal, Les Presses de l'Université de Montréal, pp. 231–254.
Bernier, L., Hafsi, T. and C. Deschamps (2011), *Innovation in the Public Sector. A look at the Innovation Awards of the Institute of Public Administration of Canada applications and winners*, Quebec: CERGO (ENAP), www.cergo.enap. ca/CERGO/33/Cahiers_de_recherche.enap (last accessed 10 November 2011).
Bezes, P. (2009), *Réinventer l'État. Les réformes de l'administration française*, Paris: P.U.F.
Boltanski, L. et È. Chiapello (1999), *Le nouvel esprit du capitalisme*, Paris: Gallimard.
Borins, S. (ed.) (2008), *Innovation in Government. Research, Recognition and Replication*, Washington: Brookings Institution Press and Ash Institute for Democratic Governance and Innovation (Harvard University).
Callon, M., P. Larédo and V. Rabeharisoa (1997), 'Que signifie innover dans les services. Une triple rupture avec le modèle de l'innovation industrielle', *La Recherche*, **295**, 34–36.
Chesbrough, H. (2003), *Open Innovation: The New Imperative for Creating and Profiting from Technology*, Cambridge, MA: Harvard Business Review Press.
Christensen, T. and P. Laegreid (eds) (2011), *The Ashgate Research Companion to New Public Management*, Farnham, UK: Ashgate Publishing.
Côté, L. and B. Lévesque (2009), 'L'État stratège, la citoyenneté active, la démocratie plurielle et la gouvernance partagée', in Côté, L., B. Lévesque and G. Morneau (eds), *État stratège and participation citoyenne*, Québec: Presses de l'Université du Québec, pp. 11–69.
Emery, Y. and D. Giauque (2005), *Paradoxes de la gestion publique*, Paris: L'Harmattan.
Enjolras, B. (2008), 'Régime de gouvernance et intérêt général', in CIRIEC (ed.), *Gouvernance et intérêt général dans les services sociaux et de santé*, Brussels: P.I.E. Peter Lang, pp. 23–38.
Esping-Andersen, G. (1990), *The Three Worlds of Welfare Capitalism*, Princeton, US: Princeton University Press.
Evers, A. and J.-L. Laville (eds) (2004), *The Third Sector in Europe, Globalisation and Welfare*, Cheltenham, UK: Edward Elgar Publishing.
Freeman, C. (1991), 'Innovation, Change of Techno-Economic Paradigm and Biological Analogies in Economics', *Revue économique*, **2**, 211–231.
Hall, P. (1993), 'Policy Paradigms, Social Learning and the State. The Case of Economic Policy Making in Britain', *Comparative Politics*, **25** (3), 275–296.

Hall, P. and D. Soskice (2001), *Varieties of Capitalism: The Institutional Foundations of Comparative Advantage*, Oxford: Oxford University Press.

Hartley, J. (2005), 'Innovation in Governance and Public Services: Past and Present', *Public Money and Management*, **25** (1), 27–34.

Hartley, J. (2011), 'Public Value Through innovation and improvement', in Benington, John and Mark H. Moore (eds), *Public Value. Theory and Practice*, New York: Palgrave Macmillan, pp. 171–184.

Hollingsworth, J.R. and R. Boyer (1997), *Contemporary Capitalism. The Embeddedness of Institutions*, Cambridge: Cambridge University Press.

Hood, C. (1991), 'A Public Management for all Seasons?', *Public Administration*, **69** (1), 3–19.

Kamarck, E.C. (2003), *Government Innovation around the World*, Boston: Ash Institute for Democratic Governance and Innovation, John F. Kennedy School of Government, Harvard University, http://observgo.uquebec.ca/observgo/fichiers/78979_kamarck_global_innovations.pdf (last accessed 2 October 2011).

Klein, J.-L. (2008), 'Territoire et régulation', *Cahiers de recherche sociologique*, **45**, 41–58.

König, K. (1997), 'Entrepreneurial Management or Executive Administration: The Perspective of Classical Public Administration', in W. Kickert (ed.), *Public Management and Administrative Reform in Western Europe*, Cheltenham, UK: Edward Elgar Publishing, pp. 217–236.

Lévesque, B. (2003), 'Fonction de base et nouveau rôle des pouvoirs publics: vers un nouveau paradigme de l'État', *Annals of Public and Cooperative Economics*, **74** (4), 489–513.

Lévesque, B. (2005), 'A new Governance Paradigm: public authorities-markets-civil society linkage for social cohesion', in *Solidarity-based Choices in the Market-Place: a vital contribution to social cohesion*, Strasbourg: Council of Europe Publishing (Trends in Social Cohesion, 14), pp. 29–67.

Lévesque, B. (2006), 'L'innovation dans le développement économique et dans le développement social', in Klein, J.-L. and D. Harrisson (eds), *L'innovation sociale. Émergence et effet sur la transformation sociale*, Québec: Presses de l'Université du Québec, pp. 43–70.

Levy, C. (2011), *Making the most of public services A systems approach to public innovation. A Knowledge Economy programme report*, London, UK: The Work Foundation.

Monnier, L. and B. Thiry (1997), 'Architecture et dynamique de l'intérêt général', in Monnier, Lionel and Bernard Thiry (eds), *Mutations structurelles et intérêt général. Vers quels nouveaux paradigms pour l'économie publique, sociale et coopérative*, Bruxelles: De Boeck-Université, pp. 11–30.

Moulaert, F. (2009), 'Social Innovation: Institutionally Embedded, Territorially (Re)

Produce', in MacCallum, D., F. Moulaert, J. Hillier and S. Vicari Haddock (eds), *Social Innovation and Territorial Development*, Farnham (UK) and Burlington VT, US: Ashgate Publishing Limited, pp. 11–24.

Moore, F.H. (1995), *Creating Public Value: Strategic Management in Government*, Cambridge, MA, US: Harvard University Press.

Mulgan, G. and D. Albury (2003), *Innovation in the Public Sector*, London: Strategy Unit, Cabinet Office, www.webarchive.nationalarchives.gov.uk/+/http://www.cabinetoffice.gov.uk/upload/assets/www.cabinetoffice.gov.uk/strategy/pubinov2.pdf (last accessed 28 October 2011).

Nambisan, S. (2008), *Transforming Government Through Collaborative Innovation*, Washington: IBM Center for the Business of Government, http://www.businessofgovernment.org/sites/default/files/NambisanReport.pdf (last accessed 14 November 2011).

O'Flynn, J. (2007), 'From New Public Management to Public Value: Paradigmatic Change and Managerial Implications', *The Australian Journal of Public Administration*, 66 (3), 353–366.

Osborne, S.P. (1994), 'Naming the Beast: Defining and Clarifying Service Innovations in Social Policy', *Human Relations*, 54,1133–1154.

Osborne, D. and T. Gaebler (1993), *Reinventing Government: How the Entrepreneurial Spirit is Transforming the Public Sector*, New York: Penguin.

Osborne, Stephen P. and Kerry Brown (2005), *Managing change and Innovation in Public Services Organization*, London: Routledge.

Paradeise, C., Y. Bleiklie, J. Enders, G., Goastellec, S. Michelsen, E. and D. Reale and F. Westerheijden (2009), in Huisman, Jeroen (ed.) *International Perspectives on the Governance of higher education: alternative frameworks for coordination*, New York: Taylor and Francis Books US, pp. 88–106.

Parker, R.L. (2007), 'Networked governance or just networks? Local governance of the knowledge economy in Limerick (Ireland) and Karlskrona (Sweden)', *Political Studies*, **55** (1), 113–132.

Pollitt, C. and S. Dan (2011), 'The impact of the New Public Management in Europe: A Meta-analysis', www.cocops.eu/publications/working-papers (last accessed 2 December 2011).

Rhodes, R.A.W. and J. Wanna (2011), 'The limits to Public Value, or Rescuing Responsible Government form the Platonic Guardians', *The Australian Journal of Public Administration*, **66** (4), 406–421.

Simard, Carole and Luc Bernier (1992), *L'administration publique*, Montréal: Boréal.

Stoker, G. (2006), 'Public Value Management: A New Narrative for Networked Governance?', *The American Review of Public Administration*, 36 (1), 41–56.

Thelen, K. (2004), *How Institutions Evolve: The*

Political Economy of Skills in Germany, Britain, the United States and Japan, New York: Cambridge University Press.

United Nations (2006), *Innovations in Governance and Public Administration. Replicating that Works*, New York.

Vaillancourt, Y. (2009), 'Social Economy in the Co-Construction of Public Policy', *Annals of Public and Cooperative Economics*, **80** (2), 275–313.

Van de Walle, S. and G. Hammerschmid (2011), 'Coordinating for Cohesion in the Public sector of the future', COCOPS Working Paper, 1, www.cocops.eu/publications/academic-publications (last accessed 6 December 2011).

Verhoest, K., B. Verschuere and G. Brouckaert (2007), 'Presssure Legitimacy and Innovative Behavior by Public Organizations', *Governance:*

An International Journal Policy, Administration, and Institutions, **20** (3), 469–497.

Von Hippel, E. (2005), 'Democratizing Innovation: The Evolving Phenomenon of user innovation', *Journal für Betriebswirtschaft*, **55**, 63–78.

Vries, J. (de) (2010), 'Is New Public Management Really Dead?', *OECD Journal on Budgeting*, **1**, 1–5.

Wilkins, J. (2011), 'Alternative Service Delivery Revised', Discussion paper, 10, London: Commowealth Secretariat, www.publications.the commonwealth.org/alternative-service-delivery-revisited-870-p.aspx (last accessed 2 December 2011).

Wood, Christopher (1995), 'The New Public Management in the 1980s: variations on a theme', *Accounting Organizations and Society*, **20** (2/3), 93–109.

3. Social innovation, social economy and social enterprise: what can the European debate tell us?
Jacques Defourny and Marthe Nyssens

3.1 INTRODUCTION

Organizations corresponding to what we now call 'social enterprises' have existed since well before the mid-1990s when the term began to be increasingly used in both Western Europe and the United States. Indeed, the third sector, be it called the non-profit sector, the voluntary sector or the social economy, has long witnessed entrepreneurial dynamics which resulted in innovative solutions for providing services or goods to persons or communities whose needs were neither met by private companies nor by public providers. However, for reasons which vary from region to region, the concept of social enterprise is now gaining a fast growing interest along with two closely related terms, namely 'social entrepreneur' and 'social entrepreneurship'.

Social innovation, or at least innovation to provide answers to social needs, seems to be at the heart of the fast developing literature around those 'SE concepts'. So it makes sense to question more deeply the actual links which may exist between the corpus of social enterprise research and the social innovation dynamics as defined in this book's introduction through three major features: the satisfaction of human needs, the relations between humans in general and between social groups in particular, and the empowerment of people trying to fulfil their needs, this third feature being seen as a bridge between the first and the second.

For doing so, we first contextualize the emerging SE concepts, especially highlighting their different roots and subsequent schools of thought both in the United States and Europe. While doing this, we try to show the extent to which social innovation has a place and a role in such streams of literature (Section 3.2).

Then, we analyse more deeply the EMES conceptualization of social enterprise. The EMES approach to social enterprise has been developed by a group of European scholars and is anchored in the European tradition of social economy (Section 3.3). The specificity of the EMES approach is to approach social enterprise dynamics both by its aim, the primacy of social aim and its process through democratic governance echoing the different dimensions of social innovation (Section 3.4). Finally, we develop the issue of the links between public policies and the diffusion of social innovation in the field of social enterprise. For that purpose, we rely on one of the main EMES research projects in the field of work integration social enterprise (Section 3.5).

3.2 SOCIAL INNOVATION IN THE VARIOUS SOCIAL ENTERPRISE SCHOOLS OF THOUGHT

While social innovation emerged as a specific field of interest in the early 1980s, through pioneering works like those of Chambon et al. (1982) among others, the concepts of social entrepreneurship and social enterprise only attracted a clear research interest more than a decade later, mainly in third sector studies and then well beyond that specific field to embrace a wide range of business strategies to address social challenges. Probably because they are recent and try to cover a wide range of initiatives, current conceptions and theories of social enterprise/social entrepreneurship do not form an integrated body, rather a cluster of theories where different schools of thought can be identified (Defourny and Nyssens 2010). This is why we first develop a brief historical and contextual analysis of those schools of thought in order to better identify their respective links with the social innovation debate.

3.2.1 The 'Earned Income' School of Thought

The first school regarding the conceptual debate on social enterprise refers to the use of commercial activities by non-profit organizations in the United States. Indeed, the bulk of its publications focus on strategies for starting a business that would earn income in support of the social mission of a non-profit organization and that could help diversify its funding base in a context of increased competition for philanthropic and public resources (Weisbrod 1998; Kerlin 2006). However, we suggest a distinction between an earlier strand in this school focusing on non-profits, and which we call the 'commercial non-profit approach', on the one hand, and a broader and more recent strand embracing all forms of business initiatives, and which may be named the 'mission-driven business approach', on the other hand. The latter approach also deals with social purpose ventures encompassing all organizations that trade for a social purpose, including for-profit companies (Austin et al. 2006).

Within this 'earned income' school of thought, no link is explicitly made with social innovation. Its earlier version however is deeply rooted in the tradition of non-profit studies which, for several decades, have tried to understand the role and the *raisons d'être* of non-profit organizations within market economies. More precisely, among such raisons d'être, some authors have identified the socially innovative capacity of non-profits in the field of social services: indeed, an historical perspective shows that non-profit organizations played a pioneering role by meeting emerging social demands, which clearly corresponds to the first dimension of social innovation. They reveal, to some extent, collective benefits associated to the provision of goods and services (Salamon 1987).

Although closer to the 'mission-driven business approach', the notion of social business as understood by M. Yunus (2010) also has an implicit dimension of social innovation: defined as a non-loss, non-dividend, fully market-based company dedicated entirely to achieving a social goal, his notion of social business always involves an innovation which allows the meeting of a basic need of poor populations (for instance, a highly nutritive yoghurt distributed at a very low price by a large number of disadvantaged female sellers).

3.2.2 The 'Social Innovation' School of Thought

This second SE school puts the emphasis on social entrepreneurs in a typical Schumpeterian perspective. The early writings of this school came first of all from 'reflective practitioners who saw themselves as civic entrepreneurs working in collaborative arenas to improve the resilience of specific communities with an ambition of systemic change' (Hulgard 2010, p. 295). This was also the approach adopted by Bill Drayton and Ashoka, the organization he founded in 1980 in the United States. Ashoka's mission was (and still is) to find and support social entrepreneurs who 'have innovative solutions to social problems and the potential to change patterns across society' (http://www.ashoka.org/fellows, last accessed 7 December 2012). Ashoka therefore focuses on the profiles of very specific individuals (first referred to as 'public entrepreneurs') able to bring about social innovation in various fields. Although many initiatives launched by social entrepreneurs result in the setting up of non-profit organizations, most recent works of this school of thought tend to underline blurred frontiers and the existence of opportunities for entrepreneurial social innovation within the private for-profit sector and the public sphere as well.

Whether the work of these social entrepreneurs is to deliver solar energy to Brazilian villagers, to improve access to college in the United States or to start a home-care system for AIDS patients in South Africa (Bornstein 2004), the centre of attention is their capacity to develop innovative ways to address pressing social needs, thus reflecting the first dimension of social innovation as understood in this book, i.e. the satisfaction of human needs.

For this school of thought, social entrepreneurship is therefore more a question of outcomes (Dees 1998; Mulgan 2007; Murray et al. 2010) than a question of incomes, as it is in the 'earned income' school. Moreover, the systemic nature of innovation involving new frameworks (technologies, institutional forms, regulatory and fiscal frameworks . . .) is underlined as well as its impact at a broad

societal level through a process of scalability (Kramer 2005; Martin and Osberg 2007; Mulgan 2010). However, if the satisfaction of human needs is at the core of this school, the key actors of innovation are seen in a rather individualistic perspective and therefore the issue of relations between different social groups is not part of the debate.

3.3 SOCIAL ENTREPRENEURSHIP AS OBSERVED BY THE EMES NETWORK IN EUROPE

In Europe, the social enterprise debate took place in the mid-1990s through the identification of new entrepreneurial dynamics at the very heart of the third sector, primarily arising in response to social needs that were inadequately met, or not met at all, by public services or for-profit enterprises. Before looking at this phenomenon, let us stress that a strong European tradition sees the third sector as bringing together cooperatives, associations, mutual societies and increasingly foundations, or in other words, all not-for-profit organizations (organizations not owned by shareholders) that are also labelled the 'social economy' in some European countries (Evers and Laville 2004). This legal-institutional approach of the social economy is usually combined with a normative or ethical approach which underlines the essential common features of these different types of organizations: their aim is to provide a good or service to their members or to a community, rather than generating profits, and their specific governance rules (independent management, democratic decision making process and primacy of people and labour over capital in the distribution of income) thereby expressing a long historical quest for economic democracy (Defourny 2001).

Why did it make sense to talk about a new social entrepreneurship and not simply an evolution in third sector or social economy organizations? In 1996, scholars from the 15 EU member states got together to study and compare the 'emergence of social enterprise' in all their respective countries (and to form the EMES European Research Network).[1] The background of this major research project was the classic work of Schumpeter, for whom economic development is a 'process of carrying out new combinations' in the production process. Following the work carried out by Young (1983) and Badelt (1997), the Schumpeterian typology of innovation was reinterpreted to identify innovating dynamics in the third sector (EMES 1999; Defourny 2001).

3.3.1 New Products or a New Quality of Products

There are many theoretical and empirical works showing that third sector organizations have often invented new types of services to take up the challenges of their time (Salamon 1987; Defourny et al. 1999). Therefore, many of these organizations can be said, nowadays as in the past, to be born or have been born from an entrepreneurial dynamics. But have the last two or three decades been different in any specific way? The answer is clearly affirmative as the crisis of the European welfare systems (in terms of budget, efficiency and legitimacy) has resulted in public authorities increasingly looking to private initiatives to provide solutions that they would have implemented themselves if the economic climate and the collective willingness to redistribute had been as good as in the 1945–1975 'golden period'. The two main fields of activity covered by the works of the EMES European Research Network, namely work integration of low-qualified

jobseekers (Nyssens 2006) and personal services (Borzaga and Defourny 2001), have seen multiple innovations in terms of new activities better adapted to needs, whether in regard to vocational training, childcare, services for elderly people, or aid for certain categories of disadvantaged persons (abused children, refugees, immigrants, etc.) referring to the first dimension of social innovation i.e. the satisfaction of human needs.

Such a social entrepreneurship seemed all the more innovative as, even within the third sector, it sometimes contrasted sharply with the bureaucratic and only slightly innovative behaviour of certain large traditional organizations.

3.3.2 New Methods of Organization and/or Production

What is most striking in the current generations of social enterprises is the involvement of several categories of actors. Salaried workers, volunteers, users, support organizations and local public authorities are often partners in the same project, whereas traditional social economy organizations have generally been set up by more homogeneous social groups. If this does not necessarily revolutionize the production process in the strict meaning of the term, it nevertheless often transforms the way in which the activity is organized. In some cases, one could even talk of a joint construction of supply and demand, when providers and users cooperate in the organization and management of certain proximity services (Laville and Nyssens 2000). The setting-up of childcare centres run by parents in France or in Sweden is just one of many examples of such cooperation. In this case, social innovation not only refers to the satisfaction of human needs (e.g. childcare) but also to the relations between different social groups in the entrepreneurial process (for example users, workers and volunteers) and to the empowerment of users themselves trying to fulfil their needs. Users are no longer considered as consumers but as central actors of the development of the service itself.

3.3.3   New Production Factors

One of the major but long-standing specific characteristics of the third sector is its capacity to mobilize volunteer work. In itself, the use of volunteers is thus not innovating. However, volunteering has profoundly changed in nature over the last few decades: it seems to be not only much less charitable than 40 or 50 years ago, but also less 'militant' than in the 1960s or 1970s. Today's volunteers are fairly pragmatic and focus more on 'productive' objectives and activities that correspond to specific needs. It is not unusual, indeed, that the entrepreneurial role, in the most common meaning of the term (launching an activity), is carried out by volunteers.

Paid work has also seen various innovations. For instance, many third sector organizations have been at the forefront of experiments regarding atypical forms of employment, such as hiring salaried workers in the framework of unemployment reduction programmes. This is the case with work integration social enterprises (WISEs) which were pioneers in promoting the integration of excluded persons through a productive activity. The first WISEs actually implemented active labour market policies before they came into institutional existence. More precisely, the philosophy of innovative social enterprises which emerged in the 1980s clearly resided in the empowerment and integration of excluded groups through participation in WISEs whose aim was to offer the disadvantaged workers a chance to reassess the role of work in their lives by supporting them while they gained control over their own personal project. This conception implies not only giving an occupation to these persons but also developing specific values, for example through democratic management structures in which disadvantaged workers are given a role, and/or through the production of goods and services generating collective benefits (such as social services or services linked to the environment) for the territory in which the WISEs are embedded (Nyssens 2006).

Once more, what is at stake in both cases is not only satisfying needs (for volunteers, providing social services, for unemployed persons, having a job) but also the relations between social groups as volunteers and workers in integration initiatives are not considered as underling agents but instead are mobilized with other stakeholders in the entrepreneurial process itself through specific organizational structures which favour empowerment of these groups.

What is striking from this brief overview is the multiplicity of facets of social innovation, from dynamics in social enterprises related to new services satisfying basic human needs, to the relationships between social groups involved in the entrepreneurial process as well as the empowerment of groups formed by users, workers or volunteers, among which there are often vulnerable persons.

3.3.4   The EMES Conceptual Approach of Social Enterprise

Against this background, the EMES European Research Network built a working definition to identify organizations likely to be called 'social enterprises' in all 15 countries that then formed the EU. Guided by a project that was both theoretical and empirical and instead of seeking an elegant short definition, EMES preferred from the outset the selection of various indicators based on an extensive dialogue among several disciplines (economics, sociology, political science and management) as well as among the various national traditions and sensitivities regarding social enterprise within the European Union. Through the nine indicators presented hereafter, it is easy to recognize usual characteristics of social economy organizations, which are refined in order to highlight new entrepreneurial dynamics (Borzaga and Defourny 2001). Those indicators allow the identification of brand new types of social enterprises, but they can also lead to designate as social enterprises older organizations being reshaped by new internal dynamics.

Such indicators were never intended to represent the full and precise set of conditions that an organization should meet to qualify as a social enterprise. Rather than constituting prescriptive criteria, they describe an 'ideal-type' in Weber's terms, i.e. an abstract construction that enables researchers to position themselves within the 'galaxy' of social enterprises. In other words, they constitute a tool, somewhat analogous to a compass, which helps the researchers locate the position of the observed entities relative to one another and eventually identify subsets of social enterprises they want to study more deeply.

The indicators have so far been presented in two subsets consisting of four economic indicators and five social indicators (Defourny 2001, pp. 16–18). However, it now seems more appropriate to classify these nine indicators into three subsets rather than two, to highlight particular forms of governance which appear to be specific to the EMES ideal-type social enterprise when compared to the other SE schools of thought presented here above

(Defourny and Nyssens 2010). As it will be shown, this governance pillar has a profound impact on the way social innovation may be theorized and observed in social enterprises.

Three criteria reflect *the economic and entrepreneurial dimensions* of social enterprises.

a) A continuous activity producing goods and/or selling services: social enterprises, unlike some traditional non-profit organizations, do not normally have advocacy activities or the redistribution of financial resources (as, for example, many foundations) as their major activity, but they are directly involved in the production of goods or the provision of services to people on a continuous basis. The productive activity thus represents the reason, or one of the main reasons, for the existence of social enterprises.

b) A significant level of economic risk: those who establish a social enterprise assume totally or partly the risk inherent in the initiative. Unlike most public institutions, their financial viability depends on the efforts of their members and workers to secure adequate resources.

c) A minimum amount of paid work: as in the case of most traditional non-profit organizations, social enterprises may combine monetary and non-monetary resources, voluntary and paid workers. However, the activity carried out in social enterprises requires a minimum level of paid workers.

Three indicators encapsulate the *social dimensions* of such enterprises:

d) An explicit aim to benefit the community: one of the principal aims of social enterprises is to serve the community or a specific group of people. In the same perspective, a feature of social enterprises is their desire to promote a sense of social responsibility at the local level.

e) An initiative launched by a group of citizens or civil society organizations: social enterprises are the result of collective dynamics involving people belonging to a community or to a group that shares a well-defined need or aim; this collective dimension must be maintained over time in one way or another, even though the importance of leadership – often embodied by an individual or a small group of leaders – must not be neglected.

f) A limited profit distribution: the primacy of the social aim is reflected in a constraint on the distribution of profits. However, social enterprises not only include organizations that are characterized by a strict non-distribution constraint, but also organizations which – like cooperatives in many countries – may distribute profits, but only to a limited extent, thus allowing to avoid a profit-maximizing behaviour.

Finally, three indicators reflect the *participatory governance* of such enterprises:

g) A high degree of autonomy: social enterprises are created as autonomous projects which are governed by the people involved and not, directly or indirectly, by public authorities or other organizations (federations, private firms etc.) even though they may rely partly on public subsidies/funds. Those involved in the governance of such enterprises have the right both to express their ideas ('voice') and to terminate their activity ('exit').

h) A decision-making power not based on capital ownership: this criterion generally refers to the principle of 'one member, one vote' or at least to a decision-making process in which voting power is not distributed according to capital shares in the governing body which has the ultimate decision-making rights.

i) A participatory nature, which involves various parties affected by the activity: representation and participation of users or customers and of various stakeholders in the decision-making process and a participative management often are important characteristics of social enterprises. In many cases, one of the aims of social enterprises is to further democracy at the local level through economic activity.

3.4   WHAT LINKS THE EMES APPROACH TO THE CONCEPT OF SOCIAL INNOVATION?

It seems social innovation does not appear explicitly in these various EMES indicators, which may be surprising as we showed that SE's dynamics have been a vehicle for social innovation throughout Europe. The reason is that the focal point of EMES work has been the identification of entrepreneurial dynamics driven by social aims. If social enterprises have been pioneering in various fields (work integration, ethical banking, recycling industries, personal services . . .), they also provide an organizational form that contributes significantly to the scaling up of innovation and its replicability. For example, in the European Union, the pioneering WISE initiatives were launched in the late 1970s/early 1980s, without any specific public scheme to support their objectives. As a matter of fact, in a context of increasing unemployment and social exclusion, social actors did not find public policy schemes adequate to tackle these problems. Initiatives thus emerged as a protest against established public policies and pointed at the limits of institutional public intervention practices towards those excluded from the labour market. In that early stage, many such WISEs were quite innovative and, in a second stage, they contributed to shaping innovative public policies in the field of work integration (Defourny and Nyssens 2008). In turn, the existence of such specific public programs fostered the development of work integration social enterprises which are now the result of a scaling up process of social innovation but can no longer be qualified as fully innovative in many countries.

If social innovation is not present as such among EMES indicators, it should be stressed, however, that the governance pillar, which distinguishes the EMES approach to SE from other SE schools, allows us to highlight specific links with social innovation. To do this, let us come back again to the different components of social innovation dynamics as stated in the introduction of this book: the satisfaction of human needs, the relations among human beings in general, and among social groups in particular, as well as the empowerment of people trying to fulfil their needs, this last feature being considered as a bridge between the first and the second.

The first element – the satisfaction of human needs – is at the intersection of the criteria of 'a continuous activity producing goods and/or selling services' and 'an explicit aim to benefit the community'. Indeed, the goal of SE is not the maximization of profit but the provision of goods or services which matter for the development of a community (even if they are especially addressed to a specific target group in the community). In fact, this characteristic is shared by the vast majority of SE schools. In traditional business entrepreneurship, the key motivation is to build a profitable company and to earn an attractive return on investment, while in social entrepreneurship the drive is to create social value (Austin et al. 2006).

The other two dimensions of social innovation – the relations between social groups and the empowerment of people – are deeply linked to the governance pillar of the EMES approach as the latter's ideal-type SE involves a collective dynamics. More precisely, the participatory governance pillar can be seen as a set of institutional characteristics designed to ensure that the initial collective impulse will be maintained over time. First, the organizational autonomy and a distribution of voting power not based on capital ownership are certainly in line with the cooperative tradition for which there is a primacy of members as persons over any logic of profit accumulation and maximum return on investment. Second, these features add to constraints on the distribution of profits with a view to strengthening the non-capitalist nature of the enterprise. Third, within such a cooperative-like tradition, the EMES social enterprise may be seen as innovative: while most cooperatives are typically organizations fostering the interests of one category of stakeholders (workers, consumers, savers, farmers . . .), social enterprises often represent a new type of cooperative or cooperative-like enterprise, i.e. involving various types of stakeholders in their governance structures and/or focusing on the needs of target groups who are not necessarily part of the membership. These institutional characteristics reflect the fact that social innovation doesn't solely concern outcomes, but processes as well – and most especially the social relations between groups.

The EMES ideal-type SE suggests that the production of social value through the provision of goods and services meeting important needs of a community and the implementation of specific governance patterns are deeply interrelated. Moreover, a great deal of EMES empirical works confirms that social enterprises with such structural features are more likely to be vehicles of social innovation (Gardin 2006b; Brandsen and Pestoff 2009). In this sense, we fully share the point of view of Moulaert and Nussbaumer (2005, p. 2071) stating that:

> social innovation at the local level rests on two pillars: institutional innovation (innovation in social relations, innovations in governance including empowerment dynamics) and innovation in the sense of the social economy – i.e. satisfaction of various needs in local communities . . . Yet both pillars are intimately related.

3.5   SOCIAL ENTERPRISE AND PUBLIC POLICIES

The analysis of social innovation can't be limited at the level of the organization. As noted by Moulaert and Nussbaumer (2005), it is insufficient to design specific modes of governance without taking into account higher spatial scales and their impact on the meso level.

In the European context, the process of institutionalization of social enterprise has often been closely linked to the evolution of public policies. As already mentioned, a historical perspective shows social enterprises have contributed to the development of new public schemes and legal frameworks, which in turn became channels for social innovation. Especially, social enterprises built platforms and federative bodies to advocate for a better recognition of their specificities. As a result, laws were

passed to promote new legal forms, better suited to social enterprises, and public schemes were designed to target more specifically work integration social enterprises (Defourny and Nyssens 2008).

Italy has clearly been a pioneer in such a move: as early as in 1991, the Italian parliament passed a law creating a new legal form for 'social cooperatives' and the latter went on to experience an extraordinary growth. In the second part of the 1990s or in the early 2000s, 11 other European countries also introduced new legal forms reflecting and promoting the entrepreneurial approach adopted by an increasing number of 'not-for-profit' organizations, even though the term of 'social enterprise' was not always used as such in those legislations (Roelants 2009). The emergence of these social cooperatives and social enterprises are more or less explicitly related to the cooperative tradition (Defourny and Nyssens 2008) characterized by a quest for democracy through economic activity, which has been at the heart of many pioneering initiatives of the 19th and 20th century across Europe.

3.5.1   Scaling up of Social Innovation or Trend towards Isomorphism?

In turn, legal frameworks tend to shape, at least in part, the objectives and practices of social enterprises. So it is relevant to raise the hypothesis of a possible trend towards 'isomorphism' in such organizations – isomorphism being understood as a progressive loss of their inner characteristics under the pressure of legal frameworks or professional norms spilling over from the for-profit private or public sectors (Di Maggio and Powell 1983). If they could actually be observed, isomorphism pressures could curb the innovative dynamics of social enterprises.

This question, among others, has been

analysed by the EMES Network in the field of work integration through a large empirical survey covering 160 WISEs in 11 EU countries over four years (Nyssens 2006). On the basis of such a detailed field study, one of the largest to date, Bode et al. (2006) conclude that there is no overall tendency towards isomorphism understood as an evolution in which WISEs completely lose their initial identity. This said, however, external pressures generate strained relations between the different goals of WISEs.

Both public authorities and governing bodies of WISEs agree on the fact that the hiring and professional integration of disadvantaged workers are at the very heart of WISEs' mission, but differences arise regarding how this integration is to be understood. The dominant model of public recognition of WISEs tends to only acknowledge one kind of benefits – namely those benefits linked to the work-integration goal in the framework of active labour market policies – and through a very specific target, i.e. the integration of workers into the 'first' labour market.

Getting workers back into the first labour market was actually not the priority of the pioneering WISEs. However the institutionalization and professionalization of the field over the years, through public schemes increasingly linked to active labour market policies, has generated a clear pressure to make the social mission instrumental to the integration of disadvantaged workers into the first labour market. As a result, a strained relation can often be observed between the objective of empowering excluded groups through participative decision-making processes and the mission of integrating the beneficiaries into 'normal' jobs. Regarding the production goal, the first challenge for WISEs is to find a type of production suited to the capacities of the disadvantaged groups they employ while making it possible to train these workers through the production process. To meet this challenge, developing market niches has proven a successful strategy. However, 'WISEs which have successfully entered into niche markets may discover that, from the moment these markets become more stable, private competitors (with fewer social concerns and constraints) are keen to make money in them as well' (Bode et al. 2006, p. 239). As a result, WISEs can be driven to adopt the norms of these for-profit competitors.

3.5.2 A Genuine Hybrid Identity or an Impossible Combination of Conflicting Logics?

In various regards, social enterprises can be seen as hybrid organizations and their hybrid nature is reflected particularly clearly in their mode of governance and sources of income. Such a hybridity could be qualified as an institutional innovation. However, does this hybrid character of social enterprises constitute a bulwark against isomorphism, or is it rather a threat for their identity, embedded in different, contradictory logics?

Their mode of governance could be seen as hybrid insofar as it relies on a dynamics of linking people with different backgrounds. Indeed, most WISEs surveyed by the EMES network were founded through a partnership among different categories of civil society actors. Local public bodies were sometimes associated with this dynamics as well. Fifty-eight per cent of European WISEs were described as involving more than one category of stakeholders on their board, these categories being defined as users, volunteers, workers, local businesses, public bodies, other non-profit organizations (Campi et al. 2006). These features highlight the collective and hybrid dynamics underlying many social enterprises and contrast with some literature on social entrepreneurship just emphasizing the leadership of individual social entrepreneurs without any attention towards the role of other stakeholders in the enterprise's governance.

Hybridity is also reflected by the resource mix mobilized by European WISEs (Gardin 2006a). The latter indeed show a particular capacity to articulate resources coming from different sources. The sales of goods and services represent on average, at the European level, 53 per cent of WISEs' resources – of these 53 per cent, one third are socially motivated sales i.e. the result of public purchases decided where explicit social objectives of WISEs are taken into account in the choice of the provider by the public authorities, for example through social clauses. Redistribution resources account for 38.5 per cent of resources. Voluntary resources, which are most probably undervalued, represent on average 8.5 per cent of total resources. This last kind of resource somehow reflects the degree of embeddedness of WISEs in civic networks: social enterprises which are more strongly embedded in civic networks are usually better able to mobilize voluntary resources than social enterprises launched mainly with the impulse of public bodies.

Public schemes, though, do not usually recognize such a hybrid character of social enterprises. Indeed, one of the most visible effects of the institutionalization of WISEs in the different European countries is that it pushes them to reduce the variety of their resources mix and to position themselves, most of the time, either in the 'market economy' or, when they employ very disadvantaged workers, in the 'redistributive economy'; as to the role of voluntary resources, it is in neither case recognized. Such a too narrow approach puts social enterprises into 'boxes', denying one of their fundamental characteristics – namely the fact that they are located in an intermediate space between the market, the state and civil society.

3.6   CONCLUSION

The social enterprise debate is on the rise. The diversity and openness of the concept are probably some of the reasons for its success. The perspective we have adopted in this chapter suggests that the various SE conceptions are deeply rooted in the social, economic, political and cultural contexts in which these organizations emerge. These conceptions have obvious links with the social innovation debate. A focus on the satisfaction of human needs is shared by all SE schools as each one in its own way, is discovering or rediscovering new opportunities to promote, simultaneously, entrepreneurial spirit and the pursuit of the public good. The specificity of the EMES approach which is embedded in the European social economy tradition is to highlight the central place of participatory governance which paves the way for the empowerment of various groups of stakeholders – users, workers, volunteers . . . – involved in the activity.

In the European context, the process of institutionalization of social enterprise has often been closely linked to the evolution of public policies. In fact, social enterprises significantly influence their institutional environment and they contribute to shaping institutions including public policies. If this dynamics can be seen as a channel for the diffusion of social innovation, the key role of public bodies in some fields of social enterprises may also reduce them to instruments to achieve specific goals which are given priority on the political agenda, with a risk of bridling the dynamics of social innovation.

Empirical evidence shows that the involvement of various categories of stakeholders in social enterprises constitutes a channel for developing relations and trust among these groups. Analysis also tends to show that such a multi-stakeholder nature may in turn be a resource to pursue a complex set of objectives and may consequently support the innovative capacity of social enterprises. Finally, the reliance on a variety of resources, both from the point of view of their origin (e.g. from private customers, from the business sector, from the public sector or from the third sector) and regarding the mode of resource allocation (e.g. sales of services, public subsidies, gifts and volunteering), also appears to be a key element to enable social enterprises fulfilling their multiple-goal missions. Keeping and managing such a hybridity nevertheless constitutes a daily challenge for social enterprise.

3.7 QUESTIONS FOR DISCUSSION

- Social innovation doesn't concern the sole outcomes but the process of social innovation as well and more especially the social relations between groups. A key research question in the field of social enterprises is therefore the analysis of governance structure inside the enterprise. Which ones do you think foster social innovation?
- What are the links between economic value, social value and social innovation? Do you think they are substitutes or complementary dimensions in social enterprises?

NOTE

1. www.emes.net (last accessed 7 December 2012).

REFERENCES

(References in bold are recommended reading.)

Austin, J.E, B. Leonard, E. Reficco and J. Wei-Skillern (2006), 'Social Entrepreneurship: It's for Corporations too', in A. Nicholls (ed.) *Social Entrepreneurship, New Models of Sustainable Social Change*, New York: Oxford University Press, pp. 169–180.
Badelt, C. (1997), 'Entrepreneurship theories of the non-profit sector', *Voluntas*, **8** (2), 162–178.
Bode, I., A. Evers and A. Schultz (2006), 'Social Enterprises: Can Hybridisation be Sustainable?', in M. Nyssens (ed.), pp. 237–258.
Bornstein, D. (2004), *How to Change the World: Social Entrepreneurs and the Power of New Ideas*, New York: Oxford University Press.
Borzaga, C. and J. Defourny (eds) (2001), *The Emergence of Social Enterprise*, London and New York: Routledge.
Brandsen, T. and V. Pestoff (2009), 'Public governance and the third sector: opportunities for co-production and innovation?', in S. Osborne (ed.) *The New Public Governance? New Perspectives on the Theory and Practice of Public Governance*, London and New York: Routledge, pp. 223–236.
Campi, S., J. Defourny and O. Grégoire (2006), 'Multiple Goals and Multiple Stakeholder Structure: The Governance of Social Enterprises', in M. Nyssens (ed.), pp. 29–49.
Chambon, J.-L., A. David and J.-M. Devevey (1982), *Les innovations sociales*, Paris: Presses Universitaires de France.
Dees, J.G. (1998), 'The Meaning of Social Entrepreneurship', Working Paper, Kauffman Center for Entrepreneurial Leadership.
Defourny, J. (2001), 'From Third Sector to Social Enterprise', in C. Borzaga and J. Defourny (eds), *The Emergence of Social Enterprise*, London and New York: Routledge, pp. 1–28.
Defourny, J. and M. Nyssens (2008), 'Social Enterprise in Europe: Recent Trends and Developments', *Social Enterprise Journal*, **4** (3), 202–228.
Defourny, J. and M. Nyssens (2010), 'Conceptions of Social Enterprise and Social Entrepreneurship in Europe and the United States: Convergences and Divergences', *Journal of Social Entrepreneurship*, 1 (1), 32–53.
Defourny, J., P. Develtere and B. Fonteneau (1999), *L'économie sociale au Nord et au Sud*, Bruxelles: De Boeck.
Di Maggio, P.J. and W. Powell (1983), 'The iron cage revisited institutional isomorphism and collective rationality in organizational fields', *American Sociological Review*, **48**, 147–160.
EMES European Network (1999), *The Emergence of Social Enterprises in Europe. A Short Overview*, Brussels: EMES.

Evers, A. and J.-L. Laville, (eds) (2004), *The Third Sector in Europe*, Cheltenham, UK and Northampton, MA: Edward Elgar Publishing.

Gardin, L. (2006a), 'A variety of resource mix inside social enterprises', in M. Nyssens (ed.), pp. 111–136.

Gardin, L. (2006b), *Les initiatives solidaires. La réciprocité face au marché et à l'Etat*, Toulouse: Editions Erès.

Hulgard, L., (2010), 'Social Entrepreneurship', in K. Hart, J.L. Laville and C. Cattani, (eds), *The Human Economy, a Citizen's Guide*, London: Polity Press, pp. 293–300.

Kerlin, J. (2006), 'Social Enterprise in the United States and Europe: Understanding and Learning from the Differences', *Voluntas*, **17** (3), 247–263.

Kramer, M. (2005), *Measuring Innovation: Evaluation in the Field of Social Entrepreneurship*, Boston, MA: Foundation Strategy Group.

Laville, J.L. and M. Nyssens (2000), 'Solidarity-Based Third Sector Organizations in the "Proximity Services" Field: a European Francophone Perspective', *Voluntas*, **11** (1), 67–84.

Martin, R. and S. Osberg (2007), 'Social Entrepreneurship: The Case for Definition', *Stanford Social Innovation Review*, Spring, 28–39.

Mulgan, G. (2007), *Social innovation. What it is, why it matters and how it can be accelerated*, London: Young Foundation.

Moulaert, F. and J. Nussbaumer (2005), 'Defining the Social Economy and its Governance at the Neighbourhood Level: A Methodological Reflection', *Urban Studies*, **42** (11), 2071–2088.

Murray, R., J. Caulier-Grice and G. Mulgan (2010), *The Open Book of Social Innovation*, Social Innovator Series, London: NESTA.

Nyssens, M. (ed.) (2006), *Social Enterprise – At the Crossroads of Market, Public Policies and Civil Society*, London and New York: Routledge.

Roelants, B. (2009), *Cooperatives and Social Enterprises. Governance and Normative Frameworks*, Brussels: CECOP.

Salamon, L. (1987), 'Partners in Public Service: The Scope and Theory of Government-Nonprofit Relations', in Walter W. Powel, *The Nonprofit Sector. A Research Handbook*, New Haven: Yale University Press, pp. 99–117.

Weisbrod, B.A. (ed.) (1998), *To profit or not to profit: the commercial transformation of the nonprofit sector*, Cambridge: Cambridge University Press.

Young, D. (1983), *If Not for Profit, for What?* Lexington, MA: Lexington Books.

Yunus, M. (2010), *Building Social Business: Capitalism that can serve humanity's most pressing needs*, New York: Public Affairs.

4. Social innovation in an unsustainable world
Abid Mehmood and Constanza Parra

4.1 INTRODUCTION

In this chapter we discuss social innovation and sustainable development as two approaches that can jointly contribute to the formulation of more harmonious human-environment relationships to address the problems of an unsustainable world. Sustainable development is a multidimensional approach that considers the social, economic, environmental, cultural and institutional aspects of human-nature interaction. However, this multidimensionality can be a weakness, as policymakers and practitioners tend to artificially disconnect its key ingredients into separate standalone 'pillars'. We believe that a social innovation perspective to sustainable development can help overcome this disconnectedness. Social innovation in this context relates to how individuals, groups and communities can take action in response to the problems of unsustainable practices and unsatisfied social needs while also focusing on the challenges of environmental degradation and climate change. As such, social innovation offers a perspective to help develop sites for grassroots movements and mobilization across different scales (see Part III of this handbook for some instructive case studies). However, social innovation literature has in general been inattentive towards issues related to sustainability, which has often been considered an *implicit* objective of any socially innovative action. We believe that the sustainable development agenda should be made more explicit in social innovation research, policy and actions.

This is because social innovation and sustainable development, once considered in conjunction, can offer clear directions towards a more sustainable living.

In the discussion below, we start with an explanation of the two approaches and their basic elements. We further identify some major weaknesses in the conventional sustainable development discourses, in particular a reductionist multidimensional view that marginalizes the social pillar, insufficient regard to scale and a limited view of 'innovation' as merely technical. Following this exposition, we map the connections between social innovation and sustainable development, and examine the cross-fertilization potential between the two approaches to show how social innovation can help to better conceptualize and promote sustainable development. Following this, we briefly present two cases as empirical evidence of potential synergies and differences between the two approaches: Local Agenda 21, a non-binding action plan for sustainable local development conceived at the global level; and the Transition Towns movement, a range of bottom-up eco-social initiatives and local actions for sustainable development. In conclusion, we stress the need for a more integrated approach to socio-environmental governance rather than a limited, functionalist multidimensionality that prevails in the conventional definitions and conceptions of sustainable development.

4.2   SOCIAL INNOVATION AND SUSTAINABLE DEVELOPMENT

Social innovation and sustainable development are not mutually exclusive, yet there has not been sufficient conversation between the two approaches in the period of their resurgence since the 1980s. It is therefore pertinent here to outline the basics of these two approaches, to see how such a conversation could further the understanding of the problems and challenges of an unsustainable world.

4.2.1   Social Innovation and its Relationship with Sustainability

We see social innovation within the context of this chapter as self-conscious collective action that seeks to address the unsatisfied needs for sustainable development. Social innovation as an approach for individual and collective wellbeing can be elaborated into three interconnected features (Moulaert et al. 2005; see also General Introduction): first, the satisfaction of human needs (both material and non-material); second, social relations between individuals and groups at different spatial scales; third, empowerment, with micro level initiatives bringing positive macro level change. Spatial scale, therefore, has a strong role in the emergence and effectiveness of socially innovative actions, especially in terms of the level of intervention. We show later how these socio-political and scalar dimensions connect to the sustainable development agenda as an interface between the core sustainability pillars and the values that promote sensitivity to societal change (Baker 2006).

Accordingly, social innovation for sustainable development can be reflected upon in two ways. First, it connects satisfaction of basic needs – including those related to the improvement in the quality of environment, innovation in social relations, governance, empowerment and social justice – to sustainability agendas. Second, it highlights local and global issues such as adaptation to climate change and unsustainable development that have thus far received relatively little attention in the social innovation literature itself. This oversight does not necessarily mean that socially innovative actions are not sustainable (Moulaert and Nussbaumer 2008). In terms of their durability and effectiveness, there is often an implicit assumption that communities or groups would continue to be innovative, and their initiatives would carry on undisrupted over prolonged periods of time. But whereas socially innovative actions are largely considered in relation to their social and economic effects, there has been less focus on their impacts on local ecologies and the environment.

Social innovation, therefore, is in need of a more explicit focus on sustainability, not only the durability of socially innovative actions but also their impact on social relations, heritage, culture, economic practices and ecological balance. Such a focus will have two-fold benefits. On one hand it will help engage social innovators (individuals, groups, communities, and governance institutions) with such objectives as climate change and resource depletion. On the other hand, it will reinforce the core sustainable development agenda. This is because with the 'social' as a starting point, the logic of development could be restructured so as to consider ecological sensitivity a basic need to be addressed through socially innovative initiatives and processes. The following section elaborates this point.

4.2.2 Sustainable Development and its Relationship with 'the Social'

'Sustainable development' calls to mind the alarming signs that in the 1970s alerted people to the contradictions between economic growth, industrialization and environmental quality. Whether or not 'growth' and 'development' could be equated was one of the fundamental questions from which the concept of sustainable development grew. The defenders of sustainability contended that development could no longer be pursued without considering the world's biophysical environment and the urgent need for its preservation, nor without taking into account the negative social consequences of capitalism in terms of equity, exclusion and poverty. From a combined socio-economic and ecological perspective, the contemporary capitalist order pursuing growth at any cost appeared as an unsustainable system, leading to mounting inequalities and therefore incapable of meeting the most fundamental human needs (WCED 1987).

Sustainable development, then, brings quality, interconnectedness and equity to the meaning of development. Whereas growth is defined as a quantitative increase in scale, development refers to the *qualitative* improvement of a system through the gradual unfolding of its potentialities (Daly 1990). Any development that is sustainable is thus supposed to improve the quality of life and wellbeing for both human and non-human actors. Based on this contention, sustainable development offers a relational view that calls for a more harmonious relationship between humans and nature. This relationship is largely explained through the tripartite arrangement of economic, environmental and social sustainabilities. *Economic* sustainability refers to the viability of a given system and touches on its capacity to grow and to be efficient in the management and distribution of resources. It can be considered as a sub-system of society and should therefore serve the ecological and social criteria. *Environmental* sustainability replaces an atomized view of nature, conceived as independent and separated from human beings, with an integrated conception of ecological systems in complex interaction and fusion with human life. The human-nature interaction view stresses the ecological limits to development that humans should respect in order to guarantee harmony with the irreplaceable natural support without which life is impossible: economic growth cannot be achieved at the expense of ecological degradation and depletion of natural resources (Costanza et al. 1997). In this respect, the debates on weak and strong sustainability essentially discuss how much natural capital should be bequeathed for future generations (see also Parra, Chapter 10). While stronger sustainability approaches press for ecological preservation and stress human responsibility for the integrity of the biodiversity legacy, weaker approaches vindicate the exploitation of nature if it brings economic growth. In the latter case, biodiversity loss might be compensated for by physical forms of capital provided by human beings (Kallio et al. 2007).

In the context of these debates over the precise ecological limits to economic growth that contemporary societies should respect, *social sustainability* has been kept in the background (Littig and Grießler 2005), being largely seen in relation to economically defined equity and/or environmental justice. More recently there have been efforts to revive the social core of sustainable development as situated in its inherent socially innovative nature (Parra 2010a, 2010b; Parra and Moulaert 2010, 2011). This stance emphasizes the role of the social in the collective resolution of tensions related to the interconnected-ness between the different ingredients that compose sustainable development as a societal goal. 'The social' here refers to how human beings interactively explore (or not) sustainability alternatives for dealing with contemporary socio-ecological challenges. However, there are certain weaknesses in the approach which have increasingly become a cause of concern.

4.3 MAJOR ISSUES IN THE CONVENTIONAL SUSTAINABLE DEVELOPMENT DISCOURSES

Sustainable development, since the Brundtland Report, has become a mainstream global discourse. Although the concept existed before in international policy discussions, albeit with a specific natural resource conservation focus (IUCN et al. 1980), the subsequent multiplicity of definitions and usages has triggered a paradoxical effect in which the omnipresence of sustainability imperatives goes hand in hand with the vagueness of their content in local and global policies and practices. We examine some of the issues as below.

4.3.1 Reductionist Interpretations

Since its inception in the 1980s, inherent weaknesses of the tripartite sustainability approach have been criticized for an inability to fully explain correlations such as those between poverty and environmental degradation, and between economic growth and participation. Rydin (2010, p. 4) identifies two objectives of these tripartite distinctions and their interrelationships. The first is concerned with resolving tensions and conflicts between any two given dimensions (such as economic vs. environmental; environmental vs. social,

etc) and effecting possible trade-offs. The second relates to the bilateral synergies to achieve win-win outcomes. We argue that such an approach for trade-offs and synergies leads to certain weaknesses. To start with, it tends to promote a reductionist view of sustainable development as constituted in discrete social, economic and environmental 'pillars' defined in functional terms as components of a 'sustainable' system. The functional construing causes a contained view of sustainability for each pillar with limited room for mutual dialogue or integration. This shifts the focus from intrinsic values of each pillar to a common sustainability objective that these, as components, should strive for. There is also a tendency for bilateral trade-offs between the ecological and the economic, seeking a win-win situation (instead of a win-win-win), demonstrating a bias at the cost of the social. The normative ramifications of this bias are that sustainability is conditioned with ideals of technology, efficiency, stability, objectivity and progress, rather than fairness, justice, equity and stakeholder engagement.

Earlier warnings over such trade-offs/synergies had predicted that the fuzziness of global sustainability discourses could actually contribute to inadequacies and contradictions in policymaking over issues such as the international trade and ecosystems management (Lélé 1991). Similar concerns led to debates about whether social, economic and environmental suffice as the three pillars of sustainability, and if there is a need to consider further dimensions to provide a more comprehensive framework for sustainable development. Hawkes (2001) has long favoured considering the role of culture – especially local/indigenous cultures – in order to give due consideration to the local histories, diversity, behaviours, path dependence, and complexities of the relationships between social and ecological (and economic) systems. Others such as Bosselmann et al. (2008) have claimed that all the pillars of sustainable development are embedded within governance, which provides means for public empowerment and wider engagement of civil society. Still, there are some sustainable development approaches that tend to classify governance as one among the many subsystems inside a wider social-ecological systemic framework (see Ostrom 2009 on natural resources, and Brondizio et al. 2009 on nature-culture preservation). We argue that such approaches reflect a functionalist 'multi-dimensional' rather than 'integrative' view of sustainable development that takes into account the full complexity of social-ecological dynamics. Hence, in such a framework, once a habitat fails to transition into a sustainable form, the lack of institutional elasticity would result in the disruption of the whole institutional setup, and governance processes will be disrupted with no provision for rebuilding the broken social/cultural relations. In this scenario, social innovation could serve to prevent the institutions from falling apart and help to address sustainability challenges.

4.3.2 Spatio-Temporal Issues

One of the key objectives of sustainable development is to define fair satisfaction of human needs through a combination of inter- and intra-generational equity aspirations (Holden and Linnerud 2007; Zuindeau 2000). The *inter-generational equity* principle refers to fairness and solidarity for the satisfaction of human needs by means of connecting rights of contemporary societies with those of past and future generations. In other words, issues such as the acceptable ecological limits to growth, pollution standards and impacts

on biodiversity should be addressed and decided upon in view of the wellbeing of the forthcoming generations. The *intra-generational equity* principle refers to the need of present societies to move towards a fairer distribution of capital and resources for wellbeing among the nations and communities around the world. One of the starting points is to find ways to rectify the unacceptable socio-economic gap between the Global North and the Global South. Sustainable development in spatio-temporal terms has simultaneously emerged as a critique to this socio-economic gap as well as a 'global' solution to the problem of unfair distribution of the planet's social, economic, ecological and political wealth.

It is worth recalling that the Brundtland Commission's perspective on sustainability governance was quite 'globalist'. It was only through the implementation of Local Agenda 21, together with other planning instruments, that sustainable development gradually reached the local level and moved towards more territorialized/ grounded strategies. In the context of the climate change debate, spatial conflicts, liabilities and concerns seem to have got a second wind especially between the local and the global and between the North and the South. Similarly, culpabilities are exchanged over the past, present and future environmental degradation, biodiversity loss, hazards and economic crises. Even the solutions, such as climate change mitigation and/or adaptation measures, become contentious. Recent dialogues over global environmental governance at COP15 Copenhagen, COP17 Durban and Rio+20 are cases in point.

4.3.3 Treatment of (Social) Innovation

Innovation is pivotal for all walks of sustainability. However, academic, policy and practice contributions drawing links between sustainable development and social innovation are both scarce in numbers and flimsy in analysing and theorizing innovation beyond the economy-ecology nexus. Due to the denial of the social and resulting absence of a coherent theoretical framework for social innovation, the scholarship looking at the role of innovation in sustainability transitions has tended to emphasize (geo-)engineering or technological approaches such as ecological modernization via the crafting of the so-called green or eco-innovations. Subsequently, the social innovation aspect became considered as a *saupoudrage* of the technical, instead of being the initiator or the driver. These approaches are closely linked to the 'weak' sustainability paradigm which advocates quantifiable economic growth and technological substitution to drive environmental change, in accordance with neoliberal discourses and aims. Such technological optimism has led global and supranational institutions to adopt environmental management and market-based measures and policies. As a result, the importance of the community in the governance of the commons does not generally receive sufficient attention (Ostrom 1990). We draw critical attention to the fact that the complexities of the role of social innovation in sustainable development go far beyond the management or the governance of the technology. It is not possible to confine social innovation – in this case social innovation for sustainable development – to the search for and the social acceptance-cum-governance of more eco-efficient technologies. This is only one part of the story.

We identify at least three problems with conventional techno-centric perspectives on innovation in sustainable development. First, there is a limited definition of innovation as a mere technical issue, which

visualizes the path towards sustainable development as mainly (or exclusively) a matter of technological refinement or change. Second, many studies tend to employ a limited functionalist view of social innovation as serving the technological improvements required for the sake of sustainability transitions (e.g. Smith et al. 2010). Third, there is opacity in and denial of the meaning and role of the social in the techno-centric views of innovation and sustainability. These problems have led to a lack of attention towards the linkages between sustainable development and social innovation, and consequently, to exploring their cross-fertilization potential. We address these below.

4.4 MAPPING THE CONNECTIONS BETWEEN SOCIAL INNOVATION AND SUSTAINABLE DEVELOPMENT

In a world system dominated by market-based and regulatory solutions where aspirations for economic growth outweigh the social and ecological costs, we pose some basic questions as below to understand how social innovation and sustainable development can help address the issues of growing inequalities and unsustainable practices in order to meet the fundamental human needs.

4.4.1 How can Sustainable Development be Socially Innovative?

As we have seen, the last two decades have witnessed a proliferation of literatures and a widespread utilization of sustainable development in different policy sectors and contexts. This has also been the case for social innovation. But strangely enough, these two streams remained indifferent to each other and hardly ever communicated.

The omnipresent buoyancy in the usage of sustainability objectives has prompted criticisms and academic debates, while at the same time it has guided various societal and institutional reorganizations to deal with the challenges of meeting strategic objectives. For scholars such as Theys et al. (2009) this progress has been meaningful yet insufficient, and reveals that sustainable development is still underdeveloped as a concept and a policy alternative. Social innovation has strong connotations in terms of the societal and institutional efforts to implement sustainability objectives especially through collective actions. The often-neglected socio-institutional component of sustainable development is, according to this view, a vital link between social innovation and the social, economic and environmental objectives. This link can potentially benefit from the operationalization of sustainable development through social innovation. This ideological shift, in the sense of ecological imperatives pressing contemporary societies to transform existing institutions and social relations, also marks the emergence of new institutions, policies and eco-social arrangements (through collaborations and negotiations etc.) to achieve sustainable development imperatives.

In its contemporary standing, at local levels, sustainable development can signify the importance of bottom-linked governance and development which strongly connects with the notion of social relations and empowerment (see Pradel et al., Chapter 11; Andersen et al., Chapter 14). Thus, it can be argued that while sustainable development makes way for technological, economic and ecological innovations, it potentially paves the way for socially conceived innovations and, simultaneously, cautions against disregarding the societal impacts of ill-conceived technical solutions. Social innovation, therefore, can

help to better understand, illustrate, and materialize collective action for sustainable development.

4.4.2 Exploring the Territorialized Cross-Fertilization Potential

One of the stronger arguments in favour of socially innovative actions is that they can become institutionally embedded and territorially reproduced (Moulaert 2000, 2009; Van Dyck and Van den Broeck, Chapter 9). Socially innovative initiatives might result from the choices and decisions made by individuals, groups and communities to negotiate the use and sharing of local resources and capacities; caring for the quality of the natural environment; and, giving priority to the equity in human needs satisfaction and sustainability values.

Table 4.1 summarizes the cross-fertilization potential between the concepts of social innovation for territorial development (through its three main features) and sustainable development (through its three conventional dimensions) with governance and institutions placed as the societal platform from which sustainable development takes place. It also highlights how both social innovation and sustainable development can jointly provide a framework to address the sustainability challenge.

Governance in this framework provides a conceptual basis for considering the social- and cultural-institutional orientations in relation to the key dimensions of sustainable development. In social terms, the satisfaction of basic needs of communities and groups can be achieved through sustainable alternatives that are both socially and environmentally effective. Actions that tend to have negative consequences on other (or neighbouring) communities cannot be considered socially

Table 4.1   Cross-fertilization potential between social innovation and sustainable development

SI \ SD	Social vulnerability	Economic viability	Environmental sustainability
Satisfaction of needs	Satisfaction of basic needs and wants; ethics	Climate change mitigation and adaptation; sustainable production and consumption	Biodiversity; balance between technological, ecological and human spheres
Changes in social relations	Social inclusion and engagement	Sustainable communities; social entrepreneurship	Social-ecological transitions
Socio-political capability	Cooperation; collaborations; citizens movements	Participative decision making	Question the effectiveness of techno-optimisms;
Governance and (social/cultural) institutions	Identity; empowerment; purpose. Reflexive governance	Adaptive management; microfinance initiatives; strategic investments	Flexible and adaptive governance regimes.

encouraging or ethical. Socially innovative initiatives, therefore, ensure involvement of a variety of stakeholders through inclusive practices and engagement. Citizenship movements are seen as a vehicle for promoting cooperation and dialogue among diverse groups and communities and can enhance the local socio-political capabilities. In economic terms, socially innovative initiatives aim to satisfy basic needs by encouraging ways of producing goods and services that are economically viable, while at the same time encouraging minimal wastage of resources and materials, as in the case of sustainable food movements. Social entrepreneurship ventures can be a source of such economic initiatives based on local production systems that are beneficial not only to individuals and groups but also to communities, society and the environment. In terms of environmental sustainability, social innovation can strive to find a balance between the natural habitat and human inhabitants to minimize impacts on local biodiversity. Such actions can also help avoid the techno-centric visions we have noted above, and support a social-ecological approach for the transition to sustainable living. Governance and institutional relations, as the facilitators of socially innovative actions for sustainable development, can help in identity building, reflexivity and local empowerment. A flexible and adaptive approach to the governance of social-ecological systems can support socio-political reforms, maintain social relations and increase social engagement.

One of the key issues raised by the Brundland Report in terms of environmental governance was the importance of community participation in the sustainable development decision making (WCED 1987, Chapter 2). From the social innovation perspective this relates to empowerment, giving due regard to the role of local communities and civil society actors, allowing them an opportunity to have their say and take part in making decisions for their social, economic and environmental needs and aspirations. It can be further argued that a social innovation approach to the governance of sustainable development would focus on such institutional arrangements that facilitate participation and engagement of those social groups and communities that, despite being the key stakeholders to the issues under considerations, tend to be left out of policy, planning, decision making and implementation processes. Such institutional or quasi-institutional arrangements can provide alternatives to the currently hegemonic vertical/hierarchical forms of policymaking. They can be organized around horizontal networks of private, public, and civil society actors while staying connected to the state and market mechanisms. Such networked forms of activism are favoured by international (UN) and supra-national (EU) institutions as well as the nation states. However, it is worth noting that multilevel governance mechanisms for sustainable development tend to confer power in different forms and ways, and be very selective in giving preferential treatment to specific stakeholders and promoting specific modes of involvement (Baker and Mehmood 2013).

4.4.3 Potential Traps

It should be clarified here that any alliance between the two approaches should give due regard to the respective complementary strengths and weaknesses. There are a few traps inherent in 'forcing' a coalition, especially in terms of social policy and governance. We mention only two. First is the 'sustainability trap' wherein sustainable development can become a normative justification for various practices, such as

a specific urban form, obscuring the complexities of trade-offs between various elements of development (Marcuse 1998). Governance arrangements, however, can help resolve these by giving particular attention to social-political dialogue so as to see how and to what extent certain actions can satisfy the local sustainability needs. Second is the 'localism trap' that may at times unjustly emphasize the local (Moulaert 2000). As Born (2008) has mentioned, scale is socially produced and may not be independent of the particular agendas of specific social actors. Here, the territorial aspect of social innovation comes into force as institutional and socio-political governance arrangements strive to promote collaborations, reflexivity, social justice and citizenship. For example, any local action that is potentially harmful to biodiversity or wellbeing of another locality or has a wider impact on (bio-) regional or national levels can be improved upon through assessment, consideration, deliberations and dialogue over its wider social, cultural, economic and environmental impacts and potential alternatives. Such scalar issues are crucial in the following two cases, which demonstrate the value of the cross-fertilization we are proposing.

4.5 TWO CASES OF SOCIALLY INNOVATIVE ACTIONS AND SUSTAINABLE DEVELOPMENT

A brief look at two examples can help us to understand how the debates on environmental uncertainty, ecological crises, social vulnerabilities and justice have catalysed institutional arrangements, multilevel governance and socially innovative collective actions at various spatial scales. First we discuss the case of Local Agenda 21 (LA21) as a non-binding action plan for sustainable local development conceived at the global level, and its implications in promoting social innovation. The second case is that of eco-community development based social innovation, using the bottom-up community-based Transition Towns movement as an example.

4.5.1   Local Development and LA21 as a Policy Framework

Local Agenda 21 was introduced as a comprehensive inter-sectoral plan of action aimed at guiding the transition toward sustainable development through the implementation of sustainability principles at the local level (UNCED 1992). Adopted at the 1992 Earth Summit, LA21 entails a societal search for alternative ways to mobilize local resources to achieve sustainable development. It seeks to combine two types of goals: substantive and procedural (Feichtinger and Pregernig 2005). *Substantive* goals denote the expected sustainable articulation between social, economic and environmental pillars of development, whereas *procedural* ones refer to the role of participation and democracy in the collective processes and negotiations leading to more sustainable paths of development. As a policy instrument, LA21 has been criticized over the recurring issues and difficulties such as political rhetoric regarding citizens' participation and/or the reduction of sustainable development to its economic or environmental dimensions in its contemporary implementation (Doyle 1998). However, it is worth calling attention to its innovative character as a policy instrument, and reflecting on the creation, implementation and outcomes of LA21 from a social innovation perspective that has thus far been overlooked in the literature. What is interesting in this respect is how an alternative form of mobilizing local resources (e.g.

social and natural capital) with the aim of bringing sustainability meets the definition of social innovation in terms of satisfaction of basic needs, inclusion and empowerment of communities.

Key aspirations of LA21 are to incorporate territorial development and socio-environmental justice issues in the policy agenda, promote participatory decision-making, and encourage collective action. LA21 can be considered innovative in terms of its character and content as a local policy tool, and as a means for societal processes to steer the implementation. LA21 plans of action and implementation have varied around the world. Putting it generally, while less developed countries are inclined to focus on local democracies and basic infrastructure and services (sewerage, waste disposal), developed countries have largely directed their efforts to reducing resource consumption and conservation of natural resources. In terms of local governance, LA21 offers a more inclusive approach towards democratic participation, strategic policy making, environmental citizenship and support for innovative actions (Selman and Parker 1999; Selman 1998). However, there are also certain downsides of the extremely localized perspectives in LA21 that tend to overlook the local adaptive capacity in policy making, the need for vertical integration with multilevel governance institutions, and the fact that many local authorities may lack the powers, expertise, capabilities and resources needed to perceive, plan, design and implement a variety of social, economic and environmental actions at the same time (Baker 2006). Thus, it can be argued that although LA21 has contributed to social development in general, it has failed to deliver on the capacity building for the local communities. This failure can be partly attributed to the fact that while many energies and resources were allocated and spent on dialogue and participation, there has been insufficient resource allocation and political support for the actual implementation of the ideas that have been deliberated and agreed upon. A disparity between the 'globalist' framing of the aims of sustainable development and the generally 'localist' approach to civic participation may underlie this gap between LA21 agreements and support from higher levels of government. As such, it may help to explain some of the difficulties we have identified in fully integrating social innovation and sustainable development. Although LA21, as a major driver of local sustainability, supports democratic values and participation, the dominant role of economy and ecology has persisted at the expense of the social.

4.5.2 Eco-Social Urbanism and Transition Towns

The present day eco-communities and ecological urbanism discourse is primarily based on an aspiration for transition to 'sustainable communities' and a low-carbon society. It also encompasses the need to adapt to potential threats from climate change by means of enhancing the adaptive capacity of vulnerable communities (Adger 2001). This eco-trend is not new and can be traced back in the ideals and problems of urban living in Western European thought. In the Renaissance period, the city was romanticized as a 'perfect body', a metaphor that in the 19th century transformed into that of a 'diseased body' (Haar 2006). To cure the harms caused by the industrial revolution, some of the forefathers of social innovation ideology (such as Émile Durkheim and Max Weber) favoured a closer human-nature relationship. It was Ebenezer Howard who broke away from the authoritarian and industrial frameworks of late 19th-century Britain to radically reform urban thought through his Garden City movement (Howard 1898, 1902). His perceived 'social city' offered an innovative socio-technical approach to the integration of social interaction and economic self-sufficiency with the natural environment while setting a precedent for an eco-socialist agenda (Hall and Ward 1998; Roelofs 1999). Howard's social reformist ambitions can therefore be seen as socially innovative in its approach to bringing humans closer to nature. Today there is a broad (and spreading) spectrum of eco-communities, which range in scale from eco-cities to eco-villages and from eco-neighbourhoods to eco-quarters around the globe. Most of these initiatives are actually being conceived and planned from top-down with limited public participation. Barton (1998) has argued that although top-down, proactive support is essential for the success of any sustainable development action, it is not the sole prerequisite; local political support together with bottom-up and civil society involvement can better ensure the long-term viability of any sustainable development action.

One of the most successful range of socially innovative bottom-up eco-community initiatives has been provided by the Transition Towns movement (Scott-Cato and Hillier 2010). Loosely following Howard's garden city model, Transition Towns demonstrates how a cooperative bottom-up approach to developing or retrofitting existing infrastructure can produce socially, economically and ecologically responsive communities (Hopkins 2008). The ideology has emerged from the community concerns about impending global oil crisis (peak oil) and the need for resilience to climate change. It recommends a number of basic actions that can be undertaken by communities on their own initiative. These include, but are not limited to: switching to renewable energy sources; inducing people to use public transport, cycle or walk; recycling water; urban greening, and other environmentally responsive interventions; as well as encouraging social engagement and mutual respect (Newman et al. 2009). The movement promotes what we could call an integrated sustainable development approach through an array of people-centred community-initiated bottom-up actions. The network boasts an international membership of more than 400 communities with scores more in the process of achieving the Transition Town status (Transition Network 2012). This example suggests how socially innovative actions can attract voluntary local participation at a global scale and help 'transition' communities beyond materialistic norms and promote sustainable development. Local empowerment also means that people can make major decisions to improve their livelihoods, reduce carbon footprints, use renewable sources of energy, and become self-sufficient and self-sustained while maintaining higher environmental standards of living.

4.6   CONCLUDING REMARKS

This chapter has taken a synergetic point of view to elaborate the cross-fertilization potential between the social innovation and sustainable development approaches. We have argued that the core philosophy of social innovation has a number of features that can help achieve sustainability objectives. We have tried to address the critical question as to why the two approaches, despite being so close to each other, have hardly ever communicated, identifying as a key reason the narrow functionalist interpretation of 'social' in

many of the sustainable development discourses. As a result, the social tends to be seen as a separate dimension besides the other two 'pillars' of sustainable development, rather than an integrated part. The functionalist predominance has also resulted in social engineering approaches that consider participation as an 'added value' rather than the core philosophy. The governance implications for sustainable development, we maintain, have been more multidimensional than integrative.

Social innovation can help push sustainable development beyond the production and/or governance of technology. While acknowledging the difficult relationships between the social and the sustainable within the sustainable development and social innovation debates respectively, we favour a dialogic approach to understanding inter-linkages between the two approaches. These synergies can help determine the connections between, for example, local biodiversity loss and global environmental change, and redefine territoriality in terms of its social and ecological, besides its economic and political aspects. To elaborate the cross-fertilization potential, the two cases discussed above provide a socio-spatial perspective on environmental governance. Whereas LA21 is an instrument of local development with limited potential for capacity building, the bottom-up Transition Towns movement is shown as a community-based philosophy of sustainability. Within these multi-scalar realities the local governance level is recognized as pivotal to fostering social innovation for sustainable development. More precisely, local identity, culture and history hold the potential for socio-institutional innovation and therefore explain their capacity to bring about change and allow transition towards more sustainable forms of development.

Social innovation is about introducing new ideas and developing new social relations. However, it needs targeted institutional support and coherent policies to support community participation and dynamics for sustainable transformations. The reason for this is that overcoming the inertia of an unsustainable world demands much more than techno-centric and market driven transformations – it demands socio-institutional innovation as well. This is only possible with the will to share knowledge and promote socially innovative actions that combine efforts from a plurality of social, institutional and political actors.

4.7 QUESTIONS FOR DISCUSSION

● What are the main issues of contention and commonalities between sustainable development and social innovation?

● Think of an LA21 action that you are familiar with. How could a social innovation focus have improved its effectiveness?

● What do you think are some of the necessary conditions to encourage the sustainability of socially innovative actions?

REFERENCES

(References in bold are recommended reading.)

Adger, W.N. (2001), 'Scales of governance and environmental justice for adaptation and mitigation of climate change', *Journal of International Development*, 13 (7), 921–931.

Baker, S. (2006), *Sustainable development*, London: Routledge.

Baker, S. and A. Mehmood (2013), 'Social innovation and the governance of sustainable places', *Local Environment* (forthcoming).

Barton, H. (1998), 'Eco-neighbourhoods: A review of projects', *Local Environment*, 3 (2), 159–177.

Born, B. (2008), 'Avoiding the Local Trap: Scale and Food Systems in Planning Research', *Journal of Planning Education and Research*, 26 (2), 195–207.

Bosselmann, K., R. Engel and R. Taylor (2008), *Governance for Sustainability: Issues, Challenges, Successes*, Bonn: IUCN.

Brondizio, E., E. Ostrom, and O. Young (2009), 'Connectivity and the Governance of Multilevel Social-Ecological Systems: The Role of Social Capital', *Annual Review of Environment and Resources*, 34, 253–278.

Costanza, R., J. Cumberland, H. Daly, R. Goodland and R. Norgaard (1997), *An Introduction to Ecological Economics*, Boca Raton, FL: CRC Press.

Daly, H.E. (1990), 'Toward some operational principles of sustainable development. *Ecological Economics*, 2, 1–6.

Doyle, T. (1998), 'Sustainable development and Agenda 21: The secular bible of global free markets and pluralist democracy', *Third World Quarterly*, 19 (4), 771–786.

Feichtinger, J. and M. Pregernig (2005), 'Participation and/or versus sustainability? Tensions between procedural and substantive goals in two Local Agenda 21 processes in Sweden and Austria', *European Environment*, 15 (4), 212–227.

Haar, S. (2006), 'The Ecological City: Metaphor versus Metabolism', www.uic.edu/cuppa/gci/publications/workingpaperseries/pdfs/GCP-07-05%20Sharon%20Haar_sm.pdf (last accessed 9 February 2012).

Hall, P. and C. Ward (1998), *Sociable Cities: The Legacy of Ebenezer Howard*, Chichester: John Wiley.

Hawkes, J. (2001), *The fourth pillar of sustainability. Culture's essential role in public planning*, Melbourne: Cultural Development Network & Common Ground Press.

Holden, E. and K. Linnerud (2007), 'The sustainable development area: Satisfying basic needs and safeguarding ecological sustainability', *Sustainable Development*, 15 (3), 174–187.

Hopkins, R. (2008), *The Transition Handbook: From Oil Dependency to Local Resilience*, Totnes: Green Books.

Howard, E. (1898), *Tomorrow: A Path to Real Reform*, London: Swan Sonnenschein.

Howard, E. (1902), *Garden Cities of To-Morrow*, London: Faber and Faber.

IUCN, UNEP and WWF (1980), *World Conservation Strategy: Living Resource Conservation for Sustainable Development*, Gland: International Union for Conservation of Nature and Natural Resources.

Kallio, T.J., P. Nordberg and A. Ahonen (2007), 'Rationalizing Sustainable Development – a Critical Treatise', *Sustainable Development*, 15 (1), 41–51.

Lélé, S.M (1991), 'Sustainable development: A critical review', *World Development*, 19 (6), 607–621.

Littig, B. and E. Grießler (2005), 'Social sustainability: a catchword between political pragmatism and social theory', *International Journal of Sustainable Development*, **8** (1–2), 65–79.

Marcuse, P. (1998), 'Sustainability is not enough', *Environment and Urbanization*, **10** (2), 103–112.

Moulaert, F. (2000), *Globalization and Integrated Area Development in European Cities*, Oxford: Oxford University Press.

Moulaert, F. (2009), 'Social Innovation: Institutionally Embedded, Territorially (Re) Produced', in D. MacCallum, F. Moulaert, J. Hillier and S. Vicari Haddock (eds) *Social innovation and territorial development*, Farnham: Ashgate, pp. 11–24.

Moulaert, F. and J. Nussbaumer (2008), *La logique spatiale du développement territorial*, Sainte-Foye: Presses Universitaires du Québec.

Moulaert, F., F. Martinelli, S. González and E. Swyngedouw (2005), 'Towards alternative model(s) of local innovation', *Urban Studies*, **42** (11), 1969–1990.

Newman, P., T. Beatley and H. Boyer (2009), *Resilient Cities: Responding to Peak Oil and Climate Change*, Washington, DC: Island Press.

Ostrom, E. (1990), *Governing the Commons: The Evolution of Institutions for Collective Action*, Cambridge: Cambridge University Press.

Ostrom, E. (2009), 'A General Framework for Analyzing Sustainability of Social-Ecological Systems', *Science*, **325**, 419–422.

Parra, C. (2010a), 'The governance of ecotourism as a socially innovative force for paving the way for more sustainable paths: the Morvan Regional Park case', PhD thesis, University of Lille 1, France.

Parra, C. (2010b), 'Sustainability and multi-level governance of territories classified as protected areas: The Morvan regional park case', *Journal of Environmental Planning and Management*, **53** (4), 491–509.

Parra, C. and F. Moulaert (2010), 'Why sustainability is so fragilely social . . .', in S. Oosterlynck, J. Van den Broeck, L. Albrechts, F. Moulaert and A. Verhetsel (eds) *Strategic spatial projects: catalysts for change*, London: Routledge, pp. 242–256.

Parra, C. and Moulaert, F. (2011), 'La nature de la durabilité sociale: vers une lecture socioculturelle du développement territorial durable', *Développement durable et territoires*, **2** (2), developpementdurable.revues.org/8970 (last accessed 9 February 2012).

Roelofs, J. (1999), 'British ecosocialism: A note', *Capitalism Nature Socialism*, **10** (1), 133–136.

Rydin, Y. (2010), *Governing for Sustainable Urban Development*, London, Earthscan.

Scott-Cato, M. and J. Hillier (2010), 'How Could we Study Climate-Related Social Innovation? Applying Deleuzean Philosophy to the Transition Towns', *Environmental Politics*, 19 (6), 869–887.

Selman, P. and J. Parker (1999), 'Tales of local sustainability', *Local Environment*, **4** (1), 47–60.

Selman, P. (1998), 'Local Agenda 21: substance or spin?', *Journal of Environmental Planning and Management*, **41** (5), 533–553.

Smith, A., J.-P. Voß and J. Grin (2010), 'Innovation studies and sustainability transitions: the allure of the multi-level perspective and its challenges', *Research Policy*, **39** (4), 435–448.

Theys, J., C. Tertre, F. Rauschmayer and B. Zuindeau (eds) (2009), *Le développement durable, la seconde étape*, Paris: Edition de l'Aube.

Transition Network (2012), 'Transition Initiatives Directory', www.transitionnetwork.org/initiatives (last accessed 26 June 2012).

UNCED United Nations Conference on the Environment (1992), 'Agenda 21: Action plan for the next century', habitat.igc.org/agenda21/index.htm (last accessed 6 February 2012).

WCED World Commission on Environment and Development (1987), *Our Common Future*, Oxford: Oxford University Press.

Zuindeau, B. (2000), 'La "durabilité": un essai de positionnement épistémologique du concept', in B. Zuindeau (ed.) *Développement durable et territoire*, Villeneuve d'Ascq (Nord): Presses Universitaires du Septentrion, pp. 27–69.

5. Social innovation through arts and creativity
Diane-Gabrielle Tremblay and Thomas Pilati

5.1 INTRODUCTION

In the context of an economy based on knowledge and symbolism, researchers are increasingly interested in the 'creative society' and the essential role of creativity as a major resource for professional and recreational activities and for social innovation conducive to socio-economic development. It is hypothesized that creativity plays a fundamental role in social innovation as well as in economic and social development since it gives a competitive edge to organizations for the development of new social forms and for knowledge accumulation. (Sacco and Tavano Blessi 2005).

In this chapter, we will look at the manifestation of social innovation in the arts and culture-creative sectors. The case of Tohu will illustrate the role of territory and the creative city in relation to social innovation. Tohu, in Montreal, is an example of culture-driven urban revitalization based on a model similar to the 'evolved cluster' or 'proactive cultural district' (Sacco and Ferilli 2006), which is clearly based on social innovation in a creative sector.

Our goal is to use this case in order to highlight the extent to which cultural or creative initiatives can effectively contribute to the development of social innovations in the cultural-arts sector. We refer here to the definition of social innovation presented in MacCallum et al. (2009), that is social innovation as a social relation, as collective agency, as empowerment. In our view, social innovation is about improving social relations and tackling social problems as well as meeting social needs. In such a view of social innovation, 'concerned' people are at the interactive centre of the project and are given the means to reveal their needs and set priorities for action (MacCallum et al. 2009; Moulaert et al. 2010). This can be observed in creative/cultural initiatives and, since the concept of the 'creative city' has an important impact, a few words on this concept are in order.

5.2 LITERATURE REVIEW

The concept of the creative city was developed in the early 1960s by urban critic and sociologist Jane Jacobs. Her book, *Cities and the Wealth of Nations* (1985), was the first to talk about 'creative cities', i.e. cities which are particularly innovative, diversified and driven towards innovation. While she did not expressly mention 'social innovation', it is clear that this form of innovation was covered in her writings. Her book *The Death and Life of Great American Cities* (1961) examined the North American city and the conditions influencing urban diversity, which in turn influenced innovation and creativity. Jacobs maintained that diversity and exchanges of ideas play an important role in the creation of a powerful and dynamic urban vitality, something which we may relate to social innovation.

The presence of different ethnic and economic realities in a local context is seen as an advantage for the community, since diversity is a source of creativity as well as social and other forms of innovation. According to Jacobs, the city possesses its own 'personality' with some districts developing as a result of individuals spontaneously gathering together for a common purpose.

According to Hosper and Dalm:

> the key to creative urban environments lies in diversity – both in spatial, social and economic terms. Neighbourhoods must have several functions so that their streets are filled with activity at all times of the day. Monofunctional settings such as business districts and commuter suburbs deprive of the daily vibrance needed for restaurants, culture and retail trade to flourish. In line with this, Jacobs supports short blocks of buildings and a finely meshed street pattern. Pedestrians should be able to walk around and turn into another street from time to time. (2005, p. 10)

To build an 'urban climate' conducive to attracting new people essential to its community, the city and its cultural policies must be able to stimulate this interaction between individuals, support creativity and be enriched by cultural diversity. According to Jacobs (1961), in most cases, 'bulldozer approaches' (or top-down approaches) to planning lead to unpopular decisions and unsuitable or over-scaled development projects, with often catastrophic consequences for cities. Jacobs thus considers that creativity and exchange of ideas play an important role in the socio-economic development of cities, and we could add in social innovation in cities.

Of course, there will always be economic poverty, but more thought should be given to the parameters which help to alleviate poverty through creative forms of social innovation. Jacobs reminds us that development programs have failed (Jacobs 1985) and that we need an alter-

native to traditional policies more than ever before. Some economists have maintained that the consumption modes are no longer linked only to basic needs, but also to the accumulation of what can be referred to as an 'identity capital', associated with individuals' desire to access symbolic resources which will affect their identity (Tremblay and Tremblay 2006). Defining individuals in relation to their consumption and wellbeing only – that which they benefit from or acquire – is a limited perspective, and Sen added that 'keeping to this restrictive approach would mean missing an essential dimension of human personality. When their capacity-building initiatives are understood, they can be recognized as responsible human beings' (Sen 1999, p. 254).

Gertler (2004) mentions that cities have often been likened to 'ecological systems', in which a diverse array of organisms in close quarters interact with one another in complex ways – sometimes competitively, sometimes cooperatively, but always with 'spillover' consequences, impacting on each other. Within the rich ecology of urban life, artists have long played a key role as dynamic agents of positive transformation. Through a process that is well recognized by scholars and other urban analysts, artists play a vanguard role in colonizing underused, neglected and devalorized urban neighbourhoods and this contributes to attract other workers and to revitalize various zones (Battaglia and Tremblay 2012a, 2012b; Darchen and Tremblay 2010).

5.2.1 Creative Class and Cities

In his book *The Rise of the Creative Class*, Richard Florida (2002) indicates that ideas, knowledge and information exchange between creative workers are essential for the production of innovations (he focused on technological and production innovations, but also covers some social innovations). He also maintains that creativity is as essential to economic prosperity as natural resources and financial capital, and his writings (2004, 2005), while contested by many (see Markusen 2006a, 2006b; Markusen and Schrock 2006; Tremblay and Tremblay 2010; Peck 2005), have contributed largely to the attention now being paid to creativity and the role of the arts-creative-cultural sectors in social innovation and territorial development (see Vitale and Membretti, Chapter 13; André et al., Chapter 18). Thus, products of the creative economy involve several fields: technology, business and the cultural milieu.

Florida's theory on 'creative cities' is centred on the idea that attracting and retaining talents (professionals, people from cultural and artistic communities and from the education and training sectors) are key processes for economic development and reconversion. However, Markusen's work on neighbourhoods in some US cities shows that creativity can manifest itself under difficult circumstances and even among people who do not have high levels of education. Indeed, people at all levels of education can exercise considerable inventiveness (Markusen 2006b) and some revitalization cases clearly highlight this (Tavano Blessi et al. 2012).

While Florida can be given credit for putting cultural and artistic activities in the forefront of debates on innovation and the development of cities, his approach has also been criticized as being elitist, and possibly conducive to social segregation. For many authors (Moulaert et al. 2004; Markusen 2006a, 2006b; Klein and Tremblay 2010a), what matters is the integration of all groups of society and quality of life in general. These are necessary to an inclusive city and are essential

conditions for developing collective projects that are socially innovative (Klein and Tremblay 2010b). From this point of view, Florida's views are limited and do not take into account the social innovation dimension, in the sense that they are not apparently concerned with improving social relations, tackling social problems or meeting social needs. They are centred on economic development; however, they have also brought forward the importance of arts and creativity to this goal.

In one of the most important critiques of Creative City theory, geographer Jamie Peck has examined Florida's studies. Peck (2005, p. 741) indicates that the book *The Rise of the Creative Class*: 'mixes cosmopolitan elitism and pop universalism, hedonism and responsibility, cultural radicalism and economic conservatism, casual and causal inference, and social libertarianism and business realism.' Florida is said to be at the same time straightforward and rather elusive. His theory has also attracted criticism for its relative neglect of issues of intraurban inequality and working poverty (Peck 2005; Klein and Tremblay 2010b). Figuring out what the Creative Class wants is an urgent task, but clearly not an easy one. Indeed, this means adopting an entirely new analytical and political mindset, and developing tools to collect and understand the aspirations and requirements of these creative people. Beyond this, one has to recognize that the behaviour of creative workers and the places where they will choose to live and work will be difficult to predict, and that above all they need space to 'actualize their identities' (Peck 2005, p. 744).

Among the other main critics of Florida's theories are Kotkin at the University of California and Glaeser at Harvard University, who argue that *The Rise of the Creative Class* defends the new citizens of the Internet era (Kotkin

2000). These critics maintain that the most prosperous American cities are not those in which the creative class is particularly important, but rather those in which taxes are not too high and the bureaucracy and size of government are less intrusive (see Tremblay and Pilati 2008).

5.2.2   The Forgotten Social Dimension

While Florida's studies have mainly focused on the link existing between creativity and urban economic prosperity, other authors such as Throsby (2001) and Sacco (Sacco and Pedrini 2003; Sacco and Comunian 2006; Sacco et al. 2007) have argued that the purpose of a creative city goes beyond the economic dimension and can include social and various other forms of innovation. This is all the more true given that culture depends on a degree of attention to local and global concerns while not being destructive of local solidarity. Therefore, it may become an asset for the territory and a source of social cohesion for the community. Moulaert et al. (2004) develop this idea further and establish the link between social innovation, social cohesion and the arts and cultural sectors.

According to Sacco and Ferilli (2006), culture can be the growth factor at the source of economic competitiveness but can also contribute to the social development and environmental sustainability of neighbourhoods or cities. This is however not automatic, and one needs to address the issue directly by integrating private initiatives with public policies that ensure a 'trickle down' effect from the cultural activities to social development, as was done in the case of the Tohu and Cirque du Soleil (Tavano Blessi et al. 2012; Tremblay and Pilati 2008). Several British and North American cities have fostered the development of districts dedicated to artistic

and cultural activities, unique and creative urban revitalization projects with quite surprising results in urban areas (Battaglia and Tremblay 2012b; Tremblay and Pilati 2008). These examples show that there is a strategic relationship between quality of culture and quality of life in urban settings.

While Florida's theories have foregrounded the elements of culture and creation, several successful cases of territorial development have been observed thanks to the strategic creation of a culture-driven model of excellence. Sacco and Ferilli (2006) put forward a model of cultural clustering based on a form of horizontal integration of different initiatives or systems, which can be seen as a social innovation. The authors refer to the 'proactive cultural district', a model which is achieved through strategic complementarity between cultural and production systems; in such a context a territory specializes in a given cultural sector or product, which then has an impact on the spatial organization of the territory. Based on this concept, the loci of production and supply of culture are not perceived only as sources of profit, but are perfectly integrated into the new post-industrial 'value chain' (Sacco and Petrini 2003); this represents a departure from the traditional industrial value chain to one based on symbolic content. The 'value' thus created through symbolic content or cultural value can be related to the post-industrial economy; it contributes to individual well-being and constitutes a necessary factor in the development of a socially recognized and sustainable territorial identity (see also Chapters 13 and 18 on illustrative cases for this).

5.2.3   The Cultural District

In the 'cultural district', a high density of cultural or creative companies – which are independent from each other but complement each other – becomes a competitive asset for a territory (Marshall 1920; Pilati and Tremblay 2007). In an integrated system of small businesses, the industrial (cultural) 'atmosphere' and information exchanges within the community contribute to ensuring the endogenous growth of the cultural district (Becattini 1991). In this context, individuals identify with and develop a sense of belonging to the local culture as well as the cultural production of the district, which can eventually lead to social innovation.

Other theoretical developments on the industrial district (Becattini 1991) argue that the district, as well as other organizations that are rooted in the territory, are based on a social and human capital already present in the territory, but the district contributes to the development and the creation of new capital, creating trusting relationships that enrich the fabric of local society. The districts have the capacity to govern themselves and to evolve independently, with the right conditions (Sacco and Ferilli 2006).

Sacco and Ferilli (2006) refer to modern economic theory and cite international cases to identify the most important factors of development. Thus, quality of life, the level of innovation, and capability are highlighted. These effects are translated into three vectors of development for the 'proactive cultural district', these being: the localization of the creative class, found in Florida's theory; the development of innovation, associated with Porter's (1999) theory; and, finally, Sen's (1999) concept of 'capability' (Sacco and Ferilli, 2006, p. 20). Although this concept of capability can be criticized, particularly for its lack of interest in structural socio-political relations and the role of political movements and transformations (Dean 2009), it is used by Sacco and Ferilli (2006) to stress

the positive effects of cultural and creative development in cities. It also highlights the importance of learning, and collective learning, in the context of cultural and creative developments. The success of the 'proactive cultural district' is based on a strategic complementarity of these three elements (capability, innovation and the right localization) and a series of combined bottom-up and top-down elements (Sacco and Tavano Blessi 2005).

Concerning the relation between culture and socioeconomic development, there are various models put forward. Tavano Blessi et al. (2012) consider that Evans (2009) presents the best typology. According to Evans (2009), three different models integrate cultural capital into urban regeneration processes:

- *Culture-led regeneration*, in which culture is seen as an aesthetical and instrumental tool of regeneration;
- *Culture and regeneration*, in which culture is functional in strategic planning but it is not integrated in the plan;
- *Cultural regeneration*, in which culture is a structural part of strategic planning, fully integrated in the improvement of the environmental, social and economic spheres. (Tavano Blessi et al. 2012)

The last type is the most complete as it really blends together the economic, social and cultural or creative dimensions.

In the literature, there is a certain feeling that this new emphasis on culture- and creativity-based policies for local development is not yet supported by sufficient case studies to defend the view of culture-led development as a social innovation and as an efficient tool for socioeconomic development (Bontje and Musterd 2009). This is why it is important to complement these theoretical developments with a case study in the cultural sector, as this can help us to better understand the concept of the creative city and, especially, how we can best observe social innovation in the arts-creative sectors.

We will thus turn to the case of the Tohu, a non-profit organization located in the *Cité des Arts du Cirque* (City of Circus Arts), an urban revitalization precinct in Montreal.[1] This case highlights the essential role that cultural activities can play in social innovation and their contribution to the urban culture-driven revitalization process (Barnes et al. 2010). This calls for the definition of a broader strategy for districts or clusters[2] than that of some revitalization initiatives, which are often centred on high technology or industrial sectors and less often on artistic and cultural activities, and also often neglect the social dimension, which is very present in the Tohu case.

5.3   THE TOHU, CITÉ DES ARTS DU CIRQUE

The Cité des Arts du Cirque, in which the Tohu is a key player, can be seen as an example of a 'proactive cultural district' or social innovation in the arts-cultural sector. Using this territorial revitalization project as an example of an aggregation of clusters (Porter 1999) and the attraction of a specialized creative class (Florida 2002), we can see how the Tohu has influenced the local environment through a strategy very much centred on attracting and including the local community in its activities, but also in its workforce.

In the March–April 2005 issue of *Policy Options*, Simon Brault, Vice-Chair of the Canada Council for the Arts and Director General of the National Theatre School of Canada, noted that:

> the correlations ... between development of the creative sector of the economy and the vibrancy, quality and diversity of a

city's cultural scene confirm the conclusions of other studies conducted recently in England, Australia and Germany which affirm that the revitalization of an urban area must include beforehand an ambitious cultural project. (Interview 2 February 2005; translation)

He then cited, as an example of this type of revitalization project, the Tohu, which is part of the Circus Arts City located in Saint-Michel district in northeast Montreal. The Tohu site can be seen as a cultural district which favours relations between a diverse group of people and contributes to defining Montreal as a 'creative laboratory' and source of social innovation in the arts-creative sector.

Saint-Michel is one of Canada's poorest districts, an area of Montreal which is undergoing a complete socio-economic transformation. This district has a population of around 60,000 which is made up mostly of immigrants, young people and people with a low educational level and low income.

The creation of the Tohu results from the convergence, during the 1990s, of various territorial actors from the public and private sectors (i.e., the Saint-Michel local community, civil society and the circus movement) in a thrust to create a social innovation. Actors in the local community got together and created *Vivre Saint-Michel en Santé* (VSMS), a non-profit organization which fostered cooperation between other territorial actors of the public and private sectors. In November 1999, Cirque du Soleil,[3] École nationale du cirque (national circus school)[4] and EnPiste[5] designed a project aimed at bringing together in one place a critical mass of infrastructure needed for the creation, training, production and diffusion of circus arts, thus creating the conditions to make Montreal the international capital of circus arts, which it has now become (TOHU 2006).

The combination of the three elements that characterize the theoretical bases of the 'proactive cultural district' can be found in the Tohu. First, the Tohu is a geographical agglomeration that hosts various organizations (Cirque du Soleil, En Piste, École Nationale du Cirque, the Tohu and, also in the same district, a residential centre for artists during their training in Montreal). Thus, organizations from the same sector are concentrated here and share the same need for infrastructure, talent and technology, as in clusters (Porter 1999). Since specialized artistic human capital and know-how are needed to create innovation, this concentration has contributed to the dynamism of the area.

Second, the Tohu is a place for the presentation of artistic and cultural practices and events, not only for paying customers from Montreal and outside the city, but also towards the immediate local community of the Saint-Michel district. The City of Circus Arts attracts many creators, artists, producers and choreographers; since these individuals eat and work like everyone, other 'less creative' jobs have also sprung up, and these are reserved for the local community, to help them develop their skills and find other jobs elsewhere afterwards. Today, the Tohu has become a cultural crossroads which promotes collaboration between professional artists, specialists, associations and citizens and the local community in the creation of activities.

Finally, the Tohu has become a *creative ecosystem* that is socially innovative where the organic, cooperation-based and self-organization components are considered to be essential elements to bring out the authenticity of this district. The 'creative core' of the circus community can reach other sectors in Montreal as there are many activities bringing together the Tohu and other organizations. It has an impact on the dynamics of the whole region, not only on the specific district, although the social impact may be more concentrated within the district.

Moreover, and this is important from the social innovation dimension, the Tohu carries out activities with an important social dimension, which seek to reduce the gaps in terms of cultural capability of the local community (Sen 1999); these gaps often make it difficult for individuals to participate actively, rather than only being observers or being totally excluded from events and activities. Indeed, when events do not meet the expectations of people in the community, these individuals cannot identify with the content of these events. The Tohu makes efforts to integrate the visions of the community. In recent research, a good proportion of respondents indicated that opportunities for social activity and individual participation have increased as a result of the efforts of the Tohu, but also because of the participatory approach taken since the beginning of the development of the site, which favours human development and social interaction (Tavano Blessi et al. 2012).

The name Tohu is inspired from 'tohu-bohu', an expression which conjures up the bubbling of ideas and actions, the chaos which precedes renewal or the hustle and bustle of the big city (TOHU 2006) and certainly calls to mind the innovative and evolving nature of the project. Indeed, the Tohu's artistic programming aims at empowering the community through various activities (artistic workshops and games for kids from the neighbourhood, collective painting, and Eco-fête – an event promoting ecological awareness). The Tohu organizes various on-site activities in order to mobilize and foster the participation of residents, which is an important aspect of its social mandate. Thus, every year, the Tohu presents the 'Las

Fallas' project. Stéphane Lavoie – then Communications Director for the Tohu – explains the significance of this event:

> Las Fallas is a popular celebration, inspired from a long tradition of Valencia's Fallas, in Spain. To foster a sense of belonging to the community, we created an event related to the myth of fire, an element which is shared by all cultures. With the collaboration of an artist, citizens make a gigantic wood sculpture which is subsequently burned, thus leaving a memory as well as creating a feeling of empowerment. (Interview 21 November 2005; translation)

The Fallas brings together over 5,000 persons each year, creates some temporary jobs and involves the participation of local artists (TOHU 2006). These various events, and their attention to social cohesion, social participation and integration of the community, are where the Tohu can most apparently be seen as an important social innovation.

Another social innovation dimension is related to the environmental component which the Tohu promotes through a partnership with one of the largest urban revitalization initiatives in Canada, the Saint-Michel Environmental Complex (CESM), and through its support of bio-climatic architecture designed on the basis of international standards. Tohu has been awarded the 'gold' level in the international LEED (Leadership in Energy and Enviromental Design) certification program, as well as numerous other honours in this field.

In terms of governance, the Tohu also set up a roundtable with the major territorial stakeholders (citizens, sponsors, community representatives from various social or ethnic groups, etc). Based on practices of community planning (Jacobs 1961) and the logic of participatory democracy, the Tohu develops projects in collaboration with the City of Montreal and several other organizations (large and small community groups in the district involved in delivering direct services to citizens and families, seniors, immigrants, young mothers, etc.) in order to establish the most integrated planning program possible. The Tohu's director, Charles-Mathieu Brunelle, indicates that consultation between the 'various protagonists is obviously a difficult process, but ultimately the most democratic course of action' (Interview 31 October 2005; translation).

The Tohu also has a social policy of hiring locally which is of great interest to the local community. Indeed, this involves employing young people from the district who have had social integration problems, including maintenance and administrative staff, security guards, technicians, etc. Tohu has also organized its cleaning and maintenance services, its restaurant staff and its technicians into workers' cooperatives (TOHU 2006).

According to Stéphane Lavoie (Communications and Marketing Director for Tohu), 'it is a very important phenomenon that people come to Tohu, but what's more important is that residents from the local community welcome them. These residents are thus given responsibilities and feel that they are part of the project and of the same context' (Interview 21 November 2005; translation).

With 65 per cent of residents coming from 75 cultural groups, the social integration dimension is extremely important. In this respect, Brunelle explains that 'these people should be able to appropriate the local culture without rejecting their origins and, on the contrary, contributing to enrich it. They must re-appropriate their culture since the motto is to influence rather than to integrate' (Interview 31 October 2005; translation).

The Tohu also acts as a mediator between providers of essential services, including the City of Montreal, the borough and local commercial organizations. Tohu seeks to influence the localization of diversified activities by intervening with land owners and stores in the district in order to promote the establishment of social economy organizations, cultural and environmental companies, organic food stores and fair-trade cafés. The Tohu thus tries to have an impact on the regional dynamics, beyond the direct district impacts.

Lastly, the Tohu also seeks to curb a possible 'gentrification', since only a minority (26 per cent) of the population are home-owners. To achieve this goal, the Tohu encourages the creation of 'housing cooperatives' as a means to sustain the important social and physical characteristics of the district.

In the Saint-Michel district, even though most of the people live in poor economic conditions and have a limited level of education, the Tohu's activities have positively influenced their willingness to participate in cultural activities. Indeed, as Nussbaumer and Moulaert (2004) indicate, culture may perform effectively as both a cohesive and a networking social factor, answering various human and social needs, and to improve quality of life and wellbeing. Indeed this connection between the cultural, human and social dimensions is extremely important. However, in order for this to happen, there are certain prerequisites. A research project on human and social capital has shown that the Tohu has contributed positively to the social and human capital of some respondents, has increased their participation, social networks and relations, education opportunities, as well as cultural participation (Tavano Blessi et al. 2011).

The Tohu project as a whole seems to be effectively oriented towards the three major effects sought, that is 'exerting an attraction for individuals with a creative ethos, producing social innovations for the local territory as well as the economic and cultural system, and redirecting individuals and society towards activities laden with experiential value, while responding creatively to the challenges posed by the local context' (Sacco et al. 2005); these objectives are considered essential in cultural districts initiatives.

The Tohu project is important with regard to the development of social and cultural activities in Montreal, especially since Cirque du Soleil has contributed to defining the image of Montreal as a creative city, as has Montreal's Cité du multimedia (multimedia city) in another artistic field (Britton et al. 2009).[6] According to C.M. Brunelle, the Tohu project is a unique social innovation: 'the entire circus world behind a single project, the entire process in a single place ... here, we can train artists and put on shows, but we can also create new shows, new companies, new processes. It is a bit like the Silicon Valley of the circus' (interview 31 October 2005; translation; see also www.ccarts. ca/fr/advocacy/publications/documents/ ArtofDevelopmentFR.pdf, last accessed 7 December 2012); however, we would add that social innovation is certainly more a feature here than in Sillicon Valley.

This case study shows that social innovation – that is improving social relations and tackling social problems as well as meeting social needs of the community – can be brought about very well through creativity, arts and culture provided that the designers of the project choose to include the local population in the process and activities.

5.4 CONCLUSION

The role of culture-led development is clearly to redefine the identity of the urban system and present cultural experiences as a common language, in both a rational and an emotional dimension (Sacco and Zamagni 2002). Arts and culture make it possible to reinforce the social identity and the sense of belonging shared by citizens, which develop 'through knowing the same artifacts, using the same symbols and going collectively through the same performance experiences.' (Hutter 1996, p. 265) This human and social dimension of the experience with the Tohu is important for the local population (Tavano Blessi et al. 2012), and can have an important impact not only at the local level, but also in terms of the measures and programs developed at the regional and national levels to alleviate poverty through social innovation.

The contribution of art and culture to the socio-cultural and economic development of a given space is based on behaviours of cooperation and organization between the territorial actors (Tremblay and Pilati 2008). It can certainly play a fundamental role in the integration of excluded or marginalized individuals and communities (Greffe et al. 2005, p. 27) but also in developing social and human capital (Tavano Blessi et al. 2012). Indeed, as mentioned earlier, culture may perform effectively as both a cohesive and a networking social factor, answering various human and social needs, and to improve quality of life and wellbeing. Research has shown that the Tohu has contributed to the social and human capital of some respondents through improved social relations and participation, expanded social networks, education opportunities, and cultural participation (Tavano Blessi et al. 2012).

Long-standing and new residents in socially disadvantaged environments must be able to easily integrate into the communities and seize the new opportunities which arise in the context of the crea-tive economy. Sen observed that choices should not be determined by the 'elite guardians of tradition . . .' (1999, p. 31), but all population groups directly concerned should be able to participate in the decision-making process.

The Tohu highlights the fundamental role that artistic, creative and cultural activities can play in the urban revitalization process. This calls for a broad strategy for districts of clusters, integrating artistic and cultural activities and social innovation, as exemplified by the Tohu. This case is particularly interesting because beyond being an urban economic revitalization project, it includes the social economy dimension. Here, there is social innovation and socio-economic revitalization through activities related to creativity, arts and culture. There is a clear link between social innovation, social cohesion and the arts and creative sectors.

It is obvious that arts and culture are not a panacea that develops spontaneously to make cities more trendy and rich (Young et al. 2006) or more creative (Peck 2005). As mentioned in Tavano Blessi et al. (2012), the idea that culture can produce important effects is not without a rationale, but it is not always clear why, how and under what conditions this can be made to happen. In any case, culture-led regeneration and proactive cultural districts are clearly important social innovations that do seem to have a serious impact in many cities).

5.5   QUESTIONS FOR DISCUSSION

- How do you see the interrelations between social innovation and cultural-artistic activities?
- Do you see such social innovations in your own city, country?
- Do you think that concrete social

objectives can deter the creative-artistic dimension of projects, or make them too 'realistic'?

- Are creative-artistic projects the best solution to city development and reconversion today? Why or why not?

NOTES

1. This project results from the convergence, during the 1990s, of various territorial actors from the public and private sectors, i.e., the Saint-Michel local community, civil society and the circus movement. Actors in the local community got together as a representative governance organization and created the Vivre Saint-Michel en Santé (VSMS) non-profit organization which fostered cooperation between other territorial actors of the public and private sectors. Through meetings between key individuals and exchanges of ideas between the various territorial actors, in November 1999, Cirque du Soleil, École nationale du cirque (national circus school) and EnPiste applied their energy to designing a project whose priority is to bring together in one place a critical mass of infrastructure needed for the creation, training, production and diffusion of circus arts, thus laying down the conditions to make Montreal the international capital of circus arts (TOHU 2006).

2. For a typology of clusters, see Tremblay (2006).

3. In 1982, Guy Laliberté organized activities for the youth hostel in Baie-Saint-Paul. In 1984, he founded Cirque du Soleil in Québec as a non-profit organization. Today it is one of Canada's largest cultural multinationals and is known on the international scene for its unique circus arts-inspired choreography. Cirque du Soleil employs over 3,000 people and 900 artists in various countries (www.cirquedusoleil.com, last accessed 7 December 2012).

4. Founded in 1981, École Nationale du Cirque (national circus school) is the only institution in Canada for higher and college education specialized in circus arts. Its primary mission is to train artists and it has trained hundreds of artists in circus arts, who pursue their careers all over the world (www.enc.qc.ca, last accessed 7 December 2012).

5. EnPiste is a non-profit national association of circus arts professionals, companies and institutions. Its objectives are to develop cohesion and create initiatives to promote the circus arts community (www.enpiste.com, last accessed 7 December 2012).

6. Also see Klein et al. (2010) for the case of the Creative Lab, another social innovation in the cultural-artistic sector, which brings fashion creators together to share resources (equipment, human resources) and therefore be able to create their designs.

REFERENCES

(References in bold are recommended reading.)

Barnes, T., T. Hutton, J.-L. Klein, D.-G. Tremblay and D. Wolfe (2010), 'A Tale of Three Cities: Innovation, Creativity and Governance in Montreal, Toronto and Vancouver', presented to 12th Annual Meeting of the Innovation Systems Research Network Conference, http://www.utoronto.ca/isrn/publications/NatMeeting/Nat Slides/Nat10/Papers/Session%20VI%20Barnes HuttonTremblayWolfe%20ver%20MY10.pdf (last accessed 13 July 2012).

Battaglia, A. and D.-G. Tremblay (2012a), '22@ and the Innovation District in Barcelona and Montreal: a process of clustering development between urban regeneration and economic competitiveness', *Urban Studies Research*, 2011, Article ID 568159, http://www.hindawi.com/ journals/usr/2011/568159/ (last accessed 13 July 2012).

Battaglia, A. and D.-G. Tremblay (2012b), 'El Raval and Mile End: a comparative study of two cultural quarters in Barcelona and Montreal, between urban regeneration and creative clusters', *Journal of Geography and Geology*, 4 (1), 56–74.

Becattini, G. (1991), 'Italian Districts: Problems and Perspectives', *International Studies of Management and Organization*, 21, 83–90.

Bontje, M. and Musterd, S. (2009), 'Creative industries, creative class and competitiveness: Expert opinions critically appraised', *Geoforum*, 40 (5), 843–852.

Britton, J.N.H., D.-G. Tremblay and R. Smith (2009), 'Contrasts in clustering: the example of Canadian new media', *European Planning Studies*, 17 (2), 211–234.

Dean, H. (2009), 'Critiquing capabilities: The distractions of a beguiling concept', *Critical Social Policy*, 29 (2), 261–278.

Darchen, S. and D.-G. Tremblay (2010), 'What attracts and retains knowledge workers/students: the quality of place or career opportunities? The cases of Montreal and Ottawa', *Cities*, 27 (4), 225–233.

Evans, G. (2009), 'Creative Cities, Creative Spaces and Urban Policy', *Urban Studies*, 46, 1003–1040.

Florida, R. (2002), *The Rise of the Creative Class. And How It's Transforming Work, Leisure and Everyday Life*, New York: Basic Books.

Florida, R. (2004), *Cities and the Creative Class*, New York: Routledge.

Florida, R. (2005), *The Flight of the Creative Class. The New Global Competition for Talent*, New York: Harper Business.

Gertler, M.S. (2004), *Creative Cities: What Are They For, How Do They Work, and How Do We Build Them?* Canadian Policy Research Network (CPRN) Family Network, Background Paper F/48.

Greffe, X., S. Pflieger and A. Noya (2005), *La culture et le développement local*, Paris: OECD.

Hospers, G.-J. and R. van Dalm (2005), "How to create a creative city? The viewpoints of Richard Florida and Jane Jacobs", *Foresight*, **7** (4), 8–12.

Hutter, M. (1996), 'The Impact of Cultural Economics on Economic Theory', *Journal of Cultural Economics*, **20**, 263–268.

Jacobs, J. (1961), *The Death and Life of Great American Cities*, New York: Random House.

Jacobs, J. (1985), *Cities and the Wealth of Nations*, New York: Vintage Books.

Klein, J.-L. and D.-G. Tremblay (2010a), 'Créativité et cohésion sociale en milieu urbain; pour une ville créative pour tous', in R. Tremblay and D.G. Tremblay (eds), *La classe créative selon Richard Florida: un paradigme urbain plausible?* Québec-Rennes: Presses de l'université du Québec and Presses universitaires de Rennes, pp. 201–221.

Klein, J.-L. and D.-G. Tremblay (2010b), 'Can we have a "Creative City" without forgetting social cohesion? Some avenues of reflection', *PLAN Canada*, **50** (2), 27–29.

Klein, J.-L., D.-G. Tremblay and D. Bussières (2010), 'Community Based Intermediation and Social Innovation. A Case Study in Montreal's Apparel Sector', *International Journal of Technology Management*, **51** (1), 121–138.

Kotkin, J. (2000), *The New Geography*, New York: Random House.

Marshall, A. (1920), *Principles of Economics*, London: Macmillan.

MacCallum, D., F. Moulaert, J. Hillier and S. Vicari Haddock (eds) (2009), *Social Innovation and Territorial Development*, Farnham: Ashgate.

Markusen, A. (2006a), Cultural planning and the creative city, presented at the Annual Congress of the American Collegiate Schools of Planning, Fort Worth, Texas. November, www.hhh.umn.edu/img/assets/6158/271PlanningCulturalSpace.pdf (last accessed 13 July 2012).

Markusen, A. (2006b), 'Urban development and the politics of a creative class: evidence from a study of artists', *Environment and Planning A*, **38**, 1921–1940.

Markusen, A. and G. Schrock (2006), 'The distinctive city: Divergent patterns in growth, hierarchy and specialisation', *Urban Studies*, **43**, 1301–1323.

Moulaert, F., H. Demuynck and J. Nussbaumer (2004), 'Urban renaissance: from physical beautification to social empowerment', *City*, **8** (2), 229–235.

Moulaert, F., E. Swyngedouw, F. Martinelli and S. González (eds) (2010), *Can Neighbourhoods Save the City? Community Development and Social Innovation*, London: Routledge.

Nussbaumer, J. and F. Moulaert (2004), 'Integrated area development and social innovation in European cities', *City*, **8** (2), 249–257.

Peck, J. (2005), 'Struggling with the Creative Class', *International Journal of Urban and Regional Research*, **29** (4), 740–770.

Pilati, T. and D.-G. Tremblay (2007), 'La cité créative et le district culturel: une contribution au débat théorique', *Géographie, économie et société*, **9** (4), 381–401.

Porter, M. (1999), *La concurrence selon Porter*, Paris: Edition Village Mondial.

Pyke, C., S. McMahan and T. Dietsche (2010), *Green Building and Human Experience*, Washington: U.S. Green Building Council.

Sacco, P.L. and S. Zamagni (2002), *Complessità relazionale e comportamento economico*, Bologna: Il Mulino.

Sacco, P.L. and S. Pedrini (2003), 'Il distretto culturale: mito o opportunità?', EBLA Working Paper No. 05/2003, Dipartimento di Economia 'S. Cognetti de Martiis', Torino.

Sacco, P.L. and G. Tavano Blessi (2005), 'Distretto culturale e aree urbane', *Economia della cultura*, **2**, 153–165.

Sacco, P.L. and R. Comunian (2006), *Urban regeneration and limits of the creative city: Newcastle Gateshead*, Working paper Venezia: DADI, Università IUAV.

Sacco, P.L. and G. Ferilli (2006), *Il distretto culturale evoluto nell'economia post industriale*, Working paper, Venezia: DADI, Università IUAV WP (4).

Sacco, P.L. Ferilli, G. and Lavanga, M. (2007), 'The cultural district organizational model: a theoretical and policy design approach', Working paper, Venezia: DADI, Università IUAV.

Sen, A. (1999), *Development as freedom*, Oxford: Oxford University Press.

Tavano Blessi, G., D.-G. Tremblay, M. Sandri and T. Pilati (2012), 'New trajectories in urban regeneration processes: Cultural capital as source of Human and Social Capital accumulation. Evidence from the case of Tohu in Montreal', *Cities*, **2, 397–407.**

TOHU (2006), *Tohu: Un modèle de développement durable au cœur du quartier Saint-Michel*, Montréal: TOHU.

Tremblay, D.-G. (2006), 'Networking, Clusters and Human Capital Development', Research report, available at http://www.teluq.uqam.ca/chaire ecosavoir/pdf/NRC06-08A.pdf (last accessed 17 January 2013).

Tremblay D.-G. and T. Pilati (2008), 'The Tohu and Artist-run Centers: Contributions to the Creative City?' *Canadian Journal of Regional Science*, **30** (2), 337–356.

Tremblay, D.-G. and R. Tremblay (eds) (2006), *La compétitivité urbaine à l'ère de la nouvelle économie:*

enjeux et défis, Québec: Presses de l'université du Québec.

Tremblay, Rémy and Diane-Gabrielle Tremblay (2010), *La classe créative selon Richard Florida: un paradigme urbain plausible?* Québec-Rennes: Presses de l'université du Québec and Presses universitaires de Rennes, http://www.puq.ca/media/produits/documents/456_D2509_FPR.pdf (last accessed 7 December 2012).

Throsby, D. (2001), *Economics and Culture*, Cambridge: Cambridge University Press.

Young, G. (2006), *The Ashgate Research Companion to Planning and Culture*, Aldershot: Ashgate.

6. Microcredit as a social innovation

Arvind Ashta, Karl Dayson, Rajat Gera, Samanthala Hettihewa, N. V. Krishna and Christopher Wright

6.1 INTRODUCTION

Microcredit is considered as an innovative system of lending aimed at financial inclusion of the poor. Hailed as a messiah by some and as a demon by others, it has, nevertheless, enabled more than 150 million families to take loans.

Why is it a social innovation? And why has this social innovation gone where bankers feared to tread? Essentially, as this chapter details later, a novel system of group lending to women coupled with dynamic incentives led to steep reductions in risk and transaction costs, permitting the poor to be profitable customers.

Microfinance is conceptualized and operationalized as a means of poverty alleviation. Poverty alleviation is the act of reducing the scourges of poverty of an individual or community. Principal factors identified by the literature as being responsible for poverty include market failure (economic exclusion), regional disparities (spatial exclusion), and low-status (cultural exclusion). These factors reinforce each other as components of deprivation and exclusion and have causal and dynamic connections (on these cumulative dynamics, see e.g. Antohi 2009).

There are various ways of alleviating poverty and the use of microfinance services is suggested as one means. Microfinance programs ensure availability of funds without collateral. Microfinance has been defined as the provision of financial services to low-income clients (the poor) including those who are self-employed (Armendàriz and Morduch 2005). These financial services generally include savings, insurance and credit provisions. In the last few decades the world has witnessed a rapid growth of microfinance institutions (MFIs) to make the services accessible to the poor.

The key assumption behind all microfinance programs is that intervention will change human behaviours and practices in ways that lead to, or increase the likelihood of, desired outcomes. In a conventional microfinance project a package of technical assistance and capital changes the behaviour (and products) of a MFI which subsequently provides different services to a client, most commonly in the form of a loan. These services lead to the client modifying her/his microenterprise activities which increases expected microenterprise income. The change in microenterprise income causes changes in household income which creates greater household economic security. The modified level of household economic security reduces the morbidity and mortality of household members, increases educational and skill levels and enhances future economic and social opportunities. In turn, microfinance programs are expected to deliver behavioural and functional change at institutional, individual and household levels through a systemic process of intervention. Figure 6.1 illustrates the financial part of the above discussion in classical economic terms.

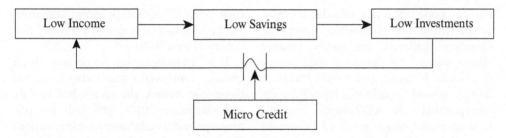

Figure 6.1   Microcredit is an external boost to the micro-economy of the poor

The first section describes the setting in which microcredit was introduced and the socially innovative characteristics of the lending system which allowed it to succeed. The second section describes the institutional changes and challenges that accompanied the expansion of microcredit. The third section indicates that technology may give a new impetus to expansion while further reducing transaction costs and changing social relationships. The fourth section warns of a difference in institutions between developing countries and developed countries and that the same forms of microfinance may not readily adapt to developed countries. The fifth section suggests limitations of microfinance. The final section looks at the how microfinance institutions may evolve in the future to overcome these limitations.

6.2   MICROCREDIT CHALLENGING MAINSTREAM VALUES

In this section, we first describe the historical background of financial services being provided to the poor in the decades before microcredit came in and then explain, in this perspective, the socially innovative characteristics of microcredit.

6.2.1   Historical Background

Despite the attention lavished on microfinance during the last 30 years, there is evidence of similar activities over many centuries. Although practiced in many cultures across the world, there are few historical accounts of its evolution. Only in Europe has there been an attempt to develop a systematic historiography of financial services to low income families (Seibel 2003). There have been sharply differentiating outcomes in different countries mainly due to the nature of the legislation passed. While Irish Loan Funds began in 1720 and served 20 per cent of households by 1840, the introduction of a legal cap on their charges ultimately led to their decline. By contrast rural and urban cooperative savings schemes in Germany, established in the 1840s, received supportive legalisation and have today morphed into savings banks with 75 million customers and in 1997 undertook 64 per cent of all financial intermediation services (Seibel 2005).

In the 1970s, this rich history was ignored and microcredit was re-invented in the developing world. The new microcredit era started with Muhammad Yunus, an economics professor at Chittagong University, making small loans to micro-entrepreneurs in two parts of Bangladesh in the mid-1970s, which led to the creation of Grameen Bank in 1983. What was remarkable was that Yunus demonstrated that the poor will repay affordable credit, contradicting an established viewpoint. Grameen achieved this partly because clients wanted to maintain their access to affordable credit and would therefore work to ensure the debt was repaid. Yunus incorporated this self-policing into his lending model which involved groups of borrowers taking it in turns to receive loans. Only after the initial recipients repaid the loan could the next members of the group receive one. Whether wittingly or not, Yunus had adopted an approach similar to the rotating savings and credit associations (ROSCAs) that operated informally around the globe, going under the name of Tontines in Africa, after an Italian banker, Lorenzo de Tonti, who invented a slightly different concept in 1653. Though involved in savings rather than credit activity ROSCAs also used peer pressure to ensure all members continued to save towards the central pot even after they had received their own share. Thus, Grameen Bank used existing bonds of collective solidarity as a means to offset their lack of knowledge about the borrowers.

At the same time that Muhammad Yunus was experimenting in Bangladesh, similar activities were being undertaken elsewhere, including Indonesia and Latin America. During the following 30 years, the range of services extended from microcredit to include a broader range of financial services and the sector was renamed as microfinance. Moreover, the industry expanded across the developing world and a few developed countries, although by the turn of the century it had begun to appear in most developed countries. According to Microcredit Summit (http://www.micro creditsummit.org/, last accessed 7 January 2013), by 2007, one Apex Agency was receiving data from 3,552 institutions (in developing countries) serving 155 million customers, 107 million of whom were from the bottom half of a nation's poverty line (Daley-Harris 2009).

This transformation has not been without controversy and today there are those that believe the sector has lost its way (Bateman 2010), although microfinance providers continue to disprove conventional wisdom that the poor cannot repay loans.

6.2.2   What Qualifies Microcredit as a Social Innovation?

The difficulties of lending to the poor can be summarized as lack of complementary inputs for the poor to productively use capital, risks and market imperfections such as information asymmetry, as well as transaction costs (Armendàriz and Morduch 2005; Ashta 2009). The transaction costs were high because the loan size was low. The risks were high, owing to asymmetric information-related problems of adverse selection, moral hazard and the lack of police to enforce contracts in poor countries. Adverse selection means that, before giving the loan, the lender is not able to distinguish between safe and risky borrowers since they have no credit history (Akerlof 1970; Stiglitz and Weiss 1981). Moral hazard means that, once the loan is given, the borrower has no incentive to make the project work and to repay the money and he may take bigger risks (Stiglitz and Weiss 1981).

In any case, it was believed that the poor were unable to use the financial capital productively since they did not have the social and human capital which were required as complementary inputs. For any social innovation to work, it had to address these three problems.

Microcredit is a social innovation, using socially available information, peer lending, social collateral, and public payments to overcome problems of information asymmetry that can cause high loan-default rates. When microfinance benefits women it contributes to empowerment, wellbeing and development, and benefits percolate to the whole family. As Antohi (2009, p. 39) puts it:

> The current enthusiasm for microfinance operations can be explained by the various significant impacts that such operations are deemed to have on individuals and local communities:
>
> • Combating poverty and exclusion (the mechanisms used give priority to those in socio-economic difficulty);
> • (Re-)injecting some dynamism into local areas by creating economic activity;
> • Supporting projects that respect human factors and the environment (ethical approach).

Moreover, the principles of social relations and proximity underlying the action of microfinance institutions vis-à-vis the beneficiaries are key aspects of microfinance as a socially innovative approach to combating poverty and exclusion: '. . . taking account of social relations . . . enables the most vulnerable customers to be included and hence become economic players in their society and recover their dignity, public recognition and self-confidence.[1] (Antohi 2009, pp. 41–42)

6.2.2.1 Using social information and women to overcome information asymmetry

Typical microcredit group lending methodology varies with the Grameen model, Indian self-help groups, FINCA's village lending and other variants (Armendàriz and Morduch 2005). In the Grameen model, a group is formed with five women. A loan is given to two women. If they repay, two more will get a loan. If all four repay, the fifth will get a loan.

The first social innovation is that the potential members form groups with people they trust and, because the group members know everyone in the village, they have information which banks lack. Therefore, the asymmetric information and adverse selection problems are solved in a novel way, without the bank getting the information.

The second social innovation is that the loans are made to women, who were traditionally kept out of the economic sphere. This is because women repay better. Moreover, they are less prone to migrate to urban areas and, thus, can be found easily.

6.2.2.2 Using social pressure to monitor and enforce

Since the group members know each other, the first two borrowers will feel guilty if due to their actions the others do not get a loan. This guilt is combined with pressure from the group monitoring to overcome moral hazard. Finally, performance in the business for which the loan was taken may improve, due to the Hawthorne effect – providing a third innovation. The Hawthorne effect comes from an experiment in which behaviour improved during a period of study and then slumped and is attributed to the observation that behaviour is modified simply because people are being observed and not because of any external manipulation (Machol 1975).

A fourth innovation is that loans are paid weekly. Weekly repayments make the reimbursement amounts small, manageable, and create the discipline of regular repayment (monthly or quarterly repayments, by increasing the repayment amount, increase moral hazard of the loan).

6.2.2.3   Using social relations to reduce transaction costs

The fifth social innovation is the elimination of physical collateral and the limiting of registering charges and taxes. In a typical group lending scheme, financial collateral is replaced by social collateral. In fact, the group may act as a guarantee in some of the schemes which are joint-liability groups. Thus, the capacity of the individual is replaced by the group's repayment capacity. Also, the lack of formalities leads to a quick processing of loan applications.

A sixth social innovation is that repayment takes place in public. A typical Grameen weekly meeting could consist of eight groups of women and the bank agent who makes the collection in public, lowering the time and cost of collections for the MFI agent. Fear of social embarrassment increases collections.

6.2.2.4   Co-creation to enhance social and human capital

Yet another beneficial impact of microfinance is that group members have a mutual interest in each other's success. As a result, they offer helpful advice and other assistance so that all are able to repay. Thus, the group goes beyond the Hawthorne effect to act as a co-creator.

In some cases, the field agents who meet hundreds of borrowers in similar situations are able to transfer this knowledge and the capacity to repay to other borrowers. Thus, the field agent is not just a lender but a co-creator in the business, similar to a venture capitalist. For example, ADIE, France Active and France Initiative in France help entrepreneurs to make their business plans and helps them to meet other investors who would ultimately provide (additional) finance for the project. In other cases, other NGOs or public programs train borrowers to improve and foster their businesses (Premalatha 2010).

6.2.2.5   Changing the role of women

Microfinance also fits into the mission of empowering women, who in poor countries did not have any claims on equality. First, many of the MFIs teach the women to at least sign their names,: a visible sign of the capacity to contract. Second, it allows them to participate in their family economics as sources of financial capital rather than merely as spenders. Third, if they use it for their business, they start participating in the economic life of their society. Fourth, women tend to redistribute the benefit of their income to the entire family and this allows the entire family to be better nourished, clothed and educated.

Thus, a series of small innovations from microcredit create multiple impacts on society. These can be reclassified in terms of the three generic features mentioned by the editors in their introduction (satisfaction of human needs, relations between humans and groups, and empowerment) as shown in the Table 6.1 below.

6.3   DIFFUSION OF MICROCREDIT AS A SOCIAL MOVEMENT

The spread of microfinance had to battle against conservative forces. Yet, the drivers of diffusion overcame this. At times, existing institutions needed to be transformed to allow microfinance to succeed. Transformation of institutions is an aspect of social innovation, and an important factor in small-scale innovations 'taking' at the broader social level.

Table 6.1   Generic reclassification of innovations of microfinance

	Satisfaction of human needs (financing)	Relations between humans and groups	Empowerment
Using social information and women to overcome information asymmetry	✓	✓	
Loans are made to women	✓	✓	✓
Using social pressure to monitor, enforce and co-create		✓	✓
Loans are paid in small weekly amounts		✓	
Using social collateral instead of physical collateral		✓	
Loans are repaid in public		✓	

6.3.1   Conservative Forces

This section describes the various challenges related to successful commercialization of microfinance.

Operating necessity and ideological contradictions have long beset microcredit. One conflict involves sustainability, e.g. a precursor microfinance institution founded in 1361, after the Bishop of London bequeathed 1,000 marks of silver to establish 'a bank to lend money on pawned objects, without interest' (The Catholic Encyclopedia 2010), failed because operating costs consumed its capital.

Thus, it is clear that microfinance institutions need to be financially sustainable in addition to being socially useful. If the MFI is donor dependent, and if donors are subject to fads, the borrower may not repay, expecting that the MFI will go bankrupt. Therefore, the MFI has to be profitable. However, people have the wrong perception that *NGOs* are working for poverty alleviation but other financial institutions are working to make profit that cannot possibly go along with poverty alleviation. In fact, operating on a non-profit basis means that most NGOs cannot

transform due to lack of required institutional capability (e.g., skilled manpower, infrastructure and cost structure) or due to a lack of a clear vision about what to achieve.

The funding capacity of donor-based microfinance is limited. This in turn limits the numbers who could avail the fund or if availed, use it to get out of the net of poverty. Similarly, microcredit programs run by government have shown a poor performance, usually because politicians trade votes for debt forgiveness, creating a culture of non-repayment.

As poor people have no assets to back their loan, non-repayment has a higher impact on MFIs than on banks who take collateral. Therefore, even if 98 per cent of MFI borrowers repay, the non-repayment of 1 per cent or 2 per cent constitutes a total write-off. A credit information bureau may reduce the risk to some extent but this would require all the necessary institutional, regulatory and legal formalities. Thus, legal and regulatory environment must be supportive and conducive with a clear vision of the respective authorities. However, such bureaus do not exist in poor countries.

The microfinance movement also had to overcome the existing money lending or usury institutions which prevailed. In developing countries, the exploiters are often village money lenders or other creditors who lend at ruinous rates and take crops or seize farms/chattels in return. Poverty is an ongoing source of profit for those who extend credit for weddings, funerals or festivals that leave families indebted for generations. Microcredit is an innovation that frequently frustrates those seeking profit from the poor, excluded and disenfranchised. As a result, microcredit is often reviled by these entrenched institutions/interests.

Another source of resistance to microcredit arises from the need of some of the more fortunate to validate their superiority by keeping the poor in poverty. Kaplan et al. (1996) and Kennedy et al. (1996) show a correlation between age-adjusted mortality and income inequality. This effect is often tied to the relative deprivation of the poor or maintaining the relative superiority of the affluent (Banerjee and Duflo 2008; Headey and Wearing 1988; Marmot 2003): 'It is not enough to succeed: Others must fail.' Thus, some resistance to microcredit programs reflects its failings but much arises from an unsavoury mix of unenlightened short-run economic self-interest or self-righteous one-upmanship. In this light, Mair and Marti (2007) indicate that existing microfinance borrowers, who will probably be relatively well off to have passed the initial screening process, have difficulty accepting that an NGO provides free assets (or interest-free loans) to the ultra-poor (the poorest of the poor) and may not admit the ultra-poor in their existing borrower groups to enable them to receive credit.

Those staffing and managing MF institutions are key MF stakeholders but little research is directed at understanding their

motives, behaviour and imperatives. In studying a similar group of individuals, Niskanen (1971) suggests that many bureaucrats, instead of representing the best interests of their constituents, seek to maximize their budgets or 'lead the quiet life' or some combination thereof. While many employees of MF institutions are truly wonderful people, as MF becomes well established, a rising number of individuals employed in MF may display *Niskanean* bureaucratic tendencies in empire building, mission drift to less poor clients, and choosing job security and institutional sustainability over providing useful client services. Thus, the purported great successes of microcredit carry a risk that MF may become a hidebound orthodoxy, protected by high-priests who brook no interference with their vision, control, and privileges.

Finally, an old economics axiom, the paradox of thrift, threatens this expanded microcredit role. As (Banerjee and Duflo 2008) note, most entrepreneurial poor run several micro-enterprises because they have few other options and often sell to their equally-poor neighbours. Thus, microcredit may be constrained to helping only a few rise – restraining the spending habits of the poor may deflate sales opportunities for the entrepreneurial poor and become a net-transfer of wealth to middle-class retailers.

6.3.2   Drivers of Diffusion

Factors for a successful commercialization of the microfinance model include external environment, financial resources and technology.

6.3.2.1   External environment
A supportive external environment where such NGOs/MFIs work is the foremost requirement. This external environment

would include legal frameworks enabling microcredit to perform; social infrastructure such as associated bodies which could provide the complementary inputs of human capital (knowledge, skills, competencies) and social capital (networks and relationships) (Carter et al. 2003; Mosey and Wright 2007; Papagiannidis et al. 2009); and physical infrastructure such as better roads, electricity and water, to enable the microenterprise to deliver.

6.3.2.2 Financial resources

For microfinance to develop, it needs initial donor capital. Thereafter, the MFIs need to either tap deposits or to obtain commercial funding. In much of West Africa, where savings and credit cooperatives are the basis of microfinance, savings deposits are the key constraints to growth of microcredit. In other countries, the NGOs are either able to raise commercial loans or transform themselves into non-bank financial institutions to acquire commercial credit. Thereafter, an evolution into banks, as in the case of Compartamos in Mexico, allows the benefits of commercial credit, equity financing and deposits. The availability of commercial funds has to be combined with a strategic capacity to ensure commercial management of funds and sustainability. Operational efficiency must be ensured through the application of commercial principles in all possible respects.

6.3.2.3 Technology

Every social innovation attempts to solve an identified problem by introducing changes in business and social models, and progresses through the stages of generation of the solution concept, transformation into usable products/services and implementation at appropriate scales. Technology plays a major role in the transformation of key ideas into products, and

in implementing such offerings in a scalable and reliable manner in the MFI sector.

The microfinance sector services large numbers of customers, currently over 130 million families, and transactions generated by the system are also correspondingly high. The repayment frequency tends to be much higher in microcredit compared to traditional banking models, leading to a much higher number of transactions per loan. This size factor makes it essential to integrate appropriate technology into any operational system, and MFIs are rapidly computerizing, with only 18 per cent currently relying on manual methods (Nyapati 2011). The availability of robust backend technology platforms, operating systems, databases, and applications coupled with data communication infrastructure, has made it possible for MFIs to rollout operations rapidly (Ashta 2011).

6.3.3 The Transformation of Institutions to Overcoming Resistance

6.3.3.1 Using existing institutions

As noted earlier, it is in the interests of moneylenders and others to keep the poor in poverty. Thus, without making institutions evolve, it is unlikely that the poor will escape poverty. Mair and Marti (2007) indicate that BRAC (a microfinance NGO) used the theatre as a medium to overcome traditional mindsets. More specifically, BRAC reminded the elites that they have a social as well as a religiously-ordained role to play in the uplifting of their people, and in creating institutions where they would have a leading role. Mair and Marti (2007) studied a situation of extreme resource constraints and an institutional fabric that is rich but often at odds with market development. They find that the crafting of new institutional arrangements, entailing negative consequences to those who are entrenched, is an ongoing process of *bricolage* to create new cultural identities by borrowing from other social areas and requiring political manoeuvring to gain acceptance.

6.3.3.2 Changing the attitudes and limitations that make people poor

Recent research on microcredit outcomes has been less than flattering. Banerjee et al. (2010) and Karlan and Zinman (2009) found, after correcting confounding factors (e.g. self-selection), that microcredit negligibly reduces poverty. Chemin (2008), Banerjee and Duflo (2008) and Coleman (2006) attribute much of microcredit's purported success to expectations, good public relations, poor internal controls and poor experimental design by researchers.

However, Servon (2006), Bhatt and Tang (2001), Pitt et al. (2006), Banerjee and Duflo (2008) and Banerjee et al. (2010) note that microcredit is more than lending money, it changes client habits and thinking, provides counselling, support and other assistance as those changes precipitate other issues. Mair and Marti (2007) also indicate that microfinance, in conjunction with the accompanying measures, improves the confidence of the ultra-poor.

6.3.4 Technology for Further Diffusion

It is also well recognized that reducing operating costs as a proportion of the total assets is a key driver for the successful adoption of the MFI model. We have already mentioned the leading role of computerization and management information systems.

Many innovative technology applications are being piloted in various parts of the world, which promise significant reductions in operational costs in the near future (Ashta 2011). One can visualize a scenario in which a large number of transactions are processed without the need for intermediation (e.g. through deployment of mobile-money transfers and ruggedized ATMs in rural areas). Indeed, as the MFI model matures, the high levels of intermediation found in current operational models will reduce sharply, as has happened through technology in multi-channel banking operations.

MFIs need to deliver a significant amount of information to their current and prospective clients, to open new markets, educate customers on new products and other sales and marketing information. They also need to engage large numbers of agents, in order to implement campaigns and to monitor operational parameters. All these information needs can benefit from the deployment of technology-based solutions, and their costs can be driven down simultaneously by reducing the role of intermediaries. Internet enabled services now reach a significant proportion of smart phone and other cell phone users in India – which is orders of magnitude larger than the internet users in India and suggests that such technologies can support information product delivery to the MFI's target segment.

A major problem faced by the MFI sector is the lack of a reliable client database, with credit related data, shared across all operators. This lacuna has allowed customers to avail themselves of multiple loans from multiple MFIs, thereby significantly increasing the risk of default. Technology has a key role to play in providing reliable credit related data to MFIs, while meeting data security and privacy requirements.

Compliance with regulatory requirements and auditability are other key system level requirements which can be effectively supported by technology. These audit needs can be effectively met only by suitable technology deployment.

Customer and transactional support are other emerging areas in which innovative solutions are being tested. One initiative is based on voice-recognition technologies, which are used to deliver automated responses and process a set of transactions. This solution is being piloted by large MFIs and banks, and potentially offers a low-cost channel for information delivery and customer support. A doctoral study on the diffusion of innovation (Hoerup 2001) identifies uncertainty of innovation as being a key inhibiting factor in the diffusion process. Hence, improving and automating information delivery and support services can help accelerate the diffusion process.

In summary, the microfinance sector is well suited to utilize technology at various phases of the innovation. The requirements of cost-effectively supporting a huge volume of transactions, delivering information and support services, reducing transaction costs, ensuring compliance with regulations, and audit, can only be supported and met by suitable deployments of technology.

6.4 THE INSUFFICIENCY OF MICROCREDIT AS A SOCIAL INNOVATION TOOL FOR DEVELOPED COUNTRIES

In modern developed countries (DCs), small loan size and high operating costs can make microcredit a bottomless pit (Hettihewa and Wright 2010). Microcredit institutions in developed countries enhanced their sustainability by evolving from resolving exclusion issues of society's poorest to facilitating less desperate working-poor. As a result, funding stakeholders should be warned that microcredit is not a poverty panacea but part of a poverty-reduction strategy.

In both Renaissance Europe and contemporary Less Developed Countries (LDCs), defaulting on obligations risked damage to vital social capital (e.g. family honour, social standing and/or other networks). In modern developed countries, mobility, small nuclear families and state-managed social-safety nets make social capital less relevant to survival and less viable as collateral. This relative irrelevancy of social capital in developed countries minimizes the opportunities to indenture families across generations; at the same time, the poor are exploited by a growing array of cheque-cashing operations, payday lenders and hire-purchase firms seeking short-run profits from effective annual interest rates ranging from 40–70 per cent. While LDC informal lenders may also charge similar rates, much of their rates pass on interest costs of financing (32.5 per cent) that are three times those of mainstream lenders.[2]

Peer's Law, i.e., the solution to the problem changes the problem, suggests that facilitating entrepreneurial aspirations of the working-poor may resolve sustainability in developed country microcredit institutions by creating new issues (e.g. helping clients through a minefield of business, welfare and other regulation). Thus social innovation creates a mixed bag of opportunities and new conflicts.

6.5 FUTURE INSTITUTIONAL TRANSFORMATIONS

After over 30 years in its current incarnation, microfinance is reaching a point where greater specialism and professionalism are producing a wave of consolidation. This has been accompanied, in recent years, by a number of criticisms (Bateman 2010; Shil 2009). These criticisms range from accusations of profiteering from the poor through excessive interest rates to allegations that microfinance simply does not reduce poverty.

These criticisms and inappropriate government responses could result in a fragmentation of the sector but could also prove beneficial. The transformation of predominately commercial providers into fully-licensed banks may supply the necessary infrastructure for emergence of a mainstream banking sector in developing world nations. As new fully-professional banks, former MFIs could serve the needs of the growing middle and working classes. They will face much criticism and will need to develop codes of conduct and quality benchmarks to reassure their public and other stakeholders.

By contrast, those MFIs that wish to remain focused on poverty reduction will need to adapt and contribute to sustainable economic growth. In most cases, this will involve incorporation into national and regional networks for economic development. They may still retain their independence but future subsidies (and most will require ongoing subsidisation) will be linked to their capacity to support and promote profitable SMEs and business clusters. In some cases, the MFIs will target loans at enterprises most likely to contribute to local employment, or work with mainstream funders to offer syndicated credit. Another model may involve offering business training services or working with those who provide such services. Ironically, these approaches are already evident in Europe, where the microfinance sector is at its weakest. But it's precisely because European MFIs deal with market failure within a mature financial sector that this will be the future for many MFIs across the world as their nations develop.

6.6   CONCLUSION

As transformations bring microfinance a long way from small loans to poor women in Bangladesh, there will still be a need for affordable alternatives to local moneylenders. Thus, the essence of microfinance – to design products for people who are unable to access conventional credit and employ social knowledge to ensure repayment – will remain. To overcome rising criticism, it will have to adopt social innovation as a continuing process of empowerment, social and institutional transformation.

6.7   QUESTIONS FOR DISCUSSION

- Loans to poor people have existed from times immemorial. What is so innovative about microfinance?
- What technologies can boost the growth of microfinance? Would these technologies lead to new social relations? Will they lead to empowerment?

NOTES

1. Whether microfinance reaches the most vulnerable or the poorest of the poor is disputed in the literature: see, for example, Hulme (2000) and Navajas et al. (2000). However, such critiques could stimulate NGOs to go further. See also the section on future institutional transformations and Bateman (2010) for further discussion on the limitations of the effectiveness of this social innovation.
2. For a discussion of the multifaceted nature and role of 'social capital' and its differentiated impacts in developed countries as compared to developing countries, see Antohi (2009).

Microcredit as a social innovation   91

REFERENCES

(References in bold are recommended reading.)

Akerlof, G.A. (1970), 'The Market for "Lemons": Quality Uncertainty and the Market Mechanism', *Quarterly Journal of Economics*, **84** (3), 488–500.

Antohi, M. (2009), 'Microfinance, Capital for Innovation', in D. MacCallum, F. Moulaert, J. Hillier and S. Vicari Haddock (eds), *Social Innovation and Territorial Development*, Farnham: Ashgate, pp. 39–61.

Armendáriz, B. and J. Morduch (2005), *The Economics of Microfinance*, Cambridge, MA: MIT Press.

Armendáriz, Beatriz and Marc Labie (2011), *The Handbook of Microfinance*, Singapore: World Scientific Publishing.

Ashta, A. (2009), 'Microcredit Capital Flows and Interest Rates: An Alternative Explanation', *Journal of Economic Issues (M.E. Sharpe Inc.)*, **43** (3), 661–83.

Ashta, A. (ed.) (2011), *Advanced Technologies for Microfinance: Solutions and Challenges*, Hershey, PA: IGI Global.

Banerjee, A.V. and E. Duflo (2008), 'The Experimental Approach to Development Economics', Working Paper, Cambridge, MA: MIT Department of Economics.

Banerjee, A.V., E. Duflo, R. Glennerster and C. Kinnan (2010), 'The Miracle of Microfinance? Evidence from a Randomized Evaluation', presented at *Universities-Research Conference on Economic Development*.

Bateman, M. (2010), *Why Doesn't Microfinance Work? The Destructive Rise of Local Neoliberalism*, London: Zed Books.

Bhatt, N. and S.-Y. Tang (2001), 'Making microcredit work in the United States: Social, financial and administrative dimensions', *Economic Development Quarterly*, **15** (3), 351–67.

Carter, N., C. Brush, P. Greene, E. Gatewood and M. Hart (2003), 'Women entrepreneurs who break through to equity financing: the influence of human, social and financial capital', *Venture Capital*, **5** (1), 1.

The Catholic Encyclopedia (2010), http://www.newadvent.org/cathen/10534d.htm (last accessed 13 July 2012).

Chemin, M. (2008), 'The benefits and costs of microfinance: Evidence from Bangladesh', *Journal of Development Studies*, **44** (4), 463–84.

Coleman, B.E. (2006), 'Microfinance in Northeast Thailand: Who benefits and how much?', *World Development*, **34** (9), 1612–38.

Daley-Harris, S. (2009), 'State of the Microcredit Summit Campaign Report 2009', Washington, DC: Microcredit Summit Campaign.

Headey, B. and A. Wearing (1988), 'The Sense of Relative Superiority – Central to Well-being', *Social Indicators Research*, **20**, 497–516.

Hettihewa, S. and C.S. Wright (2010), 'Socio-Economic Differences and Deployment of the LDC Micro-Finance Bottom-up Approach in DCs', *Journal of Electronic Commerce in Organizations*, **8** (2), 41–53.

Hoerup, S. (2001), *Diffusion of an Innovation: Computer Technology Integration and the Role of Collaboration*, Virginia: Virginia Polytechnic Institute.

Hulme, D. (2000) 'Is microdebt good for poor people? A note on the dark side of microfinance'. *Small Enterprise Development*, **11** (1): 26–28.

Kaplan, G., E.R. Pamuk, J.M. Lynch, R.D. Cohen and J.L. Balfour (1996), 'Inequality in income and mortality in the United States: analysis of mortality and potential pathways', *British Medical Journal*, **312**, 999–1003.

Karlan, D. and J. Zinman (2009), 'Expanding Microenterprise Credit Access: Using Randomized Supply Decisions to Estimate the Impacts in Manila', Working Paper, New Haven: Yale Economics Department.

Kennedy, B.P., I. Kawachi and D. Prothrow-Stith (1996), 'Income distribution and mortality: cross sectional ecological study of the Robin Hood index in the United States', *British Medical Journal*, **312**, 1004–7.

Machol, R.E. (1975), 'The Hawthorne Effect', *Interfaces*, **5** (2), 31–2.

Mair, J. and I. Marti (2007), 'Entrepreneurship for social impact: encouraging market access in rural Bangladesh', *Corporate Governance*, **7** (4), 493–501.

Marmot, M.G. (2003), 'Understanding Social Inequalities in Health', *Perspectives in Biology and Medicine*, **46** (3), S9–S23.

Mosey, S. and M. Wright (2007), 'From Human Capital to Social Capital: A Longitudinal Study of Technology-Based Academic Entrepreneurs', *Entrepreneurship: Theory & Practice*, **31** (6), 909–35.

Navajas, S., M. Schreiner, R. Meyer, C. Gonzalez-Vega and J. Rodriguez-Meza (2000), 'Microcredit and the Poorest of the Poor: Theory and Evidence from Bolivia', *World Development*, **28** (2), 333–346.

Niskanen, W.A. (1971), *Bureaucracy and Representative Government*, New York: Aldine-Atherton Inc.

Nyapati, K. (2011), 'Stakeholder Analysis of IT Applications for Microfinance', in A. Ashta (ed.), pp. 1–17.

Papagiannidis, S., F. Li, H. Etzkowitz and M. Clouser (2009), 'Entrepreneurial networks: A Triple Helix approach for brokering human and social capital', *Journal of International Entrepreneurship*, **7** (3), 215–35.

Pitt, M., M. Shahidur, R. Khandker and J. Cartwright (2006), 'Empowering women with micro finance: Evidence from Bangladesh', *Economic Development and Cultural Change*, **54** (4), 791–831.

Premalatha, U.M. (2010), 'An Empirical Study

on the Impact of Training and Development on Women Entrepreneurs in Karnataka', *IUP Journal of Soft Skills*, **4** (3), 49–64.

Seibel, H.D. (2003), 'History matters in Microfinance', *Small Enterprise Developmemt*, **14** (2), 10–12.

Seibel, H.D. (2005), 'Does history Matter? The old and new World of Microfinance in Europe and Asia', Working paper, University of Cologne, Development Research Centre, No. 10, http://hdl.handle.net/10419/23654 (last accessed 7 January 2013).

Servon, L.J. (2006), 'Microenterprise development in the United States: Current challenges and new directions', *Economic Development Quarterly*, **20** (4), 351–67.

Shil, N.C. (2009), 'Micro Finance for Poverty Alleviation: A Commercialized View', *International Journal of Economics and Finance*, **1** (2), 191–205.

Stiglitz, J.E. and A. Weiss (1981), 'Credit Rationing in Markets with Imperfect Information', *American Economic Review*, **71** (3), 393–410.

7. Social innovation for People-Centred Development[1]

Lars Hulgård and P.K. Shajahan

7.1 INTRODUCTION

If the unstable condition of the world today is directly attributable to human failure, the stabilization of society can be accompanied through intelligent human effort. As social idealists we are faced with a tremendous task – a task which is by no means lightened by the apathy and pessimism of so many of our fellow men. But I am firmly convinced that if thought . . . could be given to morally creative efforts towards mobilization of social welfare, our problem would be solved . . . If we can play but a small role in this process, our training here shall not be in vain. (Clifford Manshardt, Founder Director of TISS, 20 June 1938)

Social innovation is closely related to the people-centred development (PCD) framework of knowledge production and intervention as developed by the Tata Institute of Social Sciences (TISS) in Mumbai.[2] The three features of social innovation emphasized in this handbook are satisfaction of human needs, the role of social relations, and empowerment or socio-political mobilization by people trying to fulfil their needs. The discussion of people-centred development in this chapter particularly expands on the third feature of social innovation mentioned above, i.e., the empowerment or the socio-political mobilization of people.

The insistence of social innovation theory on uniting the fulfilment of human needs to active engagement and changes in social relations is based upon two fundamental goals: the aim of creating 'a people's democracy' and a desire to address issues of social injustice, such that innovations target 'the fundamental needs of groups of citizens deprived (*démunis*) of a minimum income, of access to quality education and of other benefits of an economy from which their community has been excluded' (Moulaert 2009, p. 18). At TISS, a similar approach has been defined as people-centred development (PCD), first in social work (due to the fact that the university was originally established as a Graduate School of Social Work) and in more recent years within the social sciences in general. PCD, as the benchmark adopted and refined by TISS, since its foundation in the late 1930s, is an attempt to realize many of the basic features of social innovation, by changing the oppressive social relations that are barriers to social justice and human dignity through participatory processes.

This chapter discusses the PCD model used by TISS as a contribution to social innovation. First, we give an introduction to the meaning of PCD as a partnership-based model of social innovation (see also Fontan et al., Chapter 23). Secondly, we present a number of people-centred interventions performed by TISS, with an emphasis on the M East Ward[3] Project. And thirdly we discuss these interventions and the concept of PCD in relation to social innovation frameworks.

7.2   THE MEANING OF PEOPLE-CENTRED DEVELOPMENT

In its 75 years of existence, TISS has adopted and elaborated a learning and intervention profile with a clear linkage to contemporary approaches in social innovation, particularly emphasizing the process dimension of social change (Moulaert and Sekia 2003; Moulaert et al. 2005; MacCallum et al. 2009; Phills 2008; Defourny et al. 2010; Hulgård 2011). People-centred development has been a core concept in TISS's model since its foundational period. This refers both to the model of learning and knowledge building that integrates research, education and field interventions, and to the way TISS tries to position itself as a change agent. By this, it aspires to go beyond its conventional university mandate, to promote sustainable, equitable and participatory development, social welfare and social justice. This is reflected in TISS's vision statement:

> ... to be an institution of excellence in higher education continually responding to the changing social realities through the development and application of knowledge, towards creating a people-centred and ecologically sustainable society that promotes and protects the dignity, equality, social justice and human rights for all, with special emphasis on marginalized and to vulnerable groups.[4]

Drawing from this people-centredness in its approach, TISS has adopted the PCD vocabulary from the UN Development Programme, where it is defined as 'development of the people, by the people and for the people' (Cox 1998, p. 518). Cox identifies five foundations of PCD as an approach: awareness-raising, social mobilization, participation, self-reliance and sustainability. Cox further argues that 'it is an approach which emphasizes process

over outcome' (Cox 1998, p. 519), an emphasis we understand in relation to issues of power and inequality in conventional models of economic development and globalization. This requires an alternative mode of co-construction of knowledge between academia and the communities that we work with.

The concept of PCD has been used to position social work and social workers as change agents in situations where they may be constrained by norms of professionalization and goals of economic efficiency. Desai et al. argue that the professional model of social work may have led to a depolitization of social work that 'retards the social worker's ability to engage in political struggle and movements' (Desai et al. 1998, p. 531). They further stress that the process of professionalization during the first half of the 20th century led to an assumption that social workers were working on behalf of 'the establishment' without contributing or perhaps even noting the major social movements of the 20th century (for instance the civil rights movement in the US, the labour movement and the women's movement across the world). Instead, social work was dominated by a clinical paradigm, and social work research 'suffered from scientism brought in by professionalization' (Desai et al.1998, p. 534). Yuen (2010, p. 17) further argues that no other factor has distorted social work more than the prevailing hegemony of managerialism and its associated approach to measure effectiveness in restricted economic terms. The search for an alternative social work paradigm, questioning the insidious trends to professionalization and managerialism, is closely linked to the development of the PCD approach.

Souza Santos radicalizes the critique of economic and managerial dominance by arguing that it represents part of a process

which 'aimed at reducing the understandings of the world to the logic of Western
epistemology' (2008, p. xxxiii), a process he
terms 'epistemicide' – a metaphor for the
complete submission of indigenous knowledges to Western colonization and world
views. The solution suggested by Souza
Santos is, first, to recognize that 'there is
no global social justice without global cognitive justice' (2008, p. xix) and, second,
to engage in communication, dialogue
and negotiations from the perspective that
the epistemic diversity is potentially infinite (2008, p. xivii). The call for cognitive
justice and the recognition of epistemic
diversity is an important source of inspiration for the elaboration of people-centred
approaches to development, which attempt
to 'stag[e] dialogues and alliances between
diverse forms of knowledge, cultures, and
cosmologies in response to different forms
of oppression that enact the coloniality
of knowledge and power' (Souza Santos,
2008, p. xiv). Similarly, PCD is inspired
by Gadamer's notion of 'dialogical understanding', in which the 'Western model of
monological understanding' is substituted
by a model of co-operation, which changes
the interpreter as well as the interpreted
towards a situation based upon mutual
understanding, even extending to a 'fusion
of horizons' (Yuen 2010, pp. 34–42). Such
a fusion of knowledge horizons forms the
cornerstone of PCD, where knowledge is
co-created and development is collectively
designed.

7.3   TOWARDS PEOPLE-CENTRED SOCIAL INNOVATION

PCD links to social innovation (SI)
through its emphasis on empowerment as
intrinsic to the development process. This
means that PCD is produced in collaborative arenas which bring socially desir-

able outcomes by adopting processes that
put faith in diverse forms of knowledge.
Thus, we adopt an integrated approach
that observes 'process' and 'outcome' as
being equally important in enabling social
innovation (Borzaga and Defourny 2001;
Moulaert and Sekia 2003; Moulaert et al.
2005; MacCallum et al. 2009; Chesbrough
2006; BEPA 2010; Hulgård 2011).

This process-outcome integration links
to an emphasis throughout the social
innovation literature on participatory
governance. For example, from the perspective of social enterprise, the EMES
Network[5] has defined social innovations
especially in the area of social services
and work integration as initiatives that
combine economic risk, social value and
participatory governance (Borzaga and
Defourny 2001; Nyssens 2006; Defourny
and Nyssens, Chapter 3). Similarly, from
the perspective of territorial planning
and development, Moulaert et al. (2005)
have argued that unmet needs could be
satisfied if neighbourhood development
strategies pursued innovation in governance relations within the neighbourhood
and the wider community. Such practices
contain a transformative potential that
goes beyond local contexts. They can transcend mere micro-public spheres to obtain
greater transformative power on the wider
society.

From a policy-based perspective, the
Bureau of European Policy Advisers
(BEPA) argues that to ensure Europe's
position in the global economy there is a
need to reform society in the direction of
a more participatory democracy. BEPA
defines social innovation as new ideas for
products, services and models that meet
social needs and are based on participative social interactions (BEPA 2010). It
is further emphasized that empowering,
learning and network processes are in
themselves to be understood as outcomes

which can generate 'improvements in the way people live and work' (BEPA 2010, p. 28).

Thus, the integrated approach being discussed in this chapter emphasizes the importance of participatory processes, as reflected in several conceptualizations of social innovation. It is further inspired by a turn in technological innovation research from a so-called old 'Closed Model of Innovation' (CMI) to the new 'Open Model of Innovation' (OMI) (Chesbrough 2006). In the CMI, products and outcomes of innovation originate from within the boundaries of the innovating enterprise or organization. Here the focus is on the end results; innovation is about the introduction of new products and services to be launched by the organization. OMI transcends the borders of the innovating organization, since neither the process nor the outcomes are fully controlled by the organization. Networks and inputs from the outside are important features of the innovation process (Chesbrough 2006; Eschweiler and Hulgård 2011) in OMI. Such inputs and networks from outside can be interpreted for the purpose of conceptualizing and analysing as giving impetus to the process dimension of social innovation.

The approach to social innovation presented in this chapter is an effort to combine an epistemological alternative to *coloniality of knowledge and power* in the context of marginalized communities. Its significance lies in how this epistemological alternative is able to address failed social needs through a process of enhancing participatory social interaction, knowledge production and participatory governance. As we shall see in the following sections, the way TISS practises people-centred development is an example of a socially innovative strategy which rests upon its ability to engage in dialogue and networking with the multiple stakeholders (Nyssens 2006) to produce material outcomes too. Here the process-outcome duality is made to disappear; knowledge is collectively created and shared and set to inform the change process, thus presenting a case of people-centred social innovation.

7.4   TISS MODEL OF PEOPLE-CENTRED SOCIAL INNOVATION

One of the ways in which TISS has engaged in people-centred action for social change has been direct involvement in crisis situations as well as in situations of development deprivations and livelihood vulnerabilities. TISS has always reached out to support people affected by natural and human-induced crises. In 1948, in the aftermath of the Independence and Partition of India, the Institute deployed a team of students and faculty to work in the refugee camps in Kurukshetra where the team was actively engaged in relief coordination and camp management. TISS's engagement after the earthquake in 1993 which devastated two districts in Maharashtra, located approximately 250 miles from Mumbai, was another large scale intervention using a people-centred approach. In this case, TISS had conducted an independent baseline survey of damages covering approximately 35,000 households spread over 69 villages, which significantly contributed to the assessment of rehabilitation needs of the affected community. In recognition of this, TISS was later appointed the Community Participation Consultant in long-term rehabilitation planning and implementation by the government-run Maharashtra Emergency Earthquake Rehabilitation Programme (MEERP), funded by the World Bank.

While addressing the emergent social and economic needs triggered by crisis situations, emphasis on participatory processes has made such interventions unique and socially relevant. The process of engagement with the affected communities right from damage assessment to participatory rehabilitation planning and resolution of community conflicts has been an intense process of *social value creation*, socially innovative in the sense suggested by Moulaert et al. (2005) and MacCallum et al. (2009) where innovation in social relations is achieved as well as in satisfying human needs.

Another very important aspect of social innovation lies in the degree of *strategic repositioning* which entails the creation of benefits or reductions of costs for society 'through efforts to address social needs and problems in ways that go beyond the private gains and general benefits of market activity' (Phills et al. 2008, p. 39). Second, it requires *novel combinations of ideas, resources, and capabilities*; the process of creating social value is deliberate, effortful, and unusually demanding (Schumpeter 1951[1934]; Phills et al. 2008). The strategic repositioning in these cases has two facets: (i) the internal changes to accommodate the heightened demand on the institute and its people and (ii) the external repositioning of the institute vis-à-vis other actors in the field including the government. Internal changes include the suspension of teaching activities, suitable modification of academic calendar to ensure participation of students and staff alike, shortening of vacations etc. to meet the demands of human and institutional engagement in calamitous situations. Measures of process and outcomes are united in a spirit of co-operation; longer working hours are necessary to ensure that the academic schedule is not really disturbed. As far as the external reposition-

ing is concerned, TISS assumed different roles ranging from independently assisting relief operations and assessing relief gaps, assessing damages and conducting baseline surveys, to actively collaborating with government and non-governmental organizations in rehabilitation planning and implementation.

After the Indian Ocean Tsunami of 2004, intervention on a massive scale was undertaken by TISS in collaboration with a wide variety of actors ranging from academic institutions, funding organizations, government departments and non-governmental organizations. The range of engagements undertaken by the institute included assessment of loss and impact to lives, property, livelihoods, environment and infrastructure, rehabilitation and development needs; relief management, psychosocial support to women, children and other vulnerable groups and mobilization of human resources for relief and rehabilitation work. TISS also facilitated community participation in the reconstruction and rehabilitation process; policy and programme development support to government and non-governmental organizations (NGOs); coordination of civil society participation; training and capacity-building of personnel engaged in relief and rehabilitation work; publication and documentation; and conflict resolution and peace building initiatives.

In all these initiatives, the novel combination of ideas, resources and capabilities for social value creation is sought by working closely with state governments and the district administrations, NGOs, academic institutions and funding organizations. While the people-centred social innovation emphasizes the importance of active participation of the communities in question in governance and knowledge creation, it also seeks to make meaningful collaborations and establish strong networks

Table 7.1   Some critical indicators of underdevelopment and deprivation

Indicators	All India[#]	Mumbai*	M/E Ward*	Remarks
Human Development Index (HDI rank among all wards)			24.00	Lowest
Literacy Rate	74.04	76.9	66.1	Lowest
Infant Mortality Rate	50.00	34.57	66.47	Highest
Average age at death	n/a	52.16	39.4	Lowest

Sources: [#] Census of India 2011; * Mumbai Human Development Report 2009.

in the process of addressing the social and economic needs of the community. In the following sub-sections, we show how these critical features of the PCD approach – collaborative partnerships, participatory governance and epistemological openness – have shaped the planning for TISS's latest project, the transformation of M East Ward in Mumbai.

7.4.1   The M East Ward Transformation Project

In 2011 TISS celebrated its 75th anniversary by launching one of the most ambitious and creative social innovations ever performed by an academic institution. The M East Ward Transformation Project is a partnership-based intervention drawing upon the institute's longstanding experience with people-centred development. There are two specific reasons for the selection of M East Ward: firstly, the developmental deficits and vulnerabilities of communities living in this ward and, secondly, the fact that the ward forms the immediate neighbourhood for TISS.

According to the 2001 census, 54.06 per cent of Mumbai's population live in slums as against the overall percentage of 14.88 and 27.26 of slum population at the national and state (Maharashtra) level respectively. Located at the north eastern edge of Mumbai, M East Ward has over

the years become home for migrants from different parts of the country as well as resettlers from other areas of the city due to development and displacement in those areas. Currently, more than 77 per cent of the population of M East Ward live in slums, the third highest percentage among all wards in Mumbai (see Table 7.1).

Recognizing the low development indices for its neighbourhood, TISS has embarked, in partnership with the municipal administration and other stakeholders, on a participatory transformatory mission for M East Ward through strategic interventions that are expected to enhance the wellbeing of its population and bring measureable and sustainable change on the ground. Such an approach aims both to address immediate concerns of communities and individuals and to co-create a collective vision and development model where both human and economic development can go hand in hand.

Key aims of this innovative programme are to bring measurable change in health, education and livelihood. Thus, like all social innovations, it starts by recognizing the need for a change in social conditions. This requires a paradigm shift in addressing issues of urban poverty, marginalization and vulnerability, a significant transformation in thought and action that ensures the participation of the M Ward communities in the knowledge production and in upholding people's rights and entitlements and also in reworking systems and structures that perpetuate inequalities and marginalization (Lingam 2011). The idea of combining strategies to deal with economic risk, creating social value and adopting a participatory governance process has been the foundation on which this project is based.

To this end, a detailed project proposal entitled 'Transforming the M East Ward: Creating a Model of Inclusive Development' (August 2011) was prepared after a series of consultations with the representatives of local communities and different development organizations working in the area. While people's *experiences* of deprivations formed the basis of these discussions, these experiences clearly resonated with the findings of the Mumbai Human Development Report. It was interesting to note that the deliberations with community leaders brought forward (i) issues of food insecurity and malnutrition of children and women, (ii) abysmal health conditions in these settlements as a combined effect of absence of primary health care facilities and the poor living conditions, (iii) poor educational infrastructure and unfavourable conditions in the families and neighbourhoods, and (iv) the existence of precarious livelihood opportunities as major features of deprivation.

As far as general areas for action are concerned, the consultations also identified a need to generate neighbourhood-level data, as members of the local communities wanted to have these data as the beginning point for their neighbourhood-level discussions and further action. Therefore a two-phase plan was drawn, with a baseline sample household survey and community amenities assessment in the first phase, and micro-planning and community building exercises in the second phase. The baseline survey was aimed at gathering, analysing,

and presenting information on the extent, location, and conditions of poverty in M East Ward with the intention of generating a Ward poverty profile. Methods for selection of sample households from each of the slum settlements were defined collectively by the research team at TISS and community representatives; 300 community volunteers participated in the first phase of the survey, which covered 9,000 households. The remaining households were being covered with the help of 70 trained research assistants along with community volunteers.

The baseline survey is to be followed up by a participatory micro-planning exercise for collectively developing a people's plan for comprehensive development of M East Ward. This process is to be undertaken in line with the open model of innovation discussed earlier where neither the process nor the outcome is fully controlled by the intervening organization. It will begin with lane-level planning and gradually scale up to cluster level to identify needs, resources, and possible solutions. For the development of these local plans, communities will review the data collected, reflect on their conditions and the underlying causes, and take action to improve their life situations and environment. Ward Development Conferences will be conducted to share the results of the lane level and cluster level planning processes as well as the sectoral plans developed with the community and other important local stakeholders to give final shape to the people's development plan. This will be followed by a second conference involving the representatives from the community, Government departments, community-based organizations, local self-governments, public sector enterprises and TISS to present the comprehensive development plan for the ward and initiate discussion on generating resources for direct development interventions.

All these proposed processes are aimed at the collective creation by the community of relevant knowledge for necessary actions in response to different forms of oppression (Souza Santos 2008, p. xiv) and for changing conditions of marginalization and powerlessness though effective networking and collaboration. This is particularly important in the context of the preparation of a development plan for the city of Mumbai which is currently underway. As a legal document, the development plan will determine land use in the city for the next 20 years. The document also presents the need for the development of services and infrastructure in the city, currently negatively skewed as far as M East Ward is concerned. The current project is expected to provide opportunity to correct this disparity by feeding the particular needs of M East Ward into the wider development plan of the city. Moreover the people's development plan and the micro-planning data will be available for different centres and schools within TISS for planning research and field action programmes to feed into the larger engagement plan. Thus, the local innovation may have the potential to become embedded 'into the politico-administrative system of the democratic states of the countries to which communities belong' (Moulaert et al. 2005, p. 1973).

While the medium and long-term plans for engagement in the ward are expected to evolve from the participatory processes, some immediate concerns of the community are being addressed simultaneously. During the household and anthropometric surveys, women and children found to have critical nutritional deficiency and gender-specific health issues were identified. A special team consisting of doctors from School of Health Systems (SHSS) at TISS visited these households and arranged nutritional supplement with the help of non-governmental organizations working in the area, and emergency health care was provided through the municipal hospitals and health posts. Medical camps in different settlements are being organized to screen patients for a planned intervention. Several children attending unaided, private and unauthorized schools in the ward do not have access to the government's Mid Day Meal Scheme.[6] In order to address the immediate food and nutritional requirements of these underprivileged children and also to ensure their enrolment and retention in schools, an innovative scheme has been worked out with ISKON Food Relief Foundation, a private charitable organization providing cooked meals for underprivileged children in schools. The financial support for this is currently being mobilized from a public sector enterprise as part of their corporate social responsibility initiative. During the first phase of the survey, six slum pockets were identified by the municipal corporation as illegal, and thus not having access to any civic service (water, sanitation, school, child care, etc). Childcare facilities in theses pockets are being developed to provide protective and supportive environments for the children of these areas. Apart from this, a library and learning centre for children of the Ward is planned to be operational before the start of next academic year.

This innovative project recognizes the fact that a substantial section of the population in slums in M Ward have abysmal living conditions and remain invisible to the Municipal Corporation and the state government as far as provision of basic civic services are concerned. Thus the project aims to lend visibility to the invisible slum dwellers living in poverty and civic neglect and to create opportunities for enhancing their quality of life, not only by providing them with equitable access to various programmes and services, but also by empowering them through leadership development and enhancement of their capacity to collaborate with development agencies who can affect their future.

7.5   DISCUSSION: PCD ENHANCING SOCIAL INNOVATION

The TISS model of people-centred development is predicated on the need to ensure that ideas are carried into practice, thereby becoming social innovations in the real world. The model's ability to do this rests upon three pillars that potentially radicalize the way universities and other institutions of higher education engage in co-construction of knowledge, while simultaneously addressing issues of cognitive and social justice. The first pillar is the willingness to take the risk of engaging in new large-scale combinations within the university system as well as with outside partners. Following Schumpeter, development is founded on new combinations; the process of development is led by entrepreneurs who by their ability to carry out new combinations take the risk of introducing a new method of production – or they may even revolutionize an entire industry (1951, p. 66). Large-scale interventions such as the M Ward project are innovative in this sense, because they are based upon the ability to combine a multitude of layers and tangible as well as intangible resources. The PCD model of social innovation challenges the way universities generally work as big bureaucratic organizations with a sectorized departmental structure; its success relies to a large extent on TISS's ability to combine different actors and ways of working in an open model of innovation (depending on resources and relations both within the boundaries of the university and outside). In the M Ward

project, carrying out new combinations had internal as well as external dimensions – this is often the case in social innovation, since social entrepreneurs seldom control all the resources needed for the innovation (Austin et al. 2006). Internally, the university removed or at least ignored the departmental structure for a while. At the same time the disciplinary focus and practice strengths of each of the schools and centres, as well as those of community volunteers, were effectively utilized to create useful combinations of ideas, knowledge and skills. Simultaneously capitalizing on the strengths of each of the disciplinary areas, specific tasks were undertaken by different groups. Such tasks included the gathering of anthropometric measures and related data by the students of health system studies, collection of oral histories and audio as well as video documentation of narratives of the life of people in communities by a team from the centre for media and cultural studies etc.

The second pillar of social innovation presented here is the process dimension in social change, with particular emphasis on community participation. This is as critical for the success of sustainable people-centred social innovation as the ability to carry out new combinations. Critical analysis of the role of varied stakeholders and a firm belief in participatory processes point to the importance of a non-linear approach to addressing pressing social concerns. Social innovation presents respect for the *life world*, and for the knowledge and convictions that people draw from it, which help them to comprehend their world and to develop action strategies based on a common language (Eschweiler and Hulgård 2011). The M East Ward project, as well as other people-centred interventions discussed earlier, shows a strong process orientation right from conceptualization to the various mechanisms it proposes for operationalizing the change process. This process orientation cannot be reduced simply to the engagement of the community in question (say, the M East Ward community) but should also involve varied stakeholders including the Municipal Corporation, civil society groups and industries. Multistakeholder participation at various levels of the project has played a very important role in this case.

The third pillar is epistemological openness, which is an extension of the other two aspects discussed above and involves the willingness to challenge the knowledge base of academics, experts and professionals and to engage in genuine dialogue and deliberation with the community and other stakeholders to determine the trajectory of actions for social transformation. This means reducing reliance on expert views in changing conditions of marginality. The idea of developing a people's plan for the ward through a micro-planning exercise and feeding this into the Development Plan for the city demonstrates this aspect of people-centredness in the innovation. The M East Ward project is both a development and a research project, which aims to apply collective learning, energies and experience to explore new dimensions of knowledge, to develop innovative pedagogies, to demonstrate TISS's skill repertoire and, in so doing, to reinforce the relevance of an academic institution with a social mission. The challenge is to bring all disciplines within TISS to focus on research, theory, teaching and practice for social change and development, sourced from and led by the M East Ward community. This clearly presents an alternative to the *coloniality of knowledge and power* discussed earlier in this chapter, because the M East Ward community plays a dominant role in sourcing the data and generating ideas for action.

Thus, the university's engagement with the community produces new knowledge and understanding of vulnerability and marginality. As such, this project could be considered to be what Fontan et al. (Chapter 23) define as a partnership-based research contribution to social innovation, one in which the researchers are engaged with stakeholders in bottom-up efforts to democratize knowledge. Both the PCD model discussed in this chapter and the partnership-based model defined by Fontan et al. contribute to a rethinking of how scholars and research institutions can contribute to social innovation, firstly by providing a democratic and collaborative arena of social creativity to resolve human and social problems, and secondly by developing a concept of social relationships that integrates knowledge, resources and people (see also Dubeux, Chapter 22).

7.6   CONCLUSION

In people-centred social innovation, as presented in this chapter, the commonality and complementarity of the two frameworks of people-centred development and social innovation are foregrounded, showing the importance of developing meaningful social relations, collaborative networking and participatory processes of engaging with marginalized communities. Through an exposition of the current M East Ward Transformation Project, the chapter identifies three important pillars of people-centred social innovation. It argues that for an academic institution to engage in socially relevant innovation programmes, it must display a *willingness to take the risk of engaging in new large scale combinations* within the institution as well as with outside partners; it must have respect for *the process dimension in social change*; and it must exhibit an *epistemo-*

logical openness, allowing knowledge to be taken out of the domains of experts.

TISS has a long history of engaging in large-scale interventions for people-centred development in a variety of contexts since its inception, as demanded by its mission to continually respond to changing social realities with special emphasis on marginalized and vulnerable groups. Amidst the increasing bureaucratization and departmentalization of universities, as well as declining resource availability, TISS remains significant in its ability to generate resources and forge alliances with government, academic communities, NGOs, industry and other civil society groups through dialogue, networking, policy making and awareness raising to produce innovative, socially relevant and people-centred development projects. Skilfully implemented, such projects may create the conditions for long-term social innovation, as we hope the M Ward project will show.

7.7 QUESTIONS FOR DISCUSSION

- How compatible are the frameworks of PCD and SI? What are their main differences?
- How important is the co-creation of knowledge to social innovation?
- As a university, how can we best operationalize epistemological openness in our social engagements?

NOTES

1. We wish to express our thanks to Professor Surinder Jaswal for her comments on an earlier version of this chapter.
2. TISS was founded as a graduate school of Social Work in 1936 and has been a fully-fledged deemed university within the Social Sciences since 1964. Deemed university is a status of autonomy granted by the University Grants Commission of Government of India to high performing universities, and is a proof of recognition of quality.
3. Municipal Corporation of Greater Mumbai is divided into 24 administrative wards and are named with alphabets and some with east and west directions. M East Ward is one such ward in the Municipal Corporation where the project under discussion is initiated.
4. See http://tiss.edu/TopMenuBar/about-tiss/vision-mission (last accessed 8 December 2012).
5. The EMES European Research Network (EMES) was established as a cross-European research network in 1996. EMES is considered as a leading European network on the third sector and social enterprise. EMES has a strong international position and cooperates with centres of excellence in Asia, North America and Latin America. Its goal is to build a corpus of theoretical and empirical knowledge around social enterprise, social entrepreneurship, social economy, solidarity economy, social innovation, and the third sector. EMES organizes research programs as well as bi-annual research conferences and bi-annual doctoral summer schools. See http://www.emes.net (last accessed 6 December 2012).
6. Mid Day Meal Scheme is the world's largest school feeding programme run by the Government of India reaching out to all children studying in Government, Local Body and Government-aided primary and upper primary schools. The main objects of the programme are to reduce drop-out rates and enhance retention rate of children from poorer families and to enhance their nutritional intake.

REFERENCES

(References in bold are recommended reading.)

Austin, J., H. Stevenson and J. Wei-Skillern (2006), 'Social and commercial entrepreneurship: same, different, or both?', *Entrepreneurship: Theory and Practice*, **30** (1), 1–22.

BEPA Bureau of European Policy Advisers (2010), *Empowering people, driving change: Social innovation in the European Union*, Bruxelles: European Commission.

Borzaga, C. and J. Defourny (2001), *The Emergence of Social Enterprise*, London & New York: Routledge.

Census of India (2011), *Provisional Population Totals*, New Delhi: Office of the Registrar General and Census Commissioner of India, Government of India.

Chesbrough, H. (2006), *Open Innovation: The New Imperative for Creating and Profiting from Technology*, Boston: Harvard Business School Press.

Cox, D. (1998), 'Towards people-centred development: the social development agenda and social work education', *The Indian Journal of Social Work Education*, **59** (1), 513–530.

Defourny, J. (2001), 'From Third Sector to Social Enterprise', in C. Borzaga and J. Defourny (eds), pp. 1–28.

Defourny, J., L. Hulgård and V. Pestoff (eds) (2010), 'Social Enterprise, Social Entrepreneurship, Social Economy, Solidarity Economy: An EMES Reader on the "SE Field"', Liege: EMES European Research Network.

Desai, M., A. Monteiro and L. Narayan (1998), *Towards People-Centred Development*, Mumbai: Tata Institute of Social Sciences.

Eschweiler, J. and L. Hulgård (2011), 'Social Innovation and Deliberative Democracy', Paper presented at the 3rd EMES International Research Conference on Social Enterprise, 4–7 July 2011, Roskilde University, Denmark.

Hulgård, L. (2011), 'Social economy and social enterprise: an emerging alternative to mainstream market economy?' *China Journal of Social Work*, 4 (3), 201–215.

Lingam, L. (2011), 'Ethical Considerations for the baseline socio-economic survey of households in M-Ward', unpublished discussion note, Mumbai: TISS.

MacCallum, D., F. Moulaert, J. Hillier and S. Vicari Haddock (eds) (2009), *Social Innovation and Territorial Development*, Farnham: Ashgate.

Moulaert, F., (2009), 'Social Innovation: Institutionally Embedded, Territorially (Re)Produced', in MacCallum et al. (eds), pp. 11–23.

Moulaert, F. and F. Sekia (2003), 'Territorial Innovation Models: A Critical Survey', *Regional Studies*, **37** (3), 289–302.

Moulaert, F., F. Martinelli, E. Swyngedouw and S. Gonzalez (2005), 'Towards alternative model(s) of local innovation', *Urban studies*, **42** (11), 1969–90.

Municipal Corporation of Greater Mumbai (2010), *Mumbai Human Development Report 2009*, New Delhi: Oxford University Press.

Nyssens, M. (2006), *Social Enterprise: At the crossroads of market, public policies and civil society*, London: Routledge.

Phills, J.A., K. Deiglmeier, and D.T. Miller (2008), 'Rediscovering Social Innovation', *Stanford Social Innovation Review*, **6** (4), 34–44.

Schumpeter, J.A. (1951[1934]), *The Theory of Economic Development*, London: Oxford University Press.

Souza Santos, B. (ed.) (2008), *Another Knowledge is Possible*, London: Verso.

Yuen, S.-P. (2010), 'Towards a Hermeneutic Conception of Social Work Practice' in Y. Ho, and S. Yen (eds) (2010), *Reconstitution of Social Work – Towards a Moral Conception of Social Work Practice*, Singapore: World Scientific Books, pp. 1–107.

PART II

SOCIAL INNOVATION THEORY: ITS ROLE IN KNOWLEDGE BUILDING

Introduction: social innovation – an idea longing for theory

Stijn Oosterlynck

The concept of social innovation has a long and chequered history, going back to the early 19th century and the emergence of socialist experiments like those of Fourier and Saint-Simon (Godin 2012). It started off as a derogatory label to criticize those who proposed 'schemes' that ignored the limits imposed on social arrangements by the dynamics of capitalist development. As Godin shows, over the past two centuries the concept of social innovation has been used in a variety of contexts by a range of different authors writing for diverse audiences. However, until recently the concept lacked a clear and univocal definition and proper grounding in a broader theoretical framework. The chapters in this part are testimony to some of the sustained and stimulating attempts of the past several decades to provide social innovation with conceptual clarity and theoretical foundations.

The rich variety of perspectives on social innovation and the elaboration of its manifold linkages to related concepts displayed in this part shows how social innovation has been developing into a broad body of knowledge with a strong interdisciplinary and transdisciplinary character. It proves the value of theorizing social innovation and its diverse meanings and of putting it in dialogue with related concepts. Since progressive social change can have many roots and follow different trajectories, this part does not offer a definitive theory of social innovation. Instead it provides a number of conceptual elaborations and

theoretical explorations that, together, begin to satisfy the longing for theory of a concept the use of which has up until recently been too isolated and vague.

The contributions start with a chapter by Bob Jessop, Frank Moulaert, Lars Hulgård and Abdelillah Hamdouch, who provide a view on where the concept of social innovation comes from and where it is heading today. They observe a distinction between the 'old' theories of social innovation in the 19th and first half of the 20th century, which were firmly focussed on macro-social change, and the 'new' theories of social innovation that were developed over the course of the last four decades and that are more concerned with transformative social practices and microsocial dynamics. The authors argue for a mutual enrichment of these two traditions in social innovation theory in order to challenge the narrow market-based ontology in which social innovation is increasingly grounded in official discourse. On this basis, the authors develop a number of basic methodological criteria for social innovation research.

The second chapter in this part, authored by Barbara Van Dyck and Pieter Van den Broeck, zooms in on one critical dimension of social innovation, namely its nature as a territorial process. The authors are critical of the way the concept of social innovation is increasingly being used in a reductionist manner in business innovation frameworks focusing on coalitions and networks and organizational forms, using a containarized view of space. Such narrow perspectives ignore the ethical dimensions and treat social innovation as a decontextualized managerial approach aimed at stimulating growth in an era of crisis. Van Dyck and Van den Broeck instead ground the concept of social innovation in local and regional development studies, highlighting the inherently territorialized nature of socio-economic development dynamics. Central here is the reproduction and transformation of community social relations.

In the third chapter of this part, Constanza Parra equally highlights the territorial nature of social innovation and analyses territorial practices of social innovation as a meeting ground with the increasingly popular concept of social sustainability. In this chapter, Parra puts social innovation in a fruitful dialogue with social sustainability. She argues that the social is not the weakest pillar of the triad of sustainability, but is instead its driving force. In order to make this case, Parra reinforces the social dimension of sustainable development by moving beyond issues of social justice and equity and including the concern of social innovation with the transformation of social relations. Conceiving of social dynamics as the driving force behind sustainable development brings governance to the fore. Governance, according to Parra, in this context refers to the manifold ways in which societies collectively organize to pursue sustainable development and to the question who takes responsibility for steering this process.

Marc Pradel, Marisol García and Santiago Eizaguirre further reflect on the relationship between governance and social innovation in Chapter 11. They analyse how socially innovative practices can transform governance mechanisms through the creation of new mechanisms to provide resources, new collective actors and ways to influence decision-making on the one hand, and how existing governance arrangements influence the capacity of different actors to develop socially innovative practices on the other hand. They explore this double process with regard to multilevel governance and propose a methodology to understand the interrelationship between social innovation and multilevel governance. One of the issues that Pradel et al. pay specific attention to is the tension between institutionalization and innovation.

The final chapter of this part is by Jean Hillier, who develops a post-structuralist perspective on social innovation drawing on the work of Deleuze. Hillier is attracted to the latter's work because of Deleuze's concern with how the production of something new might be possible. Instead of seeing social structures as the main drivers of social innovation, she claims that social innovation emerges from challenges to 'institutionalized and normalized legitimacy'. This implies a relational approach, in which social innovation stems from the development of new connections between heterogenous elements in a pragmatic response to problems or a perceived lack of something. On the basis of this Deleuzean inspired framework, Hillier develops a methodology of strategic navigation to assist social innovation practitioners with applying a 'what might happen if . . .?' approach. This methodology starts with the tracing of the conditions of possibility for things and places as they currently are. It then suggests to map the possibilities for innovation and creation and makes a diagram of the relational forces that play out for each of these possibilities. The last step in the methodology of strategic navigation is the outlining of a programme of what might take place.

REFERENCE

Godin, Benoît (2012), 'Social innovation: utopias of innovation from c.1830 to the present', Working Paper 52, Project on the Intellectual History of Innovation, Quebec: INRS.

8. Social innovation research: a new stage in innovation analysis?
Bob Jessop, Frank Moulaert, Lars Hulgård and Abdelillah Hamdouch

8.1 INTRODUCTION

Social innovation is '*à la mode*'. It figures prominently around the world in diverse policy programmes, and is a strategic reference point for social movements and organizations that aim to fight poverty, overcome social exclusion, empower minorities, etc. It has a key role in the Millennium Agenda, in Barack Obama's Office of Social Innovation and Civic Participation, in the EC's Innovation Union Programme (BEPA 2010), in OECD policy advice on the role of social entrepreneurship in combating social exclusion and socioeconomic restructuring (Noya 2009; OECD 2010) and in the strategies of organizations and foundations such as Ashoka Innovators for the Public, the Skoll Foundation, and the Schwab Foundation for Social Entrepreneurship with a global outreach promoting market driven social innovation (Elkington and Hartigan 2008; Reich 2011).

The significance that various mainstream strategy and policy documents accord to social innovation (hereafter SI) varies greatly. Nonetheless, one commonality stands out: they interpret it in economic, indeed often in narrowly market-economic, terms. This perspective is strongly influenced by management science, innovation economics and a micro-economic interpretation of social innovation strategies (see for example Young Foundation and SIX 2010). While social innovation certainly has economic aspects, stressing them too strongly can easily lead to a reductive interpretation of SI and its potential – especially where a narrowly market-economic approach prescribes how economic practices and relations should be analysed. The resulting economistic view in these documents of the relationship between economy and social innovation becomes evident from their account of the relations between social problems and how SI initiatives would address them, the overly organizational view of innovation in social relations, and the uncritical privileging of firms as the (potential) carriers of social innovation. The last feature prioritizes the social business over the social movement as a vehicle for social innovation and thereby misrepresents the functioning of the social economy.

An important aspect of the biased approach to the relationship between economy and society is the recurrent tendency in much of the cited literature to consider the social economy as an aggregation of individual social enterprises. This conception of the social economy – and therefore also the socially embedded economy as a whole – does not adequately reflect its advanced degree of institutionalization, its market dynamics, its typical relations of production and cooperation, etc. (Hamdouch et al. 2009), or its articulation with the wider social world. This economistic and reductivist account of the social economy has three mutually reinforcing weaknesses. On the one hand, it tends to ignore the distinctive macroeconomic aspects of social innovation as an interactive ensemble of practices; in addition it neglects the economic aspects of social innovations that are not immediately economic in their objectives – such as the democratization of the educational system, the pursuit of gender equality, or the psychiatric liberation movement (Chambon et al. 1982); and, finally, it puts so much emphasis on *economic* agency that it pushes *other types of socially innovative agency*, including those in the social economy, to the background.

These weaknesses are reflected in a superficial understanding of the relations between social change, social transformation and social innovation. Overall, this narrow view of social innovation promotes a 'caring liberalism' that privileges social enterprise as the key agent for social change and the economy as the primary sphere of social life.

In this chapter we challenge this approach by situating SI in a broader societal logic and developing a methodology for SI research that is consistent with that logic. We do so in four steps.

First, we comment on some key authors and themes in the social scientific literature on SI, the factors provoking it, and the processes embodying it. Putting aside the radical interpretation of social innovation as social revolution (e.g., in the form of utopian socialism) or the more ambivalent interpretation in this period as government-sponsored social reform (e.g. addressing the social question) (see Godin 2012), we identify a marked discontinuity in the literature between the 'old' pre- or trans-disciplinary theories of social innovation and social change in the second half of the nineteenth and early twentieth centuries (Marx, Tarde, Weber, Durkheim, among others) and the contributions since the late 1980s which mark renewed interest in social innovation but are in general more discipline-bound and practice-oriented. This overview does not aim to be comprehensive but helps to locate the arguments in other chapters. Further references to SI literature can be found in Chapter 1 by Moulaert, MacCallum and Hillier. This said, we are not concerned here with post-war commentators who refer to social innovation in generic terms or have a neutral ethical position on the nature of human development (Drucker 1987; Gershuny 1987).

Second, although the mainstream literature has addressed SI agency and processes, sometimes abstractly, sometimes concretely, at different spatial scales and with regard to different levels of collective action, it largely neglects the macrosocial dimensions of social innovation. We remedy this neglect here and also indicate how different analytical entry points can be combined to facilitate a better understanding of the potential complementarity between social innovation as a series of bottom-up strategic initiatives with local roots and as a coherent set of top-down but 'enlightened' institutional reorganizations that could enable and promote bottom-up initiatives at different spatial levels. We particularly explore two tracks of social innovation following the Fordist period in the advanced capitalist economies: (i) social innovation based on a rediscovery of the social economy; and (ii) social innovation as a multifaceted movement for social emancipation and human development. Both tracks have developed in the context of new socio-political dynamics that call for more proactive institutional arrangements. They converge in the rise of community-based and grassroots-initiated initiatives oriented to a much wider spectrum of human needs than those considered by earlier generations of social enterprise, state-led social protection agencies, social movements and organizations.

Third, we examine whether SI analysis can follow the path of innovation analysis in science and technology, innovation economics, management science, etc. In many respects, the revival of the concept of social innovation in the post-war period was motivated by opposition to the concept of technological innovation and its hegemonic status in economic, social, and political discourse (Nussbaumer and Moulaert 2007; Godin 2012). While we note some similarities among different currents in innovation analysis, we also identify some major contrasts. In particular, the functional or instrumental approach in innovation systems analysis as covered in EC Framework IV, V and VI research does not work in SI research. This is mainly because social innovation oriented to human development is not concerned primarily with business innovation but with recognition of the diversity of human needs that must be met for human development to materialize. Instead SI research aims to promote innovation in social relations and socially innovative strategies in various spheres of society. Thus it requires an ontological perspective premised on the social, spatio-temporal, and substantive contingency of social relations and on the correlative human capacities for social transformation. It also requires a corresponding epistemology sensitive to the inevitable dialectics of struggle between forces pursuing radical social innovation oriented to social emancipation and those seeking to maintain an asymmetrically organized social order biased towards agencies of profit-making, efficient markets, and business-friendly social relations.[1]

Fourth, we offer some basic methodological criteria that define the scope of, and most suitable methods for SI research.

These methods should be consistent with an ontology of social transformation (as defined above), an epistemology sensitive to the dialectic of strategy and structure, social innovation and resistance thereto, opportunities and constraints, mechanisms of innovation and possible countertendencies. Given that SI research values the emancipatory potential of social innovation, this methodology should facilitate the reflexivity of its agents and observers, enabling lesson-drawing and lesson transfer. That is why we emphasize in the last section of this chapter that SI research methodology is intrinsically reflexive and transdisciplinary. This is best achieved, we argue, through a transdisciplinary approach that identifies the connections among the diverse problems of human development that social innovation must address, the questions to be researched in this connection, and a commitment to show the superiority of social innovation in these regards compared with alternative approaches. But we also make suggestions on how the research team might best be composed, what are the stages involved in the research, which stakeholders will have a role in each stage, and how the research relates to other moments of the SI process. A related set of concerns is how the SI meta-theoretical framework can (and should) be co-produced as a shared view of societal change among the actors participating in the transdisciplinary research.

8.2   SOCIAL INNOVATION: A BRIEF SURVEY OF THE SCIENTIFIC LITERATURE

The concept of social innovation is not new. It has been used in different contexts, sometimes with pejorative, sometimes with neutral, and sometimes with positive connotations, at different periods and within different disciplines. Other concepts that cover part of the same content have been used: for example, social invention (Weber 1968[1922]; Ogburn 1922; Coleman 1970), social change, transformation or regulation (Weber, Durkheim), social diffusion through imitation of new practices (Tarde1999[1893]), or changes in social practice (see Chapter 1 in this Handbook). Good but partial surveys of the use of social innovation concepts and their underlying theories as used in various social science fields are available (see, for example, Cooperrider and Pasmore 1991; Godin 2008, 2010, 2012; Hillier et al. 2004; Moulaert and Nussbaumer 2008; Young Foundation and SIX 2010). Early scholarship covered the most significant dimensions of social innovation, including many that are overlooked or subjected to a reductive interpretation in the theoretical analyses, policy paradigms, and specific recommendations promoted in the policy notes of many international organizations advancing SI today. Nonetheless significant work remains to be done on situating the pioneering analyses, concepts and theories within the history of social science and collective action.

This section explains the discontinuity in the analysis of social innovation between the 'old' theorists of social change (from the end of the 19th century up to the 1960s or 1970s), who did their research in a much more pre- or proto-disciplinary period, and the 'new lighters' in SI analysis (from the 1970s on). Although several contemporary analysts continue to work in the 'old' tradition, most of them are now more inclined to use a more micro-logical, partial or practice-oriented approach. The recent turn toward SI as a key vehicle in 'caring liberalism' that privileges social enterprise as the agent for social change and the economy as the primary sphere of social life can be connected to this change

in orientation. Our principal argument in this chapter is that the reunification of 'old' social change analysis with the more practice-oriented analyses of the last three decades is essential to give SI analysis a coherent epistemological status and to provide it with the necessary methodological tools.

From his doctoral research on the development of medieval business organization onwards (1889), Max Weber showed the power of rationalization in his work on the development of trade in free markets, the rational organization of the labour process considered from the viewpoint of its technical organization and rational capitalist accounting, and the development of the money and credit systems (e.g., Weber 1968[1922], 1961[1923]). He also considered the development of rationality (means-end calculation) and its implications for social invention and innovation in other spheres too, notably in law, the state, science, the military, religion, and the professions (1989[1915–1920], 1968[1922]). For Weber technical change only has a meaning within the context of an innovation or a renovation (Weber 1968[1922], p. 26) of the social order which endows it with significance. Still, for Weber, social agents who introduce new forms of practice, organization, or social product, although these are often initially considered deviant, can exert a decisive influence if the new behaviour spreads and becomes established social usage. These views are reflected in his own engagement in social reform through bodies such as the German *Verein für Sozialpolitik* (Association for Social Policy) as well as his work on constitutional reform (see Bendix 1978).

Émile Durkheim (1997[1893]) highlighted the role of social regulation to secure the benefits of a developing and more advanced division of labour that comes with change in the technical and social relations involved in social practices. Without adequate regulation, he argued, there would be growing symptoms of social disorder (e.g., *anomie*) and/or coercion in the societal organization (a 'forced division of labour'). Getting the balance right in this regard was essential for the *intégration du corps social*. In developing his approach Durkheim sought a 'third way' between the excesses of unregulated capitalism and the social conservatism of the Catholic tradition. He did not consider innovation an unalloyed good and, for this reason, he has been considered 'a sociologist of stability rather than change'. Indeed, he advocated a form of guild socialism as a means to harmonize social conflicts that might result from economic and social development. While we would not necessarily accept his proposed solution, there are affinities between his conditional approval of innovation and his concern about the adequacy of its social regulation. This is reflected in our ambition to reintegrate theories of societal change into SI research (see Sections 8.3 and 8.5 of this chapter). According to Durkheim, types of solidarity are related to types of society. The analysis of the passage from a mechanical towards an organic solidarity, for example, shows how stages of development, codes of social behaviour and societal systems of moral values are fundamental to understanding the breeding grounds of individual and collective change initiatives, thus for identifying potential for SI.

Joseph Schumpeter was influenced by the German Historical School – he was considered a representative figure of the fourth GHS – and Austrian economics and showed an early interest in innovation and entrepreneurship, noting the wider social preconditions and repercussions of various types of 'new combination' (innovation). He began to analyse social innovation as a fundamental moment of the economic and societal organization (Schumpeter 1934[1911]) and in his celebrated text on *Capitalism, Socialism, Democracy* (1942) linked it explicitly to the phenomenon that he labelled, following earlier scholars, 'creative destruction'. Schumpeter's theory goes far beyond the economic logic of development and innovation and makes use of an ensemble of sociologies (cultural, artistic, economic, political) which he sought to integrate into a comprehensive social theory allowing for a multidimensional analysis of development and innovation (Becker and Knudsen 2005).

We could consider the French intellectual movement of the '*Temps des Cerises*' as a turning moment between the 'old' theories of social change and the new 'social innovation' approaches. These intellectuals participated in a debate of wide social and political significance on the transformation of society and, in particular, on the role of the revolts by students, intellectuals and workers. At the same time they were interested in the sociopolitical meaning of particular social innovation. This debate was echoed in large part in the journal *Autrement*, with contributions from the likes of Pierre Rosanvallon, Jacques Fournier and Jacques Attali. Subsequently, Chambon, David and Devevey (1982) built on most of the issues highlighted in this debate. Despite the passage of three decades, this 128-page book remains an impressive 'open' synthesis on the subject of social innovation. The authors explain how social innovation signifies satisfaction of specific needs thanks to collective initiative, which is not synonymous with state intervention. In effect, these authors argue, the state can act, at one and the same time, as a barrier to social innovation and as an arena of social interaction that can stimulate social innovation originating in the spheres of state or market. They stress that social innovation can occur in different types of communities and at various spatial scales, but is conditional on processes of consciousness raising, mobilization and learning. They mainly reproduce the highlights of the French debate on SI, but also refer to experiences in the UK.

Since the late 1980s SI research has taken a different turn. The end-means relationship (e.g. neighbourhood agencies setting up actions to overcome social exclusion) has become the main focus. There is less interest in social process dynamics but it still figures in SI analysis undertaken in fields that cross-cut standard disciplinary boundaries. We address several fields.

The first is that of management science and corporate organization. For instance, in the social sciences, some authors emphasize opportunities for improving social capital (Lee 2008), which would allow economic organizations either to function better or to change, thereby promoting social innovation in both the profit and non-profit sectors. This re-reading of social capital permits – among other things – a reinterpretation of economic aspects of human development, thus facilitating the integration of broader economic concerns, such as strong ethical norms (fair business practices, respect for workers' rights) or values (justice, solidarity, co-operation . . .) into the heart of the various entrepreneurial communities (Moulaert 2009, p. 14). Other examples of fruitful sharing of concepts and approaches between management science and enterprise/corporate economics, on the one hand, and other social sciences, on the other, include the analysis of, and proposals for, social innovation through micro-credit communities, social economy networks, sustainable entrepreneurship, organization of work processes and stakeholder involvement in corporate decision-making. A very impor-

tant theme in this field is the role of social enterprise which is being analysed as a main agent of SI (see Nyssens and Defourny, Chapter 3).

The second field is that of social innovation and creativity (André et al. 2009) and the contribution of the arts to social change. In effect, the arts reinvent themselves as sociology, as in the 'Sociologist as an Artist' approach (Du Bois and Wright 2001). Michael Mumford wrote extensively about social innovation in these matters, identifying three main 'lines of work': the life history of emblematic individuals who had contributed primarily in the social or political arena; the identification of skills that leaders must possess to solve organizational problems; and the development, introduction and adaptation of process and technological innovations in industrial organizations (Mumford, 2002: pp. 253–254).

The third field concerns the well-known criticisms of the hierarchical character of political and bureaucratic decision-making systems. These have prompted proposals for change in the political system and, above all, in the system of public administration. The role of SI in governance and public administration is covered by Lévesque in Chapter 2 of this Handbook. Several modes of (re)organization have been proposed not only to give more control and influence to users and other 'stakeholders' but also to simplify procedures and release time for more creative activities than filing data (Swyngedouw 2005; Novy and Leubolt 2005). Most innovative in this field, however, is the 'bottom-linked' approach to social innovation that recognizes the centrality of initiatives taken by those immediately concerned, but also stresses the need for institutions that would enable, gear or sustain such initiatives through sound, regulated and lasting practices and clearer citizen rights guaranteed by a democratic state-functioning (García 2006; see Pradel et al., Chapter 11).

The fourth field concerns the relationships between territorial development and social innovation practices and processes. Scholars and activists alike have paid particular attention to social innovation in the 'local' space. This field is covered in detail by Van Dyck and Van den Broeck in Chapter 9 in this Handbook.

Despite their often very practice-oriented approach, many contributions to the SI literature of the last few decades show the need for, or argue in favour of, a more societal approach to social innovation agency, its institutions and cultural expressions. The literatures addressing relationships between governance and socio-political systems (see Chapter 11) and social innovation as a territorial process (see Chapter 9), especially, stress the need for such societal approach, which we develop in the next section.

8.3   THE MACRO-SOCIAL MEANING OF SOCIAL INNOVATION

Innovation is not an invention of modernity. Since hominids developed language and invented tools, social progress has been premised on social creativity, discoveries, and inventions, and their translation into successful innovation. What does seem to be *new* in the contemporary world is the self-reflexive emphasis on, and high regard for, innovation and its role in economic development and competition, political reform and revolution, and social progress more generally and, relatedly, the self-description, justified or not, of individuals, groups, organizations, institutional orders, and even whole societies as innovative rather than traditional or conformist (Nowotny 2008). This is a distinctive

feature of what is often described as modernity (e.g. by Weber, Durkheim, Simmel, Parsons) and, especially, its evolution into late, second, reflexive, or liquid modernity (Giddens 1991; Beck 1997; Bauman 2000). This second stage of modernity is said to create the conditions for a de-centred politics, no longer strongly state-centric and no longer coupled to a mixed economy in which the state is the principal means to compensate market failure. This allegedly creates the conditions for more individualistic or networked forms of social mobilization, innovation, and entrepreneurship, and for pursuing non-commodifiable use-values and models of human organization beyond the division of labour.

This provides an initial entry point into the relationship between *macro-social* developments and an increasing reflexive interest in social innovation and its implications for human emancipation and economic and political organization, going well beyond the sphere of 'civil society' or the life-world. A further step in this direction can be taken if we consider the role of social movements in reacting to changes in functional systems that fetishize reified social logics such as competitive market exchange at the expense of human interaction and sociability. A modern classic in this regard is, of course, Karl Polanyi's thick historical description of how 'society fought back' against the commodification of land, labour, and money in the 19th century. This involved a lot of social innovation – cooperatives, trade unions, friendly societies, workers' reading circles, working class 'building societies', and so on. In turn, this produced a whole proletarian social movement and public sphere that could be seen as socially innovative organizationally and as oriented to human emancipation (Negt and Kluge 1993). Polanyi also discussed different forms of social reaction to the rise of mass production in the interwar period, with fascism, communism, and social democracy representing different ways of embedding Fordism into new economic, political, and social orders (Polanyi 1944).

Fordist growth based on a capital-labour compromise (corresponding to Polanyi's account of social democracy *à la* New Deal) permitted full employment and the spread of mass consumption. Likewise, the welfare state assumed responsibility for coping with the economic and social risks (e.g., unemployment, poverty, sickness, inadequate housing) which had previously stimulated self-help through the expansion of the social economy (see Martinelli, Chapter 26). And, on the other hand, the importance of economies of scale in the dominant Fordist production paradigm encouraged firms in the social economy to move towards larger scale, more centralized, and/or hierarchical organizational forms (Carpi 1997, pp. 243–244). Weber had already noted this kind of isomorphism in the early modern social economy, when he observed that even in cooperatives (*Zweckverbandsbetrieben*):

> the civil servants rule exclusively, not the workers, who in this case can even hardly respond with strikes as they could against private entrepreneurs. The dictatorship of civil servants is on the rise, not the workers, for now anyway.[2] (Weber 2000[1918], p. 508)

On this basis Weber rejected suggestions that socialism would evolve naturally from the growing socialization of production or could be introduced by establishing various types of collective enterprise.

To update this picture, under Atlantic Fordism, as Carpi (1997) notes, there was little room for the social economy to socially innovate because there was no pressure to do so; alienation of social groups and individuals under Fordism were

often of a different kind and connected to other types of social belonging than those defined by production relations and division of labour (Massey 1995[1984]). While emancipation movements addressing different issues were mushrooming, the existent social economy institutions were mainstreamed within the Fordist system. The new movements followed a diversity of institutional trajectories ranging from becoming annexes of political parties, NGOs, loosely funded associations, etc. to anarchist action groups refuting any institutional form or funding.

The crises in the Fordist and neo-mercantilist economic development models in the 1970s and 1980s led in some cases to a neoliberal turn and, in others, to interest in economic, political, and social arrangements that depended neither on the anarchy of the market nor the top-down control of the state. It is in this context that the social economy has been (re-) discovered in connection with social innovation. But 'resetting' the social economy was only one aspect of the socially innovative initiatives and processes that pervaded the Fordist society as of the late 1960s and early 1970s. Fordism also provided the terrain for path-breaking struggles around non-class antagonisms: greater gender equality, women's liberation, the rise of anti-pedagogy, breaking down of the walls of psychiatric clinics, the criticism of clientelism in the Fordist political regimes, and the call for more direct democracy and citizen participation (see Offe 1985; Buechler 1999). It was also in this period that the excess burden of capitalism on the ecological system and sociocultural relations in communities were revealed and criticized. In later years this led to a revival of the literature on utopia and how they could play a role in social emancipation, community building and social transformation (Achterhuis 1998).

In line with the evolution of the Fordist society, the transformation of the *social economy* happened in a way that shows certain elective affinities with the transition towards post-Fordism. Carpi (1997) has observed a broad congruence between the dynamic of post-Fordism and the dynamic of a social economy in terms of three trends.

The first was the emergence of an alternative movement seeking both new forms of economic organization (democratic) and new market niches (natural and ecological goods, ideologically committed bookshops, etc.). The second was the growing weight of the service sector (*tertiarization* of the economy), the development of flexible production systems and the externalization of functions on the part of firms, which have propelled the growth of small businesses and the feasibility of productive organizations in expanding activities without any great investment. Third, a restructuring of state activity and the externalization of public service management, stimulated by the fiscal crisis and conservative ideological-political assaults, with the aim of 'rationalizing' the welfare state, has created new opportunities for the social economy to expand but unfortunately quite often within a regulatory regime based on new public management (NPM) modes of governance (see Lévesque, Chapter 2). At the same time, the recomposition of state action in social and economic affairs and the technological and economic transformation under way have created a growing number of problems and unsatisfied needs (unemployment, social exclusion, territorial decline) that have affected civil society and local authorities. Consequently, alternatives are looked for outside the capitalist sector and the state (Carpi 1997, p. 256).

This argument can be reinforced by considering the problems facing peripheral or semi-peripheral economic, political, and social spaces that cannot engage in 'strong competition' and therefore run the greatest risk of losing out in the zero-sum 'game' – 'struggle' would be a more appropriate term for such encounters – for resources from outside (see Jessop 2000). In such cases a resort to a social economy grounded in local social movements and concerned to empower the poor, deprived, and underprivileged seems to provide a more effective solution by developing a more self-sufficient economy that might then be able to re-insert itself into the wider economy or, at least, secure the conditions for a viable, local, solidary economy. Thus an expanded and recalibrated social economy could help to redress the imbalance between private affluence and public poverty, to create local demand, to re-skill the long-term unemployed and re-integrate them into an expanded labour market, to address some of the problems of urban regeneration (e.g., in social housing, insulation, and energy-saving), to provide a different kind of spatio-temporal fix for small and medium-enterprises, to regenerate trust within the community, and to promote empowerment.[3]

In this sense, against the logic of capital, the social economy prioritizes social use-value which in a competitive market may but usually does not have a high valorization potential. It seeks to re-embed the organization of the economy in specific spatio-temporal contexts oriented to the rhythms of social reproduction rather than the frenzied circulation of digitalized finance capital. It also challenges the extension of the capitalist logic to other spheres of life such that education, health services, housing, politics, culture, sport, and so on are directly commodified or, at least, subject to quasi-market forces. Indeed, extending the social economy provides a basis for resisting capital's increasing hegemony over society as a whole. For it demonstrates the possibility of organizing economic and social life in terms that challenge capitalist 'common-sense'.

Such innovation is clearly social in form and content and represents a serious challenge, at least ideationally and normatively, to the complementary logics of market and state. It revalorizes, in particular, the idea of social networks and moral communities, of reciprocity and solidarity, of negotiated consent and unconditional commitment. Therefore, we could say that the recent developments in the social economy have taken on board several of the 'other' dimensions of social innovation such as the innovation in social relations in societal and community spheres, human development targets, socio-political empowerment, etc. These developments have revived the scientific and social-political interest in the non-economic spheres of society, and strengthened the relative autonomy of social relations beyond the relations of production. They have shown that to organize communities and develop strategies to satisfy socio-cultural needs (as cited in Chambon et al. 1982) economic modes of coordination do not have to correspond either to the criteria of NPM, or the micro-efficiency of the private firm. Resulting from this it is important to understand that the social enterprise is only one type of SI actor among many others, as many of the case studies in this book show, and that its modes of 'doing economics' should not conform to those dictated by the logic of global competition.

For all types of SI actors and institutions, a key to the success of social innovation is new forms of social learning oriented to the production of knowledge as an intellectual commons organized around collective, problem-oriented learning. This requires a shift from today's hegemonic imaginaries of finance-dominated capitalism (however 'financially innovative' and 'expertise-based' it might be) and of the 'knowledge-based *economy*' (with its privileging of intellectual property rights) towards an emphasis on solidarity-based learning through sharing and cooperation. While in general this reorientation of innovation away from the prioritization of profit-oriented, market-mediated economic expansion depends on a wide range of bottom-up initiatives meant to revalorize a diversity of social use values, it also requires a wide range of institutional supports that can connect these initiatives, share good practice, and provide broader orientations. The most appropriate framework for this form of politico-institutional (re)organization is a multi-spatial (not merely multi-level or multi-scalar) pattern of subsidiarity in which there is as much local initiative and autonomy as possible and as much trans- or supra-local support as necessary to enable an equitable, ecologically sustainable social order to develop in a medium-term temporal horizon within and across the global North-global South divide. One of the most compelling arguments for this approach, apart from the moral virtues of social innovation and the solidary economy, is the urgent, imminent threat of hyperindividualism, energy, food, water, and environmental security but also to human dignity and reciprocal respect between human beings. This is both the biggest challenge and the greatest chance for a reorientation of our economic, political, and societal arrangements (see Jackson 2009; Victor 2008).

8.4   FROM INNOVATION RESEARCH TO SOCIAL INNOVATION RESEARCH

What does this socially embedded view of SI mean for SI research? Can one define criteria that distinguish an economistic approach to SI from an analysis of social innovation that is concerned with promoting human development and doing so by transforming social relations, fostering values of justice and solidarity and forms of social economy fitting the contemporary society? This is a hard task because SI has entered academic and political discourse in the last thirty years or so stepwise and through very different doors. There has been little concern about the moral virtues and ethical norms inherent to SI in the sense of human development, or about clearer definitions of SI processes and agency. Accordingly this section sketches how the gradual 'appropriation' of SI in *policy-making* spheres in interaction with *business practice* has 'mainstreamed' and apparently 'de-ethicized' the definition of SI in scientific research. It then asks whether and, if so, through which channels *academic research practice* has 'surrendered' to this mainstreaming and its proclaimed moral neutrality. The answers should allow us to set some guidelines to ensure the relevance of SI research.

8.4.1 Social Innovation in Policy Discourse and Business Practice

The scope of innovation in 'official approaches' (OECD, European Commission and national intellectual property rights offices) based on research on science and technology, innovation economics, management science etc. has been widened over the last two or three decades. This is especially clear in the highlighting of services, marketing and corporate organization as significant new domains and sources of innovation alongside more traditional formal R&D, new technological processes and products based-innovation.[4] A new wave in innovation policy has emerged from the early 2000s, when the OECD (2002) and the European

Commission began to recognize the social dimensions of innovation, with EC circles finally acknowledging the importance of SI in 2010 (The Young Foundation and SIX 2010). Even then, the policy discourse refers to SI in a rather reductionist (microeconomic) manner that does not reflect the advances made in current research programmes and in collective action practices.

This contemporary opening-up of the innovation discourse re-connects with the early-Schumpeterian spirit (Schumpeter 1934[1911]), in which innovation plays a major but problematic role in the long-term dynamics of industrial economies and societies. On the one hand, significant innovation has demanding social preconditions and, on the other, it affects the whole socio-economic system through the imitation, dissemination and collective appropriation processes that it triggers (Hamdouch 2007). However, as we saw in the introduction, the turn toward the social in contemporary innovation policy views falls short of Schumpeter's reading of the relationship between innovation and development. Since the EC showed a policy interest in it, SI has been increasingly communicated in economistic or, at best, gesturally social terms to justify and facilitate new neoliberal public policies. This posture of 'minimal social consciousness' could be summarized as follows: 'We care about social issues along with the modernization of the economy and the improvement of the economic competitiveness through R&D and technological innovation.' This discourse also underlies the latest iteration of the principles of New Public Management (NPM) that was originally promoted on efficiency grounds from the mid-1970s by the OECD (e.g. OECD 2002). Even though they intellectually take distance from the simplistic initial claims of NPM (especially the need for improving the efficiency of public administration and welfare services), many of the OECD recommendations remain in tune with NPM principles and are still widely applied by public administrations across the world – although in variegated socio-politically embedded forms.

Moreover in this business-geared policy discourse SI is often promoted as a catalyst of market-oriented ('hard'/ 'true'/ 'genuine') innovation: it should supplement innovation and competitiveness dynamics in a global competitive economy in which the 'creative destruction' process engendered by rapid technological change and the globalization of the economy requires 'social measures' in order to gild the bitter pill of the social problems it bears (de-industrialization and investment offshoring, structural loss of jobs, growing inequalities, etc.). This discourse has been translated into new policy approaches in which the progressive privatization of successive layers of public services (health, housing, education, social insurance, pension systems, etc.) and the substitution of competitive logics for collective ones have created new markets and business opportunities for the private sector ('social innovations' as sources of profit; on this, see Hamdouch et al. 2009).

These policy strategies fed into strategies deployed by the private business sector for the capture of the most profitable 'market niches' to meet needs for affordable housing, of sheltering and taking care of disabled people and the elderly, of good education and health public services in deprived urban areas, etc. With the worsening condition of the Welfare State (see above Section 8.3), the provision of these services and the (genuine) socially innovative approaches underlying them were originally developed by the 'third sector' (social economy organizations, solidarity movements, civil society associations, local communities, etc.). Economically speaking, this crisis was also

fed by the spectacular rise of fiscal benefits for the higher class, the privatization of the pension funds among other class-bound strategies to slim down the resources of the public sector needed to meet welfare needs of lower income classes (Gadrey 2012).

In this context, the distinction between 'innovation in general' accompanied by SI as a facilitator in innovation dynamics, and 'social innovation' as a core dimension of genuine economic, social, cultural and environmental human progress has been blurred. This blurring is reinforced by a growing 'import' by the business sector of ideas, 'values', terms and labels, innovative practices and services initially developed in the social field.

Still we should not confuse the official discourse about SI with the way the business sector uses the concept. Despite significant overlap with and shared ideological benefits from official SI discourse, we know that the business sector is now interested in capturing new ideas and practices developed in the social field and in valorizing new niches for the provision of services no longer supplied in a satisfactory way by the public sector. But at the same time, the business sector has applied some of the SI principles. It has turned to horizontal processes of learning through networks and horizontal interaction. It has adapted its organization and management modes in response to values and concerns initially rooted in social approaches to innovation; hence the rise of the so-called corporate social and environmental responsibility and its progressive dissemination in most (large) private firms (Moulaert and Nussbaumer 2008).

8.4.2 Refreshing the History of European Innovation Research

What then does this ambiguous status of SI in policy discourse and business practice mean for the place of SI in innovation research? Has this status affected the way in which innovation research has been led and since when? Has the academic world followed the discursive flow of high politics or the competitive market logic of business practice? Or did it adopt different positions? We try to answer this question by analysing the evolution in research of Innovation Systems as funded by the FAST and Framework Programmes up to 2000. Based on VALICORES (Moulaert and Hamdouch 2006), a survey and assessment project commissioned by the EC, we provide a brief account of how innovation has been theorized in EU funded research projects generally speaking from 1990 to 2000. First we summarize progress in the analysis of innovation dynamics realized over the period 1970–1995 and especially under the FAST programmes (1978–1983; 1983–1987; 1989–1993) and the Framework Programmes FP 4 (1994–1998) and FP 5 (1998–2002). Then we give an account of particular contributions from the VALICORES projects that could be integrated into a real theory of social innovation (11 projects that ran from 1996 to 2001). Especially the role of 'new' types of agents (research and technology organizations, knowledge-intensive business service providers, universities, intermediaries), 'new' kinds of innovation (organizational, institutional and cultural), the role of institutions and institutionalization and socio-cultural aspects of organizational learning were highlighted in the VALICORES survey.

In the course of the fourth, fifth, and sixth Framework Programmes, innovation analysis has been moving towards a dynamic approach in which innovations are analysed as processes, rather than configurations of decentralized rational (i.e. optimizing) behaviours (Lundvall and Borrás 1997). In the process approach,

routines and codes of behaviour, communication, learning and cooperation are more important than optimality norms for individual and collective behaviour. Processes are increasingly analysed as part of, but also as embodying institutional dynamics of innovation. The functional and institutional dimensions of the process dynamics are recognized as closely intertwined. Although not carefully defined in most projects, culture and cultural identity are at the core of their analysis of the institutionalization inside innovation systems. From the perspective of culture, innovation systems studied in these projects vary from strong unifying symbolic and identity systems (e.g. an institution with a strong transaction culture), to loosely coupled systems of interaction and communication between agents. In any case we learn that *innovation processes can only be properly understood if their cultural dynamics are taken into account*. This holds for innovation processes within firms and sectors, but also those involving various spatial scales (e.g. regional innovation systems including local-sectoral clusters of innovation, national innovation systems built on regional ones, industrial districts within a globalizing economy) (see also Lundvall and Borrás 1997).

In the Framework programmes, in the 1990s and early 2000s, the transfer in focus from innovation as a product to innovation as a process seems to have become irreversible (Moulaert and Hamdouch 2006). Within this processual approach room has been created for studying innovation processes as:

- the dynamic interaction between a multiplicity of agents and behavioural criteria (multi-rationality, but also irrationality in individual and collective behaviour);
- norm systems and how they affect

the reproduction of agents and institutions;
- learning and adaptation, including internal and external selection mechanisms;
- processes with significant cultural mediation and signification.

Many of the projects in the Framework programmes refer to organizational and social or cultural innovations. But what do these projects mean by these 'new' types of innovation? And if the definition of innovation should be broadened (compare e.g. with Lundvall and Borrás, pp. 29–36), what are the consequences for the definition(s) of the types of knowledge in the learning economy or society? How should the relationship between knowledge production and cultural development and emancipation be analysed? Crisscrossing these interrogations in the projects we examined is the use of various notions of 'culture', seldom defined but omnipresent when analysing organizational and social innovations and the cultural reading of the many dimensions of these innovations.

8.4.3   And SI Research Now?

Should we conclude from the above short overview of the heritage from the FAST and the fourth, fifth and sixth Framework Programmes that all concepts and theories needed to lead proper (social) innovation analysis were already available by the early 2000s, and that the new wave economistic SI approach as expressed in policy discourse and marketing oriented business approaches simply disregards this progress in innovation research to return to some of the least dynamic models of social innovation behaviour (e.g. the Young Report on Social Innovation (Mulgan et al. 2007), which takes feedback loops in SI agency into account but fails to endogenize the

societal change dynamics or consider the interaction between different types of SI agency)?

A positive answer to this question would be too simple. The 'state of the art' innovation research methodology under the cited programmes does not allow us to lead SI research according to the ontological basis we spelled out before, i.e. social innovation as innovation in social relations to foster human development – despite its strong focus on multi-agency, multi-scalarity, learning processes and institutional dynamics in innovation behaviour and processes; despite its deconstruction of the economic rationality axioms; despite the recognition of the relationships between technological, organizational and social innovation; despite acclaiming diversity and culture as drivers of real life innovation systems; despite theorizing innovation systems as part of broader economic and socio-political dynamics. Despite all these meaningful steps forward in innovation analysis, the ontological basis and epistemic underpinnings needed to lead SI analysis are missing in this innovation systems research. Can we develop a methodological framework that adopts a human development oriented ontology of (social) innovation and that takes on board the progress in innovation systems research we just flagged?

8.5   TOWARDS A METHODOLOGICAL FRAMEWORK FOR STUDYING SOCIAL INNOVATION

We suggest a methodological framework that corresponds with the 'classic' tradition of understanding social innovation in the light of social change instead of as part of a multiscalar, multi-dimensional system of innovation as analysed under the

Framework programmes. The basic difference between the complex approach to innovation systems in most of the projects we screened and social innovation research does not relate to complexity, *but to a completely different ontology*. Social innovation research starts from a social ontology that considers 'society' not as a pre-given social reality (especially given the historical challenges involved in building so-called national societies and the more recent challenges to societal integration introduced by what is often, misleadingly, described as 'globalization') but as a horizon of action defined by one or more competing 'social imaginaries' (on social imaginary, see, for example, Castoriadis 1998; Taylor 2003). This is especially relevant for research on social innovation because it highlights the constitutive, performative role of social practices and, hence, their transformative potential when linked with new economic, political, social, and other potentially encompassing social projects. In short, in adopting a contingent account of social development, space is opened for innovative connections between micro-, meso- and macro-innovation as many sites and scales of social organizations as these are realized within a hierarchically ordered system of social relations (Moulaert and Jessop 2012).

Within this approach particular attention is given to the relations and practices that promote human development through the satisfaction of basic needs and innovation in social relations, community empowerment and governance of societal structures. This ontology of socialized change practice transcends the ontology adhered to in innovation systems as analysed in the Framework projects which are in most cases geared to organizational efficiency and improved application of knowledge in different subsystems of society. Many of the features of the inno-

vation systems covered in both approaches are labelled identically. But their ontology and therefore their epistemic position are completely different. Therefore, also their ontogenesis is at least partly different (Moulaert and Nussbaumer 2008; see Moulaert and Van Dyck, Chapter 35): *social innovation research will focus on the making of social innovation processes and strategies to promote human development, whereas innovation systems research in the FP tradition will address the genesis of efficient organizations and societal structures.*

What then is specific to the methodology of human development driven SI research? Other chapters in this book present important components of research methodologies for analysing SI agency and processes. Starting from an epistemological perspective that is coherent with the SI ontology, we suggest here some criteria which SI research methodology should respect. We start by accepting that an epistemology is built around three questions, namely: *What is knowledge? How should it be acquired? When do we know that what we learned is true?* In the remainder of this chapter we will especially focus on the second question. The answers to the first and third question are also relevant to answering the second of course. The knowledge we build should fit the ontology and the ontogenesis we stand for: it should be relevant to understanding but also play a role in the genesis of social innovation. This genesis is not a functional process, but an institutionally mediated process of learning, decision-making, collective action and institutionalization among human beings. We want to understand how this genesis occurs and can be conducted in the future. This can be done with a certain degree of epistemic diversity. According to Santos, the 'epistemic diversity of the world is potentially infinite' (Santos 2008, p. xlvii). But from the perspective of SI innovation research, the notion of epistemic diversity is not a subscription to a relativistic position, it is a perception of knowledge as being spatially and institutionally embedded (Moulaert and Van Dyck, Chapter 35) and meant to learn more about the different ways of accomplishing SI.

How then should knowledge be acquired within SI research? Social innovation researchers are in different ways and also to a large extent part of social innovation processes. In order to guarantee onto-logical coherence, they should respect the ethics that are defended in these pro-cesses and act in accordance. This means among others that SI research should be *reflexive* and *transdisciplinary*; and that the object of research is SI past, present and future. These three criteria for good SI research methodology partly overlap and could be brought together under the label of *transdisciplinary reflexivity*. Still to achieve coherence among these three crite-ria we will make use of a meta-theoretical framework with at least a double purpose: situate SI within societal dynamics and its explanations; and serve as a mirror for the ethical positioning of the researchers involved (see also Moulaert et al., Chapter 1).

What do we mean by 'reflexivity'? SI researchers should not enter into SI dynamics as anthropophobic consultants but as reflexive researchers. They should be aware that the object they are studying (SI as a process and as agency) is highly subject to socialization but also that they themselves are part of the social reality in which the SI they study occurs.

Let us first focus on the *socially embed-ded nature of SI strategies and processes*, a significant aspect of reflexivity in social science in general, and SI research in par-ticular, which stresses the need to study the social relations between the elements

of reality that are analysed. In tune with the social change dynamics ontology we adopt, we place SI initiatives and processes within a meta-theoretical framework that allows us to figure out their structural and institutional dimensions, their signifi-cance within the context of social trans-formation. Such a framework could be a progressive neo-structuralist analytical framework that serves to analyse contra-dictory forces of human development as well as past and future processes and ini-tiatives of SI (Miciukiewicz et al. 2012). In such a meta-framework, strongly inspired by the reflections of social change and the role of SI therein as we unfolded them in Sections 8.3 and 8.4 of this chapter, pro-cesses of social innovation are spatially and institutionally embedded. The agency dimension of social innovation cannot be detached from society, institutional con-figuration and place. Often agents of social innovation – including scientific analysts of SI – work as 'servants' of other inter-ests than their own immediate interests in 'profit' (Hulgård 2004). They can be serv-ants of ideal motives (Weber 1989[1915–1920]); they can be concerned with the importance of community and other forms of 'conscience collective' (Durkheim 1968); and they can implement social innovation that is 'spatially negotiated between agents and institutions that have a strong ter-ritorial affiliation' (Moulaert 2009, p. 57). Social innovation occurs at diverse spatial scales as well as in communities and public spheres at the micro, meso, and macro level of society, and can hardly be iso-lated from agency related to issues such as consciousness raising, local embed-dedness, mobilization of multiple types of resources and learning. In this sense social innovation is usually not a smooth process but an arena for deliberative deci-sion making with a transformative power based upon spatial negotiation of public spheres generated through the political power of social movements. In this arena SI researchers can be active agents, as researchers or in other roles.

This leads us to the second aspect of the *reflexive* character of SI innovation research, which is that SI innovation researchers should be aware of their roles in SI research and of their place in the social relations and initiatives they analyse. As to the latter, their own role or that of their peers or predecessors could be analysed by use of the meta-theoretical framework (see above) in which their agency is defined. This is for example how it is done in the Sociology of Knowledge Approach (SoK) to SI research (Moulaert and Van Dyck, Chapter 35). The SoK approach in its 'strong program' calls for a role of a meta-framework and addresses at the same time the position of researchers, their theories and their practice from a social critical perspective. The 'strong program' of SoK could be called 'complete embeddedness': the social, political and economic context that nourished the environment in which the knowledge was developed, the socio-cultural (including the ideological) background of the scientists, their belonging to scientific and philosophical communities, the links between scientific practice and collective action, etc. should be analysed by situating it in the progressive neo-structuralist metatheoretical framework referred to above. This would allow us to understand which role theories and scientists play or have played in SI past and present; and to draw lessons for future SI research – which theories are relevant? Which political regimes are beneficial to fostering SI? What partnerships in SI research and practice are recommendable in particular conjunctures, etc?

But researchers' contribution and impact can go beyond their scientific roles. SI researchers that are in tune with the ontogenesis of SI are action researchers in many different meanings of the term (see especially Chapters 21–25 in this book). They should be aware of the diversity of roles they (may) have in SI processes. These roles can be categorized in various ways. Moulaert and Nussbaumer (2008, p. 138) make a distinction between four types of roles:

i)   *virtual* roles: the scientist as agent in theories of social innovation and in the meta-theoretical framework presented in this chapter. These virtual roles can be diverse: change agent, thinker and creator;

ii) *academic* roles: theoretician, empirical researcher, epistemologist or methodologist;

iii) *'active change'* or 'real' roles: scientist as an artist, participatory observer, change agent, democratic planner, . . .;

iv) the scientist as a *scenario-designer* of alternative development, as spokesperson for social movements, . . .

And when researchers are in such different roles they should be very aware of the consequences of these roles for SI. It is in the awareness of role diversity that the two dimensions of reflexivity in SI research meet. The meta-theoretical framework that is used should be capable of analysing at the same time: SI in accordance with its own nature and ethics; and the role of SI researchers in connection with other agents of SI within their societal setting.

This is why we argue that reflexivity in SI research is necessarily transdisciplinary. The different roles needed in SI research cannot be fulfilled by one or a few individuals. Skills, knowledge, expertise vary. And 'experts', unless they are 'experienced witnesses', cannot by themselves identify what should be the research object of a particular SI research, which human needs or change processes should be addressed, which possible collective action and policy opportunities, etc. should be explored. This makes us qualify reflexivity in the SI research approach as transdisciplinary: reflexivity that involves different actors, who are involved in different ways in the social innovation process, including the research part of it.

Applying transdisciplinary reflexivity in SI research then means setting up an interactive process of research and action which starts from a collective problematization by a transdisciplinary research group (e.g. in the case of SI at the neighbour level: inhabitants, so-called concerned citizens, local organizers, activists, researchers, policy makers ...). Such transdisciplinary problematization (Miciukiewicz et al. 2012) involves the recognition of the problems of human development to be addressed, the questions to be researched, ..., but also how the research team will be composed, what the different stages in the research will be, who will have a role in each of these stages, how the research is connected to other moments of the SI initiatives and processes, etc. (see Novy et al., Chapter 32). Also, the building of the meta-theoretical framework is part of the shared problematization: what is the view of e.g. the urban society in which the problem should be addressed? Which theories and researches from the past and present could help? But also: which criteria from a SoK perspective should be brought on board to assess the potential of particular theories, scientific roles, ...? The process dynamics of the transdisciplinary research group should be reflexively followed up with an outlook for potential power games between researchers-actors, the relations with the public institutions and the socio-political movements, etc.

8.6 QUESTIONS FOR DISCUSSION

- In your view, what are the main differences between approaches to social innovation that are societal, social transformation oriented and those that are agency-oriented? Is it possible to synthesize these approaches to enhance their explanatory power and their contribution to social innovation practices?

- How persuasive do you find the methodological criteria for social innovation research oriented to human development that were presented in the last section of the chapter?

- The macro-social meaning of social innovation is analysed in Section 8.3. Do you agree with the balance among the different dimensions? Could any dimensions be omitted, should others have been included? Have the links between social economy and other sites of social innovation been sufficiently established in this section? If not, which other links would you make?

NOTES

1. Such an analysis could also be applied, *mutatis mutandis*, to other social arrangements that are characterized by exploitation, domination, and social exclusion dynamics, whether grounded in capitalist dynamics or not.
2. In the original: 'In den öffentlichen und Zweckverbandsbetrieben aber herrscht erst recht und ganz ausschließlich der Beamte, nicht der Arbeiter, der hier ja mit einem Streik schwerer etwas ausrichtet al.s gegen Privatunternehmer. Die Diktatur des Beamten, nicht die des Arbeiters, ist es, die – vorläufig jedenfalls – im Vormarsch begriffen ist' (Weber 2000[1918], p. 508).
3. On developments in focus and organization of the social economy over the last century, see Moulaert and Nussbaumer 2005.
4. On this topic, see the evolution in official

approaches to innovation as exemplified by the successive versions of the OECD/EC Oslo Manual in 1992, 1997 and 2005.

REFERENCES

(References in bold are recommended reading.)

Achterhuis, H.J. (1998), *De Erfenis van de Utopie*, Baarn: Ambo.

André, Isabel, Brito Enriques and Jorge Malheiros (2009), 'Inclusive places, arts and socially creative milieux', in D. MacCallum et al. (eds), pp. 149–66.

Bauman, Z. (2000), *Liquid Modernity*, Cambridge: Polity.

Beck, U. (1997), *The Reinvention of Politics*, Cambridge: Polity.

Becker, M.C. and T. Knudsen (2005), 'Translation and introduction to "Entwicklung" (J. Schumpeter)' *Journal of Economic Literature*, **43** (1), 108–120.

Bendix, R. (1978), *Max Weber: An Intellectual Portrait*, Berkeley, CA: University of California Press.

BEPA (2010), 'Empowering people, driving change: Social Innovation in The European Union', Brussels, EC.

Buechler, S.M. (1999), *Social Movements in Advanced Capitalism*, Oxford: Oxford University Press.

Carpi, J.A.T. (1997), 'The Prospects for the Social Economy in a Changing World', *Annals of Public and Cooperative Economics*, **68** (2), 247–79.

Castoriadis, C. (1998), *The Imaginary Institution of Society*, Cambridge, MA: MIT Press.

Chambon, J.-L., A. David and J.-M. Devevey (1982), *Les innovations sociales*, Paris: Presses Universitaires de France.

Coleman, J. (1970), 'Social Inventions', *Social Forces*, **49** (2), 163–173

Cooperrider, L. and W.A. Pasmore (1991), 'Global Social Change: A New Agenda for Social Science?', *Human Relations*, **44** (10), 1037–1055.

Drucker, P. (1987), 'Social innovation: management's new dimension', *Long Range Planning*, **20** (6), 29–34.

Du Bois, W. and R. Wright (2001), *Applying Sociology: Making a Better World*, Boston, MA: Allyn and Bacon.

Durkheim, É. (1968), *The Elementary Forms of the Religious Life*, London: Allen & Unwin.

Durkheim, É. (1997[1893]), *The Division of Labor in Society* (trans. Lewis A. Coser), New York: Free Press.

Elkington, J. and P. Hartigan (2008), *The Power of Unreasonable People*, Boston, MA: Harvard Business Press.

Gadrey, J. (2012), 'Enquête sur un audit populaire.

La dette, quelle dette?', *Le Monde Diplomatique*, June, pp. 1, 12.

García, M. (2006), 'Citizenship practices and urban governance in European cities', *Urban Studies*, **43** (4), 745–65.

Gershuny, J. (1987), 'Technology, Social Innovation and the Informal Economy', *The Annals of the American Academy of Political and Social Science*, **493**, 47–63.

Giddens, A. (1991), *Modernity and Self-identity: Self and Society in the Late Modern Age*, Cambridge: Polity.

Godin, B. (2008), 'Innovation: the History of a Category', Working Paper 1, Project on the Intellectual History of Innovation, Montréal: INRS, http://www.csiic.ca/PDF/IntellectualNo1.pdf (last accessed 16 August 2012).

Godin, B. (2010), '"Meddle Not With Them That Are Given to Change": Innovation as Evil', Working Paper 6, Project on the Intellectual History of Innovation, Montréal: INRS, http://www.csiic.ca/PDF/IntellectualNo6.pdf (last accessed 16 August 2012).

Godin, B. (2012), 'Social innovation: utopias of innovation from c.1830 to the present', Working Paper 11, Project on the Intellectual History of Innovation, Montréal: INRS, http://www.csiic.ca/PDF/SocialInnovation_2012.pdf (last accessed 16 August 2012).

Hamdouch, A. (2007), 'Innovation', in *Dictionnaire de l'Economie*, Paris: Encyclopédie Universalis and Albin Michel, pp. 719–733.

Hamdouch, A., O. Ailenei, B. Laffort and F. Moulaert (2009), 'Les organisations de l'économie sociale dans la métropole lilloise: Vers de nouvelles articulations spatiales?' *Canadian Journal of Regional Science/Revue canadienne des sciences régionales*, **32** (1), 85–100.

Hillier, J., F. Moulaert and J. Nussbaumer (2004), 'Trois essais sur le rôle de l'innovation sociale dans le développement local', *Géographie Economie Société*, **6** (2), 129–152.

Hulgård, L. (2004), 'Entrepreneurship in Community Development and Local Governance', in Peter Bogason, Sandra Kensen, Hugh T. Miller (eds), *Tampering with Tradition: The Unrealized Authority of Democratic Agency*, Lanham, MD: Lexington Books, pp. 87–107.

Jackson, T. (2009), *Prosperity without Growth: Economics for a Finite Planet*, London: Earthscan.

Jessop, B. (2000), 'Globalization, entrepreneurial cities, and the social economy', in P. Hamel, M. Lustiger-Thaler and M. Mayer (eds), *Urban Movements in a Global Environment*, London: Routledge, pp. 81–100.

Lee, M.D. (2008), 'A review of the theories of corporate social responsibility: its evolutionary path and the road ahead', *International Journal of Management Reviews*, **10**, 53–73.

Lundvall, B-A. and S. Borrás (1997), 'The globalising learning economy: implications for innovation policy', Report based on contributions from seven projects under the TSER programme, DG XII, Commission of the European Union.

MacCallum, D., F. Moulaert, J. Hillier and S. Vicari Haddock (eds) (2009), *Social Innovation and Territorial Development*, Aldershot: Ashgate.

Massey, D. (1995[1984]), *Spatial Divisions of Labour: Social Structures and the Geography of Production*, London: Routledge.

Miciukiewicz, K., A. Novy, S. Musterd and J. Hillier (2012), 'Introduction: Problematising Urban Social Cohesion: A Transdisciplinary Endeavour', *Urban Studies*, 49 (9), 1855–1872.

Moulaert, F. (2009), 'Social Innovation: Institutionally Embedded, Territorially (Re) Produced', in D. MacCallum et al. (eds), pp. 11–24.

Moulaert, F. and A. Hamdouch (eds) (2006), 'The Knowledge Infrastructure: Analysis, Institutional Dynamics and Policy Issues', special Issue of *Innovation: The European Journal of Social Science Research*, 19 (1).

Moulaert, F. and J. Nussbaumer (2005), 'Defining the Social Economy and its Governance at the Neighbourhood Level: a methodological reflection', *Urban Studies*, 42 (11), 2071–2088.

Moulaert, F. and J. Nussbaumer. (2008), *La logique spatiale du développement territorial*, Québec: Presses de l'Université du Québec.

Moulaert, F. and B. Jessop (2012), 'Theoretical Foundations for the Analysis of Socio-economic Development in Space', in F. Martinelli, F. Moulaert and A. Novy (eds), *Urban and regional development trajectories in contemporary capitalism*, London: Routledge, pp. 18–44.

Mulgan, G., S. Tucker, R. Ali and B. Sanders (2007), *Social Innovation: What it is, Why it Matters and How It Can be Accelerated*, London: The Young Foundation.

Mumford, M.D. (2002), 'Social Innovation: ten cases from Benjamin Franklin', *Creativity Research Journal*, 14 (2), 253–66.

Negt, O. and A. Kluge (1993), *Public Sphere and Experience: Toward an Analysis of the Bourgeois and Proletarian Public Sphere*, Minneapolis: University of Minnesota Press.

Novy, A. and B. Leubolt (2005), 'Participatory budgeting in Porto Alegre: the dialectics of state and non-state forms of social innovation', *Urban Studies*, 42 (11), 2023–2036.

Nowotny, H. (2008), *Insatiable Curiosity: Innovation in a Fragile Future*, Cambridge MA: MIT Press.

Noya, A. (2009), *The Changing Boundaries of Social Enterprises*, Paris: OECD.

Nussbaumer, J. and F. Moulaert (2007), 'L'innovation sociale au coeur des débats publics et scientifiques. Un essai de déprivatisation de la société', in J.L. Klein and D. Harrisson (eds), *L'innovation sociale: émergence et effets sur la transformation des sociétés*, Québec: Presses de l'Université du Québec, pp. 71–88.

OECD (1992), *Guidelines for collecting and inter-preting innovation data*, Oslo Manual, Paris and Brussels: OCDE and The European Commission.

OECD (1997), *Guidelines for collecting and interpreting innovation data*, Oslo Manual, 2nd edition, Paris and Brussels: OECD and The European Commission.

OECD (2002), 'Social innovation and the New Economy', report of the LEED Forum on Social Innovations, Paris: OECD.

OECD (2005), *Guidelines for collecting and interpreting innovation data*, Oslo Manual, 3rd edition, Paris and Brussels: OECD and The European Commission.

OECD (2010), 'SMEs, entrepreneurship and innovation', Paris.

Offe, C. (1985), 'New social movements: challenging the boundaries of institutional politics', *Social Research*, 52 (4), 817–868.

Ogburn, W.F. (1922), *Social Change with Respect to Culture and Original Nature*, New York: B.W. Huebsch.

Polanyi, K. (1944), *The Great Transformation: The Political and Economic Origins of Our Time*, New York: Rinehart.

Reich, R. (2011), 'The Promise and Peril of the New Social Economy', http://www.youtube.com/watch?v=6Bhki3d_4Lk&feature=player_embedded#! (last accessed 7 December 2012).

Santos, B. de S. (ed) (2008), *Another Knowledge is Possible*, London: Verso.

Schumpeter, J.A. (1934[1911]), *The Theory of Economic Development: An Inquiry into Profits, Capital, Credit, Interest, and the Business Cycle* (trans. Redvers Opie from the second German edition of 1926), Cambridge, MA: Harvard University Press.

Schumpeter, J.A. (1942), *Capitalism, Socialism and Democracy*, New York: Harper & Brothers.

Swyngedouw, E. (2005), 'Governance innovation and the citizen: the Janus face of governance-beyond-the-state', *Urban Studies*, 42 (11), 1991–2006.

Tarde, G. (1999[1893]), *La logique sociale*, Paris: Synthélabo.

Taylor, C. (2003) *Modern Social Imaginaries*, Durham, NC: Duke University Press.

Victor, P.A. (2008), *Managing without Growth: Slower by Design, not Disaster*, Cheltenham, UK and Northampton, MA: Edward Elgar Publishing.

Weber, M. (1889), 'The History of Medieval Business Organisations', PhD thesis, University of Berlin.

Weber, M. (1961[1923]), *General Economic History*, New York: Collier.

Weber, M. (1968[1922]), *Economy and Society*, Berkeley, CA: University of California Press.

Weber, M. (1989[1915–1920]), *Die Wirtschaftsethik der Weltreligionen Konfuzianismus und Taoismus: Schriften 1915–1920*, Tübingen: J.C.B. Mohr (Paul Siebeck).

Weber, M. (2000[1918]), *Der Sozialismus. Rede zur allgemeinen Orientierungen von östereichischen*

Offizieren in Wien 1918. Das Werk, Berlin: Heptagon.

Young Foundation and The Social Innovation eXchange (SIX) (2010), Report prepared for the Bureau of European Policy Advisors, Brussels: The European Commission, http://ec.europa.eu/bepa/pdf/publications_pdf/social_innovation.pdf (last accessed 5 March 2012).

9. Social innovation: a territorial process
Barbara Van Dyck and Pieter Van den Broeck[1]

9.1 INTRODUCTION

In a keynote speech in Brussels in 2011 launching the Pilot Initiative 'Social Innovation Europe', José Manuel Barroso, president of the European Commission, referred to familiar discussions that define social innovation as new ways to address unmet social needs. After that, president Barroso linked social innovation to sustainable resource management; to creating behavioural changes towards more responsibility of individuals; and concluded with linking social innovation to smart, sustainable and inclusive growth (Barroso 2011). The speech is in no way exceptional or surprising but is interesting however, for the way it illustrates how social innovation has recently become embedded in a discourse that approaches development issues as de-territorialized management questions. Social innovation is addressed as something that can be 'done'; as if social innovation becomes a 'thing', a process in the best case, that can be separated from its context.

In this chapter, in contrast, we argue that social innovation, as a way to foster social cohesion, is an inherently territorialized process. Its study, therefore, is necessarily territorialized as well. To demonstrate this argument, we explore the origins of different social innovation strands and explore how territory has been addressed in different social innovation approaches, to compare and contrast them.

The prominence of the concept of social innovation in itself reflects a change in research approach and strategy in criti-cal social science. Sayer (1997) observed that debates on politics in critical social sciences partly shifted away from attacking the established powers, to a politics in which debates about desirable and existing alternatives come more frequently to the fore. In contrast to other political economy approaches that focus on the identification of false beliefs, the social innovation approach, as deployed in this handbook, is a needs-based explanatory critique, which underlines the identification of unsatisfied social needs and ways to address them (see General Introduction). It focuses on empowering innovation in social relations (Gerometta et al. 2005) as well as on how shifting spatial arrangements create the conditions for different types of social innovation (Novy et al. 2009).

Evidence of, as well as a belief in, the power of targeted spatial strategies in creating the conditions for socially cohesive development partly explain the centrality of territory as a field of action in the social innovation literature (see for example Moulaert 2000; Hillier et al. 2004; Moulaert and Nussbaumer 2008; MacCallum et al. 2009; Fontan et al. 2005; Moulaert et al. 2005). Equally, territory gained importance as an analytical concept in this literature, including studies on spatial innovation systems (Moulaert and Sekia 2003), area-based development (Fontan et al. 2005; Drewe and Hulsbergen 2007; MacCallum et al. 2009; Oosterlynck et al. 2011) and integrated area development (Moulaert 2000). Other social innovation approaches have developed analytical tools based on management based approaches which relate social innovation mainly to innovation in services through processes of good governance and social entrepreneurship (Wolk 2007; BEPA 2011; Mulgan and Pulford 2010; Murray et al. 2010).

This chapter reviews the literature, to inquire into the dimensions and features of territory that are analysed in the different social innovation strands. Drawing on insights from the fields of planning, geography and regional economics, the chapter emphasizes that it is important to further develop analytical frames in social innovation studies that take territory[2] seriously.

9.2   MANAGEMENT BASED APPROACHES TO SOCIAL INNOVATION

Recently a larger number of social innovation studies have emerged, mainly oriented towards policy advice, in Europe and the US (Wolk 2007; BEPA 2011; Mulgan and Pulford 2010; Murray et al. 2010). In the Six and Young Foundation 'Study on social innovation', social innovations are defined as:

> innovations that are social both in their ends and in their means. Specifically, we define social innovations as new ideas (products, services and models) that simultaneously meet social needs (more effectively than alternatives) and create new social relationships or collaborations. In other words they are innovations that are both good for society and enhance society's capacity to act. (Mulgan and Pulford 2010, p. 16)

This multi-dimensional definition is at first sight quite similar to the ways in which social innovation is defined in this handbook and developed in the European Framework projects 'Integrated Area Development', SINGOCOM, KATARSIS and SOCIAL POLIS (see

General Introduction, Moulaert et al. 2010; MacCallum et al. 2009; González and Healey 2005). This involves innovations in social relationships, in ways to meet social needs, and a dimension of empowerment. Different approaches also agree that social innovations can emerge from different actors or sectors. When looked at more carefully, the analytical frameworks and ethical perspectives deployed in this handbook are nevertheless quite different from the ones in management based approaches to social innovation.

Indeed, the latter approaches remain close to economic innovation studies, both in approach and goals. In reports of the Six and Young Foundation (Mulgan and Pulford 2010; BEPA 2011; Murray et al. 2009, 2010) it is argued that social agendas should be tied more closely to 'the' economic agenda and that addressing societal challenges is, as stated in Mulgan and Pulford (2010), in the first place considered a way to fight crisis by aiming to unleash new sources of growth. Social innovation in services and other fields with high impact with respect to goals of better health, education, employment or the environment is identified to open cheap possibilities for growth.

Murray et al. (2009) identify three levels of inquiry and three areas of social innovation. The levels correspond to macroanalysis, micro-analysis and the inquiry into innovation in productive systems. The three areas are institutional conditions for social innovation, the distinct processes of social innovation and systemic innovations. The shape of the social economy, constituted of sub-economies of the public, grant, market and household economy and their interfaces (state-grant, state-market, state-household, market-grant, household-market, household-grant), forms the starting point for inquiry. Impressive lists of examples of social innovation in different economic spheres are generated, but it remains unclear how these initiatives are embedded in the broader societal logic and, therefore, how they may overcome causes of inequality and injustices. Collective dynamics or articulation between spatial scales, fundamental to explaining development (Storper and Scott 1988; Becattini 2002) remain invisible. Networks and coalitions are identified as the driving factors of development (Murray et al. 2010; Wolk 2007), but it remains vague how these networks become 'a means of stimulating a more dynamic, inclusive and sustainable social market economy' as is stated in the Mulgan and Pulford report (2010, p. 5).

In management-based approaches, space is treated as a manageable entity that is accounted for through the study of allocation and administering of public space (such as 'reclaim the streets' or 'guerrilla gardening' as examples of new forms of management and multiple uses of public space). The interaction between 'innovators' and the 'environment' they are working in (Mulgan and Pulford 2010, p. 27), is stressed when explaining how social change happens, yet refers merely to individuals or organizations (the 'innovators) and other groups that have more capacity to implement or promote new ideas (the 'environment'). The approach thus starts from a diversity of social innovation actors, but remains within the primacy of a classical economic logic that lacks contextuality. Such an orthodox economic view on territorial development runs the risk of reductionism by assuming linear relationships between causes of social problems and socially innovative initiatives. From development studies we have indeed learned that it is crucial to understand how initiatives are embedded in specific socio-political and socio-economic contexts (Moulaert and Sekia 2003).

9.3 A SPATIALIZED VIEW IN STUDYING SOCIAL INNOVATION

As outlined in the introduction of this chapter, the concept of territory is central in a considerable part of the social innovation literature, both as a field of action and as analytical concept. As a *field of action*, these writings thus seek to advance territorial strategies that exemplify place sensitive modes of policy intervention. These are strategies that, according to Bradford (2003), articulate a coherent spatial logic and are constructed with local knowledge, informed by the particular circumstances on the ground, and delivered through multi-sectorial, horizontal networks crossing functional boundaries or program silos. As a field of *analysis*, social innovation mobilizes the concept of territory to understand and explain the spatial processes that obstruct or enhance the capacity of action of disfavoured social groups (Klein and Harrisson 2007; MacCallum et al. 2009). Social innovation thus does not simply happen in a spatial context, but consists of the transformation of spatial relations, which are context and spatially specific, spatially negotiated and spatially embedded (Moulaert 2009).

The centrality of territory or *territoire* is surely not unique to the social innovation literature. Next to the typical 'spatial sciences' – geography, regional economics, planning and urbanism –political sciences, policy studies, sociology and behavioural studies have also often put the territory at the heart of analysis. The spatialization of analysis and a renewed interest in spatial ontology is based on the recognition both that the outcome of social processes differ from place to place, and that space impacts on these very processes (see for example Massey 2005). The incorporation of spatial concepts in the humanities and social sciences is widely referred to as the 'spatial turn' (Thrift 2002) and is a reaction to universal single-voiced historical narratives (Warf and Arias 2009). Space is increasingly understood as a social construction relevant to the interpretation of histories and cultural phenomena. The notion of *territoire* reflects this even more explicitly.

The following section first gives a brief overview of how territory has been an important factor in development studies, and then explores specifically how it is analysed by a variety of authors dealing with social innovation.

9.3.1 Opening the Container of Space

For a long time, territory has been recognized as a necessary element in development. This becomes especially clear in the studies of industrialization and urbanization of the late 19th century. Spatial organization appeared to be crucial in sustaining capitalist development. Work and living had to be located far enough apart to create living environments, away from the unbearable environmental conditions close to the factories, but close enough to bring workforce into the factories. Since the 1930s, territory was seen as a necessary scale of action to balance out inequalities and address the crisis. Modernity itself was based on processes of territorialization. Through spatial interventions, directed by the nation state, growth had to be stimulated and homogenized throughout the regions. In the study of these processes in dominant urban studies, geography and economics, space was presented as a container or an 'unchanging box within which material events occur' (Smith 2008[1984], p. 2).

From the mid 1970s the pace of secular decline and deindustrialization of the old industrial core raised important questions in terms of understanding the ongoing social and economic transformations. It was clear that to fully understand these transformations, and to pose practical questions of what might be done to reconstruct viable futures for such areas, it was critical to relate what happened to how, why and where (see e.g. Fontan et al. 2003; Hudson 2000). Moreover, spatial strategies based on the idea of equal distribution of growth were no longer functioning (Lévesque et al. 1996). Manufacture-intensive components of the industrial chain continued to relocate away from western cities. Better off classes moved out of city centres *en masse*, leaving behind urban cores that had been stripped of their economic and demographic capital. The demographic and economic crisis of the urban cores triggered the development of new organizational models, as well as the search for new spatial strategies. Ongoing global transformations of deregulation and liberalization of the economy in the 1990s increased the complexity of those questions even more. In particular, spatial strategies now stressed competitiveness and the promotion of economic development-from-below as ways of regulating uneven development (Brenner 2004). The development of decentralized administrative authorities, special agencies, and place specific strategies aimed at reconcentrating productive capacities into strategic urban and regional growth centres (Peck and Tickell 1992). These new spatial strategies were part of an attempt to rescale regulation, based on the promotion of unequal concentrations of investment and accumulation (Brenner 2004). Unlike under spatial Keynesianism, the interrelationships between successful and unsuccessful spatial economies were not at the basis of spatial policy (Raco 2007). In contrast, discourses of global competition and the promotion of supply-side competitiveness (for example through the promotion of innovation and enhancing small and medium enterprises) at various scales evolve into a major philosophy of spatial policy and practices to sustain flexible accumulation. In contrast with entrepreneurial strategies that aimed at creation of urban environments capable of attracting mobile capital (Harvey 1989), spatial strategies based on the power of local (endogenous) resource mobilization emerged. The local scale, small and medium-sized firms and the capacity of valorizing human capital was reasserted in reaction to the failure of centralized regional planning (Stöhr 1981; Moulaert and Sekia 2003). The strength of the local, according to local development studies, is that it increases actors' capacity of action. It is through 'places' that social actors revindicate their development claims (Bellemare and Klein 2011a).

In the light of these evolutions, governance and development analyses became more spatialized, focusing explicitly on governance, and the norms and conventions in the negotiation of the distribution of wealth (e.g. Painter and Goodwin 1995; Collinge 1999; Goodwin 2001; Jessop 2001; Jessop and Sum 2006). Social innovation approaches form a particular strand belonging to the literature dealing with governance and development while developing analytical frameworks that allow us to identify factors and conditions that shape regulatory practices that benefit weaker social groups. A number of social innovation researchers caved their explanations of territorial development on place's embeddedness in wider networks of relational assets and spatial proximity, and on the particular role creative actions and strategies have in transforming spatial relations in ways that empower formally excluded people and that better succeed in addressing social needs (see for example Lévesque et al. 1996; Fontan

et al. 2003, 2005; Moulaert et al. 2005; Moulaert and Sekia 2003; Moulaert and Nussbaumer 2005; González and Healey 2005). The following discussion shows how these authors look into the 'black box' of forces, resources, activation strategies and processes that determine development processes.

9.3.2 The Social Region, Local Initiatives and Socio-Territorial Capital

In reaction to the technicist and economistic bias in the study of regional and local economic development, Moulaert and Nussbaumer (2005) link social innovation to territorial innovation models. They argue that much of the research on learning regions and innovative clusters concentrates on how to implement concepts (development models) that coincide best with the dominant growth model and market-competitive logic. This, they suggest, creates a new polarization in the development of regional and local societies. As an alternative, it is argued, broader views of development have to be included. This leads to a strand of literature that is based on the reconversion of local economies in post-Fordism that links territorial development with social innovation (Lévesque et al. 1996; Fontan et al. 2003, 2005; Moulaert et al. 2005; Moulaert and Sekia 2003; Moulaert and Nussbaumer 2005).

Moulaert and Nussbaumer (2005) propose an approach to development that is based on the reproduction of various interrelated types of 'non business' capital according to their own existential logic: ecological, human, social. Resources identified in different territorial innovation models range from traditional production factors of labour and capital, to a broad range of actors, human capital, infrastructure, institutions, culture, small firms and social capital. The capacity of activation of resources is explained as the capacity of innovation and social learning through a complex set of institutions and relations.

In the same vein, Tremblay, Klein and Fontan, throughout their work (Tremblay et al. 1998; Fontan et al. 1999, 2003, 2005; Fontan and Klein 2004) insist on the idea that social innovation is a necessary factor to explain vitality and success in local and regional economic renewal. On the basis of their observations in the Québec context, and adopting a multidisciplinary approach (sociology, geography, economy), they underline the crucial role of social actors and social or cultural 'non-productive' activities in the redeployment of zones in decline (Tremblay et al. 1998). These authors' research, all based at the CRISES Centre for Research on Social Innovations, is partly based on theories and concepts which attempt to explain the existence of certain innovative environments or innovative milieus that point to the inseparability of culture and economy (Benko and Lipietz 1998; Storper and Scott 1988). In their development analysis, territorial proximity is superimposed with relational, institutional and cultural forms of proximity, and territorial identity (appartenance) is stressed. The analytical framework is expanded with insights from 'urban regime theory' (Stone 1989), and social innovation as a way to discuss social transformation (Alter 2000; Callon 1989). Based on these strands of literature, Tremblay et al. (1998) develop reflections on territorial innovation systems, with a special interest in the role of social actors in collective learning, and its sedimentation in the construction of bottom-up innovation systems.

Furthermore, social innovation is linked to a successful combination of exogenous and locally mobilized resources. According to Klein et al. (2008) and Klein

and Tremblay (2009), the combination of local and extra-local resource-mobilization processes constitutes a crucial factor in the triggering of local initiatives into collective action. The resource-mobilization processes generate the dynamics necessary to create the conditions for partnerships and local empowerment that in turn stimulate a knowledge-building-cycle that is bound to repeat itself (Klein et al. 2008). This process is what, according to the authors, generates the power for changing institutional structures and thus enables social innovation. Klein (2008) indeed stresses the need to combine exogenous and endogenous resources through communities' participation in supra-local networks, mainly because deprived areas are typically characterized by deficient commercial and state service provision, which contributes to the increase of spatial injustices. As a consequence, a large market of unmet needs arises that is often taken up by social economy and community-based organizations.

Also essential in the work at CRISES is the notion of 'socio-territorial capital' and its mobilization by local communities in given geographical spaces. This concept suggests that a set of resources, a spatial dimension, a social frame and a capacity to create added value through institutional and organizational arrangements (Klein 2008) are all crucial in the process of socio-economic area development (Fontan et al. 2005).

9.3.3 Integrated Area Development (IAD)

The 'Integrated Area Development' (IAD) framework seeks to create opportunities to socially redress 'disintegrated areas' (Moulaert and Leontidou 1995) by bringing together different types of actors and their aspirations, solutions for the threats to sustainable development (economic, ecological, socio-cultural and political), restoring links with other areas in the city and rebuild a neighbourhood and community identity. To this purpose IAD aims to valorize the diversity of historical social, institutional, artistic cultures and traditions as resources for community based development. Furthermore it considers the transformation of governance relations from a local or bottom-up to a bottom-linked architecture, in which different governance scales (e.g. neighbourhood, city, region, national and international) find each other, as a necessary dimension of IAD. In terms of neighbourhood co-operation, inhabitants, organizations, movements, diverse public and private agents etc. are observed to come together and create opportunities to communicate with each other to build up a neighbourhood development strategy (Moulaert 2000). This cooperation often happens spontaneously through social mobilization initiated to overcome severe problems of deprivation.

IAD approaches thus focus on how different forms of fragmentation of urban space (socio-economic, physical) may be overcome. It is suggested that different actors should grasp their relations to space to improve uses of space. Different groups, actors, agents, people with area-based development agenda's have to interactively learn how to build in the spatial dimensions, for example by integrating housing functions with public space, reorganising space in order to accommodate a diversity of social relations, establishing a park hosting different functions and actively involving people coming from inside and outside the neighbourhood in socio-political networking, etc. Spatial outcomes of social innovation are found in the consolidation and reconfiguration of networks. The creation of openings for previously excluded social groups in spatially articulated governance systems or place-making decision centres is one of such an example (see e.g. Van Dyck 2010).

9.4 DEVELOPING THE TERRITORIAL APPROACH

The literature review shows that social innovation studies open new perspectives for local and regional development, both as a scale of action and analysis. It does so by stressing the use and organization of space as a new opportunity-set for change initiatives, by democratizing territorial governance dynamics and by linking local and regional bottom-up development agendas to the multi-scalar social relations that should enhance them.

The territorialized perspective of social innovation particularly allows the explanation of the relationships between the satisfaction of human needs on the one hand and social empowerment on the other through the reproduction of community social relations. With a focus on path and space dependency and interrelated socio-territorial capitals, the social innovation process is about transforming relationships in which actors are embedded in order to increase control over these relationships and so impact on development trajectories. The relation between social innovation and territory can therefore be defined as impacting on socio-spatial relationships in such a way that local autonomy is increased in the construction of futures. Actors tend to be involved in both local networks and external networks, but the size, direction and intensity of networks may vary. Hence, in this approach territorial development is considered as a complex mesh of networks in which resources are mobilized and in which the control of the process consists of an interplay between local and external forces (Klein et al. 2008).

Despite its richness in recognizing institutional dynamics as having a key role in development, territorialized social innovation approaches still remain extremely vague about the importance of spatial organization as an analytical unit in explaining social innovation or the capacity for empowerment (Van Dyck 2010; Van den Broeck 2011). To overcome this gap Van den Broeck (2011) argues that spatial capital can be analysed as part of socio-territorial capital.

Analysis of urban interventions, spatial layout and design is a field still to be explored in the social innovation literature, and interesting pathways may be opened when social innovation perspectives to territorial development are cross pollinated with design-oriented approaches. The 'social innovation approach to space through social space' indeed has important assets to offer as to the analysis of the processes that have led to the physical construction and organization of space and place, as well as to the institutional and social design of participation processes (communication, decision-making) that could lead to an improved use of space in its various dimensions, including the physical.

The weak incorporation of the material dimension of territory in social innovation is also particularly striking with regard to its failure in dealing with non-human components of territory (land, water, soil, air ...). With regard to territorial development, so far the social innovation literature has mainly focused on the reconfiguration of social, and socio-spatial, relations through exploring the interaction of bottom-up formal and informal initiatives and urban policy-making. The environment, ecological degradation, and so on, make an appearance in many studies, yet few of them truly investigate the nature-society relationship. A social innovation perspective could contribute to bridging overlapping, but too often only weakly connected environmental, social justice and environmental justice movements. It holds the potential to connect governance dynamics to practices that shape environmentally less destructive and socially just situations (see for example Parra 2010; Parra, Chapter 10).

In the wake of the current socio-economic and ecological global crisis, spatial strategies that arise from situations of social and economic decline have to take the agency of non-human actors seriously. Social innovation in territorial development will necessarily imply socio-ecological innovation.

9.5 CONCLUSION

The literature review in this chapter pointed to differences between social innovation approaches that are grounded in local and regional development approaches and those that are based on business innovation theoretical frameworks focusing on coalitions and networks and organizational forms. In the latter, space is generally approached in a reductionist container view. Economic geography and related disciplines, however, have shown the necessity of territorial analysis to explain development. De-territorialized views of social innovation run the same risks of other flat development approaches with a tendency of universalistic histories such as those common in neoclassical regional economy models.

If the aim of social innovation studies is to foster socially innovative initiatives that tackle underlying inequalities and injustices, we argue that it has to be inscribed in a development approach that takes seriously ethics as well as territory. Such an approach has the capacity to address development in all its dimensions (social, spatial, ecological . . .) while adopting an ethics of social justice. It would be shameful to lose this richness, which allows going beyond a containerized view of territory, by starting from the social dimension of territories, and by placing and considering innovation and networks in their spatio-historical context without losing sight of the material territoriality. Yet this may happen if we follow business innovation models, as expressed by e.g. the Six and Young foundation (Mulgan and Pulford 2010) and president Barroso (2011). Societal challenges, such as social exclusion or climate change impacts, will then no longer be considered as problems on ethical grounds, but problematic for they 'hamper [European] competitiveness and growth' (Mulgan and Pulford 2010, p. 6).

To contribute to meaningful and positive change it thus matters how we think about social innovation. Approaching social innovation as a solution to create new markets will not stimulate thinking and action in ways that support alternatives to market-driven development. As a matter of fact, no one could reasonably argue that adding up socially innovative initiatives instrumentally leads to changes able to tackle fundamental problems. Social innovation, as a way to go beyond business as usual, consequently, requires a broad understanding of initiatives as part of their multi-scalar contexts.

9.6   QUESTIONS FOR DISCUSSION

- What are the main differences between management based and alternative development based social innovation approaches?
- What do you think are the most

important dimensions of how territory is part and parcel of social innovation?
- How can social innovation be broadened to include innovation in socio-ecological relations?

NOTES

1. This chapter was prepared as part of WP 3.1 & WP 3.2 in the framework of the Spindus research project (www.spindus.org, last accessed 7 December 2012) financed by the Flemish government (IWT-SBO).
2. We understand territory as it is popular in *Latin* languages. From this viewpoint, territory is not related to national space, or top-down connection between state and territory. Instead it refers to the bottom-up spatial context for identity and cultural difference. We use the definition of Moulaert and Sekia (2003) – following Friedman and Weaver (1979) Territory and Function: The Evolution of Regional Planning. Edward Arnold, London – who define territory in terms of 'the clustering of social relations, the place where local culture and other non-transferable local features are superimposed'.

REFERENCES

(References in bold are recommended reading.)

Alter, Norbert (2000), *L'innovation ordinaire*, Paris: Presses universitaires de France.

Barroso, José Manuel (2011), 'Europe leading social innovation', speech at Social Innovation Europe initiative, Brussels, 17 March 2011.

Becattini, Giacomo (2002), 'Industrial Sectors and Industrial Districts: Tools for Industrial Analysis', *European Planning Studies*, **10** (4), 483–493.

Bellemare, Guy and J.L Klein (eds) (2011a), *Innovation sociale et territoire. Convergences théoriques et pratiques*, Québec: Presses de l'Université du Québec.

Bellemare, Guy and J-L. Klein (2011b), 'La question territoriale des pratiques sociales, des pratiques scientifiques et des savoirs', in G. Bellemare and J-L. Klein (eds), pp. 1–16.

Benko, Georges and A. Lipietz (1998), 'From the regulation of space to the space of regulation', *GeoJournal*, **44** (4), 275–281.

BEPA (2011), *Empowering people, driving change: Social innovation in the European Union*, Luxembourg: Publications Office of the European Union.

Bradford, Neil (2003), *Cities and Communities that Work: Innovative Practices, Enabling Policies*, Ottawa: Canadian Policy Research Network (CPRN).

Brenner, Neil (2004), *New state spaces. Urban governance and the rescaling of statehood*, New York: Oxford University Press.

Callon, Michel (1989), *La science et ses réseaux*, Paris: La Découverte.

Collinge, Chris (1999), 'Self-organisation of society by scale: a spatial reworking of regulation theory', *Environment and Planning D*, 17, 557–574.

Drewe, Paul and E. Hulsbergen (2007), 'Social innovation in urban revitalization – it might be a new experience', in M. Schrenk, V.V. Popovich and J Benedikt (eds), Proceedings of 12th International Conference on Urban Planning, Regional Development and Information Society and 2nd International Vienna Real Estate Conference, Vienna: CORP, pp. 737–744.

Fontan, Jean-Marc, J.L. Klein and D.G. Tremblay (1999), *Entre la métropolisation et le village global: les scènes territoriales de la reconversion*, Québec: Presses Universitaires du Québec.

Fontan, Jean-Marc, P. Hamel, R. Morin and E. Shragge (2003), 'The Institutionalization of Montreal's CDECS: From Grassroots Organizations to State Apparatus?', *Canadian Journal of Urban Research*, 12 (1), 58–77.

Fontan, Jean-Marc and J.L. Klein (2004), 'La mobilisation du capital socioterritorial: le cas du Technopole Angus', *Revue internationale d'action communautaire*, 52, 139–149.

Fontan, Jean-Marc, J.L. Klein and B. Lévesque (2005), 'The fight for jobs and economic governance: the Montreal model', in P. Booth and B. Jouve (eds), *Metropolitan Democracies: Transformations of the State and Urban Policy in Canada, France and the Great Britain*, Aldershot/Burlington: Ashgate Publishing, pp. 133–146.

Gerometta, Julia, H. Häussermann and G. Longo (2005), 'Social innovation and civil society in urban governance: strategies for an inclusive city', *Urban Studies*, 42 (11), 2007–2021.

González, Sara, and P. Healey (2005), 'A sociological institutionalist approach to the study of innovation in governance capacity', *Urban Studies*, 42 (11), 2055–2069.

Goodwin, Mark (2001), 'Regulation as process: Regulation theory and comparative urban and regional research', *Journal of Housing and the Built Environment*, 16 (1), 71–87.

Harvey, David (1989), 'From managerialism to entrepreneurialsim: the transformation of urban governance in late capitalism', *Geografiska Annaler, Series B: human geography*, 71 (1), 3–16.

Hillier, Jean, F. Moulaert, and J. Nussbaumer (2004), 'Trois essais sur le rôle de l'innovation sociale dans le développement territorial', *Géographie, Economie, Société*, 6 (2), 129–52.

Hudson, Ray (2000), *Production, places and environ-ment: changing perspectives in economic geography*, New Jersey: Prentice Hall.

Jessop, Bob (2001), 'Capitalism, the Regulation Approach, and Critical Realism', in A. Brown, S. Fleetwood and J. Michael Roberts (eds), *Critical Realism and Marxism*, London and New York: Routledge, pp. 88–115.

Jessop, Bob, and N.L. Sum (2006), *Beyond The Regulation Approach: Putting Capitalist Economies In Their Place*, Cheltenham, UK and Northampton, MA, USA: Edward Elgar Publishing.

Klein, Juan-Louis (2008), 'Territoire et régulation: l'effet instituant de l'initiative locale', *Cahiers de recherche sociologique*, 45, 41–57.

Klein, Juan-Louis and D. Harrisson (2007), *L'innovation sociale: émergence et effets sur la transformation des sociétés*, Québec: Presses Universitaires du Québec.

Klein, Juan-Louis, J.M. Fontan and D.G. Tremblay (2008), 'Local development as social innovation: the Case of Montreal', in P. Drewe, J-L. Klein and E. Hulsbergen (eds), *The Challenge of social innovation in urban revitalization*, Amsterdam: Design/Science/Planning Techne Press.

Klein, Juan-Louis and D.G. Tremblay (2009), 'Social actors and their role in metropolitan governance in Montréal: towards an inclusive coalition?', *GeoJournal*, 75 (2), 567–579.

Lévesque, Benoît, J.M. Fontan and J-L. Klein (1996), 'Les systèmes locaux de production. Conditions de mise en place et stratégie d'implantation pour le développement du Projet Angus', Étude réalisée sous la direction du collectif de recherche CRISES-ANGUS, en collaboration avec la Corporation de développement économique communautaire, Rosemont Petite-Patrie, Montréal.

MacCallum, Diana, F. Moulaert, J. Hillier and S. Vicari Haddock (eds) (2009), *Social innovation and territorial development*, Farnham: Ashgate Publishing Ltd.

Massey, Doreen (2005), *For space*, London: Sage Publications Inc.

Moulaert, Frank (2000), *Globalization and Integrated Area Development in European Cities*, Oxford: Oxford University Press.

Moulaert, Frank (2009), 'Social Innovation: Institutionally Embedded, Territorially (Re)produced', in MacCallum et al. (eds), pp. 13–31.

Moulaert, Frank and E. Leontidou (1995), 'Localités désintégrées et stratégies de lutte contre la pauvreté', *Espaces et Sociétés*, 78, 35–53.

Moulaert, Frank, F. Martinelli, E. Swyngedouw and S. González (2005), 'Towards alternative model(s) of local innovation', *Urban Studies*, 42 (11), 1969–1990.

Moulaert, Frank, and J. Nussbaumer (2005), 'Beyond the learning region: the dialectics of innovation and culture in territorial development', in R. Kloosterman and R. Boschma (eds) *Learning from clusters: a critical assessment*, Dordrecht: Springer, pp. 89–109.

Moulaert, Frank, and J. Nussbaumer (2008), *La logique sociale du développement territorial*, Québec: Presses de l'Université du Québec.

Moulaert, Frank, and F. Sekia (2003), 'Territorial Innovation Models: A Critical Survey', *Regional Studies*, 37 (3), 289–302.

Moulaert, Frank, E. Swyngedouw, F. Martinelli and S González (eds) (2010), *Can Neighbourhoods Save the City? Community Development and Social Innovation*, London and New York: Routledge.

Mulgan, Geoff and L. Pulford (2010), 'Study on social innovation', European Union / The Young Foundation, http://www.youngfoundation.org/publications/reports/study-social-innovation-bureau-european-policy-advisors (last accessed 25 February 2012).

Murray, Robin, J. Caulier-Grice and G. Mulgan (2010), *The open book of social innovation*, London: Young Foundation, NESTA.

Murray, Robin, G. Mulgan and J. Caulier-Grice (2009) 'How to Innovate: The tools for social innovation', draft, NESTA, www.youngfoundation.org (last accessed 15 October 2011).

Novy, Andreas, E. Hammer and B. Leubolt (2009), 'Social innovation and governance of scale in Austria', in MacCallum et al. (eds), pp. 131–147.

Oosterlynck, Stijn, J. Van den Broeck, L. Albrechts, F. Moulaert and A. Verhetsel (eds) (2011), *Strategic Spatial Projects: catalysts for change*, London and New York: Routledge.

Painter, Joe and M. Goodwin (1995), 'Local governance and concrete research: investigating the uneven development of regulation', *Economy and Society*, 24 (3), 334–356.

Parra, C. (2010), 'The governance of ecotourism as a socially innovative force for paving the way for more sustainable paths: the Morvan Regional Park case', PhD thesis, University of Lille 1, France.

Peck, Jamie, and A. Tickell (1992), 'Local modes of social regulation? Regulation Theory, Thatcherism and uneven development', *Geoforum*, **23** (3), 347–363.

Raco, Mike (2007), *Building Sustainable Communities: Spatial Policy and Labour Mobility in Post-War Britain*, Bristol: Policy Press.

Sayer, Andrew (1997), 'Critical Realism and the Limits to Critical Social Science', *Journal for the Theory of Social Behaviour*, **27** (4), 473–488.

Smith, Neil (2008[1984]), *Uneven Development*, Georgia: University of Georgia Press.

Stöhr, Walter (1981), 'Development from below. The bottom up and periphery inward development paradigm', in W. Stöhr and D. Taylor (eds), *Development from above or below?* Chichester: J. Wiley and Sons Ltd.

Stone, Clarence N. (1989), *Regime Politics: governing Atlanta 1946–1988*, Lawrence, KS: University Press of Kansas.

Storper, Michael, and A.J. Scott (1988), 'The geographical foundations and social regulation of flexible production complexes', in J. Wolch and M. Dear (eds), *The power of geography*, London: Allen and Unwin.

Thrift, Nigel (2002), 'The future of geography', *Geoforum*, 33 (4), 291–8.

Tremblay, Diane Gabrielle, J-L. Klein and J.M. Fontan (1998), 'Social Innovation, Networks and Economic Redevelopment in Montreal: New Perspectives Based on the Analysis of a Technopark Project', *Télé-université*, Université du Québec.

Van den Broeck, Pieter (2011), 'Analysing social innovation through planning instruments: a strategic-relational approach', in Oosterlynck et al. (eds), pp. 52–78.

Van Dyck, Barbara (2010), 'When the third sector builds the city: Brownfield transformation projects in Marseille and Montréal', PhD thesis, University of Antwerp.

Warf, Barney and S. Arias (2009), 'The reinsertion of space in the humanities and social sciences', in B. Warf and S. Arias (eds), *The spatial turn: interdisciplinary perspectives*, London and New York: Routledge, Introduction, pp. 1–10.

Wolk, Andrew (2007), 'Social Entrepreneurship and Government: a new breed of entrepreneurs developing solutions to social problems', in 'The Small Business Economy: A Report to the President, 2007', by The Small Business Administration, Office of Advocacy, http://archive.sba.gov/advo/research/sb_econ2007.pdf (last accessed 11 July 2012).

10. Social sustainability: a competing concept to social innovation?
Constanza Parra

10.1 INTRODUCTION

This chapter connects social innovation to social sustainability as an aspect of dialogic governance for territorial development. After a critical analysis of the subaltern status of the social pillar in sustainable development, Section 10.2 examines the meaning of the social, drawing attention to the social embeddedness of sustainable development and to the role of 'on the ground' social interactions in steering sustainable development. It is argued that the social is not – as often depicted – the weakest pillar of the triad but *the* fundamental engine of the sustainability system. Section 10.3 goes a step further, reinforcing the social nature of sustainable development with the aid of social innovation theory, highlighting the two theories' shared concern with governance, as well as their complementary role in encouraging an innovative logic of interactivity seeking a transformation in social relations oriented to define and satisfy human needs, on the one hand, and a more sustainable nature-society relationship, on the other. Socially innovative relations, social participation in governance and the production of alternative knowledge for decision-making are signalled as essential meeting points between these two approaches. The chapter concludes by examining these convergences in three examples of socially innovative practices pursuing sustainability aims. These examples show how the maturation of new forms of governance,

considered in this chapter as socially innovative for their role in pursuing sustainability, might lead toward an enhancement of social-ecological citizenship rights.

10.2 SUSTAINABLE DEVELOPMENT AND SOCIAL SUSTAINABILITY

The attempt to place and define sustainability and social sustainability from an integrated society perspective is rather recent (McKenzie 2004) and still insufficient. This section goes beyond the widespread 'globalist' sustainability explanation defining social sustainability in terms of equity and justice, and examines the 'social' signifying the modes in which human beings live together, interactively build societies and search for alternatives to address socio-ecological challenges.

10.2.1 On the Subaltern Status of Social Sustainability

Although it is gaining in status, social sustainability remains the frequent absentee in the sustainability discussion (Parra and Moulaert 2010, 2011; Lehtonen 2004). Instead, economic and ecological disciplines have concentrated most of their attention on the debate between 'weak' and 'strong' sustainability (White and Lee 2009). The difference between weak and strong sustainability relates to the 'constant capital' rule and to differing judgement about the limits to capital sub-stitution. This rule states that the total capital stock should be at least constant through time to allow future generations to enjoy a similar level of wealth as present societies. While there seems to be con-sensus that capital can take several forms – physically constructed, human, natural, social, institutional, cultural . . . – weak and strong sustainability diverge in their tolerance toward limits and choices in the substitution of one form for another. While very weak sustainability allows almost perfect capital substitutability and promotes the use of market mechanisms as drivers of change, stronger approaches are less optimistic regarding the real extent to which human made capital can (or should) substitute for natural capital in the long term. Unlike weaker approaches, strong ones reject the idea that growth of human capital can counterbalance depletion of natural capital and advocate for the sepa-rate maintenance of the different capital forms (Daly and Cobb 1989), which require interventions and regulation rather than a reliance on market mechanisms.

When we look at the discourses within the wide range between very weak and very strong sustainability, and contrast them with the genuine sustainability mission regarding needs and harmony among human beings and nature (WCED 1987), we realize that despite the lip-service paid to the social pillar of sustainability, it remains very difficult to find a consist-ent program combining humans, needs, governance and ecological sustainability. When trying to identify the reasons for this subaltern status of the social, other than the dominant influence of the economic and ecological paradigms, we should also acknowledge the still insufficient effort in properly conceptualizing the social in sustainable development. The earliest and still privileged way to deal with the social

dimension has been by using a narrow definition that restricts the meaning of 'social sustainability' to equity in the dis-tribution and access to resources. Rather than referring to the 'relational' content of the social and to the role of society and governance in dealing with the difficult interaction between the socio-economic and ecological dimensions of sustainable development, attention was directed to the material conditions of inter- and intra-generational equity, matching in this way the global macroeconomic standpoint from which sustainability was addressed in its early years.

It is logical, then, that academic con-tributions connecting social sustainability and social innovation are almost non-existent, despite the fact that both con-cepts have a similar ethical overlay and are concerned with a treatment of the social that is both normative and analytical. This chapter seeks to bring the social back to sustainable development analysis and policy implementation by reinforcing the social sustainability pillar with social inno-vation theory and research. As explored in the next sections, social innovation and social sustainability, as both conceptual constructs and social practices, are not only complementary: both are also mutu-ally reinforcing in their ethical overlays and companions in procuring grounded answers to the question of how to carry out sustainability and in examining those social practices and local capacities leading to sustainable societal transformations.

But before diving into these analyses let's briefly volunteer some explanations as to why the social sustainability pillar has been so poorly conceptualized. First, we recall the late and slow incorporation of the 'environment' in both classic and modern sociology, and in general in social sciences. The founders of sociology, in an attempt to create an independent scientific discipline, erected this new social science by keeping as much distance as possible from the already existing natural sciences (Leroy 2003). As a result, the analysis of the natural environment from a social sciences perspective came much later, and the interest of sociology in environmental issues began in earnest in the late eighties with the publication of the Brundtland report (WCED 1987) and the birth of sustainable development (Redclift 2010). Second, the ecology-centred perspective from which sustainable development has been addressed flows from an earlier anti-industrialization social movement starting in the second half of the sixties. A critical focus on economic growth and industrialization transformed an ecology concern into an economy one by shifting the attention towards the question of how to integrate the environmental variable into economic decision-making. Third, as a result of the above, a still-early transition towards interdisciplinarity in sustainable development, combined with the prominence of ecology and economy, not only left the 'social' out of the discussion but also ended up defining it in economic terms.

The section below deals with the still incomplete task of defining the social in sustainable development, first, by critically introducing the most common interpretations of social sustainability and, second, by enriching these perspectives with a more comprehensive definition of the social borrowing insights from sociology and anthropology.

10.2.2   Unpacking the Meaning of the Social

Until recently the most common attempt at defining social sustainability has been via the concepts of equity and justice within and across generations regarding the access to and distribution of wealth. According to this perspective, socio-cultural issues are defined 'as a function of equity and distribution', and discussed in terms of access to and control over resources (Stirling et al. 2007, p. 8). The pursuit of social equity goals was first approached from a globalist viewpoint and looked at economic and power disparities between the North and the South. The posterior 'territorialization' of sustainable development led to a transfer of social equity and ecological justice matters to the scale and responsibility of regions and localities (Zuindeau 2000). Nevertheless, regardless of the spatial scale from which sustainability is addressed, attention to imbalances of economic resources between rich and poor groups coupled 'social sustainability' with the struggle against poverty, inequality of income and broader human development goals. With regard to the environmental dimension, social imbalances among communities followed a comparable trend, and allied with contributions on environmental justice dealing with matters such as spatial segregation, export of ecological risks and delocalization of polluting industries to disadvantaged areas. Nonetheless, social sustainability cannot be restricted to overcoming poverty, growth disparities and justice issues (Ballet et al. 2004). If we limit the social in sustainable development to poverty alleviation and environmental justice, we risk falling again into the trap of reducing the sustainability debate to a rivalry between economic and ecologic logics. As explained in the following section, the social holds a multi-faceted role of articulation and human experiential interaction from which the quality and sustainability of societies is expected to materialize.

A relatively more recent way to approach the social has been through the concept of governance. By recognizing the inherent complexity of sustainability challenges, questions about how societies collectively organize to pursue sustainable development and who is responsible for steering this process arise. In the 1990s, governance was introduced as a fourth pillar joining the sustainability triad (Brodhag 1999, cited in Laganier et al. 2002), as also happened later with culture (Hawkes 2001). These contributions clearly express unease regarding the subaltern status of the social and make explicit the need to give social matters at least equal importance to those of economy, ecology and equity within the sustainability discussion. Yet, they present a limited view of the social and do not adequately reflect the multi-faceted social life of territories or, more precisely, the role of agency, structure, institutions, culture and plurality of interactive social relations 'on the ground' in providing alternatives and answers to the question of 'how to do sustainability'.

In an attempt to tackle such shortcomings, the four-pillar model has recently been questioned in contributions making a plea to rescue the centrality of the social dimension in sustainable development by means of vitalizing its meaning and role, starting from the concept of governance (Parra 2010; Parra and Moulaert 2011). These contributions emphasize that governance is not an addendum or fourth pillar but *the fundamental engine of the sustainability system*. The social sustainability dimension as governance symbolizes the all-embracing social thread that connects society and the natural environment, on the one hand, and opens the question about the custodians in charge of steering sustainable societal dynamics on the other. This approach gives a new balance to the sustainability triad and restores the original human and societal character inherent to the sustainability philosophy. Further, this idea of the social as governance,

which is dynamic and changing, recalls that sustainable development is a society *project* and not a 'uniquely successful' model that will be invariable along time and suitable for all territories. Sustainable development is a context-dependent concept that 'needs to be understood as a spatial concept because it is grounded in the material circumstances of people and place' (Morgan 2011, p. 88). According to this, governance, aligned with democracy and social participation, comes out as the socio-political process from which societies can learn how to deal with contemporary sustainability challenges and collectively create more sustainable paths of development.

It is important to recall that social sustainability has not only a normative but also an analytical meaning, which claims further theorization and calls for a definition of the 'social' that accounts for its complex multi-dimensional character (Littig and Grießler 2005). To this end, social innovation appears as a concept that nourishes the content of social sustainability with a renewed social dynamism. On the one hand, social innovation is meaningful to many of the most basic (social) sustainability core themes, ranging from power, political representation and institutions to the more experiential dimension of dynamic human relations. On the other hand, social sustainability as governance more explicitly opens social innovation to ecology and sustainability questions, both still embryonic themes in works on social innovation. By stimulating the development of relevant thought with an exchange of ideas between social sustainability and social innovation, we can raise issues related with the foundational role of citizens and entire plurality of actors in sustainable development.

Having introduced the basic connections between social sustainability and social innovation, let us turn for a moment to the deeper meaning of the 'social'. The social relates to the complexity of human life on this planet. It has to do with how human beings converse and interrelate across changing spatio-temporal contexts, and for that reason it alludes to the institutional, political and socio-cultural forms through which human life is being experienced and (re)produced in different places of this world. For Simmel (1909), social life is a constellation in movement through which reciprocal relationships between human beings are continuously reshaped. Interactions, associations, collaboration, as well as struggles and conflicts, produce social ties and connect individuals in a broader society (or 'togetherness') where the micro-social events of daily life are as important as the structural supports of our *vivre ensemble* (Lallement 2007). An essential implication of this characterization is that what is 'social' about sustainability and social innovation is their embeddedness in a dynamic structure of social relations. Indeed, combining social sustainability and social innovation recalls, on the one hand, the social embeddedness of governance relationships and, on the other, the values and normative choices underlying the collective action in the direction of both equity in the satisfaction of needs and integrated socio-ecological sustainability. In other words, this has to do with how societies organize taking in hand (or not) the ensemble of sustainability challenges needing and leading socio-political negotiations. Environmental matters in vogue governed in a context of uncertainty, such as climate change, energy, waste, biodiversity . . ., are examples that today generate countless social contestations, negotiations and institutional reorganizations at various territorial levels.

Going a step further in the analysis of the social tissue in which sustainability is embedded, we encounter the concept of culture, which – although it has been invoked in sustainability debates – still remains under-examined. Even if the under-examination of culture as a concept corresponds with the subaltern position of the social at the expense of economy and ecology, this omission is particularly incoherent if we recall that the overall aim of sustainability is a state of harmony between human life and nature (WCED 1987, p. 73). A division between culture and nature is paradoxical and artificial simply because human life is made up of culture and because it results from the dynamics of interaction of cultural diversity. Societal relations and governance are contingent on a relational view of culture founded on the human diversity produced from interactions of behaviours modes, worldviews and values shaping identities (Pilgrim and Pretty 2010). Believing that 'cultural systems are broadly based upon the way in which people interpret the world around them' (Geertz 1973, cited in Pilgrim and Pretty 2010, p. 3), this socialized and culturalized sustainability perspective (Parra and Moulaert 2011) breaks with the radical nature-culture dualism dominating positivist modern thinking. While being rooted in the 'moral conviction as to humankind's responsibility for nature' (Pawlowski 2008, p. 81), this socio-culturalized sustainability approach looks at how human beings consider and interrelate with nature, and retracts a groundless view of nature as unitary, pre-given and independent from human life. As an alternative, it brings out diversity and the complexities of the interactive-dialogical character of the nature-society-culture nexus.

The previous paragraphs elucidate the core role of the social in sustainable development and underlined the embeddedness of sustainable development in a dynamic structure of social relations, the indivisible continuity between society, culture and nature, and the multi-scalar interconnections among governance scales. Section 10.3 aims at further reinforcing the role of the social through a dialogue between social sustainability and social innovation. The dialogue between these two concepts calls attention to equity in the satisfaction of needs, to governance and social participation, as well as to processes of community learning and production of alternative knowledge for sustainability.

10.3 REINFORCING THE ROLE OF THE SOCIAL THROUGH COMPLEMENTARITIES BETWEEN SOCIAL INNOVATION AND SOCIAL SUSTAINABILITY

Having examined the subaltern status of the social in sustainable development and concluded that sustainability is meaningful only if understood in its socially embedded quality, this section shows how social innovation reinforces this social view of sustainable development. Social innovation in territorial development is founded on a strong link between the satisfaction of human needs and innovation in the social relationships of governance. It stresses the need to strengthen the socio-political integration of individuals and the importance of access to the necessary resources that will enable human needs satisfaction (Nussbaumer and Moulaert 2007). Social innovation consists of three dimensions: satisfaction of human needs, changes in social relationships and increasing socio-political capability. In the light of the sustainability problematic, these dimensions touch on equity issues, on the role of governance and social innovation in the col-

lective design of more sustainable paths of development that meet the satisfaction of human needs, and on the enhancement of the environmental and political rights of individuals as a basis for a new environmental citizenship (Parra 2010). The discussion about needs is doubly important. First, sustainability acts as an invitation to redefine needs via the reconnection of the social and the natural and, second, equity in the satisfaction of needs should be guaranteed from intra- and inter-generational perspectives. As to governance, social innovation provides clues to better understand the nature of collective action at different spatial levels in which the experiential dimension of sustainable development interacts with the social-ecological structure in which it operates and simultaneously moulds into different territories. The sections below further the analysis of these referents.

10.3.1 Complementarities in the Question about Needs

The first point of convergence between social sustainability and social innovation is that both concern needs. Sustainable development was originally defined as meeting human needs across and within generations (WCED 1987, p. 54). Nevertheless, even though almost every publication on sustainable development starts with a consideration about needs, the debate hardly ever goes beyond the enunciation of the tensions regarding needs satisfaction which are basically two: first, needs satisfaction for poor populations and, second, the threats that technology and human institutions impose to the capacity of the environment to satisfy needs of future generations (WCED 1987). Recognizing this deficiency, Rauschmayer et al. (2009, p. 140) state that needs, in the context of sustainable development, must include all the dimensions of human prosperity, including all the dimensions of a good human life, both objective and subjective, ranging from material exigencies to psychological states. In their definition, emotions, participation, negotiations, communication and collective learning are needs which must be taken into consideration and satisfied.

In the social innovation approach, human needs can be both material needs and intangible-existential needs – needs such as housing, work and social services are as fundamental as those for self-expression, culture, aesthetics, socio-ecological and political citizenship rights (see General Introduction). Human needs satisfaction in social innovation refers both to the processes through which communities should collectively define these needs and to socially innovative initiatives struggling for the satisfaction of needs that have not been satisfied through other channels. It is in this context that the social spaces in which new needs and aspirations or channels for human fulfilment are created and defended –for example a socially innovative and sustainability project imagined and implemented in a certain territory – claim further attention from a governance perspective addressing links between society, culture and nature.

The combination of these two 'social' approaches results in a collective definition of needs for the reproduction of the human existence and fulfilment, but subordinated to the conditions imposed by a sustainable society-nature co-evolution and to the values of fairness and democracy. This relational construction associates needs with governance and all social dynamics and socio-institutional processes reproducing social territories. For its part, the reproduction of socially sustainable territories is dependent on collective learning and community building dynamics

derived from socially innovative spatial interactions.

10.3.2 Socially Innovative Territorial Interactions and the Vital Need for Governance

With the territorialization of sustainable development (roughly from 2000 onwards), social dynamics, triggered by the commitment of governments to create Local Agenda 21 through socially participative governance, allowed the social dimension to gain importance as the societal engine of sustainability (see Mehmood and Parra, Chapter 4). This territorialization also brought embeddedness of territories and articulation among spatial scales to sustainable development to the fore. The debate started moving from an essentially a-spatial and global one towards the local level of governance, which was progressively recognized as fundamental in sustainable development (Selman 1996), finally giving way to multi-scalar approaches (Bressers and Rosenbaum 2003).

More recently, the identities of localities, their particular histories and the nature-culture nexus upon which places are built have been examined as vectors of a transformative social innovation introducing new socio-cultural dynamics nurturing adaptive transitions for sustainable development (Biggs et al. 2010). This vision of sustainability and territories as socially reproduced underscores their living, dynamic and changing nature and, accordingly, it allies social innovation in community relations with governance. This dynamic governance tissue accounts for today's multiple sustainability practices which go beyond well established Local Agenda 21 or official state programs. It is in this flourishing of territorial practices where social innovation and sustainability meet, especially in relation to the attention that both approaches give to the fundamental role of citizens and cultural plurality in the mission of imagining and designing the kind of development that we want to pursue as society. This plural and interactive governance, the foundation of what we could call 'socially innovative sustainability', involves social relations and interactions of organized groups of people, community-based organizations and socio-environmental movements, as well as individuals, leaderships, creative behaviours and plurality of nature-culture alternatives embodied in actors, institutions and territories.

10.3.3 Participation and Alternative Knowledge in Socio-Ecological Decision-Making

Sustainability projects are often highly complex, in the sense that they open new questions concerning trade-offs between socio-economic and ecological decisions. This means that broad public participation in decision-making is a prerequisite for sustainable governance (Stringer et al. 2006; Meadowcroft 2004). The distinction made by Leach and Scoones (2007, p. 7) between institutionally orchestrated forms of participation and more innovative ones is useful in revealing the variety of interactions and collective action relevant for the analysis of social innovation for sustainability. From the more orchestrated side, global collective actions led by international institutions or networks, and realized for example in the form of non-binding international agreements, transnational mobilizations and world forums, have played an important role in sustainability. As for 'grassroots movements', we find mobilizations oriented to meeting unsatisfied socio-ecological needs (e.g. provision of potable water for a commu-

nity), as well as struggles displaying novel socio-ecological demands (e.g. campaigns against genetically modified crops). An important feature of these green mobilizations is their capacity to produce socially innovative spaces of environmental citizenship, playing a part in reconnecting human cultures with nature. These forms of participation have in common their struggle for the inclusion of multiple voices and alternative knowledge in contemporary socio-ecological decision making.

The question of expertise and the production of knowledge is a major theme that connects sustainable development and social innovation and underlines the role of participation. In the past years we have seen how the current conditions of climate change and environmental uncertainty have not only put into question technically driven decision-making processes, but also unveiled the fallaciousness of the 'value independence' with which socio-ecological problems are often framed (Berkhout et al. 2003). Through a progressive recognition of the role of socio-political values, cultural beliefs and moral matters in structuring environmental problems and solutions, alternative forms of expertise and knowledge building have come to the fore: for instance post-normal knowledge, indigenous and citizens knowledge, collective learning . . . The idea behind this recognition is that learning and knowledge building cannot be limited to the technical rationality of scientific protocols. Instead, there is a need for governments and scientists to learn about and from the different social worlds, and thus to incorporate the tacit knowledge of diverse actors in the governance of territories. Here, again, we see the importance of participation and the need to build on local knowledge within civil society as a key element to foster socio-institutional capital for sustainability (Buckingham and Theobald 2003).

Social innovation for more socially sustainable communities will refer, then, to the processes by which people raise and frame socio-ecological problems, produce knowledge to deal with them and become socially engaged to address problems or transform unsustainable situations. The next section provides examples that illustrate these processes through which people take action to contest contemporary unsustainabilities and try to change them.

10.4 SOCIAL INNOVATION IN ITS CAPACITY TO PURSUE (SOCIAL) SUSTAINABILITY

The final section approaches social innovation as a mode of socio-ecological creative thinking, community knowledge and new governance relationships enhancing environmental citizenship rights. Starting from three examples, it briefly reflects on how people are currently involved in creative territorial strategies to fight for and advance sustainability.

10.4.1 Socially Sustainable 'Greener' Lifestyles

A variety of non-urban spaces with different levels of human intervention can be identified as privileged places where a variety of socially innovative community action for sustainable development has flourished. This is the case for various agro-ecological activities that combine a more sustainable use of nature with equity and justice goals, local and small-scale production and community governance. Organic agriculture, alternative agro-food networks, ecotourism, permaculture farms and sustainable energy are good examples of this (Dobson 2007; Parra 2010; Seyfang 2006; Järvela et al. 2009).

Local organic food production and alternative food networks are positioned as critical alternatives to global market driven agribusiness. This claim for bringing the food economy back home (Norberg-Hodge et al. 2002) is socially innovative, not because it makes agriculture more eco-friendly, but for the governance and value transformation that both underlies and results from the collective imagining and struggling for alternative production and consumption modes. There is a redefinition of needs and values driving people's choices and actions, from which life quality, North-South equity, healthy food and socio-ecological sustainability become very important for certain communities. This cultural transformation is also reflected in sustainable ecotourism practices, revival of local markets, launch of fair trade commerce initiatives and community experiments for alternative energy production. All these alternative voices have in common the progressive maturation of a set of values and modes of action that are foundational to a new ecological citizenship, and together they face the challenge of enhancing their capacity to transmit this local ecological knowledge and activism to consumers, visitors and public institutions.

10.4.2 Projects Reconnecting Human Beings with Nature

Revitalization projects are perhaps a positive reflection of the ongoing negotiation and recognition of the importance of ecological citizenship rights. Particularly interesting is the work of Pilgrim et al. (2009) on rural revitalization for cultural continuity and environmental quality. With a focus on indigenous communities, yet tackling an issue of great importance for society as a whole, these authors explain that the disconnection between nature and culture causes harm, particularly to those who are more vulnerable and marginalized (Pilgrim et al. 2009; Pilgrim and Pretty 2010). Therefore a reconnection with spiritual beliefs, cosmologies, traditions and deep cultural identities that interlink with nature and ecological cycles is essential to reinvigorate, socially heal and empower marginalized indigenous and non-industrial communities. This is meaningful not only for those communities directly involved in this culture-nature reconnection work, but also from a broader perspective related to the debate on learning, *savoirs* and diversity of thinking in a context where technology-driven paradigms have shown their limits. It is certainly not an easy task to rebuild social cohesion and social sustainability ties where the dynamics of social exclusion have already caused considerable harm; however community-driven reconnection projects identified by Pilgrim et al. (2009) on traditional food, ecotourism, human and community rights, culture and language, are already showing positive effects on empowerment and the recovery of identity and pride through reconnections with the land.

The philosophy of urban community gardens is very much in tune with reconnection projects. In these gardens, the goals of ecological restoration, empowerment and the healing of human and community relationships are expected to meet, as expressed by Wilson apropos community gardens (1991, cited in Irvine et al. 2009, p. 33): 'we must build landscapes that heal and empower, that make intelligible our relations with each other and the natural world'. Certainly, there is a distance between this ideal and reality, yet research shows connections between urban gardening and sustainability, including local food production, ecological impact on urbanization and social and reinvigoration and healing of communities (Irvine

et al. 2009; Silk 1995, cited in Irvine et al. 1999, p. 36).

10.4.3 Social Innovation in Research for Building Territorial Sustainability

A third interesting experience to examine through the lens of socially innovative action for sustainability is participatory action research in the field of environmental planning. This has been undertaken through stakeholder creativity workshops, scenario writing, environmental assessments scenarios and back-casting scenarios, with the purpose of stimulating a discussion with local communities about contemporary sustainability challenges and thereby triggering collective envisioning of alternative development scenarios for the future. Selman et al. (2010) present recent planning experiments of imaginative engagement as mode of citizen participation with very interesting results. The experience they describe involved inviting communities with a common socio-ecological governance problem to join a dialogue and meetings to collectively think of better alternatives for the governance and use of a river in the UK. This imaginative engagement appears as a socially innovative 'on the ground' experiential situation in the sense that it conjoins participation, knowledge building and environmental consciousness through a community (re)thinking of basic community needs in the search for sustainability.

10.5 CONCLUSION

This chapter had three interrelated intentions: i) to criticize the limited attention given to the social pillar in sustainable development; ii) to explore in detail the meaning of the social so as to explain its role as the basic engine for a sustainable socio-ecological transformation; iii) to reinforce the social nature of sustainable development with the aid of social innovation theory and practice, taking advantage of their common socially interactive logics.

For many years, the focus of many environmental studies and research has been on how ecological problems evolve and the failures of the contemporary governance of our commons. As an alternative, this chapter connects social innovation with sustainability as an invitation to change perspective and give attention to ongoing directions in collective experimentation for territorial sustainability. From this chapter we conclude then that social sustainability is more than a normative layer offering a direction for change towards equity, but rather an entire societal project inviting multiple voices to debate, think, imagine and negotiate a more sustainable transformation founded in more harmonious nature-culture relations. In this task, social sustainability and social innovation appear as complementary in providing 'grounded answers' to the question of how to encourage and carry out sustainability projects in territories, as illustrated in the governance transformations and knowledge that is deep-rooted in new countryside lifestyles, nature-culture reconnection projects and action research to collectively imagine sustainability.

10.6   QUESTIONS FOR DISCUSSION

- The social has been the great forgotten dimension in sustainable development, why is this so?
- How does social innovation reinforce the social nature of sustainable development?
- If we dispense with the idea that society, culture and nature are separate, what are the implications for socially sustainable development?
- Can you think of other cases of socially innovative practices building territorial sustainability?

REFERENCES

(References in bold are recommended reading.)

Ballet, J., J-L. Dubois and F-R. Mahieu (2004), 'A la recherche du développement socialement durable: concepts fondamentaux et principes de base', *Développement durable et territoires*, Dossier 3: Les dimensions humaine et sociale du Développement Durable, http://developpementdurable.revues.org/1165 (last accessed 15 January 2012).
Berkhout, F., M. Leach and I. Scoones (2003), 'Shifting perspectives in environmental social science', in F. Berkhout, M. Leach and I. Scoones (eds), *Negotiating Environmental Change: New Perspectives from Social Sciences*, Cheltenham, UK and Northampton, MA, USA: Edward Elgar Publishing, pp. 1–31.
Biggs, R., F. Westley and S. Carpenter (2010), 'Navigating the back loop: fostering social innovation and transformation in ecosystem management', *Ecology and Society*, **15** (2), 9, http://www.ecologyandsociety.org/vol15/iss2/art9 (last accessed 15 March 2011).
Bressers, H. and W. Rosenbaum (eds) (2003), *Achieving Sustainable Development: The Challenge of Governance across Social Scales*, London: Praeger.
Buckingham, S. and K. Theobald (eds) (2003), *Local environmental sustainability*, Cambridge: Woodhead.
Brodhag C. (1999), 'Les enjeux de l'information en langue française sur le développement durable', *Université d'Eté Francophone développement durable et systèmes d'information*, Saint-Etienne, 5–9 July.
Daly, H.E. and J.B. Cobb (1989), *For the Common Good: Redirecting the Economy toward Community, the Environment and a Sustainable Future*, Boston: Beacon Press.
Dobson, A. (2007), 'Environmental citizenship: towards sustainable development', *Sustainable development*, **15**, 276–285.
Geertz, C. (1973), *The Interpretation of Cultures*, New York: Basic Books.
Hawkes, J. (2001), *The fourth pillar of sustainability. Culture's essential role in public planning*, Melbourne: Cultural Development Network & Common Ground Press.
Irvine, S., L. Johnson and K. Peters (1999), 'Community gardens and sustainable land use

planning: A case-study of the Alex Wilson community garden', *Local Environment*, **4** (1), 33–46.

Järvela, M., P. Jokinen, S. Huttunen and A. Puupponen (2009), 'Local food and renewable energy as emerging new alternatives of rural sustainability in Finland', *European Countryside*, **2**, 113–124.

Lallement, M. (2007), *Histoires des idées sociologiques des origines à Weber*, Paris: Armand Colin Editeur.

Laganier, R., B. Villalba and B. Zuindeau, B. (2002), 'Le développement durable face au territoire: éléments pour une recherche pluridisciplinaire', *Développement durable et territoires* Dossier 1: Approches territoriales du Développement Durable, http://developpementdurable.revues.org/774 (last accessed 3 February 2011).

Leach, M. and I. Scoones (2007), 'Mobilising Citizens: Social movements and the politics of knowledge', IDS Working paper, 276, January 2007, Brighton: Institute of Development Studies.

Lehtonen, M. (2004), 'The environmental-social interface of sustainable development: capabilities, social capital, institutions', *Ecological Economics*, **49** (2), 199–214.

Leroy, P. (2003), 'Un bilan de la sociologie de l'environnement en Europe', in C. Gendron and J-G. Vaillancourt (eds), *Développement durable et participation publique*, Montréal: Presses de l'Université de Montréal, pp. 25–48.

Littig, B. and E. Grießler (2005), 'Social sustainability: a catchword between political pragmatism and social theory', *International Journal of Sustainable Development*, **8** (1/2), 65–79.

McKenzie, S. (2004), 'Social sustainability: towards some definitions', Hawke Research Institute Working Paper Series No. 27, Adelaide: University of South Australia.

Meadowcroft, J. (2004), 'Participation and sustainable development: modes of citizen, community and organisational involvement', in W. Lafferty (ed.) *Governance for sustainable development: the challenge of adapting form to function*, Cheltenham, UK and Northampton, MA, USA: Edward Elgar Publishing, pp. 162–190.

Morgan, K. (2011), 'The Green State: Sustainability and the power of purchase', in A. Pike, A. Rodríguez-Pose and J. Tomaney (eds) *Handbook of local and regional development*, London: Routledge, pp. 87–96.

Norberg-Hodge, H., T. Merrifield and S. Gorelick (2002), *Bringing the Food Economy Home: Local Alternatives to Global Agribusiness*, London: Zed Books.

Nussbaumer, J. and F. Moulaert (2007), 'L'innovation sociale au coeur des débats publics et scientifiques. Un essai de déprivatisation de la société', in J.L. Klein and D. Harrisson (eds) *L'innovation sociale: emergence et effets sur la transformation des societies*, Québec: Presses de l'Université du Québec.

Parra, C. (2010), 'The governance of ecotourism as a socially innovative force for paving the way for more sustainable paths: the Morvan Regional Park case', PhD thesis, University of Lille 1, France.

Parra, C. and F. Moulaert (2010), 'Why sustainability is so fragilely social . . .', in S. Oosterlynck, J. Van den Broeck, L. Albrechts, F. Moulaert and A. Verhetsel (eds) *Strategic spatial projects: catalysts for change*, London: Routledge, pp. 242–256.

Parra, C. and F. Moulaert (2011), 'La nature de la durabilité sociale: vers une lecture socioculturelle du développement territorial durable', *Développement durable et territoires*, **2 (2),** http://developpement durable.revues.org/8970 (last accessed 10 July 2011).

Pawlowski, A. (2008), 'How many dimensions does sustainable development have?', *Sustainable Development*, **16** (2), 81–90.

Pilgrim, S. and J. Pretty (eds) (2010) *Nature and culture: rebuilding lost connections*, London, UK and Washington, US: Earthscan.

Pilgrim, S. and J. Pretty (2010), 'Nature and culture: an introduction', in S. Pilgrim and J. Pretty (eds), pp. 1–20.

Pilgrim, S., C. Samson and J. Pretty (2009), 'Rebuilding Lost Connections: How revitalisation projects contribute to cultural continuity and improve the environment', Interdisciplinary Centre for Environment and Society Paper 2009-01, University of Essex.

Rauschmayer, F., I. Omann, J. Frühman and L. Bohunovsky (2009), 'Le développement durable vingt ans après: plaidoyer pour une seconde étape', in J. Theys, C. Tertre, F. Rauschmayer and B. Zuindeau (eds) *Le développement durable, la seconde étape*, La Tour d'Aigue: Edition de l'Aube, pp. 115–185.

Redclift, M. (2010), 'The transition out of carbon dependence: the crises of environment and markets', in M. Redclift and G. Woodgate (eds) *The international handbook of environmental sociology* **(2nd edition), Cheltenham, UK and Northampton, MA, USA: Edward Elgar Publishing, pp. 121–135.**

Selman, P. (1996), *Local sustainability: Managing and planning ecologically sound places*, London: Paul Chapman.

Selman, P., C. Carter, A. Lawrence and C. Morgan (2010), 'Re-connecting with a neglected river through imaginative engagement', *Ecology and Society*, **15** (3), 18, http://www.ecologyandsociety.org/vol15/iss3/art18 (last accessed 10 July 2011).

Seyfang, G. (2006), 'Ecological citizenship and sustainable consumption: examining local food networks', *Journal of Rural Studies*, **22** (4), 385–395.

Silk, D. (1985), "Urban agriculture", paper submitted to the World Commission on Environment and Development.

Simmel, G. (1909), 'The problem of sociology', *American Journal of Sociology*, **15** (3), 289–320.

Stirling, A., M. Leach, L. Mehta, I. Scoones, A. Smith, S. Stagl and J. Thompson (2007), 'Empowering Designs: towards more progressive appraisal of sustainability', STEPS Working Paper 3, Brighton: STEPS Centre.

Stringer, L.C., A.J. Dougill, E. Fraser, K. Hubacek, C. Prell, and M.S. Reed (2006), 'Unpacking "participation" in the adaptive management of social-ecological systems: a critical review', *Ecology and Society*, **11** (2), 39, available at http://www.ecologyandsociety.org/vol11/iss2/art39/ (last accessed 15 January 2013).

WCED (World Commission on Environment and Development) (1987), *Our Common Future*, Oxford: Oxford University Press.

White, L. and G.J. Lee (2009), 'Operational research and sustainable development: tackling the social dimension', *European Journal of Operational Research*, **193** (3), 683–692.

Wilson, A. (1991), *The culture of nature: North American landscape from Disney to the Exxon Valdez*, Toronto: Between the Lines.

Zuindeau, B. (ed.) (2000), *Développement durable et territoire*, Villeneuve d'Ascq (Nord): Presses Universitaires du Septentrion.

11. Theorizing multi-level governance in social innovation dynamics

Marc Pradel Miquel, Marisol García Cabeza and Santiago Eizaguirre Anglada

11.1 INTRODUCTION

Governance objectives and mechanisms have been changing in European cities in the last 20 years. This has served to maintain cities' competitive advantage, but also to preserve existing social models. Transformations in governance have implied both a state reorganization in multi-layered systems of policy-making and policy delivery (i.e. welfare and social care) and the opening up of the policy process to the input of non-state market and civil society actors (Brenner 2004; Jessop 2004; Kazepov 2010). In this changing framework it is possible to develop social innovation by public, private and civil-society actors as they find more space for intervening in the design and implementation of urban policies. They are supposed to find more room for manoeuvre given the higher degree of decentralization and the openness of decision-making processes to non-state actors. This chapter examines the relation between social innovation and governance focusing on how socially creative strategies can transform governance mechanisms and at the same time be influenced by them.

Following the definition in the introduction of this book, social innovation refers to processes that generate a) the provision, in response to social needs, of resources and services, b) the development of trust and empowerment within marginalized populations, and c) the transformation of those power relations that produce social exclusion through the transformation of governance mechanisms.

Multi-level governance is an empirical concept useful to describe new forms of state power organization based on a double process: an increase in the distribution of power between different levels of government and the creation of policy-making coalitions that only in part consist of representatives of the state (Giersig, 2008, p. 55) and that operate at different levels. These coalitions tend to blur the boundaries between the responsibilities of state, market and civil society. This generates new opportunities for civil-society and market actors to influence policy-making processes. Besides, governance coalitions change over time and the composition of actors, the goals to achieve, the structure and the internal rules of the coalition are redefined every time a network of actors is established (Giersig 2008, p. 58).

The dynamics between social innovation and governance are twofold. Firstly, the development of socially innovative practices influences governance through the creation of new mechanisms for the provision of resources, the creation of new collective actors and the influence exercised by actors on formal mechanisms of decision-making. In this sense, social innovation allows for new ways of conceptualizing and approaching policy problems that go beyond analyses centred on the individual, such as providing capabilities to individual citizens. While governments have used an 'individual approach' (Dean 2009), for instance in the implementation of welfare to work policies, the concept of social innovation pays attention to the individual embedded in social groups and focuses on the collective responses to social problems as a way to reinforce these capabilities. Secondly, governance structures and dynamics have an influence on the capacity of different actors to develop socially innovative practices. Thus the degree of centralization of decision-making, the selective participation of certain actors over others and the tradition of welfare are elements that frame the action of public, private and civil society actors.

There are many different ways in which actors promote social innovation. Public actors, for example, can innovate promoting new forms of organization and coordination, and/or more openness to other actors in the provision of services and resources. Private actors, such as companies active in the social economy, can be linked to social innovation when they promote new forms of trust and relations between citizens and develop new forms of economic exchange. Finally, sectors of organized citizens who may disagree with mainstream policy formulations can put forward alternative ways of addressing new risks that have not been taken into account by public and market institutions. Often, these different actors interplay, and social innovation takes place when there is a creative collaboration between public actors or market agents and civil society organizations pursuing the empowerment of citizens and the change of social exclusion dynamics.

Actors operating at multiple levels are not only constrained by other actors at different levels of government, but also have to deal with the pitfalls of democratic transparency in the policy making processes (Swyngedouw 2005). Therefore, the extent to which different kinds of actors engaged in social innovation can influence policy (creating bottom-link processes) in a multi-level context is an open question, subject to empirical analysis (García 2006; Moulaert et al. 2007). This chapter addresses this question from a theoretical and methodological point of view. A methodological approach to dealing with this question must focus particular attention on the action of socially innovative actors who develop practices for social inclusion that can transform governance in a direct or an indirect way (González and Healey 2005). Two related issues must be addressed: 1) the innovative processes to obtain material and immaterial resources in order to tackle social exclusion, and 2) the way this process can lead to a transformation of the governance mechanisms (and therefore might produce changes in power relations in areas that deal with social exclusion dynamics). When developing socially innovative practices, actors are framed in a particular governance context. It is in this framework that they develop innovative actions to obtain material resources. At the same time, these processes of innovation can produce changes in that framework, generating more openness in decision-making. Thus governance is at the same time a framework and a field for social innovation.

Regarding the first dimension (governance as a framework), social innovation processes take place in given governance schemes. These frameworks differ depending not only on the national governance system but also on the policy field in which they take place with different institutions and traditions in delivering policies. Following the approach adopted by the KATARSIS project[1] we have distinguished four policy fields covering human needs: labour market, housing and neighbourhood, education and training, and health and environment. In relation to the second dimension (governance as a field), governance is itself a field in which social innovation can be detected. In that sense socially creative strategies (SCS) can contain innovative practices aimed at creating more openness and participation as well as changes in power relations. In other words governance is practiced inside the collectives and in the relations between those collectives and institutions, governments as well as private actors.

The chapter follows three steps. The first step briefly addresses the first question, that is, how actors promote social innovation in a multilevel framework. The second step analyses the strategies and internal dynamics of actors involved in socially creative strategies. The last step evaluates the impact of SCS on and through multilevel governance.

11.2   A GOVERNANCE READING OF SOCIAL INNOVATION

Governance is a transversal institutionalization of social change which allows innovation in the ways of addressing social exclusion dynamics that occur in different policy fields and cause social fragmentation. This approach involves looking at governance mechanisms not only as a result of policy choices, but also as processes and outcomes of power relations and conflictive positions between social groups. Cities are arenas of conflict in which the consequences of social tensions caused by unequal life chances can take the form of collective action and translate in 'new constitutions of citizenry' (Weber 1978, pp. 1233–1380; Dahrendorf 1979). Institutional actors can promote social innovation through

reorganizing themselves and/or facilitating the participation of certain actors or adopting new approaches to policy problems. Citizens, on their side, can force institutions to change policy orientations when their political capability is strong. In the absence of strong mobilization, local organized citizens operate with modest objectives, such as influencing policy choices that affect the life conditions of their communities. This is often the case of civil-society groups involved in social innovation (Fontan et al. 2009; Lelieveldt et al. 2009).

When analysing the relation between SCS and governance we propose considering how welfare states have reorganized their welfare structures towards a multilevel frame and to what extent non-state actors are participating in policy-making processes (Brenner 2004; Jessop 2002; Le Galès 2002). The multi-level form has occurred partly because central governments have proved to be inefficient in dealing with increasing social diversity in cities and regions and with the associated new social risks (Andreotti et al. 2012). Indeed, although there has been a decentralization of welfare provisions and to some extent finances, central governments have retained control over fiscal management of resources creating multilevel frameworks in which non-state actors have to operate. Moreover, these general processes display a variety of models of multi-level governance, ranging from some federal political structures that give a stronger role to regions to more centralized political structures (Wollmann 2009). These frameworks influence the role of different government levels in developing social innovation as well as the openness to participation by non-state actors (Sintomer et al. 2008, p. 168; Röcke 2009). Thus, the policy context influences the capacity of certain non-state actors and can hinder the entrance of new actors in governance networks. In sum, there is dynamism and a tension between different actors for the participation in policy-making through multi-level governance processes, and the configuration of governance networks differs from one country to another, and from one policy field to another.

As different social actors try to calibrate various governance mechanisms, forms of 'meta-steering' or 'metagovernance' (Jessop 2002, p. 78) emerge creating a framework for the coordination between private, societal and public actors[2] (that is, between market, exchange and reciprocity mechanisms). Through the EU, national states have defined how different actors in a governance network can pursue their objectives, creating the framework for negotiation (Jessop 2002). This framework has been defined through the creation of the Single Market, the promotion of regional and local levels in policy-making or the involvement of non-state actors through local partnerships (Geddes and Bennington 2001). Although the impact of the EU is filtered in each Member State according to internal policy-making traditions, there has been a common commitment towards more decentralization and opportunities to participate for non-state actors. The EU has encouraged new opportunities for civil-society actors and for decision-making at the local level and has shared the definition of the rules and conditions of this participation with national governments. However, in most policy fields it has not guaranteed the redistribution mechanisms that would make this participation possible (Eizaguirre et al. 2012; Wollmann 2009). As a matter of fact, since the beginning of the financial crisis in 2008 we are witnessing tougher conditions for the development of policies at local and regional levels, while at the same time these levels are compelled

to continue to develop responses to avoid social exclusion. Hence, the conditions for social innovation have changed with more constraints to the contribution of socially innovative actors just when they are most needed.

To further approach the complexity of governance in its relation to social innovation we suggest taking into account the national and local traditions in addressing different policy fields (labour market, education, health, housing and the environment). In looking at the development of SCS we suggest seeing the different policy fields and their mechanisms of governance as complementary. Thus, a methodology is needed that offers an integrated approach to the study of social policy and ultimately aims at possible ways of superseding a fragmented analysis. Let us move to some examples.

Exclusion through housing and neighbourhood is an example of the close interrelation between social exclusion dynamics. Housing provision and the life conditions in the neighbourhood become a source of social exclusion: cities evolve and new waves of population enter and form segregated neighbourhoods; alternatively, de-populated areas in the city become deteriorated environments. Living in a particular neighbourhood may bring with it a range of disadvantages that may create or reinforce disadvantages at the individual or household level (Cameron 2007). Thus, housing and neighbourhood can be seen as contributing to these other forms of social exclusion. In the housing policy field, social exclusion dynamics have led to an emphasis on the need for intervention, not only in the housing conditions, but also in the functioning of schools and in the activation of labour market programs. However, rarely have integrated programs dealing with all problems been applied by local governments (Murie 2004).

In the field of neighbourhood renewal, social innovation driven by public administrations is often framed in a multilevel governance scheme. In urban renewal policies carried out all over Europe during the last decades the influence of regional, national and even supranational administrations has been crucial. These policies give attention to empowering citizens and look for their cooperation in linking physical regeneration to social intervention. When successful, such a combination between improvement on the social and the physical side contributes to the development of social capital important for neighbourhood governance (Colomb 2009). Among these practices it is possible to find innovation through governance with the covering of material needs (housing development and legal initiatives) and innovation in governance through practices aimed at fostering neighbourhood participation and new values on neighbourhood and housing (Forrest and Kearns 2001; Middleton et al. 2005; Moulaert and Nussbaumer 2005; Murie 2004; Uitermark and Duyvendak 2008).

If we were to examine in detail the actors involved in processes of neighbourhood change, for example in urban regeneration processes (Porter and Shaw 2009), we soon find markets, institutions and civil society groups operating not only in the neighbourhood, but also from outside. Thus, various city authorities and even regional or national governments are often involved, through financial arrangements and decision-making processes, generating a complex web of multilevel governance. Whereas markets and public institutions have national and local histories of interrelations ready for intervention (even if new ones are constantly created), organized citizens face the challenge of constructing networks first in the immediate community and then beyond the neighbourhood in order to achieve their objectives. It

is precisely at this point that empirical research reveals the various capacities and strategies that civil-society groups are capable of developing.

Finally, differences in cultural traditions concerning labour economy, housing, education and the urban environment are relevant in order to understand differences between socially creative strategies and their interaction with institutions in different places (Ghezzi and Mingione 2007; Leubolt et al. 2009). Those traditions are not isolated from the rest of the national regulatory systems and their transformation. In this regard, the variety of welfare regimes can explain not only differences in state redistribution but also differences in reciprocity mechanisms in society and how different actors interact (Esping-Andersen 2002).

The methodological steps we propose are therefore: (a) locating a particular creative strategy and the organization that promotes it; (b) finding the strategy (strategies) followed by the organization to engage other communities or civil-society actors; (c) studying the internal governance mechanisms followed by the actors involved in the specific organization; (d) identifying the organization's strategy (strategies) to find material resources which often means to reach local institutions or markets; (e) analysing the characteristics of the organization's objectives in relation to the multi-level governance structure and the decision-making process (such as accepting or alternatively attempting to change the definition of problems); trying to change the agenda in the decision-making process; opening up the decision-making process in such a way that other actors can participate; (f) observing the possible ways in which real changes in governance and democratic participation can transpire into the public sphere; (g) finding out if new practices of

Table 11.1   Relations between governance and social innovation

Relation between governance and social innovation	Forms of social innovation	Results
Governance as a framework for innovation	Innovation through already existing governance mechanisms	Material objectives in different fields
Governance as a field for innovation	Innovation and shifts in the governance mechanisms	Democracy, openness and participation
		Fighting autocratic practices

citizenship are crystallizing to the point of influencing the legal body of rights.

11.3   ANALYSIS OF SOCIAL INNOVATION IN RELATION TO GOVERNANCE

In order to develop the proposed methodology, we suggest not only taking into account the internal dynamics and organization of the actors promoting social innovation, but also looking at the impact of the SCS on governance mechanisms and empowerment capacity of individuals and collectives. In this section we deal with these two elements. The internal dynamics and organization includes the 'internal governance' – the mechanisms that make it possible to create a consensus within the organization on the objectives to reach – and strategy, that is the strategy followed to reach these objectives. The relation with governance summarizes the effects of social innovation on governance in terms of empowerment and impact on governance mechanisms (see Table 11.1).

11.3.1   Internal Dynamics and Organization

In dealing with issues of social exclusion, public institutions, market actors and civil-

society groups have to operate within a changing social context of constraints and opportunities. Their capacity to produce innovation in the different policy areas and in governance is therefore likely to be time and place specific (Sayer and Walker 1992, p. 211). Furthermore, these actors need internal organization and also have to create networks and coordination mechanisms with the rest of the actors with which they must relate. The internal organization and strategy (internal governance) is prior to the development of SCS. Although, as we shall show, these two dimensions are strongly interconnected:

11.3.1.1   Internal governance

This refers to the internal organization of socially innovative actors. Within local public administration there is a potential for social innovation in the way in which policy-makers reorganize incorporating formal and informal relations with other actors either at other levels of government and/or with actors from the civil society and private organizations (see Kazepov 2010 on welfare and social care). In civil society groups and market actors, internal governance refers to their organization, and to the way in which they combine universalistic principles – e.g. solidarity – guiding their action and elements such as leadership and intra-solidarity (i.e. solidarity specific to every single organization or institution). In this sense civil societies are hybrids formed from a combination of 'civil associations' and 'associations as enterprises' (Pérez-Díaz 1995). 'Civil associations' are based on universalistic values and on mutual toleration, and their objective is exclusively oriented towards ensuring the general, abstract and universalistic rules that everyone could be obliged to follow while pursuing their own individual, egoistical or altruistic drives. On the other hand, 'associations as enterprises' pursue goals of their own and require their members to contribute, and eventually to sacrifice themselves to such common goals. Those associations are based on intra-solidarity practices and sometimes show hostility towards strangers and outsiders (Pérez-Díaz 1995).

We find these two overlapping logics in civil society as actors are trying to find a balance between them when introducing innovative practices. They are moved by universalistic objectives but also by pragmatic aims. The 'election' of a certain objective over others is influenced by the multi-level national context and the policy field, and it affects the orientation of SCS. For instance, in the framework of the KATARSIS project (as mentioned above), the analysis showed that civil-society organizations studied in Southern European cities were based to a great extent on universalistic values, which gave them a wide basis of voluntary participation and engagement with other organizations with similar universalistic values. Still, some groups, especially in the social economy, which are strongly organized under the logic of 'enterprise', oriented to more pragmatic objectives (for instance job insertion enterprises). We can consider private actors promoting social innovation as more balanced towards an association-as-enterprise logic but with some degree

of universalistic values. What makes one or other logic prevail relates to the policy field, but more so to the time and place dimensions mentioned above.

11.3.1.2 Strategy

The analysis of different SCS reveals that there are two organizational elements generating different outcomes in terms of mobilization of resources: the 'sense of place', that is, the embeddedness of the SCS in their neighbourhood or city, and the networking capacity (which is a different type of embeddedness), the relational dimension of the socially innovative group that facilitates its actors' capacities to move along their nation's multi-level governance framework.

The 'sense of place' includes the promotion of community relations, the link between the group objectives and the neighbourhood or the community in which innovative actors are embedded. This is especially important in a context of decreasing public expenditures and co-production of public policies. In such a situation a socially innovative 'sense of place' has come to be seen as a valuable factor in attracting social investors when social services are being outsourced. For example, in almost all European cities, there are examples of community centres, as well as targeted programs, led by civil society organizations under the umbrella of public administrations (on behalf of them or with their support) and in many cases with their financial assistance (Vitale 2007; see Andersen et al., Chapter 14).

The networking capacity of the civil society groups and private actors refers to the connections of local actors to other public, private and societal actors outside their own local context. Whereas public actors can promote social innovation allowing the participation of new actors in policy-making and adopting new approaches to solve problems, often their capacity to developing innovative approaches depends on their autonomy vis-à-vis other government levels as well as their ability to interact with them in a mutually beneficial way. The Community Centre Gellerup in Aarhus, Denmark, analysed in Chapter 14, is an example of this kind of networking, in which public administration actors have promoted the involvement of civil society actors in improving the capacity to offer services in the centre to help citizens in a comprehensive way connecting several public offices and engaging volunteers. On their side, civil society actors have found ways and strategies to interact with administrations in order to achieve their objectives for greater social inclusion. In other cases the agreements between civil society organizations and public administrations are achieved after a period of opposition and collective mobilization followed by a concrete negotiation (Vitale 2007).

The two dimensions we have described are related to the degree of institutionalization and the opposition and criticism of actors promoting social innovation. With the aim of spreading socially innovative dynamics, civil-society organizations have to manage the balance between institutionalizing their practices and maintaining a critical perspective towards the existing governance mechanisms. The literature on new social movements has underlined this aspect during the last two decades of the 20th century when examining how social movements tend to generate civil-society organizations that then become service providers for public administrations (Cohen 1985; Della Porta and Andretta 2002).

The balance between institutionalization of socially innovative experiences and the maintenance of a critical perspective towards public administrations tends to be perceived as a zero-sum choice (Blackeley 2010). However, civil-society organizations are used to developing complex relations with public administrations, combining both tendencies: collaboration and opposition, consensus in certain issues and conflict in others. Therefore the consolidation of concrete collaboration between civil-society actors and public institutions does not imply a direct loss of their critical and ideologically oriented perspective. The achievement of partial agreements with public administrations is perfectly combined with maintaining their 'watchdog' role, developing critical attitudes towards public policies if necessary. For example, immigrants' advocacy groups may develop a close collaboration with local authorities to design inclusive local policy responses to the needs of migrants from an urban-citizenship perspective (Varsany 2006), and at the same time mobilize in clear opposition to national and supra-national authorities that regulate access to political rights.

Thus actors of SCS, including public actors, accept the contradiction between the policy aims of different levels of government as an unavoidable circumstance derived from the complexity of public administrations. Considering this, the institutionalization of socially creative practices and the collaboration with a concrete level of government can be oriented to influence other levels of government. The connectivity between levels of government, which is largely path-dependent, is crucial in order to understand the institutionalization of SCS in a multilevel framework (Giersig 2008; Yañez et al. 2008).

11.3.2   Influence of Social Innovation in Multi-Level Governance

How do the internal dynamics and organization of socially innovative actors interact with their capacity to have an impact on the multi-level governance system? After examining the strategies and the internal organization of socially innovative actors we are in a better position to investigate the multi-level context within which the actors of the innovative strategies have to interact. We suggest following the research with the analysis of local governance and local growth alliances in order to better grasp multi-level governance (Coimbra 2011, p. 79). The analysis can further look into the impact (or influence) that a particular SCS has on governance and see how far it reaches into multi-level governance. The influence may stop at the city level or may arrive at the level of regional or national institutions.

Two interrelated analytical dimensions help to see the impact of SCS in multi-level governance.

11.3.2.1 Empowerment capacity of SCS

One of the main elements of innovative practices is that they provide material and immaterial resources to individuals and communities to tackle social exclusion dynamics. It is therefore necessary to assess to what extent this empowerment improves the opportunity for individual and collective actors to participate in policy-making. The relation between empowerment and participation in policy-making depends not only on the SCS but also on the policy field and the multi-level national context. Nevertheless, as social exclusion dynamics in different policy fields are closely linked, empowerment in a given policy field can improve the ability of individuals as well as communities to tackle other social problems. As an example, the integration of ethnic minorities in labour market developed by the organization AFIP in France reinforces economic and social citizenship of members of these minorities by facilitating their incorporation into the labour

market and improving their chances to be eventually involved in company decision-making processes. However, empowering individuals does not mean a direct transformation of a wide practice of excluding young members of minorities (Dean 2009). In this sense a further step is required to ascertain if a SCS emerges in which at least a new conceptualization of a social problem (in this case, the employability of minorities' youth) is emerging. Further along the line of policy change would be an effective anti-discrimination policy to ensure the social inclusion of minorities' youth and their participation in the new policy process.

11.3.2.2 Impact of SCS on policy-making

Socially Creative Strategies can have an intended or unintended effect on governance mechanisms through the transformation of policy-making processes. Although civil-society groups are often called to participate in these processes, their capacity to influence is hindered through different mechanisms, such as selective participation, or consultation without real decision-making power. Nevertheless, through socially innovative practices, some civil-society groups, as well as public administration, can promote changes in these processes, redefining social problems, legitimating new actors to participate or forcing more accountability or transparency of institutional action. Considering policy-making as a process of definition, implementation and evaluation of a policy, we can assess the impact of SCS on policy-making processes by taking into consideration three interlinked dimensions.

11.3.2.2.1 Changes in the definition of a policy problem SCS often transform the way social needs are conceived and tackled and this has an effect on the definition of policies. This redefinition includes not only formal changes in discourses but also institutional change in terms of transformation of informal norms and practices as well as the routines of daily life (González and Healey 2005).

For instance, socially innovative actors can consider lobbying practices as a way to influence public administrations in a multilevel governance framework. The development of methods of social inclusion, by copying successful practices from other contexts, help to promote regional, national and supra-national alliances between SCS. These alliances tend to spread new ways of dealing with social-exclusion dynamics, to promote research on their structural conditioning and to reinforce criticism with current public policies. The development of such kinds of relationships, in addition to conceptual outputs in terms of knowledge of practices overcoming social exclusion, promotes direct enrolment of local actors in the fostering of institutional connectivity in a multilevel scheme.

11.3.2.2.2 Changes in policy-making processes Innovative practices can have an impact on policy-making processes, and contribute to opening up the policy process by demanding more accountability and transparency.

Looking at the impact of SCS on decision-making processes, a coherent collaboration between SCS actors is a way to facilitate a better connectivity between civil society and public administrations in a bottom-link manner. Two factors are in play: one, the congruence and internal coordination developed by civil society organizations help to have an impact in promoting open and democratic decision-making processes; two, the local welfare mix and its institutional path-dependencies are also relevant to the ways in which policy-making processes can change (Andreotti et al. 2012). The institutional

dynamics and material resources of a local welfare mix can support or hinder the participation of citizens in improving social inclusion and entering the public sphere to discuss redistributive options. There may be obstacles to wide citizen participation, especially of those located at the margins of the public sphere (Silver et al. 2010). The openness to taking into account squatters' views in Amsterdam's local administration in several instances and the equivalent closure in the Barcelona case serves as an example (García 2006).

11.3.2.2.3 Changes in policies and their results Apart from the transformation of policy-making processes, SCS can have an impact on policy content. In this regard the legislation of new and more inclusive policies and the outcomes of lobbying and changes in the policy agenda are the variables to be taken into consideration.

While participating in multilevel governance, socially innovative actors can seize an opportunity for institutional innovation. Mainly from a top-down approach, there are several examples of policies promoted by socially innovative actors at a supra-national level meant to bring about changes in public administration at the national, the regional or the local level. Examples include the promotion of social employment markets or 'action social clause' led by the European Union through EQUAL funds. These initiatives promoted the involvement and networking of third sector organizations at the European level, and steered the spread of these practices within local and regional public administrations. These processes stress the confidence of SCS in the engagement at supra-national levels as a way to influence governance. In these processes of institutional innovation, in which citizenship practices achieve some kind of influence in the legal body of rights, again the connectivity between levels of government, as well as between civil society and public administrations, becomes crucial.

Through the combination of these three analytical dimensions it is possible to assess the impact of SCS on policy-making, which can transform the multi-level governance framework depending on the degree of institutionalization of practices and the level of governance in which the changes in policy-making take place.

The capacity of SCS to transform the conceptualization of problems, the policy-making processes and the policies themselves depend to a great extent on the multi-level context, that is the degree of decentralization and participation of non-state actors in a given policy field. In some cases, regional, national or supranational institutions can promote the institution-alization of socially innovative practices from the regional or national levels. Thus, the transformation of governance through Socially Creative Strategies depends not only on the capacity of networking with the local community and external actors, of socially innovative actors but also on the governance framework in which they are embedded.

11.4   CONCLUDING REMARKS

The methodological approach suggested in this chapter deals with the relation between social innovation and govern-ance. The approach allows for the under-standing of two interrelated aspects: how multilevel governance frameworks influ-ence the organization and emergence of SCS and how socially innovative actors contribute to transform this framework with their actions. Multi-level governance has a clear influence on the strategies followed by socially creative actors pro-moting social innovation, and in order to survive and reach their objectives these strategies experience a tension between innovation and institutionalization. Nevertheless, institutionalization and innovation are not necessarily antagonis-tic. The impact of social innovation on multilevel governance in terms of policy-making, transforming values or providing more transparent and democratic pro-cesses needs to be sustained and renewed in a dynamic context. In this sense, socially innovative actors need to adapt their organizational logic and their actions to develop and sustain their practices and their achievements over time. Innovative practices play a key role by providing new social resources and generating oppor-tunities for gaining relevance in a multi-level governance context. The approach presented here is useful to understand how socially innovative actors try to have an impact on governance regimes through socially innovative strategies. Depending on the national context and the strat-egy followed, socially creative groups can have an influence as service providers or as actors transforming the institutional framework of policy-making. In the first case they try to put innovations in practice through existing governance mechanisms, whereas in the second case they try to transform the existing governance mecha-nisms. These two approaches are compat-ible, and in most of the experiences the two objectives can be pursued at the same time. Moreover, actors involved in social innovation usually embrace both imme-diate material purposes and long-term objectives of transformation of govern-ance. As we have pointed out organiza-tional strategies are path-dependent but have also a strategic dimension.

Finally, there is not necessarily a direct antagonism between democratic bottom-up strategies from civil society and institutional changes in governance towards social justice. There are many different modes of participation and citizenship practices. Depending on the local context and multi-level framework, relationships between these both forms of innovation can change. Given these complementarities, we argue that the term 'bottom-linked initiatives' becomes more useful for the study of SCS. In most of the cases SCS against exclusion depend on the ability of coordination of different actors at different levels.

inequality and social exclusion exchanged their knowledge and work with the aim of better integrating their research programs and methodologies. For methodological purposes, the project analysed four distinct policy fields. Nonetheless, as we shall see, the four policy fields and the exclusionary dynamics linked to them are closely related.

2. Following Kooiman (2000) and Jessop (2002), Swyngedouw defines different orders of governance: metagovernance, governance of first order and governance of second order. Metagovernance order institutions define the grand principles of governmentality, whereas first-order institutions codify and formalize these principles and second-order governance institutions implement them (Swyngedouw 2009).

11.5   QUESTIONS FOR DISCUSSION

- After the development of the analytical model proposed in this chapter, different questions for debate and further research emerge:
  - What indicators can be developed to assess the changes that SCS produce in governance mechanisms? That is, how can we measure the changes in the definition of problems, in policy-making processes and in policy results produced by Socially Creative Strategies?
  - To what extent is there a relation between modes of governance and creative strategies? What is the role of the local context and its historical development in the emergence of such strategies?

NOTES

1. KATARSIS (http://katarsis.ncl.ac.uk, last accessed 10 December 2012) was a Coordination Action funded by the European Commission under its Framework Programme 7. It provided a platform on which research teams specialized in the study of the consequences of growing

REFERENCES

(References in bold are recommended reading.)

Andreotti, A, E. Mingione and E. Polizzi (2012), "Local Welfare Systems: A Challenge for Social Cohesion", *Urban Studies*, **49** (9), 1925–1940.

Blackeley, G. (2010), 'Governing Ourselves: Citizen Participation and Governance in Barcelona and Manchester', *International Journal of Urban and Regional Research*, **34** (1), 130–145.

Brenner, N. (2004), 'Urban governance and the production of new state spaces in western Europe 1960–2000', *Review of International Political Economy*, **11** (3), 447–488.

Cameron, S. (2007), 'Housing and Neighbourhood Survey Paper 1.3', Newcastle: Katarsis, http://katarsis.ncl.ac.uk/wp/wp1/ef3.html (last accessed 5 October 2011).

Cohen, J.L. (1985), 'Strategy or Identity: New Theoretical Paradigms and Contemporary Social Movements', *Social Research*, **52** (4), 663–716.

Coimbra, D. (2011), 'Governance in new European regions: The case of Centrope', PhD thesis, Vienna University of Economics and Business, Institute for the Environment and Regional Development.

Colomb, C. (2009), 'Gentrification and community empowerment in East London', in L. Porter and K. Shaw (eds), pp. 157–166.

Dahrendorf, R. (1979), *Life Chances*, London: Weidenfeld and Nicolson.

Dean, H. (2009), 'Critiquing Capabilities: The distractions of a beguiling concept', *Critical Social Policy*, **22**, 261–278.

Della Porta, D. and M. Andretta (2002), 'Social Movements and Public Administration: Spontaneous Citizens' Committees in Florence', *International Journal of Urban and Regional Research*, **26** (2), 244–265.

Eizaguirre, S., M. Pradel, A. Terrones, X. Martínez-

Collorrio and M. García (2012), 'Multilevel Governance and Social Cohesion: bringing back conflict in citizenship practices', *Urban Studies*, 49 (9), 1999–2016.

Esping-Andersen, G. (2002), *Social foundations of postindustrial economies*, Oxford: Blackwell.

Fontan, J.-M., P. Hamel, R. Morin and E. Shragge (2009), 'Community Organizations and Local Governance in a Metropolitan Region', *Urban Affairs Review*, 44 (6), 832–857.

Forrest, R. and A. Kearns (2001), 'Social Cohesion, Social Capital and the Neighbourhood', *Urban Studies*, 38 (12), 2125–2143.

García, M. (2006), 'Citizenship Practices and Urban Governance in European Cities', *Urban Studies*, 43, 745–765.

Geddes, M. and J. Bennington (2001), *Local Partnerships and Social Exclusion in the European Union: New forms of local social governance?* London: Routledge.

Ghezzi, S. and E. Mingione (2007), 'Embeddedness, Path Dependency and Social Institutions', *Current Sociology*, 55 (1), 11–23.

Giersig, N. (2008), *Multilevel Urban Governance and the 'European City'. Discussing Metropolitan Reforms in Stockholm and Helsinki*, Wiesbaden: VS Verlag für Sozialwissenschaften / GWV Fachverlage GmbH.

González, S. and P. Healey (2005), 'A Sociological institutionalist approach to the study of innovation in governance capacity', *Urban Studies*, 42 (11), 2055–2069.

Jessop, B. (2002) *The future of the capitalist state*, Cambridge: Polity Press, pp. 49–74.

Jessop, B. (2004), 'Multi-Level Governance and Multi-Level Meta-Governance', in I. Bache and M Flinders (eds), *Multi-level Governance*, Oxford: Oxford University Press, pp. 49–74.

Kazepov, Y. (2010), *Rescaling Social Policies towards Multilevel Governance in Europe*, Aldershot: Ashgate.

Kooiman, J. (2000), 'Societal governance: Levels, modes and orders of Socio-Political interaction', in *Debating governance: Authority, Steering and Democracy*, Oxford: Oxford University Press, pp. 138–166.

Le Galès, P. (2002), *European cities, social conflicts and governance*, Oxford: Blackwell.

Lelieveldt, H., K. Dekker, B. Völker and R. Torenvlied (2009), 'Civic Organizations as Political Actors: Mapping and Predicting the Involvement of Civic Organizations in Neighborhood Problem-Solving and Coproduction', *Urban Affairs Review*, 45 (1), 3–24.

Leubolt, B., A. Novy and B. Beinstein (2009), *Governance and Democracy*, Newcastle: Katarsis, http://katarsis.ncl.ac.uk/wp/wp1/ef5.html (last accessed 5 October 2011).

MacCallum, D., F. Moulaert, J. Hillier and S. Vicari Haddock (eds) (2009), *Social Innovation and Territorial Development*, Farnham: Ashgate.

Middleton, A., A. Murie and R. Groves (2005), 'Social Capital and Neighbourhoods that Work', *Urban Studies*, 42 (10), 1711–1738.

Moulaert, F., F. Martinelli and S. González (2007), 'Social Innovation and Governance in European Cities: Urban developments between the path dependency and radical innovation', *European Urban and Regional Studies*, 14 (3), 195–209.

Moulaert, F.J. and Nussbaumer (2005), 'The Social region. Beyond the learning economy', *European Urban and Regional Studies*, 12 (1), 45–64.

Murie, A. (2004), 'The dynamics of Social Exclusion and Neighbourhood Decline: welfare regimes, decommodification, housing and urban inequality', in Y. Kazepov (ed.), *Cities of Europe*, Oxford: Blackwell, pp. 151–169.

Pérez-Díaz, V. (1995), 'The possibility of civil society: Traditions, character and challenges', in J. Hall (ed.), *Civil Society: Theory, history and comparison*, Cambridge: Polity Press, pp. 80–109.

Porter, L. and K. Shaw (eds) (2009), *Whose Urban Renaissance? An international comparison of urban regeneration strategies*, London: Routledge.

Röcke, A. (2009), *Democratic Innovation through Ideas? Participatory Budgeting and Frames of Citizen Participation in France, Germany and Great Britain*, Florence: European University Institute.

Sayer, A. and R. Walker (1992), *The New Social Economy: Reworking the Division of Labor*, Oxford: Basil Blackwell.

Silver, H., A. Scott and Y. Kazepov (2010), 'Participation in Urban Contention and Deliberation', *International Journal of Urban and Regional Research*, 34 (3), 453–477.

Sintomer, Y., C. Herzaber and A. Röcke (2008), 'Participatory Budgeting in Europe: Potentials and Challenges', *International Journal of Urban and Regional Research*, 32 (1), 164–178.

Swyngedouw, E. (2005), 'Governance, innovation and the citizen: The Janus face of governance-beyond-the-state', *Urban Studies*, 42 (11), 1991–2006.

Swyngedouw, E. (2009), 'Civil Society, Governmentality and the Contradictions of Governance-beyond-the-State: The Janus-face of Social Innovation', in MacCallum et al. (eds), pp. 63–80.

Uitermark, J., and J.W. Duyvendak (2008), 'Citizen Participation in a Mediated Age: Neighbourhood Governance in The Netherlands', *International Journal of Urban and Regional Research*, 32 (1), 114–134.

Varsany, M. (2006) 'Interrogating "Urban Citizenship" vis-à-vis Undocumented Migration', *Citizenship Studies*, 10 (2), 229–249.

Vitale, T. (2007), 'Olinda o della difficile costruzione di un pubblico', in L. Pellizzoni (ed.), *Democrazia locale. Apprendere dall'esperienza*, Trieste: ICIG, pp. 133–140.

Weber, M. (1978), *Economy and Society*, Berkeley. University of California Press.

Wollmann, H. (2009), *Modernización del Gobierno*

Local en Europa: entre continuidad y cambio. Una perspectiva comparada, Barcelona: U.P. Fabra.

Yañez, C.J.N, A. Magnier and M.A. Ramírez (2008), 'Local Governance as Government–Business

Cooperation in Western Democracies: Analysing Local and Intergovernmental Effects by Multi-Level Comparison', *International Journal of Urban and Regional Research*, **32** (3), 531–547.

12. Towards a Deleuzean-inspired methodology for social innovation research and practice
Jean Hillier

The ultimate aim is to find a place for change again, for social innovation. (Massumi 2002, p. 69)

12.1 INTRODUCTION

Gilles Deleuze claimed that the question of innovation – the production of the new, novelty or creativity – is one of the fundamental questions of contemporary thought. One of the main issues driving Deleuze's work was to discover how the production of something new might be possible. As he wrote, 'The new . . . calls forth forces in thought that are not the forces of recognition, today or tomorrow, but the powers of a completely other model, from an unrecognized and unrecognisable terra incognita' (Deleuze 1994[1991], p. 136). Resonating with Deleuze's discussion of innovation and the new, the concept of social innovation developed in this Handbook rejects traditional, technology-focussed applications of 'innovation', preferring instead 'a more nuanced reading which valorises the knowledge and cultural assets of communities and which foregrounds the creative reconfiguration of social relations' (MacCallum et al. 2009b, p. 2).

Social innovation performs an ethical re/making of social space, which affords people economic, social, governmental and/or political agency in their own development. It recognizes the potential power and interrelationships of structures (such as capital, class, gender) and agents, both human and non-human, across space and time and especially how structuring processes affect and can be affected by agents. Social innovation research and practice are interested in the networked connections between, for instance, the global and the local (e.g. how multi-national enterprise decisions in global economic market conditions may be taken in an HQ office block in New York but deeply impact on employment opportunities in southern Italy and beyond). Similarly, innovations tend to inherit some influences or impulses from the development path of a specific place and the conditions of possibility of how that place and its communities came to be as they currently are. As Moulaert (2009, p. 20) explains: 'these relationships are difficult and refer as much to the problems raised by the (structural, institutional) determinants stemming from socioeconomic history as from the potential conflicts and opportunities that the confrontation of "past" and "future" as well as "here" and "elsewhere" can generate'.

Few approaches actually tackle the dynamic and relational nature of knowledge, practices and social innovation as it is extremely difficult to capture the dynamics of innovation. In what Moulaert terms as the *va et vient* (2009, p. 20) of lived and proactive development, it is important to remember that territoriality is socially embedded. It is, therefore, vital that power relationships between strategic actors are recognized, understood and foresighted;

that 'social innovation in territorial development must be addressed through a detailed analysis of how social and territorial logics interact with each other' (Moulaert, 2009, p. 20) and how they could do so in the future. Like Moulaert, I argue that there is a need to move from regarding social innovation as mainly driven by social structures and rejecting essentialist realism, to seeing innovation as difference, constructed through dynamic, relational interplay between elements. As Gilles Deleuze's basic ontology was an ontology of difference, I suggest that a Deleuzean framework may help us transform these traditional, rather static ways of understanding (Grosz 2001, p. 7).

In this chapter I offer a brief outline of what a Deleuzean-inspired theory of social innovation might look like. I then discuss a methodology of how we might both recognize (or trace) important elements influencing social transformation to date and also how we might stimulate windows of opportunity for socially innovative strategies through a process which I term strategic navigation. Although I present a predominantly theoretical development of the methodology, I regard it as useful for researchers and practitioners in the future. The methodology of strategic navigation is intended as a management 'tool' for public, private and voluntary organizations concerned with strategically planning the new – in other words, for social innovation.

12.2   DELEUZE ON THE NEW

For Deleuze, social innovation takes place through windows of opportunity for social creativity (along what he calls 'lines of flight') which emerge as challenges to institutionalized or normalized legitimacy. Innovation often emerges from conflict.

Opportunity spaces for innovative action may well occur at local or micro-scales which make possible creative strategies at regional, national or even international macro-scale.

We can locate several instances of Deleuze claiming that the question of innovation is one of the fundamental questions of contemporary thought (Smith 2007). For instance, he argues that 'the aim is . . . to find the conditions under which something new is produced' (Deleuze and Parnet 1987[1977], p. vii). He is interested in questions of 'how are the production and appearance of something new possible' (Deleuze 1986[1983], p. 3).

In Deleuze's (and his colleague, Félix Guattari's) view, the social and the political are 'inseparable from sensation and creation, whether that creation takes place in the arts, the sciences, politics or any other sphere of human endeavour' (Bogue 2007, p. 3). Deleuze's is a relational approach, concerned with networks of 'crisscrossing diagonal paths' (Bogue 2007, p. 1) which interconnect entities. These transverse connections intensify differences and open up new possibilities of creative or innovative thought and practice. Deleuze's philosophy is concerned with immanence, or becoming; with creative transformation, experimentation and the production of the new.

Innovation is an active force which creates new forms of relationality. It is a manifestation of positive desire which makes a difference. It is an in-between; a locus for socio-cultural transformation where openness to futurity (becoming) overcomes traditional inertia and stasis. Deleuze offers us what Grosz (2001) calls a logic of innovation, an:

> understanding that is bound up with seeing politics, movement, change, as well as space and time, in terms of the transformation and realignment of the *relations* between identi-

ties and elements rather than in terms of the identities, intentions, or interiorities of the wills of individuals or groups. (Grosz 2001, p. 92, emphasis added)

Deleuze's logic is that of pragmatic creativity derived from problematization. A problem, or perceived lack of something, represents a creative possibility for Deleuze. 'Lacks' or 'differences between . . .', should not be regarded as deficiencies to be corrected, but rather as a resource of possibilities. Such an approach would look positively at assets (Asset Based Community Development approaches, for instance; see Kunnen et al., Chapter 21) rather than negatively at lacks. Deleuze was seeking a positive[1] or pragmatic, rather than a negative picture. He wanted to experiment, to explore what might happen if . . . Experimentation entails 'the creative production of new combinations of elements' (Baugh 2005, p. 91) and the discovery of how something might work, what might be its relational impact, on whom and why.

12.3   ELEMENTS GROUNDING A DELEUZIAN-INSPIRED APPROACH

Deleuze's conceptualization of society was of complex multiplicities of connectivity. Networks (assemblages) of humans and non-humans are contingent, as people and 'things' enter and leave, join together with other actors or break away from them, and so on. Networks are never 'free-standing', but are always connected to other networks across space and time. People and objects (such as buildings, places) may be part of several networks at once; for instance, a building may be used internally as a playgroup venue, a youth club, a gymnasium, offices, while its external materiality offers habitats for birds and insects, a canvas for graffiti artists and so on.

In what follows I highlight some themes which occur throughout Deleuze's work, which form the basis for developing a coherent methodology of potential value for those interested in social innovation.

I regard the most important theme as being Deleuze's *ontology of difference*. 'Difference marks the real dynamic of being' (Hardt 1993, p. 2). As Deleuze wrote, 'differentiation is never a negation but a creation . . . Difference is never negative but essentially positive and creative' (1988[1986], p. 103). Some systems, pushed to their limits, will collapse and cease to exist. Others will be more resilient, learn from the event and, perhaps, creatively adapt to changing conditions or even transform. This is a perspective that may liberate us from, for instance, the hegemonic claim that There Is No Alternative to the neoclassical market system (see Daniels 2009). An ontology of difference opens up the possibility for change – possibly through conflict – to stimulate differentiation and to create new social forms: it is the politics of the possible.

Together with difference, *becoming* – or *emergence* – is a key theme which can help us understand the ways in which social change arises. Emergence describes the continual production of difference in events (Stagoll 2005). It invokes the dynamism of change. Complex systems display behaviour that results from the *interaction* between components. Some components, or actors, will resist the behaviours of others. What Deleuze calls 'lines of flight' occur when actors have 'had enough' of one system and metaphorically flee it to creatively do/be something else, such as developing socially innovative ways of caring for the mentally ill rather than allowing institutionalization and/or chemical neuroscientific treatments to continue.

Deleuze also distinguishes between the *macro-* and *micro-political* (Deleuze and Guattari 1987[1980]). Macropolitics is concerned with those things or states of affairs, such as governmental structure, class and gender, associated with hierarchical structures. Micropolitics focuses on politics which 'transpire in areas where they are rarely perceived' (Conley 2005, p. 172), such as people talking in coffee shops or pubs. Micropolitics is a creative process, often (though not necessarily) working in small groups (Deleuze and Guattari 1987[1980], p. 215); 'stirring and escaping, eluding the guard, trickling out from under the door' (Houle 2005, p. 92).

As Houle (2005) explains, changes introduced into macropolitical systems tend to create changes in quantity rather than quality (e.g. the UK Coalition government's decision in 2010 to cut and cap welfare payments in order to save the state £1 billion[2]). Micropolitics, in contrast, tends to generate qualitative change – something which incites a heterogeneity; an 'existential mutation' (Houle 2005, p. 93). Existential mutations do not involve predetermined solutions, but enable experimentation, allowing members of a group to 'internally generate and direct their own projects': 'a reinvention of the ways in which we live' (Guattari 2000[1989], cited in Houle 2005, p. 93).

The micropolitical has an inherent capacity which is intrinsically related to time. What happens in the present and future depends somewhat on the past, but is not completely path-dependent. There is scope for experimentation, for innovation and chance. For Deleuze, micropolitics entails an expanded capacity to respond. As Houle (2005, pp. 96–97) concludes, 'micropolitics is the most viable candidate at the present time, for countering the seductive fascisms of "one size fits all" and its evil sidekick, the "single story

told as though it's the only one".' This is a view that is not anarchic, since some rules are necessary to achieve order, but which challenges the stifling and hierarchical nature of existing institutional power structures.

Deleuze emphasizes the concept of relationality through his metaphor of the rhizome. A rhizome is a decentred set of linkages between, multiple branching roots and shoots, such as ginger: 'a proliferating, somewhat chaotic, and diversified system of growths' (Grosz 1994, p. 199). A rhizome 'ceaselessly establishes connections between semiotic chains [of signs and symbols], organizations of power, and circumstances relative to the arts, sciences and social struggles' (Deleuze and Guattari 1987[1977], p. 7). The fabric of the rhizome is conjunction – 'and' – connecting elements, issues and ideas. 'AND is neither one thing nor the other, it's always in-between, between two things; it's the borderline, there's always a border, a line of flight or flow . . . [I]t's along this line of flight that things come to pass, becomings evolve, revolutions take shape' (Deleuze 1995[1990], p. 45). The rhizome maps a process of networked, relational and transversal thought (Colman 2005). It can challenge and transform structures of reified, fixed and static thought into a 'milieu of perpetual transformation' (Colman 2005, p. 233) composed of causal and/or aleatory (chance) connections and links. To think rhizomically is to reveal the multiple ways possible to assemble thoughts and actions in immanent, always-incomplete processes of becoming.

For Deleuze and Guattari, *democratic inclusion* implies a democratic space beyond the organization of others' behaviour – the conduct of conduct – which Michel Foucault (1991) famously termed 'governmentality'. The emergence of some structuring principles for democracy is not only inevitable, but necessary for a society to function coherently. The key is that they be deliberated and negotiated inclusively and democratically. As Deleuze and Guattari wrote, we need 'just a little order to protect us from chaos' (1994[1991], p. 201).

Philosophically, a Deleuzean-inspired methodology of social innovation will be grounded in pragmatism, with its focus on concrete issues in specific situations, joint development of shared understandings of problems and of actions in which people learn by experience and in deep co-operative relationships with each other, testing (experimenting with) ideas empirically. A Deleuzean form of pragmatism, moreover, is attentive to the relational force of power; to its potentially oppressive and/or creative capacities. 'Problems' cannot be solved once and for all, but are provisionally reformulated, as issues are viewed in different ways or actions taken have unanticipated consequences or side-effects. There is, therefore, no one single truth, but only possibilities.

As may be surmised from the above, there are multiple potential processes of social innovation, contingent upon circumstances and opportunities, but which are inevitably collaborative and pragmatic. The key role for the community or communities concerned is that of self-determination, while the role of government is to facilitate the innovation trajectory, perhaps through redistribution of public resources.

12.4   HOW MIGHT WE RECOGNIZE OR STIMULATE WINDOWS OF OPPORTUNITY FOR SOCIALLY CREATIVE STRATEGIES?

In this section, I offer the basis of a detailed methodology inspired by what Deleuze and Guattari (1987[1980]) term 'pragmatics'. They also refer to pragmatics as a 'cartography' of change, as it utilizes metaphors of tracing, mapping and diagramming, as I explain below. The methodology emphasizes the relational dynamics of forces, such that analysis entails detailed tracing of the conditions of possibility of how things/places/problems came to be constituted as products of particular contingencies through unfolding power-laden relations between elements and of mapping them into the future.

Deleuze and Guattari (1987[1980], p. 146) describe their cartography as comprising four components:

- the generative component – the *tracing* of stories of what happened (histories) and pointing towards the potentiality of what might emerge;
- the transformational component – making a transformational *map* of the regimes and their possibilities for innovation and creation;
- the *diagrammatic* component of the relational forces that are in play 'either as potentialities or as effective emergences';
- the *machinic* component – the outline of programs of what new assemblages[3] might emerge.

A pragmatic method of researching and/or stimulating social innovation would thus make a tracing. It would then put the tracing on a transformational map of potentialities, making diagrams of the relational forces that play in each case. It would finally outline a program of assemblages and of what might take place. This program could then function as a point of support for the task of strategic plan- and policy-making with regard to social innovation.

To *trace* entails looking back in a systematic manner. It is an investigation concerned with path-dependencies, transformations and ruptures, exploring how elements and processes (such as actors involved in social housing policy-making and provision) respond to both their own logics and to external pressures and stimuli.

Tracing is an exploration of the relations, associations and encounters between, for example, private infrastructure capital, national and international agencies of governance and interest groups, scientists, environmentalists and so on, and flows of information, actualized in materials and language such as texts, meetings, demonstrations etc. It is an 'analysis of how forces of different types come to inhabit the same field' (Due 2007, p. 145); the lines of power rather than the points. Tracing 'how did something come to be' involves asking questions such as 'what knowledges, emotions or desires drove this situation?', 'what relations existed between which actors?', 'what games of power played between actors' and so on.

Tracing overlays the product of something onto the process of its production. It can be performed at the micropolitical site level, analysing the unfolding state of affairs within which situations and sites are constituted.

Deleuzean tracing resonates with that of Michel Foucault's concept of genealogy in that it asks 'what is the nature of our present?' (Foucault 1984, pp. 34–37): how did something come to be? Researchers look not only at *what* actants (human and non-human actors) may have said, written or done, but also at *why* they said, wrote or did it in such a manner and what force relations and conditions of possibility were involved. The aim is to cut through established layers of coding of relationships between subjects, objects and words to work through how and why events came to actualize as they did, i.e. the conditions of possibility: what were the drivers? The outcome of tracing is a series of stories of what happened which look especially at the power relations between actors.

There is a difference between tracing or unfolding something in retrospect and mapping the potential innovations and trajectories through diagrams might offer opportunities for social innovation. Cartography involves *both* the deductive interpretation, especially of ruptures and discontinuities, of 'symptoms' or drivers of change (on a tracing) of an actual situation *and* the invention of innovations, experimental assemblages and pragmatic diagrams. Deleuzean *maps* are concerned with creative potential. The issue is not to attempt to define long-term detailed programs of action, but to raise questions of potential agency and of socio-economic-political and institutional conditions of change. Projected trajectories do not guarantee actual progression, however. We trace networks, human and non-human actors, their encounters, power plays, and so on, and notice where any blockages, oppositions, or resistances affect policy decisions and implementation. These tracings become part of the map. It is then a question of mapping their trajectory to see what they might be capable of. For instance, could a fringe political party acquire substantial popular support and electoral votes through association with a particular celebrity and with what implications for policy decisions?

Mapping generates a *diagram* concerned with the dynamic interrelation of relations (Massumi 1992). Diagrams act as modulators between ideas and what may become. They create possibilities; imaginary alternative worlds which promise something new; a hope of living otherwise (Bogue 2003, p. 177). By mapping connections between different relations of power or force onto a diagram, one may be able to anticipate the potential distribution of 'the power to affect and the power to be affected' (Deleuze 1988[1986], p. 73). This is a 'what might happen if . . .?' approach, not so much to predict, but to be alert to as-yet unknown potentialities. The idea is to try to anticipate the ways in which relations and alliances might be redistributed in different circumstances and situations and what they might be capable of achieving.

Deleuze and Guattari's (1987[1980]) fourth pragmatic, or machinic, component concerns the evaluative study of assemblages and their potentialities, with a view to intervening strategically. As Bogue (2007, p. 10) describes, this is 'both a process of exploring and hence constructing connections among differences, and a process of undoing connections in an effort to form new ones'. It is not a process of standing back and describing, but of intervening strategically to enter the relations between elements and 'tweaking', or manipulating, as many as possible in order to get a sense of what may emerge (Massumi 2002, p. 207). Such manipulation, or the 'art of organising encounters' (Hardt 1993, p. 110), involves guessing '*what* decisions to make, *when* to make them, *who* to involve, and *how* in a context of dynamically complex change' (Hames 2007, p. 197, emphasis in original). It would entail attempting to select and to facilitate, or strategically navigate towards, potentially 'good' encounters and to avoid 'bad' ones. This is a pragmatic exercise in which strategic planners would attempt to intervene and manipulate relational forces and their potential connections, conjunctions and disjunctions, their possible trajectories. In other words, to diagnose becomings (Bergen 2006, p. 109). This is, of course, impossible. The future is a social construc-

tion in which nothing eventuates precisely as anticipated. 'Becoming is directional rather than intentional' (Massumi 1992, p. 95). Chance is often a powerful force. Strategic planning involves 'working with odds, guesses, predictions and judgements but not ever with certainty' (Rose 2007, p. 468).

This raises several ethical issues. Who gives practitioners the authority to 'judge' which are 'good' and which are 'bad' actants, encounters and potentialities? Whose definition of 'good' or 'bad' is employed?

12.5 STRATEGIC NAVIGATION

Organizational management 'guru', Richard Hames (2007, p. 229) states that 'in a world where strategy is a commodity, navigation and imagination become the critical factors'. Hames' methodology for innovative management of change resonates strongly with Deleuzean-inspired tracing and mapping cartography. Hames (2007, pp. 228–229) defines strategic navigation as 'the art of confidently and ethically finding viable paths into the future, negotiating unknown terrain and unprecedented complexity while retaining integrity and relevance'. He advocates a methodology of 'strategy-as-process' – 'a continuous braiding of intelligence creation with insightful action' (Hames 2007, p. 81).

Strategic navigation is a collaborative conversation that weaves between specific episodes and local or micro stories, the networks and coalitions of governance processes, and the macro of governance cultures (Healey 2007, pp. 21–23). Hames (2007, p. 253) depicts this conversation as a strategic-learning spiral – which I prefer as a less closed, more open, Deleuzean rhizome – of sensing (tracing), making

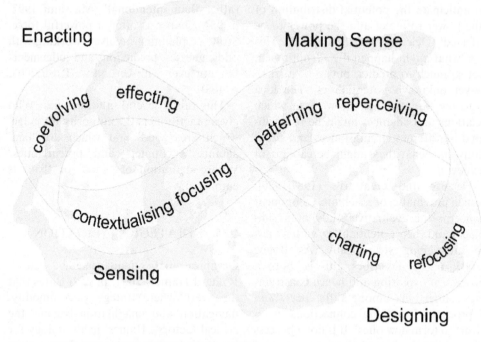

Source: Hillier 2011, p. 518 (adapted from Hames 2007).

Figure 12.1   The rhizome of strategic learning

sense and designing (mapping and dia-gramming) and enacting (machining) (see Figure 12.1).

Hames suggests that practitioners ask strategic questions aimed at uncovering not only the driving forces in play behind dif-ferent behaviours, but also why actants see and explain the world as they do (elements of *Contextualizing* and *Focusing*). The element of *Patterning* integrates the differ-ent perspectives and knowledges derived from Contextualising and Focusing into understandings of what is happening and what might happen if ... *Reperceiving* and *Refocusing* would entail scenario or *futuribles*-based diagramming of issues and implications, from which 'leverage points' are identified and pertinent responses are designed in a strategic 'plan' component

(*Charting*). The rhizome incorporates con-tinuous reflexion, re-perception and revi-sion of information, ideas and intentions as new knowledges emerge, circumstances alter and decisions change the context and issue focus (*Effecting* and *Co-evolving*).

In relation to these elements, I offer some possible questions for consideration.

Contextualizing performs understanding of the context in which strategic planning is to take place; a sensing of what is going on and how things came to be. Questions include:

● What are the key characteristics of the socio-economic-political environment? In what discourses and material manners are they actualized?

- What are the critical relationships between these characteristics?
- What were their conditions of possibility? How did they come to be? What did actants say, write, do? Why? What were the impacts on other actants?
- What were the dynamics of power or force relations between actants? Power, emotions, desires etc revealed by discourses and material objects. What were the prevailing dispositions, ideologies and imperatives?
- What changed? Why?

Focusing arrives at an initial, shared understanding of critical issues. Questions include:

- What are the most strategically significant issues requiring attention? Why? What dispositions or imperatives prevail?
- What are the relationships between these and other dispositions and issues?
- What relationships matter most? Why?
- What most concerns key decision makers? Why?
- What control or influence can be exercised over these issues and their relationships?
- What assumptions lead us to these conclusions? How do actors regard themselves and other human and non-human actors? (Do they perhaps see themselves as facilitators or critical friends of actors with valuable knowledges and skills? Or do they regard themselves as 'experts' and others as 'uninformed meddlers'?)

Patterning integrates different perspectives and new knowledges into our under-

standings of what is happening and might happen in the future. Questions include:

- What patterns of change can we identify? Are force relations changing between actors? Are dispositions, imperatives and ideologies changing?
- How and why are these patterns changing? What connections and/or disconnections are occurring? How are changes manifest by discourses and materialities?
- What are the gaps in our current thinking and knowing?
- Where can we get the information from?
- Are there other ways of perceiving the issues which raise different questions, problems, opportunities?

Reperceiving involves deepening awareness and understanding through finding new ways to view issues. Foresighting or prospective exercises can offer multiple perspectives on alternative futures. Outcomes can significantly change beliefs about what is important to actants. Questions include:

- What new insights can be gleaned from the various prospectives?
- What are the conditions of possibility of the various prospectives? What ideological commitments, assumptions, blockages, oppositions might actualize?
- What are the key relations between actants?
- How may force relations play out in the future?
- What changes might there be and why?
- What implications do these insights have for social innovation?

Refocusing examines what, from the prospectives investigated, could be more or less likely to take place and could be more or less strategically important and why. Refocusing filters attention. Questions include:

- What are the most significant issues requiring attention?
- What specific factors make these issues critical and why? What force relations are important?
- How might these issues be addressed?
- What might happen if . . .?
- Does the system have the capacities to address these issues?
- What other actors should be involved?
- What should strategies and projects address in the short-term and long-term and why?

Charting involves preparing appropriate plans. Questions include:

- What strategies are possible?
- What strategies might become possible in the short or longer-term future, how and why?
- What are the possible consequences, risks and opportunities of these strategies?
- How can the linkages between components of the strategies be described?
- Do the strategies address key leverage points?

Effecting implements the plans. Questions to consider before implementation include:

- How will we know if the plans are effective in navigating towards our strategic intentions?
- What would be an appropriate monitoring system?
- How would we accommodate

requirements for systemic change in the plans?
- What are we unaware of that may cause problems in the future?

Co-evolving enables adaptation of practice and plans in the light of changes caused by those practices and plans. Questions include:

- What signals will indicate that a fundamental change is occurring in the context from which we defined the strategies and plans?
- What may be the critical, unintended consequences of our plans?
- Do we need to think differently about our strategic intentions?
- Are we ignoring any force relations, connections or actants that might be critical?
- Do our plans need to change?

(Adapted from Hames 2007.)

Strategic Navigation can help researchers and practitioners of social innovation to assess when, if and how to initiate adaptive and transformative changes to ways of thinking and acting. There is no set formula, however, and constant reflexion is required to ensure that ideas and projects are not 'seduced' either by conventional thinking and inertia or blindly copy-pasting 'the latest flavour of the month' (Hames 2007, p. 250), whatever it may be.

12.6   IN-CONCLUSIONS

In the generative spirit of Deleuzean-inspired analysis, I advocate facilitation of social innovation by mapping assets and capacities and revaluing the subjects who perform them, rather than emphasizing needs and deficiencies (see

Gibson-Graham 2006; also Kunnen et al., Chapter 21; Gibson-Graham and Roelvink, Chapter 34). A methodology of strategic navigation is concerned with the power relations between humans and non-humans and how they were, are and could be manifest discursively and materially.

With specific regard to social innovation, a Deleuzean-inspired cartography of tracing and mapping, translated into the methodology of strategic navigation, offers 'a more *complete* model' (Houle 2005, p. 91) which folds together both human and non-human; social, psychological, natural-material, economic and political. It does not restrict social innovation to a limited number of possibilities, nor potentially 'successful interventions' to already-prescribed outcomes or solutions. It offers a more flexible approach and a more fluid and dynamic vision of the time-spaces of territorial and social innovation.

Strategic navigation is potentially an inclusive, democratic 'what might happen if . . .?' approach which allows disparate points of view to co-exist and which has a concern for multiplicity and complexity rather than systematic predictabilities. Deleuze and strategic navigation emphasize innovation, experiment, 'the spark of the new': the capacity for generating innovation through 'an unprecedented leap, the capacity of the actual to be more than itself, to become other than the way it has always functioned' (Grosz 2001, p. 130). In this spirit, I offer strategic navigation as a set of ideas and potential questions to stimulate thought; for researchers and practitioners to adapt and transform creatively into something to which they can relate and with which they can work. Strategic navigation is concerned with difference and experiments in future living: 'experiments in which those excluded, marginalized and rendered outside or placeless will

also find themselves' (Grosz 2001, p. 166). In other words, strategic navigation is concerned with social innovation.

12.7 QUESTIONS FOR DISCUSSION

- What are the main characteristics of a Deleuzean-inspired approach to social innovation?
- Why is a relational approach to social innovation important?
- How might the concept of strategic navigation assist practitioners involved in socially innovative actions?

NOTES

1. NB a positive, not a positivist.
2. Cuts in child benefit for those individually earning over £44,000 a year, together with a cap on the overall amount of benefits individuals can receive, result in a hypothetical unemployed couple with three children living in inner London losing benefits of £7,136pa while a couple with two children, earning £39,000 and £41,000 respectively, living outside London will lose nothing (Child Poverty Action Group and Chartered Institute of Housing, cited in Anon 2010).
3. The term 'assemblage' indicates a network of disparate groups of human and non-human actors.

REFERENCES

(References in bold are recommended reading.)

Anon (2010), 'Benefit changes: what could they mean for you', guardian.co.uk/money/2010/Oct04/benefit-cuts-george-osborne.html (last accessed 5 October 2010).
Baugh, B. (2005), 'Experimentation', in A. Parr (ed.), *The Deleuze Dictionary*, Edinburgh: Edinburgh University Press, pp. 91–92.
Bergen, V. (2006), 'La politique comme posture de tout agencement', in M. Antonioli, P-A. Chardel and H. Regnauld (eds), *Gilles Deleuze, Félix Guattari et le politique*, Paris: Éditions du Sandre, pp.103–114.

Bogue, R. (2003), *Deleuze on Music, Painting and the Arts*, New York: Routledge.

Bogue, R. (2007), *Deleuze's Way: essays in transverse ethics and aesthetics*, Aldershot: Ashgate.

Colman, F. (2005), 'Rhizome', in A. Parr (ed.), *The Deleuze Dictionary*, Edinburgh: Edinburgh University Press, pp. 231–233.

Conley, T. (2005), 'Molar', in A. Parr (ed.), *The Deleuze Dictionary*, Edinburgh: Edinburgh University Press, pp. 171–172.

Daniels, J. (2009), 'The Economy of Desire', *New Blackfriars*, 90/1025, 90–107.

Deleuze G. (1986[1983]), *Cinema 1: the movement-image* (trans. H. Tomlinson), Minneapolis, MN: University of Minnesota Press.

Deleuze, G. (1988[1986]), *Foucault* (trans. S. Hand), Minneapolis, MN: University of Minnesota Press.

Deleuze, G. (1994[1968]), *Difference and Repetition* (trans. P. Patton), London: Athlone.

Deleuze, G. (1995[1990]), *Negotiations 1972–1990* (trans. M. Joughin), New York: Columbia University Press.

Deleuze, G. and Guattari, F. (1987[1980]), *A Thousand Plateaus: capitalism and schizophrenia* (trans. B. Massumi), London: Athlone.

Deleuze, G. and Guattari, F. (1994[1991]), *What is Philosophy?* (trans. H. Tomlinson and G. Burchill), London: Verso.

Deleuze, G. and Parnet, C. (1987[1977]), *Dialogues* (trans. H. Tomlinson and B. Habberjam), London: Athlone.

Due, R. (2007), *Deleuze*, Cambridge: Polity Press.

Foucault, M. (1984), 'Polemics, politics and problematizations', interview with Paul Rabinow (trans. L. Davis), http://foucault.info/foucault/interview.html (last accessed 2 February 2007).

Foucault, M. (1991), 'Governmentality' (trans. R. Braidotti and C. Gordon), in G. Burchell, C. Gordon and P. Miller (eds), *The Foucault Effect: studies in governmentality*, Chicago, IL: University of Chicago Press, pp. 87–104.

Gibson-Graham, J.K. (2006), *A Postcapitalist Politics*, Minneapolis, MN: University of Minnesota Press.

Gibson-Graham, J.K. and G. Roelvink (2009), 'Social innovation for community economies', in D. MacCallum et al. (eds), pp. 25–37.

Grosz, E. (1994), 'A thousand tiny sexes: feminism and rhizomatics', in C. Boundess and D. Olkowski (eds) *Gilles Deleuze and the Theatre of Philosophy*, London: Routledge, pp. 187–210.

Grosz, E. (2001), *Architecture from the Outside*, Cambridge, MA: MIT Press.

Guattari, F. (2000[1989]), *The Three Ecologies* (trans. I. Pindar and P. Sutton), London: Athlone Press.

Hames, R. (2007), *The Five Literacies of Global Leadership*, San Francisco: Jossey-Bass.

Hardt, M. (1993), *Gilles Deleuze: an apprenticeship in philosophy*, Minneapolis, MN: University of Minnesota Press.

Healey, P. (2007), *Urban Complexity and Spatial Strategies: a relational planning for our times*, London: Routledge.

Hillier, J. (2011), 'Strategic Navigation across Multiple Planes: towards a Deleuzean-inspired methodology for strategic spatial planning', *Town Planning Review*, 82 (5), 503–527.

Houle, K. (2005), 'Micropolitics', in C. Stivale (ed.), *Gilles Deleuze: key concepts*, Chesham: Acumen, pp. 88–97.

MacCallum, D., F. Moulaert, J. Hillier and S. Vicari Haddock (eds) (2009a), *Social Innovation and Territorial Development*, Aldershot: Ashgate.

MacCallum, D., F. Moulaert, J. Hillier and S. Vicari Haddock (eds) (2009b), 'Introduction', in D. MacCallum et al. (eds), pp. 1–8.

Massumi, B. (1992), *A User's Guide to Capitalism and Schizophrenia: Deviations from Deleuze and Guattari*, Cambridge, MA: Massachusetts Institute of Technology Press.

Massumi, B. (2002), *Parables for the Virtual: Movement, Affect, Sensation*, Durham, NC: Duke University Press.

Moulaert, F. (2009), 'Social innovation: institutionally embedded, territorially (re)produced', in D. MacCallum et al. (eds), pp. 11–23.

Rose, M. (2007), 'The problem of power and the politics of landscape: stopping the Greater Cairo ring road', *Transactions of the Institute of British Geographers* NS, 32, 460–476.

Smith, D.W. (2007), 'The conditions of the new', *Deleuze Studies*, 1 (1), 1–21.

Stagoll, C. (2005), 'Event', in A. Parr (ed.), *The Deleuze Dictionary*. Edinburgh: Edinburgh University Press, pp. 87–89.

PART III

INSTRUCTIVE CASE STUDIES IN SOCIAL INNOVATION ANALYSIS

Introduction: social innovation experience and action as a lead for research

Stuart Cameron

In talking of the small town of Montemor-o-Novo below, André and Abreu describe this as a 'virtuous' case study. This term might well be used for all the case study examples in this part. They represent impressive and inspiring stories of success in the generation of socially-creative strategies and social innovation, often in difficult and unpromising circumstances. It is important in reading these chapters, though, to look beyond the case study stories, interesting and uplifting as they might be, to the analytical dimensions of the discussion in each chapter. The purpose of this handbook is to furnish and refine conceptual and analytical tools for researching and understanding how socially-creative strategies can develop to address social exclusion, and the purpose of the authors below is to utilize these tools in the context of the particular case studies they discuss. Looking across these case studies, a number of key analytical themes can be identified.

Space and spatial scale are important analytical dimensions. The account of an innovative approach to housing for Roma people in North-West Italy by Vitale and Membretti starts with a spatial issue – the segregation and physical isolation of Roma communities in 'nomad camps'. Social innovation in the use of space is described by the authors as 'performative'. The 'Dice' housing project included housing for Roma and non-Roma families together to challenge this pattern of spatial segregation. The project also included a community and arts space, the 'Dado', used to further the connection of Roma families with the wider community, and involving a participatory design process to balance openness of the space with the need for privacy and sense ownership of families' homes. In their chapter on the regeneration of Brugse Poort in Ghent, Oosterlynck and Debruyne also provide an example of the design of space as an element in social innovation. Negotiation by the city council to create access from a variety of civil society organizations on to a new green public space provided a stronger spatial context for bringing together the community and local organizations.

Vertical relationships of scale and institutional structure are discussed in several of the chapters, with a particular emphasis on the linkage of local civil society at grassroots level to more formal institutions at a wider scale. Andersen, Delica and Frandsen use the term 'bottom-linked' to indicate this relation. The main focus of their chapter is on formal public institutions, in this case library services in Denmark, which may both support social innovation and through this process themselves be changed. As Pradel et al. suggest in Chapter 11 (p. 155), 'institutionalization and innovation are not necessarily antagonistic'. The Danish case evidences a successful combination of 'strong formal institutional support' and 'a high level of active involvement of civic society and associative networks'. The Italian case study also traces the spatial interactions from an impetus for change beginning at the most local level of family interaction moving through the mediation of NGOs up to institutional levels where the resources for innovative action can be found. This well illustrates the model suggested by Vicari Haddock and Tornaghi (Chapter 19) with two dimensions of social innovation: the search for progressive social change as the 'fuel' and the institutionalization of organizational forms as its 'engine'. In Chapter 16 Calzada suggests a biocentric model which makes a similar distinction between the 'bees' – the active agents of social innovation – and the 'trees' – the institutional frameworks which host and support them.

Not-for-profit civil society organizations are seen to be a key element in 'bottom-linking' in a number of the case studies. Forms of not-for-profit organization may in themselves be a focus of social innovation. The case study by Midheme of settlement upgrading in Kenya provides an excellent example. Faced with the experience that conventional upgrading programmes based on individual ownership of land can often lead to improved housing being taken over by the more affluent, displacing existing residents, the solution developed was to establish a form of civil-society organization new to Kenya – a Community Land Trust – to retain ownership of the land and thus prevent this gentrification process. The importance of professional support to grassroots community action is also seen in various aspects of this case study. In particular, given a land-law regime in Kenya unsympathetic to innovative, collective forms of land ownership, creative legal expertise was essential to craft legal instruments for the Community Land Trust. Calzada discusses one of the most internationally-celebrated examples of non-profit social enterprise, the Mondragón network of co-

operatives originating in the Basque region of Spain. In doing so, though, he points out the dangers of declining communitarian social capital and the emergence of an individualistic form of social innovation: termed 'triumphalist talent'.

The governance and welfare regime within which social innovation occurs is an important theme. In some cases its favourable nature is clear. In the Danish case study, social innovation primarily involves a public agency, the public library, and its professional staff operating within a strong social democratic national welfare regime. In the Brugse Poort case study, the existence in Flanders of a 'neo-communitarian' regime is identified as an important context for the development of coalitions to promote urban regeneration.

Conversely, social innovation can take place through the process of struggle with less favourable contexts. In the Italian case study, Vitale and Membretti describe the established policies of the Italian State of housing Roma people in 'nomad camps', as increased their segregation and marginalization and being 'part of the problem they are supposed to solve'. The Kenyan example clearly involves a level of unmet needs and of resource constraints of a different order to the European case studies, and also what Midheme describes as a political context 'hampered by a top-down planning framework, excessive bureaucracy and political interference'. Nonetheless, these case studies share with the others positive lessons regarding the possibilities of progressive social innovation.

The role of arts and culture in socially-creative strategies is an important concern of this handbook and an important element in the examples and experiences described in this part. The potential of arts, and of celebration, in opening segregated communities and spaces, explored in the account of the Roma housing project in Italy, is one example, while in Ghent the desire to include a cultural dimension in renewal projects led, for example, to the long-term involvement of a theatre group in providing a 'socio-cultural trajectory' supporting the population through the process of neighbourhood change.

The role of arts and culture is represented most of all by the example of Montemor-o-Novo. As noted above, Vicari Haddock and Tornaghi speak of the search for progressive social change as a 'fuel' driving social innovation. Cultural creativity may be seen as another such 'fuel', though as is made clear in the discussion of Montemor-e-Novo there must be a link to social values for artistic creativity to become socially creative. The 'fuel' must also be complemented by elements of the 'engine' of organizational forms, in this case involving key artistic animateurs but also a progressive municipal government.

13. Just another roll of the dice: a socially creative initiative to assure Roma housing in North Western Italy

Tommaso Vitale and Andrea Membretti

13.1 INTRODUCTION: A CASE OF SPACE PRODUCTION AND EMPOWERMENT

This chapter concerns how social innovation relates to the social production of space (MacCallum et al. 2009). Usually, the scholarly literature on local welfare, social work, and 'social cohesion' at the urban level mostly fails to consider the relevance of space (Bifulco and Vitale 2003; Ranci 2010; Andreotti et al. 2012). The spatial dimension of a socially creative strategy is constituted in physical and symbolic boundaries, in the built environment, in situated objects and relationships. Space can significantly contribute to stigma and exclusion, notably in segregated places. In fact, space performs: it has social effects on people's opportunities and on their self-esteem (van Ham et al. 2012). Nonetheless the space is itself a social product; it is the object of strategies. Most social innovators invest in space, trying to shape it, to modify it, to make it more inclusive. They aim to use it as a lever for social innovation. Some such innovations use art as a tool to produce change in the spatial configuration for deprived groups.

In this chapter we observe a case of a socially creative strategy in which a particularly difficult housing problem was solved thanks to a holistic approach to the production of space. More specifically, we observed how a network of NGOs was able to manage a situation of housing exclusion for some highly stigmatized Roma families. In the small town of Settimo Torinese (47,494 inhabitants), the network was able to satisfy the housing needs of 35 people, to open up a process of wide and inclusive democratic governance within the community, and to empower all the actors involved in the project, especially the beneficiaries. Yet the true character of this social innovation lies precisely at the level of the production of space. The main problem that the network sought to address was the issue of segregation that housing for Roma usually reproduces (Sigona 2005). Welfare provisions for Roma in Italy are traditionally part of the problem they are supposed to solve: they maintain segregation and fail to support Roma inclusion in broader urban life.

This network therefore decided to design a project and implement it in a very collaborative way. They did not provide a specialized shelter for evicted Roma people, or for Roma housing emergencies; rather, they invented a participative path within the Turin metropolitan area to produce a space that could *also*, but not exclusively, welcome Roma families, without labelling them and without separating them from the wider local community.

13.2 ROMA IN ITALY: A CRISIS OF TERRITORIAL EMBEDDEDNESS

Housing conditions for Roma groups in Italy are a particularly weighty and worrying problem. This is an alarming situation all over Europe, but there are some particular problems in the Italian case (FRA 2009). Here, local policies for Roma and Sinti groups are mostly based on a singular 'policy instrument' (Lascoumes and Le Galès 2007), the so called '*campo nomadi*' (Nomad Camp). This is a highly segregating public housing provision that forces very different Roma groups (we are not dealing with a *single* ethnic group when we speak of Roma) to live together in highly isolated areas, in poor prefabs, subject to special regulations and differential administrative treatment (Membretti 2009a). In the late 1970s, this policy instrument was developed as an adaptation of an earlier urban policy tool dedicated to 'carnies', with the idea that all the Roma groups were travellers, with a nomadic behaviour which requires only temporary settlements for caravans. It has been diffused in the absence of any kind of national legislative framework or regional policy coordination (Vitale 2009a). Thirty years later, the Nomad Camp remains the mainstream local policy for housing Roma and Sinti groups, with a lack of integration between housing policy and other social policies. The current estimated Roma 'population' living in Italy is between 170,000 and 200,000, but only a dozen or so towns in Italy have experimented with some form of social innovation to replace the Nomad Camps (Vitale 2009b).

In reality, the performative[1] outcomes of this policy instrument are profound in terms of decreasing Roma voices (Dean et al. 2005) and degrading both Roma identities and intergenerational relationships by effectively criminalizing their traditional uses of space. What is at stake, and what forms the main point of crisis, is precisely relations between these groups and territory. It is a crisis of spatial embeddedness due to settlement segregation.

In Italy the contradictions presented by Roma and Sinti groups' presence fall on local authorities that lack adequate tools to face them;[2] besides, they are rarely backed by higher level public authorities. However, there is a degree of freedom to manoeuvre at the local level, allowing authorities to bend policies in many possible directions. Public policy choices that can be enacted at the local level strongly circumscribe opportunities for action regarding primary and secondary education, work placement, healthcare, sociability and, above all, housing. They can either favour or hinder the conditions of 'recognition' (Pizzorno 2007, pp. 275–95) of these communities in a 'necessarily complex and self-contradictory' social order (Jobert 1998, p. 25).[3]

Policies implemented at the local level are always the result of situated interaction between various actors with different interests, within common constraints. Despite the crucial role of policies and instrument inertia (especially the 'Nomad camp' device), it is nonetheless possible that social innovation can happen. What is at stake for scientific knowledge is to understand why and how socially creative strategies arise in such a constrained area, and what forms they take (Moulaert et al. 2010). The next two sections will consider these questions in relation to the 'Dice', an innovative housing project which reversed the effects of segregation in Settimo Torinese.

13.3   WHERE DOES SOCIAL INNOVATION COME FROM?

In the small town of Borgaro (13,000 inhabitants) near Turin, the presence of Roma newcomers from Romania was perceived as a threat to 'city security'. Some came in 1999, when the first Roma migration from Romania began. They built a shantytown on the land surrounding farmhouse called La Merla. After the summer floods of 2004 and 2005 in Romania, some other Roma groups arrived in Borgaro. The settlement was illegal, composed of wooden hovels and shacks, without sanitation, gas, electricity or a water supply. The housing conditions were ghastly. At the same time, the children of this community went to school, a very important element in the construction of broader social ties. School dynamics and urban space are closely intertwined and increasingly interact in producing or alleviating segregation (Oberti 2007). Parents of Roma children's classmates who had not before done so began to consider Roma as people worthy of respect, and formed relationships with them.

On 16 November 2006 the shantytown burned down, and 110 people lost everything they had. The municipality did not want to offer them shelter, but the friendly relationships that had developed between parents of classmates helped to mobilize two local NGOs – Acmos and Terra del Fuoco (TdF) – neither of which was involved in aid for the homeless, but both were able to welcome the victims in their ordinary offices. They remained there for only one week in what was certainly a heavy and exhausting situation. After that week they were moved to a Nomad Camp in Turin for 10 days, and then an emergency camp was organized in collaboration with the Red Cross until June 2007. Nevertheless, the experience of that first week was a catalyst to activate these two NGOs, and especially TdF, to think about a better housing solution for this Roma group.

They mobilized their political resources and attracted the interest of the National Ministry of Social Affairs, who promised to sustain any housing solution found, on the condition that it could be considered 'innovative'. In fact the money from the Ministry financing never came, but its promise provided legitimacy to the issue raised by the two NGOs. It was a risky game: the two NGOs used the Ministry promise as leverage to mobilize other institutional and social actors; through positive use, they made it a self-fulfilling prophecy.

The process was long and thick with various dynamics. They asked for a building, or a field or an area to promote a project within the town of Borgaro, but the mayor was averse to the idea and opposed it. When the Municipality of Borgaro proved unwilling, the TdF association instead formed an alliance with the Province of Turin to try to find another town inclined to welcome at least a small number of Roma families. This they finally found in the Municipality of Settimo Torinese, a small town with a large building previously used as social shelter. At the same time, the public and visible call for an open municipality produced a widespread consensus around the claim, and enlarged the network of organizations providing support: the large third sector association 'Gruppo Abele', the Milanese organization '*Architettura delle Convivenze*' (AdC, or Architecture of Living Together), the Turin Catholic Pastoral Office for Migrants and, most importantly, the Regional Bank Foundation.

In brief, during this process two main mechanisms stand out as crucial: (1)

the relevance of social ties built at the most local level, thanks to social proximity through Roma school inclusion, and (2) the prominence of scaling up, finding alliances at higher levels. Both of them produce the multiplication of ties as a by-product.

Using the analysis of Vicari Haddock and Tornaghi in Chapter 19 of this Handbook, we can say that the relationship provided by the inclusion of Roma children in schools offered a source of visibility and motivation that countered political and moral indifference and nihilism. At the same time, the embeddedness of two local NGOs in solid and stable structures of governance allowed them to 'exploit' and mobilize previous political ties to claim and push for an innovative solution to empower Roma and to satisfy their housing needs.

13.4 THE DICE: SOCIALLY CREATIVE APPROACH TO PROVIDING HOUSING AND MORE

The municipality of Settimo Torinese offered the TdF association the use of a 700 square metre, two-floor building, a former gymnasium built in the 1970s and used, from 2003 on, by the social services as a shelter for people with social and mental diseases. The place was highly stigmatized in the neighbourhood because of its inhabitants, and, in recent years, progressively decayed, also due to squatting by homeless people and heroin addicts.

The network of organizations involved in the project was very aware of this stigma: a stigmatized population in a stigmatized building could make for an explosive situation.[4] Thanks to the impetus of AdC, they decided to implement a non-specialized project: a shelter devoted not only to Roma families, in which some Roma families

could find temporary reception (for three years at the most), but where non-Roma families could also find a warm welcome. It was also to be a housing shelter used for more than just shelter: the organizations decided to 'sacrifice' some Roma dwelling space in view of the urgent need to reduce the risk of segregation and isolation. They constructed apartments for 8 Roma families (17 children and 18 adults), but also apartments for non-Roma families, an office for 'social mediators' (educators skilled in managing neighbourhood conflicts), a temporary shelter for refugees, and a flat that could be rent to students and workers active in broader social and political initiatives throughout Turin's metropolitan area. At the same time, the large patio was allotted as an open space for the local community, with a conference room and a space designed for art exhibitions and other cultural activities for artists from the region.

The restoration of the building, carried out according to the project authored by the AdC, was financed by the Compagnia di S. Paolo bank foundation, with an initial budget of 150,000€ (later increased); the Province of Torino supported the restoration, offering several job-grants to the Roma people directly participating in the refurbishment. This process was organized by the AdC as a 'building site-school', in which the Roma involved (and to whom the project was addressed) could gain on-the-job training, thus obtaining a qualification useful in the labour market. This was a particularly important outcome: it encouraged the education of children. In fact, several studies (Alietti 2009; Vitale and Cousin 2011) have shown that education policies for underclass migrant Roma children only work if their parents are involved in vocational training projects too, with experiencing first-hand direct access to the labour market, and therefore the relevance of education for their sons and daughters.

The entire project was 'interesting' in the peculiar sense that it attracted interest (Callon 1986). To name but a few, when the Ministry of Social Affairs finally decided not to finance the project, an influential local Bank Foundation stood alone in financing the 'Dice', 'interested' in the kind of innovation the 'Dice' was making.

Nevertheless, what seems more interesting is not the process of finding a good way of providing shelter for some of the Roma families, but the *way* in which the social housing intervention was provided. 'The way' is understood as the style and method through which the project was realised. The main question here is 'how?' and not only 'why?' or 'what?' Even the way in which the Dice was constructed contained an idea to contrast ghettoization effects.

First, the same Roma to be housed were engaged to restore and refurbish the building. They were hired by a social cooperative, and worked on building their own houses, but were paid and learning a job. The network of organizations involved provided a guarantee that the Roma builders would continue working after the end of the Dice project. The possibility for the Roma to demonstrate, through work, their capabilities and worth was a powerful means for them to gain a self-confident attitude (empowerment) with respect both to themselves and to 'outside' society: in fact, the concrete action of building their houses also promoted a positive public image of the Roma, usually suffering from the widely held prejudice that labels them as 'unable' to work, or unwilling to work.[5]

Second, at each step of the building's restoration an open party was organized involving the local community: schools, parishes, associations, sports teams, and so on. The result was to show the quality of the work, to permit the formation of new ties, to incrementally reduce the stigma attached to the building, and to engage a larger population in the aims of the project, producing a feeling of community ownership. Indeed, the building provided very different services: housing requires that the privacy and intimacy of each family be retained, while the open space needed to allow for circulation and attraction for the local community. Celebrating each step in the building of the Dice was a way to manage the plurality of functions, discussing them cheerfully.[6]

Thirdly, the building yard was also conceived as open. The building yard simplified the processes of mutual acquaintance between Roma builders, social workers, citizens, neighbours, and other local agencies. We can find here a vision of space based on the 'introvert-extrovert' polarity (Membretti 2007): the tension between these two opposite poles that becomes the field of experimentation for an idea of society and of social relations, a space considered as a meeting point between community and society, and between several communities. In this sense – both symbolically and actually – the 'court' (communitarian place) and the 'square' (public space) tend to coexist in the building and interface continuously through the practices carried out there. Openness towards the outside and an inner 'protection' are therefore elements that coexist within the Dice project.

Fourth, the Dice project was not designed by some architects looking in from the outside, but was continuously discussed, co-planned, negotiated and revised together with each of the Roma families. In fact, following the participative methods of AdC, the construction period was intended as the centre of a process of building 'social fabric' in which all the people involved (inhabitants, members of associations, etc.) make their contribution to the concrete realization of the spaces and, moreover, to their inter-subjective transformation in places. In this sense, the building activity nourishes, brick by brick, a sort of material public sphere, or, we may say, a very concrete and basic community of discourse.

Last but not least, the active role played by the Roma was very important in the process of consensus-building driven by the mayor and the TdF association. One of the main stereotypes against Roma is that they are idle and layabouts, 'bumming around' (Vitale and Claps 2010). The direct employment of Roma builders was a central point: they worked on a self-building project, therefore reducing costs and public expenditure; their work meant it was difficult to criticise the project as charity; what is more they worked to provide an exhibition space for the town.

13.5   THE ROLE OF ARTS IN CREATING A BRIDGE BETWEEN THE COMMUNITIES

The empowering approach to the restoration and rehabilitation of the building created a style that has been preserved by the TdF association in its daily work with the Roma people living in the Dice. Their social workers provide help in finding work, connect with parishes, theatre schools and sporting and musical associations, but also with informal groups of volunteers, to provide some educational support, to find economic opportunities in new niches (such as the 'last minute market'), to support children with mental health problems, and mount public campaigns against racism and discrimination.[7] Schooling provides an excellent source of positive relationships to foster and encourage community embeddedness.

At the very heart of the Dice project, and a continuing part of its daily life, are arts and cultural activities. These work to maintain and foster community relationships and multiply social and economic opportunities for the people involved. In the Dice project, the housing exclusion problem of Roma and the possibilities for alternative modes of space production were expressed and addressed through creative arts. AdC pushed the Dice project to face the trial of (re)constructing identities that could be shared by many different groups. TdF has insisted on realising this difficult task in artistic performance and activities, provoking communication within communities and among groups, a key aspect of the project's success as a social innovation (see also Tremblay and Pilati, Chapter 5, and André et al., Chapter 18).

Since 2007, AdC has been co-operating with the *Centro Studi Assenza* (Absence – Study and Research Centre), a scientific and cultural association founded in Milan in the 1970s by the psychologist and artist Paolo Ferrari. The *Centro Studi Assenza* has been promoting and hosting a dialogue between different cultures and disciplines of Social Sciences and Humanities, and a focus on neuro-sciences. The centre stresses activities and reflection on the relationship between art and science, developing and following a complex psychological and philosophical approach called *in-Absence*.[8]

The multi-disciplinary team of the centre is composed of several professionals from different disciplines such as psychiatric medicine, psychology, architecture, urban studies, and modern arts; the team is involved in artistic-scientific-architectural projects, developed in public and private spaces in metropolitan areas, often as symbolic elements of wider socio-territorial interventions aiming to respond to basic

Source: Archive of *Terra del Fuoco* association, Turin, Italy (reproduced with permission).

Figure 13.1   *The Dice, main entrance, showing the* Wandering Knight

needs, and usually expressed by ethnic minorities or populations with social problems.

In the Dice project, the artistic dimension plays a role of primary importance: the redecoration of the façade, focused on an artistic-scientific composition by Ferrari entitled *Il cavaliere errante* (the Wandering Knight; Figure 13.1), is the lever for the transformation of the building – in the perception of both its inhabitants and a wider public sphere – from a place characterized by marginality to a point of reference for the surroundings. The artistic installation is constituted by a sculpture in fibreglass, placed on a cement and iron base, made by people living in the Dice, with two big photographic prints on aluminium plates, placed on the façade of the building.

The artistic installation – promoting an aesthetic dimension of living – aims to dismantle the negative and stereotypical image usually associated with Roma housing as shantytowns or abandoned buildings. Art here is concerned as an element of opening towards the external – that is a communicational bridge between the several different groups populating the town – but, at the same time, as a support in the construction of new forms of identity and belonging, involving inhabitants of the Dice and other users of the building. So, arts may offer the basis for a territorial rooting, focused on a universalistic system of symbols, opposite to every defensive and residual form of closing, even of ethnic nature. And, as seen in the previous paragraph, the process of art making is relevant as a process, when it is conducted as catalysts for a territory's broad opening-through.

Through the use of arts, the Dice project displays its intention of marking the post-industrial territory of the suburb in a positive way, giving it a new social and cultural form of recognition, and a new and 'invented' spatial centrality at local and metropolitan level. The character of the artistic intervention could therefore be considered as performative, as it promotes identity creation processes based on complexity that involve not only the inhabitants and other users of the Dice, but also – since it is not a specialized and segregated shelter – people living in the local and extra local environments. The Dice should be considered as socially innovative in this sense too: that in its structural and cultural constitution the artistic dimension is at the centre of a creative process, essentially intended as the social construction of spaces for mutual recognition between different communities, on the base of a common and shared place to live.

13.6 HOUSING (AND HOSTING) SOCIAL CREATIVITY: SOCIAL INNOVATION AND THE PRODUCTION OF SPACE

Roma and Sinti groups are very different and cannot be considered as a single homogeneous population. Hostility against these groups is higher in Italy than anywhere else in Western Europe (Vitale and Claps 2010). Prejudices against 'gypsies' are continuously fed by a highly segregating urban policy, which has confined these groups to special 'nomad camps' at the margins of urban life. This ethnically differentiated treatment has rarely been denounced by international institutions, and remains the dominant policy type in the country, espe-

cially in the north-western regions (Open Society Institute et al. 2008; Enwereuzor and Di Pasquale 2009).

It is precisely in this part of the country that the 'Dice' was born: as such, it not only faces contestation from xenophobic groups, but also has to struggle with politicians who seek electoral advantage by opposing Roma and Sinti settlements, despite having encouraged and approved them before.

The social innovation promoted by the project is therefore noteworthy because it has been able to *differentiate* and personalize the housing offered to Roma groups, beginning from their wishes and projects rather than from previous stereotyped categorizations. It works on three elements of social innovation: (1) looking at each person in an empowerment perspective (especially in terms of labour market insertion); (2) taking care to mobilize private and public resources to build 'decent' customized housing; (3) strong engagement to promote inclusive governance and widen spaces for excluded voices, with a strong commitment from the Municipality.

The case of the Dice is also socially innovative because it demonstrates the incremental and intersubjective production of a space that is perceived, both by inhabitants and users, as a place of social inclusion and, thanks to its artistic dimension, as an inter-cultural expression of their life together. This was a very soft and tricky process: the housing needed to be conceived as a space for encounters, but could not become a completely 'public space' – it had to remain a space where families lived, with privacy, ownership, and invisibility for reasons of confidence and familiarity (Breviglieri 2006). At the same time it needed to be conceived to be used in an open way *also*, to attract and not detract from sociability. It was not a problem that could be fixed defining stable and definitive public or private functions to each physical space of the building. As we observed in our research, it was a problem of planning and promoting a process of empowerment that allowed those involved to learn how to manage tensions.

In such dynamics of empowerment, physical space plays a significant role, moving from the articulation of a variety of spaces inside the building: spaces devoted to different, but not discrete, functions (living, exhibitions, hostel, offices . . .), producing important interactions between different needs and different people (Roma and non Roma people, inhabitants and users of the building, etc.).

The sustainability of the housing project was reinforced by a way of doing things based on mutual recognition of individual uniqueness, and reciprocal respect, in which the border between inhabiting and opening up to the local community could always be negotiated by the same beneficiaries. And, as we have seen, the arts played a special role in this sustainability. It helped to open the housing shelter to the outside world, but also qualified that opening and contributed to learning how to manage tensions between different logics and development directions. It allowed the 'disgraceful' image of a slummy, degraded place – as Roma settlements are usually stereotypically considered – to be reversed. Artistic elements modify relationships between the building, potential inhabitants, the territory, and citizens. Meanwhile, artistic facilities within the 'Dice' are considered – not only by the promoting organizations, but also by the Roma – as creating a new sort of identity. Roma are recognized not for their assumed criminal behaviour or their deprivation, hardship and begging but for their cultural production and capabilities. Arts sustain the memory of

long-term traditions and support voice, reducing fear of self-expression.

The 'Dice' is therefore a noteworthy case of social innovation because it has allowed Roma welfare to be addressed not only as the satisfaction of basic needs, but also as empowering them in their capacity to make a cultural contribution to urban life. Furthermore, this case study is very useful to highlight the relationship between social innovation and the production of the space. We saw that in this case, activists, artists and social workers join together in a coalition against Roma exclusion, to produce a space of ties that bind. The 'Dice style', has been a social innovation in the design *and* management of the boundaries of a welfare shelter. It is a creative mode of space production: the space allows identities to be expressed not in order to divide and close, but as a stimulus for encounters and urban dialogue. This socially-creative process had two aspects: first, providing housing and, second, integrating the housing and the Roma residents into the local community. Both of them concern the spatial dimension of social innovation. Activists were aware of this, and they designed the Dice to try to cope with some of the major problems other empowering agencies have faced. Problems have not all been solved for all time in the designing of the space of the Dice. But the artistic sensibility and the performing activities realized in the Dice contribute to open room for reflection on the social effects of space, and on how to produce inclusionary changes.

13.7   QUESTIONS FOR DISCUSSION

- In your country, are there any ethnic minorities that face problems similar to those of Roma in Italy? Why? What do you think are the main mechanisms that prevent them from accessing housing?

- Why were arts and culture so important in the Dice case? More generally, how can arts and other sociocultural practices help to reduce the stigma of marginalized spaces?
- How is the production of space important to the social aims of an innovation for disadvantaged groups?
- Do you think that the 'celebratory style' of the Dice project is just a detail, or a necessary ingredient for community involvement? Are festivals and parties really policy instruments, or just a social work technique, not to be accounted for in policy design and implementation?
- What are the main tools and processes that are used in your town to build consensus around projects for socially unwanted groups? How do they differ or otherwise to those discussed in the Dice case?

NOTES

1. About the performative power of images, see Membretti (2009b).
2. An innovative attempt to create social and technical tools – in a participative approach – to overcome the spatial segregation produced by the Nomad Camps was made in 2009 at the workshop 'I Sinti abitano Pavia' ('Sinti people live in Pavia'), held at the University of Pavia, Faculty of Engineering (Co-ordinator: Andrea Membretti). The results of the workshop, involving the local Sinti community, the Municipality, several NGOs and a large group of students and scholars, are published at: www.sociability.it/sintiapavia. Some interesting social innovation in local policies in Trento is described in Vitale (2010a).
3. The reflections made by Ambrosini (2008, p. 212) are particularly interesting from this point of view. It is noted that, in the case of the Roma, conflicts surface within 'territorial mobility practices of transnational minorities and social benefits still regulated by bonds of affiliation to

nation-states, whose result is to dig deep inequalities within the various groups that constitute Roma and Sinti complex'.

4. This is an issue highly discussed by contemporary urban movements, and by networks of innovation in mental healthcare; see Vitale (2010b). But the high level of reflexivity on this point is not specific to the Italian context: see Duyvendak (2011, pp. 63–73).
5. It should be noted that Italy is the most racist country in the EU with respect to Roma: according to the European Values Survey, in 2008 62.8 per cent of the Italian population did not want Roma as neighbours (compared to 33.8 in UK and 25.5 in France; see Vitale et al. 2011).
6. Celebration remains a very important habit in daily life of Dice: for each child's birthday there is a party with schoolmates and their families.
7. In testimony to one anti-racist campaign 'No fear', one of the Roma children living in Dice was honoured by meeting the President of the Italian Republic, Giorgio Napolitano.
8. More details are available at: www.in-absence.org (last accessed 10 January 2013).

REFERENCES

(References in bold are recommended reading.)

Ambrosini, Maurizio (2008), 'La sfida più ardua: costruire politiche di integrazione per (e con) le minoranze rom e sinte', in Osservatorio Regionale per l'integrazione e la multietnicità, *Gli immigrati in Lombardia. Rapporto 2007*, Milano: ISMU, pp. 199–222.

Alietti, Alfredo (2009), 'Generazioni nomadi tra tradizione e mutamento', in Tommaso Vitale (ed.), *Politiche possibili. Abitare le città con i rom e i sinti*, Roma: Carocci, pp. 38–46.

Andreotti, Alberta, Enzo Mingione and Emanuele Polizzi (2012), 'Local Welfare Systems: A Challenge for Social Cohesion', *Urban Studies*, **49**, 1925–40.

Bifulco, Lavinia and Tommaso Vitale (2003), 'Da strutture a processi: servizi, spazi e territori del welfare locale', *Sociologia Urbana e Rurale*, **25** (72), 95–108.

Breviglieri, Marc (2006), 'La décence du logement et le monde habité', in Jacques Roux (ed.), *Sensibiliser. La sociologie dans le vif du monde*, La Tour d'Aigues: Ed. de l'Aube, pp. 90–104.

Callon, Michel (1986), 'Some Elements of a Sociology of Translation: Domestication of the Scallops and the Fishermen of St. Brieuc Bay', in John Law (ed.), *Power, Action and Belief: a New Sociology of Knowledge?*, London: Routledge, pp. 196–223.

Dean, Hartley, Jean-Michel Bonvin, Pascale Vielle and Nicolas Farvaque (2005), 'Developing

Capabilities and Rights in Welfare-to-Work Policies', *European Societies*, **7** (1), 3–26.

Duyvendak, Jan Willem (2011), *The Politics of Home*, London: Palgrave MacMillan.

Enwereuzor, Udo C. and Laura Di Pasquale (2009), *Italy: Thematic Study on Housing Conditions of Roma and Travellers*, COSPE (RAXEN National Focal Point).

FRA (European Union Agency for Fundamental Rights) (2009), 'Housing conditions of Roma and Travellers in the European Union. Comparative report', http://fra.europa.eu/fraWebsite/attachments/ROMA-Housing-Comparative-Report_en.pdf (last accessed 11 July 2012).

Jobert, Bruno (1998), 'La regulation politique: l'émergence d'un nouveau régime de connaissance?', in Jacques Commaille and Bruno Jobert (eds), *Les métamorphoses de la régulation politique*, Paris: LGDJ.

Lascoumes, Pierre and Patrick Le Galès (2007), 'Understanding Public Policy through Its Instruments. From the Nature of Instruments to the Sociology of Public Policy Instrumentation', *Governance: An International Journal of Policy, Administration, and Institutions*, 20 (1), 1–21.

MacCallum, Diana, Frank Moulaert, Jean Hillier and Serena Vicari Haddock (eds) (2009), *Social Innovation and Territorial Development*, Aldershot: Ashgate.

Membretti, Andrea (2007), 'Centro Sociale Leoncavallo. Building Citizenship as an Innovative Service', *European Journal of Urban and Regional Studies*, 14 (3), 252–263.

Membretti, Andrea (2009a), 'Pavia: la negazione istituzionale di una questione pubblica', in Tommaso Vitale (ed.), *Politiche possibili. Abitare le città con i rom e i sinti*, Roma: Carocci, pp. 69–79.

Membretti, Andrea (2009b), 'Per un uso performativo delle immagini nella ricerca-azione sociale', *lo Squaderno*, **12**.

Moulaert, Frank, Eric Swyngedouw, Flavia Martinelli and Sara González (eds) (2010), *Can Neighbourhoods Save the City? Community Development and Social Innovation*, London: Routledge.

Oberti, Marco (2007), 'Social and School Differentiation in Urban Space: Inequalities and Local Configurations', *Environment and Planning A*, 39 (1), 208–227.

Open Society Institute (OSI), European Roma Rights Centre (ERRC), Roma Centre for Social Intervention and Studies (Romani CRISS), Roma Civic Alliance (RCR) and Centre on Housing Rights and Evictions (COHRE) (2008), *Security à la italiana. Fingerprinting, Extreme Violence and Harassment of Roma in Italy*, Budapest: OSI, http://www.opensocietyfoundations.org/sites/default/files/fingerprinting_20080715.pdf (last accessed 10 January 2013).

Pizzorno, Alessandro (2007), *Il velo della diversità. Studi su razionalità e riconoscimento*, Milano: Feltrinelli.

Ranci, Costanzo (ed.) (2010), *Social Vulnerability in Europe. The new configuration of social risks*, London: Palgrave MacMillan.

Sigona, Nando (2005), 'Locating the "Gypsy problem". The Roma in Italy: Stereotyping, Labelling and Nomad Camps', *Journal of Ethnic and Migration Studies*, **31** (4), 741–756.

van Ham, Maarten, David Manley, Nick Bailey, Ludi Simpson and Duncan Maclennan (eds) (2012), *Neighbourhood Effects Research: New Perspectives*, Berlin: Springer Verlag.

Vitale, Tommaso (2009a), 'Politique des évictions. Une approche pragmatique', in Federico Cantelli, Marta Roca i Escoda, Joan Stavo-Debauge and Luca Pattaroni (eds), *Sensibilités pragmatiques. Enquêter sur l'action publique*, Bruxelles: P.I.E. Peter Lang, pp. 71–92.

Vitale, Tommaso (2009b), 'Sociologia dos conflitos locais contra os Rom e os Sintos na Itália: pluralidade de contextos e variedade de *policy instruments*', *Revista Cidades. Comunidades e Terrritórios*, **18**, 76–103.

Vitale, Tommaso (2010a), 'Le basi cognitive degli interventi educativi con i sinti. Eredità, continuità, stratificazioni e cambiamenti', *Animazione Sociale*, **241**, 34–43.

Vitale, Tommaso (2010b), 'Building a Shared Interest. Olinda, Milan: Social Innovation between Strategy and Organizational Learning', in Frank Moulaert, Eric Swyngedouw, Flavia Martinelli and Sara González (eds), *Can Neighbourhoods Save the City? Community Development and Social Innovation*, London: Routledge, pp. 81–92.

Vitale, Tommaso and Enrico Claps (2010), 'Not Always the Same Old Story: Spatial Segregation and Feelings of Dislike against Roma and Sinti in Large Cities and Medium-size Towns in Italy', in Michael Stewart adn Márton Rövid (eds), *Multi-Disciplinary Approaches to Romany Studies*, Budapest: CEU Press, pp. 228–253.

Vitale, Tommaso and Bruno Cousin (2011), 'En Italie. Scolarisation des Roms et des Sintis', *Cahiers pédagogiques*, HSN, **21**, 164–166.

Vitale, Tommaso, Enrico Claps and Paola Arrigoni (2011), 'I sondaggi e il loro uso. Problemi di cecità logica a partire dal caso dei Rom', *Comunicazione Politica*, **12** (2), 167–195.

14. From 'book container' to community centre

John Andersen, Kristian Delica and Martin Severin Frandsen

14.1 INTRODUCTION

The case study discussed in this chapter concerns the design and development of a community centre in the disadvantaged neighbourhood of Gellerup located in the city of Aarhus in Denmark. The case illustrates that it is possible for formal public institutions to be creatively and socially innovative and bridge the gap between bureaucratic modes of organization and the human needs and social relations of marginalized people. It is an example of a creative institutional set-up that supports citizen empowerment and advocacy for the neighbourhood and represents an alternative to mainstream new public management modes of organizing public sector institutions.

Community Center Gellerup (CCG) was initiated by a local public library branch, community workers and local civil society organizations (CSOs) with the objective of developing a multifunctional community centre uniting library services, health promotion and a counselling service for ethnic minorities, the latter being the majority among the local residents. The idea behind the community centre was to bring public welfare services 'back (or closer) to the people', and the aim was to create daily practices and strategic capacities that in an integrated yet flexible way should respond better to citizens' needs compared with mainstream fragmented bureaucratically organized social services. CCG represents a concrete version of an institution working with social innovation in relation to meeting basic human needs as outlined in the general introduction to this Handbook. As a socially innovative institutional set-up CCG emphasizes commitment to practical sharing of knowledge and learning across different professional groups (social workers, nurses, librarians and so forth) working directly with the citizens' daily needs in the neighbourhood. Furthermore, the community centre is a common platform for active networking and capacity building among community activists and civil society organizations in the neighbourhood.

14.2 FROM LIBRARY TO COMMUNITY CENTRE

Libraries in disadvantaged neighbourhoods across the globe are redefining their role from that of serving as 'containers for books' to acting as agents in innovative community empowerment processes. Libraries engage in a wide range of activities from creating open learning centres for information technology to bridge 'the digital divide'[1] to providing homework assistance for local children from ethnic minorities. In the process of repositioning themselves, libraries can bring about empowering networks to local welfare institutions and voluntary associations, housing associations and citizens and sometimes create new institutional forms.

In Denmark a national program for transforming public libraries into community centres was established in 2008 following some pioneering 'first movers' amongst public libraries based in disadvantaged neighbourhoods. This suggests that in Denmark, libraries in disadvantaged neighbourhoods are taking major steps to support improvement of the life situation of the local community and marginalized ethnic minority groups.[2] On the basis of the experiences from CCG, the Danish Agency for Libraries and Media have, by securing a grant of approximately 2.5 million Euros of government funding, established a development program for libraries in disadvantaged neighbourhoods willing to participate in a process of institutional transformation. At the time of writing (fall 2011), 16 public libraries were taking part in the project.

The development of the community centre in the neighbourhood of Gellerup was studied through an empowerment evaluation (Fetterman and Wandersman 2005) running from 2005 to 2007 (Andersen and Frandsen 2007; Andersen et al. 2007). Gellerup is, in terms of income, the poorest district in Denmark and has one of the highest concentrations of immigrants in Aarhus (Andersen 2008). The community centre development project was linked to a seven-year long integrated area renewal program financed in part by the European URBAN 2 program and inspired by the Imagine Chicago and the Asset Based Community Development approaches (Kretzman and Rans 2005; Urbanprogrammet 2007; Andersen 2008).

Before we proceed to the case study the following section discusses the framework used in analysing CCG, which builds on insights from the literature on empowerment and social innovation in relation to local community development. We then take a look at the lessons learned from the reinvention of Chicago's public libraries, which show a striking resemblance to the development of community centres in Denmark. We move on to further introduce CCG and by way of a short historical perspective on the genesis of the case, we highlight the specific local conditions for this innovative institutional transformation. We conclude by summing up some of the lessons learned from CCG as an institutional platform aimed at addressing social exclusion and supporting citizens in need.

14.3 COMMUNITY EMPOWERMENT STRATEGIES

In this section we provide a brief introduction to the concept of empowerment and its extension to a community development context. The function of this section is twofold, as 'empowerment' functions both as an analytical concept in our research guiding the case study *and* as a 'practical' point of orientation in the everyday working life for the staff at CCG. From the onset the development of the community centre was based on norms and values collectively and continuously developed by the staff inspired by empowerment approaches to community development. In CCG empowerment thus forms a strategic frame for dealing with and responding to the needs of (often) marginalized groups in the neighbourhood.[3]

The concept of empowerment was brought to the fore in the 1970s with Paulo Freire's book *Pedagogy of the Oppressed*. Freire defined empowerment as 'learning to understand social, political and economic disparities and to act against these elements of reality' (Freire 1974, p. 19). A more recent important contribution to the theory of empowerment was John Friedmann's *Empowerment: The*

Politics of Alternative Development. For Friedmann empowerment was the ability to direct one's own destiny and the restoration of initiative to those in need in contrast to centralized and bureaucratically devised development policies (Friedmann 1992). In prolongation of this tradition we define empowerment as processes of mobilization and change 'that improve underprivileged individuals' and social groups' ability to create and handle mental, material, social, cultural and symbolic relevant resources' (Andersen et al. 2003, p. 7). Empowerment strategies range from the strengthening of individual self-confidence to the enhancement of the ability (from the local community level) to influence society's developmental direction over a longer period of time (Andersen et al. 2003).

Mobilization and processes of capacity building in social groups and local communities can be described as *horizontal empowerment*, which among other things includes creating social relations of trust and mutual recognition within neighbourhoods, overcoming negative stereotypes, lack of confidence and respect between various groups of residents. One important aspect here is the relations of trust and reciprocity between local residents and the local welfare professionals (the staff in day-care institutions, schools, crime prevention work and so forth). This is by no means a foregone conclusion, as part of the problem of social exclusion in disadvantaged neighbourhoods consists in the fact that local welfare professionals not only lack resources, but also work in bureaucratically organized and fragmented systems without common visions and spaces for ongoing learning. In many cases, the professionals 'burn out', and do not (or do not have the opportunity structures to) see themselves as active agents and innovators for positive social change in local community life.

Vertical empowerment has to do with developing the impact, governance networks and channels for needs articulation upwards and outwardly to influence important decision-making centres outside the local community (that is City Hall or national or EU policies). Sustainable empowerment based strategies have therefore not only to do with getting the citizens involved from below. Over time they also require a positive, dynamic interplay between government or municipal 'top-down' policies and local 'bottom-up' movements.

Community empowerment strategies are deliberate strategies for the strengthening of citizens' involvement and positive affiliations to the local area. Common to community empowerment strategies in deprived urban areas is a long-term and holistic perspective – typically a combination of physical town development and social, cultural, education and employment focussed development projects.

Community empowerment can thus be seen as akin to the broader development strategy in the so-called Integrated Area Development approach (Moulaert and Nussbaumer 2005). This approach:

> stresses the necessity to connect a socially innovative view of development (basic needs satisfaction, cultural emancipation, social and political empowerment) to an active networking of agents and resources across various spatial scales and institutional settings, but with a strong focus on improving the quality of life in area-based communities . . . (Moulaert et al. 2007, p. 196).

14.4 THE LESSONS FROM CHICAGO

As mentioned above the community development projects in Aarhus were initially inspired by approaches and methods developed in Chicago, and the development paths for libraries in disadvantaged neighbourhoods in the two cities show a parallelism in many respects. The Chicago public libraries have over the past decade turned an ominous development into a success story. The secret behind the success has been the exploitation of the library's potential as catalyst for social networks in the local community (Putnam and Feldstein 2003). A study from the Asset Based Community Development Institute (Kretzman and Rans 2005) also points to the fact that libraries can contribute with a wealth of resources: a 'free' meeting place, the most recent information technology, knowledge, a feeling of ownership among local citizens as well as a relationship of trust between people. On the basis of this study, the following recommendations to libraries were formulated:

1. Be investigative (outreach work).
2. Find the community leaders. A coordinated effort to find leaders and community activists in the local community makes all the difference.
3. Be visionary in relation to what the library can do.
4. Make visible and contribute to the local community's unique strengths and conditions.
5. Support local institutions and business life.
6. Turn the library building into a local community centre.
7. Create a local-community-orientated culture among staff and volunteers.
8. Investments in libraries can kick-start local community development.
(Kretzman and Rans 2005, pp. 28–31)

Some of these recommendations can be drawn from the CCG case as well. However it is important to stress the specific Scandinavian context of the CCG. Compared to the US the Danish public sector is larger and better funded. Furthermore, since the late 1980s a com-plicated system for state funded (or co-funded) relatively open experimental programs in social work and neighbourhood development has emerged. Hence there is a tradition for CSOs and public agencies working together in hybrid institutional platforms like CCG.

14.5   COMMUNITY CENTRE GELLERUP

CCG was created in 2005 by a local public library branch in collaboration with a health visitor centre and an immigrant CSO. The objective was to develop what could be termed a new type of *bottom linked institution*: a community centre uniting library services, health promotion, job counselling, educational and other direct citizen oriented counselling services for ethnic minorities (the majority among the local residents), CSO activities and community activism (Andersen and Frandsen 2007).

The strategic objectives of the project were: (1) practical knowledge sharing and learning across the different professions (social workers, nurses in the role of health visitors and librarians) working for and with the citizens in the urban neighbourhood; and (2) to develop a robust platform for improved neighbourhood or *internal governance* in the form of close cooperation and horizontal empowerment between the local welfare professionals, associations, and community activists (on internal governance se Pradel et al., Chapter 11). Hence the type of social innovation in this case can be characterized by a high degree of formal institutional support and at the same time a high level of active involvement of civic society and associative networks. The case could be seen as an attempt to re-embed or re-link public services and meeting places (like the library) to the active parts of civic society and in this process to establish both informal meeting and counselling spaces potentially creating bridging social capital (Svendsen 2010).

In the case of CCG, the agents of change were both professionals in public institutions and the local CSOs and community activists. They were able to draw on a particular path dependency, namely the close collaboration between the public welfare institutions in the area, which has been developed since the beginning of the 1990s in the so-called Gellerup Model. This model entails that new public employees in the area are introduced to common basic values of active citizenship and inclusion and to the particular history of the area. The core values for the welfare professionals are loyalty, commitment, multiculturalism and solidarity with the urban neighbourhood and its citizens – rather than identification with the formal administrative bodies of the City Hall. Furthermore regular monthly meetings at the management level are arranged between the public service providers: schools, day-care institutions, social centres, crime prevention work and so on. In periods of troubles and social unrest in the area (like the riots during the 'Cartoon Crises';[4] Andersen et al. 2009), this network also meets with community leaders. In other words, the core of the model is an attempt to develop territorial decentralization by promoting increased *horizontal communication and commitment* among public servants, citizens and CSOs.

14.6 ORGANIZATIONAL AND STAFF DEVELOPMENT

Since the start in 2005, the CCG employees have worked on organizational and staff development, which has resulted in the adoption of a common vision, a set of shared values and different collaboration models. In the project period all employees participated in joint courses on appreciative inquiry (see Kunnen et al., Chapter 21), empowerment, conflict solving techniques and learning and on study tours to other local communities. Improving public service and recruiting volunteers have also been on the agenda, as well as the ability for the CCG to play the role of facilitator in the neighbourhood. CCG thus strives towards realization of the common vision by:

- developing models and methods for cross-sectoral cooperation;
- focusing on civic inclusion and civic involvement;
- supporting local community based initiatives, projects and local businesses and industry;
- contributing to creating social cohesion between the urban area of Gellerup and the city of Aarhus.

CCG builds on an organizational concept of knowledge and experience sharing, where collaboration takes place across professional borderlines in order to accomplish specific tasks, such as cultural activities, information services and informal learning activities. This might include language assistance, courses in IT, homework assistance, club activities, as well as individual, anonymous advice on health, housing, the labour market, family matters and so forth. It might also include advice to parents on their parental role. In this respect, the CCG and the staff employed there commit themselves to act both as *detectives* trying to spot the needs that are to be fulfilled amongst citizens in the neighbourhood, and as *advocates* in helping citizens and groups in dealing with possible problems and getting them through an often complex bureaucratic system in regard to the structure of the Danish public sector.

In organizational terms, CCG is a collaboration project between Gellerup Library (including a Job Corner), the Community Health Centre, and People's Information. These three institutions work closely together with voluntary organizations, associations and community activists. The Community Health Centre is a collaboration between a number of municipal institutions and the Aarhus Midwifery Centre. Health visitors had been experiencing encouraging results from their home visits to families, but had also, for a long time, been missing a place which parents could visit for instruction and guidance. When new premises had to be found, Gellerup Library offered to make a corner of its premises available. The Community Health Centre got a site, which helped to support local anchorage, and provided the chance to combine activities with the library, for example theme days on health-related subjects.

People's Information offers open and anonymous advice to the citizens in the Aarhus area, but primarily citizens with an ethnic background other than Danish. They work in several languages helping people for whom knowledge of Danish is an obstacle to their ability to manoeuvre between the different public systems and authorities. Advice is available on social rights, labour market conditions, education, citizenship and residence permits, housing allowance and so forth. Advice is also offered on communication with the authorities. Apart from that, members of staff in People's Information act as bridge-builders and mediators between citizens and the system.

Finally the job and education counselling office, the Job Corner, provides personal advice concerning job seeking, job training and ongoing contact to potential public and private employers.

In terms of the SINGOCOM project (Moulaert et al. 2010), CCG also resembles a flexible institutionalization where the constant mediation of the tension between a flat, flexible organization of the centre and a need for steerable, firmer structures have been a central part of the development process (Membretti 2010, pp. 71–72).

A short example can illustrate how citizens can benefit from this flexible institutionalization: a woman approaches People's Information to talk about her cash benefit in relation to a recently introduced piece of legislation, stipulating that after one year one must have worked a minimum of 300 hours to maintain one's right to cash benefits. She is advised to go to the Job Corner to look for feasible vacant jobs. The member of staff in the Job Corner helps her to examine her resources and to apply for a job. The woman then prepares a job application, which she can discuss with the adviser. The application is sent off, or the woman may be advised to make direct contact with the employer. If she gets the job, she can return to People's Information to learn about the consequences for her social benefits.

14.7   PARTNERSHIPS WITH CSOS

When establishing CCG, there was an important focus on the development of citizen-oriented and citizen-driven activities. Together with local citizens the CCG organized courses providing knowledge about the local community, in the Danish language. There were theme days such as a health day and an IT open learning day as well as campaigns against the use of khat[5] organized by young Somalis, a clean-up day, a concert against arson in the area and debate evenings on Palestine just to mention a few examples. During the process CCG have engaged in more formal partnerships with different civil society organizations in the area:

- The IT guide association, which is a multi-ethnic association with a double purpose: to bring together everyone with an interest in IT, and to make the members' knowledge available to citizens without IT literacy by way of free courses.
- The Homework Help Association 'Tusindfryd' under the Danish Refugee Council, which consists of young people offering help with homework on a voluntary basis. One does not have to book an appointment, but can just turn up. Homework help is for all citizens, whether they attend a language school, are studying to pass the theory test for their driving license, attend primary or secondary school or are doing an upper secondary course.
- The Voluntary Centre, the purpose of which is to establish contact between all voluntary associations and people who wish to do voluntary work.
- The Local-historical Archive, which collects pictures, association documents, maps, memoirs and so on.

What is important to stress here is the common denominators agreed upon by the different professional groups (librarians, nurses, health workers, job training officers) working with the human needs recognized in the area. This takes the form amongst the CCG staff of a certain professional ethic based on empowerment and Appreciative Inquiry. This is for instance pertinent when the staff facilitates empowerment processes with local citizens, viewing them not as administratively defined client groups but as resourceful human beings capable of collective action.

14.8 SOME LESSONS FROM COMMUNITY CENTER GELLERUP

CCG is an example of a multi-functional local community centre where a library service is combined with an advisory service, voluntary work, health work and help with job applications. The collaboration between the professionals has created a flexible network-based, 'ready-for action' attitude in relation to the local community and generated cross-disciplinary competences. The interplay between staff and volunteers is also of great importance. CCG employees maintained that during the project period they became better at discovering and acknowledging each other's particular knowledge in their contact with the citizens, in relation to health, job seeking and more extensive use of the employees' linguistic talents (Andersen and Frandsen 2007). This 'synergy advantage' has two sides.

Firstly, in relation to the employees it is a question of learning from each other and building up common competences to the benefit of the citizens in the local community. One universal challenge of innovative development processes is that over time they can be perceived as stressful, but this is not necessarily the case. If the organization and the management prioritize joint activities for the employees where they take stock of day-to-day experiences, this stress seems to be (more) limited. If you get better at using each other's various areas of competence, as in the case of CCG, it can, in fact, be stress reducing, because 'tricky' cases outside one's own field of competency can be passed on to those who are more familiar with such cases. In this way one avoids the individualized 'borderless work', and turns it instead into a collective, unbureaucratic and flexible division of labour between employees.

Secondly, it means that the citizens experience a more flexible and coherent contact with various public systems and with voluntary organizations. One may contact or be referred to another person in the community centre without having to contact another authority, make new appointments and so on.

The evaluation report concluded that in order to secure the long lasting dynamics in such development work it is important:

- to work on organization development that prioritizes the social well-being and collectivity of the staff and joint competency development;
- to encourage relevant further education of the staff that supports the development of a *community centre professionalism*, where the keywords are knowledge of the local community, civic inclusion and cooperation between professionals;
- to develop a strategy for staff recruitment in the form of clarifying which professional competences support CCG's objectives;
- to ensure creative frameworks for dialogue between voluntary work and community centre staff;
- to develop simple evaluation and user-satisfaction tools that can be used internally in the organization as well as to meet the decision-makers' demands for documentation of 'value for money'.

As an analytical, and more general, reflection on the case discussed in this chapter, we highlight, that the concept of *bottom*

linked innovation seems to capture the type of social innovation characteristic of the CCG project. The concept serves to designate socially creative strategies that in governance terms are neither strictly 'bottom up' nor 'top-down', but where there is a positive interplay across governance scales between institutional initiatives from 'above' and active and empowering involvement from 'below' (García et al. 2009; see also Pradel et al., Chapter 11). According to García et al. (2009, p. 12) public institutions can 'lead and promote social innovation looking for involvement by the Civil Society Organizations.' Successful social innovation thus depends on the coordination of different actors at different scales.

14.9   CONCLUDING REMARKS

CCG is an example of public sector bottom-linked innovation in a close interplay with the local neighbourhood and its civic associations. The multifunctional community centre is an example of social innovation in (parts of) the public sector creating better accessibility to public institutions and meeting different human needs at the neighbourhood level.

In the context of neobureaucratic and neoliberal public sector restructuring reforms CCG is an example of a practical and proactive alternative (see Lévesque, Chapter 2). This is because the institutional setup is focussed on improving outreach towards human needs, better use of public resources and the revitalization of a humanistic ethos and commitment among the welfare state professions.

One of the huge challenges facing CCG and similar initiatives, is that public sector budgeting and the core bureaucratic structure – often associated with New Public Management – are far from geared to supporting such cross-sectoral and civic community-inclusive innovations.[6] Even in the case of CCG, and more broadly speaking in relation to the national Danish development program, there still remain some hurdles to surmount for this type of bottom-linked innovation to become part of a realistic, sustainable development trajectory.

14.10 QUESTIONS FOR DISCUSSION

• What special role can public libraries play in community development and social innovation compared to other local welfare institutions and to civil society organizations?

• In what way can multifunctional and creative institutional hybrids like Community Center Gellerup mediate the gap between bureaucratic and sectoral modes of organization and the human needs of local communities and marginalized people?

NOTES

1. The term 'the digital divide' came into use from the mid-1990s and refers to the gap between people with effective access to digital and information technology and those with very limited or no access at all. See for example Servon (2002).
2. International examples of libraries reinventing their roles are Chicago's public libraries (Putnam and Feldstein 2003), Queens Library in New York (www.queenslibrary.org), Idea Store in Tower Hamlets in London (www.ideastore.co.uk) and Toronto Public Library in Canada (www.torontopubliclibrary.ca). Recently £80 million in funding has become available through the Community Libraries Fund for public libraries in UK engaging in partnerships within the local communities (Goulding 2009, p. 80). (All websites last accessed 10 December 2012.)
3. Alongside the empowerment approach the staff at CCG work with Appreciative Inquiry-methods

that function as an additional compass guiding how to meet, help and counsel the local citizens (see Kunnen et al., Chapter 21, for a discussion of Appreciative Inquiry).
4. The so-called 'Cartoon Crises' began in 2005 after the Danish newspaper *Jyllands-Posten* published 12 editorial cartoons picturing the prophet Muhammad. It was an attempt to contribute to the debate about criticism of Islam and sparked a range of protest and riots in many Muslim countries (for instance Syria, Lebanon and Iran), including the bombing of the Danish Embassy in Pakistan. In Denmark this resulted in a fierce public debate on 'free speech' and how to talk about religious minorities in the press.
5. Khat is a drug used by many African immigrants which is illegal in Denmark.
6. This was exactly the case in the large-scale German federal program called Social City initiated by the Schröder administration. One of the aims of the program was to develop community centres placed in disadvantaged neighbourhoods (Evers et al. 2006, p. 187). The experiences from this project was that management practices formed a barrier for the progress and building new forms of cooperation in the public sector: '. . . to some degree the style and the content of the new forms of cooperation are rivalling the logic of administrative reform as represented by the international philosophy of "New Public Management".' (Evers et al. 2006, p. 190)

REFERENCES

(References in bold are recommended reading.)

Andersen, John (ed.) (2008), *Ressourcemobiliserende beskæftigelsespolitik*, Frederiksberg: Samfundslitteratur.
Andersen, John and Birte Siim (eds) (2004), *The politics of inclusion and empowerment – gender, class and citizenship*, New York: Palgrave MacMillan Ltd.
Andersen, John and Martin Frandsen (eds) (2007), *Fra bibliotek til lokalsamfundscenter – evaluering af Community Center Gellerup*, MOSPUS Research Paper 1/07, Department of Environmental, Social and Spatial Change, Roskilde University, Denmark.
Andersen, John, Anne-Marie Tyroll Beck, Catharina Juul Kristensen and Jørgen Elm Larsen (eds) (2003), *Empowerment i storbyens rum – et socialvidenskabeligt perspektiv*, Copenhagen: Hans Reitzels Forlag.
Andersen, John, Martin Frandsen and Lone Hedelund (2007), 'From "book container" to community centre: Lessons from Community Centre Gellerup', *Scandinavian Public Library Quarterly*, **40** (3), 6–10.
Andersen, John, J.E. Larsen and I.H. Møller (2009),

'The exclusion and marginalisation of immigrants in the Danish welfare society: Dilemmas and challenges', *International Journal of Sociology and Social Policy*, 29 (5/6), 274–286.

Evers, Adalbert, Andreas Schultz and Claudia Wiesner (2006), 'Local policy networks in the programme Social City: a case in point for new forms of governance in the field of local social work and urban planning', *European Journal of Social Work*, 9 (2), 183–200.

Fetterman, David M. and Abraham Wandersman (eds) (2005), *Empowerment evaluation principles in practice*, New York: The Guilford Press.

Freire, Paulo (1974), *Pedagogy of the Oppressed*, New York: The Seabury Press.

Friedmann, John (1992), *Empowerment: the politics of alternative development*, Oxford: Blackwell Publishers.

García, Marisol, M.P. Miquel and S.E. Anglada (2009), 'Citizens' creative strategies facing social exclusion: towards innovation in local governance?', conference paper, Understanding and Shaping Regions: Spatial, Social and Economic Futures, Regional Studies Association Annual Conference, 6–8 April, Leuven, Belgium.

Goulding, Anne (2009), 'Engaging with community engagement: public libraries and citizen involvement', *New Library World*, 110 (1/2), 37–51.

Kretzman, Jody and Susan Rans (2005), *The engaged library. Chicago Stories of Community Building*, Chicago: The Asset Based Community Development Institute, Public Libraries Council.

Membretti, Andrea (2010), 'Social Innovation in the wake of urban movements. The *Centro Sociale Leoncavallo* in Milan: a case of "flexible institutionalisation"', in Moulaert et al. (eds), pp. 68–81.

Moulaert, Frank and J. Nussbaumer (2005), 'The Social Region: Beyond the Territorial Dynamics of the Learning Economy', *European Urban and Regional Studies*, 12 (1), 45–64.

Moulaert, Frank, Flavia Martinelli, Sara Gonzales and Erik Swyngedouw (2007), 'Introduction: Social Innovation and Governance in European Cities. Urban Development Between Path Dependency and Radical Innovation', *European Urban and Regional Studies*, 14 (3), 195–209.

Moulaert, Frank, Flavia Martinelli, Eric Swyngedouw and Sara González (eds) (2010), *Can Neighbourhoods Save the City? Community Development and Social Innovation*, Abingdon, UK and New York, US: Routledge.

Putnam, Robert D. and Lewis M. Feldstein (2003), *Better Together: Restoring the American Community*, New York: Simon and Schuster.

Servon, Lisa J. (2002), *Bridging the Digital Divide: Technology, Community and Public Policy*, Malden: Blackwell.

Svendsen, Gunnar L.H. (2010), 'Socio-spatial Planning in the Creation of Bridging Social Capital: The Importance of Multifunctional Centers for Intergroup Networks and Integration', *International Journal of Social Inquiry*, 3 (2), 45–73.

Urbanprogrammet (2007), *En bydel blev sat i bevægelse. Urbanprogrammet Gellerup-Hasle-Herredsvang 2002–2007*, Århus: Århus Kommune.

15. Venturing off the beaten path: social innovation and settlement upgrading in Voi, Kenya
Emmanuel Midheme

15.1 INTRODUCTION

Access to land in Kenyan towns is severely constrained by supply (Yahya 2002; Bassett 2005). The official land delivery processes premised on conventional state and market mechanisms have proved inadequate in coping with the demands imposed by rapid urbanization (Midheme 2010). The result has been a steady proliferation of informal settlements in major towns, particularly as poor households seek alternative spaces for housing and livelihood opportunities.

Meanwhile, policy makers are confronted with the twin challenge of improving the quality of housing already existing within informal settlements and expanding access to land and housing for those without it. Accordingly, informal settlements upgrading has been advocated as one way of improving both the quality and quantity of the urban housing stock (Bassett 2005). It has been claimed for example that settlement upgrading, particularly where it adopts the 'assisted self-help' model, 'is the most affordable and intelligent way of providing sustainable shelter for the urban poor' (UN-Habitat 2005, p. 166). Proponents further argue that compared to conventional turnkey housing projects, settlement upgrading is cheap as it often adopts practical standards regarding material and construction methods. It also incorporates substantial amounts of sweat equity which cuts down on construction costs. Upgrading is also considered resourceful because households engaged in it acquire precious skills (both technical and organizational) in the process of constructing their dwellings. Moreover, it is flexible since dwelling units are designed to accommodate phased consolidation over time. More importantly, upgrading is deemed practical as it responds to the poor's actual shelter needs, and at a cost they can afford (UN-Habitat 2005; Midheme 2010).

Despite this optimism, upgrading initiatives in Kenya have often been hampered by a top-down planning framework, excessive bureaucracy and political interference, poor coordination among concerned agencies and inadequate community involvement in project design and implementation (Midheme 2010). Of greater practical concern is the phenomenon of post-project displacement, through which higher-income classes swiftly buy out poor households soon after project completion (Bassett 2005). The urban poor thus remain largely excluded in the housing market as the state lacks the resources and/or political will to decisively respond to their plight, while the market lacks the profit incentive to do so. It is becoming increasingly clear therefore that the issue of access to land and housing for the urban poor is a form of social exclusion which cannot be addressed simply at the level of material needs by individual households. Instead, it is a far larger social problem that requires innovation on a grand scale.

This chapter discusses how innovative ideas on landholding, together with collaborative planning frameworks, can be assembled in altering the trajectory and benefits that accrue to low-income households in settlement upgrading projects. A recent upgrading initiative in the town of Voi, Kenya, is used to illustrate how socially innovative practices can be mobilized creatively in seeking lasting solutions to the problem of pro-poor housing.

15.2   SOCIAL INNOVATION AND URBAN DEVELOPMENT POLICY

According to Scott-Cato and Hillier (2010), the phrase 'social innovation' emerged primarily from the transatlantic Francophone intellectual community in the 1970s. It has since been used increasingly to refer to intellectual activity that engages actively with contemporary social problems, with the aim of achieving socially beneficial outcomes (MacCallum et al. 2009a; Scott-Cato and Hillier 2010). The principle behind social innovation is however an old one, traceable to Joseph Schumpeter's seminal work on social transformation in the 1930s (MacCallum et al. 2009b). In contemporary social analysis, the concept retains a central theme among its proponents: that 'social innovation is innovation in social relations, as well as in meeting human needs' (MacCallum et al. 2009a, p. 2).

Urban development policy is one field in which social innovation has been systematically and extensively mobilized (Moulaert et al. 2005; Drewe et al. 2008; MacCallum et al. 2009b; Headlam and Hincks 2010; Moulaert et al. 2010). The concept has therefore become not only an important anchoring device for analytical work in urban development policy; it has in fact blossomed into an alternative

view of urban development (MacCallum et al. 2009b). Moulaert et al. (2005) have identified three important dimensions that socially innovative initiatives strive to accomplish within the context of urban development. These are: (1) satisfaction of human needs currently unmet by the market and/or state; (2) changes in social relations which enhance the level of political participation by traditionally marginalized groups; and (3) empowerment, through increasing the capacity and access to resources by deprived groups. In settlement upgrading, the utility of social innovation lies in the concept's ability to reinterpret the roles and social relations among the state, market, civil society and local communities in crafting new forms of social organization and co-production, as a logical response to existing forms of exclusion in housing provision (Midheme 2010).

15.3   VENTURING OFF THE BEATEN PATH: TOWARDS A NEW APPROACH TO SETTLEMENT UPGRADING IN VOI

Voi is a small town of 50,000 inhabitants situated in south-eastern Kenya. It is located 350 km southeast of Nairobi. Established in 1898, Voi's colonial heritage has made a lasting imprint on the town's spatial form. The state-sanctioned racial segregation of the time saw Voi grow into separate enclaves for Europeans, Asians and African natives. The colonialists enacted vagrancy laws that excluded Africans from the town altogether. The natives thus opted to settle on dormitory sites on the urban fringe, from where they could sneak into the town in search of work during the day, and retreat back in the evening for the night. This led to the development of extensive informal settlements. These settlements occur on land belonging officially to private entities (Yahya 2002). As a result, the local authority is limited in the range of remedies it can proffer, owing to insufficient resources and the complicated tenure situation (Midheme 2010).

15.3.1 The Tanzania-Bondeni Settlement: Pre-Project Characteristics

The upgrading project presented here was carried out between 1991 and 2004 in Tanzania-Bondeni, a squatter settlement in Voi. The settlement has been in existence since the 1950s and covers approximately 22 hectares of land. At the launch of the upgrading project, Tanzania-Bondeni had a total of 4,370 people housed in 530 structures (Yahya 2002). The living environment was poor, as most dwellings consisted of dilapidated and overcrowded hovels. Residents lacked proper access roads, potable water or sanitation facilities. There were also environmental health concerns occasioned by indiscriminate disposal of grey water. Besides, industrial effluent discharged by an adjacent sisal factory flowed through the settlement into the nearby Voi River, from where oblivious residents routinely fetched water for domestic use (Bassett 2005). The dwellings were typically modest 100 square-feet rooming apartments accommodating household sizes as large as seven persons. The residents were generally poor, with 70 per cent either unemployed or earning less than US$8 a month. With neither access to financial credit, nor security of tenure, households' prospects for housing improvement were severely limited.

The settlement was however characterized by internal stability. At the beginning of the project, up to 47 per cent of the residents had lived on the site for more than 30 years (MoLG 2004). But a latent fear

of eviction still lingered among the occupants, as reflected in the poor condition of the settlement's housing stock. Of the 530 structures present at the time, 62 per cent was constructed of temporary material consisting of earthen floors, wattle-and-daub walling and tin roofs. There were environmental risks as well. The Voi River, on which residents depended as a source of water and livelihoods, had been heavily eroded due to uncontrolled sand-harvesting, brick-making and cultivation on river banks. The banks had been breached at several points, exposing residents to displacements, destruction of property and loss of life each time the river flooded. Meanwhile, brick-making had left behind huge gullies which filled up with water in rainy weather, becoming breeding grounds for the malaria-causing mosquito. Coupled with the absence of municipal services such as piped water, garbage removal, or medical facilities, and the fact that households lived in overcrowded quarters, health conditions were bad with high incidences of malaria, tuberculosis and diarrhoea being reported (Yahya 2002).

On the political front, there was no coherent community organization to spearhead local development initiatives. This translated into weak forms of community mobilization and hence under-representation in local democratic processes. Furthermore the community lacked official recognition from the local authority, meaning its members were excluded from the formal democratic practices of local governance. Instead there developed an adversarial relationship between residents and the local authority, as the community lived in constant fear of eviction. Besides, lack of community facilities like schools, health facilities or public spaces contributed to poor standards of living and stood out as examples of social exclusion that residents suffered for not being recognized by the authorities.

15.3.2   In Search of a Solution: the Origins of the Upgrading Project

In 1988, the Kenyan Ministry of Local Government (MoLG) initiated the Kenya Small Towns Development Programme (STDP) with the aim of assisting Kenyan small towns in enhancing local revenues, using their resources more prudently, and promoting local economic development. The programme was funded by the German agency for technical cooperation, *Deutsche Gesellschaft für Technische Zusammenarbeit* (GTZ). It is under the institutional framework of the STDP that the Voi upgrade was conceived.

In a bid to improve their living conditions, residents of Tanzania-Bondeni petitioned the Voi municipal council to have their settlement upgraded in early 1991. After preliminary consultations, the local authority agreed to facilitate the upgrade. However, it lacked the necessary resources and therefore approached MoLG to assist with the upgrade under the STDP framework. Following initial deliberations among residents, the municipal council, MoLG and GTZ, it became apparent that tenure insecurity was the main hindrance to housing development in the settlement (Yahya 2002). Any solutions proposed would thus have to address the question of land tenure reform as a matter of priority. This realization was to have a profound effect on the project design and implementation, as will be explained in subsequent sections.

15.3.3   Project Objectives and Institutional Design for Implementation

The project set out to achieve four main objectives: (1) to legalize the settlement

by providing tenure security and thereby an enabling environment for occupants to improve their dwellings; (2) to improve the delivery of municipal services to the settlement; (3) to improve environmental quality in the project area; and (4) to enhance the local authority's revenues through improved land rates (MoLG 2004).

These objectives were to be realized within the framework of a number of guiding principles agreed upon at the start of the project, among the donor (GTZ), MoLG, Voi municipal council and the local community. In summary, these principles recognized that the upgrade would be a gradual, step-by-step process to ensure residents' participation, education, ownership and long-term community sustainability. Secondly, it was agreed that all spatial plans would be prepared in a dialogic process, with full participation of the community. Third, external interventions would be in support of, and supplementary to local efforts, rather than in replacement of it. Fourth, a consultative mechanism would be established to ensure structured communication between the community and the other project partners. Fifth, the necessary mechanisms for cost-recovery would be established collectively between residents and the local authority. Finally, it was also agreed that residents would decide on the landholding system they preferred, in order to facilitate the creation of long-term benefits and community-building (Yahya 2002; Bassett 2005).

15.3.4   Post-Project Displacement and Measures to Forestall it in Voi

Aware of the dangers of post-project displacement, the Voi project team sought an alternative form of landholding. Accordingly, the Community Land Trust (CLT) – a common property form of land ownership – was floated by GTZ staff as a viable alternative to individual tenure (Yahya 2002). The proposal was then followed by extensive deliberations involving representatives of the community, the local authority, GTZ and various land administration agencies in Kenya. The deliberations dwelt on practical issues, including possibilities of the model's fit within the Kenyan legal framework and the ability of the community to effectively administer land under the CLT.

15.3.5 The Community Land Trust and the Project Implementation Process

A CLT is a model for acquiring and holding land in perpetuity for the benefit of a predefined community, usually for purposes of providing affordable housing, workspace or other community facilities (Gray 2008; Bailey 2010). Under the CLT, landed property is divided into its two constituent parts: land, and the improvements upon it. Land is taken out of the market and separated from its productive use so that the impact of its appreciation is eliminated and 'locked' into a community trust (Bailey 2010), thereby enabling long-term affordable and sustainable local development. Homeowners own their dwellings, but not the land which remains collectively owned by the community.

This form of landholding was new and hitherto untried in Kenya, meaning the Voi upgrade would be a pilot project. Aside from the novelty in landholding, the Voi upgrade was also conceived from the start as a multi-stakeholder project involving several actors drawn from various agencies (Bassett 2005). The project adopted a multi-disciplinary and multi-sectoral approach, bringing together spatial planners, land economists, community development experts and lawyers drawn from the state, civil society and the corporate sector. Other key players included the Kenya Railways Corporation and Voi Sisal Estates, the two legal owners of the land on which the settlement stood (Yahya 2002).

Given the multiplicity of stakeholders involved, the novelty of landholding and the dialogic approach that characterized actual implementation, the Voi initiative unravelled intricate power relations, negotiations and multi-stakeholder accommodation previously unseen in the Kenyan planning arena. We now turn our attention to the activities that took place in the main phases of the project.

15.3.6 Project Initiation and Community Mobilization

The project began with a baseline survey carried out in March 1991. This was conducted to assess the socio-economic profile of the residents, as well as views of local authority and state officials. An intensive community mobilization exercise then followed, led by NGO-based partners, which was meant to enhance awareness and the ability of residents to organize themselves and rally around the project. The mobilization also aimed at pooling local resources from within the community (MoLG 2004). Residents were then facilitated in forming a residents' committee and its subsequent registration as a self-help group. The committee consequently became the official voice of the community in all formal negotiations with other project partners.

15.3.7 Spatial Planning and Plot Allocation

With sufficient community mobilization, the project partners embarked on spatial planning. Residents were inducted into the planning process, with a team of planners leading practical demonstrations and explanations on the importance of spatial planning for orderly community development. To enable active engagement, deliberations were conducted in non-technical language and incorporated real-life examples and role-play. In the process, a number of space standards from official sources were modified to reflect local needs and realities. Through patience and iteration, various physical layout options were generated, culminating in the final spatial plan. The average size of residential plots in the plan was 8 × 15 m. A market and other public utility sites including schools, health centre and open spaces were also provided. Furthermore, a riparian strip was set aside in strategic areas along Voi river to provide space for subsistence gardening and to serve as a buffer zone against flood risks. Internal accessibility was greatly improved, with each individual plot opening up to some form of public realm (Midheme 2010).

The plan realized a total of 818 residential plots, far beyond the 530 claimed by original homeowners. Once the original claimants had their share, the extra plots were democratically allocated to other residents, with preferential treatment accorded to the less-advantaged (the elderly, the sick and the very poor), followed by long-term tenants. The plan then became the basis for subsequent cadastral surveys and post-project land administration (Bassett 2005).

15.3.8 The CLT Architecture and Post-Project Land Administration

Despite their misgivings about individual landholding, the project team still considered the opinion of the residents crucial in arriving at the final choice of land tenure. Accordingly, the project team commissioned concept papers on various land tenure models as proposals for consideration by residents. This was done with the assistance of NGO-based lawyers, who introduced residents to three main tenure types: housing cooperative, individual titles, and the CLT. Each model was presented alongside its respective abilities in meeting project goals as outlined earlier. Following extensive deliberations, a vote was finally called in which residents overwhelmingly picked the CLT as the preferred tenure model. Out of the 258 structure owners who took part in the vote, 239 voted for CLT, with individual titles attracting the remaining 19 members.

The next task involved setting up the necessary structures for land administration under the new tenure model. Important to note is that the classic CLT model as implemented elsewhere could not easily fit within the Kenyan land administration system, owing in part to a lack of adequate policy and legal support for communal landholding. Moreover, the land administration bureaucracy is accustomed to issuing individual titles under standardized provisions. Any attempts at crafting titles with radically new provisions would therefore predictably meet bureaucratic roadblocks (Yahya 2002). The project team therefore had to explore alternative avenues of embedding the CLT into the existing legal framework, while maintaining the model's original objectives.

One outstanding obstacle that the CLT faced from the outset is the 'perpetuity rule' which prevents land from permanently being removed from the market under Kenyan law – an express objective of the CLT (Bassett 2005). To circumvent the rule and still achieve the broader goal of the CLT, lawyers had to craft two separate legal instruments. The community was first organized into a legally-recognized settlement society, complete with its own constitution and rules, developed through a series of workshops facilitated by legal experts. The constitution and rules were then reviewed and approved by the state. The society was subsequently registered as Tanzania-Bondeni Settlement Society, under the Societies Act, Cap 108. To date, this body remains the mass membership organization to which all residents can belong. The second instrument established for purposes of the CLT was the trust. Again, with the help of legal experts, the community crafted a trust deed, which spelt out guidelines on the appointment of the board of trustees and the board's responsibility in managing the society's resources. The trustees were then appointed and subsequently registered as the Tanzania-Bondeni Community Land Trust, under the *Trustees (Perpetual Succession) Act*, Cap 164.

Next, the community applied for a head-lease from the Commissioner of Lands. Based on this head-lease, the trust could award sub-leases to individual homeowners as proof of property-holding within Tanzania-Bondeni. For long-term operations, the CLT is administered by a nine-member board of trustees. The board is assisted by a residents' committee, which is responsible for the day-to-day running of the society. There are 13 members elected into this committee, with three seats reserved for women (Midheme 2010). The membership is charged annual fees to enable the trust to meet its recurrent expenditures and audited accounts are approved by members during the annual general meeting. To ensure housing remains within the community, the CLT reserves pre-emptive rights of purchase whenever a member opts out. A resale formula was adopted for determining the purchase price in such cases. The formula ensures fair compensation to the seller while keeping affordability within reach of trust members. All lessees are required to make contributions towards the cost of

infrastructure over a period of time and there is considerable flexibility in making these payments. The money so collected is converted into a development fund for long-term community development (MoLG 2004).

To cushion members from displacements instigated by high building standards, the head-lease incorporates conditions that bind the state and the local authority in recognizing the existing dwellings as they are. The owners are however required to gradually improve their houses to conform to local authority building by-laws over time. As a new source of financing, individuals may also charge their sub-leases against bank loans (Yahya 2002).

15.4 THE STRENGTH OF SOCIAL INNOVATION: UNDERSTANDING THE VOI CASE

Employing Moulaert et al.'s (2005) three dimensions of social innovation, it is possible to identify salient features of socially innovative practice as unrolled in Voi. We can pick out instances in which the project endeavoured to satisfy unmet human needs, effect changes in social relations that enhance community participation, and bring about empowerment and improved access to resources by the residents of Tanzania-Bondeni.

15.4.1 Satisfaction of Unmet Human Needs

The project has met a need that the local authority and the housing market have long failed to satisfy. It has expanded access to homeownership by poor households. All the original inhabitants were accommodated. New housing stock has also been created as homeowners erect higher-capacity structures capable of absorbing more tenants. Fundamentally, the CLT has met the poor's needs in a distinct way. By ensuring protection against post-project displacement, the model has facilitated the poor's access and retention of land and housing in a manner that could never have been possible in the open land/housing market. An additional merit is the special arrangement for financial guarantees to avert incidences of foreclosure among community members. Moreover, the elimination of absentee landlordism and the various community institutions spawned by the project are good ways of fostering social capital among residents as they promote associational co-existence and long-term community-building (Midheme 2010).

The project has also brought about other indirect benefits. The boost in tenure security has alleviated residents' fear of eviction and led to increased construction activities. Accordingly, the residents have put up new dwellings and social facilities. In doing so, they make use of appropriate techniques and building materials introduced under the project. Because the local authority has undertaken to recognize all dwellings as they exist, occupants have ample time to gradually improve their housing as their means allow. The project has also made valuable investments in local infrastructure including improved roads, storm water drainage and a piped water supply system. Environmental conservation components have also been implemented to prevent flooding. Furthermore, openings have been created for on-site employment and other livelihood opportunities in and around the settlement. Social facilities have also been provided. All these improvements have substantially contributed to the betterment of the residents' quality of life.

15.4.2 Negotiated Social Relations and Enhanced Community Participation

The mobilization of multiple stakeholders with diverse interests certainly brought with it specific demands, power relations, negotiations and accommodation previously unseen in the local planning arena. But it was also a major achievement in terms of getting community members to fully participate in effecting change within their locality. The ability to bring the community and the local authority to work together was itself a major achievement given the hostility that had long characterized their relations. Furthermore, the active engagement of residents throughout the project is a fine example of how deliberative democracy can be mobilized in seeking solutions to social problems by creating new spaces for citizens to directly influence decisions that affect their lives (Headlam and Hincks 2010). In Voi, there was always an attempt to seek greater reflection on the new interventions proposed, together with their practical implications. This earned the project a high level of acceptability among residents. By mobilizing and meaningfully engaging multiple actors from diverse backgrounds and on such a drawn-out process, the project generated new power relations that clearly went beyond what ordinarily obtains in planning practice in Kenya (Midheme 2010).

This case demonstrates how social justice and democratic governance can be enhanced when policy formulation and design of new interventions involve the ultimate users within a framework of inclusive deliberation. That way, users – in this case poor, marginalized groups – become active 'makers and shapers' (Cornwall and Gaventa 2000) of their destiny, as opposed to passive supplicants of state munificence. The upshot is that the debate on governance and democracy is recast and extended. Governance ceases to be the administrative procedures employed by the state. It becomes the systematic shift from a monopolistic state sponsorship of social projects, to the delivery of these through strategic partnerships involving the state, market, civil society and local communities working together in non-hierarchical and flexible alliances (Midheme 2010).

We also see in Voi the utility of external support in building grassroots structures and innovative mechanisms. This is vital in propping up a nascent community agency. It must not be forgotten however that successful participatory engagement relies on community interest and enthusiasm. In Voi, the overwhelming endorsement of the CLT was partly born of the many years of neglect and animosity that had characterized relations between the community on the one hand, and the local authority and legitimate land owners on the other. It is this collective desire for change and community improvement among residents that provided an enabling environment for project success.

15.4.3 Community Empowerment and Improved Access to Resources

As a result of project design and implementation, house owners and tenants have organized into one strong community. Sensitization and capacity-building during the project have contributed in transforming the residents into a self-conscious settlement society, competent enough to run local community affairs (Midheme 2010). It is noteworthy that the effects of community mobilization have gone beyond the project area. Other informal settlements in the neighbourhood have since mobilized their residents, registered themselves as self-help groups and petitioned the local authority to get them started on

similar paths to settlement upgrading. As an example, Maweni – a neighbouring informal settlement – has since undergone a successful upgrading exercise initiated and largely financed by the residents themselves (Midheme 2010).

The upgrading initiative has further enabled the Tanzania-Bondeni community to marshal resources from hitherto untapped sources. Housing cooperatives have been formed by residents to assist in housing consolidation. To facilitate access to institutional funds, these cooperatives have been formally linked to the National Cooperative Housing Union (NACHU), from where they have been able to draw funds (Midheme 2010). Housing construction has further been financed through individual savings and loans from financial institutions, and enabled by a strong tradition of self-help. Kenya has a long history of self-help movements steeped in the *harambee* culture. *Harambee* is Swahili for 'pulling together', and denotes the concept of people coming together relationally to provide solutions to collectively felt needs. The concept embodies ideas of mutual assistance, joint effort, social responsibility and community self-reliance, and is characterized by tacit notions of interdependency and reciprocity. In Voi, the concept has taken various forms, including collective house-building, fund-raising and construction of community facilities. In essence, residents collaborate rather than compete, and believe that the community is only as strong as its weakest member. Today, the Tanzania-Bondeni CLT is sustained largely through funds raised locally by the community.

The CLT also confers other unique benefits. Intuitively, homeownership, elimination of absentee-landlordism and incorporation of all residents into the settlement trust should all promote wealth accumulation, property maintenance, neighbourhood stability and social cohesion over time. All these contribute to the building of stronger communities. Moreover, the CLT has provided a vital springboard for expanding civic engagement by building upon the bases of social organization created under the project. This has long-term impacts on social action and community development, besides broadening the range of resources available to residents. Lastly, the CLT has afforded the poor residents of Tanzania-Bondeni an avenue to the coveted status of homeowners. With this comes the satisfaction of 'making it' (Gray 2008), a feat that most households could never have hoped to achieve, unaided.

15.5   CONCLUSION

The Voi case is an example of how socially innovative strategies can be gainfully deployed in seeking practical answers to the pressing problem of urban housing. The uniqueness of the case lies not just in its ability to gather actors beyond the traditional state and market sectors in responding to the housing need; the innovation that went into the land tenure and the collaborative engagement that informed project design and implementation are both significant. The 'minimum intervention approach' (MoLG 2004) employed in the project rests on the logic that communities have innate capacities and resources to solve their own problems. All they need is technical assistance and political empowerment to enable residents marshal those resources towards meeting their social needs. In that respect, the Voi initiative has been a major departure from the conventional settlement improvement initiatives carried out in Kenya before. The upgrade has been a major attempt to venture off the beaten path of conservative centralized planning frameworks and standardized forms of property that have long informed housing policy in the country (Midheme 2010). The CLT is therefore an apt example of creative re-conceptualization of property rights, viewing them principally as instruments for social purposes and trying to (re)design them to meet real social needs, rather than being contented with conventional 'off-the-rack versions of property' (Kennedy 2002, p. 86). The result has been a modification of the sticks in the property bundle, in order to attain more socially just results quite different from those that have flowed from conventional models (Midheme 2010).

In many ways, the case demonstrates that a shift from bureaucratically-controlled project design and implementation to substantive stakeholder participation through collaborative processes can improve the handling of problems facing local communities, whether through mobilizing resources or promoting socially sustainable local development. In many cities the neoliberal logic has created a major source of economic and social inequity, consigning low-income households to the fringe of society. This adversely affects the poor's level of achievement and integration in the wider urban community. However social innovation presents a viable means through which alternative social relations may be re-created in a bid to assuage the socio-economic excesses of the neoliberal project (Moulaert et al. 2005; MacCallum et al. 2009b).

From a housing rights perspective, this case has shown that settlement upgrading can play a vital role in improving the existing housing stock, while cushioning the poor from the vagaries of the market. More importantly, upgrading is not only useful in improving tenure security: the method and process employed can be vital in achieving a whole structure of social re-organization necessary for long-term community building and social cohesion. The case further proves that if empowered, communities are able to embrace workable options, develop plans which reflect their aspirations and create community obligations linked to the improvement of residents' quality of life. The CLT further shows that achievement of equity is possible if the negative effects of the market are curtailed and the community's cohesion is maintained for purposes of long-term local development. As of April 2010, the housing situation in Tanzania-Bondeni had vastly improved, with the settlement housing close to 8,000 people in decent housing. But by the same token, about 20 per cent of the original structures are yet to record meaningful consolidation, owing to high levels of poverty among the homeowners. This confirms the disparities that exist in household capabilities to improve their dwellings. It is this same reason that reinforces the need for special arrangements to cushion such 'slow consolidators' from the onslaught of 'marauding gentrifiers' seeking to benefit from the windfall of upgrading initiatives.

15.6   QUESTIONS FOR DISCUSSION

- In what way is the housing crisis in developing world cities a problem of social exclusion?
- What role did participatory governance play in creating social innovation in Voi?
- In view of the Voi case-study, what problems are you likely to face in implementing socially innovative community land trusts in your own city?

REFERENCES

(References in bold are recommended reading.)

Bailey, N. (2010), 'Building Sustainable Communities from the Grassroots: How Community Land Trusts Can Create Social Sustainability', in T. Manzi, K. Lucas, T. Lloyd-Jones and J. Allen (eds), *Social Sustainability in Urban Areas: Communities, Connectivity and the Urban Fabric*, London, UK and Washington, DC, USA: Earthscan, pp. 49–64.

Bassett, E.M. (2005), 'Tinkering With Tenure: The Community Land Trust Experiment in Voi, Kenya', *Habitat International*, 29, 375–398.

Cornwall, A. and J. Gaventa (2000), 'From Users and Choosers to Makers and Shapers: Repositioning Participation in Social Policy', *IDS Bulletin*, 31 (4), 50–62.

Drewe, P., J.-L. Klein and E. Hulsbergen (eds) (2008), *The Challenge of Social Innovation in Urban Revitalization*, Amsterdam: Techne Press.

Gray, K.A. (2008), 'Community Land Trusts in the United States', *Journal of Community Practice*, 16 (1), 65–78.

Headlam, N. and S. Hincks (2010), 'Reflecting on the Role of Social Innovation in Urban Policy', *Journal of Urban Regeneration and Renewal*, 4 (2), 168–179.

Kennedy, D. (2002), 'The Limited Equity Coop as a Vehicle for Affordable Housing in a Race and Class Divided Society', *Howard Law Journal*, 46 (1), 85–125.

MacCallum, D., F. Moulaert, J. Hillier and S.V. Haddock (2009a), 'Introduction', in D. MacCallum et al. (eds), pp. 1–8.

MacCallum, D., F. Moulaert, J. Hillier and S.V. Haddock (eds) (2009b), *Social Innovation and Territorial Development*, Aldershot: Ashgate.

Midheme, E. (2010), 'Laying the Foundations for the "Just City": Collaborative Spatial Planning and Settlement Upgrading in Voi, Kenya, MaHS Thesis, *ASRO*, Leuven: Katholieke Universiteit Leuven.

MoLG (Ministry of Local Government) (2004), 'Guidelines for Upgrading of Informal Settlements Based on Minimum Intervention Approach', Nairobi: Ministry of Local Government, Kenya.

Moulaert, F., F. Martinelli, E. Swyngedouw and S. González (2005), 'Towards Alternative Model(s) of Local Innovation', *Urban Studies*, 42 (11), 1969–1990.

Moulaert, F., F. Martinelli, E. Swyngedouw and S. González (eds) (2010), *Can Neighbourhoods Save the City? Community Development and Social Innovation*, London, UK and New York, USA: Routledge.

Scott-Cato, M. and J. Hillier (2010), 'How Could We Study Climate-Related Social Innovation? Applying Deleuzean Philosophy to Transition Towns', *Environmental Politics*, 19 (6), 869–887.

UN-Habitat (2005), *Financing Urban Shelter: Global Report on Human Settlements*, London, UK and Sterling, USA: Earthscan.

Yahya, S.S. (2002), 'Community Land Trusts and Other Tenure Innovations in Kenya', in G. Payne (ed.), *Land, Rights and Innovation: Improving Tenure Security for the Urban Poor*, London: ITDG Publishing, pp. 233–263.

16. Knowledge building and organizational behavior: the Mondragón case from a social innovation perspective
Igor Calzada

16.1 SOCIAL INNOVATION: THE PRESENT, PAST AND FUTURE

The new conceptualization of innovation in postmodern management studies has generated quite some *marketecian* noise. Still, other community-embedded approaches to innovation bypassing a unilateral global competition logic are possible. To this end, Geoff Mulgan and his colleagues contextualize the challenges and issues that territories and business nodes confront in a globalized world, offering the idea of 'creative ecosystems' and the metaphor of the Bees and the Trees (Mulgan 2007; Murray et al. 2010). According to this idea, socially innovative experiences are based on an 'alliance' between active agents of innovation (creators, innovators and entrepreneurs) – the 'bees' – and active agents of validation (universities, companies and institutions) – 'trees'. When bees and trees live together in the same urban area they can, through their mutually beneficial interactions, create creative local communities. Presently, at grassroots level in cities, such 'alliance' is required between the post-crisis large-scale projects investors and social entrepreneurs. Without an alliance between these two types of agents, it is not possible for social innovation to occur, because the resources and structures needed to generate the emerging dynamics that would lead to innovation would not be available. In this chapter, this approach

of a 'bees and trees' alliance (Figure 16.1) is referred to as a biocentric approach – it represents an 'ecologization' of the economy and its relations with the local community and civic society as a whole. As the chapter will show, the biocentric approach in the Mondragón case relates to the critical value of land and territory as primary sources of social innovation.

Castells (2009) bases his prediction for the future of cities and territories on the belief that the social networks (Christakis and Fowler 2011) that are currently a part of people's daily lives do not differ greatly from power or 'censorship in the age of freedom' (Cohen 2012). Therefore, rather than leaving the market and its forces to their own devices, one must consider a vision for civil society in which institutions intervene in market forces. The primary issue is to offer protection from the market, rather than be 'bullied' by the influence of the globalization, and to show how to 'survive' and function in it. Thus, it is now appropriate to reintroduce great discoveries such as those that led Jane Jacobs (1984) to propose slowing economic growth for the sake of other social and community benefits. More recently, contributions on the relationship between urban development and community dynamics include David Harvey's concept of 'rebel cities' (2012), Edward Glaeser's ideas on urban and rural complementarities in cities (2011), and Nick Cohen's critique of the superficially 'free'

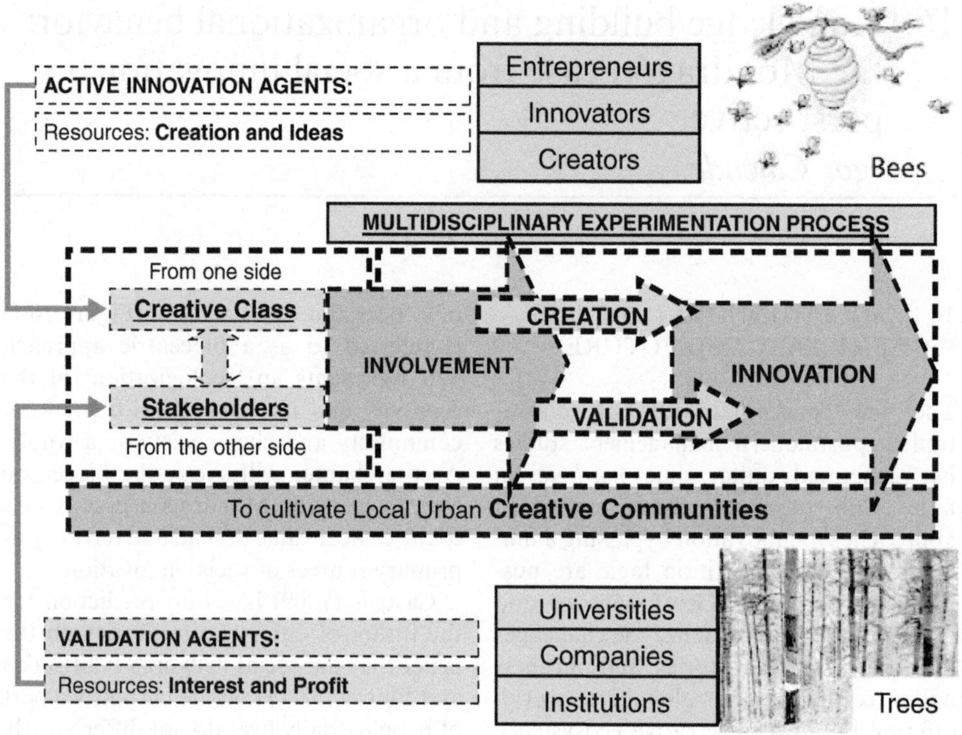

Source: Calzada (2011a, p. 44).

Figure 16.1 Social innovation creative ecosystem: bees and trees

connected world made by digital social networks (Capra 1996; Cohen 2012). The future of social innovation is already being written in terms of a return to the past, through the revival of essential values such as authenticity, identity and local community.

It is not likely that Jose María de Arizmendiarrieta had heard of Jacobs's ideas when he founded one of the world's most-studied cooperative experiences in 1956 in Mondragón, a Basque town with a population of 30,000 people. However, this town had all of the community characteristics that Jacobs had established for an environment to be 'fertile' for social innovation, which is what occurred. Currently the seventh largest business group in

Spain, the Mondragón group employs 83,869 people in 256 cooperatives with an export rate of 60 per cent of its total €14.8 billion (Mondragón Corporación Cooperativa 2011).

16.2 THE DECREASE IN COMMUNITARIAN SOCIAL CAPITAL (CSC) IN THE BASQUE CITY-REGION

To paraphrase the founder of the Mondragón cooperative, Jose María Arizmendiarrieta, '[n]othing differentiates individuals and people as much as their respective attitudes to the circumstances in which they live. Those who choose to make history and change the course of events for themselves have advantages over those who decide to wait passively for the results of change' (Azkarraga et al. 2012, p. 76). In today's globalized environment, we require an affirmative but critical examination from within the Mondragón experience. Globalization promotes individualism with the result that the cooperative *modus operandi* is changed and risks losing its cooperative identity. As Azkarraga states:

[w]e have experienced an ideological emptying and the reinforcement of a new human profile that is more shallow, pragmatic and individualistic. The process of de-ideologization has affected the whole of society and, as members of that society, the co-operative social body as well. (Azkarraga et al. 2012, p. 78).

In this context, the original vision of the Mondragón cooperative provides valuable lessons for the present. Figure 16.2 shows the presence of Mondragón cooperatives worldwide, including 94 production plants and nine corporate offices. The challenges for this network due to globalization are immense. The internationalization of the cooperatives (Luzarraga et al. 2007), the emergence of the BRICS (Brazil, Russia, India, China and South Africa) countries, the ways in which China and India are revolutionizing global business patterns, the decrease in communitarian social capital (CSC), the rise of individualism, the gluttony of unfettered consumerism, and the growing individualization of life through virtual networking (e.g. the use of mass social networks) all contribute to the urgency of critically recovering the foundations of the cooperative experience, which is the core of social innovation. Hence, we need a strategic vision that accounts for both local and global realities.

The present is uncertain: it is reasonable to think, as Azkarraga argues, that 'the cooperative lung needs more oxygen than that provided from the new masks distributed in the name of postmodern management. The Mondragón Experience requires a closer connection with the renewed paths of humanization being proposed in today's world' (Azkarraga et al. 2012, p. 79). In the Basque region, with the emerging dynamism of 'Chindia' (a term used to describe two of the five BRICS countries, namely China and India), the financial crisis has reinforced the need to innovate beyond a business-centered view. In this context, the Mondragón Corporación Cooperativa (MCC) group has defined its response to global markets over several years. In the past, during periods of growth, a technocentric approach prevailed. Now, however, from the more holistic stance of corporate social identity, the MCC must abandon this outdated approach and move forward. The MCC is being branded globally as social entrepreneurship (Hulgård 2006), and in this chapter I attempt to demonstrate the importance of restoring communitarian social capital to the business and academic agendas. In other words, we believe that once the technocentric approach is superseded by one based on an anthropocentric view of social entrepreneurship, there is a risk that this view will prove no more than a veneer for the threat of modern individualism: 'triumphalist talent'. By 'triumphalist talent', we refer to the cases in which entrepreneurial action succeeds in an individualist manner and as a consequence of one-to-one competitiveness (Calzada 2011a, p. 235). To understand this better, we can refer to the provocative and best-selling book *Funky Business* (Riddestrale and Nordstrom 2000), which shows how companies are changing their size and methods of management and operation. When we examine cooperative companies, we can also observe organizational changes

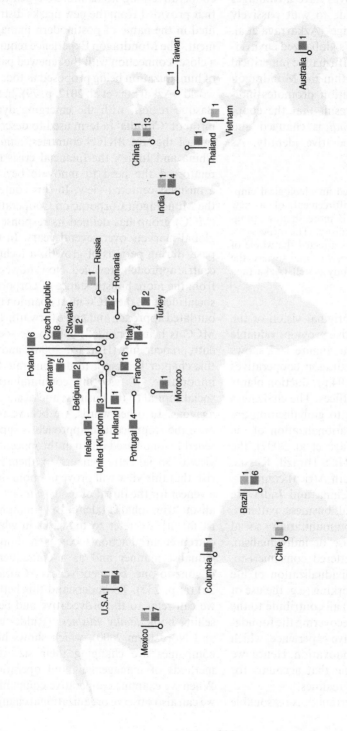

Source: Mondragón Corporación Cooperativa (2011).

Figure 16.2 The international manufacturing presence of the Mondragón cooperatives

from industrial conventional post-Fordist companies to entrepreneurial-networked atomized business units. Moreover, a new generation of cooperative members is threatened by individualism. Thus, how can we avoid the temptation to encourage 'triumphalist talent,' which encourages individualism and organizational anemia in universities and companies? How can we establish a new generation of social entrepreneurs according to the cooperative traditional synergy with the biocentric approach, who can respond creatively to the current economic, social and environmental challenges?

We must strike a balance between encouraging individualist and triumphalist forms of 'social' entrepreneurship with the need to structure communities, which are the basis of the cooperative economy. When we speak of communities, we refer to self-governing actions that are initiated by a business, university or the scientific and technological world and that can extend to the level of public institutions and civil and associative society. Ultimately, social entrepreneurship should serve local communities. For example, universities are active agents of validation (trees) that host many active agents of innovation, or social entrepreneurs (bees).

If the Mondragón experience is to adapt to today's challenges, then it must initiate a biocentric path in which sustainability is not an addition but permeates the way business is conducted, with the involvement and proximity of local communities. The biocentric approach reminds us why the Mondragón experience has been socially innovative in a communitarian manner, both economically and sustainably, and why we should recover those values and activities to adapt them to the present. This chapter's analysis of the Mondragón experience shows how the biocentric approach can save cooperativ-

ism, which was originally too anthropocentrically oriented.

16.3   COMMUNITARIAN SOCIAL CAPITAL (CSC) BUILDING IN MONDRAGÓN

The Mondragón experience was based on the idea that community development is more important than economic progress. As a result, a number of small entrepreneurial businesses gradually created a dense business network in a single valley. However, the increased sizes of the cooperatives, the greater degree of internationalization and a move towards more individualistic patterns of community and civic life have lowered the levels of communitarian social capital (CSC) to historic minimums. Today, therefore, the cooperative model faces a potential crisis, and there is a need to reformulate it from the ground up while preserving its cooperative essence. In other words, there is an urgent need to build a new biocentric model of development that does not harm the ecosystem but fosters lifestyles with a strong post-materialist element based on responsible consumption, self-containment and austerity. Let us examine some inspiring experiences connecting past and present in Mondragón.

ORONA is a leading MCC international cooperative company that is compatible with a biocentric perspective. This company is a world leader in elevation systems and is currently developing an ambitious strategic project called ORONA IDeO, Innovation City (http://www.orona-group.com/en/sections/we-are-orona/innovation/orona-ideo-innovation-city.php, last accessed 9 January 2013). The aim of this project is to build a research hub led by an international company and the University of Mondragón to initiate a dialogue with the stakeholders of the Basque city region. The practical approach of ORONA IdEO is a good foundation from which to valorize the territory as a biocentric unit of the society, economy and environment.

For the University of Mondragón, though, the primary effort in recent times has been the promotion of projects and initiatives not in international companies, but in junior cooperatives. Although job maintenance is supported by 'traditional' business and cooperative structures, the original driving forces behind the firms belonging to the Mondragón group (some of them: Orona, Maier, Eroski, Fagor and Ulma), today we should explore the possible replacement of these 'traditional' structures with global, dynamic, young, open, networked and sustainable initiatives (similar to the business model promoted by Riddestrale and Nordstrom (2000). This is the impetus behind the university's LEINN (Enterprising and Innovative Leadership) degree, which is contributing to the formation of a new talent pool of social entrepreneurs which is consistent with the vision of the Mondragón experience and that will enhance truly reticular cooperative entrepreneurial business models (Calzada 2011a, p. 235). The future of social innovation lies not with large companies but with networked structures of social entrepreneurs.

An interesting historical experience is the civil movement of support for the *Ikastolas* (schools in Basque) and the revival of the Basque language (Calzada 2011b). In the closing years of the Franco dictatorship, the Basque society experienced major upheavals, with a strong social response on the streets. In addition to numerous other demands, the element that largely united Basque society (despite differences over ideological strategy) was the revival of the Basque language as a

key social asset. Civil organizations for the creation of Basque schools united people with different ideologies to create a high level of CSC.

Finally, the case of *Auzolan* (Calzada 2011a, p. 243), or neighbourhood community work, represents an historical ideal and an experience from which important lessons can still be learned today. The roots of this civil movement began in the Basque Country and are based on the same idea on which the Mondragón experience was founded. A revival of neighbourhood community work in several towns and areas throughout the Basque country has recently begun. One way of reviving this practice today to increase the level of CSC for towns and districts, which are micro-territories (Calzada 2011a, p. 241), is to upgrade the concept of *Auzolan* to that of the *Auzolab*, a community laboratory for the development of neighbourhoods and villages.

16.4   CONTEMPORARY OPPORTUNITIES FOR THE BASQUE CITY REGION

No analysis of the deterioration of CSC in the Mondragón experience and in the Basque country can ignore the political violence suffered by the Basque people. The consequences of this violence include social withdrawal, the creation of closed communities (archipelagos) and a damaged moral and social fabric that has led to citizens' disempowerment and demoralization. As Bauman (2001) and Putnam (2001), noted, the loss of community values is inexorably linked to the erosion of CSC. In the Basque country, such erosion certainly influenced and even paralyzed civil society (Innerarity and Gurratxaga 2009; Elzo and Silvestre 2010; Echeverría and Gurrutxaga 2010).

However, at the time of writing, a number of covert developments point in the direction of a possible peace process. After two years without attacks and a defusing of the dynamics that created vicious circles of political violence, there is increased hope and opportunity for socio-political change. This context offers an opportunity to break the cycle of stagnation and deterioration and to begin a new period of openness and inclusive work. The time may be right for the Basque country, as a geostrategic cross-border territory within the EU, to take ownership of the decisions that affect it and to emerge as a Basque city region that we shall call 'the Basque City'.

These changing socio-political conditions point to a scenario of 'normality' against a backdrop of economic crisis and recession. Combined with a commitment to strategic projects in emerging industries, new CSC may generate opportunities for development. A specific opportunity is presented by new technologies, in the form of trans-local social connectivity.

16.4.1 Strategies of Social Innovation: Social Connectivity, Social Networks and Reconfiguration in New 'Glocal' Communities

With the rise in online social networks (for example, Facebook, Twitter and Linked In), there is a tendency to confuse the emergence of new relational patterns with the consolidation of CSC. In other words, increased interaction on social networks does not necessarily lead to a substantial increase in CSC. Evidently, social networks are creating relational flows that would have been inconceivable only a few years ago and constitute an essential phase of recombination and intersections (Johansson 2004) for innovation. However, after a first step of recombina-

tion and remixes (Lessig 2008) between entrepreneurs in search of new opportunities and unexplored niches, creative ecosystems must undergo the consolidation/institutionalization (Calzada 2005) of relations and relationship patterns. When we speak of institutionalization, we refer to the transition from an informal social network to an institutional cluster. The necessary condition for CSC is not the mere presence of active (online) social networks. Another condition, which now also constitutes a new category of scientific analysis, is necessary: 'Social Connectivity' (Calzada 2011a, pp. 58, 215, 220). Social connectivity should be understood as the linking of social networks at the community level with the purpose of activating consensus among diversity.

Ultimately, a creative ecosystem needs its networked relationship patterns to become dynamic and representative of the structure of the system itself. Unfortunately, an explanatory model has not yet been devised from the perspective of social innovation. However, we can observe that without social connectivity, social networks will rise and fall without creating lasting community value and without generating CSC through dynamic social networks that practice social connectivity on a daily basis.

Let us now examine the three constituent elements of CSC (Burt 2005) *bonding*, *bridging* and *linking* for the Basque City:

- Bonding: an important starting point is to overcome the scenario of political violence to create the necessary conditions for bridging the gap between different agents. We assume that *bonding* through social entrepreneurship in the university-company-public institution triad is now bearing its first fruits. In the past, the distances between the elements of this triad were immense; however, the collaborative work being conducted by the university is playing a leading role in strengthening this triad.

- Bridging: one disturbing aspect of bridging is the style of social entrepreneurship being promoted, which conflicts with the creation of CSC because it demands a profile of 'triumphalist talent'. This conflict is also paradoxical because it is unrelated to the basic principles of the Mondragón experience. We encounter the risk of encouraging the emergence of an individualistic entrepreneurship with no bridging and no CSC-building process.

- Linking: social networks are leading us towards new 'glocal' scenarios in which social innovation seeks to deal with similar questions in geographically different points: 'glocal' means that the local and global are interlinked. Thus, we are building arrangements in trans-local parameters in which the power of the local territory acquires a new dimension on the global map. In other words, we are increasingly interested in experimenting with local *Auzolabs*, which are inter-connected to favor trans-local learning. Linking has prime importance in this dimension. Given that it is essential to recover CSC, social innovation must be implemented today with strategies that include the glocal dimension (Calzada 2011a, p. 220).

16.4.2   Glocalization, Social Entrepreneurship and Cooperativism in Mondragón

This section examines new paradoxes and problems that may serve to spark an articulation and response mechanism. We begin by quoting Azkarraga, who insists that '[i]t clearly seems inconsistent to set up a cooperative metropolis with a capitalist periphery. (. . .) But the cooperative group does not yet have a model of internationalisation of its own, a model that also in one way or another internationalises the cooperative idea.' (Azkarraga 2007, p. 5)

The great challenge for social innovation research lies in the formulae, methodologies, case studies and lessons to be learned from the processes of internationalizing the cooperatives (see Figure 16.2) that currently form the flagship of the Mondragón experience. These cooperatives alone do not create a competitive advantage for strategic positioning in global markets. Considering this situation of maximum global uncertainty, we must explore a new concept of social entrepreneurship in different emerging industries: entrepreneurs with large glocal networks who are highly specialized and prepared to form or lead culturally and thematically diverse teams.

However, some questions remain unanswered: what specific organizational/cooperative form would provide coverage, projection, autonomy and freedom of movement to these new social entrepreneurs, individually, in teams or in glocal cells? Is it possible to speak of 'intrapreneurship'? Are the 'driving' cooperatives willing to encourage social entrepreneurs to join their structures? Does the Mondragón experience currently allow these social entrepreneurs to work towards the future of the Mondragón brand? Is there not a risk that their efforts will be dissipated into small and unconnected initiatives? Is there a way to maintain two speeds of development (one traditional and mature and the other emerging but voluntary or idealist)? Is it possible for these speeds to converge?

Let us recall that the Mondragón experience originated with a few social entrepreneurs under the protection of the local community. They were small groups with close social relations in this local community. The situation at that time was more comfortable than the current situation and was characterized by social, cultural, communicative and psychological proximity. Today, in contrast, the Mondragón case comprises 83,859 individuals in a cooperative group of more than 256 companies with a high degree of complexity, social differentiation and organizational architecture. There has been a move from a geographical concentration to a clustered relocation on a global scale.

This new geography of clustered relocation affects the social networks (Cohen 2012) generated in the socio-business world: relationships between cooperative workers, social entrepreneurs, researchers, consultants, managers, teachers, and the entire community network in which they operate. The following essential questions must be answered: how will those social networks initially be created? How will they be consolidated to create new communitarian social capital? Could these networks build a new cooperative horizon for social entrepreneurs based on cooperative principles?

Azkarraga identified a key challenge to these new social and spatial configurations stating that:

> an ideological horizon was lacking that would embrace the different self-managing social scenarios within an integrating framework. The cooperative valley has not been nourished by the necessary ideological, symbolic and intellectual impetus. There has been no comprehensive project and no vision to mark this orientation since the death of Arizmendiarrieta. This new vision offers a real possibility of overcoming this shortfall. (Azkarraga 2007, p. 6)

Here, we can identify the first obstacle. One cannot simply propose that a new

entrepreneurially based 'cooperativism' should ignore the community or make the individual the primary driving force behind all change (i.e. an anthropocentric vision). In a social innovation approach, we employ a biocentric focus that involves social entrepreneurship in a variety of cooperative roles.[1]

The real issue for the Mondragón experience today is that no cooperative forms of society currently articulate the new creative ecosystem on a systematic basis. One of the great challenges for cooperative firms is to adopt this articulation as a prelude to being a true social innovator.

16.4.3 Social Entrepreneurship vs. Public Sector? Noise and Silence

A related matter – and without wishing to enter a slippery polemic but rather to examine the real situation directly – is the paradox of the current socioeconomic system. In the midst of a crisis and recession, there is support for entrepreneurship, but which type of entrepreneurship is being discussed? Moreover, is entrepreneurship the most important type of agency in the current crisis? This tension is expressed in the contrast between the 'noise' generated by the frustration of the Spanish 2011 protest movement, the '*Indignados*' (Harvey 2012), and the silence on the part of many agents in the system who have the social responsibility both to survive the recession and to take on a new approach to social transformation. I am essentially referring to the leaders of private financial institutions and the politicians who apply only partial measures in their areas of influence, with the excuse that global issues are beyond their reach.

When one considers the discourse of entrepreneurship for the sake of entrepreneurship, there is a tendency to overlook the necessary public service reforms. The

Basque city region has an oversized public administration that is bureaucratized and sometimes inefficient because of redundancy and overlap (Calzada 2011a, p. 265). How can this problem be addressed?

Social innovation strategies should encourage a spirit of social entrepreneurship within a wider dynamic of cooperativism. In this regard, companies and public institutions must commit to the new dynamic biocentric approach based on the creative ecosystem. Furthermore, a review of the forms and functions of public service is imperative, both from the perspective of management and efficiency and in terms of citizen solidarity and democracy.

16.5   CONCLUSION

Articulating the Mondragón experience with the territorial and community-based development of the Basque city region involves a move from a technocentric and anthropocentric approach to a biocentric one.

We must identify how to make the transition from an experiment in socio-economics to one in eco-socioeconomics. As noted above, this transition requires the companies of the Mondragón group, the University of Mondragón's research projects and students, and the Basque country, as a networked territory known as the Basque city region, to consider this territory a primary asset. The ORONA IdEO, Innovation City and LEINN projects are good examples of the practical consequences of social innovation. New green economy jobs, projects, companies and public policies ought to be supported through the pollination and co-creation processes of the urban local creative ecosystem. In the case of Mondragón, this support should take the form of collective action shared by companies, universities and public administrations.

However, this transition undoubtedly requires five key changes: (a) the change in the energy matrix and the transition towards a greater self-sufficiency; (b) business reorientation towards the creation of 'green' products; (c) job creation policies; (d) policies related to innovation, science and technology; and (e) a profound cultural change in the cooperativist social body. The biocentric approach will produce a new eco-socioeconomic paradigm in which social innovation is the strategy and the city region is the territorial concept for the post-2008 crisis scenario.

In summary, we aimed to propose from a social innovation approach stepping stones, not only to allow the Mondragón cooperative group to meet new challenges but also to empower the hopeful reality of the Basque country as it establishes itself as a Basque city region.

16.6   QUESTIONS FOR DISCUSSION

- How can we design more social innovation projects, like IDeO and LEINN, in which companies and universities develop a new biocentric approach to cooperativism? In doing so, can we avoid the triumphalist and individualistic entrepreneur's 'dangerous' business style?
- Are these two projects the seeds with which to plant local urban creative communities in the Basque city region?
- What role could an academic perspective on territorial development and social innovation (MacCallum et al. 2009) play in the future design of services, and even products, in a new eco-socioeconomic paradigm in Mondragón?

● How can the University of Mondragón develop its sensitivity to the value of territory and business design simultaneously?

NOTE

1. In this context, we can revisit the University of Mondragón's new LEINN degree, to ask whether the pool of social entrepreneurs it is creating is consistent with the vision of the Mondragón experience? How can we ensure a truly reticular cooperative entrepreneurial business model?

REFERENCES

(References in bold are recommended reading.)

Azkarraga, J. (2007), *Mondragón ante la globalización: la cultura cooperativa vasca ante el cambio de época*, Eskoriatza, Gipuzkoa: Cuadernos de LANKI, no 2, Mondragón Unibertsitatea.
Azkarraga, J., G. Cheney and A. Udaondo (2012), 'Workers Participation in a Globalized Market: Reflections on and from Mondragon', in Maurizio Atzeni (ed.), *Alternative work organizations*, London: Palgrave.
Bauman, Z. (2001), *Community: seeking safety in an insecure world*, Cambridge: Polity.
Burt, Ronald S. (2005), *Brokerage and Closure: An Introduction to Social Capital*, Clarendon Lectures in Management Studies, Oxford: Oxford University Press.
Calzada, I. (2005), *Cultura, Conocimiento, Innovación y Gestión: Las Clases Creativas en la Euskal Hiria*, Vitoria, Revista Vasca de Economía, Ekonomiaz and Euskonews.
Calzada, I. (2011a), *¿Hacia una Ciudad Vasca? Aproximación desde la Innovación Social*, Vitoria-Gasteiz: Edit. Servicio Central de Publicaciones del Gobierno Vasco.
Calzada, I. (2011b), *Towards the Basque City? Comparative Territorial Benchmarking from Social Innovation: Dublin (Ireland) & Portland (Oregon)*, Bilbao: Innobasque-Basque Innovation Agency.
Capra, F. (1996), *The Web of Life: A New Synthesis of Mind and Matter*, London: Harper Collins.
Castells, M. (2009), *Comunicación y Poder*, Madrid: Alianza.
Christakis, N. and J. Fowler (2011), *Connected: The Amazing Power of Social Networks and How They Shape Our Lives*, London: HarperPress.

Cohen, N. (2012), *You Can't Read This Book: Censorship in an Age of Freedom*, London: Fourth Estate Press.
Echeverría, J. and A. Gurrutxaga (2010), *La luz de la luciérnaga: Diálogos de Innovación Social*, Donostia-San Sebastián: Edit. Ascide, pp. 121–123.
Elzo, J. and M. Silvestre (eds) (2010), *Un individualismo placentero y protegido: Cuarta Encuesta Europea de Valores en su aplicación a España*, Bilbao, Universidad de Deusto.
Glaeser, E. (2011), *Triumph of the City*, Oxford & London: Pan Books.
Harvey, D. (2012), *Rebel Cities: From the Right to the City to the Urban Revolution*, London: Verso.
Hulgård, L. (ed.) (2006), *Social Enterpreneurship and the Mobilization of Social Capital in European Social Enterprises: A Public-Third Sector Partnership*, London: Routledge.
Innerarity, D. and A. Gurratxaga (2009), *¿Cómo es una sociedad innovadora?* Bilbao: Innobasque-Innovación Social.
Jacobs, J. (1984), *Cities and the Wealth of Nations*, New York: Random House.
Johansson, F. (2004), *The Medicci Effect. Breakthrough Insights at the Intersection of Ideas, Concepts and Culture*, Boston: Harvard Business School Press.
Lessig, L. (2008), *REMIX: Making art and commerce thrive in the hybrid economy*, New York: Penguin Press.
Luzarraga, J.M., D. Aranzadi and I. Irizar (2007), 'Understanding the Mondragón Globalization Process: Local Job Creation through Multi-Localization: Facing Globalization Threats to Community Stability', paper presented at the 1st CIRIEC International Research Conference on Social Economy, Victoria, Canada.
MacCallum, D., F. Moulaert, J. Hillier, S. Vicari Haddock (eds) (2009), *Social Innovation and Territorial Development*, Aldershot: Ashgate.
Mondragon Corporación Cooperativa MCC (2011), *Annual Corporate Profile*, http://www.mondragon-corporation.com/mcc_dotnetnuke/Portals/0/documentos/eng/Yearly-Report/Yearly-Report.html (last accessed 9 January 2013).
Mulgan, G. (2007), *Social Innovation: What it is, why it matters and how it can be accelerated*, London: The Basingstoke Press.
Murray, R., J. Caulier-Grice and G. Mulgan (2010), *The Open Book of Social Innovation*, Social Innovator Series: Ways to design, develop and grow social innovation, London: Nesta.
Putnam, Robert D. (2001), *Bowling Alone: The Collapse and Revival of American Community*, London: Simon & Schuster.
Riddestrale, J and K. Nordstrom (2000), *Funky Business*, London: Pearson.

17. Going beyond physical urban planning interventions: fostering social innovation through urban renewal in Brugse Poort, Ghent[1]

Stijn Oosterlynck and Pascal Debruyne

17.1 INTRODUCTION

In this chapter we analyse the scope for socially innovative forms of strategic urban agency at the neighbourhood scale. Our focus here lies on integrated area development (Moulaert 2002) and socially creative strategies in post-industrial neighbourhoods that are subject to severe forms of socioeconomic decline and are confronted with increasing degrees of ethnic, cultural and socioeconomic diversity. What we are particularly interested in is how particular local social needs are identified and integrated in an urban renewal project for this type of neighbourhood. We will show that this requires a socially innovative approach to urban renewal, i.e. an approach that goes beyond mere physical urban planning interventions but also transforms existing localized social relations and community dynamics in ways that empower local communities to collectively identify and meet its needs.

In what follows, we briefly engage with the literature on neo-communitarian strategies for urban renewal and community development and relate it to the social innovation literature. We then assess the social innovation potential of neo-communitarian urban renewal strategies in the Belgian city of Ghent, which has invested in community-based forms of urban planning for more than two decades and has developed quite a reputation in it (Stad Gent 2009). We zoom in on a recent large-scale experiment in community-based planning in the neighbourhood Brugse Poort, namely the urban renewal project 'Oxygen for Brugse Poort', and analyse how community-based planning led to the identification and integration of particular local social needs in the urban renewal project and assess to what extent this amounts to the project acquiring socially innovative dimensions.

17.2 THE SOCIAL INNOVATION POTENTIAL OF COMMUNITY-BASED PLANNING

Jessop (2002) argues that neoliberalism, despite being the general tendency, might not be fully accepted and implemented in each place and on each spatial scale, particularly not at the urban scale where its social tensions and contradictions are most apparent. Post-industrial neighbourhoods, confronted with social, cultural and economic problems for which conventional state or market-based solutions seem less than adequate, often adopt what he calls 'neo-communitarian' strategies (Gerometta et al. 2005). Neo-communitarian strategies put community building, civic engagement and social economy and third sector initiatives at the centre of urban revitalization and redevelopment (DeFilippis and North 2004; Jessop 2002; Lepofsky and Fraser 2003; Moulaert et al. 2010). Community-based action is proposed as a third way between the state-based collectivism of socialism and the market-geared individualism of liberalism (DeFilippis and North 2004). For DeFilippis (2004), communities are a potentially emancipatory category because they build capacity for collective action in urban space on the basis of the social relations in a particular geographic setting.

This provides a bridge to the social innovation approach, which is rooted amongst others in debates on local economic development and the new urban policy and in which social innovation implies a critique on technologically determinist, accumulation-centred and elite-driven views of local development and technocratic approaches to urban planning (Moulaert 2002; Swyngedouw et al. 2002). The social innovation approach centres on the quality of social relations between individuals and groups, and is particularly focussed on creating social relations that allow disadvantaged socioeconomic groups to participate in those production processes that satisfy their basic needs (see General Introduction).

Those basic needs are not well served by large-scale market-oriented urban development projects and technocratic urban planning approaches. Large-scale urban redevelopment programmes have become the privileged vehicles through which cities are repositioning themselves within global political-economic networks and the international spatial division of labour now that national states have withdrawn from their previous Keynesian ambition to spread development equally over their territory (Brenner 2004). The problem with these large-scale urban development projects is that they focus on physical spatial interventions and do not start from local human needs, but form those local development 'assets', often highly spatially con-

centrated, of cities that can be marketed at wider spatial scales (Moulaert 2002; Moulaert et al. 2001). This narrow market-oriented and spatially selective focus is strongly related to the urban governance configurations that steer these kinds of urban development. More often than not those governance configurations are autocratic, focussed on the commercial interests of a limited number of state and private sector actors and closed off from broad civic participation.

Socially innovative urban development hence requires a social transformation of the urban governance mechanisms, i.e. the relations of power across state and civil society in the city, through which human needs are defined and strategies to allow inhabitants to satisfy them are developed (see KATARSIS project in Moulaert et al., Chapter 1). Only by creating new and more inclusive social relations can another, more integrated urban development agenda be put forward. It requires the 'social production of power' through the creation of a collective capacity to act, as urban regime analysts would put it (Stone 1993). Neo-communitarian strategies focus on place-based communities as vehicles for the social production of power. However, the mobilization of the ideal of the community does not necessarily lead to social innovation, i.e. the formation of new, inclusive social relations that empower local people to satisfy their own needs. As DeFilippis and North (2004, p. 84) argue, 'the emancipatory potential of community-based collective action in urban space collides with attempts to instrumentally impose an ideal of community in which there is no space for collective action.' Community-based planning strategies often are no more than a compensatory strategy to address the worst effects of the market-based restructuring of the city and the disinvestment of governments in social and spatially just policies in disadvantaged urban areas throughout the last neoliberal decades.

From a social innovation perspective, then, it is crucial that community-building is not instrumentally imposed as a means of socially controlling disadvantaged neighbourhoods fraught with political tensions (Uitermark 2003), but that it transforms localized social relations in such a way that local people are empowered to voice and organize around their own needs. In the words of DeFilippis (2004, p. 29): 'For local-scale actors to be autonomous, they must therefore transform relations they are embedded in to allow themselves greater control over those relationships.' The community, as the focal point through which a collective capacity to act on shared local needs are created, is hence something that needs to be built and which, according to DeFilippis, can only maintain its emancipatory potential when the differences and conflicts within it are not denied. Socially innovative community-based planning efforts should therefore not be treated as a formal planning model applied by the local state and bureaucracies, but as a local development practice grounded in concrete multiscalar relations of power, social struggle and bottom-up mobilization.

17.3   THE DEVELOPMENT OF COMMUNITY-BASED PLANNING IN GHENT

This section explores the social innovation potential of community-based planning by zooming in on the urban renewal project 'Oxygen for Brugse Poort' in the Belgian city of Ghent. The city of Ghent has, over the last three decades, pioneered a tradition in social urban renewal, using participatory mechanisms to involve citizens in urban planning processes. This social urban renewal approach is applied to the post-industrial neighbourhoods in its 19th-century belt, which are confronted with a concentration of socio-spatial problems: lack of green and open space, unemployment, poverty and social exclusion, tensions between immigrants and the original labour class inhabitants, bad quality of housing, high density, etc. The project 'Oxygen for Brugse Poort', launched by the city council in 2002, was the first in the most recent series of large scale social urban renewal projects in Ghent.

17.3.1   Brugse Poort: a Neighbourhood in Need of Urban Renewal

The popular neighbourhood Brugse Poort, situated to the north-west of the city centre, has a rich industrial history. Over the course of the 19th century, especially after the *octroi*[2] levied at the city walls had been abolished in 1860, the neighbourhood expanded rapidly. Large textile factories set up shop in the neighbourhood and to accommodate the factory workers, new streets and houses were built. This happened in an unplanned and speculative way, leading to a chaotic and very dense urban tissue, which largely remains until today. The neighbourhood developed a lively socio-cultural life, albeit pillarized[3] and segmented along ideological lines, and a strong local identity, embedded in the strongly knit local community that was reproduced on the factory floor, the local church and the many pubs, clubs and associations in the neighbourhood.In the 1960s the neighbourhood lost many of its factories through de-industrialization, while most of its middle-class residents moved to the suburbs. From the 1970s onwards, migrants started arriving in the neighbourhood, initially mainly of Turkish and Moroccan origin, but in the

1990s Eastern European immigrants and, increasingly, also 'illegal' immigrants. In the second half of the 1990s, new urban middle classes, mainly former university students, were attracted by the revival of the city and moved into the neighbourhood, often because of the availability of affordable housing. Suburbanization, de-industrialization and the arrival of migrants led to the disintegration of the tightly-knit local community, the erosion of its socio-cultural life and associations and the weakening of the local identity and pride of the neighbourhood. Next to this weakened 'traditional' associational life, and of more recent origin, were a range of civil society organizations such as social workers, neighbourhood workers, youth workers, theatre groups, neighbourhood and street committees, environmental actions groups, etc. These can loosely be described as the heirs of the anti-authoritarian movement of the late 1960s and often entertained close (financial and other) relationships with the state. As a result, the local civil society was characterized by fragmentation, inter-organizational competition and lack of coordination. Meanwhile, the housing stock in the neighbourhood, which had never been of good quality, deteriorated, while the population density remained very high. Given problems of drug use and alcoholism, poverty, unemployment, illegal immigrants and intercultural tensions, the neighbourhood has a bad reputation as a residential area.

In 1999 the city council asked the urban design companies NERO and Stramien to analyse the urban tissue of the neighbourhood and draft an urban design to address the identified spatial problems. The urban design ('Stadsontwerp West') suggested 25 urban interventions in the neighbourhood (NERO and Stramien, 2000). Amongst others, they proposed a maximum and minimum (or 'essential') scenario in which respectively 582 and 186 bad quality houses would be demolished and 953 and 180 new houses would be built. In 2001, the city's spatial planning department developed an urban renewal vision for the area, taking over some – but by no means all – of the suggested urban interventions. The vision was called 'Oxygen for Brugse Poort' and mainly addressed the lack of green and open space, the bad quality of the housing stock and road safety for pedestrians and cyclists. The city council aimed to create more space and improve the housing stock by demolishing three out of 13 poor quality housing blocks and building new and qualitative social and private houses. Open and green space was to be created through the designing of a number of parks (Pierkespark, Fonteinenplein, Luizengevecht and Groene Vallei), while a 'red ribbon' was built as an alternative and safe pedestrian and cycle route connecting different neighbourhood functions. The main aim was to make to improve the 'liveability' of the neighbourhood and make it more attractive to middle-class residents in order to create a better 'social mix'. This rather technocratic physical spatial planning approach was, as the urban renewal project proceeded, coupled with a neo-communitarian approach, which aimed to involve the local population and civil society via various participation mechanisms. In this way, the city council wanted to mobilize support for the urban renewal project (given the unpopular measure to demolish a large quantity of houses of bad quality), revive community dynamics and create a new neighbourhood identity that would break with the neighbourhood's bad reputation.

In the remainder of this chapter, we analyse how through this neo-communitarian approach (or community-based planning as the city council calls it), existing social relations were transformed, new social relations were built and local social needs became more central to the urban renewal project. We will explore to what extent various participation processes contributed to put local social needs more central in urban planning interventions, show how the transformation of social relations triggered by the urban renewal project involved moments of social struggle, analyse the socially innovative role played by social-artistic actors in building identity and community and identify public spaces and parks as places where the need for socially creative strategies to improve social relations in post-industrial neighbourhoods is most acutely felt and addressed. We will not develop an exhaustive analysis of the urban renewal project 'Oxygen for Brugse Poort', but focus on four different community-based planning processes or moments within it: a) the negotiations with the neighbourhood council over the content and focus of the urban renewal project; b) the struggle to turn Groene Vallei into a large urban park; c) the social-artistic strategy to revive community dynamics; and d) the participation processes for the redesigning of the parks.

17.3.2   The Neighbourhood Council: Beyond Physical-Spatial Planning

When the spatial planning department launched the urban renewal project, their vision had yet to come together with the vision being developed by the existing neighbourhood council. This neighbourhood council, which had been in existence since the 1980s and originated in previous phases of social urban renewal, gathered a number of mainly white middle-class residents of the neighbourhood and was revived to provide feedback to the city council's urban renewal plans (De Meyer 2010). Three representatives of the neigh-

bourhood council were involved in an advisory board where the urban renewal project was discussed. This led to a charter between the neighbourhood and the city council (Stad Gent and Buurtraad Brugse Poort 2002). When the city council proposed its urban renewal program for the neighbourhood, it clashed with the vision that the neighbourhood council had been developing with the assistance of social workers. The neighbourhood council demanded interventions which were much more in line with the urban design that had been made by the design companies Nero and Stramien (see above), but the city council argued that they did not have the financial means to implement those plans. For the neighbourhood council, the project was also too much directed at attracting new residents, while they wanted the urban renewal investments to be focused mainly on the living conditions of the existing residents. It called for more social housing in order to avoid the problem of weaker inhabitants being pushed out of the neighbourhood through gentrification. Although the neighbourhood council was not against the urban design interventions, they wanted the city council to give priority to improving the bad quality of much of the housing stock and the creation of 'socially safe' open and public space. Eventually, agreement was reached and formalized in the aforementioned charter and the neighbourhood council acquired its status as an advisory body to the city council for the urban renewal project. As representative of the neighbourhood, the neighbourhood council was closely involved in the further development of the urban renewal project and was regularly allowed to voice its vision and concerns.

What is important about this participation process is that the neighbourhood council clearly demanded an approach that 'goes beyond stones' since 'the proposed plans focus pre-dominantly on the [physical] urbanism story' (Stad Gent and Buurtraad Brugse Poort 2002, p. 3). The neighbourhood council argued that the effects of the urban planning interventions will only have maximum effect if measures are taken for the neighbourhood on other terrains as well. They referred for example to the overpopulation of some houses, the need for employment and training projects and the development of services tailored to the local needs. The neighbourhood council also stressed the importance of supporting the participation of disadvantaged groups such as immigrants and people with weak reading skills and who are less vocal. The attempts of the neighbourhood council in the initial phases of the urban renewal project to make social needs more central highlights the role of path dependency in social innovation. In this case, the presence of a 'representative' local forum to communicate and promote local social needs added socially innovative features to the urban renewal project.

17.3.3 Green Valley: The Struggle For Green and Open Space

When a new city council gained power after the municipal elections of 2000, it gave itself one year to study the urban design plan made by Nero and Stramien and develop the urban renewal project for Brugse Poort. One of the main challenges for the city council was to find support for its plans in the neighbourhood, particularly with regard to the demolishing of a number of poor quality housing blocks. A long standing struggle of a local action committee to turn an adjacent brownfield site into an urban park provided a unique, if rather costly, opportunity for the city council to show that it was serious about urban renewal and the neighbourhood's demand for more green and open space.

In 1964 a flax spinning factory which occupied a large area in between Brugse Poort and the adjacent neighbourhood Ekkergem was demolished and the land was sold. The real estate developer Amelinckx who bought the land initially planned to build high-rise luxury apartment blocks and a shopping mall. Between 1969 and 1976, three apartment blocks and a supermarket were built, but then the real estate developer went bankrupt due to the economic crisis in the late 1970s. The remainder of the brownfield site stayed vacant and gradually turned into a wild and 'unofficial' urban park as people started using it in informal ways. The lasting uncertainty over its future use led to the establishment of the action committee Groene Vallei Groen ('Green Valley Green'). When the real estate market revived in the 1980s, the committee resisted further construction on the brownfield site and asked the city council to turn the area into a park. The action committee was mainly populated by middle-class residents from Brugse Poort and the adjacent neighbourhood. However, because some of its members entertained close links with the city administration, the local Green Party and the Flemish umbrella organization for environmental movements, the action committee was able to mobilize supra-local support and networks. Ten proposals of real estate developers – for example the proposal to build a big private broadcasting network tower – were fought off successfully.

In the middle of the 1990s the city council eventually announced, much to the disapproval of the action committee, that only two thirds of the area would be reserved for a green area, with the remaining one third being earmarked for real estate development. The city council then started to look for a real estate developer who would be given building permission on the condition of financing the building of an urban park in the rest of the area. However, all proposed real estate plans ran into resistance of the neighbourhood and the action committee because in order to make a profitable venture high rise buildings were required, which in turn would lead to extra traffic. The neighbourhood and the local action committee argued that buildings of 18 to 28 storeys were too high for the area. Eventually, in 2000, the city council decided to leave the decision on the most recent real estate proposal to the future council, which would have to develop and implement a global vision for urban renewal of Brugse Poort and could hence adapt its plans for the Groene Vallei to fit this global vision.

The next city council was quick to recognize the opportunity and took action immediately after its instalment. It rejected the plans of the real estate developer, took the expensive[4] decision to buy the land and pay for the design of the park and only allowed 10 per cent of the land to be used for housing construction of a moderate height. It also involved the members of the action committee in the participatory design and building of the park. It should be noted, however, that attempts by social workers paid by the city council to organize participation in the urban renewal project failed to involve the inhabitants of the social housing blocks near the park. The latter's conceptions of a park did not match those of the ecologically minded middle classes active in the local action committee and the members of the action committee overwhelmed the much less vocal social housing residents (De Meyer 2010). For example, requests by inhabitants of the social housing block for the park to be lit at night so that they would feel safe walking there were rejected on the grounds that the light may disturb the birds.

For the city council the building of the park offered an opportunity to gain support for its urban renewal plan. It would have been virtually impossible to justify abolishing the houses in the neighbourhood, to create new parks among other reasons, if it would have allowed real estate development on what had become an informal park. What is also important is that by incorporating the new park into the urban renewal project, the city council automatically involved the local action committee in the project as well. By allowing them to be involved both in the designing and building of the park, the antagonistic relationship between the city council and the local action committee was transformed into a more cooperative one. Their struggle paid off as the city council had recognized the local need for green space. The local action committee's leadership in bringing about the park was recognized through their continued involvement in the park's management (see e.g. the organization of the annual Green Valley celebration). The Green Valley episode highlights the importance of social struggle in bringing about social innovation, especially when it finds the urban development interests of market and local state interests on its way. At the same time, however, it shows how social struggle may also work to exclude other local groups and their needs, particularly those with less capacities to organize themselves.

17.3.4   Cultural Strategy to Revive Community Dynamics

As we highlighted above, the urban renewal project was initially predominantly oriented towards (physical) spatial planning. Although spatial planners acknowledged the social, economic and cultural needs of the neighbourhood, the institutional barriers between the various policy sectors proved difficult to overcome. However, both the project communicator and coordinator were strongly convinced of the need to couple spatial and social interventions and used the autonomy they received from the city council to experiment with different ways to bring this in practice. The then mayor Frank Beke was a strong believer in the role of culture (Beke and Renson 2006; Van de Steene 2006). For him, cultural infrastructure in the neighbourhood is important to fight the disintegration of the social tissue and isolation and helps to soften intercultural tensions. From the 1980s onwards, he was keen to include cultural elements into every urban renewal project in the city. With the involvement of the theatre group 'De Vieze Gasten' ('The Dirty Pals') the urban renewal project acquired a separate socio-cultural trajectory. This socio-cultural trajectory started from the idea that urban renewal projects have a big impact on the neighbourhood and that the neighbourhood has to grapple and come to terms with the changes wrought on it and appropriate the new spaces that are created. The theatre group, with decades of experience with socio-artistic work, was subsidized to develop a socio-cultural trajectory that would assist the neighbourhood to cope with and appropriate the changes in their area. To that end, they assisted people from the neighbourhood to photograph and write about the changes in the area, had their brass band write a neighbourhood theme song and performed at many neighbourhood events to create neighbourhood specific cultural expressions, etc.

Because of their role in the urban renewal project De Vieze Gasten have become a central actor in the neighbourhood. They connect other actors in the neighbourhood by making their theatre infrastructure available for use by the local schools and organizations, have their brass band or photographers playing and exhibiting on local events, etc. Their central role as social innovation agent was not planned, but came about through the creation of a new central place in the neighbourhood as part of the city council's attempt to revive the local community dynamics in the area. Before the urban renewal project many local civil society actors in the area did not have much contact with each other. The urban renewal project aimed to change this by spatially linking and concentrating several neighbourhood services around a newly created central place for the neighbourhood (called Pierkespark). Pierkespark is traversed by the new circulation route for pedestrians and cyclists through the neighbourhood, which guarantees ease of movement for the inhabitants. But in order for the public green space to function and be experienced as a central place in the neighbourhood, the city council attempted to convince De Vieze Gasten and a social economy firm, both adjacent to Pierkespark, to relocate their entrance to the side of the park. The city council also gave another building adjacent to the park to the local organization Trafiek to run a coffee house and neighbourhood centre. By locating the social economy firm, the theatre and the neighbourhood centre at different sides of a new public green space, it effectively acquired a central space function that brings together the inhabitants of the neighbourhood, thus supporting social innovation through the strengthening of community.

In conclusion, the organization of a socio-cultural trajectory that assisted and supported the neighbourhood in grappling with and appropriating the physical-spatial changes in the neighbourhood caused by the urban renewal project transformed the fragmented local civil society. New communication channels and relations were forged between actors that were previously not in contact with each other. The socio-cultural actors operating as nodes in the reinvigorated local social networks also served to create a new identity for the neighbourhood as a vibrant and creative socio-cultural space. Social-artistic actors hence have the potential to develop and pursue socially creative strategies that revive community dynamics.

17.3.5   Living Together in Public Parks

One of the central aims of 'Oxygen for Brugse Poort' was to create more open space in order to increase the liveability of the neighbourhood. Several new parks were planned. Following a long tradition of participation in the city and keeping its promise to the neighbourhood council, the city council contracted social workers to organize a range of participation trajectories for the design of new small parks in the neighbourhood (De Meyer 2010; Dewart 2009). The participation trajectory for the first new park (Kokerpark) did not go well. The social workers used the rather conventional method of a survey to collect the views of the inhabitants on how the park should be redesigned. It turned out that the residents were less concerned about the specificities of the physical redesigning of the park (e.g. where benches should be placed), but were concerned about the possible occupation and appropriation of the park by particular groups to the exclusion of other groups (e.g. migrant youth), drug dealing and use, rubbish dumping, noise from children playing late at night, etc. These concerns were not taken into account when designing the park. The newly designed park was vandalized after a couple of weeks.

For the design of the next park (Boerderijpark), the city council only organized a meeting to present the plans to the inhabitants. Because this meeting was poorly attended the social workers decided to organize an event in the park. The social workers co-operated with youth workers to organize events for children and teenagers from the neighbourhood, temporarily designed the park as it was planned so that neighbouring residents could directly experience it and give feedback and gave it a festive touch by also providing music and a bar. This event was highly successful as it attracted many inhabitants, with a good social mix, and took place in a less grim and more relaxed atmosphere. The success of this event, combining neighbourhood participation and activities for children and youngsters, gave rise to 'BabbelBabbel' (literally 'TalkTalk'), a network consisting amongst others of youth organizations, neighbourhood and social workers and the city council department of arts. BabbelBabbel aims to organize activities in the parks to intensify the use of public parks by different social groups and organizations and give people practical experience on how to live and use public space together (Samenlevingsopbouw Gent 2008). They also wanted to promote communication between the children and teenagers playing in parks and the neighbouring residents, who often see these children and youngsters as a nuisance. Given that social relationships around the parks in the area remain fraught with tensions and living together within and around some of the parks is hampered by inappropriate park designs (e.g. Fonteineplein, which was designed to be 'football unfriendly', but which is still used by children to play football), BabbelBabbel has been lobbying, unsuccessfully until recently, for funds to appoint one or more youth welfare workers. The Babbelbabbel network is often called upon by the city council, often after complaints of local residents, 'to do something about the nuisance' caused by children and teenagers in the parks, which poses a real threat to its socially innovative potential and may serve to exclude some young people from the community. However, the approach of organizing neighbourhood activities in public spaces still carries a distinctly socially innovative potential that may be further developed in the future and put the social safety of the parks and living together in public space firmly on the agenda of urban renewal.

17.4 CONCLUSION

The analysis of the urban renewal project 'Oxygen for Brugse Poort' in Ghent suggests a number of conclusions regarding the relationship between community-based planning and the various dimensions of social innovation. Firstly, the case study shows how in post-industrial neighbourhoods, which due to the lack of private investments and the concentration of social and spatial problems have become non-competitive urban spaces, neo-communitarianism can emerge as an integral part of urban renewal strategies. In this case, it was mainly through the confrontation between the spatial planning-based vision of the city council and the community dynamics and organization in the neighbourhood that the project acquired a strong community-based planning dimension. This confrontation could take place because of the long tradition of participation in urban renewal in the city and was supported by functionaries who were open to local civil society and used the autonomy they had to experiment with community-based planning and link it to the planned physical-spatial interventions.

Secondly, in general, but certainly not always, this coupling of physical-spatial interventions and community work con-

tributed towards an improvement of local social relations and a greater focus on local social needs. More specifically, in Brugse Poort it brought more social cohesion and shared sense of purpose in the social networks of local civil society. The fragmentation along ideological lines, mutual disinterest and competitive relationships have given way to a more constructive and cooperative approach, in which the socially creative strategies of the social-artistic organization De Vieze Gasten played a crucial role. The neo-communitarian approach also allowed particular local social needs, for example the shared use of public space by different social and cultural groups, to come to the fore and be integrated in the urban renewal project. The fact that despite extensive delays of some physical-spatial interventions (e.g. the building of new parks and social housing) there is a shared feeling in the neighbourhood that 'things have changed for the better' testifies to the impact of the neo-communitarian strategy on the identity of and community dynamics in the neighbourhood.

Thirdly, the neo-communitarian approach also opened up institutional opportunities for local actors who had been organizing and mobilizing around particular local needs for a long time (González and Healey 2005). One example of this is the integration of the Green Valley action committee in the urban renewal project through the city council's decision to acquire the land and involve them in the design of the park through participation. The creation of institutional opportunities for local actors to join in the urban renewal project significantly enlarged the space for socially innovative actions.

Fourthly, despite the clear social innovation tendencies embedded in the urban renewal project through the neo-communitarian approach, it is important to pay attention to the heterogeneity of the community, or risk some of the most marginalized groups and pressing local needs being only weakly or insufficiently integrated in the renewal project. As local communities are never homogenous, every neo-communitarian strategy should attend with great care to the diversity within each local community. The exclusion of the residents of an adjacent social housing block from the participatory design of the Green Valley park is just one example. This highlights the fact that the empowerment of certain groups and their needs potentially implies the disempowerment of other groups and their needs. Analysis of processes of social innovation should hence not only focus on empowerment but also pay attention to possible processes of disempowerment, especially of marginalized groups.

Finally, it seems that the transformation of social relations in the local civil society and between the local state and civil society is more difficult when clear private property and market-based interests are involved. Perhaps the greatest local need is the improvement of the quality of housing in the neighbourhood. Several scientific analyses of the quality of the housing stock in the 19th-century urban belt have shown that more than half of the houses have serious deficiencies (e.g. unsafe electricity, moisture problems, risk of carbon monoxide intoxication, unsafe gas pipes, etc.). The number of old houses demolished and the number of new housing units constructed is clearly insufficient to deal with this massive problem. Because of a lack of financial resources, the local city council counts on private capital to regenerate the neighbourhood, which is why the attraction of middle-class families figures so centrally in the urban renewal project. This seriously weakens the social innovation potential of 'Oxygen for Brugse Poort', which is reflected by the hostile responses of the city council with which action groups against the demolition of houses were met.

Overall, community-based planning has great potential for social innovation. Participation of local community actors helps to put local social needs central to urban planning interventions and socially creative strategies revive community dynamics and transform existing social relationships. Attention should be paid however to the processes of inclusion and exclusion that inevitably underlie processes of community building. Sociopolitical mobilization and struggle does not only empower, but can equally well serve to disempower certain groups and their needs. This should be taken as an important reminder that social innovation is always an unfinished undertaking.

17.5   QUESTIONS FOR DISCUSSION

- Community building is a powerful vehicle for transforming local social relations. How can social innovative strategies avoid community building further disempowering marginalized groups?
- Under what conditions do participation processes allow local social needs to become more central to urban renewal projects?
- In post-industrial neighbourhoods it is in public spaces that the need for social innovation is often most acutely experienced and addressed. Which socially creative strategies may help to improve living together in diversity in public space?

NOTES

1. Part of the research in this paper was financed by a post-doctoral research fellowship of the Fund for Scientific Research – Flanders (held by Stijn Oosterlynck). We are grateful to the many people that shared their knowledge about social urban renewal in Ghent and especially Brugse Poort with us. The authors remain solely responsible for the facts and arguments presented in this chapter and any factual errors or omissions it may contain.
2. A tax or toll levied on the passage of goods into/out of a city.
3. Pillarization (*verzuiling* in Dutch) is a term used to describe the organizational segregation of Belgian society along political-ideological lines (Christian, socialist and to a more limited extent liberal).
4. The council effectively bought expensive building land on a prime location close to the city centre to build a park on.

REFERENCES

(References in bold are recommended reading.)

Beke, Frank and Ine Renson (2006), *Mijn Gent*, Antwerpen: Manteau.

Brenner, Neil (2004), 'Urban governance and the production of new state spaces in western Europe, 1960–2000', *Review of International Political Economy*, 11 (3), 447–488.

De Meyer, Patrice (2010), Interview by Stijn Oosterlynck, 5 August, Gent.

DeFilippis, James (2004), *Unmaking Goliath. Community control in the face of global capital*, London: Routledge.

DeFilippis, James and Peter North (2004), 'The emancipatory community? Place, politics and collective action in cities', in Loretta Lees (ed.) *The emancipatory city?*, London: Sage, pp. 72–88.

Dewart, Sylvie (2009), 'Participatie en diversiteit: "Zuurstof voor de Brugse Poort" revisited', unpublished Masters thesis, Brussels: Ruimtelijke planning en stedenbouw, Erasmushogeschool Brussel.

Gerometta, Julia, Hartmut Häussermann, and Giulia

Longo (2005), 'Social innovation and civil society in urban governance: strategies for an inclusive city', *Urban Studies*, 42 (11), 2007–2021.

González, Sara and Patsy Healey (2005), 'A Sociological Institutionalist Approach to the Study of Innovation in Governance Capacity', *Urban Studies*, 42 (11), 2055–2069.

Jessop, Bob (2002), 'Liberalism, neoliberalism and urban governance: a state-theoretical perspective', *Antipode*, 34 (3), 452–472.

Lepofsky, Jonathan and James C. Fraser (2003), 'Building Community Citizens: Claiming the Right to Place-making in the City', *Urban Studies*, 40 (1), 127–142.

Moulaert, Frank (2002), *Globalization and integrated area development in European cities*, Oxford: Oxford University Press.

Moulaert, Frank, Erik Swyngedouw and Arantxa Rodriguez (2001), 'Social polarisation in metropolitan areas. The role of new urban policy', *European Urban and Regional Studies* (special issue), 8 (2), 99–102.

Moulaert, Frank, Flavia Martinelli, Erik Swyngedouw and Sara González (2010), *Can neighbourhoods save the city?*, Abingdon: Routledge.NERO and Stramien (2000), *Stadsontwerp Westsector Eindrapport*, Gent: Stad Gent.

Samenlevingsopbouw Gent (2008), *Jaarverslag 2008: Zuurstof voor de Brugse Poort*, Gent: Samenlevingsopbouw Gent.

Stad Gent (2009), Urban Renewal and Community Based Planning, Gent: Stad Gent.

Stad Gent and Buurtraad Brugse Poort (2002), Charter tussen het stadsbestuur en de buurtraad Brugse Poort: Zuurstof voor de Brugse Poort, Gent: Stad Gent.

Stone, Clarence N. (1993), 'Urban regimes and the capacity to govern: a political economy approach', *Journal of Urban Affairs*, 15 (1), 1–28.

Swyngedouw, Erik, Frank Moulaert and Arantxa Rodriguez (2002), 'Neoliberal urbanisation in Europe: large-scale urban development projects and the new urban policy', *Antipode*, 34 (3), 542–577.

Uitermark, Justus (2003), '"Social mixing' and the management of disadvantaged neighbourhoods: the Dutch policy of urban restructuring revisited', *Urban Studies*, 40 (3), 531–549.

Van de Steene, Sonny (2006), 'Interview met Frank Beke', *UVV Info*, 23, 10–16.

18. Social innovation through the arts in rural areas: the case of Montemor-o-Novo

Isabel André, Alexandre Abreu and André Carmo

18.1 INTRODUCTION

Culture and the arts have been taking on an increasingly important role within the context of local development strategies in the last couple of decades (Landry et al. 1996; Lowe 2000; Newman et al. 2003). It is often thought, or assumed, that culture and art can provide a veritable 'sleight of hand' capable of turning run-down, degenerated areas into dynamic, prosperous, 'nice' places. But to what extent are those regenerated places also equitable, fair and cohesive? And what does it take for culture and art to play a positive role in this respect as well?

This chapter puts forth two main arguments in this regard: i) the promotion of culture and art within the context of local development strategies may provide a crucial contribution to harmonizing the goals of economic competitiveness and social cohesion (as well as those of economic innovation and social innovation), but does not *always and necessarily* have that effect; and ii) the 'virtuous' outcome is dependent on a broad-based, participatory approach to culture and arts that is able to (re)combine collective memory and collective creation (see Tremblay and Pilati, Chapter 5; Cornwell 1990; Puype 2004; Markusen and Gadwa 2010).

This discussion is illustrated by drawing on a 'virtuous' case study from Southern Portugal: Montemor-o-Novo, a rural municipality in the largely depressed Alentejo region, where the municipal government has, over the last three decades, implemented a local strategy of which culture and art constitute a central pillar. This has made it possible for an interesting and dynamic local 'cluster' to emerge based on the interaction between various forms of artistic expression, including dance, theatre, sculpture, photography and video art. Alongside the artists and art-promoting organizations themselves – most of which belong to the third sector – the municipal government has played a very important enabling role by promoting and financing the creation of a network of cultural facilities and services (exhibition gallery, art schools, concert halls, etc.) which has further contributed to drawing in numerous creative agents. One of the most interesting features of this case study is the relationship between the cultural and artistic agents and the local community – a relationship that has significantly enhanced social innovation and creativity.

The chapter is organized as follows: Section 18.2 contains a brief theoretical discussion on the topic of the creative city from a critical perspective, which highlights, among other things, the exclusive and elitist character of many initiatives undertaken under this banner. Then, Section 18.3 addresses the role of arts in the promotion of social innovation and creativity in adverse milieus, with a particular emphasis on the specificities of rural contexts. Section 18.4 contains the case study, which gives a concrete expression to the general arguments put forth in the preceding sections. Finally, Section 18.5 puts forward a number of concluding remarks with regard to what the necessary conditions are for socially creative and innovative milieus to arise in rural contexts.

18.2 CREATIVE CITIES: A CRITIQUE

The concept of the creative city – as developed and explored by Charles Landry (2000), Richard Florida (2002, 2005, 2008) and other authors (Hall 2000; Hospers 2003; Pratt 2008; Smith and Warfield 2008) over the last couple of decades – has come to be regarded as a true 'treasure map', the 'egg of Colombus' that makes it possible to raise post-industrial cities out of the doldrums in which they have increasingly found themselves. Drawing in creative and talented people has become a key goal for numerous cities – and with that goal in mind, public authorities throughout the world have financed a variety of urban projects both in the cultural and artistic sphere and in those infrastructural domains that are required to keep creative cities running (e.g. transports, communications, environmental rehabilitation).

The remarkable popularity that these strategies have come to enjoy in recent times should be understood against the background of the increasing importance of aesthetics and the 'spectacular' in daily life – most especially in the case of cities, with their highly distinctive character (as argued, among others, by Jane Jacobs (1993[1961]) and Guy Debord (2006[1955])). This is, of course, a deeply ambiguous project. On the one hand, it has raised many relevant questions and enabled truly creative accomplishments in the cultural and artistic field *per se*, as well as, on a broader societal plane, on matters to do with the appreciation of diversity and

tolerance – particularly in what regards civil rights issues and the formulation of alternative visions of society. On the other hand, and as has been increasingly acknowledged, the creative city has often turned out to have a very elitist and exclusive character. This is a consequence of the fact that the 'creative cities' discourse has little time or consideration for the aims of social justice and spatial cohesion, and that the strategies adopted in the pursuit of this vision are more often than not driven by the interests of private capital.

Creative cities tend to disregard social creativity and social innovation, not least because the latter emphasize equity, empowerment, social justice and changes in social relations, and thereby pose challenges to the prevailing social order. Indeed, it is the contrary that is often the case: many actions and initiatives undertaken within the ambit of the standard, mainstream approach to creative cities have given rise to the exclusion and expulsion of some of the poorest and/or most vulnerable groups from city areas undergoing regeneration (Ley 2003; Moulaert et al. 2004). Private capital is quick to seize the value generated by the 'creative class' – both directly within the creative industries sector and indirectly (but not less importantly) through such ways as the increase in the price of urban land and housing, or its role as a magnet that attracts other firms with an interest in sharing in the creative environment as 'form'.

It is therefore ironic that myriad 'creative' urban regeneration projects have flourished in recent times which could themselves hardly be less creative, insofar as they often 'carbon-copy' each other. And that adds to an even more serious cause for concern: the fact that these projects often trample land use laws and regulations, and disregard the will of the local communities. As eloquently argued by Moulaert et al.

(2004, p. 2344), 'maybe the term beautification should be avoided in this context [of urban regeneration]: it has been burnt by its strong connotation of socially destructive gentrification, including the destruction of poor quarters, the dislocation of poor people, the polarization between chic and outskirt neighbourhoods.' Basically, the creative city often walks hand in hand with the fragmented and socially exclusive city. Moreover, we should be careful to distinguish between the various senses of the word 'creativity', their respective implications and their interrelationships: as argued by Scott (2006, p. 10), 'the mere presence of "creative people" is certainly not enough to sustain urban creativity over long periods of time. Creativity needs to be mobilized and channelled so that it can develop into practical forms of learning and innovation.'

In reality, the effects of attracting 'creative professionals' are often illusory, given that the high mobility levels of the people in question prevent their full integration into, and commitment *vis-à-vis*, the milieus to which they are temporarily attracted. More often than not, they are just passing by, living their daily lives within a relatively close social circle, engaging more in long-distance social relations than in neighbourhood and proximate ones, and thus hardly leaving any 'creative seeds' behind them in their places of residence/work. This is an issue that is seldom addressed, and usually disregarded, in the context of urban policies aimed at giving rise to 'creative cities'.

The Canadian public authorities seem keenly aware of this debate, including the criticisms that have been levied against the more simplistic views of creative cities. In a publication entitled *Creative Cities: What Are They For, How Do They Work, and How Do We Build Them?*, published by the Canadian Policy Research Networks,

Gertler (2004, p. 1) puts forth a number of recommendations for public policy-makers that seem particularly relevant in this context:

> First, we should support the development of creative cities because they play an ever more important role in enhancing the dynamism, resilience, and overall competitiveness of our national economy. Second, we should nurture the development of creative cities because they have the potential to enhance quality of life and opportunity for a broad cross-section of Canadians. [Debates on the creative cities remind us of] the importance of adapting the creative class thesis to the Canadian context in an active and critical (rather than passive) way, by making our aspirations very clear. The goal for public policy in Canada should be – and can be – to enhance the formation of socially inclusive creative places.

This issue has been almost always discussed in the context of large European and North American cities and especially in the case of deprived neighbourhoods, given that it is at the local scale that socially creative strategies have taken on their greatest expression. Many local development initiatives have been undertaken (and debated) that have sought to pursue social inclusion and empowerment through music (e.g. the Birmingham opera company, UK; El Sistema, Venezuela; Tocárufar, Portugal), street art (with many cities organizing a wide array of artistic events in public space, with a special focus on 'alternative' expressions), theatre (e.g. Theatre of the Oppressed, Brazil; Stut Theatre, Holland) and circus (Chapitô, Portugal; Fekat Circus, Ethiopia; Machincuepa Social Circus, Mexico). Indeed, arts have come to play an increasingly relevant role in the promotion of creativity in general, and of socially creative strategies in particular. Arts do not necessarily provide 'the solution', but they help to 'illuminate the way' by inspiring people and communities.

18.3   ARTS, SOCIAL CREATIVITY AND SOCIAL INNOVATION IN RURAL AREAS

Artistic creation, to a greater degree than other forms of creativity – product design, for example – plays a central role in the context of social creativity and social innovation, given its unique ability to challenge habits and social structures and to (re)construct collective memories and identities. Art's inherently metaphoric character makes it possible to transcend the obvious and facilitate the communication of deep values and feelings (Smiers 2005). As both a product and a source of inspiration, it has the capacity to produce 'transcendence' (Ruby 2002). And public art, in particular, is especially relevant to the promotion of individual and collective self-esteem, to the (re)construction of local and social identities and to strengthening the sense of belonging – a crucial condition of urban social cohesion (Miles 1997).

Especially in the case of deprived contexts, arts have emerged as key promoters of critical thinking and facilitators of communication (Campbell and Martin 2006; Belfiore and Bennett 2008; André and Carmo 2010), by stimulating the creativity of community members and facilitating the emergence of new answers to unsolved (political, social, economic and environmental) problems. Moreover, the promotion of artistic activities can also become a means to counter or reverse the reproduction of inequality and disadvantage, by constituting a stimulus to social innovation, increasing personal and collective confidence, and contributing to eliminating the negative connotations associated with certain communities and places (André and Abreu 2009). Artistic creation has thus been increasingly recognized as constituting a key lever for the construction of creative milieus, based on the assumption that artistic creativity will inspire and stimulate creativity in other spheres of human activity.

Nevertheless, and contrary to what seems to be implied by the literature on creative cities, it is apparent that creativity – social, economic, cultural, etc. – also exists outside of large cities, including in the context of rural regions experiencing decline. Rural tourism (nature, adventure, cultural, etc.) is often suggested as a possible way for overcoming the obstacles and adversities that characterize these territories. In the case of the European Union, the support to the development of rural areas has been mainly targeted towards social issues, the preservation and valorization of the environment and the landscape, and the diversification of the economic basis – an orientation that is apparent in the encouragement and support to rural tourism, biological agriculture and initiatives associated with heritage and culture (Borrup 2006; Markusen 2006).

Still, despite the attempts by rural development policies to counter this perception, it is undoubtedly the case that, for most people, innovation and creativity continue to be mostly associated with cities and, especially, with large metropolises. Critical mass, mobility and accessibility, and social and cultural diversity are all typically considered to be crucial factors for creativity and innovation – and they are also essentially urban features (Törnqvist 2004; Meusburger 2009). Nevertheless, as exemplified by the case study presented further on in this chapter, that is not necessarily the case: small-sized cities in rural areas may very well exhibit very favourable conditions for the emergence and consolidation of socially creative milieus. So which conditions are these that we are referring to?

As we have argued elsewhere, the key pre-conditions for social creativity to be nourished and sustained are *diversity, tolerance, collective learning and critical thinking* (André and Abreu 2006). Diversity is crucial insofar as (socially) creative actions and activities typically emerge as a consequence of bringing diverse experiences, ideas and perspectives into contact. It may come about as a consequence of mobility, of culturally different groups coming and going and sharing the same space, or of the interaction between different social groups who are compelled to work together in order to come up with solutions to various forms of adversity. These contacts and interactions between diverse groups and individuals typically give rise to conflicts and tensions that can either bring about negative and destructive outcomes or, on the contrary, constitute a positive and creative stimulus to finding shared solutions and new compromises. Additionally, a high level of acceptance and appreciation of that which is different and/or unexpected is another pre-condition of socially creative milieus – and tolerance and open-mindedness are also critical to the extent that risk-taking is only encouraged and nourished in milieus that do not systematically penalize failure. Finally, collective learning and critical thinking make it possible for novelty to introduce information and knowledge which needs to be appropriated, deconstructed and reconstructed in order for existing institutions and structures to be recreated and provided with new meanings. It is especially important that learning does indeed take on a collective character – otherwise those who hold a relative 'monopoly' over knowledge are able to impose their own rules upon others.

Social innovation – a concept that is closely related to, but distinct from, social creativity – takes the latter a step further, in the sense that it places greater emphasis on the social appropriation and dissemination of socially creative 'novelties', to the *relative* detriment of the creative act *per se*. It is no less essential for social cohesion and social justice, however (Fincher and Jacobs 1998; Tremblay et al. 2005; Moulaert et al. 2007). Indeed, the very distinction between these two logical moments is little more than a conceptual aid, given how inextricably interwoven the two must be in order for the aforementioned objectives to be attained. Still, pre-conditions for social innovation to occur may be formulated somewhat differently from those identified above for social creativity. They include: i) *participation*, or the encouragement of collective cooperation, dialogue and, whenever necessary, conflict (in a critical and positive understanding of the latter); ii) *collective references and memories*, which provide the necessary anchors that ensure the resilience of places and their ability to embrace what is new without degenerating into fragmentation and 'negative' conflict; (iii) *leadership*, which has been empirically shown across a variety of contexts to provide the spark for consequent collective action; and iv) *an adequate geographical scale* making it possible for the previous pre-conditions to be met without the introduction of tensions too significant for the places in question to be able to withstand and resolve. When the previous conditions are met to a sufficient degree – which, admittedly, is particularly hard to test *ex-ante* – we speak of *'plastic* places', in reference to the concept of plasticity from physics, which denotes the ability to change shape without losing internal structure and coherence (Lambert and Rezsohazy 2004).

Thus, generally speaking, the conditions that foster and enable social creativity and social innovation in different socio-territorial contexts may assume different configurations, but gravitate around a common core. In order to illustrate just

Table 18.1   Social creativity and social innovation in urban and rural milieus

		URBAN AREAS	RURAL AREAS
SOCIAL CREATIVITY	DIVERSITY	Different lifestyles and sub-cultures Different national and ethnic backgrounds	Different social groups, as a consequence of an accumulated history of class and labour relations Different age groups Outsiders Return migrants
	TOLERANCE	Based on citizenship principles and rules Lesser sensitivity to alterity	Based on personal relationships Greater sensitivity to alterity
	COLLECTIVE LEARNING AND CRITICAL THINKING	Importance of school and of the interpersonal networks established there Specific qualifications for creativity Critical thinking as an individual attitude (contestation)	Importance of tacit knowledge and of the experience passed from one generation to the next Critical thinking in association with political ideologies and affiliations
SOCIAL INNOVATION	PARTICIPATION	Virtual social networks Goal-oriented cooperation	Neighbourhood networks and relationships Cooperation based on personal trust
	COLLECTIVE REFERENCES AND MEMORIES	Based on the 'official' discourse Materially-expressed (squares, buildings, events, . . .)	Non-material heritage (stories, poetry, music, . . .)
	LEADERSHIP	Importance of the mass media Role of competences translates into the effectiveness of the actions	Importance of personal charisma and of personal ties
	GEOGRAPHICAL SCALE	Multiscalar space (neighbourhood – metropolis – the world)	Place (daily spaces of the local community)

this, Table 18.1 puts forth an attempt, largely but not exclusively based on the Portuguese reality, to illustrate how the various general pre-conditions for social creativity and social innovation may take on different forms in different contexts – in this case, depending on whether we are referring to urban or rural contexts.

Thus, to sum up the ideas underlying Table 18.1, the construction of socially creative and innovative milieus in the case of rural contexts largely depends on the ability to overcome pre-existing social fractures and to reconstruct social relationships. Local policies and their ideological orientation are critically important insofar as the cleavage between the conservative outlook (associated with tradition and stability of social relations) and the progressive one (which seeks to promote change) exerts a profound impact on the trajectory of the local community. On the other hand, leaders play a very important role, too, given that the ties that bind them to the local community have an 'emotional' character, and are often capable of overcoming the difficulties and contradictions that more strictly rational approaches are unable to come to terms with. Finally, one of the key assets of rural contexts in terms of social innovation consists of the geographical scale at which the actions, initiatives and relationships take place. Proximity seems to be a fundamental condition as far as processes of social innovation are concerned – one which has a transversal character *vis-à-vis* the other conditions, by: i) enabling levels of trust that clearly foster a sense of the 'collective'; ii) turning small features and details into identity references shared by the community as a whole; and iii) stimulating and encouraging feelings and emotions, to the detriment of strictly rational thought (Moore 2008).

In view of all this, the central questions driving the case study to which we shall now turn may be formulated as follows: which concrete factors have played the most critical roles in stimulating socially creative strategies and driving social innovation in the case of this particular instance of a rural milieu experiencing decline? To what extent have arts fostered and assisted these processes?

18.4 MONTEMOR-O-NOVO: SOCIALLY CREATIVE POLICIES AND INITIATIVES

Montemor-o-Novo (MoN), like many other towns and cities in the Alentejo region, has had to face a remarkably adverse economic and social context. A city of 9,000 inhabitants (2001 Census), it experienced a natural demographic balance of −5.4 per cent between 1991 and 2001. About one quarter of the population is over the age of 64 and its traditional economic base – agriculture – has undergone a severe secular decline, currently accounting for barely 15 per cent of the workforce. In addition, one third of the adult population has had no schooling whatsoever, and only about 5 per cent have a university degree. At first glance, this hardly depicts the trappings of a typical 'creative city'. Nevertheless, the recent 2011 Census seems to indicate some changes in MoN: in a local context that continues to show signs of demographic decline (the municipality as a whole lost 6.3 per cent of its population during the last decade), two parishes exhibit a different tendency. In the most urban parish of the municipality, Nossa Senhora da Vila, the population grew by 7.9 per cent and the number of buildings increased by 13.4 per cent (indicating a significant number of new secondary residences). Even more surprising is the similar tendency experienced in one of the rural parishes, Foros de Vale Figueira, where the population registered a slight increase, by 0.4 per cent, and the number of buildings increased by 13.8 per cent. It is not a coincidence that the only instances of positive demographic dynamics in this municipality correspond to those parishes where three of the key initiatives that we will be referring to further on in this text are located: the urban parish of Nossa Senhora da Vila (Convent Workshops and

The Space of Time; see below) and the rural parish of Foros de Vale de Figueira (Freixo do Meio Farm). Next, we will try to illustrate the extent to which socially creative strategies based on cultural and artistic activities devised and undertaken in MoN have contributed to reversing the cycle of adversity.

Despite the unfavourable context, the local authorities have over the past three decades been able to mobilize resources and pursue a strategy that has significantly advanced community development. One of the main pillars of this local strategy has consisted in the promotion of cultural and artistic activities – on the one hand, by seeking to combine and cross-fertilize memory and creation (i.e. using the historical heritage as a crucial resource for the promotion of creative initiatives and the attraction of creative professionals); on the other, by pursuing economic development, social inclusion and urban cohesion in an integrated manner. Biological and organic agriculture, rural tourism and cultural activities have been elected by the local authorities as the main strategic axes of MoN's development strategy. Among the latter, however, one towers above all others: in a context of adversity, MoN is increasingly recognized as a centre of artistic production and creative activity of international renown.

The roots of this are to be found in its historical trajectory, in which the city council played the key leadership role. Just four years after the democratic revolution of 1974, the municipal government founded an Arts Gallery and a Library, located in the ancient Convent S. João de Deus. The 1980s witnessed the creation of a municipal socio-cultural office and the launching of arts workshops for children. Then, in the 1990s, European Structural Funds made it possible to undertake a range of innovative local projects combining culture, arts and social aims. From the mid-1990s onwards, a new stage followed that has corresponded in a sense to the 'maturity' of this development strategy, as the focus turned to the attraction of artists and creative professionals from outside the municipality, region and country. In return, these artists and creators have been explicitly asked to commit to preserving the historical heritage, undertaking partnerships with schools, the local elderly, etc., and holding their *premières* in MoN. In sum, under a democratic but determined leadership, virtuous synergies have been gradually fostered between various local agents. From the perspective of social innovation, a number of local initiatives sharing a commitment to the valorization of heritage through artistic creation and to the promotion of strong connections with the local community can be found in MoN.

Amongst the wide range of initiatives that have given shape to this strategy, there are three that illustrate its crucial features particularly well: i) a choreographic centre – The Space of Time – located in a 15th-century monastery within the MoN castle; ii) a visual arts association – Convent Workshops – that functions in an old monastery in the centre of the town; and iii) a biological agriculture unit – Freixo do Meio Farm – that promotes an integrated approach to rural activities, including eco-tourism, permaculture and land art exhibitions. Table 18.2 synthesizes the main characteristics of each of these initiatives.

In the case of MoN, the arts have become central drivers of the local development strategy, as well as an important way of improving the social recognition of the municipality among outsiders. This has taken place through the activities of the cultural and artistic entities themselves, but also via institutions that are primarily

Table 18.2 Profile of the three initiatives analysed

	CONVENT WORKSHOPS	THE SPACE OF TIME	FREIXO DO MEIO FARM
FOUNDATION FOUNDERS	1996 Virgínia Fróis (fine arts teacher – sculptor) and Vasco Silva (cultural programmer for the City Hall). Established in MoN in the aftermath of the 1974 Revolution, connected to socio-cultural action.	2000 Rui Horta (choreographer and dancer). Horta returned from Germany wanting to start a choreographic centre in a rural area away from the large metropolises. He received support from the MoN mayor who allowed him to use a 15th-century monastery located in the MoN Castle.	2001 Alfredo Cunhal Sendim (zootechnical engineer). Heir to a family of large agricultural property owners. Uses his 650ha farm to develop a multifunctional and integrated rural project.
VISION	To convert the constraints that characterize Montemor-o-Novo into cultural added value for the local residents (artistic creation-heritage link). To deepen the relation between the local residents and the urban space, the surrounding landscape and traditional architecture.	To provide creators with the necessary distance for the elaboration of creative works: contemporary art is essentially an urban phenomenon; however, distance is required for reflection and the creation of the artistic object.	To foster local development in the sense of respect for the needs and desires of local communities, while seeking to mobilize available resources and to create new ones. It has an integrated vision of social, economic, and cultural activities in this rural milieu. Biological and sustainable production techniques have been adopted.
MAIN OBJECTIVE	To valorize local culture and to promote a closer relationship between citizens and their shared spaces. To promote public art and qualify the landscape, as well as the natural, architectural and environmental heritage.	To create a 'laboratory' for the innovation and renewal of scenic languages, by building a structure that is simultaneously professional and flexible.	To promote environmental sustainability, seeking to create conditions that will allow for its continuous self-sufficiency.
SPECIFIC OBJECTIVES	To recover the S. Francisco monastery in order to set up an artistic centre. To collaborate with other agents in local development initiatives. To promote artistic and professional training.	To create new audiences. To establish dialogue and cross-fertilization between different genres of performing arts. To promote research and experimentation. To prioritize investment in technical materials,	To invest in alternative energies. To develop permaculture methods and techniques. To protect and valorize the region's specific landscape (i.e. the *montado*).

	CONVENT WORKSHOPS	THE SPACE OF TIME	FREIXO DO MEIO FARM
ACTIVITIES WITH LOCAL COMMUNITY	Training, artistic promotion and production of works of art by newcomer artists.	production team qualification and recovery of spaces. Training of children, youths and teachers (in collaboration with schools). Opening up of the Saudação monastery to the local population as a meeting point.	Incubator to firms related to permaculture and agriculture (e.g. honey, wine, olive oil, cheese, soups).
AREAS OF WORK	Sculpture (ceramics and metals); Image (photography and multimedia); Music; Multidisciplinary event production.	Dance; Theatre; Cinema and Video; Architecture; Visual arts; Installations.	Animal production (main resource); Environment; Energy; Tourism; Arts & Culture.
MOST RELEVANT INITIATIVES	Recovery of the Almansor river and one of its windmills (Ananil). River Project (2004/2005): artistic production/land art, conferences, courses, publications. Margins Project (2006): landscape intervention, workshops, conferences.	Regular cinema and music concerts program (during the Summer). Performing arts throughout the year. Over the last six years, a total of 260 shows have been performed in either MoN or Évora (the regional capital).	Events and projects aiming to disseminate the results and products of the work being made in the FMF, and others that are directly linked to the need to strengthen the relationships with local communities. Since 2005, the "Spring Festival" has been held, seeking to open channels of communication between local communities and outsiders. Land art exhibitions. Eco-Camping.
Networks	Host of foreign artists. Artistic residences. Internship for fine arts students. Joint actions with local schools.	Hosting foreign artists. Artistic residences. Collaboration with the Viriato Theatre (Viseu), the CCB (Lisbon) and the Rivoli Theatre (Oporto). Collaboration with the Lisbon Upper School of Dance, the Dance Forum of the Aveiro University, University of Évora and the NOVA University of Lisbon.	Cooperative relations established with the Lisbon Upper School of Dance, with the aim of providing space for the development of performing arts.

dedicated to other activities but which ended up including artistic expression as a pivotal element for their own strategy (as in the case of the Freixo do Meio Farm). Likewise, some of the places that constitute MoN seem to favour the development of creative artistic processes. In fact, underlying the Space of Time initiative is an understanding that art is not just a mere repetition of reality, but a *reflection* (*or re-creation*) of it. Thus, the existence of a distance between urban inputs and creative reflection makes sense, as it facilitates the encounter with the artistic object. Montemor-o-Novo is a 'haven'; an old space of religious (Dominican) enclosure is now a space for creative 'enclosure'. The architecture of the place, with its private, semi-private and public spaces, was made for encounters with oneself as well as with thoughts and ideas. It was, right from the start, created for others and most of all having in mind the necessities of creators.

The initiatives presented above exhibit two shared features that seem to be decisive from the point of view of creativity and social innovation. On the one hand, an integrated and transdisciplinary vision, in which a specific nexus, a relational meaning, is found to connect different activities; on the other, strong local community integration in articulation with national and transnational networking.

Another aspect that is worth stressing is the existence of intense relations of cooperation and collaboration between different local agents. A good example of this densification and qualification of local-based social relations can be seen in the 'Concerned City' event. Between 2005 and 2008, the Convent Workshops organized a large cultural event in the Ananil windmill, on the banks of the small Almansor River, in which visual arts and music played a pre-eminent role. The event quickly became famous beyond the region and started to attract a growing number of participants. In 2009, it turned into a more structured and transdisciplinary event, named 'Concerned City', which includes not only exhibitions and shows, but also workshops and colloquia. It started being produced by the Convent Workshops, the Space of Time and the MoN municipality, thus bringing together in a single joint initiative the three main cultural agents present and active in MoN. Beyond these three agents, the event has also involved several sponsors, including the Freixo do Meio Farm, and the participation of various local agents – including organizations and actors that have established themselves in MoN in the last couple of years, but also historical entities such as the Sociedade Carlista (see Table 18.3). Arguably, the 'Concerned Cities' event has become a milestone in the socially creative trajectory initiated by MoN in the aftermath of the 1974 revolution. It has further deepened the local networking processes, thus contributing to the success of MoN's socially creative strategies.

18.5   CONCLUDING REMARKS

The case of Montemor-o-Novo is especially interesting and useful as a narrative of socially creative success, whereby culture and art have crucially contributed to social cohesion and to social innovation, in addition to fostering economic development, in the context of what would otherwise have been just another small, deprived city in a depressed rural region. While extrapolations of the 'best practice' sort are usually over-simplistic, this narrative does provide food for thought on the conditions and determinants of social innovation and social creativity in analogous contexts. What we find here, among other things, is the virtuous coming

Table 18.3 '*Concerned entities*' *in 2011*

NAME	IDENTIFICATION
9Ocre	Art gallery founded in 2005.
ADL Brand	Local development association created in 1996.
Alma d'Arame	Cultural association created in 2008 by students and a professor of the Cascais Professional School of Theatre.
	Objective – performing arts with special emphasis on puppetry (the Puppetry Festival of Montemor-o-Novo is in its 3rd edition).
Children Workshop	Initiative created in 1981 by the MoN municipality with the aim of valorizing the free time of children.
Citizenship Network	Citizenship network created in 2010 for the promotion of participatory citizenship (cities in transition movement).
Convent Workshops	See Table 18.2.
Entranhas	Cultural association founded in 1999.
João Cidade House	Socio-therapeutic community – social gathering, rehabilitation, education and insertion of young people and adults with mental disabilities.
MontemorEnsemble	Chamber music group (trumpet quartet) founded in 2006.
Ruins Project	Theatre project initiated in 2001 with the aim of creating original texts, shows written from improvisation (devising) and individual memories.
S. Domingos Choir	Choir founded in 1987 (MoN).
Sardinha em Lata	Created in 2007, it is an enterprise dedicated to the development of audiovisual and cinematographic projects and the production of animated works (series, short films, and publicity).
Sociedade Carlista	Founded in 1861 under the regency of Carlos Simões, 'Master Carlos'. It has a music school with approximately 40 students.
The Space of Time	See Table 18.2.

together of: i) an inspired, determined and democratic leadership; ii) constant attention and recourse to the memory and identity of the place, namely in terms of its landscape and historical and architectural heritage; iii) the stimulus provided to creative activities, not least through the ability to draw on the existing natural and cultural resources; iv) the creation of significant new landmarks; and v) the firm requirement that artistic creation does not become an elitist endeavour and that the artists and creators do not become an enclave. Rather, the ultimate goal has consistently been to ensure that creativity does indeed become *social* creativity, by taking on a collective character driven by the collective (re)construction of iden-tity and the empowerment of vulnerable groups.

Another key element to be retained consists of the decisive effect of geographical scale. In Montemor-o-Novo, interpersonal relationships have a decisive influence upon the collective trajectory of the community. This collective trajectory is not simply planned in a strictly rationalist way, but rather understood and negotiated as a function of feelings and emotions that often become diluted at other scales. The fact that the members of this community generally know each other and are able to come together to negotiate and (re)construct their collective trajectory seems to us the decisive factor that has consistently enabled social innovation at this local level.

This is, to sum up, a case study that challenges the conventional creative class paradigm in two ways. Firstly, by providing an example of cultural regeneration which is democratic and inclusive, instead of being about the attraction of an elite and the transformation of places to accommodate that elite. Secondly, by challenging the assumption of creative quarters as central city localities and by providing an example of cultural regeneration in an un-gentrified and rural setting.

18.6 QUESTIONS FOR DISCUSSION

- To what extent has globalization (and its associated space-time compression) affected the conditions for social innovation in rural milieus?
- Are rural milieus intrinsically less (or more) creative than urban ones?
- To what extent do rural areas in developing countries exhibit different characteristics and constraints compared to those in the developed countries, in terms of social innovation and creativity?

REFERENCES

(References in bold are recommended reading.)

André, I. and A. Abreu (2006), 'Dimensões e Espaços da Inovação Social', *Finisterra*, **XLI** (81), 121–141.
André, I. and A. Abreu (2009), 'Social Creativity and Post-Rural Places: The Case of Montemor-o-Novo, Portugal', *Canadian Journal of Regional Science/Revue canadienne des sciences régionales*, **32** (1), 101–114.
André, I. and A. Carmo (2010), 'Régions et villes socialement créatives: étude appliquée à la péninsule ibérique', *Innovations*, **33** (3), 65–84.
Belfiore, E. and Oliver Bennett (2008), *The Social Impact of the Arts: An Intellectual History*, New York: Palgrave Macmillan.
Borrup, T. (2006), *The Creative Community Builder's Handbook: How to Transform Communities Using*

local Assets, Art, and Culture, Saint Paul, MN: Fieldstone Alliance.
Campbell, M.S. and R. Martin (eds) (2006), *Artistic Citizenship: A Public Voice for the Arts*, New York: Routdlege.
Cornwell, T. (1990), *Democracy and the Arts: The Role of Participation*, New York: Praeger.
Debord, G. (2006[1955]) 'Introduction to a Critique of Urban Geography', http://www.bopsecrets.org/SI/urbgeog.htm (last accessed 15 September 2011).
Fincher, R. and J. Jacobs (eds) (1998), *Cities of Difference*, New York: Guilford Press.
Florida, R. (2002), *The Rise of the Creative Class*, New York: Basic Books.
Florida, R. (2005), *Cities and the Creative Class*, New York: Routledge.
Florida, R. (2008), *Who's Your City? How the Creative Economy is Making Where to Live the Most Important Decision of your Life*, New York: Basic Books.
Gertler, M. (2004), *Creative Cities: What are they for, how do they work, and how do we build them?*, Ottawa: Canadian Policy Research Networks.
Hall, P. (2000), 'Creative Cities and Economic Development', *Urban Studies*, **37** (4), 639–649.
Hospers, G. (2003), 'Creative Cities: Breeding Places in the Knowledge Economy', *Knowledge, Technology and Policy*, **16** (3), 143–162.
Jacobs, J. (1993[1961]), *The Death and Life of Great American Cities*, New York: Modern Library.
Lambert, D. and R. Rezsohazy (2004), *Comment les pattes viennent au serpent. Essai sur l'étonnante plasticité du vivant*, Paris: Flammarion.
Landry, C. (2000), *The Creative City: A Toolkit for Urban Innovators*, London: Earthscan.
Landry, C., L. Greene and F. Matarasso (1996), *The art of regeneration: urban renewal through cultural activity*, Stroud: Comedia.
Ley, D. (2003), 'Artists, Aestheticisation and the Field of Gentrification', *Urban Studies*, **40** (2), 2527–2544.
Lowe, S. (2000), 'Creating community: art for community development', *Journal of Contemporary Ethnography*, **29** (3), 357–386.
Markusen, A. (2006), 'An Arts-Based State Rural Development Policy', *Journal of Regional Analysis and Policy*, **36** (2), 47–49.
Markusen, A. and A. Gadwa (2010), 'Arts and Culture in Urban or Regional Planning: A Review and Research Agenda', *Journal of Planning Education and Research*, **29** (3), 379–391.
Meusburger, P. (2009), 'Milieus of Creativity: The Role of Places, Environments, and Spatial Contexts', in Peter Meusburger, Joachim Funke and Edgar Wunder (eds), *Milieus of Creativity: An Interdisciplinary Approach to Spatiality of Creativity*, Heidelberg: Springer and KTS.
Miles, M. (1997), *Arts, Space and the City: Public Art and Urban Futures*, London: Routledge.
Moore, A. (2008), 'Rethinking scale as a geographi-

cal category: from analysis to practice', *Progress in Human Geography*, **32** (2), 203–225.

Moulaert, F., H. Demuynck and J. Nussbaumer (2004), 'Urban renaissance: from physical beautification to social empowerment', *City*, **8** (2), 229–235.

Moulaert, F., F. Martinelli, S. González and E. Swyngedouw (2007), 'Introduction: Social Innovation and Governance in European Cities', *European Urban and Regional Studies*, **14** (3), 195–209.

Newman, T., K. Curtis and J. Stephens (2003), 'Do community-based arts projects result in social gains? A review of the literature', *Community Development Journal*, **38** (4), 310–322.

Pratt, A.C. (2008), 'Creative cities: the cultural industries and the creative class', *Geografiska Annaler: Series B*, **90** (2), 107–117.

Puype, D. (2004), 'Arts and culture as experimental spaces in the city', *City*, **8** (2), 295–301.

Ruby, C. (2002) 'L'art public dans la ville', http://www.espacestemps.net/document282.html (last accessed 20 September 2011).

Scott, A.J. (2006), 'Creative cities: conceptual issues and policy questions', *Journal of Urban Affairs*, **28** (1), 1–17.

Smiers, J. (2005), *Arts under pressure, promoting cultural diversity in the age of globalization*, London: Zed Books.

Smith, R. and K. Warfield (2008), 'The creative city: a matter of values', in Phillip Cooke and Luciana Lazzeretti (eds), *Creative Cities, Cultural Clusters and Local Economic Development*, Cheltenham, UK and Northampton, MA, USA: Edward Elgar Publishing, pp. 287–312.

Törnqvist, G. (2004), 'Creativity in time and space', *Geografiska Annaler: Series B*, **86** (4), 227–243.

Tremblay, D.-G, J.-L. Klein and J.-M. Fontan (2005), *Innovation socio-territoriale et reconversion économique: Le cas de Montréal*, Paris: Editions L'Harmattan.

PART IV

SOCIAL INNOVATION ANALYSIS: METHODOLOGIES

Introduction: 'reality' as a guide for SI research methods?

Abdelillah Hamdouch

This part focuses on the methodologies that can be mobilized to be effective from a social innovation (SI) perspective. The key idea underlying the part is that SI analysis should be guided by what is going on in the 'real' social world: new initiatives, people's responses to new socioeconomic challenges, perception and interpretation of such experiences by the stakeholders, forms of interaction, negotiation and collaboration among social actors, learning patterns and strategy-building in SI initiatives, etc. But should SI analysis be instructed by 'reality' only, or are there also methodologies that have something to say about how reality should be interpreted, analysed and, potentially, 'transformed'?

For researchers, therefore, a key challenge is to think of how new knowledge about the reality of SI initiatives and dynamics can be built and, at the same time, contribute to changing the reality. To put it another way, researchers are confronted with three intertwined major issues: 1) knowledge from 'where' and gathered/ produced by 'whom'? 2) knowledge for 'what' and for 'whom'? 3) what are the roles of the researchers in SI processes?

The first issue is related to the way new knowledge is obtained/ produced: historical-institutional analysis, case studies, surveys, quantitative and qualitative analysis, interactive field work with/among stakeholders, action and partnership-based research, etc. are all eligible methods. It equally raises the question of the 'origin' and 'nature' (the-

oretical, practice-rooted, 'utopian' ...) of knowledge on SI. Finally, the type of actors (academics, practitioners, communities, social movements, public authorities, policy makers, etc.) who collect, generate, disseminate or (co)-produce the knowledge is not neutral, as this also determines to a large extent the final uses of the new knowledge that is made available.

This connects directly to the second issue. Is the aim of research just 'knowledge for knowledge's sake' (at best, knowing better what exists), or is it also to imagine, promote and implement socially innovative policies, new governance practices, creative strategies and experiences? Is this new knowledge just a pre-conditional 'input' for action, or is it also an outcome of the action itself, co-produced through interactive learning and collaborative processes among various stakeholders?

It is here that the relationship between SI analysis (the 'research' side) and the 'reality' (the 'action' side) poses its ultimate challenge for researchers. How does a researcher analysing SI position her/himself vis-à-vis the other stakeholders, especially the people and communities concerned by/involved in socially creative initiatives? Is the researcher just a 'lesson-concept-method provider', even a simple 'photographer' reflecting on what exists? Or is she/he also a potential co-producer of a 'workable knowledge' about new imaginaries and social perspectives? What 'social value' and legitimacy have the methods and researchers' commitment in concrete SI processes? Are the researchers mere (yet potentially useful) 'facilitators' helping the 'field actors' in the production/exchange/use of new knowledge and in fostering their (cross-)learning capabilities? Or might they also be genuine 'active actors' contributing to the (co-) design and/or the (co-)implementation of new socially creative strategies, policies and experiences?

The chapters in this part address these crucial questions and dimensions from different but convergent viewpoints. In particular, they all insist on the fact that if the researcher can contribute (and learn also) by being involved in socially innovative initiatives, actions and processes, his/her role is not to replace the 'field stakeholders' nor to provide them with ready-to-use ideas and methods. It is rather, and mostly, to help stakeholders become aware of their existing/potential powers, capabilities and resources and assist them in the design and implementation of democratically co-created solutions that could 'work' for them. Equally emphasized is the irreplaceable importance of qualitative, context-sensitive, interactive and 'open-minded' methodological approaches to/within socially innovative initiatives and processes. Finally, the chapters stress the central challenge for all actors, and particularly for researchers, of finding a balance between the need to institutionalize socially innovative initiatives as a condition for their visibility, recognition and dissemination in the public and policy-making spheres while, at the same time, avoiding the risk of inhibiting or sacrificing the creative power of the 'actors in the field' on the altar of 'politically correct'/'acceptable' approaches.

In Chapter 19, Vicari Haddock and Tornaghi suggest a reading grid of forms of social innovation. The approach builds on a comparative analysis of 20 case studies

extracted from two major research projects (SINGOCOM and KATARSIS; see Moulaert et al., Chapter 1) and on several rounds of discussion with the researchers who carried them out. This material leads to the classification of these cases along two main axes: the nature of societal values that underlie socially innovative initiatives and practices, and the degree of institutionalization of such experiences in the social, public and policy-making spheres. The chapter discusses the role of researchers and scholars in the initiation, implementation and dissemination of socially creative actions in specific local contexts. Here the 'positionality' and reflexivity of academics and experts in their interaction and collaboration with the various stakeholders of the 'social field' are crucial as they condition the way new knowledge about how to overcome social exclusion problems is co-produced, used and disseminated through territorialized cross-learning processes.

In Chapter 20, Konstantatos, Siatitsa and Vaiou stress the role of qualitative approaches in understanding bottom-up socially creative initiatives. The authors also build on a sample of case studies carried out in the KATARSIS Project and on collective-interactive-open work with the promoters and actors of the initiatives. Here, 'reality' is seen as a 'local praxis' that can be revealed through the 'lens' of the interaction with/among these actors, gathered in a focus group. This approach has yielded several methodological lessons. Firstly, the participants have proved able not only to exchange and co-learn about their respective experiences, but also to co-decide on the relevant way to exchange the knowledge accumulated from their various contextual 'realities'. They have collectively engaged in a kind of 'bottom-up methodological process' as they have re-shaped the criteria for comparison of experiences and the interaction process ('method') initially proposed by the researchers. They have also raised new topics to be discussed and helped in identifying 'invisible relations' that guide socially innovative initiatives. Secondly, they have shown that one can learn not only from the 'reality' as such (i.e. as observable), but also both from the 'visions' they have of their respective 'realities' and from the initiatives they have taken within the interactive process. Finally, this exercise has shown that researchers and 'users' have been involved in a dynamic process in which learning has proved to be as horizontal (among users themselves) as transversal and symmetric (learning by researchers from practitioners and vice versa).

Chapter 21 by Kunnen, MacCallum and Young is informed by critical, appreciative inquiry or action research methods and practices with the aim of enhancing individual and community capacity through the research process. In the past 10 to 15 years community development theory and practice have adopted approaches that aim to recognize the skills, resilience and knowledge available within local communities. These approaches have variously been described as assets or strengths based community development (ASBCD) perspectives. A brief case scenario (the 'Balingup Model') is used to illustrate the research practices enacted. The authors argue that, firstly, all communities and the people and organizations within them, have assets, skills, capacities and networks; and, secondly, effective community development begins with the identification of those assets, the building of relationships with and within communities and the use of assets and relationships in achieving the visions and plans emerging from the process. Research strategies are therefore integral to assets and strengths based development practice. The chapter

outlines the key features and limitations of these approaches, arguing that ASBCD practice and social innovation analysis can enrich one another in both theory and action.

In Chapter 22, Dubeux offers a complementary illustration of the usefulness of participatory approaches to solving social exclusion and poverty problems. In the context of Brazilian society, marked over the last decades by structural marginalization of large parts of rural and urban populations, Dubeux shows how, thanks to the development of a long-standing tradition of solidarity economy initiatives and the key role played by trade unions movements and many other stakeholders, innovative approaches and strategies have emerged that have yielded original forms of collaboration with the marginalized groups. Among these initiatives, the creation of Technological Incubators of Solidarity Economy in the mid-1990s, with the pioneering role played by universities, has been among the most decisive. About 70 universities, organized within two major networks, have developed such incubators and contributed to the production of new knowledge about solidarity economy initiatives, to inclusive processes of the people through 'popular education', and to the nurturing of many socioeconomic initiatives rooted in the solidarity-based economy. One key outcome of the cross-learning developed within these incubators is that the universities and the researchers themselves have been 'transformed' as a strengthened conscience of their sociopolitical role in the Brazilian society has emerged.

The insistence on the key role of learning in socially innovative processes is also at the core of the approach privileged in Chapter 23. Fontan, Harrisson and Klein analyse the processes that make partnership-based research (PBR) a powerful approach for techno-production of knowledge that contributes both to social innovation theorizing and to the promotion, incubation and dissemination of socially innovative solutions to exclusion and poverty problems. PBR, they argue, is an approach that allows the co-construction of knowledge by academic researchers and social actors. As such, it may be considered as an important driver in redefining the knowledge society as a fairer model, democratizing the production of knowledge and giving civil society a place in it. The contribution of PBR depends on the mutual recognition of needs, shared definition of problems, and a common search for solutions by academic researchers and social actors. The challenge then is to orient academic research toward a stronger connection with society. Building on the Québec experience in the social action field, the authors present the origins and the development of PBR, then discuss more specifically the role of collaboration between universities and the social economy as well as its implementation in local development experiences. They finally show that the PBR model contributes to social innovation only if it is part of an institutionalized development process.

In Chapter 24, Andersen and Bilfeldt go a step further by showing how participatory approaches can address societal problems rooted in the conservative functioning of publicly managed social and health services. Building on the 'Critical Utopian Action Research' (CUAR) perspective, the authors describe the way this approach has been initiated and implemented in a public elder care facility in Denmark where both residents and employees were unsatisfied with the quality of the service delivered. The project was structured using interactive/iterative methods promoted by the CUAR approach, notably a 'future creation workshop' and a feedback 'network

conference'. The keys to the process were giving voice, empowering, imagining new ways of doing things, democratic negotiation on the priority solutions to be implemented, and collective learning through dialogue. What has been crucial in the success of this experience is the fact that the researchers have in no way substituted for the key stakeholders (employees, residents and their relatives, and the management team of the nursery), who, from the beginning of the project, have been encouraged by the researchers (as facilitators and co-producers of a new shared-knowledge) to think, discuss and act as 'self-masters of the game' for changing their reality.

Finally, Chapter 25 by Arthur provides, in a sense, a 'reflective-forward looking' view on how the endeavour of 'changing the reality' through research *and* socially innovative action should be calibrated. Arthur argues that although action research (AR) and participatory action research (PAR) originated as methodological processes intended to make a contribution to social emancipation, over time the methodology became separated from the original radical context and incorporated into the business processes of change management. To escape this trap, he proposes that AR and PAR can be re-claimed for radical purposes if clearly re-connected to emancipatory research questions. Moreover, Arthur suggests that such an approach is both ethically and scientifically 'reasonable' (as proposed by the neo-pragmatist philosopher of science Hilary Putnam), and draws several avenues through which AR and PAR can provide a sound basis both for research and emancipatory social innovation. As such, Arthur's thoughts and convictions not only offer a balanced assessment of the contribution over the last decades of participatory and interactive approaches to the promotion of social innovation, both in terms of concept and practice, but also open the window for a necessary *re-rooting* of social innovation research and action in the 'hard foundations' of the reality. From a methodo-

logical viewpoint, this is probably the most challenging 'innovative move' facing the researchers on social innovation.

19. A transversal reading of social innovation in European cities
Serena Vicari Haddock and Chiara Tornaghi

19.1 INTRODUCTION

In this chapter we aim to contribute to a methodology for research on social innovation with a particular interest in developing a comprehensive reading of its forms and a critical reflection upon its constitutive dimensions. Our starting point is a transversal reading of various socially innovative and creative initiatives across a number of domains of experience that the literature has identified as loci of processes of social exclusion. We draw in particular on 20 case studies[1] in European cities, and analyse the role played by actors, looking at which kind of actors succeed in resisting and overcoming processes of social exclusion, examining their vision of the causes of social exclusion and the problems they confront, and investigating the strategies they pursue to find solutions to these problems.

This investigation allows us to characterize social innovation initiatives according to two main dimensions (Section 19.2). The first refers to value orientation; our cases cover a very wide range of values that are negated by processes of social exclusion and which are, on the other hand, pursued and established as central in the various initiatives. These values pertain to the realms of social justice and equity, gender equality, environmental care, democracy and empowerment; they are oriented toward progressive social change in the direction of the 'just city' (Fainstein 2010) where alternative, radically democratic, socially just and sustainable forms

of urbanism are taking shape (Brenner et al. 2009). The second dimension measures the extent to which these practices have penetrated the public sphere.

In Section 19.3, we build upon our work and draw from this analysis three crucial issues that should be taken into account in social innovation research, practice and promotion. In particular we discuss the role of academics and experts in socially innovative organizations and associations, as researchers, managers and activists bring complementary resources for sharing and reinforcing reflexivity, a necessary factor in the successful evolution of social innovation.

In the final section, we point to issues that need to be addressed in order to gain a better understanding of the dynamics of social innovation in relation to the context in which socially innovative practices emerge and evolve.

19.2 TWO DIMENSIONS OF SOCIAL INNOVATION

The analysis of an extremely large and diversified array of programs, projects, initiatives and practices and the consequent identification/construction of different forms of social innovation in different fields of experience has increased our understanding and appreciation of how social change is produced as a result of the dynamics of social exclusion and the reactions brought about by it.

When we read these forms across fields of experience, two main dimensions emerge as constitutive of social innovation. The first is the value orientation that motivates people to pursue progressive social change and legitimizes their action; it is constitutive of social innovation insofar as it is a value orientation in conflict with mainstream hegemonic values that privilege the market economy, representative democracy, formal education systems and traditional cultural definitions, for example around gender issues. Progressive social change is promoted as the result of alternative models centred on non-profit economic activities, people's empowerment and their direct involvement in decision-making processes, the pursuit of social justice, equal opportunities and gender equality. This first dimension serves as a 'fuel' for social innovation, as it provides the motivation to act.

The second dimension concerns the process of institutionalization and serves as the 'engine' of social innovation, i.e. the mechanism by which social innovation is produced and reproduced over time. We use an extensive definition of institutionalization which includes two levels of change: a first level is reached when innovative practices prove able to penetrate the public sphere and inform the public discourse and culture with different visions and models; a second level of institutionalization is achieved when innovative practices enter into relatively stable and sustainable arrangements with the public administration.

In our empirical analysis we have seen this process of institutionalization at work, sometimes with one level setting the stage for the other; this is not always the case, however. Thus we believe the two levels should be kept analytically separate, even though in the majority of our cases the initiatives analysed have become institutionalized at the two levels in strictly intertwined ways, i.e. at the same time by influencing the public discourse in the direction of more inclusive and effective citizenship rights and by entering into governance relationships with public governmental bodies at various scales. Depending on the context, an impact on the public sphere can be achieved in different ways: civil society organizations can act as innovative service provision agents, which identify and respond to new needs and demands, thus giving legitimacy to new claims in the public discourse; civil society organizations can also transform the institutional governance framework, changing values and norms to generate new policies and practices. In both ways it is the link between civil society organizations and different public and private actors at different scales that has proven to be the crucial element for the success of those strategies labelled '*bottom-linked*' (see also Pradel et al., Chapter 11).

In the following chart (Figure 19.1), these two dimensions are represented as orthogonal axes framing a space where the instances of social innovation analysed in our research projects are positioned.

A word of caution is necessary before discussing the results of our exercise. Positioning different practices, organizations and programs along these two dimensions is a task fraught with difficulty; it is evident from the case studies that the degree of institutionalization and the innovative strength of value orientation need to be measured against the specific local and national contexts that each organization or initiative confronts. For example, a citizens' group planning a public space deserves a higher score both in terms of progressive value orientation and in terms of its impact on the public sphere if it is active in a city such as Naples, where criminal organizations tend to restrict their

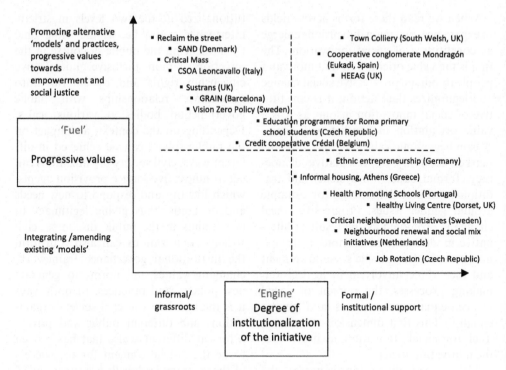

Figure 19.1   Chart representing socially innovative initiatives

rights to citizenship and even to a normal life, than in other cities where the right to make decisions impacting public space is taken for granted.

The context-dependent nature of these 'measurements' implies that we have to rely on the assessment made by the 'local' researchers for the positioning of the innovative practices. In order to reduce the highly subjective character of the assessment, we had several rounds of discussion with the researchers who originally provided the case studies, designed to provide us with some degree of confidence in a context-sensitive but shared measurement matrix. We believe this chart to be a useful analytical device, which generates interesting questions for future research.

In the space charted by these two axes we find that innovative initiatives are mainly concentrated on the *upper left*

and *lower right* sides of the chart. Before analysing the meaning of these two concentrations it is worth clarifying that the *lower left* quadrant is empty because of the specific definition of social innovation and the selection process of the initiatives studied which derives from it; events or initiatives which remain highly informal, have no visibility and do not challenge mainstream values fall outside the field of social innovation study. The field of housing provides a case in point. Practices of informal occupation or squatting are a constant presence in European cities where suitable housing has become unavailable to a growing number of social groups; in addition to the high degree of informality, these practices are episodic, involve a very small number of people, are hardly visible to the public (except when 'criminalized') and are rarely able to connect to wider networks of collective action. As a result, these practices are not included in our analysis. A completely different profile is presented by self-managed renewal projects having different degrees of institutionalization (from informal to social economy initiatives to public area based regeneration programs) or by homeless organizations such as S.A.N.D. in Denmark. A borderline case, positioned just outside the lower left quadrant, concerns the practices of informal housing in Athens where, like in many Southern European cities, weak regulation and law enforcement allowed illegal housing developments that have since been formally recognized. These experiences have been included because they serve as examples of collective mobilizations successfully challenging traditional models.

The *upper left concentration* is made up of initiatives in which citizens, in differently organized forms, play a leading role and engage in activities with a robust value content that motivates them and strongly informs the practices. These initiatives have multiple links with social movements and often find in 'the movement of movements' their main cultural reference; they are able to take part in alternative 'associative networks' (Eckstein and Wickham-Crowley 2003) which they form and operate on their own terms, with or without outside support, on the basis of a shared orientation of self-organization and direct action and involvement. This orientation implies a critical stance, with a varying degree of radicalism, towards representative democracy which is perceived as ineffective in addressing new forms of social exclusion. Alternatives to the existing social order are then articulated in a plurality of visions in which value orientation toward social justice, environmental concerns, democracy and empowerment are called upon in different combinations. Moreover, each

context shapes a specific combination and shows how conceptions of social justice or environmental concerns, for example, are socially constructed and historically contingent, shaped by people's values and institutionally grounded in real-life experience.

As a consequence of this radical/alternative cultural orientation, initiatives in this first concentration often maintain an unstable relationship with public actors and encounter difficulties in engaging with institutional structures of governance; this relationship varies from an oppositional and confrontational stance to forms of reciprocal recognition and cooperation, although often based on precarious and temporary arrangements and subject to unending negotiations. Moreover, a limitation also arises from the high level of instability and turnover that characterizes this type of initiative: some may have a short life, but new ones appear continuously, and old and new actors coalesce in new ones. Examples of this type are 'Critical Mass' and 'Reclaim the street'. While firmly rooted within a radical/alternative cultural framework claiming the collective ownership of public space, they are not cohesive organizations with a well-defined structure, but rather a constellation of groups able to mobilize themselves and other groups such as 'Edible Public Space' (see http://www.foodurbanism.org/edible-public-space/, last accessed 21 January 2013) around similar but not always overlapping aims. Activists who are present in different groups of this kind facilitate communication and coordination and facilitate both general forms of mobilization and specific single-issue initiatives.

A contrasting type is identifiable in the *lower right concentration*. These initiatives are characterized by strong and formal links among institutional actors in the public, private and non-profit sectors, and the primacy of governmental actors at different scales in governance structures. Civil society organizations and associations and third sector foundations, agencies and enterprises are involved as co-producers of public policy, contributing to the success of the initiatives by their direct and situated knowledge and their capacity to partake in complex networks of different actors. Take, for example, the various neighbourhood renewal initiatives often implemented jointly by several third sector organizations in cooperation with local institutions, in a mix that varies according to each context. Among these initiatives the commitment to progressive values may not be as strong and paramount as in other cases or it may not contribute so strongly to the group and individual identity of the participants; the focus is on service provision or even effective production of goods, and more radically inclusive strategies must be sacrificed to this objective.

All this is not to say that there are no initiatives and practices to be located outside these two main concentrations or types; quite the contrary, some of the most interesting cases are in the *upper right* side of the chart as they have strong progressive and inclusive value orientations and, at the same time, are embedded in solid and stable structures of governance. These initiatives resemble 'working utopias' (Crossley 1999) or 'spaces of hope' (Harvey 2000) that sustain cultures of resistance vis-à-vis the hegemonic consensus on neoliberalism, commodification of urban spaces and market values. By doing so, they broaden and reinforce the social innovation front. The experience of Town Colliery is, in this respect, exemplary. One of the oldest deep-coal mines in the United Kingdom, it has been the object of a workers' buy-out and continues to function as a self-managed cooperative, with many links to the social-green economy of

the area (Arthur et al. 2006). We can argue that in these cases strong social innovation is produced within a solid frame of institutional relations, albeit subject occasionally to conflicts and repeated negotiation. As such these initiatives are particularly interesting because they appear to have found a dynamic balance between institutionalization and grass-roots action: they are able to maintain strong links with civil society organizations and at the same time with different public and private actors at different scales. They demonstrate not only that this two-pronged strategy is possible but that it is also necessary if a strong innovative content is to be maintained over time.

Summing up and going back to the two concentrations analysed above we can say that, when looking at the initiatives in the *upper left* side of the chart, one is struck by the vitality and resilience of these projects and organizations and at the same time by their arduous struggle to penetrate the public sphere as they fight against the commodification of public spaces, for example, or the pervasive impact of car dependence.

Similarly, the initiatives of the *lower right* side of the chart call our attention to the tension between social innovation and institutionalization and to the resistance encountered when new needs and demands ask for recognition.

These two concentrations or types speak of an inverse relationship between institutionalization and alternative, socially progressive values; in other words, they support the generalization that radical social change tends to be promoted outside (if not against) existing institutions. This is hardly news. But the overall distribution with some cases also in the upper right side of the chart depicts a more complex picture and brings up additional questions, which need to be raised and answered if we want to improve our understanding, build abstractions and generalizations, and eventually devise policy recommendations.

19.3 ORIENTING RESEARCH ON SOCIAL INNOVATION

The above analysis points to crucial issues that should be taken into account when approaching social innovation research and promotion work.

The first concerns societal values. We have identified value orientation as one constitutive dimension of social innovation and our reading of social innovation has exposed a wide variety of values permeating the analysed socially innovative and creative practices. Researching and promoting social innovation requires that researchers acknowledge and appreciate the whole set of values which bring about progressive social change. One must also maintain an attitude of particular sensitivity to all instances where these values find expression and nourish processes of mobilization, however small or informal the resulting collective and associative forms may be.

The wide variety of values present in contemporary society, along with hegemonic values, implies a plurality of models of local development, which are shaped to different degrees by diverse configurations of values according to the local context. Researchers must be aware of the local specificities in terms of historically determined cultures and resources. But they should also recognize new collective energies emerging in the local context as a result of pressing demands and needs, which are able to redirect and modify a hitherto path-dependent route of socioeconomic development.

Finally, the valorization of progressive social values cannot be decoupled from the assessment of hegemonic values and the structure of interests and power with which they are connected. These structural factors work against progressive social change and empowerment, and this conflict needs to be recognized and accepted. Because social exclusion is related to structural constraints, the struggle against these constraints needs to have a central place in social innovation discourse and practices. Researchers should pay attention to the risk of separating social issues from political ones, a de-politicization of civic life that makes empowerment little more than a rhetorical device. A second crucial issue is strictly related to the first because it calls into question the role of academics and experts as they bring their own values and attitudes to the social innovation research project. Academics and experts work outside civil society organizations and associations as researchers carrying out Action Research, for example, or within such organizations, as activists. Peter Marcuse's work (2009) constitutes a useful point of departure for this discussion; it is a manifesto calling on critical scholars to work in three directions: a) 'exposing' issues of social injustice, b) 'proposing' alternatives on the basis of their work with social actors, and c) 'politicizing' justice claims in the frame of the right to the city. The analysis of social innovation initiatives should go further in exposing the micro-dynamics of the activists-scholars interaction. Building on the recent debate in critical and radical human geography (Cahill 2007; Cahill et al. 2007; Maxey 1999; Routledge 2004; Fuller and Kitchin 2004), we believe it is crucial to pay attention to the performative and empowering effects of researchers *on the trajectory* of socially innovative initiatives. The lively debate on the researchers' values, social commitment, political views, awareness of their embodied identity, and their effects on research design, research methodology selection and human interaction during field work, which in literature is referred to as 'positionality' (see references above), is particularly relevant for our reflection on social innovation. The assumption here is that researchers, managers and activists can often effectively bring complementary resources to these initiatives, and that sharing and reinforcing reflexivity on their positionality can contribute to the successful evolution of social innovation.

Even though we are aware that the boundaries between these actors' roles are often blurred, with researchers sometimes being active members or initiators of these initiatives, or co-authors of innovative policies (as government consultants, for example), to the point that a demarcation line is not always possible or appropriate, we call for a reflection on these roles and identity overlaps. Researchers involved in grassroots movements and highly informal initiatives will have to deal, for example, with different communication styles, or with a constant negotiation of the role of their professional knowledge in the map of the overall knowledge informing the discussions and decisions of the group. This is not just a matter of individuals' frustration, but rather of reflecting on how such identity conflicts, communication styles, knowledge questioning and exchange, and the timeframe in which they happen, can become vehicles and tools for social innovation.

Far from adopting a technocratic view, in claiming the need for more reflexivity we stress the importance and the differential impact of a different kind of knowledge. A better understanding of the role of researchers as activists-academics in communicating and shaping visioning processes is necessary. We need to investigate and make more explicit the politics of positionality, the performative power of discourses around social innovation,

its codification and its empowering effects (Cahill 2007; Maxey 1999). As a consequence, researchers are called upon to confront the following questions. How do researchers represent the range of possibilities for the development of these initiatives? What skills do they mobilize for enhancing internal communication? And how do they contribute to shaping the dialogue between the groups in which they are involved and the wider range of actors they encounter? How do they share their access to information, freedom of expression, and ability to make a difference on the ground (Fuller and Kitchin 2004, p. 4) with other participants? In short, how do they contribute to structuring the system of opportunities and the structure-agency dynamics? Another way to pose these questions is to investigate the extent to which their contribution is not just a matter of knowledge transfer, or facilitation in creating transnational networks of support: it is embedded in systems of co-production and generates learning circuits of empowerment.

Our third and final issue regarding the task of orienting social innovation and action concerns the relationship between social innovation and government: it is critical that researchers approaching social innovation do not take for granted that social innovation is successful and sustainable only if institutionalized by local government. As we have seen, the relationship between civic society associations engaged in social innovation practices is much more complex and poses different challenges for researchers interested in the furthering of social innovation. These challenges are structured differently in every context (in relation to the level of associative life, the role of the third sector and the structure of the national and local welfare regime; see Pradel et al., Chapter 11) but they all refer to the problem of maintaining links between these associations and organizations and different public and private actors at different scales. Their success and resilience is due to the capacity to build and sustain over time a strong network of relationships where material and symbolic resources may circulate and produce synergies. Rich associative networks are then a premise and an outcome of the activity of researchers on social innovation. Once these networks are created and consolidated, researchers confront the challenge of maintaining the inclusion and empowerment character and this challenge assumes a different nature according to the context. In contexts where the social innovation strategies are institutionalized, the risk is that civic society associations transform themselves into agencies of services provision where the potential for empowerment is sacrificed on the altar of efficiency. But as empowerment requires time and repetition, it is at risk also in contexts of low institutionalization, because forms of associative life are instable, mainly due to the project-based system of financing and the consequent constant grant-hunting demands.

19.4 CONCLUSIONS

We have discussed above the role of values, the position of researchers and the institutionalization process as constraining or enabling elements which socially innovative and creative initiatives encounter in their development. As highlighted in other parts of this handbook (see for example Van Dyck and Van den Broeck, Chapter 9) the role of territory and context is crucial in understanding the emergence and consolidation of socially innovative initiatives. Researchers have begun to identify the contextual factors facilitating socially innovative initiatives in relation to differ-

ent welfare regimes and diverse regulatory frameworks governing the social economy and social enterprises, but a lot of work lies ahead; from what we have learned from our investigation we believe our understanding of the dynamics of social innovation would be greatly enhanced by future research in three specific directions.

In the first place we believe that future research should be based on a *historically grounded approach*, which must take into account socio-cultural models and institutional change. How do the different local cultures and traditions in which these institutional frameworks are embedded shape and nourish the visions of future trajectories? We think social innovation analysis has so far been limited to a short timeframe, which has confined our understanding of the paths along which a particular form of social innovation may take shape and evolve. A historically grounded approach would incorporate long and medium term change in culture and civil society arrangements in the understanding of the dynamics of social innovation. Much energy should be devoted to the development of such an approach.

The second direction for broadening the understanding of the context of social innovation points to the analysis of the *role of social capital and social networks*. In analysing the network of relations that facilitate mobilization and underlie social action we have primarily looked at public realms emerging from proximity and face-to-face contacts. But contemporary associational life depends on multiple technological, informational, personal and organizational networks that link locations in a very complex way. In this respect our understanding remains unsatisfactory on two grounds: firstly, because we need a better understanding of the working of social capital, which, embedded as it is in webs of power and inequality, has both inclusionary and exclusionary aspects (Blokland and Savage 2008), and secondly, because our work has so far failed to take seriously the combination of local and trans-local social networks that are held to produce collective action and mobilization. We ought also to look at the use of online social networks to initiate and organize grass-roots action. A more theoretically grounded view of the physical and digital context is needed. Theories centred around the social infrastructure of a city provide a promising framework for the understanding of the nature of social networks and the significance of voluntary associations for contemporary urban life. Appropriately tailored it would point out that in each context 'we need to understand the specific mechanisms through which social capital operates through people and groups crossing borders, forming borders and maintaining borders' (Blokland and Savage 2008, p. 14).

A final direction we want to point out relates to *the scales on which socially innovative and creative initiatives operate*, and their relation with the broader processes of neoliberal transformation and State rescaling (Brenner and Theodore 2002). Much of the existing literature on scale has concentrated on the politics of rescaling from above, i.e. devolution of regulation to sub-national institutional levels. Less has been written about rescaling initiatives from below. We have observed forms of social innovation based on connecting the local with the national and EU levels and argue that such links increase the resilience of innovative forms. What remains to be investigated is the relationship between the multi-scalar dimension of social innovation and contemporary transformations: are these local projects able to address issues of power distribution and, more generally speaking, to harness neoliberal restructuring? A critical view

portrays innovative projects as a temporary 'fix' to amend the cracks in the system and avoid escalating conflicts; others claim that structural changes are produced and consequently that they have the potential to radically change neo-liberal and capitalistic societies (see, for example, Holloway 2002, 2010). The actual impact of these projects at different scales needs to be assessed. How can this analysis be carried out? What is the most appropriate methodology for this assessment? We leave these questions open as a challenge to social innovation theorists and methodologists.

19.5 QUESTIONS FOR DISCUSSION

- Do the two dimensions of social innovation operating as 'fuel' and 'engine' enable a better understanding of the initiatives you are familiar with? How?
- How and why is the penetration into the public sphere a crucial process for socially innovative strategies?
- How do you think that the 'positionality' and 'reflexivity' of activist-academics might affect the process of institutionalization of socially innovative initiatives?

NOTE

1. These case studies have been analysed in two European Framework Programme funded projects: the international research project SINGOCOM (Social Innovation, Governance and Community Building 2001–2004, see http://users.skynet.be/frank.moulaert/singocom/) and the coordination action KATARSIS (Growing Inequality and Social Innovation: Alternative Knowledge and Practice in Overcoming Social Exclusion in Europe 2006–2009, see http://katarsis.ncl.ac.uk/, websites last accessed 13 March 2013).

REFERENCES

(References in bold are recommended reading.)

Arthur, L., M.S. Cato, T. Keenoy and R. Smith (2006), 'Where is the social in social enterprise?', conference paper, 3rd International Social Enterprise Conference, University of the South Bank, http://www.lsbu.ac.uk/bcim/cgcm/confer ences/serc/2006/speakers/arthur-serc-2006.pdf (last accessed 13 December 2012).

Blokland, T. and M. Savage (2008), *Networked urbanism: social capital in the city*, Farnham: Ashgate.

Brenner, N. and N. Theodore (2002), 'Preface: From the "New Localism" to the spaces of neoliberalism', *Antipode*, **34** (3), 341–347.

Brenner, N., P. Marcuse and M. Mayer, (2009), 'Cities for people, not for profit', *City*, **13** (2–3), 176–184.

Cahill, C. (2007), 'Repositioning Ethical Commitments: Participatory Action Research as a Relational Praxis of Social Change', *ACME*, **6** (3), 360–373.

Cahill C., F. Sultana, F. and R. Pain (2007), 'Participatory Ethics: Politics, practices, institutions', *ACME*, **6** (3), 304–318.

Crossley, N. (1999), 'Working Utopias and Social Movements: An investigation using case study materials from Radical Mental Health Movements in Britain', *Sociology*, **33**, 809–830.

Eckstein, S.E. and T. Wickham-Crowley (eds) (2003), *What Justice? Whose Justice? Fighting for Fairness in Latin America*, Berkeley and Los Angeles: University of California Press.

Fainstein, S. (2010), *The Just City*, Ithaca: Cornell University Press.

Fuller, D. and R. Kitchin (eds) (2004), *Radical Theory/Critical Praxis: Making a difference beyond the academy?*, Vernon and Victoria: Praxis (e) Press.

Fuller, D. and R. Kitchin (2004), 'Radical Theory/Critical Praxis: academic geography beyond academy?' in D. Fuller and R. Kitchin (eds), pp. 1–20.

Harvey, D. (2000), *Spaces of hope*, Los Angeles: University of California Press.

Holloway, J. (2002), *Change the World Without Taking Power*, London: Pluto Press.

Holloway, J. (2010), *Crack capitalism*, London: Pluto Press.

Marcuse, P. (2009), 'From critical urban theory to the right to the city', *City*, **13** (2), 185–197.

Maxey, I. (1999), 'Beyond boundaries? Activism, academia, reflexivity and research', *Area*, **31** (1), 199–208.

Routledge, P. (2004), 'Relational Ethics of Struggle', in D. Fuller and R. Kitchin (eds), pp. 79–91.

20. Qualitative approaches for the study of socially innovative initiatives

Haris Konstantatos, Dimitra Siatitsa and Dina Vaiou[1]

20.1 INTRODUCTION

Social innovation, as it is conceptualized by the contributors to this volume, valorizes the knowledge and cultural assets of communities and prioritizes the creative reconfiguration of social relations (MacCallum et al. 2009, p. 18). In this sense, it is sought not only in bottom-up initiatives linked to particular places, but also at a multiplicity of spatial scales and intersections of institutional and everyday practices.

Socially innovative initiatives often develop as a response to growing inequalities and processes of social exclusion, mobilizing resources of various kinds in novel ways. As such, they call for particular methodologies to approach, and learn from, the actors, aims and practices involved. Such methodologies are part of the broad field of qualitative research, which has gained a hard won acceptance in many disciplines since the 1970s.

In this chapter we reflect upon the usefulness and relevance of qualitative methodologies for the study of social innovation. Our focus on socially innovative initiatives that cope with social exclusion in various local or communal contexts, places this work within a tradition of approaches towards knowledge production which problematizes the role of research and researchers in relation to social needs and problems. It relates to a praxis-oriented process of knowledge production, which acknowledges tacit (as expressed in everyday practices) and collective knowledge as relevant for academic research. Knowledge, in this context, is a socially constructed and socially distributed phenomenon (see the pioneering work of Berger and Luckmann 1966).

In what follows, we argue that qualitative methods are appropriate for the study of socially innovative initiatives, their characteristics and potentials. We also argue that qualitative methods based on interactive procedures and participatory techniques (such as focus groups, participatory research or action research) may support the transdisciplinary character of research on social innovation, by bringing together, and fostering the interaction of, the multiple actors involved. A particular consideration when examining initiatives to combat social exclusion is that interactive methods may also contribute to empowerment and self-determination of the subjects of research. In this sense these methods themselves may prove socially innovative.

The first section of the chapter provides a brief overview of the emergence of qualitative methodologies. In the second section we describe and reflect upon an example drawn from the KATARSIS Coordination Action (see Moulaert et al., Chapter 1), a focus group held with actors from a number of socially creative organizations across Europe. This is followed by a discussion of the methodological questions arising from this experience and of their relevance for social innovation research. Finally, some comments are put forward about the scope, advantages and limitations of such methods and their relevance for policy and other forms of collective action.

20.2 FROM THEORETICAL FORMULATIONS TO THE RESEARCH FIELD

Qualitative approaches developed out of the critique of logical positivism, particularly after the Second World War, in heated debates about how valid knowledge and truth claims are constituted.[2] Qualitative methodologies are related to the need of scientific enquiry to develop questions beyond the single aim to broaden the base of empirical evidence, focusing not simply on quantifiable variables, but on the qualities of entities/phenomena and on processes and meanings that do not lend themselves to measurement (Denzin and Lincoln 2005). Qualitative methods, then, represent a different ontological and epistemological approach to knowledge and data, and are used to answer different questions, in different ways and from different (but not necessarily opposed) grounds, compared to quantitative methods (DeLyser et al. 2010).

Going to the field, techniques deployed include participant observation and ethnography, interviewing, life histories, focus groups, visual analysis, landscape interpretation, archival research, textual and discourse analysis – often used in combinations that are unique to each research project. The methodological focus of such techniques turns to the object/subject relationship and its dynamics, in relation to social context. The researcher does not stand on some imagined Archimedean vantage point, but is often immersed in the field. It is no longer the researcher alone who decides in advance what s/he is going to 'measure' and how. People and their practices, places and phenomena are studied as much as possible *in situ* and the effort is to understand and engage with the meanings and priorities of those involved in the research process. Although research is planned in advance, the complex and intersubjective nature of these techniques calls for adaptations and the invention of new combinations (DeLyser et al. 2010). A small and flexible set of questions is usually a starting point to look at what happens within a social situation or group, the latter contributing to determine what is important or not. This set of questions is initially formulated based on bibliographical research, theoretical enquiry, study/knowledge of the context – a pre-research phase which helps develop questions and topics. Hence, analytical categories are adaptively constituted and evaluated based on the material that comes out of the research experience (interview, focus group discussion, participant observation, case study and so on), and are subject to many readings. The need for a theoretical perspective and the emphasis on the positioning and self-reflexivity of the researcher in relation to the object of his or her research is at the core of the longstanding debate advocating the use of qualitative approaches for the study of human and social matters: 'The gendered, multiculturally situated researcher approaches the world with a set of ideas, a framework (theory, ontology) that specifies a set of questions (epistemology) that he or she then examines in specific ways (methodology, analysis)' (Denzin and Lincoln 2005, p. 21).

It is out of the scope of this chapter to summarize the voluminous literature on qualitative methodologies. Rather, we focus more closely on the use of such methodologies in the study of bottom-up, socially innovative initiatives which aim to cope with situations of social exclusion. Such initiatives originate from a variety of theoretical standpoints and political priorities, include complex practices and mobilize a multiplicity of skills. As the analysis in the following sections of the chapter indicates, contextual differentiation is crucial for understanding such priorities, practices, organizational structures and activities. In this complex scene, the chapter does not seek to uncover regularities or approach questions of a quantitative character; it is rather a reflection on some of the issues raised by the use of qualitative methodologies for social innovation research.

20.3 SOCIALLY INNOVATIVE INITIATIVES: INSIGHTS FROM THE KATARSIS PROJECT

In this section of the chapter we draw together and reflect upon the methods used in the context of the KATARSIS project to come to grips with the contributions of a number of bottom-up initiatives towards the development of socially innovative strategies to cope with and perhaps overcome social exclusion. Bringing together diverse experiences from different places across Europe, with different languages, research traditions and contexts of practice, the project proposed innovative perspectives for the formulation of research questions and for policy design. Those methodological choices did not aim to 'verify' or 'falsify' already formulated hypotheses, but rather to address a number of questions arising from the coming together of different 'languages' and practices of academics and practitioners and to identify innovative ways of contact and communication.

20.3.1 Research Process

One of the goals in this context has been to analyse how a range of place- or community-specific material practices and knowledge can foster dynamics to overcome situations of deprivation and social alienation. To this end, a group of practitioners active in innovative initiatives in many European countries was mobilized.[3] These included members of NGOs, grass roots organizations, and so on, who work with questions and experiences of social exclusion/inclusion in different places. Most of the participants in this project were identified by the researchers within the KATARSIS project, either from previous collaborations or as an impetus for new research partnerships. The constitution of this group as a 'field' or resource for research material was, therefore, subject to a high degree of randomness and individual choice; in this sense it does not lend itself to easy generalizations. On the other hand, the experiences and practices that this project brought together form a rich, diverse source of material on social innovation.

Underlying methodological choices in this kind of research influence how to tap into this rich source without compromising its potential and diversity: directed, but also leaving room for interaction and exchange among participants. Taking into account the limitations of such a project, we proposed a focus group discussion. This is a method used in marketing as well as in the social sciences and is considered to have high apparent validity (see, among many, Marshall and Rossman 1999; Lydaki 2001; Lofland and Lofland 1984; Hay 2005). Major issues involved are related to the constitution and size of the group, the standardization or not of questions and procedures, the level of moderator involvement (see Morgan 1996). In any case, information about such issues and choices is mentioned in detail when presenting the findings; in this way findings can be assessed and the methodology can be improved in future research.

In our case the group of practitioners participating in KATARSIS formed the focus group. They were asked about their practices within and attitudes towards socially creative strategies to overcome social exclusion. The logic of this choice was twofold: on the one hand people involved in day-to-day praxis were expected to respond more eagerly in a discussion environment, rather than through formal interviews; on the other hand, the co-presence and interaction was expected to create a different dynamic and bring out issues that perhaps had not been considered on an individual basis, either by the focus group participants or by the research team.

A discussion outline had been pre-circulated, so that participants could be prepared about the issues to be discussed, but the discussion was rather loosely structured, encouraging interaction and the free flow of ideas. Members of the KATARSIS team acted as moderators of the discussion, reminding participants occasionally of the general topics that had to be covered. Not all issues and questions proposed in the initial outline were regarded by participants as being important or relevant for the description and analysis of their own experience, while others were introduced by them, thereby modifying the initial outline. The discussion was recorded, and later transcribed, and many photos were taken. In addition, moderators observed and later analysed more than spoken words: who spoke, from what subject position, body language, expressions, group dynamics. These were noted in detail and helped to interpret the transcripts. The relative disadvantage of having less control over the flow of the discussion (than would perhaps be the case with a one-to-one interview) was compensated by the development of a group dynamic which brought out interesting, previously unthought-of aspects of the discussed topics and clarified many context-related practices.

20.3.2 Processes of Knowledge Production

Qualitative methods in processes of knowledge production are inherently present in social initiatives like the ones mobilized in the KATARSIS focus group. Such initiatives call for socially sensitive, context-specific approaches and put at the centre of their actions participatory and democratic ideals, the empowerment of 'minor' voices, the valorization of contextual grassroots practices. These aims call – among others – for alternative and collective processes of new knowledge production and access to it. Novy and Leubolt (2010) put the socialization of knowledge in innovative and creative ways at the centre of experimentation and strategies for democratization and equal empowerment. Socially innovative initiatives and organizations mobilize the full range of knowledge available in society by improving the integration of local ideas and needs and the use of local knowledge and creativity.

We discuss below some of the main issues raised by practitioners who participated in the KATARSIS focus group related to processes of knowledge production: local embeddedness, open governance, orientation to specific social needs and fostering social change.

- Innovative social initiatives tend to mobilize in their work practices which have their analogies in qualitative research methodologies: understanding and incorporating local tacit knowledge in qualitative research, stronger or looser territorial bonds, relations with the neighbourhood, the community and/or the targeted group emerged as of major importance for the effectiveness and sustainability of locally embedded social projects.

- Issues of democracy also come out in relation to governance and methods of internal organizational form. Openness in the setting up and function of bottom-up creative strategies, as well as participation in decision-making are also crucial for the constant redefinition and advancement of social innovation. For social organizations and initiatives empowerment through networking, bottom-up coalitions and exchange are also very crucial.
- Such organizations address the social body in qualitative ways, in the sense that they do not target large groups or beneficiaries of social policies in general (such as, for example, all homeless people in a region); rather, they seek to address people who participate in groups with qualitative criteria (a common interest, for example artistic issues, or some special skills which they have or have not been able to develop, or a common territorial bond). Their goal, rather than delivering quantitative outcomes (as is the case with the welfare state structures), is to develop collective action and identity based on personal (but collectively acknowledged) qualities.
- As we have argued in the relevant KATARSIS reports, the question of "how bottom-up" is an initiative can (and probably should) be rephrased as "how the targeted group of people has control over the content and

process of the initiative". The bottom-up/bottom-linked component of social initiatives (see Pradel et al., Chapter 11; Andersen et al., Chapter 14) targets issues of democracy and empowerment, openness and creative social experimentation that can forge changes in socio-spatial relations towards the transgression of social exclusion and deprivation.

20.4   LESSONS FROM THE FOCUS GROUP EXPERIENCE

The choice of a focus group discussion in which actors from bottom-up initiatives are brought together, re-directs research interest to the dynamics of the group and to the possibilities of experience exchange. In such a group, situations and relations develop which are very interesting to register and describe; in fact, dense description yields rich findings and contributes to new knowledge. Diversity within a focus group is, in principle, an asset for the purposes of the research, in that it provides a broad range of 'cases' from which to approach questions of creativity and social innovation in different contexts. Prior knowledge/contact on the other hand is another asset, in that it establishes a level of trust, which is necessary for the deployment of methods based on personal interaction.

In the case of KATARSIS, most of the participants had been previously involved in research providing instructive case studies of social innovation, and they were therefore somewhat familiar with the aims of the project. Their participation has been crucial to our understanding of how diverse initiatives, across different socio-political and economic contexts, contribute to addressing conditions of social exclusion in various fields shaping the everyday life of social actors. Three key lessons emerged from the focus group, as summarised below.

20.4.1 Group dynamics and Contextual Contradistinction: an Approach to Difference and New Knowledge Production

Qualitative methods support the effort to uncover relations which are not readily visible, but which nevertheless guide socially creative initiatives. Physical co-presence and interaction of the participants in the focus group, the verbal expression of arguments, ideas and beliefs, and the dynamics of interaction among participants of various backgrounds all contributed to the same end: the dilemmas, problems and difficulties which actors often face (and handle in socially innovative ways) seem to gain a renewed impetus when expressed in relation to other similar ones; their active involvement led to understandings which would otherwise be difficult or impossible, given the diversity of the issues raised.

These dynamics are related to what has been called the 'group effect':

> Focus groups are more than the sum of separate individual interviews, since participants both query each other and explain themselves to each other. Such interaction offers valuable data on the extent of consensus and diversity among the participants, as it gives the ability to observe the extent and nature of interviewees' agreement and disagreement. Furthermore the researcher can ask for comparisons among their experiences and views, rather than aggregating individual data. (Morgan 1996, p.139)

Individuals who participated in the KATARSIS focus group were themselves representatives of groups (NGOs, grassroots initiatives etc), thus introducing to the whole exercise different levels of complexity.

20.4.2 Empowerment and Coalition Building

Direct meetings and interaction in dialogue forums and network meetings are practices that organizations choose in their everyday operations as appropriate ways to exchange experiences, increase visibility and empower their participants through coalition building. The role of researchers is then to acknowledge and take advantage of this rich source of material that can inform both research questions and policy proposals.

Carefully and sensitively used, focus groups (much like qualitative methods in general) have been acknowledged for their ability to 'give a voice' to marginalized groups, not only in the sense of listening to others but also serving as a platform for empowering people, groups, and wider communities (Morgan 1996). In this sense, they seem to be well suited to social innovation research. They are commonly used by researchers wishing to break down the division between researcher and researched. In this way, focus groups can actually:

> facilitate the democratization of the research process, providing participants more dialogic interactions and the joint construction of more polyvocal texts. While functioning as sites for consolidating collective identities and enacting political work, they also allow for the proliferation of multiple meanings and perspectives as well as for interactions between and among them. (Kamberelis and Dimitriadis 2005, p. 904)

The tradition of feminist research is instructive here: it has incorporated in its repertoire of methods 'consciousness-raising groups' – a practice of the feminist movement aiming to empower women – building 'theory' from the lived experiences of women (Harding 1987). In an analogous way, 'focus groups constitute spaces for generating collective 'testimonies' and these testimonies help both individual women and groups of women to find or produce their own unique and powerful voices' (Kamberelis and Dimitriadis 2005, p. 893).

20.4.3   Weaknesses and Limitations

The discussions amongst KATARSIS researchers and other participants revealed also some of the limitations of the focus group method: as in all group exercises that rely on verbal interaction the issue of language has a central, even determinant, position in the process. The necessary choice of English as the working language of the debate might have had two important consequences: firstly, at a personal level, not all participants were fluent or felt confident enough to participate equally in the discussion; secondly, it structures the vocabulary and the terms of the debate in ways which not everyone can relate to their own experiences and fields of action; at the same time, it constitutes experiences and practices developed in Anglophone environments as 'norms' from which other participants feel that they 'deviate'.

Following from the KATARSIS focus group, both the role of the moderator in generating research material and the impact of the group itself on that material have been discussed as weak aspects of the focus group method. On the one hand, and despite efforts to minimize 'moderating', 'the moderator's efforts to guide the group might disrupt the interaction of the group. It is often noted that it is the moderator, rather than the ongoing work of the group, that determines the agenda and form of discussion' (Morgan 1996, p.140). On the other hand, group members, and particularly the most vociferous ones, have affected group dynamics and each other, more than would have been the case in

face-to-face interviews or other methods of communication.

20.5   QUESTIONS OF METHODOLOGY

The experience presented in this chapter raises complex methodological issues to do with 'representativeness' and relevance for further research and policy formulation. It is clear from the constitution of the 'population' (or number of 'cases') that the focus is not on statistical representativeness, comparative study or general theoretical claims. The interest of the process lies rather in the micro-events and in difference (or otherness), while lived experience plays a key role in the formulation of truth claims (Harding 1987; see also Horkheimer 1974). Validity and credibility are judged in different terms than in quantitative methodologies: the process of the research is important (and hence its transparency has to be made explicit when presenting research findings), while self-reflexivity of the researcher and consciousness about context and positionality also matter (see, for example, Lydaki 2001).

20.5.1   On 'Objectivity'

Qualitative methods have often been criticized on the grounds of relativism and subjectivity, summoning arguments around the explicitly theoretically informed nature of the questions posed and the non-generalizability/non-transferability of findings or research outcomes. Such criticisms, however, are also pertinent in quantitative methods: here as well the researcher chooses the questions and analytical categories, the variables into which findings are broken down, as well as the relative weight of these variables – all of which imply a theoretical (and subjective) standpoint (see for example Wallerstein 1983 on the constitution of statistical categories). Data (in the case of quantitative methods) and material or findings (in the case of qualitative methods) are not objectively produced they are rather socially situated and dependent on the interaction between researcher and researched: 'No single method can grasp all the subtle variations in ongoing human experience' (Denzin and Lincoln 2005, p.21).

It is in the context of such debates on methodology and truth claims that qualitative approaches have stressed the importance of consciousness about context and power relations between the researcher and the researched, and have called for reflexivity and consideration of the researcher's positionality along the research process. The epistemological approach adopted by the authors of this volume, considers social innovation research not as a doctrine of scientific knowledge creation but as an inquiry into and a negotiated consensus on the way to develop knowledge; SI epistemology is:

> an interactively unrolled manual on how to connect questions about social change to scientific interrogation (*problématique*), how to lead this interrogation, and how to decide on the relative "verity" or "truth" of the answers. From the social innovation perspective, "truth" is concerned about the (socially accepted) relevance of the scientific answers for the satisfaction of (non-revealed) needs, the transformation of social relations, and the empowerment of populations and communities. (Moulaert and Van Dyck, Chapter 35)

20.5.2   Positionality and Reflexivity

As feminist and post-colonial theorists have persuasively argued, the research process involves power relations, which have to be taken seriously into consideration in the research design and in the inter-

pretation of findings. The research process begins long before the physical encounter between researcher and respondents, with theoretical and political concerns, formulation of research questions, setting up thematic areas, establishing a context – many decisions are taken by the researcher alone (Igglesi 2001). It also continues long after the encounter, with the analysis of material, its presentation in written or other forms, its communication to different audiences. 'How one chooses to frame things, how one tells a story' (Nagar 2002, p. 179) is decided by the researcher who is, therefore, in many ways in a position of power.

However, power is in no way unilateral; the respondents also determine in many ways the conditions under which the researcher may penetrate beyond a certain point: the answers that the subjects give are rarely in accordance with the answers they would give when they face similar issues in their everyday lives; they place a number of filters in the communication, beyond which the researcher is not allowed to reach, thereby protecting their own 'personal space' (Petronoti 1998).

On the other hand the researcher runs always the risk of interpreting and categorizing the subjects' experience according to his/her own perceptions. The meanings constructed by/through the relationship between researcher and respondents have to be put into a language which is meaningful to different audiences – that of one or many academic communities, 'local' or 'international' – and here language and words carry different meanings and connotations, according to the social context in which they are used (Vaiou 2004).

Reflexivity in this sense is proposed as a necessary engagement: a constant effort on the part of the researcher to transgress biases or pre-conceptions of his/her experience of, and position in, the world and at the same time be aware of the human inability to achieve this task. In various types of interviews within the tradition of qualitative approaches, the issues put forward by the researcher are ignored or marginally perceived as such by the respondents, since they are very often generated in a different context and often within different sets of values, aims and priorities, a problem that our example also indicated.

The 'ontology' of knowledge in social innovation analysis and practice, calls for a researcher's positioning towards the genesis of the views of the world as a social process and the outcome as socially reproduced, therefore never reaching completion and always critically reinterpreted (Moulaert 2009, p. 6; see Moulaert and Van Dyck, Chapter 35).

20.5.3   Context, Difference, Innovation

The differences in socio-political histories and systems, in welfare state regimes and in civil society formation define in different ways why, where, when and how socially creative strategies and social innovation develop, or which is the innovative element in each case. In this sense and apart from the many forms and the wide spectrum of these initiatives, their main differences are context-related. Even within the western European common philosophical heritage and historical development of social movements there are variations echoed in the different focus, the degree of politicization and relation to social affiliations (see also Moulaert et al. 2010; MacCallum et al. 2009). Those variations are further pronounced when southern European traditions of civil society and state organization are also included.

What is most important then, in order to draw useful lessons out of such a multiplicity of examples, is to develop tools which will help understand the details of their constitution and functioning and the context in which they operate, including the different terminologies and traditions of thought. A process like this, which ultimately highlights differences rather than looking for similarities, would enrich knowledge and help pose more relevant questions to be further investigated (Greenwood and Levin 2005, p. 51).

Qualitative inquiry is capable of taking account of contextual differentiation: 'qualitative data can redress the imbalance provoked by quantification and exclusionary research designs, by providing contextual information' (Guba and Lincoln 1994, p. 106). However, qualitative methods such as case studies and focus groups do not necessarily allow for a strict comparative analysis of socially creative strategies in relation to the contextual specificities, institutional frameworks and path dependencies that lead to diversified praxis. And in this sense they do not allow 'universal' and generalizable conclusions to be formulated. A more composite and global understanding requires a combination of quantitative and qualitative methods and a procedural and dialectical position towards the findings of the research. Qualitative methods, however, provide thick descriptions and therefore deeper understandings of the context in which particular experiences are formed; in this sense they contribute to a deeper understanding of responses to particular questions or of issues raised by participants during the research process.

20.6   CONCLUSION: TOWARDS A CONTEXTUALLY RELEVANT POLICY BUILDING PROCEDURE

The project from which this chapter draws, KATARSIS, was a practice-oriented one – focused on practices to cope with and address conditions of social exclusion, which are created by a multiplicity of factors. Hence the methodological inclination to describe relations and dynamics around which social innovation develops and leads to praxis as political intervention. Moreover, KATARSIS aimed to promote more efficient ways of communication among researchers, policy makers and socially active persons and groups, and ultimately to contribute to the development of a shared language for the groups involved. These aims can only be realized by reaching a consensus over a shared language on a commonly accepted field, in this case 'overcoming social exclusion'. The dialogue around such a shared language cannot take place only among institutionalized representatives, nor through standardized practices. Here, individuals and ad hoc created groups may have a decisive role, while multiplicity and diversity are at the same time an asset and a limitation of the process.

Acknowledging and working with multiplicity and diversity brings out a number of issues which would otherwise remain hidden; it requires methodologies that will incorporate and build upon these issues in order to formulate further research questions and policy guidelines. This raises an important question for policy development: how to make space for diverse organizational forms that will respond, in different contexts, to various aspects and forms of social exclusion and promote self- and community empowerment. Policy guidelines cannot be uniform as this could lead to the narrowing and bureaucratization of areas of activity that draw their value from bottom-up creativity. An institutional environment for innovative initiatives, including funding mechanisms and assessment methods, should try to support open space for imagination and creativity rather than assuming a standardized model.

As individuals and groups subject to situations of social exclusion multiply, in the EU and beyond, innovative bottom-up initiatives are actively proposed as effective processes in civil society to cope with, and perhaps overcome, marginalization and deprivation. In this context, it becomes methodologically opportune to promote qualitative research into Social Innovation and multiple ways to disseminate its findings. This would involve developing processes which favour interaction among different environments and initiatives, thus contributing to the production of new knowledge. To this end, practice-oriented research and qualitative methods not only enrich academic knowledge but also contribute to develop connections, new ideas and practices among those involved in the field.

20.7   QUESTIONS FOR DISCUSSION

- It is widely acknowledged that socially innovative initiatives differ in their territorial and historical context; how could interactive qualitative methods contribute to turn diversity into an asset for the research?
- Given the existing power relations between researcher and researched, how can qualitative methodologies lead to the development of a shared language around questions of social innovation?
- Qualitative methods and knowledge production through the study of bottom-up initiatives are often seen as having localized and partial validity. How can we permeate policy formulation based on such material in order to foster social innovation and combat social exclusion?

NOTES

1. The authors would like to thank Professors Maria Mavridou and Maria Mandouvalou for their valuable contribution in previous stages of this work.
2. A voluminous literature is related to the discussion of philosophical currents (for example phenomenology or hermeneutics) connected to this critique. See, among many: Mueller-Vollmer 1986 (with texts by Gadamer, Husserl, Habermas and others); Halbwachs 1997; Kuhn 1996; Feyerabend 1993.
3. Arsis (Greece), Pedestrians (UK), Freire centre (Austria), Olinda (Milano/Italy), Promo Cymru (Wales/UK), Afip (France), Laurens-Stiftung (Hamburg), SMAK (Belgium), City mined (Brussels, London, Barcelona), Ateneu Popular de Nou Barris (Barcelona/Spain), Groundworks (Wales/UK).

REFERENCES

(References in bold are recommended reading.)

Berger, L. and T. Luckmann (1966), *The social construction of reality: a treatise in the sociology of knowledge*, New York: Doubleday.
DeLyser, D., S. Herbert, S. Aitken, M. Crang and L. McDowel (eds) (2010), *Handbook of Qualitative Geography*, London: Sage.
Denzin, N.K. and Y.S. Lincoln (2005), 'Introduction: The discipline and practice of qualitative research', in N.K. Denzin and Y.S. Lincoln (eds), pp. 1–33.
Denzin, N.K. and Y.S. Lincoln (eds), *The Sage handbook of qualitative research* (3rd ed.), Thousand Oaks: Sage Publications.
Feyerabend, P. (1993), *Against Method* (3rd ed.), London: Verso.
Greenwood, D. and M. Levin (2005), 'Reform Through Action Research', in N.K. Denzin and Y.S. Lincoln (eds), pp. 43–64.
Guba, E.G. and Y.S. Lincoln (1994), 'Competing paradigms in qualitative research', in N.K. Denzin and Y.S. Lincoln (eds), pp. 105–117.
Halbwachs, M. (1997), *La mémoire collective*, Paris: Albin Michel.
Harding, S. (ed.) (1987), *Feminism and Methodology*, Bloomington: Indiana University Press and Open University Press.
Hay, I. (ed.) (2005), *Qualitative Methods in Human Geography*, Melbourne: Oxford University Press.
Horkheimer, M. (1974), *The Eclipse of Reason*, London & New York: Continuum.
Igglesi, Ch. (ed.) (2001), *Reflexivity in feminist research* (in Greek), Athens: Odysseas.
Kamberelis, G. and G. Dimitriadis (2005), 'Focus groups: Strategic articulations of pedagogy, politics, and inquiry', in N.K. Denzin and Y.S. Lincoln (eds.), pp. 875–895.
Kuhn, T.S. (1996), *The Structure of Scientific Revolutions* (3rd ed.) Chicago: University of Chicago Press.
Lofland, J. and L. Lofland (1984), *Analysing Social Settings: A Guide to Qualitative Observation and Analysis*, Belmont: Wandsworth.
Lydaki, A. (2001), *Qualitative methods in social research* (in Greek), Athens: Kastaniotis.
MacCallum, D., F. Moulaert, J. Hillier and S. Vicari Haddock (eds) (2009), *Social Innovation and Territorial Development*, Aldershot: Ashgate.
Marshall, C. and G. Rossman (1999), *Designing Qualitative Research*, London: Sage.
Morgan, D. (1996), 'Focus Groups', *Annual Review of Sociology*, 22, 129–152.
Moulaert, F., F. Martinelli, E. Swyngedouw and S. Gonzàlez (eds) (2010), *Can Neighbourhoods Save the City? Community Development and Social Innovation*, London and New York: Routledge.
Mueller-Vollmer, K. (ed) (1986), *The Hermeneutics Reader*, Oxford: Blackwell.
Nagar, R. (2002), 'Footloose researchers, "travelling" theories and the politics of transnational feminist praxis', *Gender, Place and Culture*, 9 (2), 179–186.
Novy, A. and B. Leubolt (2009), 'Scale-Sensitive Socioeconomic Democratisation', presented to the RSA-conference: Understanding and Shaping Regions: Spatial, Social and Economic Futures, Leuven, 6–8 April 2009, http://regional-studies-assoc.ac.uk/events/2009/apr-leuven/papers/Novy.pdf (last accessed 18 December 2011).
Petronoti, M. (1998), *Portrait of an intercultural relationship* (in Greek), Athens: UNESCO/EKKE/Plethron.
Vaiou, D. (2004), '(Re)constituting the "urban" through women's life histories', in G. Cortesi, F. Cristaldi and J. Droogleever Fortuijn (eds), *Gendered Cities: Identities, activities, networks. A life-course approach*, Rome: Home of Geography, pp. 171–182.
Wallerstein, I. (1983), *Historical Capitalism*, London: Verso.

21. Research strategies for assets and strengths based community development
Nola Kunnen, Diana MacCallum and Susan Young

21.1 INTRODUCTION

Among the fields that link the satisfaction of human needs to empowerment and social-economic change is the tradition of community development. This chapter considers how social innovation research can both contribute to and be informed by a particular set of community development approaches which emphasize recognition and mobilization of existing skills, networks and knowledge within local communities – rather than cataloguing the problems they face – as the key principle guiding research and development activities. These approaches, referred to broadly as 'assets and strengths based community development',[1] can contribute to social innovation research for the satisfaction of human need. They draw on a variety of theoretical and practical traditions, and resist any strong delineation between scholarship and practice. That is, assets and strengths based development approaches have research strategies within their practice which link general and local relations and conditions to knowledge to enable action. The strategies most commonly used derive from qualitative, critical action research methodologies (Craps et al. 2004; Kemmis and McTaggert 2005) and appreciative inquiry methods (Dick 2004, 2006; McNamee 2004), methods which we believe resonate strongly with the concerns of social innovation research as understood in this handbook (see also Gibson-Graham and Roelvink 2009).

The chapter draws on inclusive community research practices enacted by colleagues at Curtin University with the aim of enhancing individual and community capacity through the research process (e.g. Kunnen and Martin 2004, 2005; Stehlik and Buckley 2008). It provides a brief introduction to assets and strengths based community development, describes some core features of the research approaches involved, and identifies cautions for research practice within these emerging approaches. Finally, it discusses these processes and issues in relation to social innovation research, concluding that the two practices have much to learn from each other.

21.2 OVERVIEW: ASSETS AND STRENGTHS BASED COMMUNITY DEVELOPMENT

Community development, at its broadest, refers to the actions and practices employed by various parties to improve conditions and build development capacity within communities. The impetus for particular projects may come from communities themselves; from public policy or non-government organizations charged with services, economic health, or social wellbeing within a defined population; from private sector actors concerned with ensuring the capacity of a market or labour base, or, these days, with demonstrating 'corporate social responsibility'; and/or

---

BOX 21.1   FEATURES OF A STRONG COMMUNITY

Hughes et al. (2007, pp. 113–114) explore a variety of strengths oriented community development approaches concluding that a resilient or strong community is not only safe (for residents), welcoming, environmentally aware and sustainable but is also:

- *a learning community*: where knowledge, skills and confidence can be gained through community activity;
- *fair and just*: upholding civic rights and equality of opportunity and recognizing and celebrating diverse cultures;
- *active and empowering*: involving people in local organizations and having a clear identity and self-confidence;
- *influential*: people are consulted and provide input into decision-making;
- *caring*: aware of community members' requirements and providing good quality services;
- *Economically strong*: creating work opportunities and retaining a high proportion of its wealth.

---

from research efforts to better understand the needs and aspirations of particular groups of people. However, since the 1970s, participatory decision making has been accepted as a necessary feature of community development projects.

Traditionally, much community development practice has begun from the identification of needs, problems or deficits that the project in question must seek to address; however, in recent decades another model offers a different approach which reflects a strengths-based orientation. 'Asset Based Community Development' (ABCD) is the terminology applied by Kretzmann and McKnight (1993) from Northwestern University, Illinois. 'Strengths based community development' perspectives draw on theories and practice within mental health and social work (Saleeby 1996) and share many similarities with ABCD, including the recognition that justice, fairness and equality are *essential* components of a healthy human society (Beilharz 2002;

Young 2006; Hughes et al. 2007; see Box 21.1).

The ABCD and strengths-based approaches include varying perspectives that resist concise distinctions. However, two underlying principles are common to all approaches: firstly, that all communities – and the people and organizations within them – have assets, skills, capacities and networks; secondly, that effective community development begins with the identification of those assets, the building of relationships with and within communities, and the use of assets and relationships in achieving the visions and plans emerging from the process. Irrespective of the terminology and origins of these approaches, the common emphasis is on capacities and abilities rather than shortcomings. This chapter does not attempt to resolve the overlap or lack of clarity between these approaches. Rather, the term 'assets and strengths based community development' (ASBCD) is used as an all-encompassing term, and the discussion below pertains to both.

ASBCD perspectives recognize that communities where marginalization and exclusion occur will require external resourcing; that the creation of strong local institutions, democratic processes and economic opportunities (see Box 21.1) cannot occur in a financial vacuum (e.g. Beilharz 2002; ABCD Institute 2008). However, where they differ from some other approaches to community development is in their insistence that communities cannot be empowered, nor can they empower themselves, when they are treated as helpless or dependent on authorities. ASBCD approaches have emerged from a shared critique of traditional community development policies and practices 'focusing on a community's needs, deficiencies and problems' (Kretzmann and McKnight 1993, p. 1). They argue that such problems-focused approaches inform a 'mental map' (Kretzmann and McKnight 1993, p. 2) held by policymakers, practitioners and professionals interacting with communities, which blinds them to the potentials within the communities themselves. Even worse, such ideas are said to contribute to an ongoing process of marginalization and exclusion by becoming embedded within the attitudes of local community members who then enact a deficit-oriented perception of themselves, their neighbours and communities (Gardner and Jamieson 2000; Young 2006; Cameron and Gibson 2005). Such a positioning defines people and their circumstances by the things which they lack (as in resources) or are deficient in: for example, poor skills, imperfect understanding of, say, parenting, and limited knowledge. This orientation then constructs people as incompetent, unable, unknowing and incapable rather than having the skills, knowledge and attributes they can contribute to improving their own and others' circumstances. ASBCD approaches offer an antidote to these vicious cycles of dependence.

21.3 ASBCD STRATEGIES: TRANSFORMATION THROUGH RESEARCH

21.3.1 Methodological Influences and Considerations

A number of key methodological influences for ASBCD can be identified: action research, social constructionism, appreciative inquiry and reflexivity. Action research, more particularly, critical action research (Kemmis et al. 2005; see also Dubeux, Chapter 22, and Andersen and Bifeldt, Chapter 24) has been an important part of the community development repertoire since the 1970s. Influenced in part by Paulo Freire's critical pedagogy (1970), its aims emphasize not only knowledge production, but also social transformation. As knowledge production, it prioritizes 'macro-social' research that accesses community knowledge in order to understand how local 'sub practices are constitutive of lived social realities' and aims to inform 'a critical theory of social life' (Kemmis and McTaggart 2000, p. 579). As a form of social change, it draws on the interaction between localized and macro-social knowledge to empower marginalized groups to influence the distribution of resources (both within and towards their communities) and, as Maguire (1987, p. 28) puts it, 'not merely to describe and interpret social reality, but to radically change it'. Kemmis (2005, p. 414) identifies a need to direct research toward discovering, investigating, and attaining 'intersubjective agreement, mutual understanding and unforced consensus about what to do'. To this end, an especially important strand of action research, in relation to ASBCD approaches, is Participatory Action Research (PAR), which emphasizes the committed involvement of those 'researched', not only in data collection but also in setting the research agenda and informing analytical frameworks (McTaggart 1991; see also Arthur, Chapter 25).

In a similar vein, McNamee (2004) draws attention to the relevance of integrating praxis-oriented and reflexive processes and techniques that facilitate a 'transformative dialogue' through the research process. To this end, she advocates social constructionist analysis which acknowledges the 'coherent forms of practice and sense-making that emerge from the differing day-to-day activities of participants' (McNamee 2004, p. 407), rather than assuming a particular theory of the social order from the start. Furthermore, and key to the inductive knowledge-building process relevant to community development, a social constructionist methodology allows for knowledge building through a 'practical and generative' process (McNamee 2004, p. 408).

McNamee's method, drawn from earlier work in organizational development (Cooperrider et al. 2000), is known as an 'Appreciative Inquiry' because it begins with positive observations – valorizing the 'best of what is' (Bushe 1998, p. 41) as a basis for visioning and improving systems. Here, we see also the influence of poststructuralist and feminist research approaches which acknowledge the power of *representation* in creating worlds of experience and possibility (Cameron and Gibson 2005; see also Gibson-Graham and Roelvink, Chapter 34), and which recognize and actively seek to resist the potential for all relationships – including those between researcher and 'subject' – to be exploitative and/or disempowering (Doyle 1999). As such, appreciative inquiry and ASBCD are research approaches that seek alternative, counter-hegemonic discourses through which to imagine action – discourses which, in Scraton's (2004, p. 175) words, speak 'the truth from below'.

To capture and communicate the rich experiences and multiple perspectives of participants requires an analytical approach that accommodates multiple accounts of shared experiences, both positive and negative. In relation to this, developing and retaining a strengths orientation requires ongoing reflexivity by researchers (Martin and Kunnen 2008). Just as community members can readily adopt deficit-oriented perspectives in relation to their skills and capacities if authoritatively presented, researchers too can fall into this trap, which is shaped by a long tradition of policy and development practice. It is therefore essential for researchers to actively maintain the habit of avoiding a deficits focus. One strategy that we have found effective is to incorporate regular debriefings with community researchers and within research teams to provide space for reflexive dialogue processes. In these spaces, researchers and other participants, including funders of the research, are encouraged to reflect critically on their positionality and their conceptions of framing ideas such as 'vulnerability' or 'resilience' (Martin and Kunnen 2008).

21.3.2   Research Activities

An ASBCD process comprises four key moments (Green and Haines 2008, pp. 12–13, citing Kretzmann and McKnight 1993): asset mapping; relationship building; motivation and capacity building; and mobilization[2] – though generally undertaken in this sequence, some activities will often overlap. Usually they are part of an ongoing action, akin to the

BOX 21.2   FOUR STAGES/ACTIVITIES FOR ASBCD

Asset mapping: the asset mapping process commences with a multi-layered and comprehensive inventory of a community's capacities, resources, networks, and organizations and infrastructure. The process of identifying information that otherwise remains unrecognized assists in building interest, involvement and confidence that capacities and assets are available within that community.

Relationship building: the aim is to establish and cultivate rapport, confidence and trust. At all stages, relationships remain strength- rather than deficit-focused; they are not relationships of dependence. An ASBCD approach seeks to continually build relationships with and within communities and through these relationships to engage people in developing visions, priorities and action plans, as well as in capacity building opportunities.

Motivation and capacity building: to varying degrees, ASBCD processes create opportunities for community members to increase their involvement, to build their skills and capacities, to extend their networks, and to use their identified skills, talents and abilities to respond to identified needs, whether this be via voluntary or paid activities. Mathie and Cunningham (2003b, p.478) propose that one explanation for the capacity building potential of asset-based perspectives is that 'communities and organizations move towards what gives them life and energy. To the extent that memory and the construction of everyday reality offer hope and meaning, people tend to move in that direction.'

Mobilizing resources: the purpose of the mapping process is twofold, firstly to identify resources that are readily available within the community and secondly to identify assets, such as connections, networks and knowledge that can assist in securing the required external resources.

Action Research spirals (Stringer 2007; see also Arthur, Chapter 25). A brief description of each activity is provided in Box 21.2; however our discussion below focuses in particular on the asset mapping stage, as this represents the key *research* activity of the process, on which the success of the approach largely hangs.

21.3.3   Asset Mapping

The 'core' of any community's assets (Mathie and Cunningham 2005), within which the skills and attributes of the people can be identified and supported, are its formal and informal associations, networks and links. The process brings to the fore information about assets and knowledge of networks that are unlikely to be identified by needs- or problems-focussed community profiling or survey methods (Green and Haines 2008, p. 10; Kretzmann and McKnight 1993). This particularly means 'social assets, the particular talents of individuals, as well as the social capital[3] inherent in the relationships that fuel local associations and informal networks' (Mathie and Cunningham 2003, p. 474).

But such social assets both shape and are shaped by institutional, economic and physical environments. A comprehensive understanding of assets for research purposes would comprise:[4]

1. **People**: the knowledge, skills, talents, experience and expertise of individuals. Asset-based perspectives emphasize the importance of identifying the skills and talents of all groups and sub-groups within a community through engagement with the people. This includes all age groups and specifically people most likely to experience exclusion and marginalization.

2. **Places**: the places, natural resources, physical assets such as community buildings and meeting spaces, and the services and programs where people live, work and visit.

3. **Informal gathering spaces**: social networks and spaces – including people's homes – where people can interact informally, particularly those where people discuss and explore ways of responding to local issues.

4. **Partnerships and collaborative networks:** more formal collaborative networks and partnerships, connections and agreements that link the community and its members (i.e. stakeholder network groups, youth networks, local adult or community education networks, regional social or economic development forums, regeneration or revitalization partnerships). Of particular importance are those organizations and connections that promote and facilitate positive changes.

5. **Associations, groups, organizations and services:** local associations (i.e. local commercial, professional or business networks, community centres),

community groups, committees, recreational groups, clubs, residents' or tenants' organizations and institutions and services (i.e. schools, local government, community health, churches, emergency services).

6. **Local Business:** economic linkages, local businesses and business leaders.

7. **Culture:** mapping significant places, customs, behaviours and activities that have meaning to people and groups within the community, and that contribute to local identity.

8. **History and/or heritage:** sites, stories and records that help communicate the community's lived experience and local knowledge. These might include previous processes, plans and efforts in community and economic development, such as community campaigns, community planning proposals, community economic development projects, previous community visioning activities, other community development/involvement activities.

An inventory of individual assets can be completed by engaging people on an individual basis, as well as through contact at household, street by street, or place of employment level. The process of engagement is crucial because many marginalized communities have had negative experiences with both policy and academic inquiry, and treat researchers with some suspicion (Smith 1999; Martin 2008). For this reason, ASBCD enquiry is often realized in relatively long-term projects, involving extensive periods in which relationships, shared concerns and common languages are built (Stringer 2008). However, the imperatives faced by both policy and university researchers frequently work against such long-term engagement. In the following section, we briefly visit a model for ASBCD research which has evolved in this contemporary 'on-time and on-budget' environment.

21.3.4 The 'Balingup' Model

The Balingup model is named after the town in which it was first trialled, a small rural town in the southwest of Western Australia. In 2004, Curtin University's Alcoa Research Centre for Stronger Communities was approached by a group of Balingup community representatives to help develop an understanding of the needs and hopes of the town's elderly and aging residents. As such, it could have been the traditional *needs assessment* process characteristic of some community development practice. Instead, as shall be seen, because attention was paid to engagement and inclusion, it used the strengths and assets already present in the location, and assisted in developing these further. The project had a limited budget and time frame, which necessitated the use of volunteer researchers and a clear program of activities. It was considered highly successful by its participants, including the elderly community of Balingup, and the resulting report has served as a resource for local planning.

The process developed, described in detail by Stehlik and Buckley (2008) and summarized briefly in Table 21.1, provided a number of useful lessons and has since been applied in a number of other places in which service providers are concerned to engage 'hard to reach' communities. It focuses particularly on capacity building as an integral part of the research, and puts community assets to immediate work.

21.3.5 Cautions and Limitations

A number of important cautions emerge in the asset mapping process. Firstly, although the asset and strengths orienta-tion is crucial to the success of ASBCD programs (Gardner and Jamieson 2000), asset mapping is not a means for masking or ignoring contested issues, inequities or conflicts within communities. Instead, the process emphasizes the importance of commencing dialogue and research by recording what is present, rather than what is absent. To reiterate, commencing with a focus on conflicts, problems, negatives or tensions replicates the deficits-oriented approach that has historically been the starting point of policies and programs; ASBCD approaches instead give their initial attention to goals, strengths and potential (Green and Haines 2008, p. 8). It is through the recognition of these that the community's issues of exclusion can be approached with a positive view towards solutions, rather than a reinforcement of dependence.

Secondly, community-oriented praxis requires an awareness that aims, programs and terminology wax and wane with shifts in policy. For example, many policies and programs have been influenced by the concept of 'social capital', but have used it fairly uncritically, and often disconnected from the social theory that supports it.[5] This has led to a shift in social policy discourse to the extent that 'community' has been described as the 'modern elixir for much of what ails ... society' (Sampson 2008, p. 163). Yet 'community' is a 'slippery' concept (Green and Haines 2008, p. 1; Mathie and Cunningham 2003, p. 475) extending beyond communities of locality or place, and with tendencies that may be exclusionary or divisive as much as they are inclusive (Young 1990; Baumann 2002). Any community practice requires a caution that communities, even those most enthusiastically engaged in development projects, can exhibit such divisive processes from within, in addition to marginalizing influences arising from external

Table 21.1   The Balingup model in summary

Project aims	• Build relationships • Facilitate wide community input and involvement • Establish and maintain trust • Improve research capacity of both the Centre and the community • Provide actionable, relevant and informed research findings
Key emphases guiding the process	• Minimizing demands on community resources and time • Ensuring that local skills, knowledge and assets are integrated into the research process • Caution about relying on limited community input given multiple interests and opinions inevitably present within even small communities.
Strategies	• Early identification of key local contact person • Use of community-based researchers with a personal interest in the issue • Provision of suitable training for community researchers – ensures both scholarly rigour and capacity building • Community input into the design of the instruments to ensure that they are locally relevant, suitably worded, and appropriately targeted • Research team undertakes the 'office' work (preparation of instruments, data entry and analysis) • Ongoing feedback and debriefing between community and research team • Different approaches contribute to knowledge building • Public recognition of community researchers' input (through publicity, celebration and payment of an honorarium) • Continual building of trust in the research process, leading to good participation rates and incorporation of findings in future plans
Main methodological steps	1. Establish initial connections and relationships 2. Community profiling from secondary sources (demographic data, previous surveys and reports, other relevant literature) 3. Appoint a local project manager/facilitator 4. Community Workshop 1: contextual orientation including preliminary asset mapping; designing the research instruments 5. Preparation of research instruments by research team 6. Community workshop 2: test and refine instruments and information packages; emphasis on identification of community assets and strengths 7. Information gathering: volunteer researchers complete asset mapping through surveys and interviews 8. Analysis and writing up of results by the research team in consultation with key stakeholders 9. Public event: report findings and celebrate community researchers' achievements

and contextual factors (Sampson 2008, p. 163). In addition, as well as communities almost never being homogeneous, community interactions are increasingly fragmentary and diverse, often requiring consideration of multiple communities of interest (Hughes et al., 2007, p. 115). The implementation of assets and strengths based perspectives is not limited to communities defined solely as communities of place, and practitioners need to remain aware that, for most people, several 'communities' overlap, with potentially conflicting loyalties and orientations.

Finally, and relatedly, experience reinforces the importance of the relationship-building, consultation and planning phases of the research process. For many years, community development theory and practice have grappled with difficulties surrounding tokenistic participatory strategies (Jordan 2004; Kothari 2001; Kunnen 2005). The complexity of community connections and the need to maintain a realistic perspective on possibilities and constraints underpin the importance of building relationships with and within community, engaging the diverse range of stakeholders and mapping fully available knowledge, resources, skills and networks as the first stages of research practice.

21.4 CONNECTING ASBCD AND SOCIAL INNOVATION

While both the academic and grassroots traditions of ASBCD and social innovation differ, there are clearly important similarities in their orientation, concerns and problems. In particular, both emphasize the need to broaden ideas about and approaches to development beyond the economic, to challenge the conventional 'recipes' for addressing problems of marginalization, and to consider political participation and empowerment as non-negotiable elements of any attempt to improve conditions for needy or excluded communities. Both, too, foreground a research ethics that attends – in one way or another – to the lived experience of often marginalized subjects. What, then, can each learn from the other?

One key difference between social innovation and community development research is the *position of the researcher*. In ASBCD, the emphasis is on achieving concrete practical outcomes; the researcher is always, explicitly and directly, an agent of social change and research strategies such as asset mapping are oriented to this end. By contrast, much social innovation scholarship has been written from an observer's perspective. Even in cases where the researcher has been an actor within a socially innovative movement (see for example Moulaert 2000; also Vitale and Membretti, Chapter 13; Andersen et al., Chapter 14; Novy et al., Chapter 32;), their role as documenter and analyst has tended to be somewhat distinct from their role as practitioner. This difference has important methodological implications: for the protocols under which research projects are initiated and undertaken; for the place of theory and, in particular, for the emphasis given to geographic, institutional and temporal scale; for the ethics of commitment and dissemination.

Social innovation theory sees innovation in socio-political realms – empowerment being a crucial element of this – as emerging from the actions that communities take to meet their needs and alter their condition. In this model, power is not *conferred* on people or community organizations (for example through the establishment of decision-making mechanisms), but generated by creative interactions between the various actors experiencing marginalization or exclusion from the dominant, market-driven mode of development. For an ASBCD project initiated and/or managed by a public or academic institution, these interactions constitute precisely the foundation of resources for alternative modes of development; for example, the social movements and social economy organizations that have been the traditional focus of social innovation research are frequently important foci for the communities they mobilize and/or serve. No asset mapping process could ignore such resources. Thus, social innovation provides a conceptual lens for understanding the potentials inherent in communities. Conversely, ASBCD as a methodological framework can help to operationalize the ideal of 'bottom-linked' praxis (see Pradel et al., Chapter 11) by normalizing the establishment of respectful and productive relationships and protocols between funding, research and development agencies on the one hand, and socially innovative movements within communities on the other. A creative conversation between these two practices, then, can help to soften the traditional dichotomy between 'bottom-up' and 'top-down' initiatives.

Related to this, and as noted under 'cautions and limitations' above, ASBCD practice needs to sustain an awareness of the embeddedness of community, and of its own projects, within a political and social environment characterized by complex networks and histories. One of the strengths of the social innovation project (see Moulaert et al., Chapter 1) is its theoretical focus on exactly this issue. In exploring the dynamics of the relationship between social exclusion and the evolution of creative strategies against it, it has brought into the foreground of our attention issues such as path-dependency and multi-scalar governance relations – as limitations to, as sites of, and as concentrations of resources for social change. ASBCD can usefully mobilize these concepts and, indeed, actively use the resources they highlight in shaping new paths and modes of governance, including new opportunities for the institutionalization of social innovations.

Finally, ASBCD's long commitment to, and its particular development of, action research and appreciative enquiry methods can be a contribution to the emerging picture of social innovation research as a trans-disciplinary project,

a picture that is further elaborated by Novy et al. in Chapter 32 of this volume. Community development research has always been centred on addressing real-world problems; ASBCD approaches provide concrete strategies for incorporating experiential knowledge and representations in the construction of alternatives. As such, they represent a mode of social innovation in themselves. J.K. Gibson-Graham and Gerda Roelvink, in Chapter 34, show how current critical issues (such as climate change and the global financial crisis), leading to increasing doubts about conventional models of economic growth/wellbeing, require new ways of thinking about the future – ways in which experimentation, affect and the performativity of discourse[6] are foregrounded. This also means that careful attention should be paid to how researchers become and remain part of these 'other worlds', as Gibson-Graham and Roelvink put it, as well as to how practitioners within communities share in the ownership and dissemination of the knowledge produced within such projects. The difficulties of 'short-termism' are well recognized in community development studies (Liamputtong 2007), as are issues of access to academic and policy discourse, and what happens to community knowledge in translation (MacCallum 2008, 2009). These are significant ethical questions, which must remain central to the development of the dialogue we have started here.

21.5   CONCLUSION

Social innovation as a process and purpose has at its centre the imperatives of inclusive self-directed action to satisfy human needs within a socially just environment. As such, it demands action at the interpersonal, group and structural levels. Addressing social exclusion, as a broad concept encompassing varied social and economic relations, is a concern shared by a range of actors: researchers, policy makers, service providers and, especially, the people experiencing the exclusion. Some community development practice has seen practitioners and scholars seeking to bridge the gap between these actors' very different ways of understanding and responding to socio-economic problems, emphasizing the centrality of empowerment to achieving this. Researchers' attention to structural change as well as to local transformative actions has been informed by various models and theoretical perspectives. In this chapter we have shown ASBCD to be predominantly a model of, for and with the local, yet with the potential to establish the foundations from which an active citizenry can influence action towards meeting collective human needs. Theoretically then, this model may be seen to share much with social innovation research in its focus on empowering practices undertaken by social groups in meeting their needs. A crucial element in our example of Balingup and ASBCD in general, which can contribute to social innovation analysis and practice, is the grouping of research strategies which may be known collectively as action research, in which democratic involvement and activity generates change. Together they have much in common with social innovation research in principle and in purpose, and can add to its practice.

21.6 QUESTIONS FOR DISCUSSION

- Asset and strengths based community practices are collaborative endeavours, yet some worthwhile projects initiated by organizations rely on a single worker. Using the Balingup Model discuss/reflect on possibilities for developing an ASBCD team for practice and research.

- How might the concept of social innovation assist in making the connections between systemic and local change?

- How might you introduce the concept of social innovation and its connection to ASBCD to a community group with whom you are working?

  - How might you explore the possible cautions to their use with the group?

  - How might you suggest ways to overcome concerns?

  - What challenges can you see arising for practitioners, and how might these be responded to?

NOTES

1. For ease of reference this chapter refers to 'assets and strengths based community development', or 'ABSCD' approaches as an all encompassing term to refer to community development practice and research strategies which draw on aspects of either asset based community development (ABCD) or strengths based practices. The authors do not intend to imply that there exists, either in the literature or in practice, a singular approach which draws together ABCD and strengths based perspectives into one approach: the use of 'ASBCD' by the authors is limited to this chapter only.

2. On occasions, additional steps may be required. For example, in a case study of one three year project, Beilharz (2002, pp. 14–26) reports that a process of rapport building and information dissemination about the proposed project was undertaken for six months prior to the asset mapping or other activities, during which time a steering group was convened.

3. 'Social capital' is an ambiguous and often contentious term. Mathie and Cunningham use it in the sense first promoted by Putnam et al. (1993) and taken up by many policy, service and advocacy practitioners since: the formal and informal associations within a geographically-defined community, which support the sustainability of

that community and facilitate civic action. In this sense, social capital is not seen as 'belonging' to an individual (see for example Bourdieu 1984), but is a collective asset.

4. This list has been compiled and adapted from several sources including Building & Social Housing Foundation 2003; Central Coast Community Congress Working Party 2003; Green and Haines 2008; Kretzmann et al. 1993; MSU Outreach Partnerships 1999; Thompson 2005.

5. The Communities for Children (CfC) initiative of the Stronger Families and Communities Strategy was one such programme to have social capital as a foundation concept. Yet the idea was little explained and therefore understood by the practitioners in charge of the implementation even at the same time as 'community' was lauded as the place and process for change. Much in the way of other resources external to the locality, skills and knowledge, and developmental processes were needed to provide substance for change which social capital theory on its own could not achieve (Hendrick 2011).

6. This idea is explained in Chapter 34. Briefly, performativity refers to the capacity of language to bring real change into being – for instance, when a marriage celebrant pronounces a couple 'husband and wife', saying it makes it so. ASBCD approaches accept the poststructuralist observation that performativity has profound and far-reaching implications beyond such trivial examples.

REFERENCES

(References in bold are recommended reading.)

ABCD Institute (2008), *About ABCD*, Evanston, IL: Institute for Policy Research, Northwestern University 2007, http://www.sesp.northwestern.edu/abcd/about/ (last accessed 12 February).

Bauman, Z. (2002), *Community: Seeking Safety in an Insecure World*, London: Polity Press.

Beilharz, L. (2002), *Building Community – The Shared Action Experience*, Bendigo: Solutions Press.

Bourdieu, P. (1984), *Distinction: a social critique of the judgement of taste*, Cambridge, Mass.: Harvard University Press.

Building and Social Housing Foundation (2003), *Agents Rather Than Patients: Realising the potential for asset-based community development*, London: Building & Social Housing Foundation.

Bushe, G.R. (1998), 'Appreciative inquiry in teams', *The Organization Development Journal*, **16** (3), 41–50.

Cameron, J. and K. Gibson (2005), 'Building community economies: A pathway to alternative 'economic'

development in marginalised areas' in P. Smyth, T. Reddel and A. Jones (eds) *Community and Local Governance in Australia*, **Kensington: UNSW Press, pp.172–191.**

Central Coast Community Congress Working Party (2003), *Making HeadWay Building your community: An Asset Based Community Development ToolKit*, Sydney: NSW Government.

Community Strengthening Branch (2006), *Asset Mapping Guide*, Melbourne: Department for Victorian Communities, Victorian Government.

Cooperrider, D., P.F. Sorensen and D. Whitney (2000), *Appreciative Inquiry: Rethinking Human Organization Toward a Positive Theory of Change*, Champaigne IL: Stipes.

Craps, M., A. Dewulf, M. Mancero, E. Santos and R. Bouwen (2004), 'Constructing Common Ground and Re-creating Differences Between Professional and Indigenous Communities in the Andes', *Journal of Community & Applied Social Psychology*, **14**, 378–393.

Dick, B. (2004), 'Action research literature: Themes and trends', *Action Research*, **2** (4), 425–444.

Dick, B. (2006). 'Action research literature 2004–2006: Themes and trends', *Action Research*, **4** (4), 439–458.

Doyle, L. (1999), 'The big issue: empowering homeless women through academic research?', *Area*, **31**, 239–246.

Freire, P. (1970), *Pedagogy of the Oppressed*, New York: Herder and Herder.

Gardner, F. and B. Jamieson (2000), *Building Community, Strengthening Families: Shared Action in Long Gully*, Melbourne: The Ian Potter Foundation, La Trobe University, St Luke's.

Gibson, K. and J. Cameron (2000), *Transforming Communities*, Melbourne: Australian Housing Urban Research Institute.

Gibson-Graham, J.K. and G. Roelvink (2009), 'Social Innovation for Community Economies', in D. MacCallum et al. (eds), pp 25–37.

Green, G.P. and A. Haines (2008), *Asset Building & Community Development*, 2nd ed., Los Angeles: Sage Publications.

Hendrick, A. (2011), *Place management: social policy, government authority, community responsibility*, PhD, Curtin University.

Hughes, P., A. Black, P. Kaldor, J. Bellamy and K. Castle (2007), *Building Stronger Communities*, Sydney: University of New South Wales Press.

Jordan, B. (2004), 'Emancipatory Social Work? Opportunity or Oxymoron?', *British Journal of Social Work*, **34** (1), 5–19.

Kemmis, S. (2005), 'Knowing practice: searching for saliences', *Pedagogy, Culture & Society*, **13** (3), 391–426.

Kemmis, S. and R. McTaggart (2000). 'Participatory action research', in N.K. Denzin and Y.S. Lincoln (eds), *Handbook of Qualitative Research*, 2nd ed., Thousand Oaks, CA: Sage, pp. 567–605.

Kemmis, S., R. McTaggart and J. Retallick (2005),

The Action Research Planner, 2nd ed., Karachi: Aga Khan University Institute for Educational Development.

Kothari, U. (2001), 'Power, Knowledge and Social Control in Participatory Development', in B. Cooke and U. Kothari (eds), *Participation: The New Tyranny?*, London: Zed Books.

Kretzmann, J.P. and J.L. McKnight (1993), *Building Communities from the Inside Out: A Path Toward Finding and Mobilizing a Community's Assets*, Evanston, IL: Institute for Policy Research.

Kunnen, N. (2005), 'Participation in Australian Community Practice: Karaoke and Fugue', PhD in Social Work & Social Policy, Curtin, 2006.

Kunnen, N. and R. Martin (2004), *'Getting back on my feet': Exploring self-reliance in the context of supported accommodation and homelessness*, Perth: Australian Housing and Research Institute, Western Australia Research Centre.

Kunnen, N. and R. Martin (2005), 'Self Reliance and Homelessness in Australia: Challenges of Definition', in S. Darby, P. Flatau, I. Hafekost (eds) *Building for Diversity* (refereed proceedings of National Housing Conference), Perth: Department of Housing and Works.

Liamputtong, P. (2007), *Researching the vulnerable: a guide to sensitive research methods*, Thousand Oaks: Sage.

MacCallum, D. (2008), 'Participatory planning and means-end rationality: a translation problem', *Planning Theory and Practice*, **9** (3), 325–343.

MacCallum, D. (2009), *Discourse Dynamics in Participatory Planning: Opening the Bureaucracy to Strangers*, Aldershot: Ashgate.

MacCallum, D., F. Moulaert, J. Hillier and S. Vicari Haddock (eds) (2009), *Social Innovation and Territorial Development*, Aldershot: Ashgate.

Maguire, P. (1987), *Doing Participatory Research: A Feminist Approach*, Amherst, MA: Center for International Education, University of Massachusetts.

Martin, K.L. (2008), *Please knock before you enter: Aboriginal regulation of outsiders and the implications for researchers*, Teneriffe, Qld: PostPressed.

Martin, R. and N. Kunnen (2008), 'Reinterpreting the Research Path', in Paul J. Maginn, S. Thompson and M. Tonts (eds), *Qualitative Housing Analysis: An International Perspective*, Bingley, UK: Emerald, pp. 61–89.

Mathie, A. (2006), 'Does ABCD Deliver on Social Justice?' Civicus. Glasgow: unpublished, http://coady.stfx.ca/tinroom/assets/file/Does%20ABCD%20deliver%20on%20social%20justice%20%28FINAL%20July20%2006%29.pdf (last accessed 7 January 2013).

Mathie, A. and G. Cunningham (2003), 'From clients to citizens: Asset-based Community Development as a strategy for community-driven development', *Development in Practice*, 13 (5), 474–486.

Mathie, A. and G. Cunningham (2005), 'Who is Driving Development? Reflections on the Transformative Potential of Asset-Based Community Development', *Canadian Journal of Development Studies*, **26** (1), 175–186.

McKnight, J. (1995), *The Careless Society: Community and its Counterfeits*, New York: Basic Books.

McKnight, J. (2003), 'Regenerating Community: The Recovery of a Space for Citizens', in *The IPR Distinguished Public Policy Lecture Series*, Northwestern University, Evanston, IL: Institute for Policy Research, Northwestern University.

McNamee, S. (2004), 'Imagine Chicago: A Methodology for Cultivating Community Social Construction In Practice', *Journal of Community & Applied Social Psychology*, **14**, 406–409.

McTaggart, R. (1991), 'Principles for Participatory Action Research', *Adult Education Quarterly*, **41**, 168–187.

Moulaert, F. (2000), *Globalization and integrated area development in European cities*, Oxford: Oxford University Press.

MSU Outreach Partnerships (1999), 'The Several Forms of "Community Mapping" 2'. Best Practice Briefs Number 4, East Lansing: Michigan State University, http://outreach.msu.edu/bpbriefs/issues/brief4.pdf (last accessed 14 December 2012).

Putnam, R.D., W.R. Leonardi and R.Y. Nanetti (1993), *Making Democracy Work: Civic Traditions in Modern Italy*, Princeton, NJ: Princeton University Press.

Saleeby, D. (1996), 'The strengths perspective in social work practice: extensions and cautions', *Social Work*, **41** (3), 296–305.

Sampson, R.J. (2008), 'What Community Supplies', in J. DeFilippis and S. Saegert (eds) *The Community Development Reader*, New York: Routledge, pp. 163–173.

Scraton, P. (2004) 'Speaking truth to power: experiencing critical research', in M. Smyth, and E. Williamson (eds), *Researchers and their 'subjects'*, Bristol: Policy Press, pp. 175–194.

Smith, L.T. (1999), *Decolonising Methodologies: Research and Indigenous Peoples*, London, Dunedin: Zed Books and University of Otago Press.

Stehlik, D. and A. Buckley (2008), 'Participative inquiry using a community-as-researcher approach: the Balingup model', *Sustaining Gondwana Working Paper Series* Issue 9. Perth: Alcoa Foundation's Conservation and Sustainability Fellowship Program, Curtin University.

Stringer, E.T. (2007), *Action research*, Thousand Oaks: Sage.

Stringer, E.T. (2008), '"This Is So Democratic". Action Research and Policy Development in East Timor', in P. Reason and H. Bradbury (eds), *Handbook of Action Research*, 2nd ed., Thousand Oaks, CA: Sage, pp. 550–561.

Thompson, H. (2005), 'Fostering Community Engagement and Participation Through Local Skills Audits', in 2nd Future of Australia's

Country Towns Conference, Bendigo: Centre for Sustainable Regional Communities, La Trobe University.

Young, I.M. (1990), 'The ideal of community and the politics of difference', in Linda Nicholson (ed.), *Feminism/Postmodernism*, Routledge, New York, pp. 300–323.

Young, S. (2006), 'What is the best modern evidence to guide Building a Community?' Australian Research Alliance for Children and Youth, http://www.aracy.org.au/publications-resources/command/download_file/id/167/filename/What_is_the_best_modern_evidence_to_guide_building_a_community.pdf (last accessed 7 January 2013).

22. Technological incubators of solidarity economy initiatives: a methodology for promoting social innovation in Brazil[1]

Ana Dubeux

22.1 INTRODUCTION

Like many emerging economies, Brazil has long suffered from the consequences of a colonial development pact (Prado Junior 2006).[2] It is a society marked by social exclusion, whose consequences are apparent in the country's very high unemployment and under-employment rates. Between the 1960s and the early 2000s, accelerating industrial growth, the rise of the global market and reorganized global production processes deepened the impact of exclusion throughout Brazil. One small segment of Brazilian society inherited the land and, with it, the country's wealth and political power; a much larger segment lives in conditions of acute poverty, even destitution. This in turn leads to social and economic marginalization, a situation clearly demonstrated by data gathered from the country's main cities (IBGE 2010).

For the people living mainly on the outskirts of the major cities, this marginalization is reproduced territorially. Far from the city centres (sometimes up to 40 km out), these people live without access to the basic infrastructure usually provided by the state (public transport, paved roads, electricity, clean drinking water, sewerage and domestic waste handling services, etc.). As a result, the country consists of two opposing realities: the residents of the 'mainstream' city have access to public infrastructure that ensures their baseline wellbeing, whereas those who live on the margins suffer major deficits of public policy. Brazilian society can thus be said to be one of extremes, from those who form part of the official economy, to those who suffer marginalization and social deprivation: the excluded. Economic constraints make the latter second-class citizens, but their numbers are such that they have the potential to drive the country towards either social chaos, or far-reaching change.

Between 2003 and 2010, Brazil experienced what some researchers and political analysts call the 'Lula period'. In this period of recent history, which has yet to be studied in depth, the country embraced a policy of growth (in terms of GDP); compensatory social policies were also implemented to support growth by promoting consumption. As a result, Brazil became the world's seventh largest economy in terms of GDP, but continued to underperform in terms of education, public infrastructure, and policies to combat social inequality. The United Nations Human Development Index puts Brazil in 84th place (PNUD 2011).

Prior to the Lula period, the efforts of Brazilian workers in the 1980s led to an increasing number of solidarity economy initiatives. As these efforts helped create a movement around demands for equal citizenship, numerous solidarity economy initiatives were implemented in both urban and rural areas,[3] notably by cooperatives, informal production groups, economic cooperation networks and worker-managed businesses, and these initiatives were supported by networks that included NGOs, church representatives, trade union movements and, notably, universities. Because of this wide range of stakeholders, Brazil's solidarity economy has significant overlaps with the merchant, non-merchant and non-monetary economies, and has thus acquired a form that is very different from that in developed countries.

Some Brazilian analysts view solidarity economics as a response from the urban labour movement to declining Brazilian industry in the 1990s (Singer 2000). Others, more Marxist in standpoint, promote solidarity economics as an alternative to the capitalist production system, introducing 'new forms of production, labour organization, market structure, or even an alternative economy' (Todeschini and Magalhães 1999, p. 7).[4] The analysis provided in this chapter is based on concepts developed by Latin American writers who view solidarity economics as a form of worker resistance, rooted in the working-class economy (Coraggio 2007; Migliaro 2011). According to these authors, an economy must be based on labour and the logic of reproduction. The idea is to replace an exchange value with use value, and give collective needs priority over individual accumulation.

In this context, universities have been under various pressures, both political and academic, to support social projects that tackle marginality across territories, notably through implementing solidarity economy initiatives rooted in the dynamics of territorial development. This process helps foster social innovation, because it requires researchers, teachers and students to adopt new conceptions of science and technology and to consider how the out-comes from their work fit in with the everyday lives and social relations of the people it is meant to support. At the same time, close collaboration with excluded workers enables the joint creation of a new kind of knowledge, one that goes beyond the usual applications to drive deep-seated transformation and sustainable territorial development.

This chapter discusses the role of universities in building an arena for public debate on the economic change required to create a new societal paradigm in Brazil. The principles of solidarity economics orient university action and, as universities are involved in territorial organisation, they produce knowledge that stems directly from the everyday concerns of their partners.

22.2 THE SOLIDARITY ECONOMY IN BRAZIL: THE ROLE OF UNIVERSITIES

Since the 1990s, the increasing prevalence and visibility of social solidarity economy initiatives across Brazil led universities to step up their scientific research programmes in this domain. By the late 1990s, solidarity economics was acknowledged as a viable research topic by national research funding bodies (CNPq and Capes), thus generating further interest from researchers, students and lecturers. This was a significant achievement for researchers, a large majority of whom are involved in incubator projects and who are gradually requiring state institutions to take a stand in this domain.

Alongside this primarily institutional battle to institute solidarity economics as a development strategy recognised by research bodies, it is important to clarify the conceptual debate surrounding solidarity economics in Brazil, as it differs from similar debates in Europe in certain key details. In Brazil, as in many Latin American countries, the solidarity economy is largely rooted in the 'popular economy' ('economia dos setores populares'), that is, economic activities which are oriented to meeting the needs of people rather than generating profit. Kraychete et al. (2000) define the solidarity economy as being socially responsible. It is nourished by numerous activities involving the innovative restructuring of social and productive relations within rural and urban communities and territories, grounded in the popular economy. It influences the reproduction conditions for the lives of ever-increasing numbers of social groups (e.g. urban production groups, associations of craftswomen, 'recyclers', fishermen, etc.). As such, it provides a way for 'rural and urban workers, native populations and immigrants to leverage their traditional support networks and promote a sense of community that contrasts with the disorder produced by capital' (Laville and Gaiger 2009, p. 163).

Until the early 1990s, Brazil's support and funding for science and technology had little apparent basis in social concerns, particularly as regards excluded populations, because these policies were based on a development model that promoted capital-based strategies. However, public debate about development drew Brazil's universities into wide-ranging scientific discussions about the needs and specific characteristics of the groups involved directly in the lifestyle reproduction of thousands of people; people who were themselves responsible, through the production and exchange of considerable goods and services, for creating new, embryonic forms of production and social interaction. It is important to note that since colonial times research in Brazil, as in many countries, has primarily worked for corporate inter-

ests with state support, rather than for associative initiatives based on territory and local needs.

What is evident in the Brazilian dynamic is the potential to change circumstances and drive social innovation, made possible by the coming together of many players with a significant role in the everyday life of local communities, despite the difficulties experienced. This obliges universities to consider new and innovative ways of meeting the social needs of disadvantaged populations. At the same time, through their role in incubators, universities acquire a key position within a new mode of territorial development, in which the production and exchange of knowledge promote social innovation.

With this in mind, it seems appropriate to refer to the vision of territorial development defined by Moulaert and Nussbaumer (2008). Using a multi-dimensional approach, Moulaert and Nussbaumer define a concept of territorial development that is based on a 'broad understanding of human liberties and the capacity of human beings to meet their needs', an understanding which reasons that 'human needs can be met through multi-partner initiatives, and this is facilitated by building development on innovative social relationships' (2008, p. 67).

Collaboration between numerous stakeholders from different social movements, all campaigning for a new kind of development, obliges universities to step out of academia and into society, thereby helping to build and democratize a new type of knowledge and thus foster empowerment. The Technological Incubators of Solidarity Economy Initiatives were created to meet a need that was expressed not only by a few of the most committed universities but primarily by large groups of actors demanding greater interaction between research institutions and society.

As such, universities were compelled to open their doors and leverage their structural and scientific resources to facilitate effective and diverse exchange across all sectors of society. The aim was clearly to exchange knowledge, but also to fulfil the primary mandate of a university: producing and disseminating knowledge.

22.3 TECHNOLOGICAL INCUBATORS OF SOLIDARITY ECONOMIC INITIATIVES: A METHODOLOGY FOR PROMOTING SOCIAL INNOVATION AND SOLIDARITY ECONOMY

22.3.1 Building a New Scientific Paradigm

We currently see universities as an integral part of the modern paradigm: 'the multiples crises experienced by universities relate to the crisis of the modern paradigm itself, and can therefore not be resolved other than in this context' (Souza Santos 1997, p. 223). As such, if we assume that the modern paradigm has reached its limits, it follows that universities as they are currently conceived must also have reached their limits. Universities must therefore 'revise their traditional roles and look within themselves to identify new practices that will help break with the modern paradigm and drive a sea-change, to achieve a situation where innovation will constitute a driving force' (Braga 1997, p. 23).

The transition from modern to postmodern science, and from the modern paradigm to post-modernity involves ruptures. Indeed, Souza Santos (1997, p. 224) claims that 'universities find it difficult to reach a compromise whereby citizens and academics can come together in authentic interpretive communities and go beyond

standard interactions to challenge standard perceptions of their social reality.' The drivers of such ruptures can be found in the launching of trans-disciplinary discussions on the paradigm crisis, the current transition period, and the possibilities for the future. Discussions of this kind within each university should trigger the creation of new concepts and must be communicated widely to stimulate further and wider discussions. Challenging today's dominant epistemological foundations involves incremental innovations that help to change various levels of thought at the local scale, even if no one instance results in global change.

It was discussions of this kind that led to the creation of Technological Incubators of Solidarity Economy Initiatives (ITCP) in Brazil as of 1995, as well as to greater cooperation between universities and the social movements engaged in fighting poverty, hunger and destitution. These incubators form protected environments for integrating university research, teaching and *'extensão'*,[5] with a view to creating and disseminating knowledge, educating a new generation of professionals to embody a new style of leadership, and developing methodologies that support the dynamics of innovative solidarity economics. The incubators are used to produce knowledge that is rooted in the reality of solidarity economy initiatives. They also promote transformation within the universities themselves, notably as regards their relationship with development, thereby injecting a substantial political element into their action.

Brazil's incubators are currently organised into two university networks: the ITCP network, which includes 40 universities working through their own incubators, and the UNITRABALHO network, which has a membership of over 30 universities. In addition to their scientific work, both networks actively campaign for greater government involvement in Brazil's solidarity economy, particularly as regards joint public policy-making through the Brazilian Forum for Solidarity Economics.[6]

22.3.2 The Conceptual Basis behind the Incubation Methodology

Brazil's first incubators were created in the mid-1990s. Of the five universities that pioneered the concept, only one had previous research and teaching experience in the field of associations. As such, the initial impetus came primarily from the popular education experience of various lecturers involved in the incubator project, and the standard business incubator model, heavily revised for this purpose (Dubeux 2004).

The concept of popular education is rooted in the theories and methodologies of Paulo Freire (1967, 1987, 1996).[7] Popular education is achieved through permanent, ongoing training processes that aim to enable people to transform their own reality. It results from the collective actions of popular educators, movement leaders, social organisations and networks that are rooted with the people, and teams responsible for creating and overseeing public policies within society. Training activities are based on theoretical-methodological practices. They take place in cultural arenas where it is possible to 'read the world', extend theory and draw up strategies for action. It is a reflexive process whereby the subjects gain awareness and empowerment through formative interaction with their physical and social environment (Gadamer 1996).

The role of incubators may also be analysed according to the work of Souza Santos (2009), who encourages us to go beyond the conventional distinction between subjects and objects. Experience, common sense, and interaction between researchers and the 'objects' of their research form the basis of a new scientific paradigm whereby the 'autobiographical nature of knowledge is fully assumed: comprehensive, intimate knowledge that does not cleave us apart but, better still, unites us with the realities that we are studying' (Souza Santos 2009, p. 84).

The incubators use a wide range of technical support and teaching methods and, as a result, they implement their expertise in very different ways as regards the core aspects of the methodology. The main differences in approach concern: a) the relationship with knowledge; b) involvement in different levels of education; c) involvement in social movements; d) domains or areas of interest; e) students' roles and training; f) the length of the incubation period; g) profiles of incubated groups; h) systematizing research results. However, emphasis on action research process and a focus on participative methods are central tenets of all incubators.

After 15 years, the current incubation methodology is such that incubators incorporate and implement new concepts every day, based on interaction with incubator stakeholders. This is primarily achieved by building, as part of the process, something that we call '*social technologies*', understood as products, techniques and/or methodologies that are developed through interaction with residents, and which represent effective solutions for social transformation. (Dagnino et al. 2004). Conceptually, social technology means an understanding of social intervention that is inclusive in all stages of its construction; it is a participative process of generating knowledge and conceptualizing science and technology. In practice, social technology is developed and communicated according to the possibilities inherent in each neighbourhood, city or country, and may be used to build solutions to a wide range of social issues.

Building social networks is another key tenet of the group incubation methodology. In the incubation process, networks are built not only within the university between researchers, students and technicians from different departments, but also and more importantly between groups of incubation process stakeholders, and with other players in the solidarity economy movement. These networks constitute important articulations between different entities that use these links to exchange a range of resources. And, in a process of education for cooperation, the starting point is the exchange of knowledge. Exchanges mutually reinforce each 'node' in the network, at the same time being themselves reinforced by all the actors involved in the network's various flows.

Building networks certainly gives a powerful boost to territorial development, notably because bringing stakeholders together implies a need to work around one of the pillars of modernity, according to which the state, in cooperation with the market, has responsibility for curbing social conflicts. Instead of being handled by a welfare state, social problems and needs can be managed through self-organizing social movements through various mechanisms, notably that of association. Over the last 10 years, various instruments for collective bargaining and social control over public policy have been developed in Brazil. These promote articulation between the various social subjects and, at the same time, stimulate relatively dynamic forms of territorial development (França Filho 2007).

A closer look at the incubators currently established in Brazil shows a change in their methodology, with a noticeable shift from support for enterprise to support for territorial development. When building social technologies with incubated groups, researchers and students are placed at the heart of stakeholders' issues. Consequently, as the reality studied is not an academic subject, they are compelled to interact with other stakeholders when discussing this reality and work together to formulate alternatives. As such, the role of researchers in this process can perhaps best be analysed according to the sociology of knowledge (see also Moulaert and Van Dyck, Chapter 35). Using this epistemological framework, Moulaert and Nussbaumer (2008) suggest that researchers working on the ontology of territorial social innovation may adopt one of four role types: virtual, academic, real or discursive. In the incubation process, however, researchers assume all four roles simultaneously. Furthermore, in each role, one of their primary tasks is to mediate between the university and the outside world.

The incubation process involves knowledge exchange at several levels, using the incubators as mediators: a) between groups and the solidarity economy movement; b) in creating a network of stakeholders; c) between groups and the various university departments; d) between groups, solidarity economy movements and the public authorities; e) between groups and other support organisations.

The action of incubation is a complex socio-political methodology, developed by universities, that encompasses multiple dimensions (technology, social culture, political ideology, economics, etc.) and different sites and scales for action (individual, family, neighbourhood, business, social solidarity economy initiative, territory), and which is also affected by various cross-cutting elements (gender, generation, ethnicity, environment, culture and leisure). Figure 22.1 below schematises the

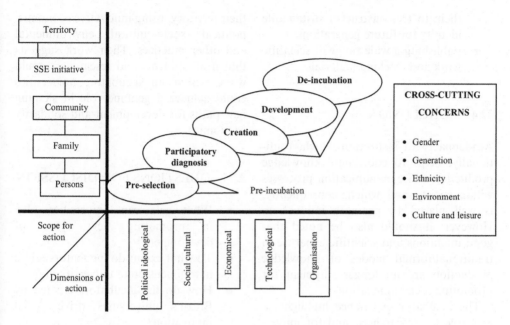

Source: Created by the author.

Figure 22.1 The incubation process: components, flows and stages

relationship between all these factors over the various stages of the process (pre-incubation and incubation).[8]

22.3.3 Incubator Outcomes

Incubators obtain results through their activist campaigns and actions. These results reflect the political-pedagogical nature of their methodology:

● building economic opportunities outside the market economy;
● fostering relationships with social movements engaged in a joint transformation and social innovation processes;
● undertaking discussions with public authorities in relation to implementing policies to promote solidarity economics;
● helping to forge relationships between solidarity economy initiatives, notably through networking;
● training students to think about building a new social and economic paradigm;
● democratizing access to the knowledge generated by the university;
● promoting sustainable development and dialogue between holders of traditional and scientific knowledge (popular education);
● working with the families of incubator group members;
● developing a process for recovering cultural memories from incubator groups in relation to food, traditional medicine, productive procedures, traditions, customs, etc.;
● increasing school attendance rates among incubator group members;
● supporting or initiating practices that involve young people and enable

them to (re)construct a sustainable identity for future generations;
● publishing a wide range of scientific work and teaching materials.

22.4   CONCLUSION

Academia is an institution which, traditionally, helps to coordinate knowledge production and communication processes within society and which, consequently, is well placed to promote innovation. However, it should also be noted that good intentions and scientific expertise in traditional/formal modes of knowledge production are no longer sufficient for promoting social innovation.

The incubator experience highlights a new role for researchers, and for universities in general. Beyond concerns with the production-oriented indicators used by research funding bodies, and the policy of classifying researchers as productive or unproductive, the incubators place students and researchers in a dynamic that challenges their very experience within the university. Seeking scientific knowledge that is rooted in real, everyday needs seems self-evident to all those involved in incubator projects.

Appropriating and adapting existing technologies is not in itself enough to reduce social inequality. The greatest challenge facing incubators is to develop technologies that incorporate, from inception to application, a commitment to promote social inclusion and sustainable development. A desire to meet human needs, notably by building socio-economic relations across society, lies at the heart of the incubator experiment in Brazil. Incubators are socially innovative insofar as they empower participants in solidarity economy initiatives to help drive socio-political transformation processes in

their territory, using innovative economic, political, socio-cultural, environmental and other practices. Their work suggests that if all students and researchers could work within an incubator, universities could achieve a genuine role in shaping new paths for development and solidarity economics.

22.5   QUESTIONS FOR DISCUSSION

● What role can universities play in promoting new types of development?
● To what extent do incubators add a new dimension to university life?
● How do the incubators created by Brazil's universities drive social innovation?
● When promoting social innovations with a view to creating new opportunities for socio-economic development, what place should be accorded to discussions about building knowledge?

NOTES

1. This chapter, including all quotations within it, has been translated from French.
2. The development pact in colonial times was based on exclusivity in commercial changes between colonies and metropolis. Even after decolonization, the characteristic of having two poles of political and economic decision making is reproduced internally in Brazil, with some regions (south and southwest) being more powerful than others (north and northeast). This dynamic increases the differences between regions, as well as putting the capitals and major metropolis in the control of the most important economic and political decisions of the country.
3. Through the National Secretariat for Solidarity Economics, and in partnership with the Brazilian Forum for Solidarity Economics, the Ministry of Labour and Employment created a National Solidarity Economy Information System to map such initiatives (Ministério do Trabalho e Emprego 2009) Although all groups have yet to

be listed, some 21,859 solidarity-based companies have been identified across Brazil.
4. This diversity of conceptions is also apparent
   within the solidarity economics movement in
   Brazil. In March 2011, movement members with
   trade union ties agreed to a government proposal to transfer the National Secretariat for
   Solidarity Economics to the Ministry for Small
   and Medium Enterprise. This decision caused a
   major rift within the movement, as most stakeholders see solidarity economics as a means of
   transforming the economy and building relationship across society.
5. The term university 'extensão' refers to external
   training initiatives, generally short-term, implemented by universities in Brazil. The incubators
   extend understanding of this term, because they
   require longer-term university inputs of time and
   commitment to support incubator groups.
6. The Brazilian Forum for Solidarity Economics
   (FBES) brings together solidarity economy
   stakeholders from across Brazil. It is the government's main partner in joint efforts to build
   public policies that promote solidarity economics. Both incubator networks are members of
   FBES. For more information, see www.fbes.org.
   br (last accessed 13 December 2012).
7. Paulo Freire was a leading Brazilian educator,
   known world-wide for his published works on
   education, particularly popular education. His
   work criticised the 'banking' model of education,
   whereby teachers 'deposit' information with students who then 'withdraw' it to pass tests.
8. This incubation flow diagram was developed by
   the incubator at the Federal Rural University of
   Pernambouc. However, most incubators use a
   similar methodology.

REFERENCES

(References in bold are recommended reading.)

Braga, A.M. (1997), 'Universidade Futurante: inovação entre as certezas do passado e incertezas
do futuro', in D. Leite and M. Morosini (eds),
*Universidade Futurante: produção do ensino e ino-
vação*, Campinas: Papirus, pp. 21–37.
**Coraggio, J.L. (2007), 'La Economia del Socialismo
del siglo XXI', http://www.itcp.usp.br/drupal/
node/300 (last accessed 21 November 2011).**
Dagnino, R., F. Cruvinel and H.T. Novaes
(2004), *Sobre o marco conceitual da tecnologia
social*, http://www.ige.unicamp.br/site/publica

coes/138/Sobre%20o%20marco%20anal%EDtico
-conceitual%20da%20TC.pdf (last accessed
21 November 2011).
**Dubeux, A.M. (2004), 'Education, Travail et Economie
Solidaire: le cas des incubateurs technologiques
de coopératives populaires au Brésil', PhD thesis,
Université de Paris I, Panthéon, Sorbonne.**
França Filho, G. (2007), 'Definindo gestão social', in
R.T. Jeová Torres Silva (ed.), *Gestão social: práti-
cas em debate, teorias em construção*, Juazeiro do
Norte: Imprensa Universitária, pp. 35–47.
Freire, P. (1967), *Educação como prática de Liberdade*,
Rio de Janeiro: Paz e Terra.
**Freire, P. (1987), *Pedagogia do Oprimido* (17th ed.),
Rio de Janeiro: Paz e Terra.**
Freire, P. (1996), *Pedagogia da Autonomia. Saberes
necessários à prática educativa* (25th ed.), São
Paulo: Paz e Terra.
Gadamer, H.-G. (1996), *La philosophie herméneu-
tique*, Paris: PUF.
IBGE (2010), 'Resultados do Censo 2010', Instituto
Brasileiro de Geografia e Estatística, http://www.
censo2010.ibge.gov.br (last accessed 5 April 2012).
Kraychete, G., F. Lara and B. Costa (eds) (2000),
*Economia dos setores populares: entre a realidade e
a utopia*, Petrópolis/RJ: Vozes.
Laville, J.-L. and L.I. Gaiger (2009), 'Economia
Solidária', in A. Catani, J. Laville, L.I. Gaiger and
P. Hespanha (eds), *Dicionário Internacional da
Outra Economia*, São Paulo: Almedina.
Migliaro, L.R. (2011), 'Os caminhos da economia de
solidariedade', http://www.luisrazeto.net/content/
os-caminhos-da-economia-de-solidariedade (last
accessed 21 November 2011).
Ministério do Trabalho e Emprego (2009), *Atlas
da Economia Solidária no Brasil 2005–2007*, São
Paulo: Todos os bichos.
Moulaert, F. and J. Nussbaumer (2008), *La logique
sociale du développement territorial*, Québec:
Presses de l'Université du Québec.
PNUD (2011), *Relatório de Desenvolvimento Humano
2011*, New York: ONU.
Prado Junior, C. (2006), *História Econômica do
Brasil*, São Paulo: Brasiliense.
Singer, P. (2000), *A Economia Solidária no Brasil*, São
Paulo: Contexto.
Souza Santos, B. (1997), *Pela mão de Alice. O social
e o político na pós-modernidade*, São Paulo: Cortez.
**Souza Santos, B. (2009), *A crítica da razão indolente:
contra o desperdício da experiência* (7th ed.), São
Paulo: Cortez Editora.**
Todeschini, R. and R. Magalhães (1999), 'A CUT e
a Economia Solidária', in *Sindicalismo e economia
solidária*, São Paulo: Central Única dos trabal-
hadores, pp. 5–22.

23. Partnership-based research: coproduction of knowledge and contribution to social innovation

Jean-Marc Fontan, Denis Harrisson and Juan-Luis Klein

23.1 INTRODUCTION

Partnership-based university research has an important place in today's knowledge society. The building and maintaining of a knowledge society is supposed to be based on the mutual recognition of needs, a definition of the shared problems, and a common search for solutions by the university and community sectors. (Sajnani and Mendell 2007; Wiewel and Broski 1997, p. 2). However, in practice, today's knowledge society has increasingly evolved into an elitist 'knowledge economy'. As a marketed good, knowledge is a central component of 'information capitalism', or even of a technical-productive paradigm, which is neither neutral nor objective (Lundvall 2002; Foray 2000). In that sense, information and knowledge are key parameters of social justice and citizenship (Castel 2008). The more they are used to serve the selfish interests of an elite, the more society is unequal and exclusive. Conversely, the more they are shared between different types of actors, the more society is potentially cohesive and inclusive.

This chapter concerns the expansion of the network of knowledge producers through partnerships between researchers and practitioners. Our insistence on the importance of the co-production of knowledge is consistent with our notion of social innovation. Rethinking social innovation means formulating a concept of social creativity to resolve human and social problems, addressing the flow of knowledge, ideas and resources to tackle the difficulties, and developing a concept of social relationships that integrates knowledge, resources and people. We proceed in four steps. First, we present the issue of knowledge production in relation to social innovation. Second, we discuss partnership-based research as the combination of a method and an organizational model. In a third step, we feature the case of Québec by presenting an example of a partnership-based modality of collaborative knowledge production from this society. And in conclusion, we point to the challenges associated with implementing a partnership-based research that can contribute to knowledge production and find solutions to social problems.

23.2 KNOWLEDGE PRODUCTION AND SOCIAL INNOVATION

As has been amply demonstrated, neoliberalism has undermined the significance and potential of collective action by imposing the commodification of many public services. Invariably, such a strategy of commodification has created more losers than winners. The link between knowledge production and social innovation must be seen in the context of this antagonism between social actors defending diverse, or even opposite, interests concerning the production of and accessibility to knowledge and information. The social innovation approach presented in this chapter sheds light on this social transformation and on the way knowledge is being produced and disseminated.

The value and potential of knowledge production for finding solutions to social, economic and cultural problems has been widely recognized since Michael Gibbons' (and colleagues) cornerstone volume *The New Production of Knowledge, The Dynamics of Science and Research in Contemporary Societies* (1994), on the co-production of research outcomes through interdisciplinarity and the collaborative search for solutions to problems, and Henry Etzkowitz and Loet Leydesdorff's seminal work *Universities in the Global Economy: The Triple Helix of University-Industry-Government Relations* (1997). These authors seek to position research and its applications in a transdisciplinary and evolving framework that guides efforts towards solutions. This framework includes the collaboration of heterogeneous practitioners as well as academic researchers who together create knowledge that addresses problems occurring in specific and local contexts and timeframes. The outcomes are easily transferred to all those participating in their production, and the mode of research is adaptable and flexible. The triple helix metaphor points to the links between university, business and government and to the ways in which these links co-evolve to form a durable model for producing and transferring knowledge between different stakeholders to promote technical innovation.

Such a model is also applied to promote social innovation, thereby addressing civil society, social movements and social entrepreneurs. Research-funding public agencies are increasingly encouraging alliances between government bodies, academics and practitioners in order to spur a type of knowledge production that is appropriate for practitioners. Such alliances are ideally transferable and open to the dissemination of innovation at local, regional, national and international levels. Such modes of knowledge production also lead to the transformation of institutions, wherein the learning process evolves according to a dynamic and non-linear path. Therefore, understanding the significance of knowledge production is crucial for understanding post-industrial social and economic development (Lundvall and Johnson 1994).

Social innovation is above all a process in which a set of actors collaborate to develop practices for solving specific types of problems (Klein and Harrisson 2007; Mulgan 2007). The process presupposes a common understanding about the social significance of the production of knowledge and ideas by the actors. It is generally initiated by a transfer of activities into concrete applications, and only then are the results thereof disseminated within an organization or a territory (Fontan et al. 2005; MacCallum et al. 2009). Although individual effort is by no means excluded or discouraged, creativity is seen largely as the outcome of interactions and collaboration of a heterogeneous ensemble of social actors. Social creativity is stimulated by the meeting and interaction of actors in a social environment that is open to diversity and sufficiently stable to guarantee the continuity of the efforts. This social creativity, at the root of social innovation, is understood as a complex cognitive process consisting of identifying problems, gathering information on phenomena, and conceptualizing and combining concepts (Mumford et al. 2003). However, reaching the level at which social creativity is actually generated relies on the contribution of many actors in the community as well as extensive research.

In that context, engaging in knowledge production through the social innovation approach is important for two main reasons. First, although knowledge production is generally driven by profit motives, it can also be advanced by other incentives. It can also contribute to the development of a more just and inclusive society through the implementation of values and practices that characterize collective action. Second, the social innovation process relies on the development of social capital created by people who circulate in many networks and who are willing to share their knowledge, influence and social links with the goal of finding original solutions to complex problems (Moulaert and Nussbaumer 2008). To innovate, the social actors must transform the modes of knowledge production imposed by neoliberalism so as to serve the public interest. Social innovation is thus a particular combination of production and interconnection of knowledge and information.

23.3   ACTION RESEARCH AND PARTNERSHIP-BASED COLLABORATION: TWO PILLARS OF PARTNERSHIP-BASED RESEARCH

Most mainstream-oriented methodologies view social-scientific research and analysis as occurring in either one of two constituent areas of activity – fundamental research or applied research – which are portrayed as separate entities. According to that perspective, fundamental research aims to create scientific knowledge on social or organizational processes and facts with the goal of establishing overriding principles and rules for their understanding and explanation. The objective here is to produce new knowledge, including the discovery of new relations between concepts, and to establish a framework for understanding new phenomena in order to

be able to predict results. Applied research, for its part, whether conducted for private capital, public agencies or social actors, seeks to understand a social or organizational problem in order to contribute to decision-making. In this type of research, concepts are mobilized for a utilitarian purpose. Researchers are supposed to adjust the theory to the stated problem and to try to gain access to the milieus experiencing and seeking to address the given problem.

Thus, the conventional, mainstream methodologies distinguish and compare two forms of research and impose a hierarchy according to which fundamental research ranks at the top and applied research as a secondary and residual form of the latter, and where both of these are exclusive of each other. The first type of research reserves the circulation of knowledge to academia, while the second orients knowledge production for the benefit of specific users, namely those who have paid for it. The authors of this chapter advocate the rethinking of this approach, with the view to a democratization of knowledge production. From that perspective, partnership-based research must be seen as the basis for a recomposition of these main scientific and social constituents of knowledge production. This recomposition rests on two pillars: one is a research method, namely action research, and the other an organizational form based on cooperation, namely partnership-based collaboration.

23.3.1   Action Research

Kurt Lewin (1948) was the first researcher who investigated action research in more depth. According to his 'collaboration model', collaboration in decision-making promotes change more than the passive participation of the actors in knowledge production. With this approach, actors directly affected by a problem can find solutions by becoming involved in the process of knowledge production. In the case of action research, a researcher collaborates with practitioners in the effort to change a situation and resolve a problem experienced in a milieu, community or organization, and to improve the understanding of the phenomena in question.

Action research is determined by social needs and builds on the systematic communication between a diversity of stakeholders (Bawden 1991). A division of labour exists among the latter, with the researchers being more preoccupied with research, the problematic, the methodology, the training of students and the dissemination of results, while the actors are more concerned with the possibility of changing a concrete predicament they face. However, both are engaged in the same research unit and process of knowledge production. The research is performed according to the standard practices and procedures of the research milieu and involves a review of scientific literature; the identification of the scientific problem; the development of the theoretical framework, the model and the appropriate methodology; and the dissemination of results in peer-reviewed scientific journals and within user networks. The possibility exists to pursue fundamental research while at the same time pursuing practical objectives, which generally respond to economic, political, cultural and social issues. In this dynamic, the two objectives/logics influence each other, comprising a combined process of action and theoretical analysis. The research takes shape and evolves through the interaction between the researchers and practitioners (Lavoie et al. 1996), and the results qualify as socially legitimate due to the fact that both parties, i.e., the researchers and the practitioners, play an active role in their production.

Action research does not distinguish itself for its information gathering techniques, which can be qualitative or quantitative. Rather, its specificity lies in its practical objective and the constant communication between researchers and practitioners. In short, action research is a process that integrates research and practice into a system of intervention. It is a comprehensive activity which breaks with the classic typology that draws a sharp line between fundamental research and applied research, as well as between researchers and users. The action research method is applied and above all systematized in partnership-based research, which is characterized by specific institutional arrangements In the following section we will describe and define partnership-based collaboration, the second pillar of partnership-based research.

23.3.2   Partnership-Based Collaboration

Partnership is the practice of inter-organizational collaboration, pursued with the assumption that problems are better resolved in a team than alone (Agranoff and McGuire 2003). A complex organizational form, it can be viewed as a network offering creative solutions to problems facing the organizational actors (Swan and Scarborough 2005). Its practice demands the continuous involvement of the actors, who are generally dealing with changing conditions and multiple sources of authority. Inter-organizational collaboration aims to resolve social problems more efficiently by building the capacities of organizations through the sharing and better use of resources, qualifications and knowledge (Hardy et al. 2003). The challenge here consists of ensuring that partner organizations respect the boundaries that are negotiated and discussed in a relationship built on cooperation (Tsasis 2009).

Partnership thus facilitates innovation by unravelling a problem on the basis of results co-produced by a variety of actors. Co-production, for its part, is a process by which the user is led to participate in the production of the service that she/he requests (Vaillancourt 2009). In partnership-based research, knowledge is likewise co-produced by the users, in this case practitioners and researchers.

Partnership is efficient if both parties see an advantage therein (Gazley 2010). This pragmatic perspective is influenced by the institutional context as well as by the stakeholders' interests, their mandates and expectations, and the traces left by former experiences, such as conflicts and efforts to build connections. Partnership is thus the result of a combination of forces that have incentive and normative influences. It contributes to collective and organizational learning, because the actors develop new capacities and a new sense of responsibility as well as an ability to frame and contextualize sources of uncertainty and conflict.

The goal of this vision of partnership-based research is to serve not market interests, but rather the collective interest through partnership-based agreements. In that context, social innovation holds a distinct place with regard to defending the general interest and the common good and to promoting modes of knowledge acquisition that are founded on solid alliances between researchers, universities, public sources of funding and civil society-based organizations working towards the same goal.

23.4 PARTNERSHIP-BASED RESEARCH AS A CREATIVE APPROACH

Partnership-based research is a creative approach based on a dynamic that matches a research method with an inter-organizational type of relationship (Hackney 1994). It adopts a specific modality of knowledge production in which the barriers between the researchers and actors are less pronounced, if not entirely eliminated. Adopting this approach involves a learning curve and a change of attitude, especially on the part of the researchers. The two parties work together in a research approach characterized by a synchronicity of knowledge production and knowledge transfer (Klein 2007). In a quasi-simultaneous process, the actors provide their organizations and projects with new knowledge immediately upon producing it. In this way, partnership-based research serves to accelerate the speed at which hypotheses are confirmed or refuted, initiating a dialectic process of research and action. Moreover it promotes the full exposure of knowledge, in turn allowing participants to co-produce new knowledge and to initiate actions for development (Bussières and Fontan 2003; Benson and Harkavy 2000). In this approach, academic research is assigned a role that is more complex as well as stronger. Contrary to fundamental research, conducted *on* or *about* actors and actions, and applied research, conducted *for* the actor, partnership-based research is conducted *with* the actor (Klein 2007).

23.4.1 The Bases of a New Approach

At the beginning of the 1970s, the innovative 'science shop' system was developed by student movements in the Low Countries (Netherlands, Belgium) with the goal of helping non-profit organizations meet scientific challenges. Eventually, the system gained recognition by Dutch universities and some European governments, which set up science shops that served to create links between civil society and scientific groups (European Commission 2003). The science shop system made its way beyond European borders, to countries such as Canada, Israel and the United States. At the interface of science and society, and applying ambitious and direct research approaches, the science shops thus contributed to channelling the focus of research organizations to the needs of the community. Under the impetus of the emerging knowledge society during the 1980s, universities then further developed this community approach from a new angle. Especially in the United States, activities between society and universities experienced a new vigour (Soska and Butterfield 2005; Vidal et al. 2002).

Hackney (1994) and Walshok (1995) introduced yet another new approach that seeks to coordinate and align the competencies of the university milieu with those of civil society organizations. Unlike former approaches, wherein academics, considered the experts, tended to discredit the importance of the more practical skills developed by social actors (Bussières and Fontan 2003), this new approach aims to match and combine the skill sets required for co-producing new knowledge in a perspective of political involvement, democratic change and social transformation (Benson and Harkavy 2000; Fontan 2008). The approach thus recognizes the importance of the knowledge held by the social actors and contends that a true understanding of social reality requires a combination of different types of knowledge and actors. The approach developed by Hackney and Walshok thus asserts that, to achieve the co-production of knowledge, a new research culture must be developed that will allow researchers and practitioners to bridge the cultural gaps that separate them.

23.4.2 The Québec Experience

The Québec experience is rooted to those various practices, albeit with some specificities. As Klein et al. show in Chapter 28, the role of the social actors and partnership-based research in Québec is linked to the expansion of the social economy and the organizations representing it (Sajnani and Mendell 2007). For half a century now, university researchers have contributed to building the Québec social economy, which has its origins in the 1960s, when models of knowledge exploration and production were developed by scholar-practitioners who linked academia with the cooperative sector. Since then, the collaboration between academia and the social economy in Québec has been characterized by two big waves (Fontan 2008). The first took place between 1960 and the 1980s and was distinguished by the active involvement of many academics in various social movements. During that time, researchers and practitioners also collaborated in the establishment of organizations and associations, many of which were to become long-standing, important institutions, stimulating the development of the collective economy. For instance, in 1970, the Université du Québec à Montréal created the *Service aux collectivités* (SAC), launched in partnership with unions, women's groups and community groups to give them access to university resources.

The second wave, from the end of the 1980s on, was characterized by government funding programs for new research structures at the federal and provincial levels. Research teams (1980s) and larger centres (1990s) were supported by the main funding agencies. The first public organization to finance the development of partnership research in human sciences was the *Fonds des services aux collectivités*, with the support of the *Ministère de l'Éducation du Québec*. It was in that context that the *Centre de recherche sur les innovations sociales* (CRISES) was founded[1] – the first Québec research centre with the mandate to focus on the social economy and to conduct research together with community-based stakeholders, namely social movements, not only to find solutions to their problems but also and above all for a better understanding of the society.

From the early 1990s on, in a spirit of the co-production of knowledge, the Québec society may count on a pole of excellence in partnership-based research (Fontan 2008). The research groups aligned with this research model comprise more than 250 Québec, Canadian and international researchers from multidisciplinary, inter-university, interregional and partnership-based organizations working on social innovation, social development and the social economy.

23.4.3 New Modes of Financing

In Canada and Québec, research in human and social sciences is mainly financed by public funds, which have been subject to major reforms over the last decade. New programs oriented towards partnership-based research were implemented, such as the *Alliance de recherche universités-communautés* (Community-University Research Alliances), a program created by the Social Sciences and Humanities Research Council of Canada (SSHRC), and the *Programme d'actions concertées*, set up by the *Fonds québécois de recherche sur la société et la culture* (FQRSC).

These programs reconcile the needs of researchers to carry out fundamental research with the demands placed on research from actors of the public, private and community sectors. In keeping with utilitarian principles, these programs

perform two evaluations: one concerns the social relevance, and is conducted by actors from the organizations participating in the program and who finance it in all or in part (multiple variants of this model exist); the other is a scientific evaluation and is conducted by peers according to standard, rigorous scientific conventions. The researchers must therefore develop design tools and research plans that comply with the expectations of both of these milieus. They must also develop a language and tools for disseminating results in ways that are appropriate for both the scientific and the socio-organizational milieus.

23.4.4 ARUC-ES: a Social Economy-Oriented Partnership Research Experience

The *Alliance de recherche universités-communautés en économie sociale* (ARUC-ES) is an example of a Québec partnership-based research experience. In operation from January 2000 to December 2010 and financed by the SSHRC, this project brought together a network of researchers and practitioners from different milieus of intervention involved in the development of the social economy in Québec. Its objectives were to support and advance research on the social economy, promote knowledge sharing between universities and the community, and produce knowledge that serves social development. Its network included four universities: Université du Québec à Montréal (UQÀM), Université du Québec en Outaouais (UQO), Université du Québec à Chicoutimi (UQAC) and Concordia University. More than 40 professors of these four universities were associated with ARUC-ES. Six principal partners as well as some 30 sectoral partners participated. The main partners were: the *Chantier de l'économie sociale*, the *Confédération des syndicats nationaux* (of Québec), the *Fédération des travail-*

leurs du Québec (FTQ), the labour funds *Fondaction* (CSN) and *Fonds de solidarité* (FTQ), founded by the workers' unions federations FTQ and CSN, and the *Réseau d'investissement social du Québec* (RISQ). The network was co-directed by a professor at UQAM and the head of the *Chantier de l'économie sociale* (an umbrella organization for social economy-oriented organizations in Québec).

The activities of ARUC-ES were carried out and coordinated by the following nine thematic committees, here referred to as Committees of Partnership Action (CPA): evaluation; financing; the service sector; community housing; recreation and social tourism; jobs and integration into the workforce; sustainable development; local and regional development; and exchanges and international comparisons. Each CPA was managed by and involved researchers as well as actors. The matching was done on the basis of the milieus of practice or fields of interest. Within these committees, the research, dissemination or transfer of projects then took place on the basis of the concerns that were defined jointly by the partners.

While the range of ARUC-ES activities was quite varied, to meet the needs identified in each CPA, their goals were complementary. Overall, the CPAs responded to a need for the improvement of knowledge and for the development of operational tools for organizations. Among these were:

- sectoral portraits of the new social economy;
- surveys on innovative practices for the financing of community housing projects;
- assessments of working conditions in social economy enterprises from the service sector;
- identification of operational practices and challenges to be met by

the environmental consultation committees;
- monitoring of civil society-led industrial conversion initiatives;
- international watch group activities on solidarity-based financing initiatives;
- organization of seminars on the dissemination and transfer of knowledge; and
- implementation of a distribution network for fair trade and social economy products.

The originality, dynamism and productivity of ARUC-ES were directly related to its mode of coordinating research, in which practitioners were given a place in the overall research process and researchers were given the chance to acquire practical knowledge and participate in social experiments. Overall, this action research framework allowed for the efficient dissemination and transfer of knowledge while ensuring a democratic management mode. For example, at ARUC-ES, activity contents, dissemination methods and budgets were decided and implemented collectively through diverse instances that gave equal representation to all parties involved (CPAs, coordination committee and the management committee).

Between 2000 and 2010, the research works of ARUC-ES involved 150 practitioners from the field, representing 100 organizations. Approximately 60 researchers and about 130 students of a dozen universities were mobilized. The alliance has conducted some 200 research projects, of which 150 are documented with research reports that are available online.[2] A networking newsletter informs the community of researchers and practitioners of the various achievements and results.

ARUC-ES also trained students in the process of partnership-based research, and many of these students then went on to write their master's theses or doctoral dissertations on projects submitted or proposed by actors from the social milieu. Some students even built their subsequent careers on the partnership-based research they conducted in the context of their involvement with ARUC-ES.

In sectoral and territorial terms, the research pursued by ARUC-ES allowed for a better understanding of what the social economy represents in Québec, both domestically and in relation to the rest of Canada, Europe and the United States. This was revealed, in particular, by means of comparisons with other economic sectors in Québec.

Overall, partnership-based research of ARUC-ES contributed considerably to the development of a broad political consensus, both in Québec and Canada as a whole, on the definition and pertinence of the social economy sector as a democratic development tool for society. The alliance's targeted research activities have strengthened the relational skills of the network of organizations and businesses of the social economy, which culminated in a 'regional social innovation system' (Klein et al. 2009) offering diverse types of services to social economy organizations and businesses.

The partnership-based research activities of ARUC-ES have also facilitated the encounter and mediation between different historical cultures of the social economy. This includes the establishment of a common language, the adoption of rules for collaboration, and the determination of conventions between practitioners. Moreover, a consortium of experts at ARUC-ES has been involved in building the identity of the overall movement of the new social economy.

Lastly, the research led by ARUC-ES has contributed to the formulation of new public policies. From 2000 to 2010, funding provided to sectoral or territorial social economy projects, together benefiting from an annual budget of C$1 billion, led to the development of some nine new public policies in Québec. In 2004, the federal government announced investments of C$100 million to support the development of social economy-based businesses at the Canadian scale. In 2008, the Québec government launched the *Plan d'action gouvernemental pour l'entrepreneuriat collectif* and, in 2009, the city of Montreal entered into the *Partenariat en économie sociale pour un développement solidaire et durable*.

The research experience from ARUC-ES clearly indicates that research results differ when practitioners are involved, for a number of reasons. For one, the concerns raised by a research project defined cojointly by academic researchers and practitioners are different from those developed only by academic researchers. Secondly, research questions that are defined cojointly are more likely to give rise to an overall conceptual framework of the research interests. Thus, the intersection of a diversity of concerns and points of view, together with a wide range of experiential knowledge, enrich and add value to scientific contributions. Thirdly, throughout the realization of the research activity, the dialogue between the researchers and practitioners allows both to validate how the data is processed, with regard to both its collection and its analysis. Finally, the involvement of practitioners adds a cultural dimension that is important for arriving at a meaningful interpretation of certain data or events. Partnership-based research teams, as places where different points of view are expressed, thereby comprise laboratories where cultural mediation and translation take place.

23.5 CONCLUSION

Partnership-based research offers many advantages. Encompassing a wide range of social actors from the economic, political, cultural and social sectors, the model offers a means for researchers to pursue fundamental research while responding to practical goals (Harrisson 2006). However, certain conditions must be met to ensure that this type of research is efficient in terms of (a) producing knowledge that is socially relevant and (b) guaranteeing the immediate effect of the production/transfer process. Importantly, these conditions also call for a sufficient level of trust between the academic and non-academic members of the research team. They also presuppose a flexible and open attitude to collective learning by the team members (Klein 2007).

Nevertheless, the utilitarian orientation of partnership-based research elicits reactions and concerns. Some researchers argue that a 'utilitarian and instrumental logic' of organizations poses a threat to the independence of research (Pelletier 2006). Care must therefore be taken that the research model does not compromise the rigour of the research process so as to favour the interests of one actor or one set of actors (Harrisson 2006). That is why the partnership-based research model only evolves if it is also part of an institutionalized development process that meets the expectations of those who collaborate in the realization of a project, be they the government, the university, associations or the community. In order to prevent undue instrumentalization of research, researchers must strive to maintain their academic freedom. Independence of thought and freedom of action are thus necessary components for a critical reflection on a research topic and a key condition of the success of partnership-based research.

Partnership-based research requires mutual respect, the refusal to subordinate the interests of one partner to those of another, and the development of a common project. Moreover, it requires rigour. Government intervention, through the new policies of the granting agencies, must also work to maintain research that is independent and autonomous from immediate political or economic concerns and resistant to any force that may pressure researchers to skew or interpret results in favour of certain interests. This explains the importance of the presence of a third party that ensures the rigour as well as the transparency of the research agreements. Bolstered with such government support, partnership-based research can engage in a research process that, as shown by the ARUC-ES case, has proven relevance and suitability for the development of scientific knowledge and is considered legitimate and meaningful by academia and practice alike. This research approach is consistent with the practice of social innovation, wherein citizens participate in finding solutions to problems in a spirit of co-construction with other social actors who hold power (Vaillancourt 2009). Partnership-based research is thus a novel way of conceiving social action.

23.6 QUESTIONS FOR DISCUSSION

- Under what conditions is it possible to produce partnership-based research outcomes that are relevant for academics as well as for community?
- The co-construction of knowledge, can it favour a better understanding of social issues and a more innovating society?
- How important is it for social innovation to produce scientific

knowledge on the basis of a partnership-based research design?

● How to assure that knowledge produced on the basis of partnership-based research is as valuable as knowledge generated by a conventional research process?

NOTES

1. CRISES: http://www.crises.uqam.ca/ (last accessed 17 December 2012).
2. See: http://www.aruc-es.uqam.ca/ (last accessed 17 December 2012).

REFERENCES

(References in bold are recommended reading.)

Agranoff, R. and M. McGuire (2003), *Collaborative Public Management: New Strategies for Local Governments*, Washington, DC: Georgetown University Press.
Bawden, R. (1991), 'Towards action research systems', in O. Zuber-Skerritt (ed.), *Action Research for Change and Development*, Aldershot: Avebury, pp. 10–35.
Benson, L. and I. Harkavy (2000), 'Higher education's third revolution: The emergence of the democratic cosmopolitan civic university', *Cityscape, A Journal of Policy Development and Research*, **5** (1), 47–57.
Bussières, D. and J.M. Fontan, (2003), 'L'expérience de recherche de l'Alliance de recherche universités-communautés en économie sociale', *Interventions économiques*, **1** (32), www.teluq.uquebec.ca/interventionseconomiques (last accessed 17 December 2012).
Castel, R. (2008), 'La citoyenneté sociale menacée', *Cités*, **35**, 133–141.
Etzkowitz, H. and L. Leydesdorff (1997), *Universities in the Global Economy: A Triple Helix of University-Industry-Government Relations*, London: Cassell Academic.
European Commission (2003), *Science Shops – Knowledge for the Community*, Luxembourg: Office for Official Publications of the European Communities.
Fontan, J.M. (2008), 'Innovation sociale et territorialité', in G. Massicotte (ed.), *Sciences du territoire, perspectives québécoises*, Québec: Presses de l'Université du Québec, pp. 137–161.
Fontan, J.-M., J.-L. Klein and D.-G. Tremblay

(2005), *Innovation socioterritoriale et reconversion économique: le cas de Montréal*, Paris: L'Harmattan.
Foray, D. (2000), *L'économie de la connaissance*, Paris: La Découverte.
Gazley, B. (2010), 'Why not partner with local government? Non-profit managerial perceptions of collaborative disadvantage', *Non-Profit and Voluntary Sector Quarterly*, **39** (1), 51–76.
Gibbons, M., C. Limoges, H. Nowotny, J. Schwartzman, P. Scott and M. Trow (1994), *The New Production of Knowledge. The Dynamics of Science and Research in Contemporary Society*, London Thousands Oaks and New Delhi: Sage Publications.
Hackney, S. (1994), 'Reinventing the American university: Toward a university system for the 21 century', *Universities and Community Schools*, **4** (1–2), 9–11.
Hardy, C., N. Philips and T. Lawrence (2003), 'Resources, knowledge and influence: the organizational effects of interorganizational collaboration', *Journal of Management Studies*, **40** (2), 321–347.
Harrisson, D. (2006), 'La recherche partenariale: pour concilier la recherche universitaire et les besoins des organisations et des collectivités', paper presented at the conference: Intervenir dans le monde du travail: la responsabilité sociale d'un centre de recherche en science humaines, Lentic, Belgium.
Klein, J.-L. (2007), 'La recherche-action en développement local: possibilités et contraintes', in M. Anadon (ed.), *La recherche participative*, Québec: Presses de l'Université du Québec, pp. 31–45.
Klein, J.-L. and D. Harrisson, (eds) (2007), *L'innovation sociale. Émergence et effets sur la transformation des sociétés*, Québec: Presses de l'Université du Québec.
Klein, J.-L., J.-M. Fontan, D. Harrisson and B. Lévesque (2009), *L'innovation sociale au Québec: un système d'innovation fondé sur la concertation*, Montreal: Cahier du CRISES ET0907, http://www.crises.uqam.ca/publications/etudes-theoriques.html (last accessed 17 December 2012).
Lavoie, L., D. Marquis and P. Laurin (1996), *La recherche-action: théorie et pratique*, Québec: Presses de l'Université du Québec.
Lewin, K. (ed.) (1948), *Resolving Social Conflicts: Selected Papers on Group Dynamic*, New York: Harper and Row.
Lundvall, B.-Å. (2002), *Innovation, growth and social cohesion: The Danish Model*, London: Elgar Publishers.
Lundvall, B.-Å. and B. Johnson (1994), 'The learning economy', *Journal of Industry Studies*, **1** (2), 23–42.
MacCallum, D., F. Moulaert, J. Hillier and S. Vicari Haddock (eds) (2009), *Social Innovation and Territorial Development*, Aldershot: Ashgate.
Moulaert, F. and J. Nussbaumer (2008), *La logique*

sociale du développement territorial, Québec: Presses de l'Université du Québec.

Mulgan, G. (2006), 'The process of innovation', *Innovations*, Spring, 145–162.

Mumford, M.D., W.A. Baughman and C.E. Sager (2003), 'Picking the right material: Cognitive processing skills and the role of creative thought' in M.A. Runco (ed.), *Critical and Creative Thinking*, **Creskill, NJ: Hampton, pp. 19–68.**

Pelletier, J. (2006), 'L'université: intellectuel collectif ou entreprise?', *Analyses et discussion*, **8**, 1–6.

Sajnani, N. and M. Mendell (2007), 'La recherche partenariale: le cas de l'ARUC en économie sociale', *Organisations et Territoires*, **16** (1), 115–122.

Soska, T.M and A.K. Johnson Butterfield (2005), *University-Community Partnerships. Universities in Civic Engagement*, Binghamton: Haworth.

Swan, J. and H. Scarbrough (2005), 'The politics of networked innovation', *Human Relations*, **58** (7), 913–943.

Tsasis, P. (2009), 'The Social processes of interor-ganizational collaboration and conflict in non-profit organizations', *Non-Profit Management and Leadership*, **20** (1), 5–21.

Vaillancourt, Y. (2009), 'Social economy in the co-construction of public policy', *Annals of Public and Cooperative Economics*, **80 (2), 275–313.**

Vidal, A., N. Nye, C. Walker, C. Manjarrez and C. Romanik (2002), *Lessons from the Community Outreach Partnership Center Programme*, Washington: The Urban Institute, www.oup.org/files/pubs/lessons_learned.pdf (last Accessed 28 July 2011).

Walshok, M.L. (1995), *Knowledge Without Boundaries*, San Francisco: Jossey-Bass.

Wiewel, W. and D. Broski (1997), *University Involvement in the Community. Developing a Partnership Model*, **Great Cities Institute Working Papers, GCP-97-3, Chicago: University of Illinois at Chicago, http://www.qub.ac.uk/ep/research/cu2/data/bib_wiewel-broski_university-involvement.pdf (last accessed 28 July 2010).**

24. Social innovation in public elder care: the role of action research
John Andersen and Annette Bilfeldt[1]

24.1 INTRODUCTION

This chapter addresses the role of action research in social innovation related to elder care work at public nursing homes in Denmark. The case is part of a development project based on the principles of critical utopian action research (CUAR), a distinct type of knowledge creation which is appropriate to social innovation because of the way it improves social relations between participants, contributes to the empowerment of weaker participants, and builds knowledge essential to improving their quality of life and sense of cooperation. The chapter shows how critical utopian action research can contribute to changing a negative spiral of increasing inhumanity in elder care, and to developing practical and collective utopias to improve human social relations for both residents and employees. Utopian action research has the potential to challenge the dominant neo-bureaucratic and (quasi) market oriented modes of work organization models and governance currently dominant in elder care.

The chapter starts with an introduction to action research and a brief outline of some of the historical roots of action research in Europe including its origins in critical theory. Thereafter we describe the concrete methodology of CUAR (e.g. the use of future workshops) and how it was employed at the nursing home. We then present the experiences gained and some of the concrete outcomes. Finally we discuss how CUAR can be applied at other workplaces, what its contribution to social innovation in elder care is and how CUAR can be diffused and qualified in broader governance networks.

24.2 WHAT IS ACTION RESEARCH?

Action research is an umbrella term for research based on democratic and inclusive values where 'democratically developed knowledge' contributes actively to socially innovative, collective actions. Action research is characterized by researchers and practitioners joining in promoting democratic and social changes in 'a shared commitment to democratic social change' (Brydon-Miller 2003, p. 8). Basically, action research contributes to empowerment processes. It tries to link three aspects of theory and practice: 1) critical societal diagnosis; (2) democratic knowledge building from the bottom up; and (3) the facilitation of processes of long-term social innovation.

Action researchers see themselves as *co-producers* of knowledge with social actors based on trust and free agreement to participate. Together with the participating citizens, practitioners, users or stakeholders, action researchers should define the research questions and the agenda for collective action based on the participants' needs, experiences and visions (Reason and Bradbury 2008). Thus optimal knowledge creation is generated through shared learning cycles of problem definition, design and implementation of strategies for social change (Nielsen and Svensson 2006a; compare with Miciukiewicz et al. 2012).

Action research is not a fixed method or a collection of principles, theories and methods (see also Arthur, Chapter 25), but should be understood as a research *perspective* in which research should support collective action and social innovation while at the same time producing new knowledge (Reason and Bradbury 2008). In this respect action research has some affinity with the sociology of knowledge perspective on social innovation (see Moulaert and Van Dyck, Chapter 35). In the following we shall develop this line of thought in greater detail in relation to the CUAR tradition.

24.3 ROOTS OF CRITICAL UTOPIAN ACTION RESEARCH

The roots of critical utopian action research go back to Kurt Lewin (1890–1947), who is considered one of the founding fathers of action research in Europe and the US. Lewin was one of the many critical intellectuals who went into exile in the US to escape the German Nazi regime. His main research objective was to develop 'democratic forms of organization' and cultures. The human experience with authoritative systems made democracy a concept which according to Lewin should not be taken for granted, but a practice to be learned. He was inspired by critical theorists like Horkheimer and Adorno (the Frankfurt School), who argued, in opposition to traditional, particularly positivist social science, that '*what is*' should be understood in the light of a 'classical utopian idea of a un-reified society articulated in the Philosophy of Enlightenment'

(Nielsen and Nielsen 2006, p. 77). Critical theory insists upon the need to deconstruct 'frozen reality' and culture by means of historical utopian categories (Nielsen and Nielsen 2006, p. 83).

Critical theory can be considered as an advocate for a critique of unjust and reified social structures. In CUAR this critique is supplemented by the creation of proposals and the construction of new democratic common structures in society (Nielsen and Nielsen 2006, p. 84), a concern which underlines the importance of practical social innovation by linking the production of knowledge with social change: 'The best way to understand things is to change them . . .' (Lewin 1946, p.22).

An important theoretical inspiration for the CUAR tradition derives from Ernst Bloch's (1985) approach in which history is about 'utopian flows' and Marcuse's (1941) concept of 'reality power', which focuses on how the horizons of human possibilities and social imagination are restricted by the 'reality power' of every day practice and routines. For CUAR, developing utopian flows is an essential tool for overcoming the 'reality power' of everyday practice and for changing reality.[2] Further inspiration came from the American sociologist C. Wright Mills' manifesto *The Sociological Imagination* (1958), in which it is argued that social science should be able to link everyday troubles with societal issues.

One of the concrete methodologies developed by Robert Jungk at a later stage for overcoming 'reality power' was *Future Creating Workshops*, a practical methodological tool for socially innovative experimentations. (Jungk and Müllert 1987). The Future Creating Workshop – or 'future workshop' as it has come to be known – is an arena for the development and concretization of utopian ideas in terms of action and an important instrument used in CUAR (as will be explained later).

Paulo Freire's (see also Novy et al., Chapter 32) concept of empowerment as the ability to 'understand social, political and economic contradictions and the ability to act against the oppressing elements of reality' (Freire 1974, p. 19) is closely connected to CUAR. Paulo Freire's classic *Pedagogy of the Oppressed* spread the concept of empowerment throughout the world. In line with Freire's thought, empowerment can be defined as processes through which social groups improve their ability to create, manage and control material, social, cultural and symbolic resources (Andersen and Siim 2004). Critical utopian action research contributes to empowerment processes. Firstly, it fosters horizontal empowerment, strengthening trust, commitment and networks between different groups at the workplace (e.g. employees and residents at a nursing home). Secondly it concerns vertical empowerment, strengthening power and the possibilities of multilevel influence outwards and upwards, e.g. in relation to power centres outside the workplace, including governmental policies. Successful action research implies robust empowerment which often results from a mix of horizontal and vertical empowerment processes and become mutually strengthened over time (Andersen 2005).

24.4   THE WORKPLACE AS CONTEXT FOR CUAR

The Australian action researcher Stephen Kemmis further strengthens the links between action research and critical theory. To this purpose he employs a concept of praxis that is divided between (1) 'practice' based on ingrained path dependent habits and behaviour (much in line with Bourdieu's concept of habitus); and (2) the social, reflexive and collective morally obliging 'praxis' which can arise as a result of critical and self-critical reflection and dialogue (e.g. within the critical action research process). Kemmis argues that the aim of action research is to reframe 'practice' so that it becomes 'praxis' (Kemmis 2008, p. 123).

Action research in working life gives the participants an opportunity to increase their understanding of their own practice – the individual and collective practice as well as the structural conditions of this practice. Through cooperation with the researchers, employees gain a twofold perspective on work related practice – an insider experience-based perspective which has its origins in their own and their colleagues' work experiences, and an outsider perspective added by the researchers' participation, e.g. as workshop leaders, process facilitators and research knowledge communicators. The process in CUAR projects where practice becomes praxis can be a useful step to social innovation.

24.5   THE FUTURE WORKSHOP METHODOLOGY

As explained above, the future workshop is an important instrument of CUAR. Within the future workshop, local stakeholders, citizens and workers are the driving forces in the production of future visions, actions and scenario building. It makes use of specific rules of communication in order to minimize the influence of power relations within the group, and it applies specific rules of visualization and creativity (Drewes Nielsen 2006).

The methodology of the future workshop gives the opportunity to 'think outside the box': to develop utopias that are not limited by the everyday comprehension of what actually can be done. A future workshop is organized with plenum and group sessions. The participants' statements are presented and commented upon by using posters. The researchers' role in the future workshop is to act as facilitators and referents (Jungk and Müllert 1987). A future workshop has three phases (here illustrated with examples from public elder care).

The first is the *critique phase* which asks the question: what's wrong? It involves a brainstorming session aimed at producing critical statements. All critical statements about, in this case, public eldercare are listed, for instance poor working conditions for the employees (daily stress and lack of time), life quality problems, and social isolation of the residents The facilitator finally summarizes prioritized themes, and the participants vote about which of the critical statements are the most important.

Thereafter follows the **utopian phase** which asks the question: where would we like to go? The participants are asked to imagine a perfect nursing home, where everything is possible (for instance about more time and less stress for the employees, better life quality and social activities for the residents). The utopian dreams and visions are listed on posters and commented on. As in the critique phase, the themes are prioritized through voting, in order to find out which utopias about the ideal nursing home and good care should be developed in utopia groups.

Finally, the *realization phase* asks the question: we keep our dreams – but ask how can they become reality? First the participants are organized in working groups which are given the task of developing the utopian ideas gained from the former phase and make them into concrete proposals, which are critically commented upon and further developed in a plenary meeting. Second, the groups make agreements about plans of concrete implementation for the future.

The concrete outcome is a written protocol of 'utopian sketches' and a plan of action, to which participants have committed themselves to work with in the future. This writing process is facilitated by the team of action researchers. Following that, more concrete plans for social experimentation can be further developed by the employees in dialogue with the residents, their relatives, other colleagues and the leader in order to be implemented by the leader, the local authorities and the employees.

Importantly in the CUAR methodology the researcher has an obligation to keep a focus on a democratic interest that goes beyond narrow group interests:

> first of all, the researcher has to support the awareness of the emerging *common* – general and universal – dimensions of the proposals and sketches, thus encouraging a break with the dominant narrow interest groups perspectives. Such a break is, at the same time, a precondition for and a result of *social* imagination. (Nielsen and Nielsen 2006, p. 83)

24.6 THE QUALITY IN ELDER CARE PROJECT

The project 'Quality in Elder Care' (QEC) initiated in 2008 and carried out in 2009/10 was a joint project between university action researchers (Roskilde University and The Technical University of Denmark) and the Union for Public Employees (FOA, *Fag og Arbejde*). The context for the project was an increasingly negative discourse in the public media about neglect in elder care. Scandals were reported in the media, which included cases where the employees were accused of incompetence and inhumane care practices. The wider political context for these 'care scandals' was that during the last two decades the public social services and the health sector in Denmark has been increasingly subject to the implementation of different types of quality control systems and strict budget control under the flag of New Public Management (NPM) (Hjort 2009). This control regime is based on standardized measurements in which self-determination of the residents and social relations of care are not valued (High and Rowles 1995; Eliasson-Lappalainen and Motevasel 1997; Szebehely 2005; see also Lévesque, Chapter 2). Against this background, FOA urged their members to raise a public debate about progressive alternatives to the NPM regime and the lack of resources in elder care (Andersen and Bilfeldt 2010). To this end, the QEC project was initiated.

In this project, the CUAR methodology was applied in a public Copenhagen nursing home, where it involved dialogues and interviews with employees, residents, relatives, elder organizations and the municipal Elder Council. From the beginning it was an important challenge to keep the focus on the integration of both the employees *and* residents' needs and perspectives displaying an awareness of the elderly residents' relative lack of power. Hence there was particular concern to give the residents voice by interviewing them about their opinions during every phase of the project and by involving their organizational representatives throughout the project.

Before starting the QEC project, six months was dedicated to preparing, planning and fine-tuning the process plan. The researchers had meetings with Union representatives, the leader of the nursing home, the shop steward and represent-atives of the employees in the nursing home. This was followed by stage 1 which involved group interviews with employees and the creation of a problem catalogue. Stage 2 consisted of a future workshop (as described above) and meetings with the residents and others. Stage 3 of the project (four months) was improving and fine-tuning the suggestions at a network conference. We now discuss the project in greater detail.

24.6.1   Stage 1

In the group interviews, the employees expressed strong feelings about stress and work overload. The employees stated that they felt trapped between the needs of the residents and lack of resources. For instance, they felt personally responsible for having failed to take notice of residents with dementia leaving the nursing home and going into the streets in the evenings. The new quality standards (part of the NPM) which were based solely on the physical abilities of the residents were not consistent with the employees' ideas of quality of care. They felt that they had to rush the residents and that they did not have sufficient time to interact and empathize with them.

Based on the group interviews, the researchers developed a 'problem catalogue' about the problem fields that had been emphasized by the employees in the interviews. The employees read and made amendments to the problem catalogue and presented it to the residents who then added their comments. Residents said that they felt isolated especially in the afternoons when no activities took place. They were dissatisfied because the employees very seldom took time to talk with them. Some of the residents said that they were not asked about their needs, they wanted more influence on the nursing home and over their own daily lives. For instance, they claimed that lunch was served on their plates without them being asked which food they wanted from the choice available.

The outcome of stage 1 was the identification of a number of problems: lack of resources, employee stress, inadequate care giving, a lack of real dialogue between employees and elderly, the residents feeling isolated, and a lack of influence on the nursing home.

24.6.2 Stage 2

Stage 2 started with a two-day future workshop following the three phases described above (a critique phase, a utopian phase and a realization phase). Based on the group interviews, the researchers were able to begin the critique phase of the future workshop using themes from the problem catalogue and from the residents' comments.

As a kick starter to the critique phase the researchers/facilitators listed all the problems mentioned by employees from the problem catalogue and the residents' comments on large sheets of paper hung on the walls. Thereafter the employees supplemented and developed the critical themes with more examples and perspectives. Additional points included, for instance, having colleagues on sick leave without getting substitutes made them feel as though they were working against time. The critique phase in the future workshop opened a new communicative space by making it possible to collectively criticize the conditions for the care work instead of feeding feelings of personal inadequacy and individually handling the ambivalences between time pressure and care needs of the residents.

In the utopian phase, a number of 'utopias' were developed to improve the quality of care; these included new ways of communicating with the residents, regular meetings with the residents and suggestions for involving them in the solution of problems and decisions at the nursing home. In the future workshop, the most significant utopia concerned a plan for the reconstruction of the home with a new living room. This idea originated from the interviews with the residents about feeling bored and isolated in the afternoons, observations of the everyday practice of the residents 'bunching together' in the hall around the lift. Another utopia was developed about a physical/spatial reconstruction of the nursing home in order to host gatherings, informal communication and more social activities. The purpose was to encourage spontaneous socializing among the residents and the employees by redesigning the architectural framework. Other outcomes included the reinvention of the social dimensions of care (for instance informal talk), cooperation between residents and employees such as making solutions in common about everyday problems at the nursing home, and the inclusion of residents in decision making about organizational development.

In the realization phase of the future workshop, task forces were formed. The groups' mandates were to present the ideas to the management and to develop them in more detail together with the residents and their relatives. After the future workshop, meetings were held with the management, staff, trade union representatives and residents, at which the employees presented their utopias and suggestions and received responses. The suggestions discussed included: renewing communication with the residents; involvement of the residents in decision making; spatial reconstruction of the building; social activities; improving social dimensions of the care; cooperation with residents about solutions to problems; inclusion of the residents in organizational development.

24.6.3   Stage 3

This stage of the project concentrated on improving the suggestions made in the future workshop. Initially a two-day network conference was held within working hours. The network conference is a methodological framework for a cooperative knowledge creation process. The participants at the network conference were the employees who had joined the future workshop, the management from the nursing home, invited employees from other retirement homes and invited experts, including representatives from elder organizations and the municipal elder council, union representatives, elder care researchers and working life researchers. At the conference the participants collaborated in thematic groups and plenary meetings in order to qualify the suggestions and innovation initiatives from the future workshops (Nielsen and Nielsen 2006; Drewes Nielsen 2006).

The conference started with the employees presenting their suggestions emerging from the future workshop. For example, the living room utopia group presented the developed idea: the new living room should be relocated and transformed into a 'town square' where the residents could talk to people passing through to take the lift, greet relatives visiting the home, and have continuous contact with the employees who, whilst undertaking their work, passed the 'town square' several times a day. The residents would gather at the 'town square' instead of spending time in the current living room. By doing this, the possibility for spontaneous social interaction would be promoted. Following the presentations, the external participants asked questions concerning clarifications and raising doubts about the utopias and action suggestions.

The researchers also contributed to the network conference, by presenting research-based knowledge about, for example, stress and control tools in the public sector. One researcher was invited to speak about power structures in elder care. He introduced the theme of how the rules and regulations of the institution can limit the residents' life quality and self-determination. (e.g. inflexibility to spontaneous wishes of the residents to come home late or to make spur-of-the-moment invitations for visitors to come and eat or sleep overnight). This started a discussion amongst the employees about being aware of the power structures of the nursing home. An employee concluded the discussion by stating: 'We must not hide behind the rules, we have to find out how we can meet the wishes of the residents – even if it means that we have to "bend" a rule now and then'. The representatives from the elder municipal council introduced themes about the residents being included in dialogues about care quality. An employee argued for the importance of understanding: 'Every resident can give his opinion about what he wants, but it requires that the employees take the time to ask [questions] and to listen to the answers.'

Another important input at the network conference came from a group of employees who had visited Hyllie Park Äldreboende, which is a pioneering nursing home in Sweden.[3] The home is famous for taking the elderly people's needs and views into consideration. A group of employees spoke about the impressions they had gained from the visit, which had made them become aware of the fact that the residents are living at a work place.

24.7   WHAT WAS THE OUTCOME OF THE CUAR PROCESS? THE IMPLEMENTATION OF THE NEGOTIATED SUGGESTIONS

In order to involve the residents in decisions about daily life at the nursing home, the employees decided to arrange a monthly meeting in each apartment at the nursing home with residents, employees and relatives eating together in order to frame a continuous dialogue about everyday life at the nursing home. Taking their inspiration from the visit to Sweden, the management decided to put the theme about 'how to change the nursing home to be a private home for elderly people rather than to be a working place for the employees?' on the agenda of the monthly meeting for residents, relatives and employees. Some concrete outcomes from these meetings included:

- One of the first meetings resulted in the residents developing new strategies for preventing residents with dementia from leaving the nursing home. One idea was to cover the lift button with a piece of paper, as the residents had noticed that those with dementia could not work out how to press a button that was not visible (only residents without dementia attended these meetings).
- Another move was to have residents represented at the staff recruitment meetings. This turned out to be a good idea because the residents looked for other qualities than the employees and the director. For the residents it was important that the care worker was polite (shook hands, and maintained eye contact with the residents during the meeting) and honestly interested in the residents.
- The residents' criticisms about how

food was served on their plates also led to change. It was decided that the employees should begin a praxis of always asking the residents about what they wanted to eat. The motto was: even the weakest resident can express what he wants to eat if the employees take time to ask and to listen. Furthermore the new praxis proved to be just as fast as the previous way of serving food.

- The living room was painted as the first step to redesigning it. The tables were moved together and lamps were purchased to help replicate the architectural character of the town square. The 'town square' idea replaced an earlier renovation plan that had been developed by the director and the local municipality, had not involved residents and employees and had consequently overlooked the nature of social life in the home (Andersen et al. 2012).

24.7.1   Empowerment Perspectives: From Practice to Praxis

The living room utopia is a manifestation of the employees' increasing empathy for the needs of the residents, an example of the way that the QEC project contributed to the movement to transform their ingrained, path-dependent, habitual 'practice' into a more social, reflexive and collective morally obliging 'praxis', along the lines proposed by Kemmis (2008). The practical and needs based knowledge which the employees had gained through their daily work and interviews with the residents, as well as their reflection about the residents' needs for social interaction, was the point of departure for changing the interior design and the location of the common space. The employees and residents were empowered to contribute to decisions within the nursing home, and had a huge influence on the home's interior design. This suggestion could only be implemented because the employees focused on quality more than routine, thus challenging and disrupting the trend to specialization and standardization of daily work tasks in the new public management regime.

The living room opened up the possibility for the employees to sit down for a while and have a talk with the residents without spending too much time doing so, thus framing an informal dialogue between residents and employees. A new praxis of informal social interaction replaced the former organized social interaction that only took place at times dedicated to social activity; this better met the needs of the residents for everyday forms of social contact. From the horizontal empowerment perspective, it was about the employees being able to gather their practical knowledge from observations and interviews with residents and transforming this knowledge into a new vision and a proposal for change. From the vertical empowerment perspective (upwards and outwards), the living room example was about the proposal reaching management and the local planning authorities and was actually used as the basis for an architectural redesign of the nursing home.

Thus, the employees' experiences of elder care work, the interviews with the residents and the debate on the network conference had made the employees become more aware about integrating the residents' perspective, transforming daily practice to reflective praxis. At the same time, it enabled a form of social innovation.

The critical utopian action research approach and experiences holds many lessons for improving the relationship between shared knowledge creation and social innovation. The improvements

through CUAR in the understanding of unequal power relations, the role of conflicts of interest and how they can be overcome through democratic voice giving are also critical elements in a social innovation process.

The work on the production of concrete utopias in a context like a nursing home, where the stakeholders (residents, relatives, staff and management) have very unequal resources and powerbases is not without problems. Some of the spontaneous 'utopias' put forward by employees turned out to be 'dystopias', containing elements that had no connection to better the needs of the residents. An example of this is a 'utopia' about 'helping' the residents go to bed at half past eight in the evenings in order to prevent the night watch colleagues from being too busy. Hence an important part of the process in the future workshops is to criticize and eliminate suggestions which might be implemented only at the expense of the residents' empowerment and self-determination.

This underlines the importance of facilitating the voice and interests of the elderly residents in the process, and that the suggestions developed in the action research processes were communicated and discussed with residents and their organizations. Thus the participants at the QEC project became more sensitive to including the views of others. A precondition for sustainable improvement of working life quality at nursing homes is a focus on the common interests between residents and employees when bettering the everyday lives of the residents. This places a demand on the researchers to make sure that all actors in the field have a legitimate voice in the development process. Even though the CUAR is no guarantee against twists of power, interviews and dialogues with the residents and the network conference are concrete methodologies to reduce the risk of reproducing unequal power relations between employees and residents and give a voice to all stakeholders (Gaventa and Cornwall 2008).

Within the QEC project, this testing of new ideas basically meant two things. First, it is about managing scarcity in a creative, solidarity way. The QEC project could neither offer more economic resources to the nursing home nor increase the number of employees. But as the conditions were thematized collectively, this empowered the employees to be better at dealing with situations collectively. Instead of blaming themselves individually, and sticking to a catch 22 position – running faster, getting more stressed, rushing and disempowering the residents – they had started socially innovative praxis initiatives to support the social life and empowerment of the residents while improving slightly their own working conditions.

Thus, action research design can contribute to the development of practical visions, the implementation of change strategies over which both employees and residents have ownership. For the researcher, action research can make practice-related contributions to a critical diagnosis of society: what is the reality and everyday life in, for example, the elder care sector? Furthermore, action research can also develop knowledge on how social changes can be designed and implemented. Researchers' participation in sustained change processes – from the identification of problems and vision development to the mobilization of change agents and handling of barriers and conflicts along the way – offers unique possibilities to develop knowledge on innovative processes and what inhibits and encourages the possibility for better quality in the care sector.

24.8 CONCLUSION

In this chapter we have argued that action research can contribute to social innovation in care work. We have described the process, the methodology and some of the results of a Quality in Elder Care project at a nursing home. In a context of scarce resources and (re)bureaucratization of public service institutions, it is vitally important to counteract a negative spiral of individualization and disempowerment. In the future workshop methodology, the first step was to 'collectivize' the frustration and critique at the workplace. The second step was to articulate and develop visions for alternatives and the third step was to try to fine tune and implement changes.

The QEC case demonstrates how researchers can engage with employees, residents and representatives from elder organizations in democratic bottom-up processes. Such processes can create socially innovative alternatives for bettering the life quality of the residents, as well as challenging the principles of the neo-bureaucratic new public management regime (NPM) which currently dominates social services/public sector.

The case shows that action research can be an important tool for empowerment by creating democratic and empowering platforms in public institutions such as nursing homes and, through the participative process which it involves, can be helpful in convincing management to see action research as a relevant and legitimate way of developing the quality of life of the residents as well as of developing the organizational frame of care giving.

One of the ways to encourage a more systematic link between (1) capacity building, the development of good practices and action research in work places (nursing home work places) and (2) a societal perspective, could be by making action research a *direct part of training programs* for employees and shop stewards in the public sector. Action research in, for example, the nursing home sector could be an important contribution to life-long learning programs from a democratic and change-oriented perspective. Unions and forward-looking managers could play an important role in developing practical models for the utilization of action research experiences in future training programs. This could be one of the democratic answers to the NPM wave in the public nursing home sector which is reaching a crisis point.

24.9   QUESTIONS FOR DISCUSSION

● Can you identify any other examples of how action researchers can work with trade unions to contribute to social innovation in public services?
● How can 'clients'/citizens depending on public elderly care (or other social services) get a voice to express and articulate their needs and take part in social innovation?
● How important do you think alliances between employees and 'clients'/citizens (e.g. the elderly at nursing homes) are to success in the search for better welfare and social rights?

NOTES

1. This chapter is dedicated to the Danish action researcher, Professor Kurt Aagaard Nielsen, Roskilde University, who died in April 2012. Kurt Aagaard Nielsen has been a huge source of inspiration for a lot of intellectuals for the development and implementation of action research in Denmark and Scandinavia. He was one of the driving forces in establishing the Center of Action Research at Roskilde University.
2. CUAR was also theoretically inspired by the

concept of 'proletarian public sphere', developed by the German sociologist Oscar Negt.
3. See www.hylliepark.se (last accessed 17 December 2012).

REFERENCES

(References in bold are recommended reading.)

Andersen, John (2005), 'Empowermentperspektivet – vejen frem for kritisk handlingsorienteret socialfor-skning?' *Tidsskriftet Social Kritik*, **15** (101), 60–76.
Andersen, John and Birthe Siim (eds) (2004), *Politics of inclusion and empowerment – gender, class and citizenship*, Houndsmills: Palgrave.
Andersen, J. and A. Bilfeldt (2010), 'Aktionsforskning på plejehjem – et al.ternativ til new public management?' *Tidsskrift for Arbejdsliv*, **11** (1), 67–82.
Andersen, J., A. Bilfeldt and M. Soegaard Joergensen (2012), 'Det urbane plejehjem – empowerment-planlægning i praksis', in John Andersen, Malene Freudendal-Pedersen, Lasse Koefoed and Jonas Larsen (eds) *Byen I bevægelse, Mobilitet – Politik – Performativitet*, Frederiksberg: Roskilde Universitetsforlag, pp. 96–115.
Bloch, Ernst (1985), *Das Prinzip Hoffnung*, Frankfurt: Suhrkamp.
Brydon-Miller, Mary (2003), 'Why Action Research?', *Action Research*, **1** (1), 9–28.
Drewes Nielsen, Lise (2006), 'The Methods and Implication of Action Research', in Kurt Aagaard Nielsen and Lennart G. Svensson (eds), pp. 89–117.
Eliasson-Lappalainen, Rosmari and Nilsson Motevasel (1997), 'Ethics of Care and Social Policy', *Scandinavian Journal of Social Welfare*, 6 (3), 189–106.
Freire, Paulo (1974), *Pedagogy of the Oppressed*, New York: Continuum.
Gaventa, John and Andrea Cornwall (2008), 'Power and Knowledge', in Peter Reason and Hilary Bradbury (eds), *Handbook of Action Research*, London: Sage Publications, 2nd edition, pp. 172–189.
High, Dallas. M. and Graham D. Rowles (1995), 'Nursing Home Residents, Families and Decision Making: Toward an Understanding of Progressive Surrogacy', *Journal of Aging Studies*, **9** (2),101–117.
Hjort, Katrin (2009), 'Competence and Development in the Public Sector: Development or Dismantling of Professionalism?', in Knud Illeris (ed.), *International perspectives on Competence Development. Developing Skills and Capabilities*, London: Routledge, pp.112–124.
Jungk, Robert and Norbert R. Müllert (1987), *Future Workshops: How to Create Desirable Futures*, London: Institute for Social Inventions.
Kemmis, Stephen (2008), 'Critical Theory and Participatory Action Research', in Peter Reason and Hilary Bradbury (eds), pp. 21–138.

Lewin, Kurt (1946), 'Action Research and Minority Problems', in *Resolving Social Conflicts. Field Theory in Social Science*, Washington DC: New York American Psychological Association.

Marcuse, H. (1941), 'Some social implications of Modern Technology', *Studies in Philosophy and Social Science*, **9** (3), 414–439.

Miciukiewicz, K., F. Moulaert, A. Novy, S. Musterd and J. Hillier (2012), 'Introduction: Problematising Urban Social Cohesion: A Transdisciplinary Endeavour', *Urban Studies*, **49** (9), 1855–1872.

Mills, C. Wright (1958), *The Sociological Imagination*, New York: Oxford University Press.

Nielsen, Kurt Aagaard and Birger Steen Nielsen (2006), 'Methodologies in Action Research', in Kurt Aagaard Nielsen and Lennart G. Svensson (eds), pp.63–88.

Nielsen, Kurt Aagaard and Lennart G. Svensson (2006a), 'A Framework for the Book', in Kurt Aagaard Nielsen and Lennart G. Svensson (eds), pp.13–44.

Nielsen, Kurt Aagaard and Lennart G. Svensson (eds) (2006b), *Action and Interactive Research. Beyond practice and theory*, Maastricht: Shaker Publishing.

Reason, Peter and Hilary Bradbury (2008), *The Sage Handbook of Action Research*, **2nd edition, London: Sage Publications.**

Szebehely, Marta (2005), 'Care as employment and welfare provision. Child and elder care in Sweden at the dawn of the 21st century', in Hanne Marlene Dahl and Tine Rask Eriksen (eds) *Dilemmas of care in the Nordic welfare state. Continuity and change*, Aldershot: Ashgate, pp.80–97.

25. Reflections on the form and content of Participatory Action Research and implications for social innovation research

Len Arthur

25.1 INTRODUCTION

The history of Participatory Action Research (PAR) raises issues relating to the relationship between the form of social research, i.e. methodological processes, and its content, i.e. phenomena, social context, values and purpose. Form and content issues have, in turn, implications for the emancipatory concerns of social innovation research with respect to the relationship of epistemology and methodology. This chapter will first review form and content issues involved in the historical experience of PAR and then, second, review the epistemic warrant of case studies and the extent to which PAR may make a contribution to this through the application of transitional demands and actions, which act as a bridge between the experience of social exclusion and the implementation of emancipatory possibilities.

25.2 BACKGROUND TO ACTION RESEARCH

Action research evolved from the field of social psychology in the mid 1940s and early 1950s. Kurt Lewin, a German émigré to the USA who had worked with the critical theorists in the Frankfurt School, was commissioned under a New Deal program in the 1940s to help develop methods of reducing racial tensions in social housing estates. The outcome of this work (Lewin 1946), which involved participation of those affected in defining the problems and devising change activities, came to be described as a process of action research. Similarly, during the late 1940s and 1950s the Tavistock Research Institute in London developed research techniques drawn from anthropology, which gave a privileged position to the actor's definition and understanding of their situation (Goffman 1959) and how this related to social behaviour (Brown 1992). Much of the early Tavistock work was undertaken within the field of human relations in work situations. Essentially, it was aimed at understanding how actors saw and acted in the world of work and how improved communications might aid the reduction of conflict.

By the late 1950s and in the period of rising workplace industrial action in both the USA and the UK, Lewin's and Tavistock's methodology started to merge as 'action research' and was adopted as a management method to reduce conflict and achieve change in workplaces. Lewin's concepts of 'unfreezing' old behaviours and 'refreezing' new ones seemed particularly attractive as a management technique to improve productivity through a communications process that did not necessarily involve negotiating with trade unions. This form of action research became incorporated into the top down, more manipulative 'management of change' approaches (Grey 2005).

The methodological *form* thus became separated from its original progressive social purpose *content* of overcoming racial tensions and improving community relations. The content moved from improving solidarity between equals to being part of a process of domination by those who had more power at work (Morgan 2006). As part of this shift, there was a refinement of the methodological form of action research towards 'quasi-experimental' methods, where the change proposed by management would be the independent variable with the acceptance of the change being the dependent variable (Gill and Johnson 2010). In essence, the loss of progressive social content and the actor's understanding of the situation were sealed by a move towards positivism whereby those being studied, far from being involved participants, became an abstract variable subject to the forces of independent variables – changes introduced by those in power. Thus, the separation of form from content negatively affected both the aims of the research and its processes.

Participatory Action Research (PAR) evolved from the 1980s on, firstly as a methodological reaction to the removal of content from action research and to reclaim its roots, by attempting to put the researcher and those being researched on a more equal footing; and secondly as a parallel development led by social scientists and other researchers who were committed to more contentious and progressive social change than management consultants (McIntyre 2008). In this regard, the works of Paulo Freire (1996) and the argument of Gramsci (1971) in relation to workers being seen as 'organic intellectuals' were influential. However, the tension created by the tendency to let form dominate over content has not necessarily been resolved. For example, one of the strengths of PAR

is the cumulative spiral idea of moving forward from reflection; problem definition; develop and application of a solution; then back to evaluation and reflection as the next stage forward (Kemmis and McTaggart 1988). This approach has been adopted as a management technique known as 'double loop' thinking, considered an essential building block for developing a 'learning organization' where communication is seen to be so effective that all employees – whatever their position – will collectively work toward the improvement of quality and productivity according to technologies, such as mission statements and performance indicators, that are dictated by managerial power (Morgan 2006).

25.3   FORM AND CONTENT IN SOCIAL INNOVATION RESEARCH: QUESTIONS OF VALIDITY

Social innovation (SI) researchers have partially avoided the danger of the separation of form from content by placing an emphasis on emancipatory social innovation, firmly located within a political economic analysis of international capitalism. For example, the KATARSIS and SINGOCOM projects (see Moulaert et al., Chapter 1) explored how international capitalism creates an unequal society where a large proportion of the population are excluded from the opportunities opened up by the productive power of capitalism, despite being central to the process of production. This framework was used conceptually to describe the denial of opportunities and power in terms of lost rights, capabilities and unsatisfied basic needs which reflect and result in exclusions from social, economic and cultural capitals (Bourdieu 1986). It also allowed researchers to explore how social innovation – or more immediately, socially creative strategies – developed as forms of resistance to these inequalities and exclusions.

By defining the social context for innovation in this critical manner and seeing social innovation as actions to overcome the problems of inequality that result, SI research clearly positions itself in relation to its content. This could lead to questioning about its validity – whether the findings of such research represent 'warrantable truth claims' (Mingers 2008) – because the epistemic framework, and therefore the methodological form of the research, is informed by emancipatory *values and ethics*. The question, therefore, is to what extent are there grounds for understanding the validity of research as a process of working towards social change?

In 1922 Max Weber argued that it was possible to separate factual questions based on empirical evidence and ethical questions of 'right and wrong', but he also argued that they were interdependent (Shils and Finch 1969). He proposed that ethical values entered decisions about what the social scientist was to study but that once this decision was made, it was possible to employ a methodology that was not affected by the scientist's value system. In terms of methodological practice, Weber seems to imply that so long as the social scientist is open about the ethical starting point, a methodology can then be employed which is abstracted from these values.

Similarly, Hilary Putnam argues, from a Sociology of Knowledge perspective (see also Moulaert and Van Dyck, Chapter 35), that fact and value are inextricably tangled together in the scientific process:

> even when the judgements of reasonableness are left tacit, such judgements are presupposed by scientific inquiry . . . I have argued that judgements of reasonableness can be objective, and I have argued that they have all the typical properties of value judgement. In short I have argued that my pragmatist teachers were right . . . knowledge of facts presupposes knowledge of values. (Putnam, 2002, p. 145)

Although Putnam does not suggest a simple methodological answer, recognizing this entanglement seems more likely to provide an effective scientific way forward than one that denies the role of value – or 'reasonableness' to use his term. It seems to me that social innovation research benefits from working within the parameters of what could be described as a pragmatist discourse. It is therefore, 'reasonable' to desire social innovation that challenges social exclusion – social exclusion being 'unreasonable'. Accordingly, it is possible to produce data or findings that have the standing of warrantably valid truth claims about the nature and the extent of this exclusion and, conversely, it is possibly to produce warrantably valid data to demonstrate how social innovation can challenge such exclusion.

25.3.1 Case Studies

A key source of information used to explore the effectiveness of social and cultural strategies in social innovation research is the use of case studies (see, for example, Part III of this handbook). It is helpful, therefore, to give some consideration to their validity or epistemic warrant.

Critical Realism (CR) has re-emphasized the usefulness of categorizing the validity of methodology into different underlying logics (see also Novy et al., Chapter 32; Moulaert and Van Dyck, Chapter 35). Bhaskar (1979) argues that the phenomena attended to by sciences are such that they can be divided into those that are largely amenable to the logic of experimental manipulation through 'closed systems' and those that are not so amenable and therefore require the logic of 'open systems' of analysis. Closed systems are those in which variables can be controlled and reduced to independent and dependent in a planned experiment, so that a cause and effect relationship can be established: A causes B. Case studies are, methodologically, an example of researching 'open systems' where the phenomena can less be controlled, variables are not linear, and they interact in changing ways over time. Case study truth claims are largely based upon 'ecological validity', relying upon the richness of interaction of their various elements over a time period (Gill and Johnson 2010). They consequently tend to be unique and non replicable.

However, it is sometimes possible to analyse patterns observed over a number of studies and to study causal relationships through identifying internal and external contingencies. It may also be possible to argue, using systematic forms of analysis, that some closed system internal validity can be achieved by identifying how possible causes within case studies – reframed as independent variables – influence outcomes over time (see for example Vicari Haddock and Tornaghi, Chapter 19). Over the last 15 years, especially with the development of qualitative research software, increasing consideration has been given to systematic methods of analysing qualitative case study data and forms of presentation. What is becoming clear is that it is possible, if it is desired, to move from descriptive case study presentation to one where possible causal relationships can be identified and even established, but operating within the case study context. This can be described using the pragmatist term as a process of 'abduction' or analytical induction (Gill and Johnson 2010) – which recalls the

spiral process of cumulative understanding that characterizes PAR. More controversially, I would suggest that if casual mechanisms can be identified during such a process of analysis, then 'open system' research using case studies might be able to claim some epistemic warrant through the 'closed system' logic of internal validity.

25.4   POTENTIAL OF PAR FOR SOCIAL INNOVATION

To reiterate, the content of much social innovation research concerns the extent to which social and cultural strategies of the 'excluded' can be seen as emancipation from the 'dynamics of social exclusion' – this provides a context for understanding 'reasonableness' in analysis and, therefore, for the application of PAR processes. How the form of PAR and the emancipatory content of social innovation research may enhance each other requires recognition of the broader context of social and political power. Accordingly, I argue that the 'reasonableness' of action research for social innovation centres on the extent to which a judgement can be made about the direction or trajectory of social change – whether toward emancipation from or toward incorporation into the existing power structures.

Historically, social movements that pose a potential challenge to social and political power have constantly been confronted with the dilemma between emancipation and incorporation. It was a key issue in the first five years of the Communist International (Trotsky 1972), especially over the issue of the New Economic Plan adopted by the Soviet Government and its consequences for parties of the Communist International around the world. Within the field of industrial relations, the compromising limitations of collective bargaining as a weakened challenge to the power of the employer are well explored, for instance by Richard Brown (1992). An historical insight into the dynamic of the social processes as cycles of mobilization and retreat has been provided by Charles Tilley (1995) who, *inter alia*, provides an indication of the reasons why social movements constantly face a dilemma between emancipation and incorporation.

Tilley's findings suggest that social movements tend to move through cycles, starting with a growing collective mobilization around grievances during which the balance of power shifts toward the social movement and the possibilities of emancipation start to appear. But this process reaches a peak where the possibility of further mobilization stalls or declines, and there is growing opposition or repression from those whose social and political power is being challenged. The social movement then faces the dilemma of whether it should secure any emancipatory gains through a compromise or continue to fight. Of course the progression is not clear cut, as at every stage an understanding of the state of the 'balance of forces' depends on evidence, interpretation and judgement – a process which is difficult for a social movement dependent on the collective action of newly involved people.

What appears to emerge from this literature is that the dilemma between emancipation and incorporation is one that will emerge in all social movements with emancipatory aims that challenge existing social and political power. The first step in aiding social movements to cope with this dilemma is to recognize its existence and not wish it away – for example through myopic romanticism or blaming those that raise the problem as 'collaborators' or 'selling out'. The second step is to suggest social processes that might be adopted in which the inevitable debates can be framed in relation to long term emancipatory intentions and, in this way, enable the application of PAR in both its participatory form and its emancipatory content.

What social processes could be adopted to help frame the debates about emancipation or incorporation? A distinction between 'contained or transgressive contention' has been developed by some social movement theorists (McAdam et al. 2001) as a way of dealing with the first stage of coping with and understanding this difference between possible trajectories. By *contained contention* they mean relationships between 'established actors ... employing well established means of claim making', such that when claims are made they would if realized affect the interests of one of the actors, 'and all parties were previously established as constituted political actors' (McAdam et al. 2001, p. 7). A good example would be trade union collective bargaining, where claims are made but all parties accept there will be a settlement within the boundaries of previously established agreements. By *transgressive contention* they mean the introduction of 'newly identified political actors and / or at least some parties employ innovative collective action' ... which would be innovative if it included 'claims including collective self-representation, and / or adopts means that are either unprecedented or forbidden in the regime in question' (2001, p. 8). Extending the collective bargaining theme, claims could include a pay, conditions and benefits package that was equal for all employees; workers' control over production processes and consequent revenue; and the right to industrial action.

McAdam et al. go on to explain that their intention is to explore how social movements do and can break out of being contained and, in my terminology, become more emancipatory as opposed to being incorporated:

This book's cases fall overwhelmingly on the transgressive side of the line: they usually involve either formation of new political actors, innovation with respect to new political means, or both. We deploy the distinction contained/transgressive for two reasons. First, many instances of transgressive contention grow out of existing episodes of contained contention; that interaction between the established and the new deserves explicit attention. Second, substantial short-term political and social change more often emerges from transgressive than from contained contention, which tends more often to reproduce existing regimes. Or so we argue. (McAdam et al. 2001, p. 8)

Contained and transgressive contention are thus terms that can help frame and make conscious the dilemma that all social movements will face between a trajectory toward emancipation and one towards incorporation. As McAdam and his colleagues recognize, theirs is an attempt to come to terms with what is, in practice, a dynamic process which could have a cyclical trajectory, despite their research emphasis being on how to move forward from contained to transgressive contention.

The second stage of the process of coping with this dilemma is to explore the possibilities for reframing the inevitable cyclical judgemental debates about the balance of power and the position of the movement within a particular cycle: whether it is possible to become more emancipatory and transgressive or whether to accept that a limit has been reached and a containing and potentially incorporating agreement needs to be made. Carter Goodrich (1975[1920]) caught this position graphically when he described it – originally in 1920 – as the 'frontier of control': a boundary where the battle had temporarily stopped, to be taken up again when the balance of forces can be re-mobilized.

Gibson-Graham (2006) suggests an ethically based approach to aiding social movements to cope with the process of identifying how they might sustain a transgressive trajectory of emancipation and avoid containment. Their aim is to aid the building of a post-capitalist society by orienting mobilization through the 'development of community economies'. The alternative and transgressive routes to this trajectory are sustained by focussing on meeting *needs* locally; using any consequent *surplus* to strengthen communities; recognizing *consumption* as a viable route to development and not simply an end result; and creating, enlarging, reclaiming and sharing a *commons* as a way of tending the community. A transgressive trajectory is sustained cumulatively by defining what emancipation means in relation to both means and ends. By advocating such alternative spaces of community economies, Gibson-Graham avoids the cycle of contention experienced by social movements.

Steven Buechler recognizes that social movements can both be part of a cycle of contention and establish alternative spaces by being both political and cultural:

... from their inception, social movements have had a dual focus. Reflecting the political, they have always involved some form of challenge to prevailing forms of authority. Reflecting the cultural, they have always operated as symbolic laboratories in which reflexive actors pose questions of meaning, purpose, identity, and change. (Buechler 1999, p. 211)

He suggests that the consequential challenge that can derive from social movements as 'symbolic laboratories' can take five forms:

- De-legitimation underscores the unacceptability of existing social arrangements.
- Revelation brings power relations to the surface of social consciousness.

- Differentiation rejects false unities and identifies more fundamental lines of social cleavage.
- Solidarity creates alliances between groups who share subordinate status despite their differences.
- Relativization underscores the socially constructed nature of existing forms of domination and the possibility of their reconstruction. (Buechler 1999, p. 202; bullets added)

These themes, Buechler argues, only make sense in the 'sequencing of grievances and ideology' (1999, p. 203). The grievances, issues, problems that people experience – for example those that derive from the dynamics of social exclusion – form the reason for people to act together, but it is the ideological discourse about the causes of the grievances and their location in the wider social system that brings these themes into action and starts to create the symbolic laboratory.

To recap, the evidence from historical and contemporary research into emancipatory social movements indicates that they experience a tension, in the form of a repeating cyclical dilemma of contention, between emancipation and incorporation. The cycle is affected by the balance of forces (relative power) that the movements can bring to bear upon existing holders of social and political power. The concepts of contained and transgressive contention could help to frame this tension for actors. But recognizing it is only the first stage; social movement research can also help to provide a conceptual framework to help actors to work through this dilemma. The evidence indicates that only rarely is emancipation achieved in one revolutionary step but the transgressive trajectory can be maintained, and attention to *alternative space* plays a key role in helping to understand this. Alternative space with identifiable boundaries can be achieved by consolidating gains made in a period

of mobilization, either as a line 'where the battle has temporarily stopped' (such as through a collective agreement), through emancipated geographic boundaries where alternative development can take place, or through recognizing that both political and cultural gains are made in struggle.

Drawing upon social movement history again, it is possible to identify and develop practices that could guide practitioners through what is undoubtedly a difficult process. *Transitional demands* are closely associated with Leon Trotsky (1938) and the Fourth International but even in this context stretch back to a wider debate in the Communist International (Trotsky 1972). In fact, the idea has a longer history and was used by Robert Owen in relation to the cooperative movement in the 1840s (Arthur 2008). And more recently, without much acknowledgement to this history, the Transition Towns movement (http://www.transitionnetwork.org/, last accessed 18 December 2012) has established an international presence.

Trotsky and the Communist International argued that transitional demands were a 'bridge' between where we find ourselves and where we would like to be. They are aimed at mobilizing support for demands that capitalism would be hard pressed to meet, either by raising consciousness about how the system works – as in Buechler above – or, if conceded, by making it more difficult for capitalism to save itself at the expense of the working class. So for example, in the current financial crisis the demand for full employment achieves both ends.

Transitional demands are about applying pressure on those with power to act. However, fitting in with the emancipatory concept of alternative space mentioned above, it may also be possible to extend the concept to 'transitional space', such as the alternative economies of Gibson-Graham

(2006) or the type of action taken by the Transition Towns movement. The emancipatory trajectory is sustained in both the case of collective mobilization through transitional demands and the case of alternative space by transitional actions taken in the here and now.

The key to these actions being a possible guide through the tensions and dilemmas of contention is that both transitional demands and actions direct attention to the power context and what is required to achieve emancipation from the consequential domination and social exclusion. Moreover, they could be seen as directing attention in such a way that, by asking the question 'what can we demand or do to move toward emancipation', a process of debate about how to form a 'bridge' takes place with the aim of guiding the development of both demands and actions.

Consequently, I argue that within the purpose of social innovation research to identify the extent to which social and cultural studies are able to contend the dynamics of social exclusion, form and content can be brought together by asking further questions about the trajectories of case studies – and in particular whether, in using participatory action research processes (the PAR spiral for example), they are doing so within the context of a trajectory of degeneration or renewal: toward more contained contention or toward transgressive contention of social exclusion.

25.5 CONCLUSION

Recognizing these trends and making judgements about them is not easy. However, PAR, applied to potential transitional demands or actions that lead to a challenge to or overcoming of the power of exclusion, can be emancipatory in both form and content; it can provide a method

of both observing and explaining either how change took place or what limited its success: thus leaving the way clear for further attempts at change to build cumulatively on the earlier experience. The idea is to collectively develop a demand which would provide a solution to a problem facing people and which, if satisfied, would reduce the power or act as a defeat for elites: achieving transgressive contention. Employing PAR both in the process of developing the demand or action and in its implementation and evaluation will, within the context of agreeing to be transgressive of excluding power, provide case study evidence which is capable of collective analysis and which will be cumulatively useful and transferable to others who are challenging the same exclusionary problems.

In sum, I propose that transitional actions and demands are concepts that allow form and content to be considered together in exploring the relationship between PAR and case studies of social innovation. They direct attention both to the trajectory of the aims and strategies of social movements under study and to the extent to which members are working toward a 'contained contention' situation or one of 'transgressive contention'.

25.6 QUESTIONS FOR DISCUSSION

- How necessary is it for the emancipatory purposes of social innovation to ensure that both 'form' and 'content' are present in the application of PAR?
- How helpful is it to recognize that social movements move through a cycle of contention of forward mobilization and partial retreat?
- Can you think of an example of a social movement that is facing

a dilemma between contained and transgressive contention? How would you go about proposing a way forward?

- Do you think that transitional demands and actions represent a useful framing for PAR in social innovation?

REFERENCES

(References in bold are recommended reading.)

Arthur, L. (2008), 'Resistance, socialism and social movements: can Robert Owen still be relevant?' in R. Bickle and M. Scott Cato (eds) *New Views of Society: Robert Owen for the 21st Century*, Glasgow: Scottish Left Review Press, pp. 89–100.

Arthur, L., T. Keenoy, M. Scott Cato and R. Smith (2008), 'Social Movements and contention: an exploration of implications of diachronic and synchronic change', presented to *Transborder Laboratory from Below*, Brno: Economy and Society Trust and The Institute for the Study of the Political Economy, http://www.ipe.or.at/artikel.php?art_id=71 (last accessed 18 December 2012).

Bhaskar, R.A. (1979), *The Possibility of Naturalism*, Brighton: Harvester.

Bourdieu, P. (1986) *The forms of capital*, in J. Richardson (ed.) *Handbook of Theory and Research for the Sociology of Education*, New York: Greenwood, pp. 241–258.

Brown, R. (1992), *Understanding Industrial Organisations*, London: Routledge .

Buechler, S.M. (1999), *Social Movements in Advanced Capitalism: The Political Economy and Cultural Construction of Social Activism*, Oxford: Oxford. University Press.

Freire, P. (1996), *Pedagogy of the Opporessed*, London: Penguin.

Gibson-Graham, J.K. (2006), *A Postcapitalist Poltics*, Minneapolis: University of Minnesota Press.

Gill, J. and P. Johnson (2010), *Research Methods for Managers*, London: Sage.

Goffman, E. (1959), *The Presentation of Self in Everyday Life*, Garden City, NY: Doubleday.

Goodrich, C.L. (1975 [1920]), *The Frontier of Control*, London: Pluto Press.

Gramsci, A. (1971), *Selections from the Prison Notebooks*, London: Lawrence and Wishart.

Grey, C. (2005), *Studying Organizations*, London: Sage.

Kemmis, S. and R. McTaggart (1988), *The Action Research Planner*, Geelong: Deakin University Press.

Lewin, K. (1946) 'Action research and minority problems', *Journal of Social Issues*, 2 (4), 34–46.

McAdam, D., S. Tarrow and C. Tilly (2001), *Dynamics of Contention*, Cambridge: Cambridge University Press.

McIntyre, A. (2008), *Participatory Action Research*, Thousand Oaks: Sage.

Mingers, J. (2008), 'Management knowledge and knowledge management: realism and forms of truth', *Knowledge Management Research and Practice*, 6, 62–76.

Morgan, G. (2006), *Images of Organization*, Thousand Oaks: Sage.

Putnam, H. (2002), *The Collapse of the Fact/Value Dichotomy*, London: Harvard University Press.

Shils, E. and H.A. Finch (eds) (1969), *Max Weber on the Methodology of the Social Sciences*, New York: Free Press.

Tilley, C. (1995), 'Contentious repertoires in Great Britain, 1758–1834', in M. Traugott (ed.), *Repertoires and Cycles of Contention*, Durham, NC: Duke University Press, pp. 253–280.

Trotsky, L. (1938), *The Transitional Programme*, http://www.marxists.org/archive/trotsky/1938/tp/index.htm (last accessed 18 December 2012).

Trotsky, L. (1972), *The First 5 Years of the Communist International*, 2nd edition, New York: Monad Press.

PART V

COLLECTIVE ACTION, INSTITUTIONAL LEVERAGE AND PUBLIC POLICY

Introduction: the institutional space for social innovation
Diana MacCallum

One of the enduring questions for social innovation (SI) research concerns the relationship between the socially innovative actions that take place 'on the ground' and the broader institutional and policy environments in which such actions happen. It is a relationship that may take many forms, both positive and negative, as many of the chapters in this book illustrate. The state can be seen both as a conservative social force and as a primary provider of services which meet the needs of citizens, especially of deprived groups and persons. It is an arena within which many individuals enact daily resistance to the exclusionary forces of late capitalism – as such, it can be a socially innovative actor in its own right. And there is no straightforward causality between a 'good' political-institutional environment and successful social innovation, nor any consistent process through which socially innovative actions become institutionalized (for good or ill) either at the local or at higher scales. Hence, SI analysis continually returns to, and occasionally invents, complex conceptual constructions such as multi-level governance, 'bottom-linked innovation', 'path shaping', multi-partner networks crossing different types of institutional boundaries, and so on. Such constructions express normative positions on the relations between state institutions and socially innovative action without being prescriptive or universal. That is, they allow space for context-specific innovation.

This part includes six chapters that explore, in different ways, some of the potentials, tensions and dangers inherent in the interactions between grass-roots action, social/solidarity economies, and state institutions. They apply an SI lens to 'socially transformative' policies, governance arrangements and political events in a range of (inter)national contexts, highlighting several themes that bear further discussion. What is clear, as we have learnt from multiple case studies (see Part III of this handbook; also Pradel et al., Chapter 11; Vicari Haddock and Tornaghi, Chapter 19) and as Flavia Martinelli makes explicit in Chapter 26, is that the long-term sustainability of social innovations is very often determined by resources (especially funding) from the state, as well as by regulatory environments that constrain or enable their operation. Conversely, it is often deficiencies in the state's provision of material services and/or cultural recognition that lead to social innovation in the first place. But the synergies and tensions between the roles of state and Third sector go further than this, as socially innovative programs have helped to enable the wholesale neoliberal restructuring of welfare (see also Jessop et al., Chapter 8). Hence, Martinelli argues for a stronger role for the state in guaranteeing basic universal rights, while also supporting more context-responsive, socially innovative non-government initiatives in the field of social services.

Conditions surrounding the effectiveness of non-government actors in meeting the needs of marginalized and excluded people is a recurring theme in this part's contributions. In Chapter 27, Laurent Fraisse examines how public policies have worked to promote the social and solidarity-based economy (SSE) as a 'laboratory' for social innovation in France. He cites several factors as crucial to this relationship: political representation of SSE, leading to its establishment as a government portfolio in its own right; the sector's visibility and its capacity to promote understanding of its performance, especially in quantifiable terms. Public support for SSE helps to embed development strategies in local economies, as well as providing for economic diversity, a condition for resilience in times of crisis.

The themes of economic diversity, visibility and citizenship are taken up in Chapter 28, in which Juan-Luis Klein, Jean-Marc Fontan, Denis Harrisson and Benoît Lévesque present the 'Québec Model' as an example of how social innovations can shape the economic development system and practices of a society. The province of Québec is distinctive in North America not only for its Francophone culture, but also for a tradition of strong participation of labour and social economy organizations both in providing services to citizens and in designing the public governance arrangements under which services are provided. The authors of this chapter attribute this development model to the institutionalization of many socially innovative experiments to meet human needs in the context of the crisis of Fordism in the 1970s and 1980s. This has led to a system characterized by participatory governance, co-production of public goods and policies, and a plural economy drawing on the strengths of diverse modes of ownership.

Two chapters from Latin America further demonstrate the critical importance of history in shaping the paths of popular movements and social innovation. In Chapter 29, Ana Fernandes, Andreas Novy and Paul Singer explore the intellectual and political traditions behind contemporary solidarity economy initiatives in Pernambuco, Brazil, such as university incubators (see also Dubeux, Chapter 22). They see these initiatives as rooted in Paulo Freire's critical pedagogy, which in turn emerged from social struggles for justice and democracy in the 1950s and 1960s. Such historical perspectives can greatly enrich our understanding of the dynamics surrounding social innovation today, helping us better to see and map the complex intertwining of exclusionary and emancipatory practices.

Taking a different approach, Vicente Espinoza provides an interesting look at how protest movements in Chile have changed in form and practice since the end of Pinochet's dictatorship in 1990. In particular, he highlights a decline in the independence and vitality of collective action under democracy, attributing this to a 'reversive' process in which, while building bridges with government, popular leaders were co-opted by the new state's policymaking institutions. From this perspective, the national student revolts of 2011 can be seen as a sharp reaction not only to the new right-wing government, but also to a perceived apathy on the part of civil society. The diffuse, inclusive strategies practised by the students might be signs of a rebirth of socially innovative mobilization against long-ignored exclusionary dynamics.

In the final chapter in this part, Isabel André examines one of the most profound and far reaching social transformations affecting Western societies the last half-century – changing gender relations. In spite of its importance in shaping human needs, relations and opportunities, and in spite of the crucial role of women in advancing socially innovative strategies (see for example Ashta et al., Chapter 6), gender has traditionally been relatively neglected as a category of analysis in social innovation research. André presents a strong case for adopting such a perspective, showing that EU policies for gender equality have played a crucial role in facilitating social change in certain fields, especially labour markets, but left intact some key institutions which sustain a patriarchal form of capitalism. This chapter highlights the complexity of interactions between governance institutions and social innovation. Policies at the EU level respond to large-scale social innovation – fundamentally altered social relations resulting, firstly, from women's claims to recognition and empowerment and, secondly, from technological innovations such as reliable, affordable contraception. At the same time, they work to shape future innovations in particular ways.

26. Learning from case studies of social innovation in the field of social services: creatively balancing top-down universalism with bottom-up democracy
Flavia Martinelli

26.1 INTRODUCTION

Socially innovative initiatives (SIIs) involve collective actions that aim at improving opportunities for people threatened by a wide diversity of exclusionary processes or looking for alternative futures. However, in order to become durable, socially innovative processes and achievements need to be translated into some form of *institutionalized* rights. Since many SIIs are generated from below, this translation is far from automatic. This is most evident in the domain of social services, where, in the context of the generalized restructuring of the welfare state, a double danger emerges: on the one hand SIIs are increasingly called to *substitute* for retrenching or inadequate public provisions; on the other, since they are most often based on the mobilization of social groups characterized by hardship, they cannot be *sustained* over time.

In this chapter, based on the review of a number of case studies carried out within the SINGOCOM and KATARSIS projects (see Moulaert et al., Chapter 1) in the area of social services and education in particular, I draw attention to the fact that the growing emphasis on the socially innovative potential of bottom-up mobilization in mainstream circles can work to obscure the rolling back of the welfare state, on the one hand, and the difficulties encountered by such initiatives, on the other. Subsequently, I make two pleas: the first

in favour of the maintenance of a publicly supported and regulated system of social services that can guarantee access to basic services on a *universal* basis; the second in favour of innovative policy-oriented thinking that can ensure an institutional balance between automatic (universal) access to social services, on the one hand, and *spaces* for socially innovative, diversified, context- and user-sensitive initiatives, on the other.

26.2 SETTING THE CONTEXT: SOCIAL SERVICES, SOCIAL INNOVATION AND THE WELFARE STATE

26.2.1 Material and Post-Material Claims

A major analytical question in case study research about social movements and social innovation (see Martinelli 2010; González et al. 2010) is the *mobilizing* factor, i.e. why people mobilize, get organized and implement SIIs. The 'why' also affects the 'what', that is which goals socially innovative actions pursue and eventually achieve.

There has been much debate about whether social movements and actions starting at the end of the 1960s in all Western societies – the so-called 'New Social Movements' (NSMs) – could be considered truly 'new' and different – 'postmodern' – compared to previous social movements (see Martin 2001; Martinelli 2010 for surveys). A major discriminating element put forward to support the 'post-modern' thesis was that NSMs were based on 'post-material' claims, i.e. were more oriented to cultural, existential and ethical issues rather than material needs, to 'recognition' rather than redistribution (Fraser 1995).

In the last couple of decades, however, 'material' needs are back on stage. The end of the Fordist-Keynesian order, deindustrialization processes, increased immigration pressures and the progressive retrenchment of the welfare state throughout Europe have revived exclusionary dynamics in very material terms, more reminiscent of pre-Fordist than post-modern times. Acquired rights such as decent housing, dignified employment, basic education, health care, and assistance for the impaired are increasingly undercut. Moreover, material and post-material needs are strongly interlinked and cannot be separated either conceptually or practically. Redistribution cannot occur without recognition and – conversely – diversity can be fully recognized only in a context of universal rights.

26.2.2 Socially Innovative Initiatives as a Means to Achieve Basic Universal Rights

If we consider their main goals, SIIs can be roughly grouped into three categories:

1. Initiatives geared to satisfying *basic material needs*, such as employment, housing, social services (education and training; health assistance; care for children, the elderly, people with disabilities and other social groups at risk of exclusion).
2. Initiatives geared to satisfying *existential needs*, i.e. to obtain visibility, recognition, self-realization, and ulti-

mately *citizenship*, without necessarily forfeiting specificities and diversities, such as in the case of people or groups marginalized because of cultural or political prejudices (gender, ethnicity, education, ability, age or prior records).[1]
3. Initiatives geared to achieving *more democratic governance*, i.e. less authoritarian decision-making processes or less bureaucratic and standardized delivery of social services.

With reference to the debate on NSMs, only the latter two types of SIIs would be considered as belonging to the realm of post-material claims, whereas the former would correspond to the traditional claims for redistribution. But this artificial distinction does not make sense: all social movements – from the 19th century on (Martinelli 2010) – have been about recognition *and* redistribution, which necessarily involve empowerment and changes in relationships, together with the satisfaction of material needs. The vast majority of the SIIs examined in the SINGOCOM and KATARSIS projects were indeed geared to achieve or recover – starting from bottom-up mobilization – some basic universal rights, that were not, or no longer, ensured by contemporary institutions. In other words, socially innovative mobilization can be seen, to a large extent, as being about gaining full social citizenship. In this respect, they are no different from social movements of the past.

26.2.3 The Restructuring of the Welfare State

In this chapter I am especially concerned with a specific subset of 'basic needs', which is also a key vehicle of citizenship: *social services*. These services were a major achievement of both 'old' and 'new' social movements and a pillar of the Fordist-Keynesian welfare state. Since the 1980s, however, they have undergone a major restructuring in all European countries, although with different intensities, that has significantly undermined the 'old' notion of citizenship (Crouch et al. 2000).

Three major trends have been observed: a) a generalized reduction in the direct public provision and/or funding of such services; b) the liberalization and outsourcing of formerly public supply; c) the devolution of authority from national to local governments. These changes were brought about by several transformative pressures: on the supply side, the increasing budgetary difficulties of national governments, the alleged inefficiency of the public sector, and the rigid, bureaucratic character of public supply; on the demand side, claims for greater consumer choice, customization of services, and democratic governance. An ambiguous convergence has thus occurred between top-down neo-liberal restructuring strategies, on the one hand, and bottom-up mobilization of users and civil society for better or more effective services, on the other,[2] which has somewhat legitimized the deregulation, liberalization and privatization processes.

A large body of research has now accumulated about this 30-year-long restructuring, highlighting some common trends and outcomes, despite the great variety of national and regional trajectories. A first generalized outcome is the increased *diversification* of the supply system, with new providers – both for profit and non-profit – substituting or complementing publicly provided services, among which *third sector* organizations feature prominently. A second generalized outcome is the progressive devolution of authority over the planning, production and delivery of social services and the establishment of what have been called '*local welfare*

systems' (Ranci 2005; Andreotti et al. 2009; Kazepov 2008).

26.2.4   Social Innovation, the Third Sector and Community-Based Action in Social Services

It is against this background that the link between social innovation, third sector organizations and local, community-based initiatives in the domain of social services can be more critically examined.

In the first place, in the *specific context of social services*, the definition of social innovation provided in the General Introduction must be further articulated. Social innovation in social services – whether top-down- or bottom-up-engineered, output- or process-related, organizational, legislative, or cultural – should involve changes that:

1. *Reveal* and/or (better) *respond to social needs* – material *and* existential – by improving the quality of existing social services (e.g. adapting them to specific needs, making them more user-friendly or improving their cost/effectiveness) and/or by creating new services or delivery systems for ignored needs.

2. *Empower* users or specific social groups – that is *enhance their capabilities to act* – via better information and knowledge, and greater recognition, voice, or power.

3. *Modify social – and power – relations* among providers and users, thereby improving governance processes by e.g. making planning procedures more transparent and decision-making more participatory.

But, if we accept that social services are major vehicles of citizenship, social innovation must also:

4. Ensure, preserve and/or increase *equality of access*, the main characteristic of Fordist-Keynesian social services and warranty of social citizenship.
5. *Up-scale and 'institutionalize'* changes, i.e. make such improvements become institutionalized social achievements that can last beyond the initial mobilization/innovation moment and until the next round of innovation.

If we assume this more articulated definition, assessing the innovative role of both third sector initiatives – broadly defined[3] – and community-based local mobilization in the delivery of social services becomes more problematic.

As to the third sector, in most of the literature on social policy and social innovation – both critical and mainstream – non-profit organizations are hailed as the new protagonists in social services delivery, positively substituting for the bureaucratic, inefficient or absent public provision, while, at the same time, guaranteeing an ethical commitment. They are considered optimal carriers of an alleged 'new' model of welfare for a number of reasons. First, as the expression of bottom-up mobilization, they are supposedly more 'rooted' in the local civil society and more responsive to local needs than traditional top-down, bureaucratic public services. Second, they supposedly also ensure more democratic governance and user-friendly delivery processes than the hierarchical and authoritarian systems of old. Finally, because of their more flexible and decentralized features, they are also allegedly more cost-efficient than the rigid, centralized bureaucracies of state systems.

As to *local* mobilization, SIIs are also typically associated with the municipal, community or neighbourhood scale (Moulaert 2000; Amin et al. 2003), considered the optimal scale to play a medi-ating role between the state and citizens, thereby explaining the generalized favour accorded to devolution and the establishment of 'local welfare systems'. Locally organized supply systems and community-based organizations in the realm of social services are supposedly best equipped to understand local needs and ensure customized delivery. Moreover, they can foster empowerment, territorial identity and consciousness, whereas the proximity they afford also enables the development of relations of solidarity and reciprocity (André and Abreu 2007).

The above are, in principle, all good reasons why, within the recent debate on social services, third sector organizations and local, community-based initiatives are generally associated with social innovation and are thought to virtuously reinforce each other. But reality is less glamorous. Although heralded as a breakthrough with respect to the undifferentiated and rigid public provision of old, the liberalization and privatization of social services have increased the freedom of choice only for the better-off. While the for-profit sector has been able to capture the profitable segments of the market (i.e. the demand of the middle and upper classes), in many instances the third sector has become the main or sole provider of social services for the poor – not always with adequate financial support and personnel. In other words, the claim for diversification of supply and freedom of choice has masked an increase in inequality of access, a plight that the universal welfare state of the Fordist-Keynesian order had sought to – and had partially succeeded in – eradicating. Moreover, the focus on the local scale hides a 'subsidiarity trap' (see also González et al. 2010), since in many instances the devolution of the responsibility for social services to local governments has occurred without ensuring adequate financial transfers. In other words, what has been decentralized is not the power to deal with new responsibilities, but the management of the financial crisis of the state. At the same time, the devolution of responsibility tends to foster the erroneous belief that local problems are the result of local inadequacies and not of broader structural problems. The overall result – even allowing for notable national and regional exceptions – is a generalized reduction in social and territorial cohesion.

Thus, while the discussion on social innovation, the third sector and community-based initiatives is helpful to identify areas for improvement in social policy, it also acts as a smokescreen, hiding both the selective reduction in public expenditure on social services and the growing inability of such services to reach certain groups, that is the significant downsizing of universal coverage and the aggravated selectivism that goes with privatization. For this reason, I contend that a more critical examination of SIIs in social services is needed, paying greater attention not only to whether or not they do improve the supply-demand nexus and empower local communities, but also to how well they cope with maintaining/improving universal access in the context of a retrenching welfare state and to whether they are able to survive in the long run, beyond the socially innovative moment.

26.3   SOCIAL INNOVATION AND CITIZENSHIP IN SOCIAL SERVICES. LEARNING FROM CASE STUDIES IN EDUCATION

In the light of the observations developed in the previous section, I believe that the discussion on SIIs must be cast in a broader framework, bringing back

as a central concern the *right to welfare* – which is the basis of citizenship – and the role of the state. It is through this lens that the relationships between bottom-up community-based approaches, the third sector, the State and social innovation can be critically unfolded and placed in perspective, particularly where policy recommendations are sought.

26.3.1   The Analytical Focus

To demonstrate my points I will draw evidence from some of the SINGOCOM and KATARSIS case studies in the field of *education*. Education, in its multiple forms, lies at the heart of citizenship, as it creates and disseminates knowledge, which is the very foundation of human progress, fostering awareness, capabilities and innovation. In its Lisbon Agenda of 2000, the EC made knowledge – not just in the sense of formal school training, but in the broader meaning of 'Life-Long-Learning', self expression and socialization – the distinctive focus of its vision of the future European society, however dampened this vision was in subsequent deliberations.

This said, there are two very different views of education (Andersen and Hjort-Madsen 2007). On the one hand there is the neoliberal perspective (couched in neo-classical economic theory), which considers knowledge as a *private good* and, hence, education as an individual investment in human capital, oriented to achieve 'technological' innovation and competitiveness. The normative translation is 'hard' competitive meritocratism, which involves that schools apply sorting and reward mechanisms linked to individual achievements.[4] On the other hand, there is the social-democratic view, traditionally strong in the Scandinavian welfare model, which considers knowledge as a *common good* and, hence, education as a social investment and as a universal right: free education for all is part and parcel of social citizenship. The translation of this perspective in the educational system – which could be labelled 'soft' meritocratism – implies that sorting and reward mechanisms are balanced by other more egalitarian and non-competitive pedagogical principles, such as interactive learning, group-work, acknowledgment and valorization of diversities, etc. The neoliberal and the social-democratic/empowering approaches to education also differ in terms of objectives (Andersen and Hjort-Madsen 2007): the former asks students to 'conform' to established norms and values through a process of 'assimilation'; the latter is more oriented to valorizing students' different capabilities, through methodologies enabling self-expression, collective learning, and recognition of diversities.[5]

Thus, it is clear that the way education is organized and delivered is a key determinant of social inclusion and, conversely, of social exclusion: the greater the selectivity and stratification of the educational system, the greater the exclusionary dynamics. In many European countries recent reforms in education, couched in the neoliberal rhetoric of choice and diversity, have in fact increased inequality in supply and access (Whitty 2001; Tierolf and Nederland 2007) and in many instances local communities and the third sector are burdened with the task of facing this growing exclusion.

In reviewing the case studies I have selected in the field of education (see Table 26.1) I will address three interrelated questions, which make the bridge between social innovation, social citizenship and, later, social policy:

1. Which *social needs* do SIIs seek to satisfy, in relation to the existing

welfare system? Are they complementing or improving existing supply structures (i.e. providing more customized, user-friendly, or democratic services), or are they *substituting* for missing or ineffectual public services?

2. How is the *sustainability* of SIIs supported? In other words, do existing regulatory frameworks play an enabling or hindering role in sustaining community-based mobilization for (better) social services, i.e. in making them become a durable acquisition and right?

3. How does the *scale* of action influence the effectiveness of SIIs? Which is the best spatial/administrative scale to foster, initiate and carry out social innovation? Is it the local scale, as generally assumed?

26.3.2 Meeting Social Needs that are not or are inadequately served by the Welfare System

In all the SIIs examined, actions responded to a failure in the existing welfare system. In some cases, the initiatives provide services that the education system *does not deliver* to particular disadvantaged groups or specific areas; in others, they integrate or improve existing services that are *inadequate* to the specific needs of those groups and areas.

In fact, despite the EU discourse about Life-Long Learning, in many places even the compulsory education system either fails to reach particular groups, such as immigrant, minority or low income communities, or fails to integrate pupils in the educational process, generating early school leaving or inadequately trained diploma holders. The absence of dedicated services, the rigidity, and/or the dominant 'competitive meritocratism' and 'assimilation'

Table 26.1 Selected socially innovative initiatives (SIIs) in the domain of education services

Initiative	Social services provided	Targeted groups	Main actors(s)	Funding
Associazione Quartieri Spagnoli, Naples, Italy	Childcare, pre-schooling; training of mothers; counselling. Anti-poverty and social inclusion activities	Marginalized children, youth and women	Neighbourhood association Community organizer and volunteers University Municipality	Municipality EU
Association Alentour, Roubaix, France	Day centre for the homeless; reading & animation services for children; home care services; training classes	Immigrants, marginalized children and youth, ethnic minorities	Neighbourhood association Community organizer Volunteer social workers	National state EU
Arts Factory, Ferndale, Wales, U.K.	Life-long learning; art classes; training	People with learning disabilities, elderly, children	Social activists Private trust Membership	Membership Activities
Second Chance Schools, various European localities	Alternative education classes integrating formal knowledge and creative skills; personalized counselling for re-integrating drop-outs	School drop-outs, low-skilled youth	EU National state Local authorities and services Employers Parents	National state Local authorities Employers
Anna Polak School, Zaandam, The Netherland	Vocational training in basic skills (communication, numeracy, literacy); customized insertion programs; individual counselling	Adult women without education and with low skills	Employers and trade unions Vocational schools Local authorities EU	Employers and trade unions Local authorities EU

Organization	Activities	Target group	Actors	Funding
Social and Educational Action, Athens, Greece	Day-centre for children and adolescents; support for pre-school and school (re)integration; social, psychological and legal counselling for families; literacy and social competences programmes	Muslim Turkish-speaking and Roma children and their families	Non-profit organization; Volunteers and parents; Local schools; Private sponsors; National state	Private sponsors; National state
KESPEMs, different localities in Thrace, Greece	Centres organizing activities in schools and outside schools: Greek language, math and computer classes; books and other educational material; training of teachers; counselling to parents; 'Creative Youth Workshops'	Muslim minority children, youth and their parents; school teachers	EU; Greek Ministry of Education; Universities and local schools	EU; Greek Ministry of Education
ARSIS-Social Organization for the Support of Youth, several cities, Greece	Psychosocial support and counselling; educational programs for the improvement of skills; insertion programmes; cultural and creative expression activities; communication and socialization	Marginalized youth (school drop-outs, homeless, abused, ex-addicts, ex-convicts, refugees, etc.)	Non-government organization; Volunteers; Schools; Private sponsors; EU	Private sponsors; EU

Source: author's compilation, based on case studies investigated in the SINGOCOM and KATARSIS research projects. See especially Moulaert et al. (2007; 2010); Tierolf and Nederland (2007); Andersen and Hjort-Madsen (2007); Baharopoulou and Siatitsa (2007).

approaches of the established systems contribute to reproduce social inequality in all three moments of exclusion: access, process and outcome (Tierolf and Nederland 2007; Andersen and Hjort-Madsen 2007). The examined SIIs all seek to provide alternative educational and childcare programmes or to innovate within existing ones (see Table 26.1).

The Second Chance Schools in Denmark (Tierolf and Nederland 2007), for example, apply innovative teaching techniques, personalized counselling and empowering methodologies, to re-integrate school drop-outs and low-skilled youth, without losing sight of the need for formally recognized qualifications. The Anna Polak College for adult women in Zaandam, The Netherlands (Tierolf and Nederland 2007) targets adult women unable to access mainstream vocational schools and applies innovative teaching techniques, in partnership with prospective employers. In Athens, Greece, the Social and Educational Action association runs a day-centre providing integrated support to Turkish-speaking and Roma Muslim children, adolescents and their families, including psychological, social and legal counselling (Baharopoulou and Siatitsa 2007). In Italy, the Associazione Quartieri Spagnoli provides childcare but also counselling and educational support to young women and marginalized youth in a degraded and crime-ridden neighbourhood of Naples (Cavola et al. 2010). Similarly, the Association Alentour in Roubaix, France, integrates training classes, reading animation services and home care services targeted to immigrants and marginalized youth (Ailenei and Lefèbvre 2010). The Arts Factory in Wales (Donaldson and Court 2010) and the ARSIS initiatives in Greece (Baharopoulou and Siatitsa 2007) both make extensive use of arts and creative expression methodologies to reach people with learning disabilities and marginalized groups – such as former convicts or addicts – respectively.

26.3.3   Sustaining Social Innovation: Institutional Frameworks and Funding

A major issue with SIIs is their sustainability beyond the creative mobilization moment, i.e. the dialectic between social innovation and its institutionalization. To assess this aspect, it is necessary to look at the *institutional contexts* – more or less enabling – in which the SIIs emerged and the way their action has been – or not been – institutionalized, as well as the sources and reliability of their *funding*. These are key aspects in explaining the success of SIIs and their duration (Martinelli et al. 2010).

With regard to the institutional context, education in Europe still exhibits a great variety of regulatory and funding frameworks (Eurydice 2007), owing to the different national welfare traditions. In some countries the outsourcing to non-governmental organizations and private suppliers, as well as the relationships between these and the state system, are better regulated, whereas in others there are significant voids in public supply and regulation that are filled by both the private sector and voluntary initiatives (André and Abreu 2007; Tierolf and Nederland 2007). The same holds with regard to funding. This is consistently the chief threat to the survival of SIIs, as all of them struggle and devote enormous amounts of time and energy to secure funding in order to continue their activities. And here too, the financial contribution from the state – at its different spatial scales – exhibits great differences, while the EU provides an additional institutional and funding framework in the context of its cohesion policy.

Among the examined SIIs, those that fare better are those that enjoyed some form of institutionalization and, more importantly, managed to couple fund-raising from local and private sources with more stable public support. The Second Chance Schools that succeeded beyond the initial pilot phase are a case in point, as they are based on committed partnerships between local authorities, public social services, associations and private employers, on the one hand, and sustained funding ensured at the local level by the different partners with shared responsibilities, on the other. Similarly, the KESPEMs in Greece have been institutionally framed and funded by both the EU and the national government. In contrast, many local associations whose action is highly dependent on volunteer work and private sponsorships, and which only marginally manage to obtain some national and/or EU support, have difficulties in sustaining their activities. In the case of ARSIS, for example, national funding is virtually absent, precisely because of the lack of a national regulatory framework for addressing youth problems. The Arts Factory in Wales also consistently experienced fund-raising difficulties, whereas the Associazione Quartieri Spagnoli in Napoli, which owed its initial success to various forms of structured public support – from the municipality and from the EU – is being threatened by the recent changes in municipal social policy and the discontinuity in EU support. More importantly, in a number of cases – such as Alentour and the Arts Factory – the solidary and innovative dimension of local action is at odds with the performance criteria required by national and EU funding programmes (Martinelli et al. 2010).

26.3.4 Scale of Action and Scalar Articulation

By scale I mean both the *territorial* and the *government* scales, as the two can hardly be separated. A first concern is the principal scale of action, but a further key aspect is the *articulation* between different scales. In fact, although the *local* actors – civil society and government – are generally considered the primary, and most efficient, scale for mobilizing responses to social needs, evidence from the SINGOCOM and KATARSIS projects, as well as from the cases reviewed here, reveal that SIIs are often triggered from above. Furthermore, the examined cases clearly show the importance of multi-scalar networking and multi-level governance for the mobilization and dissemination of resources such as knowledge, information and, especially, funding. Klein (2007) stresses how the mobilization of exogenous resources enables local communities to become integrated into supra-local networks, which validate and reinforce their action. Indeed, in all the cases examined multi-level governance has proved a major enabling factor, not only in starting the initiative but also in ensuring its visibility and legitimacy, its continuity and, in some cases, its full institutionalization.

Among the initiatives triggered from above, a particularly interesting example of virtuous multi-level governance is the Second Chance Schools programme (Tierolf and Nederland 2007), promoted as a pilot project by the EU in several member states. The European scale played an essential role in initiating the projects and in the 'joint learning' process activated among them; however, the most effective cases were those that successfully mobilized both the national level – in ensuring, for example, the financial sustainability of the projects or the formal recognition of the pupil's acquired qualifications – and local actors, such as private enterprises and parents. Similar virtuous collaboration is exhibited by the KESPEMs, initiated by the EU in collaboration with the Greek national government (Ministry of Education), with the involvement of universities and local educational institutions, in the context of the Greek Operational Programme (http://www.museduc.gr/en (last accessed 18 December 2012); Baharopoulou and Siatitsa 2007). Among bottom-up initiatives that successfully involved higher scales can be mentioned the Anna Polak College in The Netherlands, which was promoted by a local partnership between local authorities, vocational schools, trade unions and employers, and is thus strongly embedded in the local context, but up-scaled through networking, becoming an international example involved in many EU projects and providing consulting to other initiatives. ARSIS, the Social and Educational Action and the Associazione Quartieri Spagnoli also all started as community-based actions, but then successfully involved the national educational system and/or up-scaled to EU programmes or networking.

26.4   LESSONS FROM THE CASE STUDIES: CREATIVELY RECOVERING A UNIVERSALISTIC SOCIAL POLICY

All the case studies analysed in the SINGOCOM and KATARSIS projects, including those more specifically concerning education services reviewed here, show that SIIs emerge in order to cope with unanswered social needs, often in the domain of very basic services, such as health, education or care, although these are also strongly linked to existential needs, such as recognition and self-expression. Thus, SIIs reveal, among other things, failures of the national welfare systems to reach particular groups or areas, whether this is because of the rolling back of public welfare services, the inadequacy of existing service delivery schemes or the generalized aggravation of social hardship. In other words, all too often social innovation is called upon to remedy for the erosion of the universalistic principle that underlay the old Fordist-Keynesian welfare system. This reading of SIIs allows me to put forward with greater strength my plea for an 'innovative' resumption of state responsibility in ensuring social citizenship.

The state – national governments and the EU in a possible future – must resume responsibility in guaranteeing universal access to social services, the only way to ensure full citizenship. This recovery of public responsibility cannot – obviously – be in the form of the old welfare state, which, while pursuing universal coverage, was often bureaucratic, paternalistic and indifferent to users' demands and specificities. But neither can we accept the neoliberal mainstreaming of social innovation, which places the burden of 'better' responding to the social needs of the excluded upon the shoulders of the third sector and community-based initiatives. The latter interpretation of social innovation becomes an alibi for the state to abdicate its social responsibility while cutting public spending and is dangerously echoed in many EU think tanks (Hubert 2010; Murray et al. 2010).

'Creative' policy-oriented thinking is thus needed, capable of conjoining social innovation with social citizenship; top-down state engagement (in terms of funding, regulation and coordination) with bottom-up action and empowerment. What kind of welfare system can then best serve the purpose of ensuring universal citizenship *together with* the recognition of differences and democratic empowerment? A number of lessons can be drawn from the case studies.

Although it is true that bottom-up, community-based, third sector initiatives in the domain of social services are potentially more innovative than top-down, hierarchical and more institutional attempts at reform, as they are more rooted in movements with explicit change agendas (André and Abreu 2007) and they devote greater attention to users' demands and quality of service, evidence from innumerable case studies also shows that they are much more vulnerable. In deprived areas and where marginalized groups are concerned, civil society and third sector initiatives are particularly difficult to mobilize and sustain. Moreover, although they aim at ensuring recognition of diversity and customization of services in response to specific needs, these initiatives often remain trapped into inequality. The case studies reviewed here also show that social innovation can be triggered from above, if appropriate spaces for experimentation are created, and, more importantly, that social innovation needs to be publicly sustained at some level (local, national, EU).

Thus, three strongly inter-related requisites seem necessary to enhance and sustain social innovation in social services while maintaining universal access: a) multi-level governance; b) availability and reliability of financial resources; c) institutional(ized) spaces for social innovation. In all three the state must maintain a major role.

1. *Multi-level governance*: although the centralized welfare state has often proved bureaucratic, authoritarian and indifferent to diversity, we cannot uncritically accept the idea that 'local welfare systems' are inherently best equipped to ensure fair and diversi-

fied social services, as they may end up reproducing inequality. Neither the central state, nor the local governments alone can assume the responsibility for answering social needs and ensuring universal coverage. Any new inclusive system of social services must involve a multi-level organization of funding, governance, and delivery. A division of labour with a 'nested' geometry of responsibility between different government scales – and also between the state and other actors – must be engineered. The central (national or EU) state should retain the responsibility of ensuring universal access to services regardless of place, origin, age, gender or social status, by guaranteeing equal resources – through re-distribution, if needed – and coordinating and regulating the supply systems, in order to ensure minimum quality standards. The local governments should ensure the 'fine tuning' of service planning and delivery, providing the spaces for democratic governance, empowerment and customization of supply, whatever service configuration is chosen, in close relation with the local communities (third sector and users associations). In other words, multi-level governance should ensure the virtuous encounter of top-down funding and regulation with bottom-up innovation. In some countries belonging to the social-democratic tradition – e.g. Denmark or Sweden – multi-scalar governance partnerships have already been introduced with interesting results, which have not attracted attention as 'socially innovative' but deserve to be better assessed.

2. *Availability and reliability of funding*: in the above division of labour the functioning of 'the bottom' must be safeguarded. A major threat to the

sustainability of social innovation is access to reliable resources. In the majority of the examined SIIs, overwhelming amounts of time and energy were spent searching for funding sources, preparing applications, lobbying and bidding for financial support – time and energy that could be more effectively used to implement the initiatives themselves. Indeed, the constant uncertainty about and the competition for funding often undermines from within, bottom-up initiatives by pitting them one against the other. Conversely, access to reliable sources of funding can 'free' other (human, organizational) resources and can contribute to overcoming the precariousness and ephemerality of SIIs. Thus, not only must the allocation of *public* resources for the provision of universal social services remain a priority of national and European social policy, but a balance must also be ensured between two types of funding: a) 'top-down' resources provided on an 'automatic' basis to sustain *basic* services for all – i.e. not subject to any potentially discretionary form of selection; and b) resources available for 'bottom-up', *innovative, context-sensitive* experiments. The latter can be discretionary to some extent – i.e. granted to specific areas, groups or service initiatives – to foster further social innovation.

3. *Institutional(ized) spaces for 'bottom-triggered' innovation*: besides funding, SIIs also need *institutional spaces* for social innovation to be sustained beyond the volunteerism and spontaneity of the initial social mobilization. How can social innovation in social services – which starts in reaction to some form of deprivation and is generally based on the mobiliza-

tion of local communities or voluntary human resources – become a *durable* social achievement? In addition to financial resources, regulatory frameworks should also be established so that room for SIIs is not won over a battlefield but is institutional(ized), i.e. recognized as spaces and rights for which people do not have to constantly fight, whether it is the satisfaction of material needs (education, health and care services), recognition of specific demands or more democratic governance. Many of the case studies examined show that the most successful and durable experiences were those framed in national legislation or EU programmes that not only funded, but also regulated, provided institutional room and legitimized the SIIs. Moreover, the national or EU institutional legitimation of initiatives often contributed to integrating community initiatives into supra-local networks, while strengthening or recreating local identity and social links within the community itself (André and Abreu 2007).

26.5 CONCLUDING REMARKS

From the above 'bottom-critical' review of SIIs in the domain of social services, both analytical and policy lessons can be drawn. First, research on social innovation cannot be limited to 'local' initiatives, but must adopt a multi-scalar perspective in order both to understand the reasons and impacts of mobilization, and to devise policy recommendations that can link bottom-up instances and actions with top-down regulation and redistribution. Second, the issue of citizenship and universal rights must be privileged in order to make the bridge between social innovation and social policy. Third, innovative policy-oriented thinking must be deployed to bridge utopian creativity with institutionalized opportunities.

In other words, we need to apply our imagination to 'reinvent the state' and envision *innovative and sustainable multiscalar institutional frameworks* capable of granting both basic rights and spaces for experimentation, involving diversified – *but regulated* – forms of co-production, partnership and responsible divisions of labour between different government scales and actors (family, community, state, and market) and in a context-sensitive way.

26.6 QUESTIONS FOR DISCUSSION

- How can universal access to social services, that is the right to good quality education, health assistance, care services, independently of income, place and origin, best be ensured?
- Is there no alternative between top-down bureaucratic and inefficient public services and bottom-up socially innovative social services? How can diversification and customization of services be attained without stratifying supply? How can social innovation contribute to better services, without superseding universal collective delivery?
- How can social innovation be sustained? What forms of public support and/or regulation can best ensure that innovations in social services become institutionalized social achievements?
- What should the role of the national state be in the realm of social services? How can we 'reinvent the state' so as to enhance both social

innovation in and universal access to social services?

NOTES

1. For instance, health, employment, drug use or criminal records which can lead to discrimination.
2. Of which Blair's 'Third way' approach was a most criticized institutionalized version, now superseded by Cameron's 'Big Society' approach.
3. The third sector encompasses a wide range of *non-governmental* organizations – from social cooperatives to associations of volunteers – producing goods and services on a *non-profit* basis, i.e. not driven by profit but on the basis of reciprocity, solidarity or other ethical motives. To a large extent it coincides with – and is the main organisational expression of – the so-called 'Social economy' (Moulaert and Ailenei 2005; Nyssens 2006).
4. The same mechanism is applied to the school system itself (in line with New Public Management principles), whereby schools are ranked according to national or international predefined standards of 'excellence', measured in terms of students' achievements, research results and/or publication records.
5. In this focus on process as well as content, education significantly overlaps with care services – child-care, care of impaired people or the elderly – where interactive learning and socialisation is part and parcel of the care function.

REFERENCES

(References in bold are recommended reading.)

Ailenei, O and B. Lefèbvre (2010), 'Social inclusion and exclusion in the neighbourhood of L'Epeule, Roubaix: the innovative role of the Alentour Association', in F. Moulaert et al. (eds), pp. 105–116.
Amin, A., A. Cameron and R. Hudson (2003), 'The Alterity of the Social Economy', in A. Leyshon, R. Lee and C. Williams (eds) *Alternative Economic Spaces*, London: Sage, pp. 27–54.
Andersen, J. and P. Hjort-Madsen (2007), 'Reflections on exclusion dynamics in education and training in the Danish context', *WP1.2 Annex C*, KATARSIS-FP6 Coordinated Action, http://katarsis.ncl.ac.uk/wp/wp1/papers.html (last accessed June 2011).
André, I. and A. Abreu (2007), 'Labour Market, Employment Strategies and Social Economy', *WP1.1 Survey paper*, KATARSIS-FP6

Coordinated Action, http://katarsis.ncl.ac.uk/wp/wp1/papers.html (last accessed June 2011).

Andreotti, A., F. Mingione and E. Polizzi (2009), 'Local welfare systems: a challenge for social cohesion', *Social Polis* Survey Paper Nr. 1. http://www.socialpolis.eu/uploads/tx_sp/EF01_Paper.pdf (last accessed December 2012).

Baharopoulou, A. and D. Siatitsa (2007), 'Education and training in Greece', *WP1.2 Annex E*, KATARSIS-FP6 Coordinated Action. http://katarsis.ncl.ac.uk/wp/wp1/papers.html (last accessed June 2011).

Cavola, L., P. Di Martino and P. De Muro (2010), 'How to make neighbourhoods act? The Associazione Quartieri Spagnoli, in Naples', in F. Moulaert et al. (eds), pp. 93–104.

Crouch, C., K. Eder and D. Tambini (eds) (2000), *Citizenship, Markets, and the State*, Oxford: Oxford University Press.

Donaldson, S. and L. Court (2010), 'Arts Factory in Ferndale, South Wales: renegotiating social relations in a traditional working-class community', in F. Moulaert et al. (eds), pp. 117–27.

Eurydice (2007), *National summary sheets on education systems in Europe and ongoing reforms*, Brussels: Eurydice.

Fraser, N. (1995), 'From redistribution to recognition? Dilemmas of justice in a 'Post-Socialist' age', *New Left Review*, **212**, 68–92.

González, S., F. Moulaert and F. Martinelli (2010), 'ALMOLIN: How to Analyse Social Innovation at the Local Level?', in F. Moulaert et al. (eds), pp. 49–67.

Hubert, A. (2010), *Empowering people, driving change: social innovation in the European Union*, Brussels: BEPA (Bureau of European Policy Advisers).

Kazepov, Y. (2008), 'The subsidiarization of social policies: actors, processes and impacts', *European Societies*, 10 (2), 247–273.

Klein, J-L. (2007), 'Social economy as a basis for local development Initiatives. A methodological reflection', *WP1.1 Annex C*, KATARSIS-FP6 Coordinated Action, http://katarsis.ncl.ac.uk/wp/wp1/papers.html (last accessed June 2011).

Martin, G. (2001), 'Social movements, welfare and social policy: A critical analysis', *Critical Social Policy*, 23 (3), 361–383.

Martinelli, F. (2010), 'Historical roots of social change: philosophies and movements', in F. Moulaert et al. (eds), pp. 17–48.

Martinelli, F., F. Moulaert and S. González (2010), 'Creatively designing urban futures: a transversal analysis of socially innovative initiatives', in F. Moulaert et al. (eds), pp. 198–218.

Moulaert, F. (2000) *Globalization and Integrated Area Development in European Cities*, Oxford: Oxford University Press.

Moulaert, F. and O. Ailenei (2005), 'Social economy, third sector and solidarity relations: a conceptual synthesis from history to present, *Urban Studies*, **42** (11), 2037–2053.

Moulaert F., F. Martinelli, S. González and E. Swyngedouw (2007), 'Introduction: Social Innovation and Governance in European Cities: Urban Development Between Path Dependency and Radical Innovation', *European Urban and Regional Studies*, **14** (3), 195–209.

Moulaert, F., F. Martinelli, E. Swyngedouw and S. González (eds) (2010), *Can Neighbourhoods Save the City? Community Development and Social Innovation*, London and New York: Routledge.

Nyssens, M. (2006), *Social enterprise at the crossroads of market, public policies and civil society*, London and New York: Routledge.

Ranci, C. (2005), 'La sfida del welfare locale. Problemi di coesione sociale e nuovi stili di governance', *Rivista Italiana di Politiche Sociali*, **2**, 9–26.

Tierolf, B. and T. Nederland (2007), 'Exclusion and inclusion in education and training', *WP1.2 Survey paper*, KATARSIS-FP6 Coordinated Action, http://katarsis.ncl.ac.uk/wp/wp1/papers.html (last accessed June 2011).

Whitty, G. (2001), 'Education, social class and social exclusion', *Journal of Education Policy*, 16 (4), 287–295.

27. The social and solidarity-based economy as a new field of public action: a policy and method for promoting social innovation
Laurent Fraisse

27.1 INTRODUCTION

Social innovation is a recent and new field of public policy in some Western countries. This concept has been used in political discourse for a few years, and has been progressively placed on political agendas. The creation of an Office of Social Innovation and Civic Participation in the Obama administration's White House, with the implementation of a Social Innovation Fund is one example. The European Commission also has introduced a strategy for social innovation through various exchanges and research programs as well as a European platform dedicated to social innovation. This chapter discusses the emergence of local public policies dedicated to the social and solidarity-based economy (SSE) in France as a case study for analysing the potential and limits of new public policies that support social innovation.

Social innovation is a broad concept. In this chapter, we refer to the Integrated Area Development definition (Moulaert et al. 2010) as grassroots initiatives based on the satisfaction of basic human needs, the empowerment of excluded social groups and communities for accessing social and citizen rights, and social changes in power relationships as well as transformations of governance practices.

Social innovation has often been associated in the literature with the social and solidarity based economy (SSE) (see Box

27.1) (Bouchard 2007; Lévesque 2007; Nussbaumer and Moulaert 2007; Richez-Battesti and Vallade 2009). Obviously, social innovation cannot be reduced to SSE because it covers a broader spectrum of individual motivations, collective actions, organization types, social networks and societal transformations that cannot be limited to materials and economic purposes, even if defined in a substantive and non formal sense (Polanyi 1983; Laville 2010). Moreover, not all SSE organizations are by essence innovative. Researchers have pointed out the permanent risk to SSE initiatives of institutional isomorphisms (DiMaggio and Powell 1983) through market pressures or instrumentalization by local government.

However, SSE is often presented as a laboratory for social innovation (Lévesque 2007). Several reasons can be highlighted to explain the close links between social innovation and SSE. First, the societal goals of economic action are distinctive characteristics of many SSE initiatives and enterprises. The motivations of entrepreneurs and groups of people to take the risk involved in starting an economic activity is not simply profit-based, and the final aim of the economic activity is often to serve the community. Second, throughout its history SSE has invented non-capitalist business statutes (co-ops, mutual societies, not-for-profit organizations) and promoted self-management practices. SSE has continued to innovate

---

BOX 27.1   SOCIAL ECONOMY, SOLIDARITY-BASED ECONOMY, SOCIAL ENTERPRISE: DEFINITIONS[2]

Social Economy
The social economy gathers enterprises from co-operative movements, mutual benefit and insurance societies, foundations, and all other types of non-profit organizations which have some common organizational and governance principles. Indeed, social economy organizations differ from the private for-profit sector as their primary goal is to serve members' needs or the broader public interest instead of maximizing and distributing profits to shareholders or members. They are also clearly distinct from the public sector although non-profit organizations may receive public subsidies to fulfil their mission: they are self-governed, private organizations with the rule 'one member, one vote' in their general assembly (Defourny 2010).

Solidarity-Based Economy
Not limited to social economy organizations, the civil and solidarity-based economy can be broadly defined as a perspective centred on all production, distribution and consumption activities contributing to the democratization of the economy based on citizen commitments and a public engagement in civil society (Eme and Laville 2006). This approach stresses the predominance of the principle of reciprocity over market and redistribution principles within the emergence of economic initiatives, as well as the hybridization of market, non-market and non-monetary resources in their consolidation and development. This balance can only be economically tenable in systems with an affirmation of public commitment and a critique of prevailing market economy standards.

Social Enterprise
According to the EMES definition (Defourny et al. 2010), social enterprises can be defined as organizations with an explicit aim to benefit the community, initiated by a group of citizens and in which the material interest of capital investors is subject to limits. They place a high value on their independence and on economic risk-taking related to ongoing socioeconomic activity.

---

during the last 20 years through the dissemination of new legal forms of social enterprises[1] (Defourny and Nyssens 2010) which include an explicit social aim of participatory organization and/or multi-stakeholder governance. Third, conceptualized from a plural economic perspective (Laville 2010) or in terms of the economy of diversity (Gibson-Graham 2008), SSE has

contributed to understanding the crucial role played by non-capitalist economic practices to achieve social well-being and environmental regeneration. The analysis of hidden and alternative economies, such as the SSE but also the economy of care, the non-monetary economy, the ecological economy, and local and complementary currencies, contribute to questioning the simple reduction of the economy to the market rules and to proposing different and broader representations of the human economy (Hart et al. 2010).

27.2 LOCAL PUBLIC POLICIES IN FAVOUR OF THE SOCIAL AND SOLIDARITY-BASED ECONOMY IN FRANCE

Whereas the 1980s were, to a certain extent, the first phase of institutionalization of the social economy at the national level, with the recognition of some national umbrella groups and the creation of a national delegation for the social economy, the 2000s witnessed the first signs of integration of the social and solidarity-based economy into public action.

Since the short-lived Secretary of State for the Solidarity-based Economy (2000–2002), a significant change has been the emergence of local public policies dedicated to the social and solidarity-based economy (Laville 2005; Fraisse 2009), with the election of hundreds of solidarity-based economy delegates in local authorities after the municipal elections of 2001 and 2008, and the regional elections of 2004 and 2010. In many cities (Nantes, Lille, Grenoble, etc.) and most regions (Nord-Pas de Calais, Provence-Alpes-Côte d'Azur, etc.), local policies mobilizing social and solidarity-based economy organizations and local networks have been gradually implemented.

For example, almost all of France's 22 regions now has an elected representative responsible for the social and solidarity-based economy and an SSE department, usually employing one or two people. Budgets run from 1 to 3 million Euros or from 7 to 20 million if employment support and 'work integration social enterprises' measures are included. Often falling under the responsibility of the department for economic development, SSE themes can also be found in departments dealing with employment, sustainable development, decentralized co-operation, etc.

27.3 SOCIAL INNOVATION AS A STRATEGIC FIELD FOR BUILDING A PUBLIC SSE POLICY

As with every new area of public action, the social and solidarity-based economy has to forge its own legitimacy within the institutional architecture framed by existing policies, which are characterized by the vertical separation that exists between economic development, employment and social cohesion, environmental protection and sustainable development. *Our hypothesis is that social innovation is one of the primary factors for legitimization of the social and solidarity-based economy as a new area of public action.*

The visibility of a policy for the social and solidarity-based economy is based on three separate strategies. The first requires a collective mobilization of stakeholders, entrepreneurs from various sectors, and other bodies in the public space via the medium of special events (forums, collective exhibitions, social and solidarity-based economy month,[3] etc.). The second strategy centres on an enhanced and quantifiable understanding of the social and solidarity-based economy in various economic and social sectors. Policies for the social and solidarity-based economy have made it easier to provide statistics[4] for the size of the social and solidarity-based economy in terms of the number of organizations and jobs, total turnover and sectors involved for any one region or urban area. Taking into account the performative impact of figures in the public debate, stating that the social and solidarity-based economy represents from 7 to 13 per cent of organizations and employment depending on the region, or that the growth rate of job creation in SSE is twice as great as the average, is a crucial argument to elected representatives and social and solidarity-based economy entrepreneurs.

The third strategy is to make use of the social and solidarity-based economy as a policy for social innovation in its own right. Support for innovative initiatives as part of the creation of local social and solidarity-based economy policies is one of the strategic lines[5] at work in many territories. This policy is primarily a response to the demands of SSE actors and organizations, which feel that the usual criteria for financial mechanisms and business creation methods are unsuited to the SSE, and sometimes even discriminating. Social and solidarity-based economy projects are often seen as atypical, which means that they are misunderstood. The co-production of services, social entrepreneurship and multi-stakeholder dynamics, the hybridization of commercial, non-commercial and voluntary resources as well as their outputs and impacts on social cohesion (job creation, internalization of social and environmental costs, social and community equity, participation in and renewal of local governance, etc.) are all aspects that do not fit in with local authorities' usual policies in supporting economic and social development.

Support for SSE initiatives is also an issue that concerns the visibility and legitimacy of a new field of public action and relies on the exemplary nature and number of initiatives in an area. Raising awareness of local initiatives and supporting their diversity in terms of sectors and statutory forms is primarily a means of making the SSE's presence felt and demonstrating its importance in the public arena. It is also the implicit counterpart in terms of the long-term involvement of stakeholders which are often asked by elected representatives to co-produce public policies. Visiting grassroots initiatives, improving their characteristics and outputs are finally pedagogical and political tools to convince elected representatives and administrative departments which are unfamiliar with SSE.

27.3.1 Diversity of Social and Solidarity-Based Initiatives

Studies of local SSE policies supported by local authorities in France (Fraisse 2008) demonstrate the diverse sectors covered by SSE initiatives. This diversity makes it difficult to summarize the variety of new activities developed by SSE entrepreneurs in different areas. This not only includes responsible consumption and fair trade, microcredit and social finance, care and personal services for elderly people, early childhood and inter-generational mutual aids, community and work integration social enterprises, micro and small enterprise creation and development, especially among the unemployed, migrants, women, but also car-sharing and mobility assistance, eco-building, social housing and access to city centre accommodation for young people and temporary workers, local exchange systems and complementary currencies, renewable energy production and energy efficiency supports, community supported agriculture and organic foods distribution, waste recycling and reuse, development cooperation and ethical tourism initiatives, collaborative web and free software, and platforms for cultural creation and exchange between artists and residents.

This diversity of sectors confirms that it is impossible to categorize the social and solidarity-based economy in one sector or industry alone. Several elected representatives have determined not to limit social and solidarity-based economy policies to the single issue of job creation and work integration of the most vulnerable population groups. This has proved decisive in producing a diversity of forms of socioeconomic innovation in the city.

27.3.2 Social Utility as a Criterion for Supporting and Evaluating Projects

Prioritizing the development of local initiatives within local SSE development programs often means redefining and broadening the criteria for supporting, funding and evaluating socioeconomic activities. Local SSE policies do not exist in isolation, and often have to collaborate with existing programs for supporting business creation, fighting against social exclusion and funding voluntary organizations.

Two strategies for supporting initiatives, sometimes complementary, have been identified. The implementation of specific SSE programs is doubtlessly the most frequently adopted approach. It often takes the form of putting out calls for projects with specific procedures and allocation and funding criteria. It can also take the form of different activity creation support programs that, depending on the area, differentiate the project design, start-up and development phases and have different funding methods for each stage. And it can sometimes be more targeted by focusing on one type of new organization, such as Société Coopérative d'Intérêt Collectif (SCIC), Business and Employment Cooperatives (BEC), social incubators (see Dubeux, Chapter 22; Fernandes et al., Chapter 29), or on the conversion of companies into co-ops.

A complementary strategy consists in integrating the SSE as far as possible into existing policies. This involves making the business start-up assistance and funding allocated by the local government to support small and medium enterprises available to SSE organizations. The goal is to progressively build a mainstreaming strategy which involves the integration of the SSE into every part of local development policy processes.

However, introducing the SSE within economic development objectives and programs or obtaining specific budgets do not suffice to promote socioeconomic innovation. Influencing elected representatives' economic representation and discourse and altering the administration's routines and methods for advising, assessing, and selecting socioeconomic projects, as well as assisting and training social entrepreneurs are also necessary.

27.4 CRITICISM AND LIMITS OF SSE POLICIES FOR PROMOTING SOCIAL INNOVATION

One of the main criticisms of local SSE policies is that they focus only on the emergence of new grassroots initiatives and small- and medium-social enterprises, rather than the development of existing and larger social economy organizations such as co-ops and mutual companies which have to face the upscaling of development strategies and competitive challenges at the national or European levels. In other words, local SSE policies marginally affect global economic players that structurally frame the main modes of production and consumption as well as capital, labour and natural flows.

A similar criticism is based on the ability of local SSE policies to consider only the entrepreneurial and organizational dimensions of social innovation without taking the institutional aspects into account.

Promoting social entrepreneurs, supporting local initiatives, allocating a specific budget to SSE etc., have only marginal impacts on the local economic system. Social innovation is often presented in the discourse of local politicians and social entrepreneurs as an accumulation of micro changes, a dissemination and reproduction of good practices rather than structural changes to the rules of competition, working conditions, norms of consumption, budget al.location systems or economic representation.

The risk of building a specific policy dedicated to SSE initiatives and organizations is the creation of an additional niche of public action which does not fundamentally modify the main decision-making process of economic and social development policies.

Limited to specific and peripheral programs, a policy of social innovation through the promotion of the SSE is confined to innovative solutions for tackling new social problems and new aspirations that neither private companies nor public administrations can meet. Social innovation remains functionally a complementary and subsidiary solution to failures by the market or the state. This narrow concept restrains the SSE as a collection of innovative initiatives and/or social enterprises without considering its potential and impacts on socioeconomic transformations.

However, several authors have emphasized the potential of the SSE as a possible way for social innovations to have positive institutional impacts. From a broader view, the SSE has been presented as a potential agent for a new social compromise (Bélanger et al. 2007) in a post-Fordist society, a means for economic democratization (Laville 2006), and key stakeholder in a local welfare mix system (Evers and Laville 2004), or in an integrated area development model (Hillier et al. 2004).

This institutional perspective of social innovation seems to be crucial to avoid the several dangers such as institutional isomorphism (Enjolras 1996) and localism (Moulaert and al 2007; Amin 2007). The recognition of innovative solutions promoted by the SSE through local public policies is not always sufficient to escape them being perceived as ordinary service providers and being co-opted by market pressures or their functional and local integration as instruments of social cohesion policies.

Studies of social innovation have also insisted on the dangers of localism (Hillier et al. 2004, p. 149). The long-term success of social innovation depends on the capacity of local SSE stakeholders to be committed in multi-level governance systems, to become part of trans-territorial networks and to mobilize monetary and non-monetary resources from beyond their immediate geographical area. Thus there is an absence of multi-level governance of the social and solidarity-based economy in France. The lack of European and national policies in support of the social and solidarity-based economy limits the opportunity for disseminating certain territorially-based innovations.

27.5 SSE: AN INNOVATIVE POLE OF RESISTANCE TO COMBAT THE EXPANSION OF PUBLIC MANAGEMENT RULES?

In spite of the persistence of doubts and criticisms of the SSE as an innovative tool for the development of new social and territorial compromises capable of creating a virtuous circle of local development linking creation of economic activities, social cohesion, and participative democracy, the existence of local SSE policies could be considered as an institutional innovation in itself. SSE could be analysed as a pole of resistance in a context of the extension of competition rules and dissemination of new public management methods. In the face of commoditization of common goods and services in particular in health and care, arts and culture, social housing, education and environmental protection fields, SSE policies preserve and foster governance spaces that are amenable to social innovation.

As underlined by González, Moulaert and Martinelli (2010, pp. 73–74), social innovation supposes transformation in local governance practices and changes in existing power relationships. Without being revolutionary, local SSE policies are a recent but useful institutional mediation for social innovation in local governance systems. Firstly, because many SSE local policies are the result of co-production and a co-construction of public action (Vaillancourt 2009) based on inclusive and permanent processes of civil society contributions. This co-construction is not only the consequence of the will of local politicians to democratize public action in conformity with SSE's values and managements principles. It is also vital to the creation of a large coalition of stakeholders able to put pressure on the local decision-making process and change local development priorities. Secondly, because SSE policies have invented criteria and evaluation methods for grassroots initiatives based not only on external evaluation frameworks that strengthen the accounting control of public authorities and limit innovation potential. Participatory and negotiated evaluation processes of projects with the commitment of SSE actors and the public authorities via mixed commissions have been proposed to avoid the risks of administrative instrumentalization and of discrimination in budgetary allocation of public resources due to dominant managerial and business representations.

27.6   CONTRIBUTING TO A HUMAN AND SUSTAINABLE ECONOMY

The first generation of policies for the social and solidarity-based economy often comprised the creation of specific mechanisms for supporting socioeconomic innovation. To go beyond this requires no longer limiting interventions to the symbolic success of a handful of projects in any particular area, but instead requires changes to local governance and the ability to influence socioeconomic development on the basis of the values of democracy, cooperation and solidarity that are both proclaimed and practised by the social and solidarity-based economy.

Social and environmental clauses on public markets, aid for economic development conditional on social and environmental criteria, responsible and sustainable public purchasing, networks and centres for multi-stakeholder cooperation and community dynamics, local funds for financing social innovation: these are some examples of socioeconomic governance that can transcend the opposition between community competitiveness and local initiatives that compensate for the social cohesion deficit.

Recent experience with social, environmental and even equitable clauses stand as examples of strategies for making the social and solidarity-based economy an engine for a plural and mixed economy. In France, purchases made in the context of public procurements account for over 8 per cent of GDP. There would be important scale and domino effects following the imposition of ecological and social requirements on these markets. Such a change requires considerable expertise as well as political awareness-raising of elected representatives and training of the technical services working for local authorities, whose long-term commitment is a decisive factor.

Existing initiatives demonstrate that one of the effective strategies for governance of the social and solidarity-based economy lies in co-constructing supply and demand upstream when setting the specifications, aiming, depending on the sector, to:

- tailor public orders to suit the size of social enterprises;
- change the scale of the offer, by providing technical support and assistance to local producer groups;
- create partnership arrangements with other local businesses, bearing in mind the employment needs of particular areas.

There are several regional initiatives of great interest as far as the conditionality of economic aid to businesses is concerned. In the Provence-Alpes-Côte d'Azur region, participation by social and solidarity-based economy stakeholders in discussions about the economic development policy was instrumental in ending the model that provided aid only to large businesses, considering their uncertain impact on local employment, moving towards a model founded on repayable loans.

In early 2007 in the Limousin region, the elected representative responsible for the social and solidarity-based economy introduced an adjustment mechanism – up to double – in the value of aid to business as a function of economic, social and environmental criteria. Every enterprise was encouraged to improve their practices in terms of employee participation in corporate governance and profit-sharing schemes, sustainable job creation

and involvement in local and regional development.

But aside from the introduction of societal criteria other than price in the regulation of local markets, *the question of the limits to competition rules* becomes an urgent issue to address. In a context where organizations in the social and solidarity-based economy are, in the name of so-called 'virtuous competition', increasingly placed on an equal footing with every other public and private (for-profit) operator, without paying attention to their different aims and contribution to the community, to their governance methods and to the limited distribution of surplus, it may well be vital to prove that the market is by no means the sole and unique prospect for local development.

The logics of competition and public service delegation – the restrictive alternative underpinned by the European framework (services directive) – leave little space for local policies for social innovation. Under either regulation, the assumption is that the broad outline of the general interest is known by the local authorities and defined under the terms of specifications that set out in advance the needs, price, public and content of the service to be performed.

Faced with the fact that calls for tender or bids appear to be becoming the norm for public action, including the management of social services of general interest, social and solidarity-based economy policies are one of the policy frames for reminding people that social innovation plays a fundamental role today, as it did yesterday, in the co-construction and co-production of the common good, based on public interventions and the demands of grassroots initiatives, as well as collective and self-managed forms of production and distribution.

Local SSE policies contribute, at their

own level, to the preservation of the ability to make direct purchases that by-pass the competitive process, to the establishment of partnerships between public authorities and the local community, to the negotiation of subsidies and other support that are vital conditions for ensuring the funding of social innovation at a time when social enterprises increasingly tend to be considered as simple providers of services rather than partners of public policies.

27.7 CONCLUSIONS

A future challenge for SSE local policies is to build a space for promoting social innovation as a strategic way to achieve local governance of a plural and mixed economy. Integrated development and social cohesion in existing urban local economies depend on the recognition of plural mechanisms of resource allocation where market mechanisms are regulated and combined with public planning as well as multiple partnership and cooperation between local stakeholders. Developing social innovation through SSE policies can contribute to the preservation of 'economic biodiversity' as a condition for reinforcing the social resilience of local economic and social cohesion to external shocks. This structural perspective of social innovation is fundamental in the current European context. The unprecedented economic and social crisis reminds us that the promotion of social innovation in political discourse and governmental programs may be combined with national and local economic austerity policies and budget cuts for mainstream social policies. The vibrant calls to the SSE to find entrepreneurial and efficient innovative solutions to tackle social issues calls into question the SSE's institutional position, whereas at the same time many traditional associations face

severe decreases in terms of funding allocated for delivering traditional community services.

27.8 QUESTIONS FOR DISCUSSION

- What are the potentials and limits of policies built on social and solidarity-based economy for the promotion of social innovation?
- To what extent is it possible to consider the social and solidarity-based economy as an innovative local governance strategy?

NOTES

1. Work integration social enterprises, social cooperatives in Italy and Poland, cooperative enterprises for the collective interest (SCIC) in France, social enterprises in Italy and Finland, community interest companies in the UK, social coops in Poland, and others.
2. For an historical, comparative and contextual review of the social economy approaches, refer to Moulaert and Ailenei's article (2005) 'Social Economy, Third Sector and Solidarity Relations: A Conceptual Synthesis from History to Present',
3. In November 2011, over 1,700 events were held across 22 regions in France (http://www.lemoiss.org/, last accessed 18 December 2012).
4. See for example, the first national atlas of the social and solidarity-based economy, compiled by the National Council of Regional Chambers of the Social Economy (CNCRES: http://www.cncres.org/, last accessed 18 December 2012). Chambers of the Social Economy are representative umbrellas gathering nonprofit organizations, co-operatives, foundations, and mutual companies at the regional level.
5. In addition to support for local initiatives, the main lines for social and solidarity-based economy policies tend to be: SSE information, awareness and communication; organizing and supporting networks of actors; budget and funding capacity for SSE organizations; horizontal inclusion of SSE in common law policies (including, in particular, economic, employment and social policies), and modifying local economic regulations (e.g. introduction of social and environmental clauses on public markets).

REFERENCES

(References in bold are recommended reading.)

Amin, Ash (2007), 'Le soutien au local au Royaume-Uni. Entre le recul politique et l'engagement solidaire', in J.-L. Klein and D. Harrisson (eds), pp. 273–298.

Bélanger, Paul. R., Jacques Boucher and Benoit Lévesque (2007), 'L'économie solidaire en Amérique du Nord: le cas du Québec', in Jean-Louis Laville (ed.), *L'économie solidaire. Une perspective internationale*, Paris: Hachette Pluriel, pp. 105–143.

Bouchard, Marie (2007), 'Les défis de l'innovation sociale en économie sociale', in J-L. Klein and D. Harrisson (eds), pp. 121–138.

Defourny, Jacques and Marthe Nyssens (2010), 'Social Enterprise', in K. Hart et al., pp. 284–292.

DiMaggio, P.J. and W. Powell (1983), 'The Iron Cage Revisited: *Institutional Isomorphism* and Collective Rationality in Organizational Fields', *American Sociological Review*, **48**, 147–160.

Eme, Bernard and Jean-Louis Laville (2006), 'Economie solidaire', in J-L. Laville and A.D. Cattani (eds), pp. 290–302.

Evers Adalbert and Jean-Louis Laville (eds) (2004), *The third sector in Europe*, Aldershot, UK and Brookfield, VT, USA: Edward Elgar Publishing.

Enjolras, B. (1996), 'Associations et isomorphisme institutionnel', *Revue Internationale de l'Economie Sociale, RECMA*, **75** (261), 68–75.

Fraisse, Laurent (2008), 'Les politiques de l'économie sociale et solidaire en France', *La Revue durable*, **33** (April), pp. 24–27.

Fraisse, Laurent (2009), 'The Third Sector and the Policy Process in France: the Centralised Horizontal Third Sector Community Faced with the Reconfiguration of the State-Centred Republican Model', in Jeremy Kendall (ed.), *Handbook on Third sector Policy in Europe*, Aldershot, UK and Brookfield, VT, USA: Edward Elgar Publishing, pp. 43–67.

Gibson-Graham, J.K. (2008), 'Diverse economies: performative practices for other worlds', *Human Geography*, **5** (32), 613–632.

González, Sara, Frank Moulaert and Flavia Martinelli (2010), 'How to analyse social innovation at the local level', in Frank Moulaert et al., pp. 49–67.

Hart, Keith, Laville Jean-Louis and Antonio D. Cattani (eds) (2010), *The Human Economy*, Cambridge, Polity Press.

Hillier, Jean, Frank Moulaert and Jacques Nussbaumer (2004), 'Trois essais sur le rôle de l'innovation sociale dans le développement territorial', *Géographie, Economie et Société*, **6**, pp.129–152.

Klein, Juan-Luis and Denis Harrisson (eds) (2007), *L'innovation sociale*, Québec: Presses de l'Université du Québec.

Laville, Jean-Louis (2005), 'Action publique et économie: un cadre d'analyse', in Jean-Louis Laville, Jean-Philippe Magnen, Genauto França Filho and Anna Medeiros (eds), *Action publique et économie solidaire. Une perspective internationale*, Ramonville: Editions Erès, pp.19–46.

Laville Jean-Louis (2010), 'Plural Economy', in K. Hart et al., pp. 77–83.

Laville Jean-Louis and Antonio D. Cattani (eds) (2006), *Dictionnaire de l'autre économie*, Paris: Folio Gallimard.

Lévesque, Benoît (2007), 'L'innovation dans le développement économique et sociale', in J-L. Klein and D. Harrisson (eds), pp. 43–68.

Moulaert, Frank and Oana Ailenei (2005), 'Social Economy, Third Sector and Solidarity Relations: A Conceptual Synthesis from History to Present', *Urban Studies*, **42** (11), 2037–2053.

Moulaert, Frank, Flavia Martinelli, Sara Gonzales and Erik Swyngedow (2007), 'Introduction: social innovation and governance in European cities: Urban development between path dependency and Radical innovation', *European Urban and Regional Studies*, **14**, 195–209.

Moulaert, Frank, Erik Swyngedouw, Flavia Martinelli and Sara González (eds) (2010), *Can Neighbourhoods save the city? Community development and social innovation*, London: Routledge.

Nussbaumer, Jacques and Frank Moulaert (2007), 'L'innovation sociale au cœur des débats publics et scientifiques', in Juan-Luis Klein and Denis Harrisson (eds), *Innovations sociales et transformations sociales*, Québec: Presses de l'Université du Québec.

Polanyi, K. (1983), *La grande transformation*, Paris: Gallimard.

Richez-Battesti, N. and D. Vallade (2009), 'Economie sociale et solidaire et innovations sociales: quel modèle socio-économique d'incubateur? Premiers résultats sur un incubateur d'entreprises sociales en Languedoc-Roussillon', *Innovation*, **2** (30), 41–69.

Vaillancourt, Y. (2009), 'Social Economy in the Co-Construction of Public Policy', *Annals of Public and Cooperative Economics*, **80 (2), 275–313.**

28. The Québec Model: a social innovation system founded on cooperation and consensus building

Juan-Luis Klein, Jean-Marc Fontan, Denis Harrisson and Benoît Lévesque

28.1 INTRODUCTION

The aim of this chapter is to present the contribution of social innovations to social transformation with a concrete example, the 'Québec Model'.[1] Let us recall that Québec is part of Canada, a confederation formed of a central government and provincial governments, and that in many respects, the province of Québec constitutes a 'distinct society'. Québec stands apart because of its culture (language and religion) and its economic development model. Québec economic structure relies on an economic and social arrangement of private companies, major public corporations and social economy based businesses.

The Québec case is a good example of a configuration in which social cohesion relies on important social innovations that have occurred since the 1960s. Social innovation takes place in the context of rationales and strategies for establishing links between individuals and communities, and among communities with each other. Social innovation thus enables us to qualify the progressive dynamic underlying the development of societies, in particular the development of their economic system. From that perspective, we will further elaborate our understanding of social innovation. As explained in the General Introduction to this Handbook, it is a process surrounding the implementation of new social arrangements, new forms of resource mobilization and new answers to problems for which available solutions have proven inadequate. Secondly, we present the main dimensions of the approach we adopted for our analysis. They are: governance, co-production of services and co-construction of public policies, and the plural character of the economy (in terms of variety of organizations and institutions and their underlying logics and objectives). We then identify the 'economic turn' of the social movements as an important source for incremental social innovations. Next, we present social innovations in three fields – labour, living conditions and local development – examining the main dimensions of innovation for each field. We then discuss the institutionalization of social innovation. In the conclusion, we reflect on the lessons that may be learned from this case with regard to social innovation and its impacts on social transformation.

28.2 SOCIAL INNOVATION: SOME CONCEPTUAL MILESTONES

Research on social innovation distinguishes between radical innovations and incremental innovations. Radical innovations represent a major rupture with the existing economic and social practices, while incremental innovations are intended to be gradual (Fagerberg 2003, p. 5). Even if incremental innovations are less spectacular, many consider their cumulative impact to be as great as or even greater than that of radical innovations (Lévesque 2006). Social innovations evolve in specific organizations and are spread through a process marked by tension and compromises. The speed and success in disseminating innovation depend on the area of activity and on the dynamic of the actors shaping the innovative organization. The spreading of social innovations to a large number of organizations, and their adoption by a range of actors, then paves the way for their institutionalization. This, in turn, gives stability and new meaning to social relationships. Social innovation brings actors occupying different positions in institutional environments to collaborate in the implementation of complementary systems of social innovation for different fields (Klein et al. 2009).

The analysis of the Québec Model reveals an entire set of social innovations that have transformed the institutional environment, thereby structuring and contributing to social transformation. Our hypothesis is that these innovations result from the participation of a plurality of actors (economic, social, political, cultural) who participate in the task of arriving at a common definition of social goals. This process of innovation thus involves the co-construction of public policies by public and private spheres in partnership with the social economy and the economic action of social movements (Enjolras 2008). Such changes are incremental and their origin lies in experiments initiated by civil society organizations. The actors deconstruct previous arrangements and adopt new practices that break with the institutional arrangements. Modes of coordination are thus modified, resulting in social transformation.

28.3 THE ECONOMIC TURN OF SOCIAL MOVEMENTS IN RESPONSE TO THE CRISIS OF FORDISM

In the early 1960s, a vast process of modernization that swept Québec, called the 'Quiet Revolution', gave rise to a centralized form of governance characterized by the predominance of the public actor (Brunelle 1978). However, starting in the 1980s, the crisis of Fordism and the questioning of the welfare state reignited a democratic fervour driven by social movements (Favreau and Lévesque 1996; Comeau et al. 2001). The response to this crisis triggered a cycle of mainly incremental social innovations that transformed the Québec Model. That cycle continued until the late 1990s, when institutionalization had progressed to the point of having a dampening effect on the innovative momentum. These innovations were also seriously questioned by the government starting in 2003, with the arrival of the Parti Libéral du Québec (PLQ), a political party with neoliberal orientations, in the Québec government. The new neoliberal forces challenged the mechanisms favouring the participation of collective actors and associations and the partnership-based forms of governance in place between 1980 and 2003, but without achieving the complete dismantling of these mechanisms, due to their institutional rootedness (Lévesque 2005).

28.3.1 The Effects of the Crisis of Fordism

The crisis of Fordism resulted in a social crisis affecting the measures introduced by the Quiet Revolution, thereby undermining the development choices that the socioeconomic actors had adhered to since 1960. Civil society was no longer mobilized only for modernization and democratization, as had been the case in the 1960s, but also by the need to respond to new social demands for economic equality.

In the domain of labour, Québec was caught up in the trend sweeping through all industrial societies. The new conditions that promoted unbridled competition generated major job losses and an increase in the proportion of precarious jobs. Many businesses, especially in the manufacturing sector, had to close their doors. Major sectors that had characterized the Québec economy, such as metalworking, textile and pulp and paper, were replaced by sectors associated with high technology. The crisis also affected the provision of public services. Under the former Keynesian system, aka the 'welfare state', the state had a monopoly on public services, in particular for education, social services and healthcare. However, that system entailed a bureaucracy and a technocracy that proved incapable of responding adequately to the demands of citizens in various respects. In efforts to make up for this failure, the urban neighbourhoods most affected by the employment crisis then began experimenting with economic community development. Thus, since the 1980s, local communities increasingly took it upon themselves to assume responsibilities for local development.

28.3.2 The New Economic Focus of Social Movements

The mobilization of the social actors was crucial in the implementation of social innovations in response to the crisis of Fordism. And that mobilization was characterized by a shift in the social actors' repertoire of collective actions.

Within the labour field, in response to unemployment and the closure of companies, the labour unions created economic development funds to invest in job crea-

tion, which marked an important turning point for the social movements and their collective actions. With regard to living conditions, citizen action began to turn to cooperation formulas. Citizens took the initiative of producing services rather than asking the state to provide them. Under the welfare state, service provision had been, although largely universal and free, centralized. The new civil society initiatives claimed democratization in the provision of services. This allowed for alliances between the users and the service providers as well as for a reconfiguration of relations of production and of consumption (Bélanger et al. 1987). The actors concerned were the new social movements (women's groups, community groups, environmental groups) but also unions and representatives of local communities and even public administrations. In local development, the crisis of 1980 caused a realignment of options for the actors concerning their territorial demands.

28.4 STRUCTURING DIMENSIONS IN THE QUÉBEC MODEL: GOVERNANCE, CO-PRODUCTION AND THE PLURALIST ECONOMY

As mentioned in the introduction, we consider that the Québec Model is characterized by major innovations that concern governance, the participation of civil society organizations in the co-construction of public policies, and the contribution thereof to the implementation of a more plural economic system. Let us now discuss those three characteristics on the basis of the types of social innovations that evolved during that time.

28.4.1 Social Innovations in the Field of Work

The main innovation in the field of work is related to worker participation in the creation of jobs and businesses. In particular, unions created pension funds intended to support job creation in Québec, but also to contribute to the development of Québec and its regions, to the training of workers and to the promotion of sustainable development and cooperation. The *Fonds de solidarité* (Solidarity Fund) was created by the *Fédération des travailleurs du Québec* (FTQ) in 1983, and *Fondaction* was created by the *Confédération des syndicats nationaux* (CSN) in 1996.

28.4.1.1 Governance

FTQ's Solidarity Fund (Fonds de solidarité) is characterized by a form of governance that calls for partnership as well as an ability to impose on businesses, in particular on SMEs, orientations favourable to the employment, training and participation of workers. It has introduced worker agents, called local representatives (LR), who represent the interests of workers. Before becoming involved in a company, the Fund conducts a type of financial audit that is complemented by a social responsibility report and sometimes by the training of workers with regard to accounting and economic matters. Since its founding, it has contributed to the creation and maintenance of more than 100,000 jobs and is a joint shareholder in private businesses, which are bound to it by restrictive shareholders' agreements. With more than 100 investment subsidiaries, the Fund is active in local and regional development as well as in the 'new economy' high-tech sectors, occasionally assisting with giving a second life to businesses threatened by closure.

As regarding governance, the links between this fund and the FTQ are very close, with the president of the FTQ also being president of the Fund. Moreover, the presidents of the diverse sector-based union federations sit on the Fund's board of directors together with socioeconomic representatives. Union representatives also sit on boards of directors of the regional and local funds. Lastly, the Fund has contributed to strengthening union action in Québec while making a significant contribution to the economic growth of Québec.

CSN's Fondaction also stands out due to the long tradition of CSN's involvement in cooperation and the social economy. The governance of Fondaction is more autonomous with regard to the FTQ. It may also be strongly networked with social economy-based organizations and businesses in which Fondaction chooses to invest. From that perspective, it strongly values its role and agency with regard to cooperation, responsible investment and the social economy. Fondaction has often and explicitly confirmed its place in the world of the social economy and promotes a plural economy dynamics.

28.4.1.2 Co-construction and co-production

From the standpoint of co-production, the partnership between union funds, the government, and social economy-oriented organizations gives rise to inter-organizational agreements between a diversity of competing actors who deliberately choose to cooperate rather than maintain confrontational relations. In Québec, many unions in the manufacturing sector and, to a lesser extent, in the service sector, participate voluntarily in this innovation process. Unions here act as intermediaries between employees and management, adding to their usual demands and influence on work organization and work safety.

At the meso level, as is the case with

sector-based labour committees where the unions sit next to employers and sometimes civil society representatives, co-construction initiatives exist, in particular for measures and programmes concerning the training of labour. However, given that they are not yet fully established, social innovations present multiple challenges even if they are promising for participative governance. One of these challenges is that social innovations are not always fully accepted, including by some of the various actors who co-produce them. Partnership is the culmination of strategic reflection and the result of various experiments. Its success depends on the presence or absence of restrictive politico-institutional arrangements and also on the capacity of the union movement to mobilize numerous and diversified resources (Harrisson et al. 2006).

28.4.1.3 Plural economy
In the labour field, the unions sit on the boards of directors of many public businesses. Moreover, they are members and shareholders of big mutual insurance companies as well as many savings banks. Also, the two workers' funds contribute to strengthening the pluralistic economy given their mission. In fact, these two funds meet practically all criteria in the definition of the social economy.

They thus contribute to the reorientation of capital investments by directing workers' savings toward sectors and territories neglected by the big capital. They have supported many community development initiatives, among them the *Fonds du développement de l'emploi de Montréal* (FDEM) supported by the Fonds de solidarité, and the *Société de développement Angus* by Fondaction. More recently, they participated in the new *Fiducie du Chantier de l'économie sociale*.

28.4.2 Social Innovations in Living Conditions

By building on horizontality and transversality to respond to concrete, localized and relatively specific problems, the production of public services raises questions of governance. For example, the production of services by the citizens' associations mobilizes reciprocity without being exclusively dependent on either public mandates or on the private market governed by supply and demand. For this reason, this production should be open to diverse rationales for action and mobilize all stakeholders (Lévesque and Thiry 2008).

28.4.2.1 Governance
Localized and autonomous production units emerge first through the voluntary commitment of users (citizens) and professionals to collaborate, often in direct link with the local community. Together, they then succeed in defining a new service project or even an existing service that is adapted to shared needs and aspirations. Public medical clinics implemented in several Montreal working-class neighbourhoods in the early 1970s are a good example of the first-generation civil society-based initiatives (Bélanger and Lévesque 1992). Those clinics were spearheaded by a citizens' committee that, questioning the individualist and passive consumption of health services, raised awareness for the influence of living conditions on health and demanded sanitary housing, a pollution-free environment and public recreational facilities.

This vision was shared by certain health and social services professionals. Many of these questioned medical practices centred on treatment rather than on prevention and also challenged the biomedical approach. The type of governance proposed by those actors involved not only the redefinition of the mode of production of health services but also their content, not to mention their accessibility. The Québec government tried to institutionalize these initiatives by creating local community service centres (Bélanger et al. 1987). This broad application of the innovative matrix comprised of community clinics was eventually integrated into the Québec health and social services network in 2003, when the public medical clinics of the 1970s had ceased to exist as such.

Experiments in public day care centres and social housing took place under comparable conditions, along with the unexpected challenges that invariably arise in such processes. It should be noted, however, that their institutionalization has not led to their complete integration to the state, at least not yet. The public day care centres, as they emerged in the early 1970s, were introduced mainly by the women's movement and initially relied on federal funds designated for job creation (Léger 1986). The extensive parental involvement which these centres rely on for their governance and service provision undoubtedly explains their superiority over for-profit centres (Kaiser and Rasminsky 1993). While the model of the public day care centres has stood the test of time (Gravel et al. 2007), their Québec-wide implementation in the form of the *Centres de la petite enfance* (CPE) in 1997 has led to major changes within their governance.

New reciprocal contractual relations between the CPEs and the *Ministère de la Famille et de l'Enfance* have been established. There was thus a transition from local day care units that enjoyed great autonomy to units belonging to a network involving a greater number of stakeholders and common rules (Gravel et al. 2007). All in all, this institutionalization made Québec the only North American society to offer day care services intended to be accessible to all families who request them. Even though it cannot be asserted whether this goal has been fully accomplished, within 10 years, from 1996 to 2006, the number of available day care places rose from 40,000 to 200,000.

28.4.2.2 Co-construction and co-production

The co-construction and co-production of social innovations by the Québec Model covers many service domains, among them social and community housing. What distinguishes the latter domain is a type of ownership and governance that allows for the participation of the users, and subsequently for the co-production of services (Bouchard 2006). To this day, non-profit housing cooperatives and organizations successfully ensure that users remain stakeholders in decisions concerning the management and maintenance of their housing. They offer not only quality and affordable housing, but also a living environment, strong social bonds and empowerment. Moreover, as these positive effects of social and community housing can even spill over to the neighbourhood, this form of housing can be considered a 'public good', in the sense that they could hardly be achieved, with the same quality, through either a public or private approach. This is because, in the latter cases, the users remain passive and thus have little interest in investing in the improvement of their housing units (and even less so in their immediate surroundings) that do not belong to them (Thériault et al. 1996). Lastly, non-profit housing organizations and cooperatives achieve greater involvement of the users, in addition to a greater socioeconomic mix of residents. In many cases, they have also contributed to enhancing certain neighbourhoods by renovating old buildings threatened by demolition.

The latter example shows that co-construction and co-production of services for people rely on the participation of users and professionals, which promotes democratic governance. In other words, they result from participatory work organization and the building and cultivation of a relationship with the users.

28.4.2.3 Plural economy

In many areas of activity involving living conditions, the plural economy exists in the form of a variety of ownership modes or a diversity of resources and rationales. Social and community housing and day care services, for example, are operated with a plurality of ownership forms, be it in the subsidized private sector, the public sector or the social economy sector. Moreover, those services benefit all of society and not only disadvantaged families. Concerning a plurality of resources and economic principles, the social economy stands out for its ability to mobilize not only market resources but also non-market (state subsidies) and non-monetary (volunteer work) resources. Thus, in the case of the CPEs, parents pay $7 per day (market resource) and contribute their time to the management and administration of the centres, while the Québec government provides subsidies ($1.3 billion per year). By the same token, in community and social housing, members of a cooperative or a non-profit organization pay a modest rent (market) and participate in management and maintenance, while the state subsidizes the cost of specific housing resources and a portion of the mortgage loan (Bouchard 2006).

28.4.3 Social Innovations in Local Development

By definition development concerns a plurality of actors and actions. In economic development, all local socioeconomic actors invariably participate in one way or another, often without identifying themselves as 'development actors' or without subscribing to any particular notion of local development. However, in our analysis in this chapter, we limit ourselves to organizations that were specifically mandated to support development in local and regional settings, a mandate that, as we shall see, targets territorial coordination and the governance of all those organizations.

28.4.3.1 Governance

Mutations within the capitalist system and demands from actors led the Québec government to modify the territorial governance modalities that had been implemented following the Quiet Revolution. The bodies in charge of applying the regional development policies implemented since the 1960s were then challenged. Centralism was replaced by a more endogenous development perspective oriented toward the development of local entrepreneurship which essentially favoured small and medium-sized businesses. This search for collaboration at the regional level between the organizations active in the economy and social development constitutes a major change in the culture of those organizations.

To meet the goal of territorial collaboration of actors at the regional level, existing territorial governance bodies were redefined, and new ones were created to respond to the specific challenges provoked by the crisis. For example, the Act Respecting Land Use Planning and Development, adopted in 1979, created a new territorial entity at the supra-municipal level, namely the *Municipalité régionale de comté* (MRC). These regional county municipalities were considered to be 'identity areas' and received the mandate to ensure territorial development in non-metropolitan settings.

378 The international handbook on social innovation

In the cities of Montreal, Québec and Hull[2], 'Urban Communities' (*Communautés urbaines*) had already been in place and functioned as the supra-municipal development entity. As a result of the Act, Québec territory was partitioned into 96 MRCs and three *Communautés urbaines*, the latter being viewed as MRCs for development purposes. This new grid turned out to be crucial for later policy shifts in support of local development.

The MRCs became the main building block for establishing the new local governance outside of the main cities. MRCs thus became the new local development units, replacing local municipalities. At another level, the administrative regions, created in the midst of the Quiet Revolution, were redefined. In the 1960s, the *Conseils régionaux de développement* (regional development councils) had been created to ensure the development planning tasks in regions and to act as the local antennas of the government. In 1983, these became the *Conseils régionaux de concertation et développement* (regional consensus-building and development councils). These new councils were composed of elected government representatives, persons in charge of local services and representatives of the socioeconomic milieu. In 1992, the government then assigned them the function of representing regional actors before government bodies. At the same time, this measure defined strategic planning as a mechanism for decision-making and resource allocation.

These reforms, which set various milestones for a partnership-based development governance of the regions, have their counterpart in the metropolitan setting, in particular in Montreal, though under different circumstances. At the neighbourhood level, a strategy took shape that was based on cooperation and partnership but prompted by social movements,

namely the community movement and unions. Communities in the neighbourhoods, including the business community, mobilized around community leaders to defend their assets in terms of services and jobs. The main result of this mobilization was the economic community development strategy and the creation of an organization dedicated to applying this intervention strategy in Montreal, the *Corporations de développement économique communautaire* (CDEC) (community economic development corporations).

The main objective of the CDECs is to promote collaboration among the actors in a neighbourhood in order to launch partnership-based development projects. Their second main objective is to support local entrepreneurship with the aim to facilitate the creation of local jobs. The third objective concerns employability, i.e. the qualification of unemployed individuals so that they can reintegrate into a job market undergoing accelerated restructuring.

In 1998, inspired by the CDEC's success in triggering local development, the government institutionalized the approach the CDECs had been experiencing by creating the *Centres locaux de développement* (CLDs) (Local Development Centres). Designed as multiservice organizations bringing together socioeconomic, political and local community actors, these centres were likewise intended to support local entrepreneurship. In the outlying regions, CLDs operated at the MRC level. In Montreal, following negotiations, the great majority of CDECs were assigned the function of the CLDs, and the territorial framework of their action became the boroughs.

28.4.3.2 Co-construction and co-production

In hindsight, government policies and measures concerning local development appear as co-constructions. On the one hand, experiments were encouraged by programmes of limited duration that often aimed to support pilot projects. On the other hand, when those experiments proved viable, even efficient, the public authorities tended to apply them over the entire territory, ready to realize hybridizations of experiments that were quite different from one another. In that sense, we can speak of a co-construction of the political approach that instituted those programmes (Lévesque 2007).

Thus, the creation of the CLDs in 1997 institutionalized innovative experiments that took place in local settings over many years and that proved efficient. CDECs were just one result of these experiments. This new entity received the mandate to mobilize all socioeconomic and political actors at the local level with the goal of promoting the creation of businesses and jobs. The definition of the role of the CLDs nevertheless remained flexible, which gave these centres broad leeway to define their own orientations.

28.4.3.3 Plural economy

Each CLD has the responsibility of devising a development strategy for local entrepreneurship that can be applied and operated within the social economy. The financing of a CLD is essentially ensured through a partnership between the provincial government and the municipalities. Each CLD at first benefits from two envelopes: the local investment fund and the social economy fund. Moreover, other funds created by specific organizations, such as the workers' funds, are also entrusted to the CLDs, who have the authority to sign production or service provision contracts with other organizations.

28.5 INSTITUTIONALIZATION OF SOCIAL INNOVATION: CONVERGENCES AND CHALLENGES

The three fields – labour, living conditions and local development – show the importance of the participation of actors representing civil society in the governance of development and in the definition of public policies in domains that matter to the community. The unions and community organizations no longer limited themselves merely to protesting against the injustices of an economic and social system; rather, they equipped themselves with tools to become actors, even stakeholders with private capital and public institutions. At the same time, the relationships between the local and the provincial levels evolved thanks to the intermediary action of the networks representing civil society, to the role of the social actors as spokespersons for governments, and to the partnership-based participation of these actors in the production of activities and services. Thus, the social actors helped build a genuine social innovation system following the reorientations achieved in the 1980s – reorientations that followed the path begun by the Quiet Revolution but that also embodied roadblocks to social innovation. The strength of these actors resides in partnership action, the ability to rally actors around issues, and the ability to get the government to take vulnerable social sectors into consideration when designing public strategies.

Even though they constitute sub-systems of social innovation, the three fields analysed are interrelated. First, sector-based organizations, as representatives of the socioeconomic actors, ensure a level of inter-sector interrelation. The *Conseil de la coopération et de la mutualité du Québec*, the *Chantier de l'économie sociale ou Solidarité rurale du Québec* and the unions and associated organizations, to mention only a few, constitute the networks of actors at the Québec level. These networks ensure a transversal coordination and a representation upstream to the government, which promotes compromises, the recognition of the social actors and the co-construction of public policies and their implementation (co-production) (Table 28.1).

Our analysis shows that the influence of the social movements on public policies results from two processes: the institutionalization of the experiments realized by civil society organizations, and the partnership between public actors and social actors. Through the institutionalization of innovations, the social movement becomes a part of the negotiation process that defines the political framework of social regulation, thereby transforming the institutions. Through partnership, civil society organizations participate in the execution of policies. The relationship of society to the state then appears as a fundamental element in a social innovation system, as illustrated by the Québec Model.

While the institutionalization of social innovations empowers civil society organizations, it also poses significant challenges to them and to society as a whole. First, in labour relations, the workers' funds created by the labour federations to intervene in business financing became key economic actors with influence on major investment projects. This allowed them to limit job losses in the many sectors in difficulty while also becoming involved in the most performing fields. Moreover, the funds supported the development of communities and projects of social economy-oriented organizations. This strengthened the position of the latter within the Québec socioeconomic system in addition to enhancing the pluralistic character of the Québec economy. Moreover, their governance favoured partnerships with private businesses, which subsequently led to more serious efforts to promote the employment and training of workers.

However, the legitimate ambition of unions to protect and create jobs and to act as an investor in businesses should not distract these organizations from their initial core mission of improving the working conditions of their members. In terms of work organization in particular, the results of the various reorganization phases triggered by the Fordism crisis too often resulted in work intensification, something the labour federations are now trying to undo by means of claims for decreased working hours and workloads.

With regard to living conditions, the main challenge resides in the link between social economy and community organizations and the state, in particular concerning the recognition, financing as well as the regulation and standardization of the actions of these organizations (Vaillancourt et al. 2003). The state agreed to embark on the decentralization of services and responsibilities, but without necessarily providing all the corresponding financial resources. In fact, the financial dependency of the organizations led them to accept, even to seek for, functions that moved them away from their original missions and that made them subcontractors rather than partners. From this perspective, the evaluation of social innovations also remains a challenge to the extent that our analysis does not take the specificity of these organizations into account.

With regard to local development, another challenge concerns the integration of two forces or movements. The first one relates to the organizations participating in governance that supports entrepreneurship, and that do so as part of autonomy claims from urban and rural social movements. The second comprises

Table 28.1   The most important innovations shaping the Québec Model in the fields studied

Dimensions	Fields			Common points
	Labour	Living conditions	Local development	
Governance	Partnership employers/ unions Participation employers/ employees Union and investment funds	Public/community partnership in the service offer Decentralization and regionalization Participation of users	Participation in neighbourhood, local and regional committees Intermediation and mediation	Partnership Regional and local governance Vertical intermediation (government/local actors) and horizontal (inter-sector interactions) Transversal role of the organizations representing civil society
Co-construction and Co-production	Work organization and training Joint definition of productivity and yields	Co-construction of social policies Policy and anti-poverty fund Forms of assistance to vulnerable persons	Community development organisations Rural pact Services offered by community organizations	Compromises between actors generate policies and recognition for consulting organizations representing civil society Participation of the social civil society in the decision-making process
Plural economy	Participation in company ownership Support of unions to social economy Partnership between private business, state, union funds	Solidarity cooperatives Health cooperatives Partnership Social and community housing Educational project	Union funds for local development Government funds Initiatives mobilizing diverse resources Intermediation section	Plurality of ownership forms: private, public and social Strategic role of the social economy Convergence of funding sources (public, private, social) Plurality of visions

the public or private investments that have impacts on the quality of life and the local economy, but that are beyond the control of local organizations and that enjoy a much greater wealth of resources. Thus, it is important that local governance organizations exercise horizontal and vertical intermediation, namely between the different actors who intervene in wealth creation and between the different levels. Moreover, the accountability of the local communities should not release the state from its responsibility for disadvantaged communities.

28.6   CONCLUSION

What does the Québec Model stand out for in terms of innovation and its relation to social transformation? The fact that social movements have switched from merely demanding actions from others to engaging, themselves, in proactive actions at the economic level can be seen as an important social innovation. Further, Québec social innovation features new combinations, approaches, ways of coordinating and regulations. From this standpoint, participative governance, co-production of services or activities, co-construction of public policies, as well as the plural character of the economy (concerning the modes of ownership and the capacity of hybridization of diverse resources) represent important dimensions of social innovation.

The examination of the Québec case also provides for a convergence of certain concepts that are generally looked at separately, in turn shedding light on the contribution of social innovations to social transformation. The notion of 'path dependency' (dependency on the institutional context) complemented by that of 'path building' (capacity of actors to break the regulatory framework and to build another one) offer a complemen-

tary avenue for understanding how innovations can be instrumental for a societal transformation. If path dependency exists in the Québec case, it is founded in part on collaboration and social cohesion as well as on the collective hope not only to survive as a Francophone society in North America but also to remain distinct with regard to its economy as well.

28.7   QUESTIONS FOR DISCUSSION

- Is it feasible to transfer the main Québec model characteristics to other societies?
- The economic turn of the social movements was a crucial milestone for the restructuring of the Québec Model. Is this important innovation likely to be adopted by other societies?
- To what extent is the consensus building mode of governance important for fighting against poverty and exclusion?
- Under what conditions could the social economy play a positive role in building a more inclusive and cohesive economy?

NOTE

1. For the concept of the 'Québec Model', see Bourque (2000) and Klein et al. (2009). For a critical analysis, see Salée (2007).
2. The name of the city of Hull became Gatineau as the result of a merging process in 2002.

REFERENCES

(References in bold are recommended reading.)

Bélanger, P.R. and B. Lévesque (1992), 'Le mouvement populaire et communautaire: de la revendication au partenariat (1963–1972)', in G. Daigle and

G. Rocher (eds), *Le Québec en jeu. Comprendre les grands défis*, Montréal: Presses de l'Université de Montréal, pp. 713–747.

Bélanger, P.R., B. Lévesque and M. Plamondon (1987), *Flexibilité du travail et demande sociale dans les Centres locaux de services communautaires*, Québec: Les Publications du Québec.

Bouchard, M.J. (2006), 'De l'expérimentation à l'institutionnalisation positive: l'innovation sociale dans le logement communautaire', *Annales de l'économie publique, sociale et coopérative*, **77** (2), 139–166.

Bourque, G.L. (2000), *Le modèle québécois de développement. De l'émergence au renouvellement*, Québec: Presses de l'Université du Québec.

Brunelle, D. (1978), *La désillusion tranquille*, Montréal: HMH.

Comeau, Y., L. Favreau, B. Lévesque and M. Mendell (2001), *Emploi, économie sociale, développement local*, Québec: Presses de l'Université du Québec.

Enjolras, B. (ed.) (2008), *Gouvernance et intérêt général dans les services sociaux et de santé*, Brussels: Peter Lang.

Fagerberg, J. (2003), *Innovation: A Guide to Literature*, University of Oslo: Center for Technology, Innovation and Culture, http://in 3.dem.ist.utl.pt/mscdesign/03ed/files/lec_1_01.pdf (last accessed 2 July 2011).

Favreau, L. and B. Lévesque (1996), *Développement économique communautaire. Économie sociale et intervention*, Québec: Presses de l'Université du Québec.

Gravel, A.R., G. Bellemare and L. Briand (2007), *Les centres de la petite enfance: Un mode de gestion féministe en évolution*, Québec: Presses de l'Université du Québec.

Harrisson, D., D. Laplante and G. Bellemare (2006), 'Innovations du travail et syndicats de la fonction publique: un partenariat à construire', *Annals of Public and Cooperative Economics*, **77 (2), 167–195.**

Kaiser, B. and J.S. Rasminski (1993), *Les services de garde pour votre enfant*, Montréal: Libre Expression.

Klein, J.-L. and D. Harrisson (eds) (2007), *L'innovation sociale. Émergence et effets sur la transformation des sociétés*, Québec: Presses de l'Université du Québec.

Klein, J.-L., J.-M. Fontan, D. Harrisson and B. Lévesque (2009), 'L'innovation sociale au Québec: un système d'innovation fondé sur la concertation', Cahier du CRISES, Collection Études théoriques, No ET0907, p. 92, http://www.crises.uqam.ca/upload/files/publications/etudes-theoriques/ET0907.pdf (last accessed 7 January 2013).

Léger, M. (1986), *Les garderies. Le fragile équilibre du pouvoir*, Montréal: RGMM-Les éditions de l'Arche.

Lévesque, B. (2005), 'Le modèle québécois et le développement régional et local: vers le néolibéralisme et la fin du modèle québécois?' in D. Lafontaine and B. Jean (eds), *Territoires et fonctions*, Tome 1, Rimouski: GRIDEQ-CRDT, pp. 15–44.

Lévesque, B. (2006), 'Le potentiel d'innovation sociale de l'économie sociale: quelques éléments de problématique', *Revue Économie et Solidarités*, **37** (1) 13–48.

Lévesque, B. (2007), 'Développement local au Québec, 20 ans d'expérimentation et d'institutionnalisation', in X. Itcaine, J. Palard and S. Ségas (eds), *Régimes territoriaux et développement économique*, Rennes: Presses universitaires de Rennes, pp. 31–47.

Lévesque, B. and B. Thiry (2008), 'Gouvernance et partenariat, deux vecteurs de la reconfiguration des nouveaux régimes de gouvernance des services sociaux et de santé', in B. Enjolras (ed.), *Gouvernance et intérêt général dans les services sociaux et de santé*, Brussels: Peter Lang, pp. 227–261.

Salée, D. (2007), 'The Québec state and the management of cultural diversity: perspectives on an ambiguous record', in K. Banting, T. Courchene and L. Seidle (eds) *Belonging? Diversity, recognition and shared citizenship in Canada*, Montréal: Institute for Research on Public Policy, pp. 105–142.

Thériault, L., C. Jetté, Y. Vaillancourt and R. Mathieu (1996), *Qualité de vie et logement social avec support communautaire à Montréal*, Montréal: Université du Québec à Montréal, Laboratoire de recherche sur les pratiques et les politiques sociales, Cahier 96-01.

Vaillancourt, Y., F. Aubry and C. Jetté (eds) (2003), *L'économie sociale dans les services à domicile*, Québec: Presses de l'Université du Québec.

29. The linkages between popular education and solidarity economy in Brazil: an historical perspective
Ana Cristina Fernandes, Andreas Novy and Paul Singer

29.1 INTRODUCTION

We argue that social innovations often emerge due to a specific context and a unique historical path pursued by social actors. The Brazilian experience with popular education and solidarity economy which have inspired a lot of social movements all over the world has its roots in popular movements and a critical and innovative form of education that emerged from the 1950s onwards. It was related to libertarian and socialist movements worldwide, but has found a unique expression whose beneficial effects have materialized in innovative forms of bottom-linked institutionalizing, social learning, knowledge production and collective action.

This chapter will apply a historical perspective on social innovation, stressing the importance of path dependency, context and history, in our case the social and political struggles in Pernambuco, a central Brazilian province during the colony, and afterwards in a long process of decline due to its dependency on sugar cane production. We will distinguish between two moments of linking education and knowledge production with the socioeconomic and political dynamics. First, before the military coup in 1964, popular education contributed to consciousness raising and the formation of a social alternative from below, an emblematic example of the counter-power challenging secular power of agrarian oligarchy. Second, due to the economic turmoil resulting from the debt crisis and the futile attempts of austerity policies in the 1980s and 1990s, solidarity economy has emerged as a socioeconomic alternative to unemployment and alienated labour, providing occupation and income to those affected by recession. This new form of cooperative economic agency has emerged in different places worldwide (Arthur et al. 2004; Altvater 2005; Altvater and Sekler 2006; Laville 2007), but with a specific socio-political dynamic and institutional support in Brazil. The movement of solidarity economy has taken up the spirit of popular education and political organization, while at the same time innovating in state-civil society dynamics acknowledging a creative role to knowledge transfer, transdisciplinary research and knowledge alliances in the form of incubators for popular cooperatives organized by federal universities.

During both the 1950s–1960s and 1980s–1990s, these initiatives were mostly brought about in the country's most industrialized state of São Paulo, birthplace of the country's strongest labour movement. In both cases, job losses have been turned into cooperatives and other sorts of initiatives by marginal as well as former industrial workers with the help of labour unions (Singer 2005).

Our argument is further discussed in five sections. The first brings about a brief historical background of social movements in Pernambuco, followed in Section 29.2 by a description of the more recent context of Brazilian popular education and solidarity economy. The third section focuses on the principles of popular education and solidarity economy and the fourth explores the particular experience of popular incubators. The last section summarizes the argument and draws conclusions for social innovations in other places.

29.2   THE HISTORICAL ROOTS OF POPULAR EDUCATION AND SOLIDARITY ECONOMY IN PERNAMBUCO

Brazilian democracy is a recent achievement of political struggle and social construction. It has been a long journey from formal liberty and democracy to a more social and substantial form of freedom and social democracy. First introduced by the republican regime in 1889, democracy remained limited to the elite until 1930. Throughout the 20th century, democracy faced several backlashes including two military coups (1937 and 1964), several attempted coups d'état and other assaults on its civic and democratic institutions. This long standing political instability is certainly related to the specific dynamics of international dependency and the deep social divide within an agricultural country formerly based on slave labour where economic and political power used to originate in large land ownership, both rural and urban, usually referred to as '*patrimonialism*' (Faoro 2001[1958]), resulting in an apparently archaic dominance of the land over the city (Freyre 2004[1936]). As for the majority of both urban and rural population, illiteracy functioned as a way of blocking access to voting.

The Brazilian Northeast, whose most important state is Pernambuco, was for centuries the socioeconomic centre of the sugar cane economy and has been a paradigmatic example of what was called the 'development of underdevelopment' (Frank 1969[1966]): dependency on a cash crop impeded the creation of a local market and resultant dynamics of a vivid division of labour (Furtado 2007[1959]). As such, even during democratic regimes, political representation usually stabilized the remarkable land concentration to the benefit of a small fraction of society as well as social exclusion of the majority of population. It is not surprising that since the very early times of the former Portuguese colony most social movements focused on getting access to land and basic civil rights. And it is also worth noting that a rigid law on land use was created in exactly the year – 1850 – when Brazil started to abandon slavery (Fiori 1995). Pernambuco housed several republican, liberal and popular movements, such as the Revolution of 1817, that proclaimed independence from Portugal and installed the short-lived *Republic of Pernambuco*, and the *Praiera Revolt* (1848–1852), both defeated, along with intense participation in the abolitionist movement as well as social and political movements mobilizing for more democratic labour relations and land reform (the so-called *Ligas Camponesas*) and the popular culture and education movements of the mid-20th century.

Extreme social disparities and extensive illiteracy are certainly at the origin of this combative character of Pernambucan poor and intellectuals. The sugar cane plantation functions as an extremely vertically integrated production unit with no relevant outsourcing apart from slave labour and cattle, thus leading to a rather reduced money circulation within the region. During its golden age, most essential ingredients and supplies were provided internally within the plantation as a self-sufficient unit, since slave labour could be used for all sorts of activities, thus paying back the high investment made in their acquisition (Furtado 2007 [1959]).

This led to a restricted local market, locking Pernambuco's economy into the traditional mono-cultural structure of sugar production. Until the 2000s, sugar has been the state's main export product. On the one hand, economic diversification and a deepening of the division of labour, as argued by Jacobs (1969), remained restricted, thereby limiting economic growth. On the other hand, wage labour after liberation from slavery remained mostly illiterate and marginalized due to small demand for labour in the regional economy outside sugar production activities, whereas political power and control of decision-making remained in the hands of the sugar landlords. The resulting extreme concentration of income, land and political power led to stagnation and concentration of commerce and other urban activities especially in the capital city, Recife (Singer 1968), a classical prime city to which population from both declining sugar regions and dry areas has traditionally fled in search of job opportunities.

Due to low levels of education, land concentration and a strong dependence on the sugar economy, industrialization only gained impetus in the 1960s and 1970s, with the help of federal public policies which induced investment from South-Eastern firms in the North-East. Newly created jobs, however, concentrated in the metropolitan region and in traditional industries (the less dynamic branches of metal-mechanics, food and beverages, clothing, retail, civil construction, domestic work), many of which remain precarious, thus restricting the growth of consumer markets as a whole in spite of relatively well paid jobs within some

industrial and public sectors (Fernandes 1998). This sugar-led economic structure has contributed to Recife lagging behind other regions in Brazil. In December 2009, the lowest average wage (R$861.90), the highest participation of military and civil servants in total occupations (10 per cent), and the second largest unemployment rate (8.4 per cent) among all metropolitan areas were recorded in Recife by IBGE (Instituto Brasileiro de Geografia e Estatística) (IBGE 2009).

Recent inward investments, however, have led to significant transformations. Expansion of the Brazilian petrochemical industry and its transportation infrastructure led by the public oil company Petrobras along with the expressive growth of the North-Eastern consumer market, both in connection with initiatives to foster the domestic economy by Lula government, have all turned the metropolitan region of Recife into an advantageous location, particularly the Suape industrial port facilities within it. Petrobras' new oil refinery (the first in over 30 years), two petrochemical mills, three shipbuilding plants, and the new factories of Fiat (with research and development facilities) and the pharmaceutical corporation Novartis, along with an impressive number of smaller firms have been reshaping the regional labour market (SUAPE n.d.). This means that Pernambuco's GDP has been growing faster than the country's in recent years (Condepe/fidem n.d.). After centuries of hegemony of the sugar cane industry, a new focus on inward investment may reshape Pernambuco, as industrial growth is raising expectations among the youth and driving many of them away from the sugar plantation which is no longer their only job opportunity.

In spite of these very recent changes, we cannot forget that Pernambuco owes to the sugar economy its backward condition, deep income concentration and very low levels of formal education so far (the average number of school years of 15 year olds and above was 6.4 years in 2008, as compared to the national average of 7.4 years, but in some regions the state still presents an average of three school years, according to IBGE). The metropolitan area of Recife, however, reached an average of eight school years in 2008, due to the higher education facilities established since the late 1800s in the city focused on the sugar related upper class (Fernandes et al. 2011). Being Pernambucos' capital city certainly accounts for this advantageous situation Recife enjoys compared to other places within the state, but it also results from the history of social and political movements, many of them inspired by liberal and socialist ideas brought in from European movements and revolutions. The importance of popular education within the social movements of the 1960s is certainly a product of the political and social actions accumulated in the face of deep social disparities, to which the wave of popular movements in post-war Europe and Latin America also contributed.

The 19 years from 1945 to 1964 – the so-called '*República Nova*' – was the longest period under democratic rule during the past century. This first period of democracy gave birth to rich experiments all over Brazil, but especially in Pernambuco. It was the fervent socioeconomic dynamics as well as the political organization of formerly excluded parts of the population which inspired some of the best Brazilian intellectuals. In economics and planning, Celso Furtado innovated in understanding Brazilian underdevelopment as well as in using planning for the transition towards a just and inclusive society. Furtado founded structuralism as a proper paradigm of development economics and was

in charge of a systematic effort of regional development policy already in the 1950s, similar to the Tennessee Valley Authority and the Casa de Mezzogiorno (Furtado 1997; Fernandes 1998). Paulo Freire, who worked in the education movement in Pernambuco in the 1950s, invented a unique form of alphabetization based on dialogue and context-sensitive didactics (Freire 2001).

It is worth noting that Paulo Freire's *Pedagogy of the Oppressed* (Freire 1996[1968]), written in exile in Chile, was elaborated within a deeply divided society in which literacy was a precondition for voting. Popular education was part of a broader movement that united diverse social and political forces in Brazil, in general, and in the state of Pernambuco in particular. Intellectuals, artists, urban labour unions, rural workers of the *Ligas Camponesas*, left wing politicians, the Catholic Church (with its *Liberation Theology* and the *Justice and Peace Commission*) were all participants in the creative wave of libertarian initiatives that sprang into life in the late 1950s and spread to other parts of the country in the first half of the 1960s (Oliveira 1987). Crucial were the so-called Movement of Popular Culture (*Movimento de Cultura Popular* or MCP) created in Recife by a group of artists and intellectuals such as Ariano Suassuna and Francisco Brennand, Hermilo Borba Filho and Paulo Freire. MCP proposed raising social and political 'consciousness' of the poor, enabling them to learn not only the alphabet, but to be able to understand and – in the words of Paulo Freire – to 'read the world', thereby interfering in the oppressive dynamics surrounding the landless and peasant classes. Emancipation was promoted through various sorts of popular artistic manifestations. MCP produced books and manuals among which the so-called *MCP*

Book for Adults Reading, the movement's guide-book. Paulo Freire's critical education methodology emerged from this experience. Brought into the state government of Miguel Arraes, within just three years MCP amassed 20,000 students (adults, youngsters and children), over 600 classes, 200 schools and radio-broadcasted classes, 450 teachers and 5 culture squares, where a great number of open air theatre sessions, art courses, workshops and expositions took place (Coelho 2002). Furthermore, the movement gained recognition by the president João Goulart – to the extent of replicating thousands of cultural circles across the country, but was wiped out by the military coup in 1964.

29.3 RECENT CONTEXT OF BRAZILIAN POPULAR EDUCATION AND SOLIDARITY ECONOMY

Until the 1980s, popular education was banished from Brazilian schools along with all sorts of emancipatory experiences. Nevertheless, such activities in rural and urban areas never stopped completely. During the authoritarian regime, urban movements such as the so-called *Comunidades Eclesiais de Base* (CEBs), in urban areas, and the *Pastoral da Terra*, in rural communities, provided forms of access to public services and resistance against persecution by the authoritarian regime (Kowarick 1979; Fernandes 1989). These diverse grassroots initiatives helped to mobilize nationwide re-democratization and to create the Workers Party as an articulation of those initiatives. Several participatory movements helped to establish a new relationship between state and civil society out of which – in the case of Pernambuco – the Special Zones of Social Interest (ZEIS)[1] and the participatory budget stand out. Several other

movements have strengthened or sprung up since then, among which the indigenous peoples movement, playing a relevant role in both the country's re-democratization process and elaboration of the so-called 'Citizen Constitution' of 1988, as well as diverse experiments with participatory governance, from participatory budgeting to models of co-management (Abers 2000; Novy and Leubolt 2005; Santos 2005; Avritzer 2006).

Re-democratization went hand in hand with socioeconomic turmoil due to the debt crisis and the resultant neoliberal turn. While the 1980s were characterized by institutionalized class struggle as well as systematic strikes, the 1990s led to a weakening of the worker's movement and strategic changes. Workers started to look for alternative sources of income creation on the basis of a solidarity economy throughout the country. As Singer (2005) points out, during the 1980s with the help of the labour unions former employees managed to create cooperatives out of bankrupt firms and slowly developed the ability to take advantage of the legislation to purchase or rent insolvent companies and preserve their jobs. In parallel, they also engaged in the process of developing so-called self-management skills to run the firm cooperatively with the contribution of *Anteag*, the National Association of Workers in Self-managed Firms, which was founded in 1994 and aimed at helping workers to fight to maintain their jobs and assist newly created firms of the solidarity economy.

Anteag has helped the creation of solidarity firms in various industrial sectors and different Brazilian states, although most of its competence has been built out of the numerous cases from São Paulo. Yet the most notorious example came to be that of Catende, a 26,000 hectare sugar plantation and industry in Pernambuco.

Catende was the largest solidarity firm of the approximately 160 assisted by Anteag in 2001, when even state and local governments were already contracting the Association in order to reduce unemployment. With the close support of socialist governor Miguel Arraes (the same politician in charge of Pernambuco's government when the MCP was created in the 1960s), the Rural Workers Union (FETAPE), the Solidarity Development Agency of CUT (*Central Única dos Trabalhadores*) and the support from the Pernambuco's government, the workers effort to turn Catende into a self-managed company, *Cooperativa Harmonia*, after its bankruptcy in 1995 allowed 3,200 families to keep their monetary income (Auinger 2007).

After the plenary session organized within the III World Social Forum in 2002, the solidarity economy movement succeeded in creating the National Secretariat of Solidarity Economy (SENAES) in 2003, and Paul Singer became the first Secretary for Solidarity-based Economy within the Ministry of Labour of the Lula government. In parallel, the National Forum of Solidarity Economy (FNES) was created to dialogue with SENAES in terms of presenting demands and suggestions, and evaluating public policies for improving solidarity economy in Brazil (Singer 2004).

Since then, solidarity economy has been fostered within the country by means of a number of new programmes for supporting solidarity entrepreneurship, from production to commercialization, banking, and restoring bankrupt firms into self-management, capacity building through formation of solidarity policy makers, educators and development agents, as well as institutional articulation within the federal government's different ministries to promote solidarity economy into diverse public policies. Among these initiatives, it is worth mentioning the programme of university-led technological incubators of solidarity cooperatives (PRONINC), created in 1998, but enhanced considerably under SENAES initiative (Ministério do Trabhalo e Emprego n.d.).

Today, solidarity economy is a nationwide movement, a form of new cooperativism based on solidarity, mutuality and self-management. In the North-East, 645,504 persons participate in the solidarity economy, making it the region with most activists. Nationwide, there are 1,687,496 members in the solidarity economy, according to the Atlas on solidarity economy, last updated for 2007 by the Ministry of Labour (Ministério do Trabhalo e Emprego n.d.).

29.4 PRINCIPLES OF SOLIDARITY ECONOMY AND POPULAR EDUCATION

Solidarity economy projects face considerable challenges though. According to Singer (2005), firstly, it is difficult to convince the workers to become partners of an insolvent firm under solidarity principles and devote themselves to turning it back into a normally solvent company. In many cases only part of the workforce agrees to engage into the venture. Secondly, getting the company's patrimony formally transferred to the workers' association or cooperative requires time consuming and complex legal and financial negotiations, which involve many actors from the private and public sector. Thirdly, the solidarity economy movement must fight to bring back clients, suppliers and credit of the former company. Fourthly, and maybe the most demanding, is finding access to credit in order to face an increasing demand. The overall process is actually a learning-by-doing process, building a new role different from being either the boss or the employee – that is, to become the bosses of themselves – is something that needs support and determination. This clearly shows the significant role that actors such as SENAES, the FNES as well as state agencies and the university incubators play by providing training, credit, facilities for exchange of experiences and other infrastructural and knowledge assistance.

However, these challenges have now entered a new phase as the impressive recovery of the Brazilian economy during the past eight years has led to sharp decline in unemployment.[2] At the same time the federal government has increased social expenditure from 11.2 per cent in 1995 to 15.8 per cent in 2009 (Barrocal 2011) and public income transfers were raised from 6.9 per cent in 2002 to 8.4 per cent in 2008 (Barbosa 2010, p. 2). Yet, the solidarity economy seems to have expanded remarkably during this period, as preliminary results of the most recent mapping of solidarity economy initiatives under way by SENAES suggests. This may indicate that the movement has gone beyond mere survival strategies and may reflect the productive and educative dimensions of the solidarity-based economy. The latter seems to have increasingly attracted the workers' preferences probably due to its superior conditions from the workers' point of view, compared to wage labour, since it offers them the means to overcome labour alienation and establish democratic decision-making processes and safe and fair workplaces.

However, the current recovery of the Brazilian economy and its increasing geo-economic importance have increased pressure on the solidarity-based economy to justify its approach. One strategy has been going beyond mere income-generation and stressing the link of economic and

vocational as well as educational initiatives. This has led some initiatives to connect solidarity economy with popular education. Inspiration comes from Paulo Freire's critical pedagogy as it develops the ability to interpret the world in order to orientate oneself and to interfere in the world (Novy 2009). This presupposes a radically different concept of education from what Freire called the 'banking' approach, in which the student is seen as an empty account to be filled with knowledge by the teacher (1996[1968]). Instead, Freire proposed thinking in terms of a mutual learning relationship in which the teacher can learn and the learner can teach. In so doing, the individuals – both the student and the teacher – encourage one another to develop autonomous thinking that leads to questioning the world and getting deep into the problems of the world, for taking part in it and transforming it (Freire 1998[1992]).

This critical attitude is based on a central idea in Freire's thinking. For him, 'Nobody educates anybody else. Nobody educates himself/herself; people educate each other through their interactions with the world' (Freire 2005, p. 78). This presupposes that 'there is no individual "I think" but a "we think" as a collective act', as Gomez (2009, p. 41) highlights, and leads to the dialectics of thinking and doing, acting and reflecting. As long as we think together and teach and learn with one another, we are in the public sphere – as exposed by Arendt (1998[1958]) – where human beings distinguish themselves, recognizing diversity and multiplicity of ideas and human differences, thus encountering conflict and contradiction. Interaction of different ideas in the public sphere fosters the ability to raise questions hence developing autonomous thinking.

Freire's essential idea is respect toward others and their way of thinking and living

(Freire 2004, p. 28). Elitist arrogance and paternalism by well-meaning experts likewise hamper not only a relationship that wants to make a difference but also one that just aims for mutual understanding. It is about the dialogue between researchers just as about the dialogue with the objects of research, which are at the same time subjects of social transformation. This interactive research praxis is transdisciplinary. Neither this implies a rejection of disciplines and their specific methods and skills nor a replacement for discipline and its strict way of thinking and acting, because 'knowledge requires discipline' (Freire and Shor 2003, p. 101).

Freire's ideas have inspired diverse social movements over the last decades, the two most important ones being the Landless Movement (*Movimento dos Sem Terra* (Wolford 2004; Stedile 2007)) and the solidarity economy. With respect to the solidarity economy, there has been a huge effort to elaborate a new democratic governance of knowledge, mobilizing universities to contribute to the local socioeconomic development (see Dubeux, Chapter 22). This implies that the authority the researcher and educator enjoy must not be allowed to degenerate into authoritarianism, hence Freire's strong aversion to the teacher-student dichotomy. Overcoming this dichotomy in human interaction as a whole and not only within the classroom experience makes the difference between creating a cooperative in order to solely provide for income and occupation and creating a self-determined collective by means of a solidarity economy initiative.

29.5 ITCP PUBLIC UNIVERSITIES' TECHNOLOGICAL INCUBATOR OF POPULAR COOPERATIVES

Two processes have merged in Brazil to create the public universities' technological incubators of popular cooperatives (ITCP, *Incubadoras Tecnológicas de Cooperativas Populares*). First, Brazilian universities have obligations in the field of teaching, research and so-called 'extension' which covers the broad range of activities which link university and society. Today, this is often reduced to getting co-financing from the private sector. Incubators are a different mechanism of linking the knowledge of the university with economic interests, which in general are for-profit organizations. Second, there is a long tradition of committed academics engaging themselves as 'organic intellectuals' in public affairs. They have played a crucial role in the re-democratization process. Betinho, an outstanding activist and intellectual who inspired the first movement for the eradication of poverty at the beginning of the 1990s, was also one of the inspiring personalities for public incubators.

The first popular incubator was created in 1995 in the Federal University of Rio de Janeiro, still without being embedded in an overall governmental programme. In 2003, the federal state secretary SENAES was created and a proper support structure was elaborated. ITCP is now present in over 100 universities, over 80 of which have been supported by PRONINC, distributed over all geographical regions and can be found in a variety of economic activities, from financial to production units, from education and knowledge exchange to commercialization, concerned with networking and social organization.

ITCP stands for democratization of knowledge and production by generating income opportunities through knowledge transfer and knowledge sharing between universities and social initiatives. ITCP stimulates the joint development of specific technologies to productive projects they support. Most ITCP have a pragmatic approach of responding to basic needs, giving know-how on technical, administrative or marketing issues. Although this is often the focus of the incubators, most ITCPs emphasize the ideological importance of popular education as a founding principle for mutual learning and respect. Popular education is introduced because solidarity economy is about collective organization and empowering. In this context 'consciousness' raising and emancipation are crucial dimensions of this social innovation, otherwise it would be just another income creation experience for the poor, stressing the content dimension of social innovations to the detriment of the process dimension (Moulaert et al. 2005). Popular education turns an ordinary economic activity for the poor into a communitarian organization whose participants jointly search for alternative models of socially just economic development by means of increasing creativity and consciousness and promoting capacities for action of individuals and social groups. Popular education contributes by bringing in operational methodologies for solidarity economy to achieve its objectives.

Today, the Ministry of Labour and Employment supports over 40 popular incubators (http://www.mte.gov.br/ecosol idaria/prog_incubadoras_proninc.asp, last accessed 5 September 2011). University incubators are not all involved in explicitly connecting solidarity economy with popular education, but those involved agree with Paulo Freire that consciousness-raising is a learning process to understand social, political and economic contradictions of contemporary societies

and taking action to change repressive life conditions. Freire's *Pedagogy of the Oppressed* inspires ITCP: instead of technology transfer, practice is oriented to joint-research of own reality and joint-knowledge creation; instead of education and knowledge for wealth creation, practice is oriented to foster creativity and learning to do together and learning to live together (Delors 1996).

In Pernambuco there are two university incubators, both located in Recife: the ITCP FAFIRE (established in a traditional catholic college), and the Federal Rural University of Pernambuco's INCUBACOOP. The latter, which links popular education and solidarity economy, has been rather influenced by the lessons of MCP (see Dubeux, Chapter 22). Its experience exemplifies the connections between popular education and solidarity economy that have been put into practice and the MCP roots upon which they might have been raised (Dubeux 2004; Hauer 2010).

In 2011, a new incubator was set up by the Federal University of Pernambuco which will deal with herbal medicines production and commercialization network. Herbs and artisanal phytotherapy drugs still are widespread popular practices in the country, particularly in the regions in the North-East and the North, but the traditional knowledge they involve has been jeopardized by the expansion of the so-called *big pharma* along with the expansion of the national health system. The activity of traditional healers, medicinal plant and phytotherapy drug popular producers and dealers is shrinking despite the richness of the well-known Brazilian biodiversity. Aware of this, the federal government engaged in an effort to preserve it, launching the Política Nacional de Plantas Medicinais e Fitoterápicos (Ministério da Saúde 2006) which proposes, among other initiatives, introducing these plants and phytotherapic drugs into the national health system following best laboratory practices and high production standards. The new incubator aims both to preserve traditional knowledge and to exchange scientific knowledge with local groups in order to improve quality, from collection and production to storing, dispensation and commercialization of these plants and drugs, thus supporting interaction among the different links of this value chain, which have acted until now in isolation, and its enlargement under solidarity principles. The new ITCP of UFPE also aims at educating the university students to interact with traditional communities enabling them to act as innovative professionals with social concerns. Territorial and individual development is expected to improve in these communities where their popular labs and the collection and production of plants and roots are starting to interconnect with popular healers, dispensers and 'natural pharmacies' that will be able to supply the public health system.

These incubators are bridges between university and society and in our case with the most excluded sectors. Popular incubators link theory and practice in various ways, because this is the only way to solve existing problems in world development. This requires a commitment, especially from the academic sector, which – in general – acts in an environment not supportive to these types of activities, forcing academics to dedicate themselves to this extension work outside official working hours.

One of the aims of incubators is to make available a broad expertise and to harness the same through dialogue and knowledge transfer. In order for popular incubators to contribute to problem-solving there must be a dialogue between expert and experience knowledge, because development is a complex and complicated process

in which people unconsciously and intentionally interfere. By collective cogitation of people with diverse experience and different expertise it becomes possible to enhance, support and to facilitate certain processes identified as eligible. This means learning from each other and building alliances for common aims.

29.6 FINAL REMARKS

There are different lessons to be learned from this innovative governance of knowledge, resulting from the interface of popular education and solidarity economy. First, the case study presented does not pretend to be a best practice, but an innovative good example of how a historical legacy, the collective memory of a social struggle and the respective knowledge of complementary actors can be mobilized in new historical situations to promote innovations in favour of social transformations towards creative ways of social inclusion.

Second, what is striking is the insistence of popular organization for full citizenship in Pernambuco, which took different forms over time. While the popular movement in the 1950s and 1960s was more militant and political, the current social movement of solidarity economy is more oriented towards self-help and the satisfaction of basic needs. However, it has always been bottom-linked and inspired by the same critical pedagogy as the popular movement decades before. While the movement of popular education stressed the antagonism of oppression and liberation, the current movement focuses on empowerment and dialogue, mobilizing socially innovative forms of the social economy as well as the governance of knowledge.

Third, popular incubators represent, beyond the specific Brazilian situation, an innovative form of theory-practice interface in favour of empowerment and full citizenship. They offer perspectives for community-oriented forms of research and training, beyond conventional forms of fostering local competitiveness via cluster formation of the so-called 'triple helix paradigm'. By bringing attention to this innovative connection, and recognizing that specific historical backgrounds make each experience unique (that is, there are no universal models) we aim to encourage other groups – particularly university teachers and students – to take action at their educational institutions to strengthen this dialogue, in spite of the significant challenges concerning the implementation of solidarity principles into real economy and society. Constructing a better world can also be achieved by knowledge alliances of diverse actors which normally do not interact.

29.7 QUESTIONS FOR DISCUSSION

- What are the contributions and limits of popular education and solidarity economy to empowerment and socioeconomic democratization?
- Can popular incubators of solidarity economic initiatives be recognized as a social innovation in the field of the so-called university-industry interaction within the national system of innovation approach?
- Does solidarity economy simply help to satisfy basic needs for marginalized populations or does it contain elements of structural change towards a post-capitalist society?

NOTES

1. ZEIS, which correspond to areas occupied by the poor in large cities, have been finally insti-

tutionalized under the urban regulation introduced in the 1988 Federal Constitution, in spite of their unmatched urban standards (size of land parcels, internal roads, formal ownership, etc.). This allowed local governments to legally provide these areas with infrastructure, public services and housing. ZEIS is a legal innovation of Recife's first master plan after the dictatorship in consequence of social housing movements with the help of the *Justice and Peace Commission*.
2. From June 2002 to June 2011 the unemployment rate in urban agglomerations has decreased from 11.6 to 6.2 per cent (http://www.ipeadata.gov.br/, last accessed 3 August 2011).

REFERENCES

(References in bold are recommended reading.)

Abers, Rebecca Neaera (2000), *Inventing Local Democracy. Grassroots Politics in Brazil*, Colorado: Lynne Rienner.
Altvater, Elmar (2005), *Das Ende des Kapitalismus wie wir ihn kennen, Eine radikale Kapitalismuskritik*, Münster: Westfälisches Dampfboot.
Altvater, Elmar and Nicola Sekler (eds) (2006), *Solidarische Ökonomie. Reader des Wissenschaftlichen Beirats von Attac*, Hamburg: VSA.
Arendt, Hannah (1998[1958]), *The Human Condition*, Chicago: University of Chicago Press, Erstaufl.
Arthur, Len, Tom Keenoy, Russell Smith, Molly Scott Cato and Peter Anthony (2004), 'Cooperative production – a contentious social space?', paper presented to the 22nd Annual International Labour Process Conference, Amsterdam, 5–7 April.
Auinger, Markus (2009), 'Introduction: Solidarity Economics – emancipatory social change or self-help?', *Journal für Entwicklungspolitik*, XXV (03), 4–21.
Auinger, Markus (2007), 'Solidarische Ökonomie und betriebliche Selbstverwaltung. Das Beispiel der Usina Catende in Pernambuco, Brasilien', in Gerald Faschingeder and Veronika Wittmann (eds), *Eigentum anders. Beiträge junger ForscherInnen*, Linz: Trauner, pp. 17–30.
Avritzer, Leonardo (2006), 'New Public Spheres in Brazil: Local Democracy and Deliberative Politics', *International Journal of Urban and Regional Research*, 30 (3), 623–637.
Barbosa, Nelson (2010), 'Latin America: Counter-Cyclical Policy in Brazil: 2008–09', *Journal of Globalization and Development*, 1 (1), Article 13.
Barrocal, André (2011), 'Gasto social ganha 4 pontos no PIB e dobra por habitante em 15 anos', *Carta Maior* website, http://www.cartamaior.com.br/templates/materiaMostrar.cfm?materia_id=18034 (last accessed 9 July 2011).

Coelho, Geraldo (2002), 'Paulo Freire e o Movimento de Cultura Popular', in Paulo Rosas (ed.), *Paulo Freire – Educação e Transformação Social*, Recife: UFPE, pp. 31–96.

Condepe/fidem (n.d.) Pernambuco government website, http://www2.condepefidem.pe.gov.br/web/condepefidem/exibir_noticia?groupId=19941&articleId=486175&templateId=82535 (last accessed 8 September 2011).

Delors, Jacques (1996), *Learning: The treasure within*, report to UNESCO of the International Commission on Education for the twenty-first century, www.unesco.org/delors/delors_e.pdf (last accessed 18 December 2012).

Dubeux, Ana Maria de Cunha (2004), 'Education, Travail e Economie Solidaire. Les cas de Incubateurs technologuices de Cooperative Populaire au Brasil Paris', unpublished manuscript.

Faoro, Raymundo (2001[1958]), *Os donos do poder. Formação do patronato político brasileiro*, Rio de Janeiro: Globo.

Fernandes, Ana Cristina (1989), *Uma imagem em negativo: considerações em torno da assessoria ao movimento popular*, MSc Thesis, Universidade Estadual de Campinas.

Fernandes, Ana Cristina (1998), 'Economic Integration of a Peripheral Region: From State Developmentism to Globalisation in Northeast Brazil', *Journal für Entwicklungspolitik*, 2, 193–212.

Fernandes, Ana Cristina, Alexandre Stamford Silva and Bruno Campello Sousa (2011), 'Demanda e oferta de tecnologia e conhecimento em região periférica: a interação universidade-empresa no Nordeste brasileiro', in Suzigan Wilson, Eduardo Albuquerque and Sílvio Cário (eds.), *Interações de Universidades e Institutos de Pesquisas com Empresas no Brasil*, Belo Horizonte: Editora Autêntica, pp. 341–402.

Fiori, José Luís (1995), *O vôo da coruja. Uma leitura não-liberal da crise do estado desenvolvimentista*, Rio de Janeiro: EdUERJ.

Frank, Andre Gunder (1969[1966]), 'The Development of Underdevelopment', in Andre Gunder Frank (ed.), *Latin America: Underdevelopment or Revolution*, New York: Monthly Review Press, pp. 3–17.

Freire, Paulo (1996[1968]), *Pedagogy of the Oppressed*, Harmondsworth: Penguin.

Freire, Paulo (1998[1992]), *Pedagogy of Hope. Reliving Pedagogy of the Oppressed*, New York: Continuum.

Freire, Paulo (2001), *Pedagogia dos sonhos possíveis*, São Paulo: Fundação Editora da UNESP (FEU).

Freire, Paulo (2004), *Pedagogia do oprimido*, São Paulo: Paz e Terra.

Freire, Paulo (2005), *Conscientização – Teoria e pratica da libertação*, São Paulo: Centauro Editora.

Freire, Paulo and Ira Shor (2003), *Medo e ousadia – O cotidiano do Professor*, São Paulo: Paz e Terra.

Freyre, Gilberto (2004[1936]), *Sobrados e Mocambos*, São Paulo: Editora Global.

Freyre, Gilberto (1992), *Casa Grande e Senzala*, Rio de Janeiro: Record.

Furtado, Celso (1997), *Obra Autobiográfica*, Vol. 1, São Paulo: Paz e Terra.

Furtado, Celso (2007[1959]), *Formação Econômica do Brasil*, São Paulo: Companhia das Letras.

Gomez, Margarita Victoria (2009), 'Emmanuel Levinas & Paulo Freire: The Ethics of Responsibility for the Face-To-Face Interaction in the Virtual World', *International Journal of Instruction*, 2 (1), 27–58.

Hauer, Michaela (2010), 'Incubadoras an brasilianischen Universitäten. Schnittstellen zu benachteiligten Bevölkerungsgruppen und Instrumente der Weiterbildung in der Solidarökonomie', *Aktion & Reflexion. Texte zur transdisziplinären Entwicklungsforschung und Bildung*, 4, Vienna: Paulo Freire Centre.

IBGE (2009), *Síntese de Indicadores Sociais*, Rio de Janeiro, IBGE, http://www.ibge.gov.br/home/estatistica/populacao/condicaodevida/indicadoresminimos/sinteseindicsociais2010/SIS_2010.pdf (last accessed 18 December 2012).

Jacobs, Jane (1969), *The economy of cities*, New York: Random House.

Kowarick, Lucio (1979): *A Espoliação urbana*, São Paulo: Paz e Terra.

Laville, Jean-Louis (ed.) (2007), *L'économie solidaire. Une perspective internationale*, Paris: Hachette Littératures.

Ministério da Saúde (2006), *Politica nacional de plantas medicinais e fitoterápicos*, Série B. Textos Básicos de Saúde, Brasilia: Ministério da Saúde.

Ministério do Trabhalo e Emprego (n.d.), government website, http://www.mte.gov.br (last accessed 5 September 2011).

Moulaert, Frank, Flavia Martinelli, Erik Swyngedouw and Sara González (2005), 'Towards Alternative Model(s) of Local Innovation', *Urban Studies*, 42 (11), 1969–1990.

Novy, Andreas (2009), The World is emerging – on the current relevance of Paulo Freire', *Aktion & Reflexion. Texte zur transdisziplinären Entwicklungsforschung und Bildung*, 3, Vienna: Paulo Freire Centre.

Novy, Andreas and Bernhard Leubolt (2005), 'Participatory Budgeting in Porto Alegre: Social Innovation and the Dialectical Relationship of State and Civil Society', *Urban Studies*, 42 (11), 2023–2036.

Oliveira, Francisco de (1987), *Elegia para uma Re(li)gião*, Rio de Janeiro: Paz e Terra.

Santos, Boaventura de Sousa (ed.) (2005), *Democratizing Democracy. Beyond the Liberal Democratic Canon*, London, Verso.

Singer, Paul (1968), *Desenvolvimento econômico e evolução urbana*, São Paulo: Companhia Editora Nacional.

Singer, Paul (2004), 'A economia solidária no Governo Federal', *Mercado de Trabalho, IPEA*, 24, 3–5.

Singer, Paul (2005), 'A recente ressurreição da econo-mia solidária no Brasil', in B. Sousa Santos (ed.), *Produzir para viver: os caminhos da produção não capitalista*, Rio de Janeiro: Civilização Brasileira, pp. 81–129.

Stedile, João Pedro (2007), 'The Neoliberal Agrarian Model in Brazil', *Monthly Review*, **58** (9), 50–54.

SUAPE (n.d.), government website http://www. suape.pe.gov.br/home/index.php (last accessed 8 September 2011).

Wolford, Wendy (2004), 'Of Land and Labor: Agrarian Reform on the Sugarcane Plantations of Northeast Brazil', *Latin American Perspectives*, **31** (2), 147–170.

30. Local associations in Chile: social innovation in a mature neoliberal society
Vicente Espinoza[1]

30.1 INTRODUCTION

Only a few years after democratic rule had returned to Chile, a scholar of grassroots democracy wondered: where did all protesters go? (Oxhorn 1994) In those days, almost any observer of the Chilean political scene had taken for granted that the popular mobilization of the 1980s would be a prominent companion to the recovered democracy. However, none of the variants of collective action that flourished under the dictatorship was able to keep its strength or appeal afterwards.

In this chapter I examine the dynamics of Chilean civil society in the last two decades stressing the changes in structural and institutional conditions and their impact on the collective action of the grassroots. I argue that during the last two decades Chile has been experiencing a change in the cycle of collective action, from a union-centred social movement towards a more diverse and horizontal mobilization. These new orientations have taken mostly fragmented expressions, having in common a preference for autonomy from institutional spaces and an open deliberation about models of society.

The elaborations here follow the Chilean case to develop a theoretical issue common to social movement scholars: the cyclic character of collective mobilizations challenging the dominant order (Cefaï 2011; Tilly and Tarrow 2007; Gunder-Frank and Fuentes 1995). Is there any continuity to be observed in protest events occurring years or decades apart? I search here for signs of continuity of recent protest mobilizations in Chile, by students and regional associations, with the democratic protests in the 1980s. I argue that current social mobilizations have shifted from a labour-centred model to a diverse network of local groups, setting the ground for a new type of collective action. In the first section I analyse the evolution of the popular movement under the dictatorial rule. The second section stresses the conditions that have inhibited collective action and conflict in the recovered democracy. Next I characterize innovation dynamics in micropolitical space. Finally I elaborate on the connections between local innovation and national mobilization as expressed by the students' movement in 2011.

30.2 UNION-CENTRED FAMILIES OF CONFLICT

Most of the social conflict in Chile during the 20th century could be understood as the attempt of popular organizations, led by workers' unions, to gain institutional standing for their demands about bettering their life conditions. Indeed, a growing group of popular associations looked for 'vertical integration' with the state apparatus by processing their demands through institutional mechanisms. Workers' unions operated within the boundaries of the Labour Code and established three-party task-forces – unions, employers and the government – for the negotiation of their demands. The poor of the city approached the state apparatus using diverse strategies and demands, until they obtained legal status for their organizations in the 1960s (Espinoza 1988). Also patron-client relationships were used as informal shortcuts to access public resources (Adler-Lomnitz 1994).

Within these 'integration dynamics' there was also a hierarchy among civil society organizations themselves. In fact, the dominant solution for the panoply of demands, associations, practices or strategies present in civil society resorted to the assumption that society had a central conflict, namely, the opposition between labour and capital. As a consequence, some demands and social actors gained centrality over the rest. Union federations at the national level – most of the time a unified body – organized demands so that income distribution to favour workers subordinated all other demands. Even schooling, health, housing or urban development were framed as 'indirect salary' (Castells 1972). In their organization, unions and their federations usually had branches for women, youth, peasants, native people or urban dwellers, but these groups could only gain national visibility or support by accepting a secondary position within labour unions; otherwise they were seldom more than scattered local organizations.

During the dictatorship the assumption of a central conflict around income distribution in society had to be relaxed, mainly because human rights became a central issue, but also because quite active social mobilizations began to acquire prominence on the national scene: cultural initiatives, student demands, women's organizations, professional associations opposing dictatorial policies or *pobladores'* land seizures.[2] The actors leading these mobilizations did not depend on unions; their organi-

zational weight was equivalent and they opposed the dictatorship while also struggling to recover democracy through more autonomous/independent channels.

The type of institutional collective action staged first by the unions then entered into crisis, as it found no institutional counterpart in the state apparatus for the processing of demands. In spite of the Catholic church's support of the movements' demands, the dictatorship was at no time open to any negotiation. The same was true for the demands of students, peasants, *pobladores*, professionals or any other group intending to channel their demands through public institutions.

30.3   A FRAMEWORK FOR THE ANALYSIS OF LOCAL MOVEMENTS IN CHILE

Unions never managed to recover the central place they occupied among popular organizations for most of the 20th century. A heterogeneous civil society, which increasingly occupied the popular space, brought forward a diversity of demands which were impossible to organize in a hierarchical way. Class identity is now only one among other possible identifications of groups and movements challenging the social order. Collective identifications no longer express the divide between class and classless groups; nowadays it seems more appropriate to distinguish between popular and organizational identities in the field of social movements. An organizational identity corresponds to an interest group, whose goals and strategies intend to benefit primarily its own members. A popular identity refers to associations or groups whose primary reference is the public interest represented by their demand, because it requires the modification of social organization in order to meet that demand. In other words, organizational identities belong to the boundaries defined by membership, while popular identities transcend those boundaries because they require linkages to other groups. According to this, no association can be conceived of as popular by definition: organizations can act either as interest groups, as parts in a specific conflict, as allies in a coalition or as members of a social movement (Diani and Bison 2004; Oxhorn 1995).

Despite the loss of prominence of class relations in social movement dynamics, the tension between inclusion and autonomy is still important to the understanding of collective action. Conflict remains the best guide to understand social movements (Touraine 1985; Melucci 1996). However, during the 1990s Chilean society appeared almost devoid of conflict around national issues, as if social movements had vanished. Moreover, situations that developed into conflicts couldn't reach legitimacy among the population. For example, the closing of Lota's coalmines, a stronghold of the workers' movement during the 20th century, provoked only solidarity statements by the national workers' associations but could not stir any further mobilization at the national level. Teachers from public schools went on strike more than once with little support from workers in other sectors, making the mobilization look like the strategy of a single interest group. These actions and the way they were societally contained were a signal of the change in the pattern of collective action that was taking place along with the installation of a democratic government.

A scenario of limited social conflict in a context of increasing inequality and no political repression was a paradox that puzzled analysts and commentators of recent Chilean socio-politics. Recently, however, we have witnessed strong mobi-

lizations contesting inequality, among students and also regional social movements. To explain the transition from one situation to another requires an understanding of the reasons that kept social conflict at low levels between 1990 and 2010. True, the struggle against dictatorship for almost 20 years placed demands about social inequalities in the background because, in the final analysis, they were the result of a model of public policy imposed by non-democratic means. Many had expected that, after the huge increase of economic inequality during dictatorship, an extended conflict on redistribution would dominate the social agenda. Neither economic inequality nor other expressions of social unfairness – ethnic, environmental, human rights – were able to mobilize people with enough strength to reach a central place in social awareness. Democratic social policies did not meet the highest expectations but were enough to initiate the payment of a 'social debt' consisting, to begin with, of about 40 per cent of the population below the poverty line.[3] Increased social expenditures, public policies intended to reduce poverty and sustained economic growth (at an average 5 per cent between 1990 and 2010) explain the fast reduction of Chilean poverty under the democratic regime (World Bank 2001). Poverty reduction and employment growth have created opportunities for the economic advancement of workers which are not associated with collective bargaining, but gained through individual positioning in the labour market. Even when capital-labour confrontations have escalated into open conflict, the government has been rather effective in dismantling mobilization using negotiation strategies. Conflicts in other fields were also deactivated by the government, usually by resorting to special funds for local development programs (Concha et al. 2001).[4] As a result of economic conditions and public policies, opportunities to form a collective action have been highly limited (Espinoza 2004). Moreover, a weakened worker identity made it necessary for other civil-society groups to devise new forms of coordination and collective action (de la Maza and Ochsenius 2010).

30.4   COLLECTIVE ACTION UNDER DEMOCRACY

Before the return of democracy, a dynamic of opposition to the dictatorship helped keep together a heterogeneous coalition of social and political movements, somehow concealing their differences. Democracy brought a renewal in the organizational panorama of the civil society such that no actor could claim centrality in the social conflict as the workers' movement had for most of the 20th century. In fact, establishing any hierarchy between associations, demands and social identities would be seen as quite arbitrary, because workers, women, ethnic groups, youth and the like would not accept subordination to another collectivity. The concept of 'organizational network' gained currency to express the coordination of diverse associations without hierarchical links among them, fostering trust and mutual support among its members. Mostly at the local level, and on a territorial basis, different organizations coordinated to foster initiatives around childhood, the elderly, violence against women, local development and others (de la Maza 2006). As democratic governments made progress in solving pressing political demands and preventing a U-turn to authoritarian rule, a new form of relationship between the government and grassroots organizations was also developing.

By the end of the 1990s, the honeymoon between grassroots organizations, NGOs and local leaders with the government withered away as democratic institutions continued to develop and consolidate. A prominent left-wing political leader, soon to become a known lobbyist, spoke metaphorically at a union meeting of the need for social organizations and the government to maintain 'separate beds'; after having relied on grassroots associations to overthrow dictatorship, this representative of the political leadership considered the relationship between social movements and political agents to be no more than a marriage of convenience which now was over. For those willing to participate in the public debate, gates were open on the condition that their contribution was instrumental to public policies.[5] Only a few social leaders declined the offer of working on a larger scale with the support and under the legitimacy of democratic institutions.

In the beginning, professionals who had been working in NGOs thought democratic governments would allow them to implement their community development, technological, health or educational programs on a larger scale. Soon, these new officers were neutralized by the bureaucratic procedures of the public sector. Those in the social movements who thought of the government as a partner replacing the external support from other movements they had received during dictatorship were also disappointed: the public sector relied on them only to implement local projects, requiring that these fit perfectly the goals of public services and also comply with regulations that burdened the rather informal practices of NGOs. Local leaders saw a window of opportunity in 1992, with the elections for mayors and local councillors. They soon found out however that they were now located on the other side of the fence, and that resource management requirements overshadowed their abilities as leaders of social movements; the latter, because of the necessity of finding resources, became instrumental to the former which drew socially innovative energies away from leading and invigorating the movements.

Moreover, and in line with the managerialism that had pervaded the movements, by the mid-1990s most of the leadership of social movements which had struggled against dictatorship had made its way into the democratic institutions: scholars left think-tanks to take high positions in the state apparatus; formerly clandestine political leaders were elected to parliament; NGO functionaries and even student leaders were to be found running public programs while grassroots leaders found a place in the local government. Social movements leadership was thus pulled apart, putting an end to a whole family of collective action associated with locally-led innovation (Oxhorn 1994).[6] Only the women's movement was to escape this fate, as its members entered the government with their own agenda and made a conscious effort to maintain contacts (Espinoza 2000).

Former social and political allies in the democratic struggle were thus growing apart as an elitist democratic project was on its way to consolidation. The situation involved more than a misunderstanding between public officers trying to do their job correctly and social organizations obstructing them. Social organizations profiled themselves as building 'new types of citizenship' (de la Maza 2010). Concepts such as social capital, local citizenship and diversity were used in an attempt to give conceptual ground to this debate (Putnam et al. 1993; Durston 2000; PNUD 1998). New relations with the public sector and the government had to be instrumental to this citizenship building.

30.5   NEW PATH FOR COLLECTIVE ACTION IN DEMOCRACY

The dimensions that framed collective action during the 1980s suffered a drastic displacement with the enlargement of the space for institutional participation during the 1990s. In fact, the 'new' social identities made almost no reference to social class, and replaced class consciousness with collective definitions that were in line with the policy aims and objectives set by the government for different social groups (Paley 2001). Strategies suggesting conflict or opposition to government also lost legitimacy as they were labelled as political violence or plain criminality. As a result, practices intended to strengthen the autonomy of the grassroots movements or to raise a critical voice about official policies were for a long time confined to rather marginal spaces, severed from the national media, denied of public funding and excluded from political representation. Social identities also lost their appeal and citizens were oriented toward integration or inclusion in the political systems.

It is worth examining the impact that the opening of institutional spaces had on local associations. There were three main types of effects: most associations decided to take advantage of the new opportunities for institutional participation; others sought to make public resources instrumental to their own goals, while still others rejected any kind of involvement with the public sector.

Although social processes do not develop as a continuous chain of events, a time-line has heuristic value to describe the historical 'cycle' of a social movement. Figure 30.1 presents characteristic events of the political system and social movement dynamics in the last four decades. During this time, social movements modified their orientations and organization from

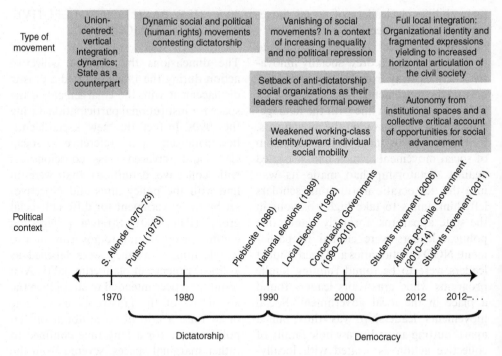

Source: Constanza Parra (2012).[7]

Figure 30.1   From a union-centred social movement towards a more diverse horizontal mobilization

a union-centred model, both in the phases of glory and decline, to a more diversified and horizontal model. While the previous sections examined collective action before and during the dictatorship, the following sections address the constitution of a collective action model under democratic rule.

30.5.1   Full Local Integration[8]

Some local associations became increasingly embedded in local politics. In fact, local authorities channelled a wide range of public funding initiatives for community development. Community development was conceived as a component of public services delivery, attending local populations with special needs which are

hard to target by national policies. Some housing programs considered hiring local workers, involving volunteers, and deliberation about design issues (Vio et al. 2010). Other funds were devised for upgrading schools, crime prevention, control of illegal drugs consumption, clubs for the elderly, other recreational activities and so on. It is usually difficult to tell whether a particular mayor genuinely encourages local participation or just uses local development funding schemes to capture votes or to reward loyal constituencies. The mayor has a strong influence in every phase of local public policy, from the selection of the target group or neighbourhood to the actual implementation of projects. Citizen participation depends, to a large extent, on the goodwill of public bodies or the mayor. The allocation of public funds is arranged through a network of relationships engineered by the organizations' leaders participating in social policies. The density of contacts and mutual acquaintance between local leaders, authorities and notables confirms them as a local elite that holds a significant stake in the distribution of local resources.

Small funds become available directly to local associations by means of contests between project proposals; these contests are by far the most typical mechanism of public service delivery in Chilean community development policies. Although initially successful, the unrestricted expansion of this system of allocation of public funds to social projects over the last two decades has led to problems. Competition for local funds has taught leaders to compete against each other, developing strategies to gain access to a limited amount of resources. Too often their discourse about cooperation among organizations, solidarity and even democratic participation is only a component of their competitive strategy. As a consequence, local associations who have become competitors over funds cannot coordinate with others in the local arena. Moreover, because of these 'funds before all' dynamics, the leaders are not really leading cohesive associations but organizations whose pragmatic affiliates only expect the leader to announce when he or she has gained access to resources. Putting an end to this mechanism of resource allocation in social policies is a necessary condition to strengthen democracy. Instead of competing, it would be preferable for the local associations to collaborate and strengthen their internal cohesion, reach consensus and set priorities: in a nutshell, they should encourage collective mobilization for the good of the larger civic community.

Social policies at the local level operate in a political arena that is more akin to a competitive market for funds among interest groups than to traditional patron-client relationships. This does not mean that patronage has been eradicated but rather that the local leaders have learned to use their resources to gain access to decision-making circles. The question, then, is whether this is a new type of citizen participation in the making. Some scholars, such as Durston et al. (2005), seem inclined to give an affirmative answer on the grounds that any system that differs from strict patronage would be democratic to some extent. My opinion in this respect is not so optimistic, because high anti-democratic hurdles persist at the local level. To begin with, leaders have become experts at devising strategies to beat other organizations rather than cooperating with them. In addition they contribute little to create Community Social Capital because they establish a network of local interest groups which, for all practical purposes, operates as a power elite (Espinoza 2009). This local elite is partly composed of democratically elected authorities such as the mayor and members of the national parliament, but also comprises some public officers, local entrepreneurs and the most powerful members of 'community' interest groups. The participation of local civil society leaders remains on the agenda as long as they have enough power to enter the circles of power, although they usually do so as members of specific interest groups, such as a neighbourhood committee, a handicapped association or the like (Espinoza 2009). This local elite makes decisions about the allocation of public funds while it largely remains invisible to local actors; thus it can operate without any control from other institutions or citizens. Finally, the structure of the local arena as a 'market for funds and votes' makes it difficult for local leaders to mobilize grassroots organizations for public purposes. In short, the local political arena seems more suited to reproducing domination than engendering democracy and participation at the local level.

30.5.2   Innovation Initiatives

By the end of the 1990s some initiatives were taken to strengthen civil society by promoting the coordination of local actors, partly as a result of public sector funding intended to take care of hard to target populations or complex social problems. Some of these initiatives defined themselves as 'associational networks' in the fields of preventing illegal drug consumption, taking actions against so called 'domestic violence' (actually, violence against women), promoting the rights of children, and dealing with health issues. Other initiatives were independent from the public sector, and in some cases acted in opposition to government policies, such as the Association of Community Broadcasters, the National Network for the Protection of the Environment, as well as some native people's groups. Whether linked to the public sector or autonomous, most coordination actions were oriented to developing community social capital. These initiatives were not defined in the strict terms of policy interventions, their primary concern being to promote contact and capacity for collective action among locals. The target population for these initiatives comprised individuals and groups facing disadvantage, discrimination or exclusion. Rather than providing direct support or assistance, these initiatives are focused on social rights, not on instrumentalizing participation to legitimize 'jack pot' public policies. Many of them have a history of groundbreaking practices in the exercise and widening of

social rights, adopting innovation in citizenship rights as the main goal of their interventions (Oxhorn 1995; Paley 2001). Innovative citizenship embraces the practices of many associations usually operating at the local level and with weak linkages among them. One of the leaders of these initiatives referred to them as an 'archipelago of social experiences' (de la Maza 2010, p. 166).

The history of socio-political innovation sparked by alienated citizenship rights harks back to the 1980s. The memory of a solidary community based on reciprocity, where the poor learned to fight for democratic values inspired the innovation initiatives of the 1990s. In fact, during the 1980s an ample community space developed among popular solidarity organizations. Mainly sheltered by the Catholic church, it coupled the search for non-economic identities with a quest for autonomy from any formal institutions. At first these groups attempted to weave a social fabric on the ashes of the solidarity bonds destroyed by dictatorial repression. These solidarity organizations put in place many forms of collective action, including those targeting a return to democracy. Some analysts stressed that this universe of local associations constituted far more than a temporary or defensive space of the working class. Some went so far as to see in them the seeds of a new economic system; but all of them confirmed that the poor had learned the value of autonomous organization, self-help and solidarity (Razeto et al. 1990; Oxhorn 1995). Without doubt they could be considered schools of citizenship and democracy. But they were weak organizations – small, with few resources and disconnected from similar initiatives – and not many survived the first years of transition to democracy.

The concept of citizenship played a key role as an intellectual driver of these local initiatives. During the late 1970s the popular education movement, which served as an umbrella in the process of association building, loosely supported the need for 'new ways of making politics' which valued subjectivity over structural determinants (Lechner 1984). Popular educators wanted an empowered 'social subject' to develop their own lines of action, rather than aligning with external strategies. Many members of political parties in that period embraced a form of political action whose main requisite was closeness to the grassroots. If counter-hegemony was the underlying rationale of a filo-Gramscian political practice, soon 'civil society' gained currency to refer to new spaces of socio-political mobilization. As of the late 1980s-early 1990s, the citizen appeared as the new socio-political subject inhabiting and organizing the space of civil society. Before this, neither militants nor popular educators had developed a concept of citizenship focused on widening or acquiring social rights, or as a practice of active involvement in public matters. Participatory democracy thus became the institutional host for citizenship innovation of the 1990s.

The associations promoting citizenship in new fields have attempted to expand their practices to the political decision-making process or simply to obtain public recognition. The ambition of these initiatives is not total autonomy but the encounter or interface between top-down public programs and bottom-up local mobilizations (Long 1999). In this respect this development is comparable to the bottom-linked approach to social innovation observed and theorised by Pradel et al. in this Handbook (Chapter 11). Even though local actors had not sought institutionalization, their practices were embedded in an institutional track, where they attempted to keep their autonomy while avoiding

conflict, without any clear view of the antagonistic forces. Such practices seem to constitute a 'reversive' (as opposed to subversive) strategy, consisting of formal recognition of the institutional rules and procedures that define them, while in practice acting against the rules (Villasante 1994).[9]

In local arenas, participation for the sake of enlarged citizenship in Chile has become a politically correct discourse trapped in a dynamic that reproduces domination. How is it possible to move from these superficial participation rituals to truly democratic practices? The starting point is difficult. Chilean citizens who believe they are moving from mere consultation to real partnership may in fact be lacking adequate information about the democratic process and how they can actually participate in it. Without adequate information and open consultation, no effective participative process is possible. Needless to say, most so-called participatory processes do not comply with these minimal requirements. The goal of a minimal scenario for participation is to set enabling conditions that will allow citizens to develop their own viewpoint through deliberation (Fung 2003). Minimal as it might seem, providing adequate information to and consultation with citizens demands deep changes to current practices. In 2005 a law of transparency in the access to public information (Nr. 20050) set new ground for control of the public sector by civil society, but no systematic initiatives of 'counter-democracy' have been implemented so far (Rosanvallon 2008). Public sector participatory initiatives, no matter how well intended, seldom go beyond the target population of specific policy actions. Even when public institutions create consultation committees involving users of the services, they tend to implement exhaustive screenings to avoid 'disruptive' practices.[10] Further, community leaders need to establish new forms of relationship with their constituencies, moving away from the instrumental role of the leader as the one who 'gets things done'. In addition, because the legal requirements for establishing new organizations are rather negligible, many local leaders restrict membership of civil society groups to loyal 'like-minds', thus avoiding diverging views, which helps them to limit democratic checks (such as regular elections) to their power.

30.5.3   Conflict and Autonomy in Collective Action

Under the recovered democracy from 1990 on, the space of conflict and autonomy, although modest, sheltered a range of actors stressing their autonomy from institutions, diverse identity principles and giving wide room to subjectivity. Conflict in this scenario was attenuated by discussions and deliberation around identities and models for social organizations. Participants in the autonomous realm had to cope with conflicted subjectivities, amid changes in their structural positions and diverse life experiences. True, many of these actors were remains of the wreckage of the traditional model of collective action. Some navigated a delicate balance between autonomy and the temptation of public funding or political positions. Others were gaining momentum: an anarchist component, long disregarded in Chilean social movements, found here a natural space for their postulates of freedom and solidarity.

Social mobilizations in Chile moved for a long time in a mode of low conflict and high innovation, usually in local spaces. Decentralized mobilizations couldn't be conceived of as part of a global strategy; they were actually partial and fragmentary, resembling Felix Guattari's (1989) 'molecular movements'. These movements do not form part of a hierarchy: they are no longer the 'mass fronts' or 'functional organizations' of political parties; nor separate branches of a larger organization. People involved in these initiatives prefer to represent themselves as a 'social network' comprising dynamic equilibria in a changing system of horizontal relationships. No group or sector could exert hegemony over the rest: power seems more plausible as potentiality than domination. The type of mobilization in the space of autonomy has radical differences with the repertoire and style of the preceding cycle. The principles of differentiation do not operate on identities defined as social positions but on a debate about models of society. Social innovations belong to what Guattari calls micro-politics of the existential territory; for some time they have expressed testimony, resistance, demand for recognition, new practices, differentiation.

30.6   THE 2011 STUDENT MOBILIZATION AS A SOCIAL MOVEMENT

Scholars of social movements in Chile didn't see it coming. The rationale of domination by a political elite seemed so perfected under Concertación[11] governments that it seemed unlikely if not impossible to witness such massive expression of unrest, supported almost unanimously by the whole Chilean population. The students' movement contradicted every assumption about the indifference of the population regarding social inequality, and showed the weakness of elitist approaches to the building of democracy. A social demand found its way into the national scenario and set the agenda for public policies: not a small feat.

The 'social debt' left by the dictatorship was paid directly with successful policies against poverty, expansion in the access to public services in education and health, employment, wage improvements and last, but not least, increased access to consumption through an expansion and diversification of credit options. Figures in these aspects are overwhelmingly positive: almost universal access to energy and drinking water, life expectancy of 80 years, absence of malnutrition and universal access to high-school are among the most outstanding (Tironi 2003). The social debt was also paid with a promise of equal opportunities, in the form of universal access to college education. For Chilean standards, being a university professional is coterminous with the highest salaries, slim chance of losing your position and also a large chance that your children will keep that standing. During the last two decades families have been moving out of poverty, gaining access to better jobs, increasing their consumption and putting their children through college. On top of this, a growing 'education market' of private universities has absorbed children of working class origin, funding their studies with preferential rates on private banks loans.[12] Chileans believe in the value of education; they have largely accepted selection tests in spite of the socioeconomic bias of such tests, and agreed to pay for their children's studies in the expectation of the winning prize – a steady position at the top of the social ladder.

The first signal that things were not going as well as promised appeared in 2006, during the first year of President Michelle Bachelet's administration: high-school students paralyzed the secondary educational system demanding equal quality of services across socioeconomic levels.[13] In Chile the educational system has three types of service delivery: fully-paid or private, which accounts for about 10 per cent of students; state-subsidized schools where students pay a variable quantity, enrolling about 40 per cent of high-school students; and free schools run by local governments, which enrol about 50 per cent of the students (Contreras et al. 2010; Cox 2007). Performance in academic tests, especially those required for college admission, shows a strong correlation with the socioeconomic origin of the student and the educational unit s/he has access to (Koljatic and Silva 2010). Only exceptionally will students from local schools reach the academic performance required to engage in college education. For this reason, students demanded a clear commitment from the state to public education. A task force was established to make a proposal for new educational regulations, but the students decided after several months of debate to withdraw from this process, because their demands were not being satisfied. The results of the high-school revolt actually became a lesson in political tactics because in 2006 the young leadership had fallen into the classic trap of co-option. They had trusted the government enough to put an end to the student's strike and participate in a committee to prepare a new law. By the time they realized that a consensus was emerging in the task-force which ignored their demands, it was too late to change tactics. In 2011 Chileans were reminded of that episode, when high school and university students led mass protests across the country, this time firmly rejecting the government's invitation to join any negotiations behind closed doors. It was only at this time that we discovered the depth of the debate among the students' leadership. They had a clear negative diagnostic of the situation of education in Chile, as well as clear proposals to address it.

A knowledgeable diagnostic of the educational system as well as mature political leadership are indeed necessary conditions for a successful mobilization, but they are not sufficient. The 'frame alignment' (Snow et al. 1986) of the movement with people's various criticisms of the current model of development can help to understand the support it gained and the impact it had on the public policy agenda. Indeed, students had the support of their families, as college education is conceived as a family endeavour of upward inter-generational mobility. There were no generational gaps here as students' demands were compatible with their parents' and professors' criticisms of the educational system. Students didn't attack the core of the development model, but pointed out how the ideology of 'equal opportunities' could be used in practice to legitimize social inequalities: college education was actually better at reproducing social positions than it was at helping the disadvantaged to improve their standing. For this reason the students' mobilization covered a wide range of socioeconomic statuses from working-class children in poor public schools to the emerging middle class in traditional universities. One of their key demands was an end to a profit-driven education; this demand could be seen to synthesize the wishes of many Chileans who, since the privatization of public services under dictatorial rule, had experienced low-quality services making profit out of user contributions.[14] For many, the most appealing aspect of the students' demands was that they established a direct link between an experience of limited opportunities and the search for profit in the production of public goods.

The repertoire of collective actions used by the students expressed a qualitative change in the character of social movement, for rallies and demonstrations comprised a panoply of carnival-like forms – dancing, juggling, street-theatre, disguises, decorated carts, marching bands and many other types of performance – along with more conventional banners and shoulder to shoulder marching. There was also a very small number of violent actions, such as fire blockades and looting. The diversity of the repertoire represented a conception of demonstrations as an open space to express their discontent. Students welcomed every group: from unions to environmentalists, from gay/lesbians to political parties, from elderly associations to sports groups. This was truly a new political style in the making, a channel for many 'molecular' or 'micro-political' practices that had been maturing for the last two decades.

30.7   CONCLUDING REMARKS

It would be difficult to assess the 2011 mobilizations in the conventional terms of interest group gains. Rather than taking advantage of a politically disoriented regime they established a new political scenario that could open the gates to other popular mobilizations. Student mobilizations first and regional upheavals later show the shortcomings of the elitist democracy built during the transition from dictatorship under the assumption that social demands would be channelled by political parties. The diversity of demands summoned by students made evident the inability of the political system to articulate social demands; under those conditions we can see the immanent social conflict underlying the otherwise stable Chilean political system. Unless political parties and authorities widen the margins of representation to new groups and social demands, grassroots mobilizations will continue to put the system under pressure.

It remains to be seen whether the 2011 student mobilizations will attain an enduring political effect, and/or whether they might herald a cycle of protest in which multiple expressions of social unrest converge to achieve common redistributive goals. However, they can be seen as socially innovative, responding to needs and exclusions through inclusionary practices of empowerment. The paths that these movements take in the immediate future, and the influence that they have on government, will be of great interest to theorists and activists alike.

30.8 QUESTIONS FOR DISCUSSION

- Do you think that it is important for civil society to sustain a voice opposing government? Why/why not?
- How should we predict the outcomes of the students' movement? For instance:
  - Will political parties in opposition to the current government continue to support the movement or will the presidential election of 2013 distract them?
  - Will the students follow the fate of other social movements and become narrow interest groups?
- What is the relationship between protest and social innovation?

NOTES

1. My appreciation to Frank Moulaert, Constanza Parra and Diana MacCallum for their encouragement and precise comments. Part of the funding for the research supporting this paper comes from Fondecyt 1120846.
2. The word '*pobladores*' means literally 'inhabitants'. Its usage in Chile refers to poor urban residents in neighbourhoods suffering problems associated with lack of housing, sanitary services or construction deficiencies. As they usually were organized and mobilized around these issues, they are also referred to as the 'social movement of pobladores'.

3. The poverty line measurement is the standard in Latin American policy. It establishes a threshold based on average nutritional requirements, the so-called 'basic-foods basket'. The line of poverty in urban Chile is set at twice the price of the goods included in the basket, and at 1.75 for the countryside (Feres 1997).
4. Funds for local development programs have never made a large proportion of the public social budget – less that 2 per cent – but are a crucial component in the delivery of public services, optimally tailoring them to suit the needs of the population and also involving local leaders (Tomei 1996). However, they are also used in the context of a modified system of patron-client relationships (Durston et al. 2005; Espinoza 2004).
5. In fact, Law 20500, which regulates the functioning of social organizations (discussed since 2004 and published on 16 February 2011), shows an unmistakable pro-governmental bias, starting from its name: *Participation of associations and citizenship in public management*.
6. De-mobilization of the civil society can be conceived of as a requisite of an elitist democratic model such as the one being staged in Chile, and some commentators have advanced conjectures about strategies of the political elite to accomplish such a goal. Appealing as the argument might be, no solid piece of evidence has been produced so far in support of these speculations. This is not to be confused with the dismantling by the government of guerrilla groups, which were still operating under democracy.
7. With grateful thanks to Constanza Parra who devised this figure in 2012 for this chapter.
8. This section is based on Espinoza 2009.
9. Villasante (1994) has proposed a colloquial formulation of this as a 'Yes, but . . .' statement, involving a formal acceptance and a challenging practice. In colonial times the sentence 'We acknowledge but we don't comply' (*se acata, pero no se cumple*) characterized the practice of American authorities.
10. Personal communication with the responsible officer of the regional health services.
11. Ruiz (1993) made an early systematic exposition about the elitist characteristics of the democratic model implemented in Chile since 1990, especially regarding the requirements to constrain people's participation. Julia Paley (2001) used ethnography to identify the mechanisms associated with public policies that prevented collective action among the poor by imposing definitions of self derived from policy definitions. Espinoza (2009) linked civil society participation in public policies to the reproduction of local economic and power elites. Durston et al. (2005) documented patron-client relationships between political parties and peasants.
12. Preferential means here 6 per cent real annual

interest; the government subsidizes the difference with the market interest rate. As a result of students mobilizations during 2011 the preferential rate went down to 2 per cent.

13. This event is widely known as the 'penguin revolution', after the bird that symbolizes secondary school students.

14. Students called to put an end to education as a lucrative activity, as opposed to education as a public good and a citizen's right. Chilean legislation does not allow profiting from college education, although allows it at other educational levels and also in higher technical education. Despite unlawfulness, in new and traditional colleges some loopholes have been found to mask for-profit activities in this sector, among them 'mirror' firms whose members are closely related to college boards – for instance real-estate agencies renting facilities for educational activities. Traditional universities have also undertaken some profitable activities through autonomous firms under university ownership, by charging for services unrelated to education such as impact assessment, market studies, certification or technological transfer; college authorities claim they do not affect the educational goals of the institutions. Consensus among students and the general public in Chile is that either for imperatives of self-funding or straight money-making, the mix of education and profit goes against the quality of the former.

REFERENCES

(References in bold are recommended reading.)

Adler-Lomnitz, L. (1994), *Redes sociales, cultura y poder: ensayos de antropología latinoamericana*, Mexico City: FLACSO.

Castells, M. (1972), 'Movimiento de pobladores y lucha de clases', technical report, Santiago: CIDU/PI/PT.

Cefaï, D. (2011), 'Diez propuestas para el estudio de las movilizaciones colectivas. De la experiencia y al compromiso', *Revista de Sociologia*, **26**, 137–166.

Concha, X., A. Pavez, D. Raczynski, C. Rojas, T. Carolina and E. Walker (2001), 'Superación de la pobreza y gestión descentralizada de la política y los programas sociales', in D. Raczynski and C. Serrano (eds), *Descentralización. Nudos Críticos*, Santiago: Asesorías para el Desarrollo/CIEPLAN, pp. 173–269.

Contreras, D., P. Sepúlveda and S. Bustos (2010), 'When Schools Are the Ones that Choose: The Effects of Screening in Chile', *Social Science Quarterly. Southwestern Social Science Association*, **91** (s1), 1349–1368.

Cox, C. (2007), 'Educación en el Bicentenario:

dos agendas y calidad de la política', *Revista Pensamiento Educativo*, **40** (1), 175–204.

de la Maza, G. (2006), 'Ciudadanía, Sociedad Civil y Participación Política', in Isidoro Cheresky (ed.), *Chile: sociedad civil, participación y política en la post dictadura*, Buenos Aires: Miño y Dávila Editores, pp. 411–442.

de la Maza, G. (2010), 'Construcción democrática, participación ciudadana y políticas públicas en Chile', PhD thesis, Universiteit Leiden, College voor Promoties.

de la Maza, G. and C. Ochsenius (2010), 'Innovaciones en los Vínculos Locales entre Sociedad Civil y Estado en Chile: su Incidencia en la Construcción de Gobernabilidad Democrática', *Revista Política y Gestión (Buenos Aires)*, **12**, 11–35.

Diani, M. and I. Bison (2004), 'Organizations, coalitions, and movements', *Theory and Society*, **33**, 281–309.

Durston, J. (2000), 'Construyendo capital social comunitario', *Revista de la CEPAL*, **69**, 103–118.

Durston, J., D. Duhart, F. Miranda and E. Monzó, (2005), *Comunidades campesinas, agencias públicas y clientelismos Políticos En Chile*, Santiago: Ediciones Lom.

Espinoza, V. (1988), *Para una historia de los pobres de la ciudad*, Santiago: Ediciones SUR.

Espinoza, V. (2000), 'Reivindicación, conflicto y valores en los movimientos sociales de la segunda mitad del siglo XX', in M. Garcés, P. Milos, M. Olguín, M.T. Rojas and M. Urrutia (eds), *Memoria para un nuevo siglo. Chile, miradas a la segunda mitad del siglo XX*, Santiago: Ediciones Lom, pp. 197–211.

Espinoza, V. (2004), 'De la política social a la participación en un nuevo contrato de ciudadanía', *Revista Política*, **43**, 149–183.

Espinoza, V. (2009), 'Citizens' Involvement in Social Policies in Chile: patronage or participation?', in P. Silva and H. Cleuren (eds), *Widening Democracy: Citizens and Participatory Schemes in Brazil and Chile*, Leiden: Koninklijke Brill, pp. 273–294.

Feres, J.C. (1997), 'Notas sobre la medición de la pobreza según el método del ingreso', *Revista de la CEPAL*, **61**, 145–163.

Fung, A. (2003), 'Survey article: Recipes for public spheres: Eight institutional design choices and their consequences', *Journal of Political Philosophy*, **11** (3), 338–367.

Guattari, F. (1989), *Cartografías del deseo* (translated by Miguel Denis Norambuena), Santiago: Francisco Zegers.

Gunder-Frank, A. and M. Fuentes (1995), 'El estudio de los ciclos en los movimientos sociales', *Sociologica*, **10** (28), 37–60.

Koljatic, M. and M. Silva, (2010), 'Algunas reflexiones a siete años de la implementación de la PSU', *Estudios Públicos*, **120**, 125–146.

Lechner, N. (1984), *La conflictiva y nunca acabada construcción del orden deseado*, Santiago: FLACSO (Ediciones Ainavillo).

Long, N. (1999), 'The multiple optic of interface analysis', Technical report, Wageningen University, The Netherlands: UNESCO Background Paper on Interface Analysis.

Melucci, A. (1996), *Challenging Codes: Collective Action in the Information Age*, Cambridge: Cambridge University Press.

Oxhorn, P. (1994), 'Where Did All the Protesters Go?: Popular Mobilization and the Transition to Democracy in Chile', *Latin American Perspectives*, 21 (3), 49–68.

Oxhorn, P. (1995), *Organizing Civil Society: The Popular Sectors and the Struggle for Democracy in Chile*, Philadelphia: Pennsylvania State University Press.

Paley, J. (2001), *Marketing Democracy. Power and Social Movements in Post-Dictatorship Chile*, Berkeley: University of California Press.

PNUD Programa de Naciones Unidas para el Desarrollo (1998), *Desarrollo humano en Chile. 1998. Las paradojas de la modernización*, Santiago: PNUD.

Putnam, R.D., R. Leonardi and R. Nanetti (1993), *Making Democracy Work: Civic Traditions in Modern Italy*, Princeton University Press, Princeton.

Razeto, L., A. Klenner, A. Ramírez and R. Urmeneta (1990), *Las Organizaciones Económicas Populares*, 3rd revised edition, Santiago: Programa de Economía del Trabajo (PET).

Rosanvallon, P. (2008), *Counter-Democracy: Politics in an age of distrust*, Cambridge: Cambridge University Press.

Ruiz, Schneider C. (1993), *Seis Ensayos sobre Teoría de la Democracia*, Santiago: Universidad Nacional Andrés Bello.

Snow Jr, D.A., S.K. Worden and R.D. Benford (1986), 'Frame Alignment Processes, Micro-mobilization, and Movement Participation', *American Sociological Review*, 51 (4), 464–481.

Tilly, C. and S.G. Tarrow (2007), *Contentious Politics*, Boulder, CO: Paradigm Publishers.

Tironi, E. (2003), 'Es Chile un país moderno?' in *Cuánto y cómo cambiamos los chilenos: balance de una década censos 1992–2002*, Santiago: Instituto Nacional de Estadísticas, pp. 15–76.

Tomei, M. (1996), 'Fondos de Inversión Social: El Caso de Chile', Cuestiones del Desarrollo Discussion Paper no. 21, Geneva: Oficina Internacional del Trabajo.

Touraine, A. (1985), 'An introduction to the study of social movements', *Social Research*, 52, 749–788.

Villasante, T.R. (1994), 'Clientelas y emancipaciones: una introducción metodológica' in *Las Ciudades Hablan. Identidades y Movimientos Sociales en seis metrópolis latinoamericanas*, Caracas: Editorial Nueva Sociedad, pp. 31–34.

Vio, A., D. Aguirre, C. Bustos, N. Morales and L. Varas (eds) (2010), *Neighbourhood Recovery Program. Lessons Learned and Good Practices*, MINVU Chile: Ministerio de Vivienda y Urbanismo.

World Bank (2001), 'Chile. Poverty and income distribution in a high growth economy. The case of Chile 1987–1998' (Report No 22037-CH), technical report, Washington DC: World Bank.

31. Gender and social innovation: the role of EU policies
Isabel André

31.1 INTRODUCTION

Gender equity is an essential dimension of social justice and welfare, comprising equal opportunities for women and men derived from structural changes in gender relations at the grand scale. Gender equity is, in itself, a fundamental human need related to autonomy and identity, a need which has been the focus of social movements throughout history. This chapter argues that the transformation of gender relations in Europe in the last four decades has been leveraged by specific public policies, stimulating social innovation in everyday practices especially in family and labour market spheres. The argument also addresses the ideological meaning of these transformations, as they represent a tension between patriarchy and capitalism. Does such change reveal the emergence or the possibility of a non-patriarchal capitalism?

Three complementary topics are considered in this chapter: (i) the deepness of gender relations dynamics in present-day Europe compelled by four decades of equal opportunity policies; (ii) the crucial focus and the main agents of social innovation that may allow for a fairer society in terms of gender equity; (iii) the transformation of gender norms as a decisive pillar of social innovation in gender relations.

In relation to the first topic, the welfare state has transformed social relations, and gender relations in particular. Whether through social support or through the regulation of labour markets, as through equal opportunity policies, there has been a significant decrease in inequalities between women and men. From the late 1960s onwards there has also been a rapid and profound transformation of the values and behaviours that guide daily lives, namely conjugality and parenthood. The liberalization of social and cultural practices, especially respecting sexual behaviour and family relationships, contributed to weakening the patriarchal system at both the material and the symbolic levels. Amplifying these changes, the emergence and adoption of contraception methods with high levels of efficiency has enabled real control over procreation and, indirectly, over conjugal relations. However, these changes are also characterized by some ambiguity in terms of gender equity (McNay 2000) and the majority of European countries and regions continue to this day to exhibit deep disparities between men and women, reflecting the endurance of patriarchal power relations. Moreover, the neoliberal turn in recent decades seems to have significantly contributed to enlarging gender inequalities. Despite the progress in terms of education the gender gap in the labour market as well as in the high decision levels of the public and private sectors remain significantly deep (European Union 2010).

The second topic concerns public policies and their role in promoting a fairer society in terms of gender equity. In this field three major drivers of change seem to be essential (Walby 2004): feminist movements, elected women in parliaments and local authorities, and the presence of women in decision-making roles in the context of the public administration. All these agents gather many different issues under the umbrella of 'gender issues'. Sexuality (and procreation) is a crucial aspect of the dependence of women, but we should not disregard other key aspects of women's disempowerment, such as education rules in school and in family, as well as fashion directions, advertising and popular media shaping the relationship of girls and women with their own bodies. Our focus in this chapter includes these various socio-cultural fields, dealing specifically with women's empowerment and autonomy and various socially innovative ways to promote them.

The third topic is related to the concept of gender norms. As in other dimensions and fields of social innovation, empowerment can come from the appropriation of hegemonic norms or from the emergence of new social orders. To be equal or different means to adopt the same or another norm. There are two clear norms, defined according to patriarchal principles, shaping gender as a social category – masculinity and femininity influence all fields of personal and social life: 'Bourdieu emphasizes that gender is a construct that differentiates according to both antagonistic and complementary principles, and operates as a highly complex, differentiated and vital symbolic order' (Krais 2006, p.120). In terms of gender equity, both norms should be reconstructed, giving place to a new gender order based on individual freedom, social justice and transformed social relations, mainly at family level but also in the labour market and other public realms, as well as in the symbolic sphere. Considering that in the last decades important changes took place in the EU forcing new arrange-

ments between capitalism and patriarchy,[1] have these really been changing the gender construct (Bourdieu 1998)?

In terms of social innovation, this question relates to the debate about how socially innovative governance can emerge from existent governance systems with their prevailing norms and values.

31.2 GENDER ANALYTICAL FRAMEWORKS

Very often frameworks for analysing social processes place the gender dimension under a shadow cast by class relations – through labour relations or consumption status. However, the lesser visibility of gender in social research has been highly contested by gender studies since the 1980s, thus drawing attention to the relevance of the gendered character of social relations (McDowell 1983; Massey 1994; Garcia-Ramon and Monk 1996). The gender debate in the first period was very pragmatic, and especially sought to stress the notorious inequalities that persisted between women and men in the case of developed and democratic countries that are purportedly built on ideals of equity. This research mainly focused on labour market and the family – certainly the main producers of gender inequality. The theoretical debate followed later on (Walby 1986).

Gender does not correspond to a social group nor to a social movement. Rather, it is a social and personal relation, combining domination, division of labour, power, sexuality and affect. This complexity – where different levels and types of links cannot be separated – makes it particularly difficult to construe gender as a social category in the way it is related to the capitalist system as well as to the patriarchal order.

A major difficulty related to the analytical framework on gender is the use of the 'family' category to describe and understand the domestic field, which is closely related to the ideological frame of patriarchy. Family is often used as a homogeneous unit where individuals cooperate and pursue common goals, e.g. where individuality is subordinated to the collective interest (defined by hegemonic rules). Even if the study of tensions and conflicts inside the family emerged as a strong topic in the social sciences, economic and social policies continue to regard the family as the essential unit, e.g. with respect to taxes, credit, social subsidies, etc.

Still, the crucial problem of the 'gender' category is that it crosses all fields of life and society, and is also related to the articulation between capitalism – regulating gender relations in the labour market – and patriarchy – controlling the domestic realm including beliefs and feelings. So what we have are gendered societies as well as gendered places and spaces, as Doreen Massey (1994) clearly stressed. Almost all human needs are gendered, meaning that most social innovations have an impact in gender relations and transform the patriarchal order even when their goals are not directly related to the promotion of fairer gender relations. A good example can be seen in the rehabilitation of urban public spaces in deprived neighbourhoods as a way to improve citizens' active participation. Apparently ungendered, such actions comprise relevant seeds of gender equity as they involve the openness of the household and the possibility for women to free themselves from the closed domestic sphere and to be part of public debates and decisions.

31.2.1   The Hidden Sphere of Social Reproduction

Under the European welfare state gender issues are often related to social reproduction vs. production (Walby 1986; Garcia-Ramon and Monk 1996; Duncan 1995; André 1996; Reay 2004). Analysing 168 papers published between 2000 and 2008, Davis and Greenstein (2009) show the relevance of topics concerning work and employment, conjugality, motherhood and household. However, the most interesting (and surprising) aspect is that those 'categories are clearly connected to the roles that women and men are expected to inhabit in married and procreative heterosexual relationships' (Davis and Greenstein 2009, p. 89). The persistence of this vision in research and, consequently, in public policies and institutions conveys in a certain way the resilience of the patriarchal system even if sometimes in tension with capitalism, namely in the context of labour market dynamics.

In 2006 Jason Jordan wrote:

> To the extent that the welfare state prevents women from having to choose between children and employment, it also frees them from economic dependence on men and marriage ... This new perspective engenders mainstream welfare state research by focusing attention on the welfare state's capacity to provide citizens with greater individual autonomy in all social relationships. (Jordan 2006, p.1112)

These arguments concerning individual autonomy illustrate quite well the conceptual foundations of European policies concerning gender equity. In general they have been based on the idea that the state facilitates women's lives and thereby women become more equal to men – the latter being the standard citizen, i.e. the hegemonic gender norm.

This political thinking places strong

barriers to social innovation in gender relations: very often public and third sector initiatives respecting for instance the flexibility or the integration of social services end up following the well known dictum by Giuseppe di Lampedusa 'If we want things to stay as they are, things will have to change.'[2]

Nevertheless, gender debates focused on social reproduction vs. production stress important gender dichotomies such as private/public, house/workspace, intimacy/publicity, and emotion/reason. Moreover, procreation and family ties (in terms of economic, cultural and social capital) seem to be the critical factors underlying biased gender relations.

In reality, family is a multifaceted field where cooperation, competition, tension and conflict are often closely related (Giddens 1995; André 1996). Even family formats are an increasingly complex issue. The conventional modern family based on parental and conjugal ties has reduced its statistical significance, giving way to monoparental arrangements, people living alone (not just elderly), same-sex couples, reconstructed families with children from different conjugal relations, etc. The greater diversity of 'the family' makes it increasingly difficult to maintain the family cell as the basic economic and social reference unit, although no other is generally envisaged. This situation of social tension – related to the (in)definition and the (ambiguous) role of the family institution nowadays – can be seen as an important leverage of social innovation in gender and parenthood relations, stimulating debate and new responses about social arrangements and their capacity to organize daily life.

The development of efficient contraception over the last 50 years, as well as scientific and civic progress in terms of assisted reproduction in the last two decades, have put great challenges to gender relations and stimulated new societal visions, including a deep rethinking of the hidden sphere of feelings and affections. The close link between sexuality and procreation has been broken and the two have become autonomous existential fields, or fields of everyday experience. This is not a minor change: it is a key social innovation with the potential to significantly affect (and perhaps decisively undermine?) the foundations of the patriarchal system. It is a social innovation that has been triggered by technological innovations (e.g. the contraceptive pill or in vitro fertilization), but which finds its highest expression at the level of social relations as well as in the sphere of culture and symbolic meanings. These new procreation possibilities make tremble the essence of patriarchy, the submission of women anchored in procreation.

In new familial contexts where procreation and sexuality are autonomous life spheres and where parenthood may be fully planned, important conditions have already been met for the decline of the patriarchal system and for decisive changes in social relations. Nevertheless, though weaker, gender inequalities remain clearly pronounced and closely related to the dichotomy between production and reproduction.

This is one of the major challenges facing gender policy in the EU. In Europe and North America, the mainstream arguments clearly point to the 'de-familialization' of care work as the key issue, and advise transferring it to the market or to the state (Esping-Anderson 2002, p.18). The ideas of Gosta Esping-Anderson in this regard are very pertinent: 'The ongoing gender revolution is both irreversible and desirable. To fully reap its advantages, we must recast the nexus between work, welfare and the family' (Esping-Anderson 2001, p.18). This argument turns on another which is even more trenchant: 'a huge part of the service economy owes its existence directly to the disappearance of house-wifery' (Esping-Anderson 2002, p. 68), underlining that the outsourcing of family services has a double job multiplier effect in terms of women's employment: the increasing availability of women in the labour market, and the growth in employment demand in the area of caring services.

Even accepting the convergence of inter-ests between gender equity and the out-sourcing of family work, the arguments related to the 'professionalization' of care work are very fragile. Jane Lewis argues that 'it is highly unlikely that all care work can be commodified. Care work can be 'active', involving some form of 'tending', but much of it is 'passive', requiring someone to 'be there' (2002, p. 347). This is also a crucial debate in terms of the way that relations between generations often remain in the shadow. Nowadays in European societies elderly people are absolutely disempowered (as they leave the labour market representing an increasing public expenditure as age advances). Very often there is a double adversity due to the fact that the majority of elder population are women.

This problem located in the sphere of social reproduction may seem minor, but it is absolutely central. Probably neither the market, nor the state, nor the third sector are able to respond (well) to the demand for children's and elderly people's 'passive' care. The ability to 'be there' with a strong emotional investment does not meet the parameters of professional work, pointing to solutions based on proximity networks of local communities. Integrated area development strategies (see also Moulaert et al., Chapter 1; Van Dyck and Van den Broeck, Chapter 9; Gibson-Graham and Roelvink, Chapter 34) seem to be an appropriate way to promote the 'renais-sance' of close links in the neighbourhood community, allowing the identification and recognition of basic needs especially of those that do not have the capacity to express their life's adversities (Moulaert 2002).

31.2.2   The Need for a Holistic View

The debates set out above clearly show the difficulty of connecting all the exis-tential fields where gender relations are manifested as well as the artificial division between social production and reproduction – the critical feature of gender relations. This suggests the need for a holistic view of gender (Connell 1985, 1987, 2005; Massey 1994; Krais 2006), from the analysis of gender in society to an understanding of society as gendered: 'Gender relations are present in all types of institutions. They may be not the most important structure in a particular case, but they are certainly a major structure of most' (Connell 1987, p. 120). The notion of gender regime (Connell 1987; Correll 2004; Walby 2004), approaches the holistic view of gender, stressing the institutional character of gender relations.

In order to identify the main 'gender regimes', Walby (2004) emphasizes the importance of understanding the con-tinuum between domestic and public, set by the market (commodification of household services, especially relevant in the USA), by the state (socialization of domestic work, especially frequent in Scandinavian countries) and through reg-ulation (conciliation between professional work and family, especially relevant in the EU). This shows important links between gender regimes and welfare regimes (Duncan 1995; Sainsbury 1999) indicat-ing points of convergence and tension. In the words of Bussemaker and Kersbergen,

'We can no longer focus only on the relation between the market, the state and the family [to understand welfare regimes]; we have to incorporate the gender structures that interlink these different spheres' (1999, p. 25).

'Gender order' also conveys the idea of gendered society, linking the various gender regimes. Connell (1987, 2002) posits four pillars supporting the gender order: (i) the relations of production (including paid and unpaid work); (ii) power relations (as part of a system of domination, patriarchy); (iii) emotional relations and sexuality, and (iv) symbolic relations (based on stereotypes and prejudices). This view raises the question of the breadth of human needs satisfaction and the desirable adoption of a broad conceptual framework for social innovation analysis, including attention to emotions, passions, beliefs and symbolic meanings. In order to understand the transformation of gender relations as a process of social innovation driven by different types of socially creative strategies, it is important to go further by adopting a multilevel view. This allows us to understand gender relations in their socio-geographic contexts, which comprise behaviour, cultural and identity patterns (Correll 2004).

These arguments point to one of the key issues in this debate: the ambiguous relations of complementarity and tension (or even conflict) between capitalism and patriarchy. Considering gender relations as the root of a social system – patriarchy – we shall discuss its relations with capitalism in order to identify both contradictions and synergies. Andrew Sayer formulates two crucial questions:

(i)   Do capitalism and patriarchy form a single system or two interacting systems? Is capitalism necessarily patriarchal or only contingently so?
(ii) Are bureaucratic organizations neces-

sarily gendered or only contingently so? Are such institutions, together with markets, neutral with respect to identities? (2000, p. 707)

In order to discuss the possibility of reconfiguring capitalism as a non-patriarchal system, and adopting a critical realist vision, Sayer (2000) stresses the need to consider: (i) associational thinking – the gendered character of capitalism based on evidence (cause-effect relations) and (ii) counterfactual thinking – there is a strong relation between capitalism and patriarchy. Sayer's contribution is crucial for linking gender with social innovation, particularly in the context of a discussion on the role of EU gender policies. It can be synthetized as follows (Figure 31.1).

31.3   GENDER AND SOCIAL INNOVATION

The changes experienced in the last few decades in the field of gender relations exhibit significant trends towards the greater inclusion of women in all areas of society (education, labour market, civic participation, political decisions, etc.), more and better responses aimed at decreasing women's workload (professional work and housework), as well as an erosion of patriarchy, implying important changes in social relations. These three trends seem to reflect and constitute combinations of various processes of social innovation, insofar as they share the fundamental constitutive dimensions of the latter (MacCallum et al. 2009; Harrison and Klein 2007), i.e. satisfaction of human needs, transformation of social relations and empowerment.

Social innovation in gender relations focuses particularly on four aspects: (i) the visibility of the inequality between men and women and the social injustice that is

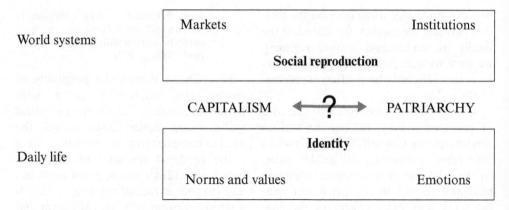

Figure 31.1   Contingent relations between capitalism and patriarchy

associated with it; (ii) the deconstruction of the complexity and multidimensionality of gender relations; (iii) the redefinition of gender norms related to masculinity and femininity, shaped in the past in the light of patriarchal principles; and (iv) the reorganization of the family institution that reproduces, even nowadays, biased gender power relations.

In spite of the fundamental social changes mentioned above, gender relations, as well as their associated inequalities and injustices, continue to be shaped in 'shadow zones' of society, especially within the domestic sphere where gender inequalities affect both conjugality and parenthood often bringing about profound injustice. Thus, social innovation concerns not just bringing gender inequalities into the 'light' – identifying hidden processes of hegemony/submission – but also distinguishing between difference and inequality in order to promote real empowerment and autonomy, or 'equity in diversity'. Under the guise of the risky right to difference, situations of social inequality or subordination often lurk. Gender stereotypes, widely publicized by the media and advertising, are frequently based on this ambiguity between difference and inequality. The complexity of gender relations –

which intersect labour relations, affections, sexuality and the symbolic dimensions of gender roles – renders their transformation more difficult, to the extent that social innovation in specific fields is not reflected in others and can even cause a reaction of resistance to change (or even hostile waves of conservatism, as these relate to contraception and abortion).

One of the fields where change has been more focused – and presented often as social innovation – is the facilitation of women's daily life, including actions aimed at the conciliation of domestic and paid work especially through the outsourcing of 'family' tasks. This reflects to some extent a patriarchal perspective on equal opportunities, whereby it is sought that women be placed at the same level as men in employment as well as in the spheres of civic and political participation. This approach to gender equity embodies the hegemony of the masculine norm – it does not undermine its foundations. If one is to adopt a truly socially innovative perspective, then daily domestic life has to be rethought as a whole and as driven by the collective of adult men and women, but also by children, youths and elder people: a collective based on dialogue and negotiation safeguarding balanced rights and duties.

Finally, family organization as a key bulwark of patriarchy should be considered a crucial target for social innovation debate and action. Under the appearance of a social unit based on cooperation, family is often an arena of competition, tension and conflict (Roussel 1989; Dagenais 2000). Social innovation in this field does not necessarily mean the end of the family, but rather the deconstruction of the 'idyllic' view of the family and the emergence of new organizational arrangements based on a negotiated equity among family members as mentioned above.

The following discussion looks at gender policies as levers of social innovation promoting social justice and new gender relations, focussing on the European Union as a case study. The analysis is guided by one overarching question: to what extent can the patriarchal system change or be changed – through socially innovative initiatives – under a capitalist order?

31.4   EU GENDER POLICIES PROMOTING SOCIAL INNOVATION

That EU policies aimed at promoting gender equal opportunities have made a significant contribution in the last few decades is beyond any doubt. But have these initiatives meant substantial structural changes in gender relations (including innovative transformation of gender order), or only a gradual decrease in the equality gap between men and women, mainly in the labour market and other related spheres such as education and training?

According to Walby (2004), there is no single answer to this question, because two different strategies can be identified in European gender policy: the *sameness model* in the 1970s and 1980s, anchored in equal pay and equal treatment; and the *plural model* since the 1990s, which stresses family and work conciliation, regulation of time, family policy, fertility, contraception and abortion, sexual preference, and violence against women. This large range of concerns has configured the gender mainstream adopted at the end of that decade.

The most recent phase clearly corresponds to a more integrated vision of gender issues, although this does not necessarily reflect an intention to promote new gender relations. However, the mere adoption of a policy of gender equal opportunities by the EC entails a recognition of 'women as a disadvantaged group in society, who deserve and require particular treatment and specialist provision in order to rectify their past experience of discrimination, which has become institutionalized.' (Booth and Bennett 2002, p. 434)

The path followed by the European gender policy has had three main stages (Booth and Bennett 2002; Stratigaki 2005; Pollack and Hafner-Burton 2000; Rubery et al. 2004): (i) equal treatment perspective, (ii) women's perspective, and (iii) gender mainstreaming.

In 1957, the Treaty of Rome stipulated in its Article 119 the equal payment principle, stating that 'each Member State shall during the first stage ensure and subsequently maintain the application of the principle that men and women should receive equal pay for equal work'. Those more sceptical about the ethical nature of this principle (Booth and Bennett 2002) state that the 'French government was concerned that differential rates of pay paid to women in the textile industry in other member states represented an unfair competitive advantage. Its objective in arguing for Article 119 was to mitigate this effect' (Rossilli 1997, p. 64). Nevertheless, the first EU directives on gender equal opportunities – equal pay, and equal treatment regarding employment, working conditions and social security – were not implemented until the late 1970s. This timing is not unrelated to the UK joining the EU and the strength of feminist movements in that country at the time.

The second stage – women's perspective – began in the early 1980s, with the First Action Program (1982–1985) but it was only fully adopted at the end of that decade under the presidency of Jacques Delors. Again, this was not just an ethical or ideological issue, but also a reaction to the greater disparities in the living conditions of women and men in the EU due to the entry into the Community of the Southern European countries – Greece in 1981 and Portugal and Spain in 1986. Taking advantage of a favourable context, a feminist vision began to be asserted at the level of European gender policy, as demonstrated by the creation of the European Women's Lobby in 1990, which currently includes more than 2,000 women's associations. Following this impetus, both the European Parliament and the European Commission created specific units to promote gender equal opportunities (Committee on Women's Rights in the European Parliament, and Equal Opportunities Unit in the Directorate for Employment, Industrial Relations and Social Affairs of the European Commission).

The various Action Programs for Equal Opportunities of Women and Men, and specific programs such as NOW (New Opportunities for Women), supported positive discrimination initiatives (positive actions) particularly in the fields of training and integration into the labour market. However, although these actions achieved significant results and impacts in terms of reducing the gap between women and men, they have also been criticised on the grounds that positive actions contradict the basic principles of equal opportunities.

Faced with acute criticism from European conservative sectors, the third step of European gender policy – called 'gender mainstreaming' – emerged in the late 1990s based on arguments that advocate a holistic view of gender equity and discourage the sectoral segmentation of policies. This new perspective was presented as an 'expansion of the EU equal opportunities agenda, focusing primarily on the potentially revolutionary, yet little studied, principle of gender mainstreaming' (Pollack and Hafner-Burton 2000, p. 432).

Theoretically and ideologically, gender mainstreaming mobilizes strong arguments: 'The gender perspective moves away from the model of women as a homogeneous group by recognizing women's diversity and difference, which relate to factors such as life course, class, age, ethnicity, religion and disability' (Booth and Bennett 2002, p. 238).

The gender mainstreaming strategy also follows the guidelines of the UN Third World Conference on Women in Nairobi in 1985, which provides it with strong political legitimacy. Generally speaking, this approach 'proposes that methods, strategies, models and studies aimed at integrating the equal opportunities dimension into all policies and activities be developed and promoted in the Member States' (COM (96) 650 final, 1997: 12). The aim was to bring a gender perspective into all EU policy-making in a 'coherent and systematic way' (ibid).

However, while this seems to constitute a qualitative change in gender relations, more careful reflection contradicts this idea. On the one hand patriarchy as a power system is not questioned by European policies (Booth and Bennett 2002) that remain at the level of civil rights enlargement and social inequalities shrinkage. It also excludes an often ignored but crucial aspect: those who implement policies and actions require specific gender-targeted training, since this is an area where the problems and solutions seem obvious from a common sense perspective, when in reality they are not. For an action to be really effective is almost always necessary to deconstruct the stereotypes that pervade our daily life.

GM certainly has the ability to promote creative gender equity strategies in many areas of European policy, but it is not itself a significant social innovation capable of transforming the bases of patriarchal relations – the crucial factor underlying gender inequalities – anchored in submission and dependency of women. The main evidence of this is the way that family, as an institution, is safeguarded from GM orientations and actions.

Positive actions developed in the last decades of the 20th century comported more seeds of social innovation probably because they represented the institutionalization of social innovations occurring across society, neighbourhoods and households. Could this be why they caused a huge reaction and were rapidly abandoned and transformed?

31.5 CONCLUSION

In conclusion, we should concede that EU gender policies have indeed stimulated social innovation in several fields. The most important of all may be the enhanced visibility of gender inequality. Until around the late 1970s, gender relations were a black box, a shadow area of social life that was hidden behind the walls of the family home. Over the last three decades, EU gender policies have brought to light the profound social inequality that exists between women and men, and thereby influenced not only the initiatives

directly undertaken with EU support, but also national policies. In many cases this stimulated social innovation at different scales, from the citizenship sphere, to labour markets and to the micro level of familial relations. At least, the European discourse on equal opportunities has been a stimulus towards new attitudes and behaviours that favour social justice. Another relevant contribution relates to the holistic view of gender comprising difference and diversity combined with equity, which has emerged as a relevant ideological debate.

Still, two crucial aspects have consistently remained absent from gender policies at the EU level. The first consists of the reconstruction of gender norms (e.g. through eliminating stereotypes in children school books) – an aspect which has never received any attention at the level of EU policies. The second (and crucial) issue regards family organization: both EU institutions and national states continue to operate on conceptual (ideological) bases that take 'the family' as the basic unit of society, overstating cooperation and disregarding competition and tension. European orientations towards the motherhood and fatherhood roles constitute a good example of this ideological basis, which constitutes a significant barrier to more decisive and profound instances of social innovation in this field.

31.6 QUESTIONS FOR DISCUSSION

- Despite relevant changes in the last decades, deep inequalities between men and women persist in the EU. What nowadays are the main gaps and why do they persist?
- In your view, is positive discrimination for women a way to weaken the patriarchal system?

- To what extent does capitalism nowadays need the patriarchal system?
- Does the EU gender mainstreaming advocate a new gender order?
- In what fields does EU gender policy stimulate real social innovation, e.g. a structural change of gender power relations?

NOTES

1. Such as the strategies for conciliation between family and paid work based on external services – provided by the state or by the third sector – and less focused in the balanced sharing of family responsibilities between women and men.
2. Giuseppe Tomasi de Lampedusa, *Il Gattopardo*, 1957 (adapted to the cinema by Luchino Visconti, 1963).

REFERENCES

(References in bold are recommended reading.)

André, I. (1996), 'At the Centre on the Periphery? Women in the Portuguese Labor Market', in M.D. Garcia-Ramon and J. Monk (eds), pp. 138–155.
Booth, C. and C. Bennett (2002), 'Gender Mainstreaming in the European Union: Towards a New Conception and Practice of Equal Opportunities?' *The European Journal of Women's Studies*, 9 (4), 430–446.
Bourdieu, P. (1998), *La domination masculine*, Paris: Ed. Seuil.
Bussemaker, J. and K. Kersbergen (1999), 'Contemporary Social-Capitalist Welfare States', in D. Sainsbury (ed.) *Gender and Welfare State Regimes*, Oxford: Oxford University Press, pp. 15–46.
Connell, R.W. (1985), 'Theorising Gender', *Sociology*, 19, 260–272.
Connell, R.W. (1987), *Gender and power: Society, the person and sexual politics*, Sydney: Allen and Unwin.
Connell, R.W. (2005), 'A Really Good Husband: Work/Life Balance, Gender Equity and Social Change', *Australian Journal of Social Issues*, 40 (3), 369–383.
Correll, S.J. (2004), 'Constraints into Preferences: Gender, Status, and Emerging Career Aspirations', *American Sociological Review*, 69, 93–113.
Dagenais, D. (2000), *La fin de la famille moderne: sig-*

nification des transformations contemporaines de la famille, Québec: Les Presses de l'Université Laval and Presses Universitaires de Rennes.
Davis, S.N. and T.N. Greenstein (2009), 'Gender Ideology: Components, Predictors, and Consequences', *Annual Review of Sociology*, 35, 87–105.
Duncan, S. (1995), 'Theorizing European Gender Systems', *Journal of European Social Policy*, 5, 263–284.
Esping-Anderson, G. (2002), 'A new gender contract', in G. Esping-Anderson, D. Gallie, A. Hemerijck and J. Myles (eds) *Why we need a New Welfare State*, Oxford: Oxford University Press, pp. 68–95.
Esping-Anderson, G., D. Gallie, A. Hemerijck and J. Myles (2001), *A new welfare architecture for Europe?*, report submitted to the Belgian Presidency of the European Union, Brussels.
European Union (2010), Gender pay gap statistics, http://epp.eurostat.ec.europa.eu/statistics_explained/index.php/Gender_pay_gap_statistics (last accessed 19 December 2012).
Garcia-Ramon, M.D. and J. Monk (eds) (1996), *Women of the European Union, the Politics of Work and Daily Life*, London: Routledge.
Giddens, A. (1995), *The transformation of intimacy: sexuality, love and eroticism in modern societies*, Stanford: Stanford University Press.
Harrison, D. and J.-L. Klein (eds) (2007), *L'Innovation Sociale – Emergence et Effets sur la Transformation des Sociétés*, Montréal: Presses de l'Université du Québec.
Jordan, J. (2006), 'Mothers, Wives, and Workers: Explaining Gendered Dimensions of the Welfare State', *Comparative Political Studies*, 39 (9), 1109–1132.
Klein J.-L. and D. Harrison (eds) (2007), *L'Innovation Sociale – Emergence et Effets sur la Transformation des Sociétés*, Montréal: Presses de l'Université du Québec.
Krais, B. (2006), 'Gender, Sociological Theory and Bourdieu's Sociology of Practice', *Theory, Culture & Society*, 23 (6), 119–134.
Lewis, J. (2002), 'Gender and welfare state change', *European Societies*, 4 (4), 331–357.
MacCallum, D., F. Moulaert, J. Hillier and S. Vicari Haddock (eds) (2009), *Social Innovation and Territorial Development*, London: Ashgate.
Massey, D. (1994), *Space, Place and Gender*, Minneapolis: University of Minnesota Press.
McDowell, L. (1983), 'Towards an understanding of the gender division of urban space', *Environment and Planning D: Society and Space*, 1 (1), 59–72.
McNay, L. (2000), *Gender and Agency, Reconfiguring the Subject in Feminist and Social Theory*, London: Polity Press.
Moulaert, F. (2002), *Globalization and Integrated Area Development in European Cities*, Oxford: Oxford University Press.
Pollack, M.A. and E. Hafner-Burton (2000),

'Mainstreaming gender in the European Union', *Journal of European Public Policy*, **7** (3), 432–456.

Reay, D. (2004), '"It's all becoming a habitus': beyond the habitual use of habitus in educational research", *British Journal of Sociology of Education*, **25** (4), 431–444.

Rossilli, M. (1997), 'The European Community's Policy on the Equality of Women: From the Treaty of Rome to the Present', *European Journal of Women's Studies*, **4**, 63–82.

Roussel, L. (1989), *La famille incertaine: essai*, Paris: Editions Odile Jacob.

Rubery, Jill, Hugo Figueiredo, Mark Smith, Damian Grimshaw and Colette Fagan (2004), 'The ups and downs of European gender equality policy', *Industrial Relations Journal*, **35** (6), 603–628.

Sainsbury, D. (1999) *Gender and Welfare State Regimes*, Oxford: Oxford University Press.

Sayer, A. (2000), 'System, Lifeworld and Gender: Associational Versus Counterfactual Thinking', *Sociology*, **34 (4), 707–725.**

Stratigaki, M. (2005), 'Gender Mainstreaming vs Positive Action: An Ongoing Conflict in EU Gender Equality Policy', *European Journal of Women's Studies*, **12 (2), 165–186.**

Walby, S. (1986), *Patriarchy at Work*, London: Polity Press.

Walby, S. (2004), 'The European Union and Gender Equality: Emergent Varieties of Gender Regime', *Social Politics*, **11, 4–29.**

PART VI

FRONTIERS IN SOCIAL INNOVATION RESEARCH

Introduction: the pillars of social innovation research and practice

Serena Vicari Haddock

This part discusses the philosophical orientations, epistemologic stances and the role of the meta-theories of societal change which have proven most appropriate to the production of knowledge in analytical and empirical work on social innovation (SI). Its purpose is to provide a proposal to advance this work.

In the first chapter of this part, Novy, Habersack and Schaller make a strong argument in favour of transdisciplinarity as the epistemological stance best suited to knowledge production, in particular in the analysis and promotion of social innovation; in doing so they also anticipate several theoretical positions presented in the following chapters. The argument is based on several propositions: first, the complexity of social problems and the highly disputed and recursive definition of their nature in contemporary societies make it necessary to take into account the plurality of both life-worlds and scientific definitions of problems. Complexity and instability in the social understanding of the world have already been captured by Giddens's double hermeneutic, which accounts for the two-way relationship between everyday 'lay' concepts and scientific definitions; people's understanding of their world shapes their practice but because people can think, make choices, and use new information they can revise their understandings, and hence their practice; in particular they can use the knowledge and insights of the social sciences to change their practices. In doing so the

'findings' of the social sciences very often enter constitutively into the world they describe and change that world in such a way that a 'new' scientific understanding becomes necessary. A transdisciplinary approach takes this epistemological stance one step further by engaging scientists, practitioners and stakeholders in a programme of joint problematization of the field in which change, i.e. social innovation, is to be produced. Secondly, the transdisciplinary approach treats ordinary citizens who experience forms of social exclusion as valuable actors and sources for problem identification, analysis and the implementation of negotiated solutions. Thus, this approach assumes that marginalized groups participate and take responsibility, along with other stakeholders engaged in SI, for the construction of arenas in which alternative definitions of social problems can be given systematic form and made accessible to a broader public. Thirdly, transdisciplinary research activity is informed by an ethical stance committed to solidarity, diversity and sustainability, on the assumption that paths toward a common good can be defined on the basis of ongoing negotiations and recursive definitions of problems and solutions. The chapter ends with the discussion of two examples of knowledge alliances as specific forms of long-term commitment and partnerships in research and action in which transdisciplinarity is embodied, and discusses the potential and limitations of these experiences.

In Chapter 33, Moulaert and Mehmood defend the methodological perspective of holism in the deconstruction of the social world and theorization of SI possibilities for progressive change. This methodological perspective is attuned to a commitment to pragmatism as the overall philosophical orientation. The focus is thus on 'what works' and on the institutional, cultural context in which people produce a certain interpretation of their conditions of existence and envision 'other worlds'; these visions of the future serve to mobilize them, i.e. to make SI work. The necessity of reflexivity on the part of all parties engaged in SI is introduced here and is developed further in the final chapter by Moulaert and Van Dyck. But here Moulaert and Mehmood intend to show the connections between holism and pragmatism on the one hand and collective action on the other, in particular how collective action is promoted by a scientific analysis informed by holism and pragmatism.

A dialogue between two research programs sharing similar theoretical and ethical orientations is the theme of the Chapter 34. Gibson-Graham and Roelvink look sympathetically at the Local/Social Innovation Project (LSIP), consisting of the Integrated Area Development-SINGOCOM-KATARSIS research trajectory (see Moulaert et al., Chapter 1), from their experience in the action research project Community Economies (CE), showing similarities and differences between the two in the ways that each conceptualizes society, the economy and their interaction. In doing so, Gibson-Graham and Roelvink defend a particular epistemological line of thought which resonates strongly with the transdisciplinary and reflexive orientations of SI research as elaborated in Chapters 32 and 35. Both research trajectories stress the role of social and economic diversity in building

other worlds. CE starts from mapping diversity in living communities, using assets-based approaches (see also Kunnen et al., Chapter 21) to reframe notions of economy and potentials, while LSIP tends rather to mirror communities' experiences onto a normative view of a just world, and to use these reflections as drivers for social change. This difference in approach provides an interesting lens through which to examine relationships between theory, meta-theory as a view of society and its transformation, and action research with its ethical commitment to social change.

The final chapter by Moulaert and Van Dyck presents new methodological lines of thought in the form of a theoretically informed discussion of the position of the researchers engaged in social innovation analysis and action and a proposal for a sociology of knowledge perspective in this knowledge production process. From a philosophy of science perspective, the authors propose a structural focus in critical realism in which pragmatism is revisited and possibilities to transcend postmodernist approaches are foreseen. The role of science and the process of knowledge building are explored as the authors deal with, first, what researchers actually do when they study, engage in research and help to draw up guidelines for collective action and policies, and to provide guidance in their implementation. In this respect, it is argued that researchers' values, social commitment, political views, awareness of their embodied identity and the effects of the latter on research design, the selection of research methodologies and human interaction during field work (referred to in the literature as 'positionality'), should be the constant object of reflection and negotiation for researchers, practitioners, activists and ordinary citizens. Thus, the issue of reflexivity, and the problem of how it should be incorporated in the overall theoretical approach, is placed at the heart of the social innovation research programme. As far as the process of knowledge building is concerned, the authors begin by showing how crucial it is in contemporary society that a rigorous assessment be performed of the role of scientific knowledge production in the understanding of social transformations and the steering of social change; they propose a sociology of knowledge perspective that addresses the role of knowledge production about or related to social innovation within the structural dynamics of society. The core of the chapter is then devoted to the exploration of what it means, for scientific work on social innovation, to take the socially constructed character of knowledge and its embeddness in society seriously. This exploration leads to the development of a meta-theoretical framework for research programs on social innovation informed by a sociology of knowledge perspective and to the discussion of its value for scientific analysis and practices. We have thus come full circle, as this perspective is meant to nurture the knowledge alliances presented in the initial chapter of this part of the handbook.

32. Innovative forms of knowledge production: transdisciplinarity and knowledge alliances

Andreas Novy, Sarah Habersack and Barbara Schaller[1]

32.1 INTRODUCTION

This chapter aims to identify effective strategies for producing socially robust knowledge for the elaboration of social innovations. Its first section exposes alternatives to monodisciplinary forms of knowledge production with a focus on transdisciplinarity, an epistemological innovation to foster multi-perspectivity, context-sensitivity and stakeholder involvement and centres on the joint problematization of the field in which actors have to act. Section two presents knowledge alliances as a specific form of transdisciplinarity based on long-term commitment and partnership. In section three and four, the trajectory, potential and limitations of two knowledge alliances, acting at different scales, are exposed: *Unequal Diversity* as a local knowledge alliance in Vienna and *Social Polis* as a transnational platform illustrate that knowledge alliances are not only a condition and cradle of social innovation towards a society based on solidarity, diversity and sustainability, but they are social innovations themselves.

32.2 TRANSDISCIPLINARY FORMS OF KNOWLEDGE AND INNOVATION

Capitalist modernization and the resultant rising complexity of society have led to increasing specialization in research and in the governance of knowledge in general. This has resulted in attempts to re-contextualize institutions and practices of science in society and a broad range of alternative proposals which aim at accommodating excellence and democratization (Siune 2009, pp. 4,16–18). While multi, inter, cross, post, pluri and protodisciplinarity focus on the transfer of methods across disciplines (Cassinari et al. 2011, p. 5), we will concentrate on transdisciplinarity, as this type of research 'is necessary when knowledge about a societally relevant problem field is uncertain, when the concrete nature of problems is disputed, and when there is a great deal at stake for those concerned by the problems and involved in investigating them' (Hirsch Hadorn et al. 2008, p. 37). In line with the Swiss Academies of Art and Science (n.d.), transdisciplinary research attempts to a) grasp the complexity of a problem, b) take into account the diversity of life-worlds and scientific perceptions of problems, c) link abstract and case-specific knowledge and d) develop knowledge and practices that promote what is perceived to be the common good. In this collaboration of researchers from different disciplinary backgrounds and practitioners with diverse experiences, expertise and objectives, the joint production of knowledge is 'about improving social relations and tackling social problems or meeting social needs' Cassinari et al. 2011, p. 11).

It is an enormous task to accommodate different languages, *modi operandi* and expectations, as it requires ongoing translation and negotiation between disciplines and life worlds (Häberli et al. 2001, p. 12). It presupposes a disposition to dialogue and valorizes the search for the new and emergent (see also Hillier, Chapter 12, and the chapters in Part IV). An open-ended cumulative-circular approach of mutual learning with diverse stakeholders has to be facilitated by trained experts (Karl-Trummer et al. 2007, p. 5). Organized professionally, transdisciplinary projects have the potential to constitute 'powerful interventions into local systems' (Thompson Klein 2001, p. 114). By the taking of ownership by non-academic participants due to joint decision making and feedback loops the chances of achieving 'socially robust knowledge' (Nowotny 2003, pp. 14–17) are enhanced.

Each context – be it a neighbourhood, a school or a development project – is composed of diverse elements and driven by different logics. Transdisciplinary research valorizes this complexity, allowing researchers to perceive contradictions and to grasp multiple perspectives and opposing interests. By fostering participation and making knowledge applicable to a local context, excluded and oppressed parts of the population can gain access to relevant knowledge for creative strategies to overcome exclusion (Moulaert et al. 2005; Moulaert 2010). Their experiences with social exclusion together with the knowledge of the researcher can improve problem identification, problem analysis and the implementation of results (Hirsch Hadorn et al. 2008, p. 37). Homeless people or migrants, feminist action groups and trade unions are actors and organizations which experience exclusion and fight for inclusion. But they have difficulties with getting heard. For them, the participation in transdisciplinary research may provide an arena for systematizing and popularizing their concerns. Therefore, due impor-

tance has to be given to the research setting in order to permit the inclusion of marginalized groups – especially if the objective of research and policies is social inclusion. This ethical commitment requires an easy access to knowledge for those at the margin of the knowledge society (Hollaender and Leroy 2001, p. 234), e.g. by making knowledge available for free via different channels (e.g. open-source technologies). In such an institutional context, place-based or at least bottom-linked knowledge can be best mobilized for social innovations in favour of inclusion and empowerment of subaltern interests of class, gender and ethnicity.

To achieve such empowerment requires a predisposition to dialogue and the exercise of a practical form of rationality which the Greek termed *phronesis* (prudence), a form of reasoning which integrates ethical and practical concerns and leads to a slower and deeper reflection on reality (Bernstein 1983; Flyvbjerg 2001). This can overcome deep divides in current thinking and acting which result from a tendency to pigeonhole problems according to disciplines and juridical competences. Such a lack of a holistic analysis often impedes 'getting the overall picture' of a situation or a problem in order to solve it. Often enough academics and policy makers who deal with economics propagate growth strategies without taking issues of distribution and the environment into consideration. Different academics, policy makers and social movements, dedicated to social and cultural policies, often stress the damage and suffering caused by social exclusion without relating socio-cultural exclusion to issues such as deindustrialization, financial liberalization or monetary policies. What do experts in different domains have to say to each other? What can they learn from each other? Dialogue would deepen understanding and empower actors to better tackle the issues (see Moulaert and Mehmood, Chapter 33 on holistic analysis). Taking the current Euro-crisis and its implications for urban development as an example: grassroots activists can deepen awareness about the resultant problems in everyday life; academics can contextualize problems by embedding them in multiscalar and multidimensional structures; and professionals can show the place-specific institutional dynamics of stigmatization and marginalization as processes of multiple deprivation. In these settings, a question-oriented educational approach can overcome departmentalization and fragmentation by empowering marginalized groups and agreeing to focus on joint problem solving.

Transdisciplinarity, although interested in changing the world, remains a specific form of knowledge production, one that is cautious about too quick solutions and too voluntarist interventions which are not aware of the complexity of the phenomena where an intervention by researchers and practitioners is planned. We suggest that the epistemological justification of transdisciplinarity as a form of high-quality knowledge production which acknowledges different forms of knowledge is strengthened by taking into consideration the work of Paulo Freire as well as the insights of critical realism (Novy 2009). 'Abstraction in cognitive conceptions is important' (Hirsch Hadorn et al. 2008, 36), as the perception of reality is concept-dependent (Sayer 1992, pp. 31–35). The contexts in which people act and the world they are part of are not given, but constructed by human agency. Neither thinking and acting, nor understanding and changing are opposites. They are linked: 'Knowledge is part of being' (Bhaskar 2002, p. 83); action and reflection go hand in hand (Freire 2004). Against fatalist res-

ignation, Freire and the critical realists perceive the world as dynamic, emerging and related, a world in constant transformation (Archer et al. 2004). Climate change, migration and social exclusion are examples of phenomena which are no fixed reality, but in a process of becoming. It is of crucial importance how reality is conceptualized and understood – whether it is perceived as static and unchangeable or constructed and open to being shaped. If not only the power of structures, but also the capacity of agency to shape reality are acknowledged the future is no longer perceived as a fate, but as emerging and co-constructed by human agency (Miciukiewicz et al. 2012; Novy et al. 2012).

32.3   KNOWLEDGE ALLIANCES

These ontological and epistemological insights show the importance of a transdisciplinary approach to knowledge production, knowledge sharing and the organization of research. The key organizational innovation for implementing transdisciplinary research in a sustainable and democratic way are knowledge alliances, i.e. sustainable learning and research partnerships composed of researchers and practitioners in all their diversity. They are based on an attitude of respect, self-reflexivity and curiosity, a disposition for mutual learning and a culture of dialogue and democracy. To organize knowledge production in such a sustainable way is a concrete utopia, a possibility emerging out of the praxis of collective agency in social movements, public agencies or solidarity economy. It is, therefore, a progressive vision of a democratic governance of knowledge, but it also describes a reality of cooperation which has evolved in rudimentary forms over the last years in diverse settings in research as well as in social mobilization and innovative learning.

Almost every transdisciplinary project is a temporary partnership, always confronted with the danger of dissolving after the project expires, thereby putting at risk the slow process of building trust and common understanding. Knowledge alliances are those partnerships which survive the single project. Their members share, produce and diffuse knowledge and build bridges between fragmented entities, be it scientific disciplines and their mono-logical explanations or single-issue policies which foster micro-efficiency to the detriment of social cohesion and socio-economic effectiveness. Knowledge alliances exist in different organizational forms and at many scales. They can be a European platform, a local neighbourhood group, a national programming initiative, etc. The common denominator is that they all want to produce relevant and robust knowledge to shape a more equal society. The term alliance directs to the starting point of any transdisciplinary research, a shared concern which a group of different actors decide to tackle. Knowledge refers not only to scientific knowledge, but to the many different forms of knowledge which can be shared in collaboration between researchers and practitioners, including:

> the interpretation in the life-world (systems knowledge); knowledge about the need for change, desired goals and better ways of acting (target knowledge); and knowledge about technical, social, legal, cultural and other means of redirecting the existing behaviour (transformation knowledge). Hirsch Hadorn et al. 2008, p. 36)

The quality and innovation of knowledge alliances come from integrating different forms of knowledge to deal with complex phenomena: Problems have to be identified, structured and analysed and research results have to be 'brought to fruition' (Hirsch Hadorn et al. 2008, p. 35), that is, realized as action. The concept of knowledge alliance includes the following features:

● *A common overall concern, specific objectives and a clear division of labour*: a knowledge alliance produces and uses knowledge to tackle a complicated and contradictory problem field. The specific objectives of the participants, however, are different according to their respective interests. It is not always useful that a researcher becomes an activist, nor do practitioners need to handle rigorous scientific methods. But the respective knowledge, abilities and skills have to be identified and valued.

● *Creating time and space for exchange*: a participative research process requires time to build trust, mutual respect for cooperation and a setting in which all participants feel comfortable expressing their views and opinions (Häberli et al. 2001, p. 12). Thereby a collective understanding and vision can be built. The provision of physical and digital spaces for encounter and exchange is preferably connected to main research phases, as for example:
  ● democratic decision making about the relevant steps in the research process;
  ● joint elaboration of research questions and aims and designing the process of knowledge production;
  ● developing a collective understanding of terms that are relevant for the problem field;
  ● collection and analysis of data and material;

- evaluation and valorization of the results and the cooperation processes (Karl-Trummer et al. 2007, p. 5).
- *Tools for communication*: enabling communication on an equal footing is the basic requirement for a democratic partnership. Translating between languages, realities of work and life and *modi operandi* is critical to identify problems correctly, to negotiate meanings of concepts and to evaluate results. Awareness of the centrality of communication and translation is a precondition for introducing effective pedagogical tools: interactive websites, blogs, material in native languages, newsletters, mailing lists, audiovisual media and interactive meeting and conference methods are options that might be used according to the context of each knowledge alliance.
- *Transparent and negotiated distribution of resources*: a fair and transparent distribution of resources is central to a respectful collaboration and enables collective thinking and acting. This not only includes allocating budget to each participant, but also taking into consideration the institutional logic and available infrastructure of each person involved.
- *Contextualized use and dissemination of knowledge*: the diverse participants have a broad range of intentions and needs for engaging in such a process. It must be clear that each actor will have the opportunity to use and disseminate the knowledge according to his/her own context (e.g. researchers writing an article for a peer-reviewed journal, policy makers for recommendations at the political level as well as the

popularization of results). A joint product is an important aim, but the collectively produced knowledge should also be customized to specific target groups and stakeholders.

32.4   UNEQUAL DIVERSITY: SCHOOL MEETS UNIVERSITY

The local knowledge alliance which we will present started six years ago between the Vienna University of Economics and Business (WU), the Kooperative Mittelschule 18 (KMS 18), a secondary school in an outer district of Vienna with pupils between 10 and 15 years old, and the Paulo Freire Centre, a centre for transdisciplinary development research and dialogical education, which organizes and documents this cooperation. The school was known to be a highly conflictive and deprived school with over 80 per cent of its pupils having a migrant background and a mother tongue other than German. The university and the school entered in a relationship of mutual learning, following Paulo Freire's argument that *'nobody knows everything, nobody knows nothing'* (Freire 1989, p. 39),[2] so we can all learn from each other. Students from the university got insights into a different and unknown milieu in their own city. They applied a development studies approach in a European context, as students from WU and pupils from the KMS 18 had to jointly research their own life realities and their city in all their diversity. Both explored spaces and experienced relationships with members of other milieus and social classes with whom they would not normally mix: pupils from popular classes got to know the university; middle class students participated in Serbian family celebrations.

In 2010, this cooperation was enlarged

within a project called 'Unequal Diversity: diversity of cultures – unequal city'. This project was financed from 2010 to August 2012 by the Austrian Ministry of Science and Research in the highly innovative programme of 'Sparkling Science: Science calls School, School calls Science', which promotes the exchange between schools and the academic community. The project includes: BG 18 (Bundesgymnasium Klostergasse), the neighbouring grammar school; Istanbul Lisesi, an elite grammar school in Turkey; and Aleska Santis, a secondary school in Secanj in Serbia, together with the Paulo Freire Center, WU and KMS 18. Its objective is to understand the conflictive relationship between cultural diversity and social inequality in cities by involving youth from diverse social and cultural backgrounds. It is well known in Austria that the segregation into secondary and grammar school at the age of 10 is one of the major causes of reproduction of educational inequality (Paulo Freire Zentrum and Österreichische HochschülerInnenschaft 2005). Therefore the integration of the BG 18, which is only 80 m away from the KMS 18, was a crucial step to widen the horizon in tackling dynamics of social inclusion. Its pupils are from middle to upper middle class with a lower percentage of pupils with a migrant background. Between the two schools, their teachers and their students, there had not been any contact until the beginning of the project, apart from some hostile encounters between pupils from the two schools in the park situated between them.

Besides the common aim of producing relevant knowledge for dealing with cultural diversity and social inequality in different institutions and life realities, each participant in this partnership has a particular set of goals according to his/her needs and interests. For the KMS

18, the contacts with students, researchers and pupils from grammar school permit a boost for the self-esteem of their pupils because their experience-based knowledge is respected and they are treated on an equal footing. The pupils of the grammar school are particularly interested in learning about research methods and getting insights into university and science, which will be the future for most of them. For both principals this project means prestige and public attention, which can bring institutional support in the form of additional resources for innovative pedagogical initiatives like bi-lingual classes. And for the researchers as well as the university students, it permits further development of transdisciplinary methodology and experimenting with social innovations in the field of social cohesion, education and intercultural learning.

The diversity of the actors involved in this project is the main source of innovation and creativity; at the same time it is the greatest challenge. This particular constellation of actors needs a transparent division of labour with clear tasks and professional management. Successfully dealing with questions of responsibility, communication and information chains like 'who has to be included in this decision?' and even very mundane questions like 'who is in charge of buying the drinks for the meeting?' must not be neglected. The organizational backbone of the knowledge alliance and a crucial democratic meeting place is the steering group, consisting of the core research team, teachers and principals from both Viennese schools and the intercultural experts that are responsible for the communication with the schools in Serbia and Turkey. Not only are organizational and financial issues discussed; it also serves as a crucial encounter of mutual learning. Preliminary research results are presented, shared and refined.

During a teaching course at WU, each summer term (March–June) small research teams, consisting of pupils from both Viennese schools and university students, are formed. They choose a research topic and develop their own research plan, including the research question, the method and the allocation of tasks to be carried out within their team. In these teams, supervised and supported by the core research team and the teachers, young people from different age groups and milieus can slowly establish trust and get to know each other in a safe setting. The task of researching their own city and their own life realities together with the methods presented by the core team, give them the frame and the tools for exchange.

To guarantee sustainability beyond the project period, tools for communication that enable the inclusion of all actors, like a website (www.ungleichevielfalt.at, last accessed 18 March 2013), interactive workshop settings and different forms of documentation (videos, photos, articles) are elaborated. For pedagogical reasons, scientific methods have to be adapted and translated for young people and the key concepts have to be clarified. To this end, tool-kits about the 'theatre of the oppressed', based on the work of Paulo Freire and Augusto Boal, and on 'interview techniques' have been produced which has facilitated the work of the small research teams. Each year a two-day research lab is organized for pupils and students, where they can experiment with methods and constitute their research teams (Fritsch 2010; Habersack 2010; Köfler 2010).

The challenge of this knowledge alliance is that each actor takes up tasks that are not part of his or her normal routine. People from milieus and institutions that normally barely cross each other's paths are working together and at best this leads to a critical self-reflection. In other

moments, this can lead to misunderstanding, frustration and a lack of clarity. For example, pupils from the grammar school had no problem in helping pupils from KMS 18, but it was very difficult to elaborate research plans 'on equal footing', as the elder pupils with middle class background could not deal with the apparent lack of discipline and knowledge of the younger pupils with popular and migrant background. The steering group learned from this joint evaluation that raising awareness of one's own position in society is a prerequisite for intercultural learning and cooperation beyond boundaries of class, ethnicity and gender.

To sum up, the development of knowledge alliances for social innovation is a slow process because all participants have to be respected with their limitations and weaknesses but also because they need time to reveal and share their assets and skills. Only by achieving mutual respect through a clear project design and a sustained trustful cooperation, a true partnership can be started.

32.5 SOCIAL POLIS: SOCIAL PLATFORM ON CITIES AND SOCIAL COHESION

The project 'Social Polis: Social Platform on Cities and Social Cohesion' is an experiment for developing a knowledge alliance at the European level (Stigendal 2010). It was a project in the 7th Framework Programme financed by the DG Research of the European Commission (see Moulaert et al., Chapter 1). It was the first Social Platform financed by the European Commission DG Research and therefore an innovative process itself. Its main goal was to elaborate a focused research agenda on urban social cohesion for the European Commission Framework Programme together with the main stakeholders in this policy and research field (http://www.socialpolis.eu/focusedresearch-agenda/, last accessed 19 December 2012). This gave researchers, grassroots activists, city officials, community workers, planners and architects from different cities the possibility to shape the future research in Europe, to foster the democratization of science and to enable an international mutual learning exercise. Social Polis created an open and multi-layered international platform of researchers and practitioners dedicated to the issue of social cohesion in the city. Since this platform was the first of its kind, it was a pilot project, a 'learning platform' to overcome mono- and multi-disciplinary research programmes and paradigms. But the most innovative element in Social Polis has been the attempt to empower stakeholders who normally are at the margin of the scientific community and powerful policy networks. Formulating a research agenda is normally a task for researchers. It is elaborated with scientific methods and written in a scientific language. But in Social Polis the experiences of grassroots activists, professionals and policy makers enriched the concepts and language of researchers. It was a collective learning process that social cohesion is related to such burning, but apparently unrelated, issues as the controversies about the use of headscarves, emerging new forms of poverty, the appropriate social mix in neighbourhoods or the appropriation of public spaces by powerful corporate interests (Novy et al. 2012). In Social Polis, there were participants focusing on intercultural learning and others who discussed urban poverty and the lack of citizenship. Instead of fragmenting the analysis by dealing with these issues as separate dimensions of social cohesion, we identified an underlying common *problématique*, resulting from the paradox of

human conviviality – to be accepted as unique as well as equal. All the above mentioned issues touch on aspects of the basic contradiction that people want to belong to and identify with a community, but at the same time desire to be accepted as full citizens, as different, but equal members of a society. Raising awareness about this paradox strengthened a common commitment to a broad concept of citizenship covering civic, political, social and economic rights and inspired collective reflection in a question-oriented way: is the ongoing fragmentation in European cities an expression of their cultural diversity or a result of increasing socioeconomic inequality? How much assimilation is compatible with basic human rights? Is the marginalization of migrants explained by their lack of citizenship or the dynamics of the labour market? Researchers who concentrate on only one dimension predefine social cohesion in a simple way and offer easy answers: some fall into the culturalist trap and embrace either multiculturalism or promote law and order; others reduce the problem to a question that can be solved by one-size-fits-all policies. But such responses are not based on a comprehensive understanding or a holistic analysis. Therefore, they remain victims of a fragmented logic and policy approach and cannot offer effective solutions.

By understanding social cohesion as a *problématique*, we acknowledge the multidimensionality and multiscalarity of cohesion as well as its context-specificity and raise doubts about simple, universal solutions. Systematic attempts to answer questions of the type cited above show that it is not easy to promote cohesive cities where people live together, enjoy equal access, rights and opportunities and acknowledge their differences. In fact, cohesive urban development is not easy to achieve. It is highly contradictory and controversial. Therefore we propose context-specific and jointly negotiated solutions to create inclusive, sustainable and diverse neighbourhoods and cities (see European Commission 2011, p. 60). It is necessary to find context-sensitive ways of linking issues of cultural diversity, social citizenship and political participation (Miciukiewicz et al. 2012).

To sum up, these methodological developments of 'problematization' could have profound implications for policy making and political activism. Just one example: to acknowledge the multi-scalarity of social cohesion helps to understand that the current urban problems – the occupation of public squares, mass youth unemployment and homelessness – cannot be dealt with at the local level alone. In line with a multi-scalar approach, maintaining urban, social and territorial cohesion in Europe requires innovative forms of place-based development strategies as well as limiting wealth concentration and offering new context-sensitive forms of European socio-ecological citizenship (Novy 2011). Transdisciplinary research cannot implement these policies, but it can show its analytical coherence and inspire grassroots initiatives, policy makers and political leaders.

The shared interest in better understanding social cohesion and in jointly elaborating strategies to tackle exclusionary dynamics has strengthened the bonds of participants in the platform. For community-based organizations Social Polis offered access to researchers and their knowledge as well as small funding for their own projects. For researchers it was an opportunity to cross academic boundaries, to learn about practitioners' knowledge and to try out new methods. The participation of representatives of city administrations was more difficult because they are used to contracting applied research to solve certain, clearly definable problems – Social Polis did not offer simple solutions, but has posed questions in a different way, due to multiple perspectives and the awareness about diverging interests.

Establishing local networks between researchers and practitioners at the city level was crucial for creating a bottom-linked European platform that is not limited to networking in Brussels. Social Polis was built on an already existing interest of core partners to work together. New stakeholders were integrated by offering funds for reflection on specific dimensions of social cohesion. Their workshops covered such diverse issues as economic micro-initiatives, intercultural competences of youth from deprived areas in Malmö or the solidarity-based economy movement in France. The workshops gave practitioners the opportunity to decide about the setting, the tools of communication and the actors invited. In the main conference, which involved over 200 stakeholders in Vienna in 2009, a dialogue-oriented setting using world café techniques facilitated the exchange of knowledge. An exhibition of good practices and intensive discussions in small working groups fostered mutual learning and contributed to the elaboration of a focused research agenda. The conference synthesized a theory-practice dialogue which was deepened afterwards in diverse settings. For example, local workshops covered context-specific issues like neighbourhood renewal in Vienna, problem-based learning in Lisbon and mutual learning dynamics in Naples. These workshops strengthened local partnerships as incipient forms of local knowledge alliances.

Pedagogical tools have been offered on the website, including a blog, a popular written version of the project (Stigendal 2010), a German website on FAQs and eight short videos on the *problématique* of urban social cohesion in the Czech republic, called VIDA (see www.socialpolis.eu, last accessed 19 December 2012). This shows the spatial, thematic and pedagogical diversity of Social Polis. To sum up, Social Polis has been a successful networking exercise, mobilizing diverse actors in favour of transdisciplinary research to foster social cohesion in the city (Cassinari et al. 2011). The main challenge associated with the project concerns its sustainability. It is difficult to maintain such a network beyond the end of project financing. In 2010, the lack of financing was compensated by a commitment of the KU Leuven to sustain the basic infrastructure. Regular updates of the website, a newsletter and workshops have kept the platform alive. In the long run, however, Social Polis can only develop into a sustainable knowledge alliance by institutionalizing the task of coordinating European transdisciplinary research activities.

32.6 CONCLUSION

Transdisciplinary research faces huge difficulties and barriers. Academic evaluation systems are dominated either by intra-academic quality criteria or – increasingly – by market geared external criteria, especially research funding and applicability of results to industry. The resultant focus on financed research leads to a short-term project logic, undermining the building of trust and sustainable partnerships. Knowledge alliances, which differ from short-term projects, need financing for the institutionalization of lasting partnerships for sharing and using knowledge. Therefore, innovative ideas are not only needed in the organization of the research process, but also in the governance of research funding. Since this implies

questioning the status quo of governing systems in politics as well as research, these efforts are not always welcome. A positive exception is the recent European Commission report 'Cities of Tomorrow', which argues in favour of encouraging 'knowledge alliances combining several kinds of "savoir"', 'a "negotiated city" which permits negotiation between apparently opposing values and visions' and the creation of urban 'laboratories' to test new policy directions (European Commission 2011, p. 99).

Knowledge alliances operationalize the transdisciplinary methodology, offer a specific form of the democratic governance of knowledge and demonstrate that they can produce scientific as well as policy- and action-relevant knowledge. In this chapter, we demonstrated their potential for social innovations in the field of social cohesion. They innovate the relationship between science and society and foster the democratization of knowledge, as practitioners and citizens engage in the decision making about research topics, voice their opinion, share their experiences and engage in mutual learning exercises. By including the knowledge and expertise of a broad variety of stakeholders, knowledge alliances not only bridge the gaps between different policy fields and disciplines and enable valuable research; the development of such alliances itself is a practical social innovation which contributes to more cooperative, sustainable and convivial places and research environments.

32.7 QUESTIONS FOR DISCUSSION

- What are the characteristics of knowledge alliances as a specific form of knowledge production, knowledge sharing and scientific cooperation?

- How can transdisciplinarity contribute to social innovation?
- What are the main challenges of producing socially robust knowledge today?

NOTES

1. The authors acknowledge the support by Sparkling Science (www.sparklingscience.at, last accessed 19 December 2012) and the European Commission which financed *Social Polis* from 2007 to 2010.
2. Translation by authors; original citation: *Ninguém ignora tudo, ninguém sabe tudo.*

REFERENCES

(References in bold are recommended reading.)

Archer, Margaret, R. Bhaskar, A. Collier, T. Lawson and A. Norrie (eds) (2004), *Critical Realism*, New York: Routledge.

Bernstein, Richard (1983), *Beyond Objectivism and Relativism*, Oxford: Basil Blackwell.

Bhaskar, Roy (2002), *Reflections on Meta-Reality: a philosophy for the present*, New Delhi, India and Thousand Oaks, US and London, UK: Sage.

Cassinari, Davide, J. Hillier, K. Miciukiewicz, A. Novy, S. Habersack, D. MacCallum and F. Moulaert (2011), 'Transdisciplinary Research in Social Polis', http://www.socialpolis.eu/uploads/tx_sp/Trans_final_web_single_page.pdf (last accessed 26 April 2012).

European Commission (2011), *Cities of Tomorrow. Challenges, visions, ways forward*, Directorate General for Regional Policy, Brussels, http://ec.europa.eu/regional_policy/sources/docgener/studies/pdf/citiesoftomorrow/citiesoftomorrow_final.pdf (last accessed 26 April 2012).

Flyvbjerg, Bent (2001), *Making Social Science Matter*, Cambridge: Cambridge University Press.

Freire, Paulo (1989), *A importância do ato de ler: em três artigos que se completam*, São Paulo: Cortez.

Freire, Paulo (2004), *Pedagogia do oprimido* (38th edition), São Paulo: Paz e Terra.

Fritsch, Katharina (2010), *Forschungslabs – Theater der Unterdrückten. Teil l*, http://ungleichevielfalt.at/article51.htm (last accessed 18 November 2011).

Häberli, R., A. Bill, W. Grossenbacher-Mansuy, J. Thompson Klein, R.W. Scholz and M. Welti (2001), 'Synthesis', in J. Thompson Klein et al. (eds), pp. 6–22.

Habersack, Sarah (2010), *Forschungslabs Sprache II*, http://ungleichevielfalt.at/article55.htm (last accessed 18 November 2011).

Hirsch Hadorn, Gertrude, S. Biber-Klemm, W. Grossenbacher-Mansuy, H. Hoffmann-Riem, D. Joye, C. Pohl, U. Wiesmann and E. Zemp (2008), 'The emergence of transdisciplinarity as a form of research', in G. Hirsch Hadorn, H. Hoffmann-Riem, S. Biber-Klemm, W. Grossenbacher-Mansuy, W. Joye, C. Pohl, U. Wiesmann and E. Zemp (eds), *Handbook of transdisciplinary research*, Dordrecht: Springer, pp. 19–42.

Hollaender, Kirsten and P. Leroy (2001), 'Reflections on the Interactive Sessions – From Scepticism to Good Practices', in J. Thompson Klein et al. (eds), pp. 217–235.

Karl-Trummer, Ursula, S. Novak-Zezula and H. Schmied (2007), *Projektmanagement im transdisziplinaren Kontext – Ein Manual zur Förderung der Lust am transdisziplinären Arbeiten*, Wien: TRAFO.

Köfler, Laura (2010), *Forschungslabs – Theater der Unterdrückten. Teil II*, http://ungleichevielfalt.at/article52.htm (last accessed 19 November 2011).

Miciukiewicz Konrad, F. Moulaert, A. Novy, S. Musterd and J. Hillier (forthcoming 2012), 'Problematising Cities and Social Cohesion: a transdisciplinary endeavour', *Urban Studies*.

Moulaert, Frank (2010), 'Social innovation and community development: concepts, theories and challenges', in Frank Moulaert, F. Martinelli, E. Swyngedouw and S. González (eds), *Can Neighbourhoods Save the City? Community Development and Social Innovation*, London: Routledge, pp. 4–16.

Moulaert, Frank, F. Martinelli, E. Swyngedouw and S. González (2005), 'Towards Alternative Model(s) of Local Innovation', *Urban Studies*, **42** (11), 1969–1990.

Novy, Andreas (2009), 'The World is emerging – on the current relevance of Paulo Freire', *Aktion & Reflexion. Texte zur transdisziplinären Entwicklungsforschung und Bildung*, 3, Paulo Freire Zentrum.

Novy, Andreas (2011), 'Unequal diversity – on the political economy of social cohesion in Vienna', *European Journal of Urban and Regional Studies*, **18** (3), 239–253.

Novy, Andreas, D. Coimbra Swiatek and F. Moulaert (forthcoming 2012), 'Social cohesion: a conceptual and political elucidation', *Urban Studies*.

Nowotny, Helga (2003), 'Re-thinking Science: From Reliable Knowledge to Socially Robust Knowledge', in Wolf Lepenies (ed.), *Entangled Histories and Negotiated Universals*, Frankfurt: Campus, pp. 14–31.

Paulo Freire Zentrum and Österreichische HochschülerInnenschaft (eds) (2005), *Ökonomisierung der Bildung. Tendenzen, Strategien, Alternativen*, Wien: Mandelbaum.

Sayer, Andrew (1992), *Method in Social Science: A Realist Approach*, 2nd edition, London: Routledge.

Siune, Karen (2009), 'Challenging Futures of Science in Society – Emerging Trends and Cutting-edge Issues', ftp://ftp.cordis.europa.eu/pub/fp7/sis/docs/sis_masis_report_en.pdf (last accessed 26 April 2012).

Stigendal, Mikael (2010), *Cities and social cohesion – Popularizing the results of Social Polis*, MAPIUS, Malmo: Malmo University.

Swiss Academies of Arts and Science (n.d.), 'Transdisziplinarität', www.trandiscinlinarity.ch (last accessed 29 April 2012).

Thompson Klein, Julie (2001), 'The Dialogue Sessions', in J. Thompson Klein et al. (eds), pp. 103–116.

Thompson Klein, J., W. Grossenbacher-Mansuy, R. Häberli, A. Bill, R.W. Scholz and M. Welti (eds) (2001), *Transdisciplinarity – Joint Problem Solving among Science, Technology and Society*, Basel: Birkhäuser.

33. Holistic research methodology and pragmatic collective action
Frank Moulaert and Abid Mehmood

33.1 INTRODUCTION

One of the privileged methods in social innovation analysis, especially when studying social innovation to address social exclusion in different but still comparable situations, is holism (Moulaert 2000). Holism as a method of research was developed in the 1920s, and has popped up periodically since then for use in comparative analysis. It has natural links with pragmatism as a social philosophy and a scientific approach (Ramstad 1986). In general terms, holism refers to a methodological perspective that gives special attention to parts-whole interactions. This makes it of particular interest to comparative case-study analysis, an essential part of social innovation research which connects collective action to the analysis of the situational and institutional conditions in which it occurs.

This chapter consists of four sections following this introduction. First we briefly explain the links between collective action and holistic analysis. In the second section we explain holism as theoretically structured comparative case study analysis. Different theories can be used to select themes eligible for analysis in holism and to identify the relations (pattern models) between them. In the next step we explain why holistic theory is so important for social innovation analysis, and how holistic theory can be used to set up a powerful framework for empirical research, such as studying social innovation as a strategy to overcome social exclusion and conditions of alienation within different yet comparable settings. In this type of analysis, both qualitative and quantitative data play an important role. We illustrate this by the use of an example from a recent research project (Social INnovation GOvernance and COMmunity building – SINGOCOM; see Moulaert et al., Chapter 1), which used a holistic-comparative approach to analyze sixteen case studies of socially innovative initiatives in nine European cities. The chapter concludes by launching the term 'social holism', thus giving holism an *explicit* ethically founded character and connecting it to pragmatism: we mobilize comparative analysis in order to build knowledge which contributes to socially progressive aims, with the specific purpose of informing and enhancing collective action and public policy. Although we are aware of the interesting theoretical debates across different disciplines about the meaning and content of 'collective action', we adopt the loose definition put forward by Tilly as 'people's acting together in pursuit of common interests' (1978, p. 7). We do not further analyse the socio-psychological and emotional dynamics feeding or embedding collective action (Emirbayer and Goldberg 2005), but consider the use of comparative analysis as part of the social learning process involved in many social actions and movements.

33.2 THE LINK BETWEEN COLLECTIVE ACTION AND SCIENTIFIC ANALYSIS

Some challenges we want to address in holistic analysis are significant for social innovation research, such as: what are the links between collective action and analysis? Why do we need analysis to prepare or to pave the way for action? Much has already been said in several chapters of this handbook on the role of theory in social innovation analysis, and in Chapter 8 on the need to analyse strategic links between 'micro' social innovation and 'macro' social transformation and the movements that guide it. In this chapter we focus on the links between theory, holistic methodology and its meaning for collective action.

First of all let us reflect a little on what collective action is about. The basic definition of collective action is that it is action coordinated between a number of agents with the objective of changing a particular situation, social relations, social conditions or policy programmes that will lead to an improvement of the condition of people in society. The desire for improvement motivating many collective actions owes a lot to collective emotions (Emirbayer and Goldberg 2005). Yet collective action is, to a large extent, rationally based because it has been negotiated between the different participating actors. According to the pragmatist approach, change agendas, policy agendas, and participation strategies are best based on (collective) practical and situationally specific judgements. Patsy Healey quotes Dewey (1993) to argue that such judgment involves:

> a combination of analytical, moral, and emotive modes of thought not conducted as abstract principles but articulated in the flow of life. And the flow of life is not lived in the splendid isolation of the autonomous individual but in the social contexts in which

what it means to live in a 'polity' are in continuous formation. (Healey 2009, p. 279)

Our own research and many cases in this handbook show clearly that collective action needs leadership to take it in the right direction. It also involves agencies, modes of behaviour, institutional codes to mobilize people, and information sharing to interpret conditions of existence and opportunities for the future. In this way, collective action is very much about social dynamics, movements and policy. Scientific analysis often plays an important role in the design of collective action.[1] Analysis is also important for the design of collective action, and therefore as a tool for problem solving, identifying solutions and predicting potential consequences of solutions that are pursued. Analysis refers to methods to reveal needs and preferences and can be used in a process of norm setting leading to collective action (see especially Kunnen et al., Chapter 21 and Gibson-Graham and Roelvink, Chapter 34) Through analysis we can, for example, understand what the human needs are, what general norms – promoting human progress – can be called upon, and also which modes of action are available to satisfy these needs.[2]

Scientific analysis can also be considered as problem solving. For example, in research as design, different types of actors are involved in shared research. Actors bring in their views and *desiderata* and actively explore potential through co-designing them. Collaborative designing, for instance, can be carried out through shared practice of drawing, mapping, narrating, installations ... (Toker 2012). Collaborative designing often requires preliminary agreement between actors on shared terms for desired spatial quality (Goethals and Schreurs 2011). Different types of analysis (fox example, involving different sets of stakeholders) can be joined to make the desired and shared ideas more concrete. Thus transdisciplinary research, combining skills and knowledge from science and fields of practice, can be used to negotiate solutions and strategies with partners and to understand how some actions, when introduced at different stages in a problem solving process, are more effective than others. Transdisciplinary research is very important in social innovation research, as several chapters in this manual explain (see especially Moulaert et al., Chapter 1; Novy et al., Chapter 32; Moulaert and Van Dyck, Chapter 35). When putting into practice an ethics of solidarity and collective pursuit of human development, transdisciplinarity reflects the deep concern of social innovation research to innovate in social relations with the purpose of building a better world.

In this context, we should stress the role of experience, contextualization, comparison, and part/whole relationships – which form the core of holism – in transdisciplinary holistic analysis (Cassinari et al. 2011). These elements all spring from the need to learn from the past, to learn from elsewhere and to learn from each other (e.g. practitioners and scientists) (Moulaert 2012). Here there is a very explicit 'process oriented' link with social learning as put forward by the pragmatist philosophers (Healey 2009, p. 281). But there is also another link with pragmatism, namely the role of feedback relationships between analysis and theory building on the one hand and collective action experience, policy and planning on the other. One of the main principles of pragmatism, as a philosophy of science and reflective intellectual agency, is that theories should be robust in the sense that they should reflect those aspects of reality that are important for our collective action agenda. In

the language of holism, that would mean that they are adaptable to significant new observations and lessons from relevant practice in collective action.

33.3 HOLISM AS THEORETICALLY STRUCTURED COMPARATIVE CASE STUDY ANALYSIS

Now, let us explain what holism is, why we would use it and how we should use it in social innovation analysis and practice. From the point of view of experience-based research, it is very important to compare cases, by paying attention to both similar and dissimilar conditions, to confront commonalities and diversities across cases and the contexts in which they occur and to explain how similarities relate to diversity while still guaranteeing comparability (see Vicari Haddock and Tornaghi, Chapter 19; Pradel et al., Chapter 11). That means that we must identify a number of concepts that allow us to make a comparative analysis. In holism terminology, these concepts are usually introduced by way of 'themes' that are common to a relatively large number of situations. As an example of a typical question in holistic analysis, we might look at how the theme of *housing occupation of a particular quality* is analysed across different neighbourhoods, localities or (as the holist would say) subsystems? Taking it further – and here emerges the link with collective action – we would ask how this analysis can lead to better grounded proposals for socially innovative housing policy.

33.3.1 The Role of Theory

In order to identify particular themes and potential relationships between those themes, theory is needed. For the purpose of this chapter, it is sufficient to say that theory will help us to select themes as well as to understand the relationships between them. We also refer to the discussion in Chapter 1 about the role of meta-theoretical structures which allow to preselect research themes and the potential productive as well as conflictive relations between them, as suggested by a diversity of theories that can be 'hosted' by a meta-theory (Novy et al. 2012; see also Moulaert and Van Dyck, Chapter 35).

We should also stress here that within our perspective of social innovation analysis, the relations between the different themes and how they materialize within case-studies should be analysed using a methodological framework that recognizes the intrinsic interaction between agency, structure institutions and discourse (ASID) (Moulaert and Jessop 2006). At the same time we should address the function of micro behaviour in particular situations such as the specific neighbourhoods studied in SINGOCOM. We must make a distinction between structural dynamics on the one hand and particular individual behaviour on the other hand. Also, we should analyse the relationships between both of them, which implies looking at the institutional mediation between structures and agency. In this mediation cultural dynamics, in which discourse is central, play a significant part. These dynamics explain why people in certain circumstances behave according to particular codes, to particular routines, and to particular norms, while in other or similar circumstances they will act in a spontaneous way, in an individual or collective way, in a creative or a codified way, and so on.

33.3.2 How does Holism Work? And what is a Holistic Theory?

Holistic theory identifies relationships between particular themes across particular subsystems and explains these relationships (or their absence) by use of partial theories fitting a meta-theoretical framework. We could say, in more conventional scientific terminology, that we are in a systems perspective but, at the same time, that we accept the role of the particular, the specific and the local, as important elements of our explanatory process – certainly as important as the generic rules or patterns which would stem from a systemic analysis. So, in holistic knowledge production, the exceptional or the particular matters as much as the structural or the systemic. Holistic theory is in this sense more like a dialectical synthesis between theorizing in its conventional meaning – as the synthesis of available knowledge in abstract terms – and empirical exploration, as well as improvement of explanatory frameworks connecting different research themes to each other.

The concepts that are used in holistic theory are first of all *systems, subsystems and analytical themes* (Diesing 1971). We already gave an example of an analytical theme, namely the condition of housing. We examine the condition of housing in different neighbourhoods (subsystems) of a city or urban region (system). The general condition of housing is measured by the provision of a particular level of housing quality, access to domestic water, sewerage and other hygiene services. So we can identify a number of variables that would express this theme. These variables are first measured for a particular neighbourhood (*subsystem*). Once the housing quality condition has been assessed for this neighbourhood, it can also be measured for other neighbourhoods. Theme one can be

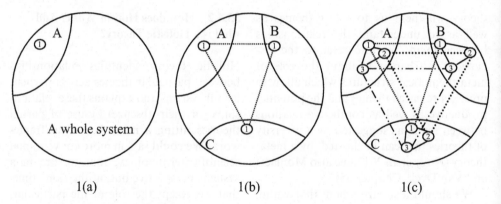

1(a)   1(b)   1(c)

Source: adapted from Ramstad (1986, pp. 1071–172, Figures 1 and 2).

Figure 33.1   Holistic analysis

subsequently connected to another theme which we expect to be relevant to its explanation or contextualisation. For example, if we consider that the quality of housing depends on public spending by the local authorities, then public spending by the local authorities could become theme two. We can argue that the quality of housing across different neighbourhoods (or subsystems) will significantly depend on the level of spending by the local authorities for the provision of the water supply network, hygiene services, etc. It is worth mentioning here that themes are not identified at random; they are subject to their place in the meta-theoretical framework, and emerge from theoretical and contextual knowledge available to the researchers. To enrich the comparative perspective, the relationship can be made more complex by looking at other themes such as the social, professional and the income position of the different households living in these neighbourhoods. So, step-by-step, significant themes are identified and connected to each other. As the cases are compared, more and more commonalities and differences emerge between different subsystems. And 'over time, a typology will be developed that summarizes the systematic differences encountered' (Ramstad 1986, p. 1072).

As themes and their relationships are identified and established empirically, the researcher then can look for linkages between different neighbourhood subsystems through the identified themes (Diesing 1971). These linkages show the interconnectedness within the system, as shown in Figure 33.1(c). Here, the themes (e.g. housing quality condition and the level of public spending by local authorities) also volunteer provisional hypotheses that can be tested through an array of qualitative or quantitative methods (such as participant observation, survey, statistics etc.) for 'contextual validation' (Diesing 1971, p. 147). Similar exercises can be repeated to validate select themes across the same neighbourhood subsystems. A group of validated themes helps in developing an interconnected network or *pattern model*. The pattern model can be complex, multi-directional and multi-causal. For example, public spending would affect the opportunities to build high quality housing while the higher quality housing may require different levels of public expenditure for maintenance. The pattern model can be simultaneously refined or modified by adding more thematic correlations, examined for each subsystem and strengthened through on-going interactions between empirical work and theoretical formulations. In such a case, the comparative analysis goes across neighbourhoods, looks at shared themes and the patterns connecting them. A typology can drastically change if variants and circumstances in individual cases display behaviours different to the generalized patterns.

What is the expected value-added of the holistic analysis presented above? First of all, it reveals general patterns that occur across all neighbourhoods. Here, theories as we know them covering the interrelationships between neighbourhood development and housing help to single out themes and universal patterns. But a more specific contribution of holistic analysis is that it sheds light on outliers or subsystems exhibiting contradictory patterns. The analysis not only reveals such outliers, but also gives them a prominent place in the holistic knowledge building process. Holistic analysis, therefore, offers a framework for a better comparative analysis, improvement of theories explaining universals and also accounting for special cases that can be of high value for both analysis and collective action. In addition, as the SINGOCOM case will show, it can be of direct utility to collective action.

33.4 THE SINGOCOM CASE-STUDY ANALYSIS

In the previous section we explained the holistic methodology using the example of the housing theme – housing at the neighbourhood subsystem within the urban system. We explained how themes are selected, connected to patterns and examined across subsystems within an urban/regional system. In the SINGOCOM research (Moulaert et al. 2011) our subsystems were neighbourhoods within their urban environment. In its selection of themes, SINGOCOM was driven by an ethical position pursuing human progress. Various aspects of social exclusion were connected to the possibilities for social innovation. These connections were established through a diversity of processes and (rational) strategies: mobilisation strategies, social economy initiatives, new governance forms ... For the comparative analysis of different cases, an analytical 'model' (ALternative MOdel of Local INnovation – ALMOLIN) was developed from a post-disciplinary perspective, using elements from various social science literatures. The role of existent theories on social innovation, originating from a diversity of disciplines, in building ALMOLIN as a pattern model connecting different themes has been significant: theories on horizontal and more democratic management structures from business science, on the social nature of economic and technological innovation, on the socially innovative character of corporate social responsibility, on the interaction between Business Administration and social cum environmental progress, on promoting social innovation through fine arts, on the role of social economy in community development (Moulaert et al. 2005) and on social innovation in spatial planning and governance (González and Healey 2005). Combined according to the ontology of community development, these theories provided the analytical pillars to frame the empirical investigation (Moulaert et al. 2010). The 16 case studies that were investigated 'in depth' in the course of the SINGOCOM research were the result of an interactive selection process, from a larger 'data bank' of 29 initiatives, set up by the network of local research teams at the beginning of the project. These cases represented a wide spectrum of socially innovative experiences in community and neighbourhood development, and allowed some interesting comparisons between countries, highlighting how the different historical and institutional contexts influence the nature of social innovation. The basic features of their socially innovative impact, historical roots and spatial reach as framed by the ALMOLIN analytical approach are charted in Figure 33.2.

ALMOLIN shows the interplay between social exclusion and the deprivation of human needs that can be countered by social innovation dynamics. These dynamics may include reactions to deprivation and exclusion, mobilization and organizing around a shared vision of change – often in the form of social movements – and reproduction of a culture of change based on the pursuit of a new identity, thereby cutting loose from the depths of humiliation and alienation. Overcoming situations of exclusion requires mobilization of resources within, or against, the existing organizational and institutional settings. Figure 33.2 does not stress the role of civil society or 'grand' political actions; these are indirectly included due to path dependency and the institutionally interconnected nature of spatial scales (neighbourhoods, local communities, municipalities, cities, and regions etc.). The boxes in the figure use a general macro-language but, when applied to case study analysis, come to hold concrete meanings. Hence, ALMOLIN exemplifies 'holism' as a scientifically established research method to address shortcomings in contemporary urban and regional development methodologies (Smuts 1926; Ramstad 1986).

The strategy for collecting the empirical information for the SINGOCOM study was entrusted to each of the local research teams, as each possessed the unique local knowledge of each case study and its context. National, regional or local statistics were gathered, policy documents were analyzed, interviews with local experts and, in some cases, participatory research (e.g. the Leoncavallo case in Milan and, to some extent, the City Mine(d) case in Brussels) were carried out. In the case of Alentour in Roubaix, a survey by questionnaire was conducted among the residents of the neighbourhood, which proved a rich source of additional information. What ensured consistency and comparability across the different cases, and the sometimes different nature and depth of quantitative and qualitative information, was the holistic analytical framework.

Nijman (2007, p. 1) maintains that authentic comparative urban research reveals 'what is true of all cities and what is true of one city at a given point in time'. The analysis in SINGOCOM moved between these two scales. As for any multi-sited research, maintaining comparability between different case studies while keeping room for the specificity of each context and research strategy was a challenge. It was clear from the beginning that social innovation, although a shared meta-theme as defined in the beginning of the project, was going to 'mean' different things for different people in different places. While, for example, collaboration between private and public institutions was considered as 'socially innovative' in southern Italy, it was seen as common practice and often as a threat to SI in the UK. But the researchers maintained their holistic 'methodological' consistency across case studies by referring back to the common definitions, analytical concepts, and theoretical bases of the socially innovative actions at the neighbourhood level.

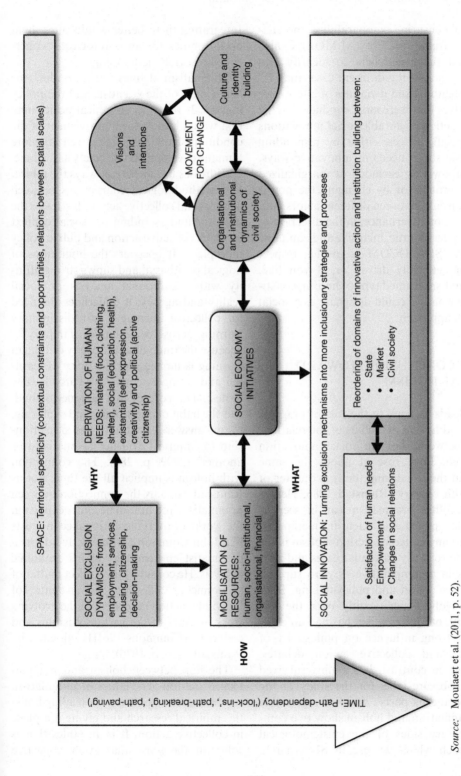

Source: Moulaert et al. (2011, p. 52).

Figure 33.2   ALMOLIN (ALternative MOdel of Local INnovation)

449

While ensuring comparability, the analytical framework of ALMOLIN also allowed the researchers to identify and assess – across the different case studies – those features and dynamics of alternative initiatives that were most conducive to the introduction of durable social innovations for specific places, either by responding to basic social needs in innovative ways, by empowering excluded or marginalized social groups, or by changing the power relationships between different actors and/or scales of governance, in the direction of a more democratic, inclusive and equitable society. SINGOCOM is in this respect a more ethically driven or, if you like, pragmatism-framed type of holism, constituting what we could designate as a social holism approach.

33.5   CONCLUSION: TOWARD SOCIAL HOLISM

This leads us back to the role of pragmatism and holism as well as of the relationship between them in social innovation research. Both rose at about the same time in the US during the first quarter of the 20th century (Ramstad 1986; Healey 2009). While pragmatism can be seen as a philosophical and scientific method to accompany collective action, holism is the method to study particular cases and situations in a comparative way, to support collective action and policymaking. Both have evolved significantly over the last century, but pragmatism has had an especially strong influence on philosophy of science and collective action debates. Holism, in contrast, has mainly survived as an obscure label for the study of the 'whole and its parts', which is regrettable as pragmatism and holism show two complementary sides of the epistemological approach which we use in SI research.

Integrating them better would offer great opportunities for an ontologically coherent SI research methodology.

Pragmatism defines the attitudes, the behaviours of the scientists and the policy makers. It refers to an ethical positioning that would lead to the improvement of the condition of human beings as well as a more humane development of society as a whole. It addresses in a variety of ways the ethical and methodological connections between analysis and collective action. It stresses the need for understanding the social context in which collective action and public policy take place. It uncovers the limitations of 'logical positivism' and shows strong affinity with institutional analysis of social reality and agency; it underlines the need for collective learning – transdisciplinary learning, across 'communities of inquiry'[3] – because the (individual) capacity of human learning is limited and the unity of learning and acting essential. As Patsy Healey writes: 'The core of this 'unique method' was the habit of questioning and exploring, testing answers and discoveries in relationship to empirical evidence of one kind or another' (2009, p. 280). The connection with holism is implicit all the time. But as Ramstad explains the connection between pragmatism and holism becomes explicit in the works of (old) institutional economists like John Commons, who clearly adopts a pragmatist epistemology in his economic analysis. He considers the subject matter of economics as 'collective action in control of individual action according to the evolving working rules of the various customs and concerns' (Commons 1961[1934], cited by Ramstad 1986, p. 1076).

The link between holism and pragmatism is natural. The ethics of pragmatism can be a starting position for leading holistic empirical research and giving it a place in collective action. It is an ethics that is solid, in the sense that every collective action that is undertaken should contribute to the progress of humanity and to the improvement of the well being of as many social groups in society as possible.

Connecting this ethical positioning to holism, we can say that we are applying what could be called 'social holism'. So, referring to the examples in this chapter, pragmatism will tell us to analyse the quality of housing because we are concerned not only about good housing and decent housing conditions for all people in the neighbourhood, but also about the role of collective action and public policy to secure such quality conditions. Holism, in complement, will tell us to identify the different themes, patterns and relations that will help to understand why the quality of housing is guaranteed, or is absent. In addition, it will establish and examine relationships between agents involved in collective action and public policy, as well as between these and their targets and objects. That is, holism will help to materialize the reflexive interrogations that are essential to pragmatism, while pragmatism will make sure that holistic scientific practice remains self-reflexive. Thus the two entries into a reflexive methodology for social innovation research will continue to revitalise each other.

33.6   QUESTIONS FOR DISCUSSION

- Holistic part-whole relationships can help generalize from specific socially innovative actions. Can you give a case study example?
- How could holistic research methodology be applied to study other social issues besides social exclusion as discussed in this chapter?
- What is the relationship between pragmatism, as a philosophy of science and reflective intellectual

agency, and social innovation? How might pragmatism contribute to the improvement/development of the analytical framework that we use for social innovation (meeting needs, social relations, empowerment)?

NOTES

1. Moulaert et al., in Chapter 1, discuss the significance of social innovation theory in the design of collective action and therefore how it should be situated in its social environment or its social conditions. This explains why so much stress is put on the role of Sociology of Knowledge (SoK) as a bridge between real life conditions, requiring collectively shared knowledge on the one hand and an embedded theory of social innovation on the other hand. Moulaert and Van Dyck's Chapter 35 is devoted to the role of SoK approaches in social innovation research and its links to other social science methods.
2. This does not mean that we are claiming in all certainty that each and every collective action needs academic analysis. Some collective actions must be immediately responsive without much reflection because there is no time for it, or because the needs are too urgent. As examples, think about dealing with sudden disaster impact (natural disaster, epidemic . . .), housing needs because of extreme temperature variations or sudden floods, or unnecessary cruelties by security, police or armed forces. Thus collective action can be spontaneous and respond to urgent need conditions without rational analysis preceding or accompanying it. In such cases gut feelings and collective intuition empathising with the urgent conditions and the environment of people facing them will probably be better guidelines than recipes drawn from logical thinking.
3. Patsy Healey explicitly referring to this Dewey concept 'communities of inquiry'.

REFERENCES

(References in bold are recommended reading.)

Cassinari, D., J. Hillier, K. Miciukiewicz, A. Novy, S. Habersack, D. MacCallum and F. Moulaert (2011), *Transdisciplinary Research in Social Polis*, Leuven: Social Polis, http://www.socialpolis.eu/the-social-polisapproach/transdisciplinarity/(last accessed 22 July 2012).

Commons, J. (1961[1934]), *Institutional Economics*,

2 vols, 2nd edition, Madison: University of Wisconsin Press.

Dewey, J. (1993), *The political writings*, Debra Morris and Ian Shapiro (eds), Indianapolis, IN: Hackett Publishing.

Diesing, P. (1971), *Patterns of Discovery in Social Sciences*, Chicago: Aldine-Argerton.

Emirbayer, M. and C.A. Goldberg (2005), 'Pragmatism, Bourdieu, and collective emotions in contentious politics', *Theory and Society*, **34**, 469–518.

Goethals, M. and J. Schreurs (2011), 'Developing shared terms for spatial quality through design', in S. Oosterlynck, J. Van den Broeck, L. Albrechts, F. Moulaert and A. Verhetsel (eds), *Strategic Spatial Projects. Calalysts for Change*, London: Routledge.

González, S. and P. Healey (2005), 'A sociological institutionalist approach to the study of innovation in governance capacity', *Urban Studies*, **42** (11), 2055–2069.

Healey, P. (2009), 'The Pragmatic Tradition in Planning Thought', *Journal of Planning Education and Research*, **28**, 277–292.

Moulaert, F. (2000), *Globalization and Integrated Area Development in European Cities*, Oxford: Oxford University Press.

Moulaert, F. (2011), 'Social Innovation and community development: concepts, theories and challenges', in F. Moulaert, E. Swyngedouw, F. Martinelli and S. González (eds), *Can neighbourhoods save the city?*, London: Routledge.

Moulaert, F. (2013), 'La région sociale dans un monde globalisant', in J-L. Klein, and M. Roy (eds), *Pour une nouvelle mondialisation: le défi d'innover*, Québec: Presses Universitaires du Québec. Chapter 22.

Moulaert, F. and J. Nussbaumer (2005), 'Defining the Social Economy at the Neighbourhood Level: a Methodological Reflection', *Urban Studies*, **42** (11), 2071–2088.

Moulaert, F. and B. Jessop (2006), *Agency, Structure, Institutions, Discourse (ASID)*, DEMOLOGOS Synthesis Paper, http://demologos.ncl.ac.uk/wp/wp2/disc.php (last accessed 19 December 2012).

Moulaert, F., F. Martinelli, E. Swyngedouw and S. González (2005), 'Towards alternative model(s) of local innovation', *Urban Studies*, **42** (11), 1969–1990.

Novy, A., D. Coimbra Swiatek and F. Moulaert (2012), 'Social Cohesion: A Conceptual and Political Elucidation', *Urban Studies*, **49** (9), 1873–1889.

Nijman, J. (2007), 'Introduction – Comparative Urbanism', *Urban Geography*, **28** (1), 1–6.

Ramstad, Y. (1986), 'A pragmatist's quest for holistic knowledge: the scientific methodology of John R. Commons', *Journal of Economic Issues*, 20 (4), 1067–1105.

SINGOCOM (2004), 'Social Innovation, Governance and Community Development', http://users.skynet.be/frank.moulaert/singocom/index2.html (last accessed 19 December 2012).

Smuts, J.C. (1926), *Holism and Evolution*, New York: The Macmillan Company.

Tilly, C. (1978), *From Mobilization to Revolution*, Reading, MA: Addison-Wesley.

Toker, U. (2012), 'The Community-base Studio: Participatory Planning and Urban Design with Students and Communities in California', paper presented at the 26th Annual AESOP conference in Ankara, 11–15 July.

URSPIC (1999) 'Urban Redevelopment and Social Polarization in the City', http://cordis.europa.eu/documents/documentlibrary/78645531EN6.pdf (last accessed 19 December 2012).

34. Social innovation for community economies: how action research creates 'other worlds'
J.K. Gibson-Graham and Gerda Roelvink[1]

34.1 BEGINNING A CONVERSATION FOR CHANGE

The Community Economies project is an ongoing effort to contribute to an emerging economic politics, one that is centred on the practice of economic self-determination, oriented by the vision that 'another world is possible' and committed to postcapitalist economic futures (Community Economies n.d.; Gibson-Graham 2006). The project seeks to 'reclaim the economy' as a situated and diverse space of ethical decision making and negotiated interdependence; through that process of reclamation, the economy – a remote and powerful sphere that seems to dictate our lives – becomes instead a familiar, even intimate, space of engagement.

Central to the project are three key elements: (1) rethinking 'economy' to create a conceptual platform for its re-enactment; (2) enrolling and re-subjecting communities and individuals (including ourselves) in new worlds of possibility; and (3) promoting collective action to build community economies. A community economy is not defined by geographic or social commonality; it is an ethical and political space of decision-making in which interdependence is constructed as people transform their livelihoods and lives.

The Community Economies project is one of many contemporary projects seeking to foster new worlds and innovative economies. In this chapter, we attempt to open a conversation between Community Economies and the Integrated Area Development Approach which has been developed in a multiphase European-based research initiative on local social innovation (see Moulaert et al., Chapter 1). This initiative started under the EC's Poverty III program as a research project on how to combat poverty through community oriented local development (Moulaert 2000). A more recent project SINGOCOM (Social Innovation and Governance in Community Development) worked around the ALMOLIN model (ALternative Models for Local INnovation) (Moulaert et al. 2005).

In this chapter and for the sake of clarity we will call it simply the Local/Social Innovation project. Like Community Economies, the Local/Social Innovation project has affinities with the politics of 'possibilities' of the World Social Forum, and highlights the ways in which social movements are starting from where they are in order to meet previously unmet needs (see Moulaert 2000). In particular, local/social innovation is seen as a way to include marginalized groups within social and political governance institutions and processes. Local/social innovators privilege participation of the needy themselves in projects that seek to harness resources in the face of contemporary economic and social crises.

So why might a conversation between these two projects be of interest or use? In *A Postcapitalist Politics*, J.K. Gibson-Graham ponders the proliferation

453

of a diverse range of economic initiatives around the globe and asks:

> ... how do we multiply, amplify, and connect these different activities? How do we trace 'connections between diverse practices ... to dissolve the distinctions between inside and outside the movement' ... and thus actualize movement goals in a transformed social order? (2006, pp. 80–81)

In beginning a conversation between two different, but related, bodies of research, this chapter offers one way of responding to the challenge of connection. The Local/Social Innovation project is oriented towards studying and theorizing movements and organizations, as well as the development trajectory of local communities and their potential community development strategies. Community Economies is more interested in activating movements and organizations through reframing strategies embedded in community-based action research. Nevertheless, both projects can be seen as promoting and supporting an economic and social order that is emergent but not fully constituted. By making this nascent and largely non-credible 'movement' an object of research, and by enhancing the knowledge and self-knowledge of the projects and subjects involved, they participate in bringing it into being as a transformative force worldwide.

In the spirit of the new politics that seeks alliances rather than mergers (or deeper divisions), this chapter inquires about the ways in which Local/Social Innovation connects and overlaps with the project of creating innovative and resilient community economies. In doing so, it develops four key themes:

1. acceptance of diversity as the starting point;

2. local ethics of individual and social needs;
3. community governance;
4. the building of innovative communities.

Each of these themes resonates with a core principle of a politics oriented to creating 'other worlds'; worlds in which alternative modes of being, thinking and acting help build equitable and resilient ways of living with each other and the planet. In the concluding section of the chapter, we highlight fundamental similarities and differences between the two projects that make them potentially fruitful contributors to each other and to the self-reflection of each.

34.2   STARTING WITH DIVERSITY: A PROJECT OF VISIBILITY

It may come as no surprise that both Community Economies and Local/Social Innovation are grounded in an appreciation of social and economic diversity. Yet for both frameworks, the recognition of diversity is not simply a matter of reflecting the truth of the world; rather it is a strategic theoretical choice. For Gibson-Graham (2006), for example, identifying and describing a rich diversity of economic practices and organizations is a key aspect of a politics of language – making space for, and giving legitimacy to, forms of social and economic activity that are obscured and devalued by a capitalocentric worldview. By bringing these to the attention of participants and stakeholders, they hope to widen the field of possibility for economic activism and development.

In a similar vein, Moulaert and his colleagues are working to broaden and diversify the dominant notion of innovation, which is limited to innovations that enhance economic efficiency (Moulaert et al. 2005, p. 1973; Moulaert and Nussbaumer 2005). They define social innovation more broadly in terms of the inclusion of the marginalized into a range of areas, including education systems, labour markets, political institutions, and socio-cultural life (Moulaert et al. 2005, p. 1970). In their research, these authors have focused primarily on innovative ways of meeting the needs of excluded groups and on innovative governance structures in organizations created by and/or serving those groups. Taken together, such organizations are understood as constituting the social economy, a concept that encompasses a wide array of initiatives oriented toward the satisfaction of needs (sometimes called the third sector, or the solidarity economy) (Moulaert and Ailenei 2005). The development of the social economy is seen as a response to the distributive failures of market and state; its presence has thus fluctuated over time with the business cycles of national and global economies, changing labour markets, the impact of world wars, the emergence and decline of the welfare state, and changes in social philosophies and their impact on collective action (Moulaert et al. 2005; Martinelli 2010). Depending on the historical and geographical context, the social economy will take diverse forms and may include initiatives that draw on the market and the state as a way to satisfy needs that are inadequately met by these institutions (Moulaert and Ailenei 2005).

SINGOCOM (centred on 'social innovation in governance for local communities') documented diverse social economy projects in Europe with the aim of providing 'these initiatives with a new synthesis of theoretical foundations' (Moulaert et al. 2005, p. 1970: see also Moulaert and Mehmood, Chapter 33). Initiatives in the SINGOCOM database include 29 cases, among others a mediating and coordinating neighbourhood organization in Berlin; an organization to support skill sharing and the development of cooperatives in Sunderland, UK; an informal social support network in Quartieri Spagnoli, a poor section of Naples; and arts projects that record local histories and feed a community identity-building process in Cardiff (Moulaert et al. 2005, 1970). All of these innovative projects are, at the same time, projects of inclusion, whether geared towards meeting the material needs of the marginalized, opening social arenas to the previously excluded, or giving 'voice' to those who have had little or no say in political life.

Community Economies is likewise interested in strategies for including the marginalized by developing diversified social economies. Their strategic entry point, however, is a reconceptualization of the *entire* economy as a diverse social arena, creating an alternative economic language of the 'diverse economy'. This language provides a discursive space and an open-ended set of categories with which to make visible the wide range of transactions, forms of work, and economic organization that have been marginalized by the discourse of the 'capitalist economy' (see Figure 34.1). The representation of economy in Figure 34.1 both ruptures the presumed unity of capitalism and calls into question its presumptive dominance, especially when we recognize that non-capitalist market and nonmarket activity constitutes well over 50 percent of all economic activity (Gibson-Graham 2006, p. 68). In particular, unpaid labour in households and neighbourhoods constitutes 30 to 50 percent of economic activity in both rich and poor countries (Ironmonger 1996). Interestingly, the social economy of Local/Social Innovation enrols many of the practices and organizational forms of

Transactions	*Labour*	*Enterprise*
MARKET	**WAGE**	**CAPITALIST**
ALTERNATIVE MARKET *Sale of public goods* *Ethical 'fair-trade' markets* *Local trading systems* *Alternative currencies* *Underground market* *Co-op exchange* *Barter* *Informal market*	*ALTERNATIVE PAID* *Self-employed* *Cooperative* *Indentured* *Reciprocal labour* *In kind* *Work for welfare*	*ALTERNATIVE CAPITALIST* *State enterprise* *Green capitalist* *Socially responsible firm* *Non-profit*
NON-CAPITALIST *Household flows* *Gift giving* *Indigenous exchange* *State allocations* *State appropriations* *Gleaning* *Hunting, fishing, gathering* *Theft, poaching*	*UNPAID* *Housework* *Family care* *Neighbourhood work* *Volunteer* *Self-provisioning labour* *Slave labour*	*NON-CAPITALIST* *Communal* *Independent* *Feudal* *Slave*

Source: Gibson-Graham (2006, p. 71).

Figure 34.1   A diverse economy

the diverse economy, including alternative market and non-market transactions, alternatively paid and unpaid labour, and alternative capitalist and non-capitalist enterprises.

Like SINGOCOM, the diverse economies framework is a tool for inventorying and describing economic diversity in an open way that begins rather than forecloses discussion. In Community Economies action research around the world, mapping the local diverse economy has allowed people to see and valorize the economic activity in which they are already engaged. Whereas conventional economic development usually starts with the presumption that a community is lacking in

and therefore needs capitalist development, the Community Economies project presumes the opposite; it affirms the presence of hidden assets and capacities that could provide a useful starting place for previously unimagined development paths. In the Latrobe Valley in Australia, the municipality of Jagna in the Philippines, and western Massachusetts in the United States, Gibson-Graham (2006) and their colleagues have shown how mapping assets and capacities rather than needs and deficiencies reveals that there is something to build upon and opens up discussions of the direction that a building process might take (see also Kunnen et al., Chapter 21). In these community discussions, there is surprise and relief at discovering existing and potential alternatives to the vision of capitalist development on offer from governments, international institutions, and many academics and NGOs.

> Shared principle for 'other worlds': making diversity visible, promoting credibility, enhancing possibility.

34.3   THE LOCAL ETHICS OF INDIVIDUAL AND SOCIAL NEEDS: A VISION OF DISTRIBUTIVE JUSTICE

Both Community Economies and Local/ Social Innovation suggest that social inclusion through innovative community initiatives can be understood as an ethical practice of locality (Gibson-Graham 2003). In the local/social innovation framework, inclusion is referenced to the needs of the excluded, seen as social groups that are in some way marginalized from society, from immigrants to the disabled. The project brings the unmet, and often unregistered, needs of marginalized groups into full view as a trigger for local/social innovation.

Although needs are recognized to be diverse and changing, they can be summed up as 'alienated basic needs', and the project itself concentrates on needs for access to resources and political participation (Moulaert et al. 2005, p. 1976). Needs are viewed as both individual and social. Thus local/social innovation sees personal and shared desires for dignified livelihoods and political voice as integrated with community development strategies. Projects of integrated area development, for example, initiate and support community enterprises that improve individual living conditions and, at the same time, strengthen the local

economy and its social, cultural and physical infrastructure (Moulaert 2000).

Social Enterprise Sunderland, one of the case studies in the SINGOCOM project, exemplifies the ways in which cooperatives can be established to meet social and individual needs. Social Enterprise Sunderland developed from a joint venture responding to local concerns about individual needs for employment and dignity in work, as well as social needs for community wealth in the form of infrastructure and housing. It offers assistance to groups wishing to develop and build cooperative and social enterprises and is beginning to link these enterprises in broader networks. It also promotes community development by managing community projects, such as a co-op centre, a sports centre, and a community primary school (Moulaert et al. 2005, p. 1970; Social Enterprise Sunderland n.d.).

Viewed through the lens of the Community Economies project, the range of needs identified by local/social innovation implies the possibility of ethical debate and local decision making about what is necessary for individual and social life, and how the common wealth (the 'commons') that defines a community is to be shared. Such ethical decision making is both the marker of community economies and the process by which they are formed; at the most fundamental level, it is both a practice and an enactment of 'being-in-common', which is Jean-Luc Nancy's phrase for the radical and unavoidable commonality of coexistence with others (Nancy 1992). For Gibson-Graham and her colleagues, a community economy is an ethical practice of being-in-common, a space of negotiated interdependence where decisions are made about what is necessary for individual and social life, and the 'question of how to live together' is openly engaged (2006, pp. 81–82).

Gibson-Graham refers to the Mondragón Cooperative Corporation in the Basque region of Spain to exemplify the kind of ethical debate that is constitutive of community economies. Reflecting on the 50-year history of the Mondragón cooperatives, which were established by the local Basque people to provide employment and allow for economic self-determination, she emphasizes how the surplus generated by each cooperative was pooled through the cooperative bank in order to capitalize more cooperatives and expand the community economy of Mondragón. The decision to use the surplus in this way and to keep wages equivalent to those of other workers in the Basque region established a certain standard of living for Mondragón workers; whatever was declared to be surplus was not available to individual workers to increase their personal and family consumption. In Mondragón, what is necessary and what is surplus are neither given by nature nor decreed by a capitalist employer; they are constituted relationally by the co-operators themselves, in the ethical process of balancing their individual desires for consumption with their goals for the Basque people and the local economy (Gibson-Graham 2006). This mode of cooperative economy is not only socially rewarding but also economically resilient. The burdens of economic crises are solidarily redistributed among the 80,000 co-operators and workers world-wide within an interdependent network of cooperatives and affiliated firms (see Calzada, Chapter 16).

From a Community Economies perspective, cooperative enterprises do not simply respond to unmet needs but provide a site in which such needs are denaturalized and opened up for discussion. In the very different context of the labour movement, we can see a similar process of denaturalization and the negotiated status of necessity; as the movement has struggled to increase

workers' wages and improve working conditions, workers have redefined what is necessary for a fair and decent way of life (Gibson-Graham 2006, p. 89). Needs are also negotiated and redefined in the process of establishing differential taxation, through which wealth is collected from some individuals and redistributed to others on the basis of a malleable and changing vision of what is necessary to support human existence. Indeed, ethical decisions around needs are made in all sorts of contexts, signalling the presence of community economies (or aspects of them) in unexpected places and at a variety of scales.

> Shared principle for 'other worlds': meeting needs directly, innovatively, democratically – distributive justice on the agenda.

34.4 COMMUNITY GOVERNANCE: CULTIVATING NEW PRACTICES AND SUBJECTS

From the perspective of local/social innovation, needs satisfaction requires changes in social relations and, in particular, relations of governance. The development of governance capacity, or the 'ability of the institutional relations in a social milieu to operate as a collective actor' (Moulaert et al. 2005, p. 1984), is thus a focus of concern for the project, which has a particular interest in the ways in which socially innovative governance initiatives emerge from the grassroots and take hold in a wider context (González and Healey 2005). When used as an 'analytical tool' in local/social innovation, a focus on governance draws attention to the people involved in decision making and also to the forms and flavours of such decision making. To resist prevailing modes of thinking and acting, innovative governance must involve a range of people, including 'non-traditional actors' (González and Healey 2005, p. 2061). The concern for social innovation in governance also suggests that the success of innovative enterprises is not simply to be measured by their life span and growth but also by the 'seeds' and 'sediments' that may influence future practice (González and Healey 2005, p. 2065). Innovation in governance is actually a useful metric for evaluating social enterprises, as the scope of success and failure extends beyond quantifiable outcomes of particular projects to more general changes in participation, practices and values.

The SINGOCOM project examines the Ouseburn Trust in Newcastle upon Tyne as an example of innovative governance. The Trust was initiated by local church and community leaders in response to development plans for the Ouseburn Valley that threatened the local commons, particularly the natural environment and industrial heritage. Over time the Trust developed networks with other local initiatives and a relationship with government, relationships that were formalized and institutionalized through the creation of an Advisory Committee. González and Healey (2005) draw on the story of the Ouseburn Trust to highlight several aspects of innovative governance. These include the role of 'non-traditional actors' such as church leaders; partnerships with other enterprises and government, which involve adaptation by innovators to formal governance rules and processes as well as the exchange of ideas; and a more general change in ideas and values of governance institutions through the inclusion of diverse participants and areas of concern. More recently, the Trust has been involved with Newcastle City Council in the elabo-

ration of a new Regeneration Strategy for the Ouseburn Valley; the delivery of a live–work co-housing 'Canvas Works' development in the Valley; and, through the 'making it' initiative funded by the European Regional Development Fund, in enabling new social enterprises set up by recent university graduates.

In the Community Economies approach, governance has been framed primarily in terms of subjectivity and subject formation, particularly the ethical practice of self-transformation that is involved in producing subjects for a community economy. The understanding that the economy is something we do, rather than something that does things to us, does not come naturally or easily. Innovative economic subjects must be nurtured and cultivated to value and act upon their interdependence.

The experience of Argentina during the early years of this century offers an inspiring example of self-cultivation as an aspect of innovative governance emerging from the grassroots. When hundreds of thousands of Argentineans became unemployed because of the economic crisis, the unemployed started to build community economies by engaging in barter and using alternative currencies, providing neighbourhood-based social services and schooling, and taking over factories and running them cooperatively. But they had to remake themselves in order to do this. To transform themselves into community economic subjects, they created a cooperative radio station; they went to the World Social Forum in Porto Alegre to see themselves reflected in others who were also engaged in projects of self-determination; they opened a school to teach themselves how to make their own history. Gibson-Graham has called this deliberate process of self (and other) transformation 'a politics of the subject' (2006), but it could just as easily be seen as a mode of (self) governance, oriented toward the creation of 'other worlds'.

Community Economies is also interested in governance processes within social and community enterprises. In order to deliver on the dual objectives of benefiting those involved in the enterprise and also the wider community, community enterprises require novel governance strategies as well as innovative ways to evaluate economic and social performance. At present, the Community Economies Collective is collaborating with community enterprises in the US, the Philippines, and Australia to produce a template for self-study for community enterprises (Community Partnering for Local Development n.d.; Gibson-Graham et al. 2013; Cameron et al. 2013). Here the governance strategies of community enterprises are being treated as experimental moves, that is, as innovations to be learned from both for the enterprises involved and for nascent or future community enterprises. One outcome of the project will be an alternative metric of success (or failure) that will clearly distinguish community enterprises from the mainstream enterprises against which they are often measured and found insufficient. This effort at self-knowledge and self-evaluation can be seen as helping to bring the community enterprise sector into the next stage of being – recognized by itself and others (including planners and policy-makers) as a crucible of social innovation and an important sector of the economy, with its own distinctive dynamics, modes of governance, and criteria of success.

Shared principle for 'other worlds': self-determination and innovative governance at every scale, from self to world.

34.5   BUILDING INNOVATIVE COMMUNITIES: A NEW ECONOMIC POLITICS

Both local/social innovation and community economies are interested in projects concerned with building new communities in which innovative governance is a central feature. In particular, scholars of local/social innovation view the inclusion of marginalized groups into the 'politico-administrative system' as a key 'political rationale' in the diverse initiatives they study (Moulaert et al. 2005, p. 1970). The participatory budgeting practised in Porto Alegre, Brazil, exemplifies the type of political empowerment they seek to understand and promote.

Andreas Novy and Bernhard Leubolt analyse the Porto Alegre experience by placing it in the context of the tension between democracy and capitalism in Latin America. From their perspective, participatory budgeting aims to strengthen the democratic state and, at the same time, contribute to an alternative economy by including local people in decision making about the distribution of public money. In order to work well, it requires a sizeable and decentralized budget and substantial public participation (Novy and Leubolt 2005, pp. 2026–2027).

Novy and Leubolt's research demonstrates that participatory budgeting has widespread benefits. In Porto Alegre, it has greatly increased transparency in budgetary decisions and has installed democratic processes, including both direct democracy and the election of representatives to participate in ongoing decision making. Like other projects collected under the banner of local/social innovation, participatory budgeting responds to local needs and tends to benefit the needy more than the well off (Novy and Leubolt 2005, p. 2028). It has seen a shift in public spending from prestigious large scale investments in infrastructure to decentralized and more socially oriented improvements mainly in deprived neighbourhoods.

From Porto Alegre participatory budgeting has been up-scaled to the surrounding Brazilian state of Rio Grande do Sul, where it has been used to promote local production systems (Novy and Leubolt 2005). Over the last decades it has been adopted by many other cities in Brazil and all over the world (Pateman 2012). The results in terms of distributive justice and empowerment of hitherto excluded groups have, however, been mixed. This indicates the importance of the governance framework for supporting experiments with participation.

As Novy and Leubolt (2005, pp. 2030–2031) describe it, the participatory budgeting process in Porto Alegre has prompted participants to articulate their individual needs in relation to community needs. Open political contestation facilitates the re-expression of 'my' needs as 'our' needs; in moving from 'I' to 'we,' participants develop and express a sense of themselves as members of a community. They become, in the language of Community Economies, communal economic subjects – open to new forms of association and to the individual becomings that arise when connection is forged and interdependence acknowledged.

In action research in the Latrobe Valley of southeastern Australia and the Pioneer Valley of western Massachusetts in the US, the Community Economies project found that building community economies entails an ongoing process of cultivating subjects who can open up to new forms of economic being (Gibson-Graham 2006). Initially this required working closely with action research participants to elicit their painful attachments to the dominant economy, giving them space to air their sense of economic injury and deficiency. As participants became involved in inventorying and representing a diverse and surprisingly vibrant local economy, their existing (narrow and relatively powerless) economic identities were destabilized, and they began (tentatively at first) to experience their economic selves in very different ways. Rather than feeling needy and deficient, isolated in an environment of scarcity, they could see themselves as having assets and capacities, embedded in a space of relative abundance. As the research process continued, revealing innovative livelihood strategies, informal transactions, and a wealth of caring connections, a sense of possibility – again, tentatively expressed – became palpable among the participants: some were motivated to take up new activities; others were able to revalue old ones, not formerly seen as economic; and still others became involved in community enterprises, showing their willingness to relate to people in unfamiliar ways (Gibson-Graham 2006, Chapter 6).

In addition to the project of opening themselves and others to economic possibility, the Community Economies project is engaged in studying and fostering collective action to construct community economies on the ground. Rather than laying out the contours of an ideal community economy (which might obscure or pre-empt the decisions of communities themselves), they offer four 'coordinates' – necessity, surplus, consumption, and commons – around which interdependence could be negotiated and explored (Gibson-Graham 2006, Chapters 4 and 7; see also Gibson-Graham et al. 2013 for an elaboration of these coordinates as key concerns of community economies). These coordinates constitute a rudimentary lexicon of interdependence, and collective decision making around them can be understood as the ethical 'dynamics' of a community economy.

Constructing the vision of a community economy around these key concerns highlights the interdependencies among what are usually targets of single-issue politics. The living wage movement, for example, concentrates on access to *necessities* of life; the simplicity movement devotes itself to lifestyle and *consumption*; the environmental movement focuses on protecting and restoring the *commons* in various forms; the union movement agitates to claim a share of privately appropriated *surplus*. Bringing these issues together creates a complex field of decision in which trade-offs and other relationships can be examined and discussed – the question, for example, among a group of migrants, of whether to pool their (surplus) remittances and, if they decide to do so, how to use the money that results. Do they want to help replenish the fisheries at home, or to shore up the incomes of the elderly and disabled, or to invest in enterprise development so that migration will not be necessary for future generations? These questions open up different ways of consuming a common store of wealth, and beg the question of who should be involved in making the decisions. For the community involved, however constituted, the decisions taken will directly or indirectly affect a variety of forms of necessity, consumption and commons, not to mention the size of a possible future surplus. What the coordinates provide is a starting place for economic decision-making that provisionally maps a complex ethical space, and creates potential connections between what are seemingly disparate and distant constituencies and issues.

Shared principles for 'other worlds': new framings for economic politics; constituting 'we' in novel ways.

34.6   CONCLUSION

Situating local/social innovation and Community Economies together in this chapter, we have highlighted areas of common concern and distilled them into widely shared principles for a politics of 'other worlds'. Yet it would be equally possible to see these two projects as very different, each with a well honed self-conception that separates and distances it from the other (and indeed from all other initiatives). For us, part of the ethical challenge of engagement with other projects lies in adopting an experimental rather than a critical stance; this means that differences are examined for what they can teach us, rather than presumed to be signs of deficiency on one or the other side. It is in this spirit of openness that we conclude the chapter with a discussion of noticeable differences between the two projects, grounded in a summary of their overlapping concerns.

Both projects are clearly concerned with redressing marginalization. Local/social innovation is primarily interested in marginalized social groups and their inclusion in social decision making (governance) and social allocation (meeting unmet needs). Community Economies conceives marginalization differently. It sees everyone as marginalized by a dominant conception of Economy that is assumed to govern itself and to disproportionately affect the surrounding social space. In the face of this general marginalization, the Community Economies project pursues a language politics that attempts to bring widespread but discursively marginalized activities to light, revaluing caring labour, informal transactions, alternative enterprises (and more) as major economic forces, and thereby revaluing the subjects who enact them.

Turning around the emphasis on marginalization, both projects are concerned about fostering its opposite – social justice and inclusion. Local/social innovation is interested in the inclusion of the marginalized in democratically governed projects that address their needs, and in strategies of connecting these innovative projects with existing governance institutions. It also is concerned to translate these connections into new democratic practice and bottom-linked governance institutions (see Pradel et al., Chapter 11). The Community Economies project focuses on rethinking economy as a social space of interdependence. Inclusion in this space requires cultivating new forms of self-recognition, new habits through which individuals and groups come to see themselves as shaping/governing economic processes rather than as simply subjected to them.

Perhaps the most interesting intersection between the two projects is their concern with theorizing the dynamics of innovation. Local/social innovation is interested in the growth and development of the social economy, which it sees as emerging both from people's changing aspirations and also in response to the crises of a larger (capitalist) economy that periodically fails to meet people's needs for employment and well-being. In this latter framing, capitalism is positioned as the principal motor of change, with the social economy and social innovation seen as responding (Moulaert et al. 2005). At the same time, social innovation is (implicitly) understood as a present and proliferative force, ready to be called into action at critical moments; it emanates from the marginalized themselves as they struggle to have their needs met, including their needs for changes in social relations and governance.

While similarly concerned with dynamics, Community Economies is interested in displacing capitalism from the driver's seat of social and economic change. It turns attention away from the so called structural dynamics of a capitalist system, and emphasizes instead the ethical dynamics of decision making involved in constructing community economies. While recognizing and admiring the capacity of the marginalized to spontaneously engage in social innovation, at the same time the Community Economies project is attuned to the resistances of those marginalized by the Economy (that is, all of us). Subjects tend to experience the Economy as an external, almost colonizing power, to which they are beholden. Even within the domain of activism and entrepreneurship, the economic imagination is often timid when it comes to thinking outside the capitalist box. This means that we need to cultivate ourselves and others (that is, everyone) as economic subjects with the capacity to innovate and the courage to explore and experiment with economic possibility (see Gibson-Graham et al. 2013).

The final shared concern of the two projects is the goal of bringing a new economy and society into being (though local/social innovation would probably not express themselves in such immodest terms). Focusing on the social economy as a site of innovation and dynamism in contemporary Europe, local/social innovation brings to bear concentrated intellectual resources on an economic sector that has only recently begun to emerge from the shadows. Bringing attention to the sector and its innovative and inclusive potentials is critical to its emergence as a potent social force, helping to attract credibility, resources, and talent to the sector, and to make it the focus of policy initiatives and political agendas. The project is an example of how attention strengthens that which is attended to, and how social research contributes to consolidating realities by making previously marginal sites and activities the focus of widespread interest and deliberate action. It also highlights clearly that SI is not in the first instance about creating new types of socially innovative economic activities but about synergising different dimensions of human development within community dynamics – social, cultural, political and economic. In this way its definition of SI is significantly different from the economic functional character attributed to it by many international organizations and think tanks (see Jessop et al., Chapter 8).

The Community Economies project is more explicit about the role of social research in helping to create the realities it also describes. Via presentations, publications, interactive websites, videos and through action research on the ground, it is involved in creating research collectives comprised of community researchers, activists, academics and institutions (Cameron et al. 2013). The Community Economies Collective sees its work as potentially 'performing' a diverse economy – that is, making it an everyday, commonsense reality by broadening and strengthening the activist imagination, inciting academic investigations among colleagues and students, and suggesting innovative directions for policy intervention. Their vision of the performativity of research foregrounds the ethical decision making of researchers, the choices we make about what to devote attention to and thus to strengthen. The process of ethical self-cultivation that is required to create subjects of community economies is also required of us as academic subjects interested in creating other worlds. This chapter could be seen as a locus and instrument for cultivating a new academic subject, one who regards the academy as an integral and active part of the new worlds being constructed and who seeks academic allies in the process of construction.

34.7 QUESTIONS FOR DISCUSSION

● In light of the economic approach laid out in this chapter can you identify different ways in which economic diversity is either encouraged or discouraged in a planning intervention you are familiar with?

● In your own local context can you identify examples of initiatives that activate one or more of the shared principles for 'other worlds' discussed in this chapter?

● Is research a form of social innovation or does it operate at arm's length from processes of social innovation?

NOTE

1. This chapter is based on the chapter 'Social Innovation for Community Economies' from the volume *Social Innovation and Territorial Development* (MacCallum et al. 2009, pp. 25–38), published by Ashgate.

REFERENCES

(References in bold are recommended reading.)

Cameron, J., K. Gibson and A. Hill (2013), 'Cultivating Post-Capitalist Community Food Economies via Hybrid Research Collectives In and Between Australia and the Philippines,' *Local Environment* (forthcoming).
Community Economies (n.d.), project website: http://www.communityeconomies.org/ (last accessed 19 December 2012).
Community Partnering for Local Development (n.d.), website http://www.communitypartnering.info/ (last accessed 19 December 2012).
Gibson-Graham, J.K. (2003), 'An Ethics of the Local', *Rethinking Marxism*, 15 (1), 49–74.
Gibson-Graham, J.K. (2006), *A Postcapitalist Politics*, Minneapolis: University of Minnesota Press.
Gibson-Graham, J.K., J. Cameron and S. Healy (2013), *Take Back the Economy: An Ethical Guide For Transforming Our Communities*, Minneapolis: University of Minnesota Press.
González, S. and P. Healey (2005), 'A Sociological Institutionalist Approach to the Study of

Innovation in Governance Capacity', *Urban Studies*, **42** (11), 2055–2069.

Ironmonger, D. (1996), 'Counting Outputs, Capital Inputs, and Caring Labor: Estimating Gross Household Product', *Feminist Economics*, **2** (3), 37–64.

MacCallum, D., F. Moulaert, J. Hillier and S. Vicari Haddock (eds) 2009, *Social Innovation and Territorial Development*, Aldershot: Ashgate.

Martinelli, F. (2010), "Historical roots of social change: philosophies and movements", in F. Moulaert, F. Martinelli, E. Swyngedouw and S. González (eds) *Can neighbourhoods save the city?* London: Routledge, pp. 17–48.

Moulaert, F. and O. Ailenei (2005), 'Social Economy, Third Sector and Solidarity Relations: A Conceptual Synthesis from History to Present', *Urban Studies*, **42** (11), 2037–2053.

Moulaert, F., and J. Nussbaumer (2005), 'The Social Region: Beyond the Territorial Dynamics of the Learning Economy', *European Urban and Regional Studies*, **12** (1), 45–64.

Moulaert, F. (2000), *Globalization and Integrated Area Development in European Cities*, Oxford: Oxford University Press.

Moulaert, F., F. Martinelli, E. Swyngedouw and S. González (2005), 'Towards Alternative Model(s) of Local Innovation', *Urban Studies*, **42** (11), 1969–1990.

Nancy, J-L. (1992), 'La Comparution/ The Compearance: From the Existence of "Communism" to the Community of "Existence"', trans. T.B. Strong, *Political Theory*, **20** (3), 371–398.

Novy, A. and B. Leubolt (2005), 'Participatory Budgeting in Porto Alegre: Social Innovation and the Dialectical Relationship of State and Civil Society', *Urban Studies*, **42** (11), 2023–2036.

Pateman, C. (2012), 'APSA Presidential address: Participatory Democracy Revisited', *Perspectives on Politics* **10** (1), 7–19.

Social Enterprise Sunderland (n.d.), http://www.socialauditnetwork.org.uk/files/1913/4917/5248/SES_Sunderland_-_Social_Report_-_2007.pdf (last accessed 10 January 2013).

35. Framing social innovation research: a sociology of knowledge perspective
Frank Moulaert and Barbara Van Dyck

35.1 INTRODUCTION

If social innovation (SI) is about transformation of institutions, overthrowing oppressive 'structures with power', collective agency to address non-satisfied needs, building of empowering social relations from the bottom-up, one can indeed wonder what leads scientists, who often have a strong theoretical interest and occasionally suffer from *forum phobia*, to social innovation analysis and social innovation practice, as advisors, theorists, activists, technicians, etc.? Is it that social innovation scientists are aware that through their work of knowledge production they – consciously or unconsciously – defend or reinforce particular positions and interests in society? They seemingly make the choice to acknowledge the inherent positionality of (scientific) knowledge and make explicit their intention of knowledge production in the interest of marginalized or disempowered voices and with the purpose of social transformation.

SI research is indeed about 'changing the world' through study, cooperation and shared intervention or collective action, often in a form of action research. Thinking about changing 'the' world necessarily implies questions about whose and which world to change. In social innovation research we thus need to look both at what is studied and how this is done. Or, as Jessop et al. argued in Chapter 8, the study of SI is intrinsically reflexive. In that regard, it also is remarkable that SI scientists, explicitly working in empathy and solidarity with interest groups, often seem to valorize the coexistence of a variety of perspectives in the definition of research questions and the ways to address them.

The confrontations of different perspectives and analytical instruments through alliances of practitioners, users, and researchers open the possibility of creating new articulations and ways of knowing. Research practices that focus on socially innovative community building and policy making contribute – as is shown in several chapters of this handbook – to transformations of social relations in and through knowledge production processes. Moreover, and despite their epistemic diversity, researchers and practitioners involved in SI research share a grand view of an institutionally complex world that is largely dominated by oppressive forces and opportunistic agencies, which can only be countered through coordinated collective action.

In this chapter, we want to reconstruct the scientific practice of knowledge building within its complex institutional dynamics. To that purpose, we opt for a 'Sociology of knowledge (SoK) approach' which puts scientists, scientific practice, theory building and methodology development in a societal context. A SoK perspective is a means to connect *what* we analyse to *how* we analyse it. We will argue that a meta-theoretical framework, incorporating the main features of the social relations and cultural dynamics in which knowledge productive is embedded, is productive in developing a SoK approach to social innovation research. It allows us to reveal the relation between political conflicts or disagreeing opinions and fundamentally different approaches about truth, reality and knowledge, within a negotiated and shared view of the social, economic, cultural and political forces that shape societal transformation. Examples of such meta-theoretical frameworks can be found in Novy et al. (2012) for the analysis of social cohesion in the city and in Moulaert (1987) for the analysis of local development institutions and strategies. Meta-theoretical frameworks share a view of the world which they address – e.g. by identifying the predominant social relations ruling that world – while remaining sufficiently 'meta' as a dialogue space for a diversity of rationales, codes of behaviour, initiatives of action, etc.

35.2   SCIENTIFIC PRACTICE SOCIALLY EMBEDDED, ANALYTICALLY UNROLLED: SOCIOLOGY OF KNOWLEDGE PERSPECTIVES

When, after about 20 years of theoretical work and grassroots participatory research, questions emerged about the 'unity' of the social innovation argument and the necessity or desirability of 'a' theory or 'a' paradigm of social innovation, the research community who worked on the projects IAD, URSPIC, SINGOCOM, VALICORES, KATARSIS and SOCIAL POLIS started collectively to reflect on the role of social science (theory, methodology, social utility) in social change debates, initiatives and analysis (also see the General Introduction of this book).[1] Through these reflections, a number of

philosophy of science concepts received a more grounded meaning.

35.2.1   Epistemology

Epistemology is an inquiry into, and a negotiated consensus on, the way to develop knowledge. It is not a doctrine of scientific knowledge creation. Epistemology is understood as an interactively unrolled manual on how to connect questions about social change to scientific interrogation (*problématique*), how to lead this interrogation, and how to decide on the relative 'verity' or 'truth' of the answers. From the social innovation perspective, 'truth' is concerned about the (socially accepted) relevance of the scientific answers for the satisfaction of (non-revealed) needs, the transformation of social relations, and the empowerment of populations and communities. The criteria for verity are therefore relationally conceived. Or, if we redefine epistemology as about the achievement of the social legitimacy of the knowledge that is developed, social innovation epistemology is about the possibility to verify the (socially accepted) relevance of the knowledge for social transformation. This relevance has to do with the recognition of the role of social forces and their discourses in the reproduction of scientific legitimacy and, therefore, with ontology. Before developing on the meaning of ontology in SI research, we briefly introduce structural-realism as a particular epistemological position in the study of social change.

35.2.2   Structural-Realist Epistemological Perspective

An epistemological perspective in SI research has to start from the idea that knowledge is socially produced, i.e. that 'it is neither an epiphenomenon of nature nor a convention of man' (Coimbra Swiatek 2011, p17). Secondly we believe that a real world exists independently of our interpretation of it, which is referred to as the independence of reality from our knowledge. Furthermore we start from the idea of the fallibility and theory-based character of knowledge. This highlights the importance of frames of meaning to mediate understanding, their impact on outcomes and the need to understand external reality in terms of its social construction. We find these features in structural realism.

We consider a structural-realist perspective as a particular stance within critical realism. A critical realist perspective, as summarised by Andrew Sayer (1992, p. 6), stresses that the view of the world 'is differentiated and stratified, consisting not only of events but objects, including structures, which have powers and liabilities capable of generating events'. This relates to a particular understanding of causation; emphasis is not on causation as such, but on causal powers or mechanisms. Causation then is studied not as a simple relationship between separate things or events. Instead the study is about what an object is like and will do under particular circumstances. This implies that for the study of SI we do not assume necessary, nor impossible, relations, but we look into the conditions, including events and structures, that make the transformation of socio-spatial relations possible.

To uncover the mechanisms causing historically contingent events, a stratified and differentiated ontology is required (Sayer 1992). Structural realism then, as a particular focus within realism, recognizes a relative hierarchy among the objects of social reality and recognizes structures in the form of relatively durable social relations as being of a potentially higher causal order. This does not mean that structures are pre-existing to social phenomena; in fact, structures are institutionally mediated and historically as well as spatially reproduced through both collective and strategic individual action. Still the conceptual nature of structures, institutions and agency is pre-informed by the theory that has analytically conceived them. Coimbra Swiatek (2011, p18), following the Baskar tradition, refers to the concept-dependent character of practices, institutions, rules, roles and relationships: 'what they are depend on what they mean to the society and its members'. The consequence is that within a critical-realist perspective several theories referring to the same or related concepts should be confronted and brought into dialogue with each other. Moreover, and relevant for SI research, structural realism presupposes a strong and interactive relationship of theory and practice.

35.2.3   Ontology

Ontology in the theory of social change has to do with 'what world' is, is desired or is to be made. Theory of social change is based both on a view of what exists, the 'logic of being' and the potential of collectively becoming. Accounts of what exists in particular places and times, recognition of core features of society and ideas of desired change are essential in ontological reasoning. Ideas of desired change are in general important for motivating change agents. They can either be a view of the desired alternative (generic or detailed), or a utopia, a *futurible*; or a procedural view of how we can move on for betterment, a mapped-out genesis of alternative becoming in which all relevant actors are involved (*transdisciplinarity*).

This tension between the 'logic of being' and the 'logic of becoming' is an issue in social theories addressing social change, transformation or innovation. A very straightforward example is neoclassical economic market exchange theory, which uses a normative view of 'the self-adapting market as the ontology of equilibrium' as a hypothesis to test how the market actually functions. In the 'desired' neoclassical economic world each agent is an optimizer and has the information and behavioural skills to optimize its individual behaviour, thus contributing to the social equilibrium. In empirical orthodox economics, then, this *aspired* ontology is used to test actual economic behaviour in actually existing markets where such optimality principles are only occasionally applied and, if they do, only in a socially (structurally, institutionally) mediated way, i.e. in an environment not meeting the assumptions of the neoclassical mental construct. The market Utopia is taken for real and by assuming that it exists or can be materialized overnight, its normative principles are translated into policy measures which have led to several of the socioeconomic failures we have known over the last few decades (implosion of the virtual economy, recurrent and deepening financial crises, . . .).

It is therefore very important to make clear distinctions between approaches to the 'construction of ontologies' relevant to social innovation (Moulaert and Nussbaumer 2008, p. 131).[2] A distinction should be made between:

1. an ontology (of the *existent* or *desired*) as the basis for a theory or meta-theoretical framework;
2. ontogenesis or process of genesis of the vision of the existent or the desired (images of the future);
3. 'flat ontology', either an ontology of a homogeneous society, or an 'open' ontology which as in (for example) a Deleuzean approach opens itself to a gradual complexification through interaction between agents;

4. structural-realist view of social reality, a view of society recognizing a structure of the economy, the political world, etc. significantly influenced by power relations and the way it constrains or facilitates collective agency.

We can apply these distinctions to territorial development and social innovation through community development (Table 35.1) (see Van Dyck and Van den Broeck, Chapter 9; Gibson-Graham and Roelvink, Chapter 34). Integrated Area Development (IAD), as an example, adopts a structural-realist ontology of a complex world dominated by social structures (capitalist economy, politics dominated by masculinity and power relations) within which institutions are reproduced in a dialectal interaction between agency and structural transformations. Such an ontology reflects the visions of society and (its) communities as starting points for theorization. But it also integrates ontogenesis as an interactive process of actors (re)producing images of society, its components and their modes of functioning. The initial view of the world (initial ontology), the ontogenesis and the ontologies developed by the social forces and the territorial actors are linked to each other.

Coherent with the socially embedded epistemological stance for SI analysis, the four concepts (*ontology, ontogenesis, flat ontology* and *structural-realism*) have analytical relevance by themselves, but should also be connected to each other. In SI research, the ontology of the existent and the desired is filled in through a transdisciplinary approach – involving concerned agents and organizations. The genesis of the views of the existent and desired world themselves are therefore approached as a social process, never reaching final completion and repeatedly critically reinterpreted as to their relevance to collective action

Table 35.1   Ontogenesis: ontologies as applied to theories of territorial development

Societal Structure Ontological Perspective	Flat ontology (3)	Structural-realist (4)
Ontology (1)	Neoclassical theory of regional growth TIM	Social Region IAD
Ontogenesis (2)	Deleuzean approach to spatial development Assembly theory	IAD

Source: Moulaert and Nussbaumer (2008, p. 131).

(see Moulaert and Mehmood, Chapter 33 on holistic research and pragmatic collective action).

35.2.4   Meta-Theory or Meta-Theoretical Framework

Meta-theory or meta-theoretical frameworks are the logical next concepts that have emerged in social innovation epistemological discussions. Meta-theory as theory of theories; or as a theory of theorizing (in sociology); or as an epistemological framework with a shared ontology and basic concepts – an overarching theoretical perspective; or, more simply, the need for epistemic reflexivity: *are the concepts and theories we are using pertinent to our problematic?* And how can we select 'a framework to host theories' that would help us to answer this question? And should this meta-theory also reflect on the role of scientific practice in social reality and social transformation? As argued by Jessop et al. in Chapter 8, ontological coherence in SI research indeed requires a reflexive positioning of the researchers in the SI research and action. This means that research agencies have to be conceptualized in the metaframework (and in some of the theories it hosts) to allow ongoing evaluation of their role in the action research. For example, by theorizing the agents in the knowledge-building complex of the society for which

SI is pursued, it becomes possible to figure out what their role could be in building alliances for new urban policy: will it be instrumental to mainstreaming 'caring liberalism' in neighbourhood development, or will it instead advise and empower radical change agendas?

Therefore, for SI analysis, it is epistemologically coherent to state that a relevant meta-theory should be based on an ontology and ontogenesis that involve relational complexity as well as all relevant types of agency that make or seek social innovation, or that make it work. Ontogenesis, or the process of genesis of the vision of the existent and the desired, then becomes intrinsically transdisciplinary, putting implicated parties/actors at its heart. A meta-theoretical structure hosting roles of scientists and science in society is an important element in building a SoK approach.

35.2.5   The Role of Science and Scientific Knowledge Building in Contemporary Society

The foregoing paragraphs dealt with criteria of verity and truth seeking in knowledge production. We now put the knowledge production process in SI studies in a societal context that could reveal its relational complexity. This societal context can then serve as a starting point for building the meta-theoretical framework that is essential to the SoK approach in SI research.

In contemporary society, with its blurred boundaries between state, market and civil society, looking at and rethinking the role of science and scientific knowledge building is crucial in understanding and enacting social transformations. Moreover, if scientific knowledge, following the enlightenment logic, may have appeared to provide the truth, standing above other forms of knowledge, scientific knowledge itself becomes now part of public debate (Stengers 2010).

Especially in what Latour (1998) refers to as 'matters of concern' or issues that matter to people, citizens voice claims for a more democratic and transparent treatment of science and its claimed truths. Practitioners and citizens who no longer believe in the myth of progress demand recognition for their part in complex knowledge-building processes. The allegory of the Cave – according to which scientists have the privilege of freeing themselves from the tyranny of the social in order to access the 'truth' (Latour 2004) – has become obsolete. Many researchers have come to or have been forced to realize that they are part of a complex world, in which society no longer simply rejects or accepts the results of science. Citizens seek to participate in formulating research questions and, in numerous cases, feel entitled to participate in setting research agendas (Miciukiewicz et al. 2012). Scientists become one actor, next to others, that add ingredients to questions about complex political issues. Next to classic scientific quality-criteria of validity and reliability, the social robustness of knowledge production becomes essential in the scientific validation process. For SI research, which typically studies innovation in social and political relations, through innovative participatory processes, this is particularly relevant.

In the epistemology section, we stressed the importance of the achievement of social legitimacy of SI knowledge and its relevance for social transformation. Achieving social robustness requires social legitimacy of knowledge and processes of democratizing knowledge (Nowotny 2003; see Novy et al., Chapter 32). Social robustness as a matter of fact involves the recognition of 'local knowledge' or 'lay knowledge' as valid knowledge as well as the approval of validity and truth of knowledge beyond university communities. In addition to 'peer review' practice – the process of internal knowledge validation – validation of knowledge is continuously negotiated with concerned parties. These can be practitioners, citizens, people in socially fragile conditions, technical experts, scientists from different disciplines.

Such processes where knowledge building explicitly materializes through the interaction of science and society is referred to as transdisciplinary research (Cassinari et al. 2011). The cooperation of scientists, practitioners and lay people from diverse backgrounds does not erase disciplinary boundaries. On the contrary, the specificities of diverse practices (including different scientific disciplines) are brought together in their heterogeneity. The possibility for innovation is created in the articulation of contrasting perspectives. Contrary to classic positivist science approaches, these hybrid knowledge platforms have the intrinsic uncertainty of knowledge at the very heart of their concerns. Knowledge, as well as the very knowledge production process, are consequently continuously debated. Issues such as social cohesion and territorial development in particular do not confront us with static problems that can be answered through linear problem-solution rationalities, neither do they lead to generalizable problems or solutions (Novy et al. 2012).

Obviously, relations of science and society have always existed. Scientific, political and economic elites have always been closely related; patterns of interaction and influence change though. Changes in context, content and organization of knowledge production are reflected in an increased emphasis on science driven by practical applications, strong influence of the market, temporary knowledge alliances and heterogenous research organizations (Hage et al. 2010). As in other sectors of society, research governance takes the form of more horizontal networks, and quality becomes a process controlled through a number of stakeholders.

However this 'horizontalization' of research governance does not guarantee transdisciplinarity as we use the term in social innovation research. Transdisciplinary research, as practised in social innovation analysis, differentiates itself from many other institutional arrangements of knowledge production in the knowledge economy in several ways. Firstly, the participants in research communities that are involved in the definition of research questions and research methods have joint interests that are not commercially oriented. Research participants in fact are usually not financially empowered, nor do they necessarily have access to cutting edge scientific knowledge. Secondly, the relation between researchers and lay people is not based on the distinction of 'those who know' (the scientists) and 'those that have to be convinced' (the people). Relations are based on the recognition of the diversity of valid knowledges that have to be brought together as a potential for socially relevant, legitimate and valid knowledge. Third, and this stems from the first two observations, the content of the knowledge-building process is oriented towards facing challenges of social and socio-ecological empowerment.

35.3   SOCIOLOGY OF KNOWLEDGE

The epistemological stance, the view of ontology/ontogenesis and the introduction of a meta-theoretical framework capable of hosting the role of scientists/science in the transformation of society spelled out before, come close to the sociology of science approach implicitly or explicitly defended by Schumpeter, inspired by Scheler (1926[1924]) and Mannheim (1936[1931]). According to Shionoya (2004, p. 340), for Schumpeter sociology of science 'views science as social activities influenced by the historical, social and cultural context of the time'.

In the structural-realist epistemological logic, the construction of concepts and theories of social innovation must be assessed within the societal framework in which they have been developed. Relational knowledge-production processes in which communities of scientists and other concerned parties cooperate facilitate the construction of concepts and theories that may be able to address societal issues. Moreover, according to Schumpeter's vision on science and as elaborated earlier, knowledge is not a monopoly of science, but (also) the object of *other forms of knowledge formation and social practice* that all have a place in the dynamics of development. Schumpeter develops arguments explaining that development should be analysed not only within a broader or general societal framework, but that the different spheres, dynamics and agency domains of society are entitled to their own sociology which together should allow to better understand the complex(ity) of development and its dimensions (knowledge, culture, economy, . . .):

Accordingly, next to economic sociology Schumpeter also has in mind a sociology of knowledge, a sociology of arts, and a sociology of the political, all of which help understand the energy and the mechanism of development, not just in general but also in each particular sphere. The question of how the sociological insights in each particular sphere can be combined into a perspective that conveys the understanding of a modern, i.e., differentiated, whole, was also Schumpeter's central concern when he attempted in TWE (1911)[3] to grasp the overall tendency of the socio-cultural development of a people. (Becker and Knudsen 2005[1932], p. 9)

Obviously, if we accept the reasoning about the role of the SoK in (the study of) scientific practice (after Scherer, Mannheim, etc.), there is no unique SoK, *and the terms of a sociology of knowledge are largely determined by the theory of society and social transformation to which it refers.* Or, from a structural realist perspective, these terms are spelled out in the meta-theoretical framework of society, the view of scientific practice, the ontology it is related to and which gives a significant role to structural dynamics in explaining change and development, etc.

We consider the literature on the sociology of knowledge as a continuum in evolution. Mannheim is a precursory voice in a social-scientific process that could be labelled as the (re)making of the SoK. He has understood that the relationships between *ideology* and scientific practice cannot only be studied through the lens of philosophy but that a sociological perspective is needed. In simplified terms, Mannheim's 'sociology of knowledge' approach follows two tracks. One more 'societal track' runs close to the Marxist way of looking at ideology formation; the other one lies closer to Scheler's microsociological analysis of knowledge institutions and practices. Knowledge for Mannheim is real, i.e., what is considered to be knowledge: *knowledge that is socially* *or individually produced, but socially accepted as being knowledge.*

Following David Bloor (1991[1976]) we could make a distinction within SoK between 'a weak program' and 'a strong program', with the 'weak program' addressing the process of knowledge creation in the limited sense: how has the relational process that led to knowledge been unrolled? Which have been the factors that have influenced the relationship between verity and bias? In the weak program the context of intellectual activity is recognized, the potential ideological bias allowed for, but no room is given to the analysis of the activity of Reason, its deductions and inductions. The 'strong program' in contrast, and which we refer to as 'complete embeddedness', includes the social, political and economic context that nourished the environment in which (the) knowledge was developed, the sociocultural (including ideological) background of the scientists, their belonging to scientific and philosophical communities, the links between scientific practice and collective action, etc.

More instrumentally or positivist oriented scientists would argue that the strong program involves 'everything' and therefore is unrealistic to pursue. This is not so, however, for several reasons.

First, it is clear that, following Mannheim's line of argument, that the 'strong program' cannot be applied without clear epistemological positioning about how to address the role of knowledge production within society. The position we adopt here, we said, is a structural-realist perspective. Scientific practice is situated with the structural dynamics of a society, e.g. as part of the knowledge infrastructure confirming the technocracy of the market economy and top-down governance systems, but also as part of counter hegemonic movements and practices of social innovation seeking to transform society and its communities in the direction of human development. The strong 'sociology of knowledge perspective' fits very well this structural-realist perspective on science and knowledge production and how it should be reflexively addressed.

A theory privileging the analysis of structures in social reality then can serve as a meta-theoretical framework hosting different epistemic viewpoints and practice-oriented interrogations. It sets the borderlines within which particular objects and their relations can be analysed. Examples of such approaches are well-known in critical geography and spatial development analysis, where the meta-theoretical framework starts from the social structures analysed in political economy – and often treats these structures as a main feature of the meta-framework's social ontology (see also Chapters 1 and 8 in this handbook).

Second, the focus is not on 'everything' but on the practices, institutions and socialization dynamics of scientific knowledge production, as embedded within societal dynamics. This consists for example of insights in the funding mechanisms of research to understand the relations between the goals of research funders, the research questions developed and preferred research methods. Another point of interest would be the social position of academics in society, and the way and type of expertise consulted in political decision-making. This is also why we believe that scientific agency should be conceptualized as a component of the meta-theoretical framework.

Third, we are looking at scientific practices producing knowledge about or related to social innovation. This means that, within the structural-realist perspective and the 'view of the world' it adopts, interrogations, concepts and theories that

address these, will be privileged. These interrogations, concepts and theories will often stem from the experience of action researchers or hybrid knowledge platforms (e.g. Social Polis; see Novy et al., Chapter 32); but also from scientific work such as critical literature surveys, action and policy oriented research from the past, etc.

Finally (for the time being) we examine these practices within their macro and micro social relations, with a particular focus on the communities, social and cultural environments, political arenas and fields of social integration and exclusion in which the knowledge institutions and scientists are involved.

35.3.1 What does the SoK Approach Mean for SI Analysis and Practice Today?

During the IAD (Moulaert 2000) and SINGOCOM projects (Moulaert et al. 2011), and from the beginning of KATARSIS (MacCallum et al. 2009), we looked at a variety of theories analysing and building-up social innovation processes, strategies, agendas. We have addressed these theories questioning their purpose: why were they developed? And according to which organizational and procedural dynamics? In a way this was the start of a SoK approach to these theories, which can be further developed now from the point of view of the 'strong' SoK program. From that perspective, the socio-political dynamics in which the scientific debate/contribution takes place and, more precisely, the links with collective action within society and communities undertaking local development action should be addressed. These socio-political dynamics should be brought in connection to politico-ideological dynamics typical of the society and the community in which the knowledge production occurs.

But if we are concerned about relevance

of 'acquired' scientific knowledge for contemporary SI initiatives and processes, we also need to address the challenges of the present – how can *contemporary* SI research and action benefit from a SoK assessment of old theories? And what about a SoK assessment of emerging theories and methods? And how does historically and institutionally embedded knowledge be(come) relevant to SI innovation challenges/strategies/processes today? Relevance for these exercises can be found in comparing contemporary societal dynamics (an 'open' SOK approach) with those in which the 'old' theories were developed. In this way 'new' theorizing, addressing contemporary challenges with their own philosophical debates and change movements, can be analysed partly by comparing them with theory building processes in an institutionally and politico-ideologically comparable past.

35.3.2 Illustration of a SoK Approach at Work

Table 35.2 gives five dimensions relevant to SoK analysis, which can be used as a 'macro' guide. This is a non-exhaustive list, but at least gives a good impression of what could be done in a balanced SoK approach according to the 'strong program'. The table shows three families of theories that are relevant for local development through SI today (see Van Dyck and Van den Broeck, Chapter 9): theories of human endogenous development; social innovation theories developed in the late 1960s; and Integrated Area Development. The following paragraphs illustrate the operationalization of a 'strong' SoK approach to social innovation theories of the 1960s (for an overview see Chambon et al. 1982).

SI analysis in the 1960s (and 1970s) should be situated in the context of the social movements and philosophies reacting against the hierarchy of capitalism and the state. The stress was very much on the democratization of institutions, sexual liberation, gender equality, respect for different cultures (multicultural society), etc. Many of the socio-political discourses considered typical of the 1960s movements could also be considered anticipatory of the post-modern philosophies, research agendas, and collective as well as individual actions. Typical for the period are intense relations between scientific communities (philosophers like Sartre, visionaries like Attali, etc.) and workers as well as student organizations. The diversity of theoretical contributions in the field of social innovation reflects the diversity of the change agendas put forward by these organizations regarding transformation of society, aspects of governance, emancipatory practices, institutional change, democratization of the educational system, humanization of welfare services, etc.

The intellectual work on social innovation in the 1960s/1970s reflects to a large extent intellectual traditions concerned about individual rights within an equitable society: social liberalism, anarchism, communitarian socialism, ... But at the same time it is concerned about the future of 'big organizations' and 'heavy institutions', making proposals to democratize them. This concern holds the modernist insight that complex societies cannot be governed without human-made governance organizations, other than the market. Thus, in a way, the social innovation analysis of the 1960s/1970s anticipated the badly needed synthesis between postmodern decentralized creativity, on the one hand, and the positive lessons drawn from the modernist governance of a complex society with its large scale institutions on the other. Thus the theories developed in those days are potentially quite relevant for theorizing

Table 35.2   Sociology of Knowledge on social innovation and local development:
illustration of the approach through three (families of) theories

Dimensions addressed in SoK Theory/School/ Approach	Socio-cultural periods: dominant philosophies, political regimes (and scientific themes stressed)	Relations with dominant scientific epistemologies-problematic addressed
Theory of human endogenous development (1970 . . .)	End of three decades of 'golden age', continuation of the values of the welfare state at local level Mixed Economy Ideology of human progress Themes: empowerment, mobilisation of endogenous resources, bottom-up development	Respond to the need of unequal spatial development that emerged from the economic crisis (half of 1970s) Refutal of neoclassic theories of regional development
Social innovation theories (1960s)	1960s + large pluralistic and emancipatory movements (progressive liberalism, democratic Marxism) Themes: anti-authoritarianism, democratisation of institutions, participation, social rights, social innovations	Reply to the excesses of capitalism and mercantile statism Try to find ways to overcome socioeconomic inequalities Dissent with modernisation theories (economy, state), rise of post-modern theories claiming creation of space for bottom-up emancipation
Integrated Area Development	1980s: rise of administrative decentralization, local social movements focused on life quality, sustainable development, improvement of life quality in deprived neighbourhood Themes: local democracy, territorial development (instead of functional), inclusion of 'new poor'	Respond to the needs of deprived neighbourhoods and their disempowered inhabitants. Refutal of theories / ideologies stressing positive effects of globalization, economic deregulation and flexibilization of labour market

Source: Moulaert and Nussbaumer (2008, pp. 134–135).

Scientific communities to which the researchers belong	Relations with collective action	Relations with scientific antecedents (continuity, antithesis, synthesis)
Economists of international development (back to the source . . .) 'Spatial' social sciences 'Old' institutionalists (influence of German Historical School (GHS))	Expertise, cooperation with local communities and development agencies . . .	Continuity: theories of development GHS, years 1960+ (Myrdal, Perroux, Hirschmann) Antithesis: development theory confronted to growth theory Synthesis: integration GHS, theory of development and empowerment, emancipation theory (Friedmann 1992)
Philosophical circles, alternative economists	Workers and student mobilization Reflexion groups on social transformation in different spheres and institutions of society. Participation in social-democratic governments (democratization of education, redistribution of income, social services)	Continuity: links with social liberalism, anarchist theories, . . . Antithesis: postmodernism versus modernism Synthesis: attempt to correct excesses of modernist institutions, growing disillusions
Reflexion groups in urban sociology, social economics, spatial planning, political science, urban and rural anthropology Important role for action research	Scientists involved in social movements project teams Experts and actors involved in local partnerships	Continuity: links with social innovation theories of 1960 Antithesis: theories which integrate the different dimensions of territorial development, moving beyond functionalism (Moulaert 2000) Synthesis: integration of TIM elements

and designing social innovation today. Still the different ideological climate, the dismantling of many Fordist institutions, the growing role of decentralized initiatives in the present contexts should be taken into account. They will necessitate, for example, reflections on bottom-linked governance (see Pradel et al., Chapter 11), the growing role of local and regional agencies and institutions in socially innovative initiatives (see Moulaert et al., Chapter 1) as well as the increased significance of ecological priorities and arenas (Parra, Chapter 10). Yet there are several similarities between the bottom-up social movements that animated the heydays of the revolutionary sixties and the political movements of today. Even if diverse issues beyond the class struggle gain in visibility, the building of decentralized alliances against oppressive powers and structures, and the belief in collective agency for social change remain.

35.4   CONCLUSION

A SoK approach to social innovation analysis shows how the contributions in this handbook, besides their value for public debate and knowledge production on issues such as social cohesion and community development, deal with a fundamental scientific yet socio-political debate. Through transdisciplinary work on matters of social concern, science itself becomes a site for social innovation. The contributions give flesh and body to democratizing the future for scientific activity in a context of blurred boundaries between the spheres of the state, the market and civil society. They propose ways to foster knowledge alliances that resist the privatization of knowledge and knowledge production to the benefit of private interests in a context where the majority of public institutions comply with the pressure for market-conformist restructuring.

The SoK approach could be considered the intellectual watchdog of the knowledge alliance approach presented by Novy et al. in Chapter 32. It provides a guideline for the reading of theory in its past context, while looking at its relevance or feasibility for addressing SI challenges today. From a structural-realist perspective it puts forward criteria to develop an appropriate meta-theoretical framework which can guide the SoK exercise in a reflexive manner, by placing the researchers in their different roles within the world they are supposed to analyse and live in. In this way, from the perspective of the role of science in social change and social innovation, the SoK approach speaks to the various grand challenges of society and communities today. And it does so by linking the lessons of the past (theory, practice, reflection, . . .) to the possibilities for the present and the future.

35.5   QUESTIONS FOR DISCUSSION

- Why would you want to adopt a sociology of knowledge approach to social innovation research?
- What is characteristic about the meaning of the concepts epistemology and ontology in social innovation research?
- What would you understand under 'socially robust' knowledge?

NOTES

1. For an overview see www.socialpolis.eu (last accessed 19 December 2012).
2. Moulaert and Nussbaumer (2008): this categorization is used to talk about the ontological status of theories of territorial development and how they incorporate social innovation.

3. TWE stands for *Theorie der wirtschaftlichen Entwicklung* (Joseph A. Schumpeter (1911), transl. by Redvers Opie (1934), *The Theory of Economic Development: An inquiry into profits, capital, credit, interest and the business cycle*, Cambridge Mass.: Harvard University Press).

REFERENCES

(References in bold are recommended reading.)

Becker, M.C. and T. Knudsen (2005[1932]), 'Translation of and introduction to "Entwicklung" (J. Schumpeter)', *Journal of Economic Literature*, **43** (1), 108–120.

Bloor, David (1991[1976]), *Knowledge and Social Imaginary*, Chicago: University of Chicago Press.

Cassinari, D., Hillier, J., Miciukiewicz, K., and A, Novy (2011), Transdisciplinary Research in Social Polis. Leuven: Social Polis, www.socialpolis.eu (last accessed 19 December 2012).

Chambon, J.-L., A. David and J-M. Devevey (1982), *Les innovations sociales*, Paris: Presses Universitaires de France.

Coimbra Swiatek, Daniela (2011), 'Governance in new European regions: the case of Centrope', doctoral thesis presented to the Vienna University of Economics and Business, Institute for the Environment and Regional Development, Vienna.

Friedmann, John (1992), *Empowerment: the politics of alternative development*, Oxford: Blackwell Publishers.

Hage, M, P. Leroy and A. Petersen (2010), 'Stakeholder participation in environmental knowledge production', *Futures*, **42** (3), 254–264.

Latour, Bruno (1998), 'Essays on science and society: From the World of Science to the World of Research?', *Science*, **280** (5361), 208–209.

Latour, Bruno (2004), *Politics of Nature: How to Bring the Sciences into Democracy*, Cambridge, MA: Harvard University Press.

Mannheim, Karl (1936[1931]), 'The Sociology of Knowledge', *Ideology and Utopia*, London: Routledge and Paul Kegan.

MacCallum, D., F. Moulaert, J. Hillie and S. Vicari-Haddock (2009), *Social Innovation and Territorial Development*, Farnham: Ashgate.

Miciukiewicz, K, F. Moulaert, A. Novy, S. Musterd, and J. Hillier (2012), 'Introduction: Problematising Urban Social Cohesion: A Transdisciplinary Endeavour', *Urban Studies*, 49 (9), 1855–1872.

Moulaert, Frank (1987), 'An Institutional Revisit of the Storper-Walker Theory of Labour', *International Journal of Urban and Regional Research*, **11** (3), 309–330.

Moulaert, Frank (2000), *Integrated Area Development in European Cities*, Oxford: Oxford University Press.

Moulaert, F. and J. Nussbaumer (2008), *La logique sociale du développement territorial*, Québec: Presses Universitaires du Québec.

Moulaert, F, E. Swyngedouw, F. Martinelli and S. González (eds) (2011), *Can Neighbourhoods Save the City? Community Development and Social Innovation*, London: Routledge.

Novy, A., D. Coimbra Swiatek and F. Moulaert (2012), 'Social Cohesion: A Conceptual and Political Elucidation', *Urban Studies*, **49** (9), 1873–1889.

Nowotny, Helga (2003), 'Dilemma of expertise. Democratising expertise and socially robust knowledge', *Science and Public Policy*, 30 (3), 151–156.

Sayer, Andrew (1992[1984]), *Method in Social Science. A realist approach*, London and New York: Routledge.

Scheler, Max (ed.) (1926 [1924]). *Versuche zu einer Soziologie des Wissens*, Munich: Duncker und Humblot.

Shionoya, Yuichi (2004), 'Scope and Method of Schumpeter's universal social science: economic sociology, instrumentalism, and rhetoric', *Journal of the History of Economic Thought*, **26** (2), 331–347.

Stengers, Isabelle (2010), *La vierge et le neutrino: les scientifiques dans la tourmente*, Paris: Les empêcheurs de penser en rond.

Index

481